HOUSING LAW:
TEXT, CASES AND MATERIALS

LM CLEMENTS, BA, LLM
LECTURER IN LAW
UNIVERSITY OF HULL

PROFESSOR PB FAIREST
LECTURER IN LAW
UNIVERSITY OF HULL

Cavendish
Publishing
Limited

First published in Great Britain 1996 by Cavendish Publishing
Limited, The Glass House, Wharton Street, London WC1X 9PX.
Telephone: 0171-278 8000   Facsimile: 0171-278 8080

Clements, Linda
Housing law: text cases & materials
1.Housing – Law and legislation – England
I Title II Fairest, Paul, 1940-
342.2'0463635

ISBN 1–85941-222-X

Printed and bound in Great Britain by
Biddles Ltd, Guildford and King's Lynn

PREFACE

Housing law is an exciting subject which has seen considerable changes over the years as different governments from different political persuasions have put their mark upon it. The Rent Act 1977, for example, reflects the political philosophy of the Labour Party, with its tenant-friendly emphasis, giving both security of tenure and rent control to tenants who are affected. By contrast, the Housing Act 1988, a Conservative government measure, has shifted the emphasis towards less protection for tenants and the creation of assured shorthold tenancies which are fixed-term arrangements with no security of tenure at the end of their duration. The 1988 Act is what may be described as more 'landlord friendly' than its predecessor.

Whatever political persuasion one adheres to, it is clear that housing law is likely to grow in importance and is becoming increasingly liable to change as a result of statutory intervention, reflecting the housing policies of the political party in power. At a time when the government is facing criticism and pressure for change in many areas, it is not unexpected that the housing issues should also figure relatively high on the political agenda. The recent Housing Act 1996 is an example of this; it has made some important changes to housing law and also contains the new homelessness legislation. The legislation was published only just before the book was completed; however, we were still able to include the relevant changes necessitated by the Act. The publication of this book therefore comes at an opportune moment.

At the same time, this book does take a wider approach to housing law than is taken by most books on the area. It includes, for instance, the area of owner occupation from the perspective of both the mortgagor and those caught up in the financial crisis of home ownership, a result of which is loss of the home being a real possibility.

The book aims to introduce the subject of housing law to the student who is new to it, and also to act as a reference work for those who work in this field. Both the areas covered and approach taken by this book make it particularly suited not only to students and academics but also to practitioners and law centres. Although a large amount of cases and materials is included, it is set in the context of substantial comment and analysis.

Both authors have read and commented upon draft chapters of the book and take joint responsibility for it, including any errors or omissions. The burden of preparing the tables of cases and statutes, as well as the index, was kindly undertaken by the publishers, to whom we are extremely grateful.

The law is stated as in force at the end of August 1996 and it should be noted that, in the future, references in this book to the Matrimonial Homes Act 1983 should be to Part IV of the Family Law Act 1996 and references to s 30 of the Law of Property Act 1925 should be to ss 14 and 15 of the Trusts of Land and Appointment of Trustees Act 1996. Both of these Acts, with the exception of certain sections, are due to come into effect at such time as the Lord Chancellor by order (or statutory instrument) appoints. The Trusts of Land and Appointment of Trustees Act 1996 replaces the trust for sale with a 'trust of land', to which overreaching will continue to apply, but abolishes the doctrine of conversion.

Linda Clements
Professor Paul Fairest

ACKNOWLEDGMENTS

Without the support and encouragement of our friends, family and colleagues, this book would not have been possible. To them we are eternally grateful. We would like to express our particular thanks to Professor Von Prondzynski, Dean of the Law School and Professor David Freestone, whose support, encouragement and patience has been immense.

CONTENTS

Contents

TABLE OF CASES

TABLE OF STATUTES

TABLE OF STATUTORY INSTRUMENTS

CHAPTER 1

INTRODUCTION

Housing law is an area of some complexity and is subject to frequent legislative change. It could be described as a 'political football', especially in relation to such areas as homelessness and the protection given to tenants in both the public and the private sectors. A change in government tends to coincide with changes of emphasis in the legislation concerning tenants in particular, exemplified by the Housing Act 1988 as compared to the Rent Act 1977, which is gradually being phased out and replaced by the former Act.

No other area of law seems to affect the average individual to the same degree as housing law, with the exception, perhaps, of family law. Much of housing law is concerned with the landlord and tenant relationship, but there are other areas which affect, for example, owner occupiers who have bought a house with the aid of a mortgage. The late 1980s and early 1990s saw an increase in the number of home repossessions by banks, building societies and other lending institutions. This had come about as a consequence of the recession following the 'Lawson Boom', with the result that interest rates rose to over 15%. Many home owners fell into heavy arrears on the mortgage and repossession became a relatively commonplace phenomenon. Small businesses borrowing on the security of the matrimonial home of the business owner or one of the partners also increased in the 1980s, often with disastrous consequences for the family which was faced with the results of bankruptcy or insolvency.

There has also been an increase in the number of actions brought against surveyors who have provided either defective valuations or defective surveys on residential properties. This increase has come about as a result of the recognition of a duty of care on the part of the surveyor towards the prospective mortgagor of residential property. Equally evident in the 1980s and 1990s has been the homeless person. Sleeping rough in the streets and begging have become noticeable in many of our bigger cities.

Traditional housing law texts have tended to concentrate on the landlord and tenant relationship. This book, however, seeks to place equal emphasis an the areas of homelessness and owner-occupation. These areas are all discussed at length. Some assumptions, however, have been made for reasons of space. It is assumed, for example, that the reader is familiar with the basic principles of contract law and the law of negligence. It is also assumed that the reader is aware of the areas of real property which form the foundations of the relationship of landlord and tenant. The emphasis of this book is, therefore, on housing and the way in which housing law both operates and impinges upon peoples' lives and aspirations.

What are those aspirations?

Most people would probably agree that good quality accommodation at an affordable price should be made available to all; and that, once acquired, that accommodation should be secure and be without threat of harassment or eviction, except, in the latter case, by legal means. However, legal protection of the tenant or home owner to the exclusion of the justifiable claims of the landlord or mortgagee would make renting out of residential property or lending on its security, unprofitable. A balance therefore needs to be struck between protecting tenants, for example, against Rackmanism and ensuring that renting by landlords does actually pay. A central question for housing law must therefore be : 'To what extent can and does housing law achieve this objective in both the landlord and tenant relationship and the mortgagor/mortgagee relationship?'. This book, in an attempt to look at this issue, discusses the areas of Landlord and Tenant both at common law and the statutory protection regimes, but, in addition, addresses the issue of protection of the family home from the consequences of financial adversity and also discusses the protection available to the most vulnerable, the homeless.

CHAPTER 2

TERMINOLOGY OF LANDLORD AND TENANT LAW AND DIFFERENT TYPES OF TENANCY

INTRODUCTION

This chapter will examine the meaning of the technical language which is used in the field of landlord and tenant law and the different types of tenancy under which a person might occupy residential accommodation.

THE LANGUAGE OF LANDLORD AND TENANT LAW

Term of years

Since 1925, when the Law of Property Act was passed, only two legal estates have been capable of existing. One of these is the 'term of years absolute' which a tenant may have, the other being the fee simple absolute in possession (or freehold) estate vested in the person who is said to 'own' the property. English land law has never recognised that ordinary people may own the land itself; that is vested in the Crown. Instead, ordinary people have an 'estate' in the land. The doctrine of estates stemming from feudal times refers to the period of time during which a person's rights in relation to the land are to continue. The largest estate, the fee simple or freehold, can theoretically last for ever, but the term of years is finite in that it can only last for a specified period of time; hence the requirement that a tenancy must have a certain beginning and ending date (see Chapter 2).

A 'term of years' is defined in s 205(1)(xxvii) to include 'a term for less than a year, or for a year or years and a fraction of a year and from year to year'. This encompasses periodic tenancies, such as the weekly or monthly tenancy, as well as the fixed term tenancy which may last for many years (see Chapter 2).

Lease/tenancy/demise

The expression 'lease' may be used in three different ways: one to refer to the process by which a tenancy is created, another to refer to the resulting arrangement, where the expression is being used as an alternative to 'tenancy' and the other to refer to the document in which the agreement is contained; these are all acceptable alternatives. The word 'demise' is a technical word which is used as an alternative to the first meaning of 'lease' above. 'Tenancy' is usually used to refer to the arrangement between landlord and tenant and is often applied to short-term arrangements, such as weekly or monthly periodic agreements or short fixed-term agreements.

Landlord/lessor and tenant/lessee

The landlord (or lessor) is the person who grants the lease, the tenant (or lessee) is the person to whom it is granted. If the person granting the lease is himself a tenant of the property, he can only grant to another a sublease (or 'underlease') unless he is assigning the entire lease to the other person. In the case of a sublease, the sublessor may also be referred to as the head tenant, and his own landlord may be called the head landlord. If there has been an assignment, however, the original tenant drops out of the picture, leaving a direct relationship of landlord and tenant between the remaining parties (see later discussion of subletting and assignment of a tenancy). This relationship is said to be one of 'privity of estate'.

Reversion

On the creation of a tenancy, the landlord retains an interest in the property. This is called the 'freehold reversion', and it represents the interest which remains vested in the owner of the freehold when that freehold is subject to a tenancy. At the end of the tenancy, the property is said to 'revert' back to the landlord, but during the tenancy the landlord has a reversionary interest in the property which he can sell by means of assignment (see later) to another person who will then take the property subject to the tenancy. (The principles mentioned here are subject to special rules relating to equitable tenancies and to the protection given to certain types of tenant by the Rent Act 1977 or the Housing Acts 1985 and 1988. See the relevant parts of this and later chapters for further discussion on this point.)

Subletting

A tenant may decide that he wishes to sublet the whole or part of the premises comprised in his own tenancy. This is a method by which a new term for a shorter period than that held by the intermediate tenant may be created out of the estate vested in the tenant. Some leases, however, restrict or prohibit subletting. A typical provision of a tenancy is for the landlord to state that the tenant can only sublet with the landlord's consent. If the tenant sublets without this prior consent, he may find that the landlord then wishes to forfeit the tenancy by relying on a term to that effect in the tenancy; so it is essential that the tenant at least seeks the landlord's consent, even if he predicts quite accurately that consent will not be forthcoming. Some assistance, however, is provided by s 19 Landlord and Tenant Act 1927.

Landlord and Tenant Act 1927

19. Provisions as to covenants not to assign, etc without licence or consent

(1) In all leases whether made before or after the commencement of this Act containing a covenant condition or agreement against assigning, underletting, charging or parting with the possession of demised premises or any part thereof without licence or consent, such covenant condition or agreement shall, notwithstanding any express provision to the contrary, be deemed to be subject–

(a) to a proviso to the effect that such licence or consent is not to be unreasonably withheld, but this proviso does not preclude the right of the landlord to require payment of a reasonable sum in respect of any legal or other expenses incurred in connection with such licence or consent; and

(b) (if the lease is for more than forty years, and is made in consideration wholly or partially of the erection, or the substantial improvement, addition or alteration of buildings, and the lessor is not a Government department or local or public authority, or a statutory or public utility company) to a proviso to the effect that in the case of any assignment, under-letting, charging or parting with the possession (whether by the holders of the lease or any under-tenant whether immediate or not) effected more than seven years before the end of the term no consent or licence shall be required, if notice in writing of the transaction is given to the lessor within six months after the transaction is effected.

(2)... (3) ... (4) ...

Examples of an unreasonable refusal of consent may be found in *Bates v Donaldson* [1896] 2 QB 241 (refusal of consent for the sole purpose of obtaining vacant possession of the premises), *Lovelock v Margo* [1963] 2 QB 786 and *Parker v Boggon* [1947] KB 346 (diplomatic immunity of proposed assignee). Consent may not be refused on grounds of either sex or race, as this is prohibited under the Sex Discrimination Act 1975 and under the Race Relations Act 1976.

It has been held that a landlord may reasonably refuse his consent if he reasonably believes that the proposed subtenant would be unable to pay the rent or to comply with the covenants in the head lease or was otherwise objectionable on personal grounds (see *Re Gibbs and Houlder Bros Co Ltd's Lease* [1925] Ch 575); or if the subtenant would gain statutory protection which was not available to the head tenant or where the subtenancy would change the nature of the tenancy from, for example, business to mixed user (see *Leeward Securities Ltd v Lilyheath Properties Ltd* (1984) 271 EG 279 and *West Layton Ltd v Ford* [1979] 2 All ER 657). For example, an assignment of a tenancy by a corporate tenant to an individual assignee may give the assignee a right to security of tenure, which the corporate tenant would not enjoy.

A covenant against subletting 'any part of' the premises will be breached by a subletting of the whole of the premises, but the reverse is not true (see *Field v Barkworth* [1986] 1 WLR 137 and *Wilson v Rosenthal* (1906) 22 TLR 233). Where the head tenancy is being forfeited by the head landlord, the subtenancy will normally fall with the head tenancy, since its very existence depends on that of the head tenancy; but relief may be granted to the subtenant under s 146(4) Law of Property Act 1925.

Law of Property Act 1925

146(4) Where a lessor is proceeding by action or otherwise to enforce a right of re-entry or forfeiture under any covenant, proviso, or stipulation in a lease, or for non-payment of rent, the court may, on application by any person claiming as under-lessee any estate or interest in the property comprised in the lease or any part thereof, either in the lessor's action (if any) or in any action brought by such person for that purpose, make an order vesting, for the whole of the term of the lease or any less term, the property comprised in the lease or any part thereof in any person entitled as under-lessee to any estate or interest in such property upon such conditions as to execution of any deed or other document, payment of rent, costs, expenses, damages, compensation, giving security, or otherwise, as the court in the circumstances of each case may think fit, but in no case shall any such under-lessee be entitled to require a lease to be granted to him for any longer term than he had under his original sub-lease.

This provision was included in the Law of Property Act 1925 because subtenants are not allowed to see details of their own landlord's title, and it would therefore be unfair on them if the sins of their landlord were visited upon them without any possibility of relief being granted to them. The subsection therefore enables the subtenant to obtain relief at the court's discretion in a suitable case, whatever the reasons for the forfeiture of their own landlord's head tenancy.

Assignment

Assignment is a process by which the interest of the tenant or of the landlord is transferred to a third party (assignee), who then steps into the place of the assignor. The tenancy may contain a clause which either prohibits (absolute covenant against assignment) or restricts (qualified covenant against assignment) the tenant's ability to assign the tenancy. If a qualified covenant, ie one which requires the landlord's prior consent to any assignment, has been included, this will be subject to the proviso that such consent must not be unreasonably withheld (see s 19 Landlord and Tenant Act 1927, above), but an absolute covenant against assignment prohibits the tenant under any circumstances from assigning the tenancy to a third party.

An assignment, to be effective at law, must be by deed. This applies to all tenancies, regardless of whether they are legal or equitable and irrespective of how they were created. Some tenancies may be created without the formality of writing or a deed, since s 54(2) Law of Property Act 1925 allows the creation of tenancies for three years or less if they take effect in possession and are for the best rent which can reasonably be obtained without taking a fine or premium. In *Crago v Julian* [1992] 1 All ER 744, a residential case, the Court of Appeal pointed out that the effect of ss 52–54 of the Law of Property Act 1925 was to draw a distinction between the manner in which a short lease may be created and the manner in which it might be assigned. Although a short tenancy (ie one for no longer than three years) may be created orally, it can only be assigned at law by deed.

To be effective as a deed, a document must comply with s 1 Law of Property (Miscellaneous Provisions) Act 1989.

Law of Property (Miscellaneous Provisions) Act 1989

1. **Deeds and their execution**

    (1) Any rule of law which:

        (a) restricts the substances on which a deed may be written;

        (b) requires a seal for the valid execution of an instrument as a deed by an individual; or

        (c) requires authority by one person to another to deliver an instrument as a deed on his behalf to be given by deed,

        is abolished.

    (2) An instrument shall not be a deed unless:

        (a) it makes it clear on its face that it is intended to be a deed by the person making it or, as the case may be, by the parties to it (whether describing itself as a deed or expressing itself to be executed or signed as a deed or otherwise); and

(b) it is validly executed as a deed by that person or, as the case may be, one or more of those parties.

(3) An instrument is validly executed as a deed by an individual if, and only if–

(a) it is signed

(i) by him in the presence of a witness who attests the signature;

or

(ii) at his direction and in his presence and the presence of two witnesses who each attest the signature;

and

(b) it is delivered as a deed by him or a person authorised to do so on his behalf.

(4) ... (11) ...

This provision has made it far easier in some respects to execute a deed than was the case before 1989.

Tenancies entered into prior to the passing of the Landlord and Tenant (Covenants) Act 1995

The law in this area has recently been changed by the Landlord and Tenant (Covenants) Act 1995 but, as will be mentioned later, the main provisions of this Act apply only to 'new' tenancies, that is to say, tenancies entered into after the coming into force of the Act. For tenancies which already were in existence, the old law will continue to apply except insofar as this is inconsistent with the provisions in ss 17–20, which apply both to 'new' and to 'old' tenancies. For 'old' tenancies, on an assignment of the landlord's reversion, the tenant must continue to comply with all the terms of the tenancy in so far as they have reference to the subject-matter of the lease.

Law of Property Act 1925

141 (1) Rent reserved by a lease, and the benefit of every covenant or provision therein contained, having reference to the subject-matter thereof, and on the lessee's part to be observed or performed, and every condition of re-entry and other condition therein contained, shall be annexed and incident to and shall go with the reversionary estate in the land, or in any part thereof, immediately expectant on the term granted by the lease, notwithstanding severance of that reversionary estate, and without prejudice to any liability affecting a covenantor or his estate.

(2) Any such rent, covenant or provision shall be capable of being recovered, received, enforced, and taken advantage of, by the person from time to time entitled, subject to the term, to the income of the whole or any part, as the case may require, of the land leased.

(3) Where that person becomes entitled by conveyance or otherwise, such rent, covenant or provision may be recovered, received, enforced or taken advantage of by him notwithstanding that he becomes so entitled after the condition of re-entry of forfeiture has become enforceable, but this subsection does not render enforceable any condition of re-entry or other condition

waived or released before such person becomes entitled as aforesaid.

(4) ...

Likewise, in favour of the tenant, the new landlord must observe the covenants entered into by the original landlord insofar as those covenants have reference to the subject-matter of the lease.

Law of Property Act 1925

> s 142 (1) The obligation under a condition or of a covenant entered into by a lessor with reference to the subject-matter of the lease shall, if and as far as the lessor has power to bind the reversionary estate immediately expectant on the term granted by the lease, be annexed and incident to and shall go with that reversionary estate, or the several parts thereof, notwithstanding severance of that reversionary estate, and may be taken advantage of and enforced by the person in whom the term is from time to time vested by conveyance, devolution in law, or otherwise; and, if and as far as the lessor has power to bind the person from time to time entitled to that reversionary estate, the obligation aforesaid may be taken advantage of and enforced against any person so entitled.
>
> (2) ...

On an assignment of the tenancy, the original tenant may continue to be liable for payment of the rent if the assignee has not paid it. (For a discussion of the law relating to the liability of the assignor, see *Deanplan Ltd v Mahmoud* [1992] 3 All ER 945.) He will, however, be able to claim an indemnity against the assignee (see s 77(1)(C) Law of Property Act 1925), but this is unlikely to be of any significance if the assignee is in financial difficulties.

Privity of contract and privity of estate

When either the landlord assigns his reversion or the tenant assigns the tenancy, the assignee will not have a contractual relationship with anyone other than the assignor; 'privity of contract' exists only as between the assignee and assignor. The new landlord (or the new tenant, as the case may be) will still have some relationship to the original tenant (or original landlord) and this relationship is called 'privity of estate'. 'Privity of estate' is a means by which covenants may be enforced between those who are not in a direct contractual relationship; it is a label used to denote that there exists a direct relationship of landlord and tenant (ie there is tenure between the parties) even though there is no privity of contract between them. Thus, there is neither privity of contract nor privity of estate between a head lessor and a sub-tenant.

Tenancies falling within the Landlord and Tenant (Covenants) Act 1995

Most of the provisions of Landlord and Tenant (Covenants) Act 1995 (ie ss 3–16 and 21) apply only to tenancies that came into existence after the date when the Act came into force: 1 January 1996. Sections 17–20, however, apply both to 'new' and to existing tenancies.

Section 2(1) of the Act makes the relevant provisions of the Act applicable to a landlord or a tenant covenant regardless of whether that covenant has 'reference to the subject-matter' of the tenancy (see ss 141 and 142 Law of

Property Act 1925) and whether the covenant is express, implied or imposed by law. Section 3(7) abolishes the rule in *Spencer's case* (1583) 5 Co Rep 16a in relation to 'new' tenancies. Such covenants which involve doing a positive act where the subject-matter is not in existence when the covenant is made, are henceforth governed by s 79(1) Law of Property Act 1925.

The effect of s 3 is that, in general, the burden and benefit of covenants in a tenancy now pass automatically on an assignment of the reversion or of the tenancy. Section 4 also ensures that the landlord's right of re-entry passes on an assignment of the reversion. Under s 5, tenants will be released from liability under the covenant on an assignment of the tenancy. A landlord, however, who assigns the reversion, must apply to be released from liability under the 'landlord' covenants by utilising the procedure set out in s 8.

The new legislation will in the future make the law in relation to the passing of the benefit and burden of covenants between landlord and tenant much easier.

DIFFERENT TYPES OF TENANCY

The common law recognises more than one type of tenancy. One significant distinction is that which exists between fixed-term and periodic tenancies, but statutory intervention has added several additional labels, such as 'assured' tenancy, 'secure' tenancy and 'protected' tenancy. These are explained below.

Fixed-term tenancies

There are three main types of fixed term tenancy:

(1) Many tenancies are expressed to last for a fixed number of years, such as a 99 year building lease. Apart from the formalities required to create such tenancies, this type presents few problems.

(2) A tenancy may be expressed to last for the duration of a certain person's lifetime. Such tenancies are converted into 90 year fixed-term tenancies by s 149(6) Law of Property Act 1925 (see Chapter 2 and the discussion in *Skipton Building Society v Clayton* (1993) 25 HLR 596).

(3) A perpetually renewable lease is one which contains an option to renew on the same terms as the present tenancy. As this will include the option to renew, the tenancy could theoretically continue indefinitely by a series of renewals and is therefore of uncertain duration. Such tenancies are converted into 2,000 year fixed-terms by s 145 Law of Property Act 1922 (see Chapter 3).

Periodic tenancies

Unlike fixed-term tenancies, periodic tenancies have no initial limit on how long they will last, since they automatically continue from one period until the next until brought to an end by the appropriate period of notice. A periodic tenancy can arise expressly, but it may also arise by implication, such as when a person has been allowed into occupation of property with the intention of creating a tenancy and rent is thereafter paid on a periodic basis. Payment of a weekly rent in such circumstances may create the inference of a weekly tenancy, although the surrounding circumstances may negative such an inference (see *Javid v Aqil* [1991] 1 All ER 243).

Periodic tenancies are not contrary to the rule requiring certainty of term, since the tenancy must last for a minimum of one period, and will then continue indefinitely until brought to an end by the appropriate notice to quit (see *Prudential Assurance Co Ltd v London Residuary Body* [1992] 3 All ER 504, *per* Lord Templeman, *Centaploy v Matlodge* [1974] Ch 1 and *Bowen v Anderson* [1894] 1 QB 164).

In the case of a yearly tenancy, the common law requires that six months' notice be given, ending on the first year or on any of its subsequent anniversary dates. A monthly tenancy may be brought to an end by a month's notice to quit, whilst a quarterly tenancy requires four months' notice at common law. A weekly tenancy only requires a week's notice at common law, but this is now subject to the requirements of s 5 Protection From Eviction Act 1977, which provides that written notice of not less than four weeks is required to be given, in the case of premises let as a dwelling, unless the tenancy is an 'excluded tenancy' (see s 3A of the 1977 Act). The common law requirements relating to notice are subject to the statutory protection which has been superimposed by the Rent Act 1977 and by the Housing Acts 1985 and 1988. This is dealt with elsewhere in this book. In the case of a joint periodic tenancy involving two or more joint tenants, notice given by any one of those tenants will bring the tenancy to an end, leaving the unfortunate remaining occupants to either negotiate a new tenancy or to find alternative accommodation (see *Hammersmith & Fulham LBC v Monk* [1991] 3 WLR 1144, [1992] 1 All ER 1 and *Crawley BC v Ure* (1995) 27 HLR 524 and below, p 287). Although hardly acceptable from the viewpoint of the other joint tenants, the rule is in line with the requirement that the 'four unities' of time, title, possession and interest for a joint tenancy remain intact.

A provision which is repugnant to the nature of a periodic tenancy will be struck down. Such provisions usually exclude either the landlord's or the tenant's right to serve notice to quit. In *Centaploy v Matlodge* [1974] Ch 1, a periodic tenancy provided that notice to quit could only be served by the tenant. This term was struck out, since it was repugnant to the nature of a periodic tenancy, which is that notice may be given by either party.

The landlord of a weekly tenant of residential premises is obliged by the Landlord and Tenant Act 1985, to provide the tenant with a rent book or similar document; otherwise the landlord commits a criminal offence unless the rent includes 'payments in respect of board and the value of that board to the tenant forms a substantial proportion of the whole rent'. The obligation to provide the tenant with a rent book and the penalty for non-compliance are contained in ss 4–7 of the 1985 Act.

Landlord and Tenant Act 1985

4. Provision of rent books

(1) Where a tenant has a right to occupy premises as a residence in consideration

of a rent payable weekly, the landlord shall provide a rent book or other similar document or use in respect of the premises.

(2) Subsection (1) does not apply to premises if the rent includes a payment in respect of board and the value of that board to the tenant forms a substantial proportion of the whole rent.

(3) In this section and sections 5 to 7–

(a) 'tenant' includes a statutory tenant and a person having a contractual right to occupy the premises; and

(b) 'landlord', in relation to a person having such a contractual right, means the person who granted the right or any successor in title of his, as the case may require.

5. Information to be contained in rent books

(1) A rent book or other similar document provided in pursuance of section 4 shall contain notice of the name and address of the landlord of the premises and–

(a) if the premises are occupied by virtue of a restricted contract, particulars of the rent and of the other terms and conditions of the contract and notice of such other matters as may be prescribed;

(b) if the premises are let on or subject to a protected or statutory tenancy or let on an assured tenancy within the meaning of Part I of the Housing Act 1988, notice of such matters as may be prescribed.

(2) If the premises are occupied by virtue of a restricted contract or let on or subject to a protected or statutory tenancy or let on an assured tenancy within the meaning of the Part I of the Housing Act 1988, the notice and particulars required by this section shall be in the prescribed form.

(3) ...

6. Information to be supplied by companies

(1) Where the landlord of premises to which section 4(1) applies (premises occupied as a residence at a weekly rent) is a company, and the tenant serves on the landlord a request in writing to that effect, the landlord shall give the tenant in writing particulars of the name and address of every director and of the secretary of the company.

(2) ...

7. Offences

(1) If the landlord of premises to which section 4(1) applies (premises occupied as a residence at a weekly rent) fails to comply with any relevant requirement of–

section 4 (provision of rent book), or

section 5 (information to be contained in rent book), or

section 6 (information to be supplied by companies),

he commits a summary offence and is liable on conviction to a fine not exceeding level 4 on the standard scale.

(2) If the person demands or receives rent on behalf of the landlord of such premises while any relevant requirement of–

section 4 (provision of rent book), or

section 5 (information to be contained in rent book),

is not complied with, then, unless he shows that he neither knew nor had reasonable cause to suspect that any such requirement had not been complied with, he commits a summary offence and is liable to a fine not exceeding level 4 on the standard scale.

(3) If a person fails to comply with a requirement imposed upon him by s 6(2) (duty to forward request to landlord), he commits a summary offence and is liable on conviction to a fine not exceeding level 4 on the standard scale.

(4) If a default in respect of which–

(a) a landlord is convicted of an offence under subsection (1), or

(b) another person is convicted of an offence under subsection (3),

continues for more than 14 days after the conviction, the landlord or other person commits a further offence under that subsection in respect of the default.

Tenancy by estoppel

A tenancy by estoppel may arise where a person purports to grant a tenancy at a time when he himself has a defective title to the property concerned. The 'landlord' may, for example, have contracted to purchase the property but not yet had it conveyed to him at the time he purports to create a tenancy of it. At that stage the 'landlord' will only have an equitable interest himself and so cannot create a legal tenancy. Alternatively, the 'landlord' may have a mortgage on the property which contains terms either forbidding or restricting his right to grant tenancies. The 'tenant' may not be aware of his 'landlord's' defect in title, because a tenant (or subtenant) is not allowed to ask to see the freehold title due to s 44(2) Law of Property Act 1925.

Law of Property Act 1925

44(2) Under a contract to grant or assign a term of years, whether derived or to be derived out of freehold or leasehold land, the intended lessee or assign shall not be entitled to call for the title to the freehold.

If the 'landlord's' title is later perfected, then the tenancy by estoppel is said to be 'fed' and ripens into an ordinary tenancy. But whilst the tenancy remains one by estoppel, certain consequences may follow. First, the 'landlord' cannot deny that he has created a tenancy, since he is estopped from doing so. Second, the tenant cannot avoid liability to the landlord once he has gone into possession and paid rent. Third, the tenancy by estoppel may not be binding on a third party, such as a subsequent mortgagee of the property. A mortgagor may create tenancies of the mortgaged property unless expressly prohibited from doing so in writing: s 99 Law of Property Act 1925 gives this power of leasing to the mortgagor.

Law of Property Act 1925

99(1) A mortgagor of land while in possession shall, as against every incumbrancer, have power to make from time to time any such lease of the mortgaged land, or any part thereof, as is by this section authorised.

(2) ...

(3) The leases which this section authorises are–

(i) agricultural or occupation leases for any term not exceeding twenty-one years, or, in the case of a mortgage made after the commencement of this Act fifty years; and

(ii) building leases for any term not exceeding ninety-nine years, or, in the case of a mortgage made after the commencement of this Act nine hundred and ninety-nine years.

(4) ... (5) ...

(6) Every such lease shall reserve the best rent that can reasonably be obtained, regard being had to the circumstances of the case, but without any fine being taken.

(7) Every such lease shall contain a covenant by the lessee for payment of the rent, and a condition of re-entry on the rent not being paid within a time therein specified not exceeding thirty days.

(8) ... (12) ...

(13) This section applies only if and as far as a contrary intention is not expressed by the mortgagor and mortgagee in the mortgage deed, or otherwise in writing, and has effect subject to the terms of the mortgage deed or of any such writing and to the provisions therein contained.

(14) ... (19) ...

Building society mortgages commonly exclude this power of leasing altogether, since such leases would cause the mortgagee problems in gaining vacant possession in the event of default by the mortgagor. But some mortgages do allow the mortgagor to lease the mortgaged property with the mortgagee's prior consent.

Tenancy by estoppel came into prominence in the 1950s, culminating in the decision in *Church of England Building Society v Piskor* [1954] Ch 553. That case decided that a mortgagor had for a very short time an unencumbered legal estate in between acquiring the property from the vendor and mortgaging it to the mortgagee. In that short interval (called the scintilla temporis), the rights of the person to whom the mortgagor had granted a tenancy in advance of completion of the sale crystallised into legal rights; the tenancy by estoppel was therefore 'fed' by the mortgagor's subsequent acquisition of the legal estate. The tenancy by estoppel then became an ordinary legal tenancy which ranked ahead of the rights of the mortgagee, preventing the latter from gaining vacant possession of the property. Little was then heard of tenancy by estoppel until 1990, when two cases involving estoppel came before the court. In *Abbey National Building Society v Cann* [1990] 2 WLR 832, [1990] 1 All ER 1085, the House of Lords overruled Piskor's case on the grounds that it was inconsistent with other authorities. *Abbey National v Cann* concerned the question whether an overriding interest under s 70(1)(g) Land Registration Act 1925, crystallised at the date of transfer (or creation) or at the date of registration of an interest, but the issue of estoppel and its 'feeding' by the acquisition of the legal estate was also raised.

The overruling of *Piskor's* case means that any tenancy by estoppel arising before the mortgage will now only be effective as between the landlord and the tenant. The tenant will be thrown back on the remedies for breach of contract against a landlord who is already in financial difficulties with a mortgagee who is seeking vacant possession. Since the only realistic remedy available to the tenant will be an award of damages, this leaves him in a very weak position. What use is such an award against someone who is unable to pay?

Abbey National v Cann does not deal with the situation in which the tenancy is created after the mortgage and in breach of its terms. This situation did arise, however, in *Britannia Building Society v Earl* [1990] 1 WLR 422, [1990] 2 All ER 469. In that case, the mortgage deed prohibited any letting of the premises without the consent of the mortgagee but the mortgagor nevertheless subsequently let the property to tenants without the mortgagee's consent. Whilst this tenancy would be binding on the mortgagor as landlord, it would not necessarily be binding on the mortgagee, since the mortgagor's title would be 'defective' in the sense that he had restricted his otherwise unencumbered title by contract with the mortgagee, and given up any power to grant leases. The mortgagor fell into arrears on the mortgage payments and the mortgagee sought vacant possession of the property. The tenants claimed, *inter alia*, to be statutory tenants under the Rent Act 1977, with the right to remain even as against the mortgagee. The Court of Appeal held that the tenants had not become statutory tenants as against the mortgagee, even though they were statutory tenants as against the mortgagor. The situation was considered to be no different in principle from that where a tenant is a contractual tenant, as in the case of *Dudley and District Benefit Building Society v Emerson* [1949] Ch 707, in which it had been held that a contractual tenancy granted after a mortgage and in breach of its terms was liable to be defeated by the title paramount of the mortgagee. The tenant therefore has no rights against the mortgagee. Of course, the tenant could always sue the landlord for breach of contract, but that will not provide him with a roof over his head and is unlikely in the circumstances to provide him with financial compensation either.

The two decisions discussed above leave the tenant by estoppel in a precarious position, dependent on the financial viability of the landlord. In times of economic recession, when home owners are encouraged or forced to make extra income from letting their property, the decisions above are a blow to the security of the residential tenant. What is the point of Rent Act or Housing Act security of tenure if it does not guarantee that you can remain in the property? It is suggested that those mortgagees who know of the letting in breach of the mortgage and have either encouraged it or have failed to do anything about it ought to be estopped from gaining vacant possession at a later date. The problem with this, however, is that the person who would wish to argue estoppel is not the same person as the one who has been encouraged by the mortgagee to meet the payments on the mortgage by letting part of the property to a tenant; there is no reliance on the part of the tenant. Any gaps in this area of the law can only be filled by Parliament, unless the House of Lords subsequently decides that the above decisions were wrong.

Tenancy at will

A tenancy at will has been described as 'where the tenancy is on terms that either party may determine it at any time' (*per* Nicholls LJ in *Javad v Aqil* [1991] 1 All ER 243 at 244, para j). In other words, the so-called 'tenant' occupies the property at the will of the 'landlord', who may ask the tenant to leave at any time without giving the usual period of notice.

A tenancy at will may be granted expressly, but it can also arise by implication. This occurred in *Javad v Aqil*, a case involving non-residential premises, where a prospective tenant was allowed into possession and made periodic payments whilst the negotiations for a formal tenancy were continuing.

Tenancy at sufferance

A tenancy at sufferance may arise where a lawful tenant remains in the property without permission after the tenancy has come to an end. A tenant at sufferance is similar in some respects to a trespasser, but with the distinction that the tenant at sufferance entered the property originally as a lawful entrant.

A tenancy at sufferance must be distinguished from a statutory tenancy under the Rent Act 1977, a statutory periodic tenancy under the Housing Act 1988 and a periodic tenancy under the Housing Act 1985. All of these forms of tenancy automatically follow at the end of the original contractual tenancy, irrespective of the landlord's wishes.

Protected and statutory tenancies

Under the Rent Act 1977, the status of a protected tenant is conferred on a tenant who falls within s 1 and whose contractual tenancy has not yet come to an end by either the passing of time or notice, but who qualifies for protection under the Act. At the end of the contractual tenancy, the tenant (or his statutory successor) if resident, may enjoy security of tenure as a 'statutory' tenant (or 'statutory tenant by succession'). These labels and their implications are discussed in more detail elsewhere in this book (see Chapter 7).

Assured tenancy and assured shorthold tenancy

The Housing Act 1988 introduced a new form of assured tenancy with the Housing Act's counterpart of Rent Act security of tenure. The Housing Act 1988, however, is far less generous to tenants compared to the Rent Act 1977, particularly in relation to grounds for possession. The Housing Act 1988, also introduced the assured shorthold tenancy (a 'shorthold' was also possible under the Housing Act 1980) which confers no security of tenure beyond that which is provided under the general law of landlord and tenant, but which enables a tenant to challenge an excessive rent payable under the tenancy.

The principle behind the Housing Act 1988, unlike the Rent Act 1977, was to disentangle security of tenure from protection of tenants against high rent levels. The 1988 Act has achieved this to a large extent through the assured and the assured shorthold tenancies. Both of these types of tenancy are discussed in more detail elsewhere in this book (see Chapter 7). However, the general principle is that an assured tenancy confers security of tenure but little protection against high rents, whilst an assured shorthold tenancy, as mentioned above, confers no security of tenure at the end of the contractual period but does provide very limited protection against excessive rent levels. The Housing Act 1996, makes amendments in relation to both types of tenancy.

Secure tenancy

A public sector tenant who enjoys security of tenure under the Housing Act 1985, is referred to as a 'secure' tenant. This status, with some exceptions, confers on the tenant various benefits, including the right to buy the freehold of the property. This type of tenancy is also discussed in more detail elsewhere in this book (see Chapter 8). The Housing Act 1996 enables local authorities to offer 'introductory tenancies' to new tenants which will last for one year and which may be terminated at the end thereof by a court order; if no such order is obtained by the end of the year, a secure tenancy will arise. (See ss 124, 125 and 130 of the 1996 Act.)

Excluded tenancy

Section 31 Housing Act 1988 created the concept of an 'excluded tenancy' for the purposes of ss 3 and 5 Protection From Eviction Act 1977. These two provisions concern prohibition of eviction without due process and validity of notices to quit respectively. The excluded tenancy is discussed in Chapter 5, but it involves the landlord or a member of his family sharing accommodation with the tenant and the landlord occupying the same building (which, in the case of sharing with a member of the landlord's family, is not a purpose-built block of flats) as his only or principal home.

FORMALITIES REQUIRED FOR THE CREATION OF A LEASE OR TENANCY

Tenancies can be either legal or equitable, but in order to create a legal tenancy certain formalities must be complied with. Under s 52 Law of Property Act 1925, a deed is required to give rise to a legal estate in land. However, there are certain exceptions to this requirement which are dealt with in s 54(2). This provision enables a short legal tenancy to be created quite informally, even without writing, if the tenancy is to last for no longer than three years, takes effect 'in possession', and is for the best rent obtainable without asking for the payment of a premium. In the case of land which remains under the old-style unregistered title system of conveyancing, there is no need to register a legal tenancy, but an equitable tenancy does need to be registered as a Class C(iv) land charge if it is to be binding on third parties (see s 2(4)(iv) Land Charges Act 1972). In the case of registered title, however, a legal tenancy itself may need to be registered on the Title Register. All tenancies in registered land which have more than 21 years unexpired term must be registered, but those for 21 years or less may qualify as 'overriding interests', either under s 70(1)(g) or 70(1)(k). Those which do not fall into either of the two previous categories should be protected as 'minor interests' through the entry of a 'notice' or 'caution' on the register; these tenancies will often be equitable tenancies (see ss 8, 48, 54 and 70(1)(k) Land Registration Act 1925).

A tenancy may arise in equity for a period exceeding three years because it was not created by deed. The application of equitable principles will save the tenancy even if the correct formalities have not been complied with. The status of 'equitable tenancy' is arrived at by going through various stages:

(1) The tenancy is invalid as a legal tenancy, since it was not created by deed.

(2) The transaction may be treated as a specifically enforceable contract to convey or create a legal tenancy at some future date.

(3) Since the transaction is treated as a contract, this brings in the availability of the remedies for breach of contract. Whilst the award of damages remains a possibility, the equitable remedy of specific performance is regarded as the more appropriate remedy where contracts concerning land are involved. Certain conditions, however, must be complied with before equity, in its discretion, will grant this form of remedy. First, the contract must comply with any necessary formalities and second, the claimant must have acted equitably, since 'he who comes to equity must come with clean hands'.

In order for the contract to be upgraded into an equitable tenancy, it must of course be supported by consideration, but equity requires more than would suffice for consideration at common law. 'Valuable consideration' must be provided and the contract must comply with s 2 Law of Property (Miscellaneous Provisions) Act 1989, ie be in writing and incorporate all the terms which the parties have agreed to. In these circumstances, equity is prepared to anticipate in advance the fulfilment of the landlord's obligation to perform the contract and therefore regards the tenancy as effective in equity; hence the label 'equitable tenancy' is applied to the agreement.

One problem which may arise is whether this equitable tenancy takes precedence over a parallel legal periodic tenancy. The parties to the contract for a tenancy may have acted upon the agreement on the supposition that a legal tenancy has already been created by it. The tenant may have gone into possession of the property and paid rent on a periodic basis. This may create the inference of a periodic legal tenancy which may be inconsistent with the terms of the equitable tenancy arising from the written contract. Rent, for example, is normally payable in arrears, but the written contract may have specified that rent is to be paid in advance. Which tenancy is to take precedence? This issue arose in *Walsh v Lonsdale* [1882] 21 ChD 9, which was decided after the Judicature Acts 1873–75, gave precedence to rules of equity. In that case, the landlord granted a seven year tenancy on the terms that the rent should be paid in advance, but the agreement was not by deed. The tenant went into possession and paid rent in arrears, thereby acquiring a yearly periodic tenancy under which the rent is payable in arrears. The landlord demanded that rent should be paid in advance in accordance with the terms of the written agreement; when the tenant refused, the landlord sought to recover the rent by levying distress (ie seizing goods on the premises in payment of outstanding rent). The tenant sought specific performance of the seven year agreement and damages for trespass and wrongful distress. The court ruled that the equitable tenancy took precedence over the legal periodic tenancy and rent was therefore payable in advance

Walsh v Lonsdale

Sir George Jessel MR: The question is one of some nicety. There is an agreement for a lease under which possession has been given. Now since the Judicature Act the possession is held under the agreement. There are not two estates as there were formerly, one estate at common law by reason of the payment of rent from year to year, and an estate in equity under the agreement. There is only one court, and the equity rules prevail in it. The tenant holds under an agreement for a lease. He holds, therefore, under the same terms in equity as if the lease had been granted, it being a case in which both parties admit that relief is capable of being given by specific performance. That being so, he cannot complain of the exercise by the landlord of the same rights as the landlord would have had if a lease had been granted. On the other hand, he is protected in the same way as if a lease had been granted; he cannot be turned out by six months' notice as a tenant from year to year. He has a right to say, 'I have a lease in equity, and you can only re-enter if I have committed such a breach of covenant as would if a lease had been granted have entitled you to re-enter according to the terms of a proper proviso for re-entry.' That being so, it appears to me that being a lessee in equity he cannot complain of the of the right of distress merely because the actual parchment has not been signed and sealed.

The application of the doctrine from *Walsh v Lonsdale* depends on the availability of specific performance; if specific performance cannot be granted, the tenancy will be governed solely by the legal periodic tenancy. But where specific performance is available, *Walsh v Lonsdale* operates to convert into an equitable tenancy both a defectively executed lease and contract for a lease.

It is sometimes said that 'an agreement for a lease is as good as a lease' due to the effect of *Walsh v Lonsdale*, but an equitable tenancy does have certain weaknesses compared to a legal tenancy:

(1) An equitable tenant is thought to be outside the realms of 'privity of estate' as against a successor in title to the landlord. This, subject to the Landlord and Tenant (Covenants) Act 1995, affects the enforceability of leasehold covenants between them; it also affects their enforceability as between the original landlord and anyone to whom the equitable tenant has assigned the equitable tenancy.

(2) An equitable tenant cannot invoke in his favour the 'general words' contained in s 62 Law of Property Act 1925, under which certain licences may be upgraded into easements (see, for example, *Wright v Macadam* [1949] 2 KB 744). An equitable lease is not a 'conveyance' within s 62.

(3) The equitable tenant's position against third parties depends on whether the equitable tenancy has been protected in the correct manner. In the case of unregistered title to land, this depends upon registration of the equitable tenancy as an estate contract land charge; in the case of registered land, the tenancy should be protected by either notice or caution on the register unless the tenant qualifies as having an overriding interest within s 70(1)(g) of the Land Registration Act 1925, by virtue of being a person in actual occupation of the land.

These problems apart, an equitable tenant is no worse off than a legal tenant.

RENT BOOKS AND OTHER INFORMATION

Landlords of residential premises are also normally required to provide each of their weekly tenants with a rent book which contains the name and address of the landlord and certain other specified information, for instance, about security of tenure (see Landlord and Tenant Act 1985 ss 4 and 5). The penalty for non-compliance is that the landlord commits a criminal offence, but the requirement does not apply in favour of a tenant whose rent includes a payment in respect of board and where the value of that board forms a substantial proportion of the whole rent.

In the case of an assured tenant under the Housing Act 1988 and a protected or statutory tenant under the Rent Act 1977, the rent book to be issued to a weekly tenant must be in a form, and contain the matters prescribed by statutory instrument (see Rent Book (Forms of Notice) Regulations SI 1982/1474, as amended).

The Landlord and Tenant Acts 1985 and 1987 further provide that in the case of any tenancy of premises occupied as a dwelling (see 1985 Act) or of premises which include a dwelling not covered by Part II Landlord and Tenant Act 1954 (see 1987 Act) certain information must be provided by the landlord for the tenant's benefit. The relevant sections of these statutes are set out below.

Landlord and Tenant Act 1985

1. Disclosure of landlord's identity

(1) If the tenant of premises occupied as a dwelling makes a written request for the landlord's name and address to–

    (a) any person who demands, or the last person who received, rent payable under the tenancy, or

    (b) any other person for the time being acting as agent for the landlord, in relation to the tenancy, that person shall supply the tenant with a written statement of the landlord's name and address within the period of 21 days beginning with the day on which he receives the request.

(2) A person who, without reasonable excuse, fails to comply with subsection (1) commits a summary offence and is liable on conviction to a fine not exceeding level 4 on the standard scale.

(3) In this section and section 2–

    (a) 'tenant' includes a statutory tenant; and

    (b) 'landlord' means the immediate landlord.

2. Disclosure of directors, &c of corporate landlord

(1) Where a tenant is supplied under section 1 with the name and address of his landlord and the landlord is a body corporate, he may make a further written request to the landlord for the name and address of every director and of the secretary of the landlord.

(2) The landlord shall supply the tenant with a written statement of the information requested within the period of 21 days beginning with the day on which he receives the request.

(3) ...

(4) A landlord who, without reasonable excuse, fails to comply with a requirement imposed upon him by subsection (3), commits a summary offence and is liable on conviction to a fine not exceeding level 4 on the standard scale.

3. Duty to inform tenant of assignment of landlord's interest

(1) If the interest of the landlord under a tenancy of premises which consist of or include a dwelling is assigned, the new landlord shall give notice in writing

of the assignment, and of his name and address, to the tenant not later than the next day on which rent is payable under the tenancy or, if that is within two months of the assignment, the end of that period of two months.

(2) ...

(3) A person who is the new landlord under a tenancy falling within subsection (1) and who fails, without reasonable excuse, to give the notice required by that subsection, commits a summary offence and is liable on conviction to a fine not exceeding level 4 on the standard scale.

(3A) The person who was the landlord under the tenancy immediately before the assignment ('the old landlord') shall be liable to the tenant in respect of any breach of covenant, condition or agreement under the tenancy occurring before the end of the relevant period in like manner as if the interest assigned were still vested in him; and where the new landlord is also liable to the tenant in respect of any such breach occurring within that period, he and the old landlord shall be jointly and severally liable in respect of it.

(3B) In subsection (3A) 'the relevant period' means the period beginning with the date of the assignment and ending with the date when–

(a) notice in writing of the assignment, and of the new landlord's name and address, is given to the tenant by the new landlord (whether in accordance with subsection (1) or not), or

(b) notice in writing of the assignment and of the new landlord's name and last-known address, is given to the tenant by the old landlord,

whichever happens first.

(4) In this section

(a) 'tenancy' includes a statutory tenancy, and

(b) references to the assignment of the landlord's interest include any conveyance other than a mortgage or charge.

Landlord and Tenant Act 1987

Information to be furnished to tenants

46. Application of Part VI, etc

(1) This Part applies to premises which consist of or include a dwelling and are not held under a tenancy to which Part II of the Landlord and Tenant Act 1954 applies.

(2) In this Part 'service charge' has the meaning given by section 18(1) of the 1985 Act.

47. Landlord's name and address to be contained in demands for rent etc

(1) Where any written demand is given to a tenant of premises to which this Part applies the demand must contain the following information, namely–

(a) the name and address of the landlord,

(b) if that address is not in England and Wales, an address in England and Wales at which notices (including notices in proceedings) may be served on the landlord by the tenant.

(2) Where–

(a) a tenant of any such premises is given such a demand, but

(b) it does not contain any information required to be contained in it by virtue of subsection (1), then (subject to subsection (3)) any part of the amount demanded which consists of a service charge ('the relevant amount') shall be treated for all purposes as not being due from the tenant to the landlord at any time before that information is furnished by the landlord by notice given to the tenant.

(3) ...

(4) In this section 'demand' means a demand for rent or other sums payable to the landlord under the terms of the tenancy.

48. Notification by landlord of address for service of notices

(1) A landlord of premises to which this Part applies shall by notice furnish the tenant with an address in England and Wales at which notices (including notices in proceedings) may be served on him by the tenant.

(2) Where a landlord of any such premises fails to comply with subsection (1), any rent or service charge otherwise due from the tenant to the landlord shall (subject to subsection (3)) be treated for all purposes as not being due from the tenant to the landlord at any time before the landlord does comply with that subsection.

(3) ...

49. Extension of circumstances in which notices are sufficiently served

In section 196 of the Law of Property Act 1925 (regulations respecting notices), any reference in subsection (3) or (4) to the last-known place of abode or business of the person to be served shall have effect, in its application to a notice to be served by a tenant on a landlord of premises to which this Part applies, as if that reference included a reference to–

(a) the address last furnished to the tenant by the landlord in accordance with section 48, or

(b) if no address has been so furnished in accordance with section 48, the address last furnished to the tenant by the landlord in accordance with section 47.

Indi
No Services

Secure for
fibre

Assured
for contrs

CHAPTER 3

THE DISTINCTION BETWEEN A LEASE AND A LICENCE

INTRODUCTION

This chapter is concerned with the distinction which the law draws between a lease (or tenancy) and a licence. The label which the parties choose to place on an agreement is not decisive; an agreement described as a 'licence' may therefore create a tenancy (see, for example, *Addiscombe Garden Estates Ltd v Crabbe* [1958] 1 QB 513 and *Skipton Building Society v Clayton* (1993) 25 HLR 596). What, then, is the essential difference between a lease and a licence?

A lease can give rise to one of the two legal estates which are possible under s 1(1) Law of Property Act 1925, the other being the freehold estate (referred to as the fee simple) which is vested in the owner of the property. A licence cannot confer a legal estate on the licensee. A lease grants to the tenant an interest in the relevant property; a licence, on the other hand, gives merely a personal permission to occupy, without which the licensee would be a trespasser. One consequence of this distinction is the ability of a tenancy to bind third parties. A licence, however, according to orthodox opinion, is merely personal to the parties, though it is accepted that in a limited number of cases a licence may bind a third party who acquires the fee simple.

The distinction between a lease and a licence is still crucial because many of the protections offered to tenants are not offered at all, or to the same degree, to persons who have been given merely a licence to occupy. This distinction is of particular importance in the private sector. Both the Housing Act 1988 and the Rent Act 1977, for instance, give full security of tenure to many tenants, but not to licensees, because of the statutory requirement that a dwelling must have been 'let' for either of the statutes to apply. Some protection is given to licensees by other statutes, such as the Protection From Eviction Act 1977.

This is not the case, however, under the Housing Act 1985 which applies in the public sector. An occupant of a council house, if in exclusive possession, may have a secure status despite being only a licensee, unless the licence was granted merely as a temporary expedient to a person who entered originally as a trespasser (see s 79(3) and (4) Housing Act 1985. Compare, however, *Westminster City Council v Clarke* [1992] 2 WLR 229).

The Protection from Eviction Act 1977, gives some protection to certain classes of licensee (see ss 1, 3 and 5). Nevertheless, it still remains true, as a broad generalisation, that the status of a tenant is more secure than that of a licensee. It is for this reason that property owners have, in the past, been keen to ensure that they created nothing more than a licence in favour of a residential occupant. This is not quite so important today, because the Housing Act 1988 is not so generous in its extent of security of tenure to tenants as the Rent Act 1977 is, and the former Act applies to most tenancies granted on or after 15 January 1989 (see Chapter 7).

There are still, however, some residential agreements which were entered into before the operative date of the Housing Act 1988 and for which the distinction between a lease and a licence remains crucial. The distinction may still be important even if the agreement was entered into after 1988, following the decision in *Skipton Building Society v Clayton* (1993) 25 HLR 596. Since 1988, a lessee will normally enjoy protection as an 'assured tenant' or have an 'assured shorthold tenancy', but in Skipton Building Society the tenancy agreement was 'rent free', which took it out of the 1988 Act 'assured tenancy' provisions.

There are also other reasons why a property owner might still wish to create only a licence even today, despite the diminution in protection brought about by the Housing Act 1988. The Protection from Eviction Act 1977, for example, excludes certain licences ('excluded licences') from the ambit of ss 3 and 5 (Prohibition without Due Process of Law and Validity of Notices to Quit) as a result of amendments introduced by the Housing Act 1988. In addition, the rules about repairing obligations under s 11 Landlord and Tenant Act 1985 do not apply to licences.

This chapter will discuss the essential requirements of a tenancy and the continuing problems that the courts have faced when applying those requirements to specific situations.

THE ESSENTIAL REQUIREMENTS OF A TENANCY

There are certain situations where an occupant is obviously a licensee rather than a tenant: a relative who comes to stay for a few weeks as a paying guest is obviously not a tenant, but other situations are more borderline. Is the student who lives with a family during term-time, for example, and who shares all but a bedroom with members of that family more accurately classified as a licensee or as a tenant? And the long-term private occupant of a hostel or residential home for the elderly is not easy to categorise either (see *Westminster City Council v Clarke* (above) and *Abbeyfield (Harpenden) Society Ltd v Woods* [1986] 1 WLR 374). The starting point for any discussion of the difference between a lease and a licence is the House of Lords' decision in *Street v Mountford* [1985] AC 809, [1985] 2 All ER 289, (1985) 17 HLR 402.

Prior to this case, the courts had often looked at the intention of the parties as being the crucial means for distinguishing a tenancy from a licence. This had been demonstrated most significantly in *Somma v Hazelhurst and Savelli* [1978] 1 WLR 1014. That case, the report of which obligingly for landlords reproduced the entire text of the agreement, had involved an agreement which was to provide a blue-print for future agreements made by those who did not want to grant a tenancy.

It was to be overruled, however, by *Street v Mountford*. *Street v Mountford* concerned an agreement by which Mr Street gave to Mrs Mountford the right to occupy two furnished rooms in a house for £37.00 per week. The agreement stated that Mrs Mountford accepted that there was no intention to create a tenancy protected by the Rent Act but there was no clause which purported to deny to Mrs Mountford exclusive occupation of the rooms, and it was conceded that Mrs Mountford enjoyed exclusive possession. Lord Templeman identified three hallmarks by which to distinguish a lease from a licence. These were:

(1) Exclusive possession;

(2) For a term; and

(3) At a rent.

If all these factors are shown to be present, it is likely that the agreement will create a tenancy rather than a licence.

Street v Mountford

Lord Templeman: ... My Lords, there is no doubt that the traditional distinction between a tenancy and a licence of land lay in the grant of land for a term at a rent with exclusive possession. In some cases it was not clear at first sight whether exclusive possession was in fact granted. For example, an owner of land could grant a licence to cut and remove standing timber. Alternatively, the owner could grant a tenancy of the land with the right to cut and remove standing timber during the term of the tenancy. The grant of rights relating to standing timber therefore required careful consideration in order to decide whether the grant conferred exclusive possession of the land for a term at a rent and was therefore a tenancy or whether it merely conferred a bare licence to remove the timber ...

In the case of residential accommodation there is no difficulty in deciding whether the grant confers exclusive possession. An occupier of residential accommodation at a rent for a term is either a lodger or a tenant. The occupier is a lodger if the landlord provides attendance or services which require the landlord or his servants to exercise unrestricted access to and use of the premises. A lodger is entitled to live in the premises but cannot call the place his own. In *Allan v Liverpool Overseers* (1874) LR 9 QB 180, 191–192 Blackburn J said:

> 'A lodger in a house, although he has the exclusive use of rooms in the house, in the sense that nobody else is to be there, and though his goods are stowed there, yet he is not in exclusive occupation in that sense, because the landlord is there for the purpose of being able, as landlords commonly do in the case of lodgings, to have his own servants to look after the house and the furniture, and has retained to himself the occupation, though he has agreed to give the exclusive enjoyment of the occupation to the lodger.'

If on the other hand residential accommodation is granted for a term at a rent with exclusive possession, the landlord providing neither attendance nor services, the grant is a tenancy; any express reservation to the landlord of limited rights to enter and view the state of the premises and to repair and maintain the premises only serves to emphasise the fact that the grantee is entitled to exclusive possession and is a tenant. In the present case it is conceded that Mrs Mountford is entitled to exclusive possession and is not a lodger. Mr Street provided neither attendance nor services and only reserved the limited rights of inspection and maintenance and the like set forth in clause 3 of the agreement. On the traditional view of the matter, Mrs Mountford not being a lodger must be a tenant.

There can be no tenancy unless the occupier enjoys exclusive possession; but an occupier who enjoys exclusive possession is not necessarily a tenant. He may be an owner in fee simple, a trespasser, a mortgagee in possession, an object of charity or an occupier. To constitute a tenancy the occupier must be granted exclusive possession fixed or periodic term certain in consideration of a premium or periodical payments. The grant may be express, or may be inferred where the owner accepts weekly or periodic payments from the occupier.

Occupation by service occupier may be eliminated. A service occupier is a servant who occupies his master's premises in order to perform his duties as a servant. In those circumstances the possession and occupation of the servant is treated as the possession and occupation of the master and the relationship of landlord and tenant is not created; see *Mayhew v Suttle* (1854) 4 El&Bl 347. The test is whether the servant requires the premises he occupies in order the better to perform his duties as a servant:

> 'Where the occupation is necessary for the performance of services, and the occupier is required to reside in the house in order to perform those services, the occupation being strictly ancillary to the performance of the duties which the occupier has to perform, the occupation is that of a servant', *per* Mellor J in *Smith v Seghill Overseers* (1875) LR 10 QB 422 at 428.

The cases on which Mr Goodhart relies begin with *Booker v Palmer* [1942] 2 All ER 674. The owner of a cottage agreed to allow a friend to install an evacuee in the cottage rent free for the duration of the war. The Court of Appeal held that there was no intention on the part of the owner to enter into legal relationships with the evacuee.

Lord Greene MR, said, at p 677:

> 'To suggest there is an intention there to create a relationship of landlord and tenant appears to me to be quite impossible. There is one golden rule which is of very general application, namely, that the law does not impute intention to enter into legal relationships where the circumstances and the conduct of the parties negative any intention of the kind. It seems to me that this is a clear example of the application of that rule.'

The observations of Lord Greene MR were not directed to the distinction between a contractual tenancy and a contractual licence. The conduct of the parties (not their professed intentions) indicated that they did not intend to contract at all.

In the present case the agreement dated 7 March 1983 professed an intention by both parties to create a licence and their belief that they had in fact created a licence. It was submitted on behalf of Mr Street that the court cannot in these circumstances decide that the agreement created a tenancy without interfering with the freedom of contract enjoyed by both parties. My Lords, Mr Street enjoyed freedom to offer Mrs Mountford the right to occupy the rooms comprised in the agreement on such lawful terms as Mr Street pleased. Mrs Mountford enjoyed freedom to negotiate with Mr Street to obtain different terms. Both parties enjoyed freedom to contract or not to contract and both parties exercised that freedom by contracting on the terms set forth in the written agreement and on no other terms. But the consequences in law of the agreement concluded, can only be determined by consideration of the effect of the agreement. If the agreement satisfied all the requirements of a tenancy, then the agreement produced a tenancy and the parties cannot alter the effect of the agreement by insisting that they only created a licence. The manufacture of a five-pronged implement for manual digging results in a fork even if the manufacturer, unfamiliar with the English language, insists that he intended to make and has made a spade.

It was also submitted that, in deciding whether the agreement created a tenancy or a licence, the court should ignore the Rent Acts. If Mr Street has succeeded, where owners have failed these past 70 years, in driving a coach and horses through the Rent Acts, he must be left to enjoy the benefit of his ingenuity unless and until Parliament intervenes. I accept that the Rent Acts are irrelevant to the problem of determining the legal effect of the rights granted by the agreement. Like the professed intention of the parties, the Rent Acts cannot alter the effect of the agreement.

In *Marcroft Wagons Ltd v Smith* [1951] 2 KB 496 the daughter of a deceased tenant who lived with her mother claimed to be a statutory tenant by succession and the landlords asserted that the daughter had no rights under the Rent Acts and was a trespasser. The landlords expressly refused to accept the daughter's claims but accepted rent from her while they were considering the position. If the landlords had decided not to apply to the court for possession but to accept the daughter as a tenant, the moneys paid by the daughter would have been treated as rent. If the landlords decided, as they did decide, to apply for possession and to prove, as they did prove, that the daughter was not a statutory tenant, the moneys paid by the daughter were treated as mesne profits. The Court of Appeal held with some hesitation that the landlords never accepted the daughter as tenant and never intended to contract with her although the landlords delayed for some six months before applying to the court for possession. Roxburgh J said, at p 507:

'Generally speaking, when a person, having a sufficient estate in land, lets another into exclusive possession, a tenancy results, and there is no question of a licence. But the inference of a tenancy is not necessarily to be drawn where a person succeeds on a death to occupation of rent-controlled premises and a landlord accepts some rent while he or the occupant, or both of them, is or are considering his or their position. If this is all that happened in this case, then no tenancy would result.'

In that case, as in *Booker v Palmer*, the court deduced from the conduct of the parties that they did not intend to contract at all.

Errington v Errington and Woods [1952] 1 KB 290 concerned a contract by a father to allow his son to buy the father's house on payment of the instalments of the father's building society loan. Denning LJ referred, at p 297, to the judgment of Lord Greene MR in *Booker v Palmer* [1942] 2 All ER 674, 677 where, however, the circumstances and the conduct of the parties negatived any intention to enter into legal relationships ...

In *Errington v Errington and Woods* [1952] 1 KB 290 and in the cases cited by Denning LJ at p 297 there were exceptional circumstances which negatived the *prima facie* intention to create a tenancy, notwithstanding that the occupier enjoyed exclusive occupation. The intention to create a tenancy was negatived if the parties did not intend to enter into legal relationships at all, or where the relationship between the parties was that of vendor and purchaser, master and service occupier, or where the owner, a requisitioning authority, had no power to grant a tenancy. These exceptional circumstances are not to be found in the present case, where there has been the lawful, independent and voluntary grant of exclusive possession for a term at a rent.

If the observations of Denning LJ are applied to the facts of the present case it may fairly be said that the circumstances negative any intention to create a mere licence. Words alone do not suffice. Parties cannot turn a tenancy into a licence merely by calling it one. The circumstances and the conduct of the parties show that what was intended was that the occupier should be granted exclusive possession at a rent for a term with a corresponding interest in the land which created a tenancy.

In *Cobb v Lane* [1952] 1 TLR 1037, an owner allowed her brother to occupy a house rent free. The county court judge, who was upheld by the Court of Appeal, held that there was no intention to create any legal relationship and that a tenancy at will was not to be implied. This is another example of conduct which negatives any intention of entering into a contract, and does not assist in distinguishing a contractual tenancy from a contractual licence.

In *Facchini v Bryson* [1952] 1 TLR 1386, an employer and his assistant entered into an agreement which, *inter alia*, allowed the assistant to occupy a house for a weekly payment on terms which conferred exclusive possession. The assistant did not occupy the house for the better performance of his duty and was not therefore a service occupier. The agreement stipulated that 'nothing in this agreement shall be construed to create a tenancy between the employer and the assistant. Somervell LJ said at p 1389:

> 'If, looking at the operative clauses in the agreement, one comes to the conclusion that the rights of the occupier, to use a neutral word, are those of a lessee, the parties cannot turn it into a licence by saying at the end "this is deemed to be a licence"; nor can they, if the operative paragraphs show that it is merely a licence, say that it should be deemed to be a lease.'

Denning LJ referred to several cases including *Errington v Errington and Woods* and *Cobb v Lane* and said at pp 1389–1390:

> 'In all the cases where an occupier has been held to be a licensee there has been something in the circumstances, such as a family arrangement, an act of friendship or generosity, or such like, to negative any intention to create a tenancy ... In the present case, however, there are no special circumstances. It is a simple case where the employer let a man into occupation of a house in consequence of his employment at a weekly sum payable by him. The occupation has all the features of a service tenancy, and the parties cannot by the mere words of their contract turn it into something else. Their relationship is determined by the law and not by the label which they choose to put on it.'

The decision, which was thereafter binding on the Court of Appeal and on all lower courts, referred to the special circumstances which are capable of negativing an intention to create a tenancy and reaffirmed the principle that the professed intentions of parties are irrelevant. The decision also indicated that in a simple case a grant of exclusive possession of residential accommodation for a weekly sum creates a tenancy.

In *Murray Bull & Co Ltd v Murray* [1952] 2 All ER 1079, [1953] 1 QB 211 a contractual tenant held over, paying rent quarterly. McNair J found, at p 217:

> 'both parties intended that the relationship should be that of licensee and no more ... The primary consideration on both sides was that the defendant, as occupant of that flat, should not be a controlled tenant.'

In my opinion this case was wrongly decided. McNair J, citing the observations of Denning LJ in *Errington v Errington and Woods* [1952] 1 KB 290, 297 and *Marcroft Wagons Ltd v Smith* [1951] 2 KB 496 failed to distinguish between, first, conduct which negatives an intention to create legal relationships, second, special circumstances which prevent exclusive occupation from creating a tenancy and, third, the professed intention of the parties. In *Murray Bull & Co Ltd v Murray* the conduct of the parties showed an intention to contract and there were no relevant special circumstances. The tenant holding over continued by agreement to enjoy exclusive possession and to pay a rent for a term certain. In those circumstances he continued to be a tenant notwithstanding the professed intention of the parties to create a licence and their desire to avoid a controlled tenancy.

In *Addiscombe Garden Estates Ltd v Crabb* [1958] 1 QB 513 the Court of Appeal considered an agreement relating to a tennis club carried on in the grounds of a hotel. The agreement was–

'described by the parties as a licence ... the draftsman has studiously and successfully avoided the use either of the word "landlord" or the word "tenant" throughout the document' *per* Jenkins LJ at p 522.

On analysis of the whole of the agreement the Court of Appeal came to the conclusion that the agreement conferred exclusive possession and thus created a tenancy ...

In the agreement in the *Addiscombe* case it was by no means clear until the whole of the document had been narrowly examined that exclusive possession was granted by the agreement. In the present case it is clear that exclusive possession was granted and so much is conceded. In these circumstances it is unnecessary to analyse minutely the detailed rights and obligations contained in the agreement.

In the *Addiscombe* case Jenkins LJ referred, at p 528, to the observations of Denning LJ in *Errington v Errington and Woods* to the effect that 'The test of exclusive possession is by no means decisive'. Jenkins LJ continued:

'I think that wide statement must be treated as qualified by his observations in *Facchini v Bryson* [1952] 1 TLR 1386, 1389; and it seems to me that, save in exceptional cases of the kind mentioned by Denning LJ, in that case, the law remains that the fact of exclusive possession, if not decisive against the view that there is a mere licence, as distinct from a tenancy, is at all events a consideration of the first importance.'

Exclusive possession is of first importance in considering whether an occupier is a tenant; exclusive possession is not decisive because an occupier who enjoys exclusive possession is not necessarily a tenant. The occupier may be a lodger or service occupier or fall within the other exceptional categories mentioned by Denning LJ in *Errington v Errington and Woods* [1952] 1 KB 290 ...

In *Abbeyfield (Harpenden) Society Ltd v Woods* [1968] 1 WLR 374 the occupier of a room in an old peoples home was held to be a licensee and not a tenant. Lord Denning MR said at 376:

'The modern cases show that a man may be a licensee even though he has exclusive possession, even though the word "rent" is used, and even though the word "tenancy" is used. The court must look at the agreement as a whole and see whether a tenancy really was intended. In this case there is, besides the one room, the provision of services, meals, a resident housekeeper, and such like. The whole arrangement was so personal in nature that the proper inference is that he was a licensee.'

As I understand the decision in the Abbeyfield case the court came to the conclusion that the occupier was a lodger and was therefore a licensee not a tenant.

In *Shell-Mex & BP Ltd v Manchester Garages Ltd* [1971] 1 WLR 612, the Court of Appeal, after carefully examining an agreement whereby the defendant was allowed to use a petrol company's filling station for the purposes of selling petrol, came to the conclusion that the agreement did not grant exclusive possession to the defendant, who was therefore a licensee. At p 615 Lord Denning MR in considering whether the transaction was a licence or a tenancy said:

'Broadly speaking, we have to see whether it is a personal privilege given to a person, in which case it is a licence, or whether it grants an interest in land, in which case it is a tenancy. At one time it used to be thought that exclusive possession was a decisive factor. But that is not so. It depends on broader considerations altogether. Primarily on whether it is personal in its nature or not: see *Errington v Errington and Woods* [1952] 1 KB 290.'

In my opinion the agreement was only 'personal in its nature' and created 'a personal privilege' if the agreement did not confer the right to exclusive possession of the filling station. No other test for distinguishing between a contractual tenancy and a contractual licence appears to be understandable or workable.

Heslop v Burns [1974] 1 WLR 1241 was another case in which the owner of a cottage allowed a family to live in the cottage rent free and it was held that no tenancy at will had been created on the grounds that the parties did not intend any legal relationship. Scarman LJ cited with approval, at p 1252, the statement by Denning LJ in *Faccini v Bryson* [1952] 1 TLR 1386, 1389:

> 'In all the cases where an occupier has been held to be a licensee there has been something in the circumstances, such as a family arrangement, an act of friendship or generosity, or such like, to negative any intention to create a tenancy.'

In *Marchant v Charters* [1977] 1 WLR 1181 a bedsitting room was occupied on terms that the landlord cleaned the rooms daily and provided clean linen each week. It was held by the Court of Appeal that the occupier was a licensee and not a tenant. The decision in the case is sustainable on the grounds that the occupier was a lodger and did not enjoy exclusive possession. But Lord Denning MR said, at p 1185:

> 'What is the test to see whether the occupier of one room in a house is a tenant or a licensee? It does not depend on whether he or she has exclusive possession or not. It does not depend on whether the room is furnished or not. It does not depend on whether the occupation is permanent or temporary. It does not depend on the label which the parties put on it. All these are factors which may influence the decision but none of them is conclusive. All the circumstances have to be worked out. Eventually the answer depends on the nature and quality of the occupancy. Was it intended that the occupier should have a stake in the room or did he have only permission for himself personally to occupy the room, whether under a contract or not? In which case he is a licensee.'

But in my opinion, in order to ascertain the nature and quality of the occupancy and to see whether the occupier has or has not a stake in the room or only permission for himself personally to occupy, the court must decide whether on its true construction the agreement confers on the occupier exclusive possession. If exclusive possession at a rent for a term does not constitute a tenancy then the distinction between a contractual tenancy and a contractual licence of land becomes wholly unidentifiable.

In *Somma v Hazelhurst* [1978] 1 WLR 1014 a young unmarried couple, H and S, occupied a double bed-sitting room for which they paid a weekly rent.

The landlord did not provide services or attendance and the couple were not lodgers but tenants enjoying exclusive possession. But the Court of Appeal did not ask itself whether H and S were lodgers or tenants and did not draw the correct conclusion from the fact that H and S enjoyed exclusive possession. The Court of Appeal was diverted from the correct inquiries by the fact that the landlord obliged H and S to enter into separate agreements and reserved power to determine each agreement separately. The landlord also insisted that the room should not in form be let to either H or S or to both H and S but that each should sign an agreement to share the room in common with such other persons as the landlord might from time to time nominate. The sham nature of this obligation would have been only slightly more obvious if H and S had been married or if the room had been furnished with a double bed instead of two single beds. If the landlord had served notice on H to leave and had required S to share the room with a strange man, the notice would only have been a disguised notice to quit on both H and S The room was let and taken as residential accommodation with exclusive possession in order that H and S might live together in undisturbed quasi-connubial bliss making weekly payments. The agreements signed by H and S constituted the grant to H and S jointly of exclusive possession at a rent for a term for the purposes for which the room was taken and the agreement therefore created a tenancy. Although the Rent Acts must not be allowed to alter or influence the construction of an agreement, the court should, in my opinion, be astute to detect and frustrate sham devices and artificial transactions whose only object is to disguise the grant of a tenancy and to evade the Rent Acts. I would disapprove of the decision in this case that H and S were only licensees and for the same reason would disapprove of the decision in *Aldrington Garages Ltd v Fielder* (1978) 37 P&CR 461 and *Sturolson & Co v Weniz* (1984) 272 EG 326. In the present case the Court of Appeal held that the agreement dated 7 March 1983 only created a licence. Slade LJ accepted that the agreement and in particular clause 3 of the agreement 'shows that the right to occupy the premises conferred on the defendant was intended as an exclusive right of occupation, in that it was thought necessary to give a special and express power to the plaintiff to enter ...'. Before your Lordships it was conceded that the agreement conferred the right of exclusive possession on Mrs Mountford. Even without clause 3 the result would have been the same. By the agreement Mrs Mountford was granted the right to occupy residential accommodation. Mr Street did not provide any services or attendance. It was plain that Mrs Mountford was not a lodger. Slade LJ proceeded to analyse all the provisions of the agreement, not for the purpose of deciding whether his finding of exclusive possession was correct, but for the purpose of assigning some of the provisions of the agreement to the category of terms which he thought are usually to be found in a tenancy agreement and of assigning other provisions to the category of terms which he thought are usually to be found in a licence. Slade LJ may or may not have been right that in a letting of a furnished room it was 'most unusual to find a provision in a tenancy agreement obliging the tenant to keep his rooms in a "tidy condition"'. If Slade LJ was right about this and other provisions there is still no logical method of evaluating the results of his survey. Slade LJ reached the conclusion that 'the agreement bears all the hallmarks of a licence, rather than a tenancy, save for the one important feature of exclusive occupation'. But in addition to the hallmark of exclusive occupation of residential accommodation there were the hallmarks of weekly payments for a periodical term. Unless these three hallmarks are decisive, it really becomes impossible to distinguish a contractual tenancy from a contractual licence save by reference to the professed intention of the parties or by the judge awarding marks for drafting. Slade LJ was finally impressed by the statement at the foot of the agreement by Mrs Mountford 'I understand and accept that a licence in the above form does not and is not intended to give me a tenancy protected under the Rent Acts'. Slade LJ said, at p 330:

> 'it seems to me that, if the defendant is to displace the express statement of intention embodied in the declaration, she must show that the declaration was either a deliberate sham or at least an inaccurate statement of what was the true substance of the real transaction agreed between the parties ...'

My Lords, the only intention which is relevant is the intention demonstrated by the agreement to grant exclusive possession for a term at a rent. Sometimes it may be difficult to discover whether, on the true construction of an agreement, exclusive possession is conferred. Sometimes it may appear from the surrounding circumstances that there was no intention to create legal relationships. Sometimes it may appear from the surrounding circumstances that the right to exclusive possession is referable to a legal relationship other than a tenancy. Legal relationships to which the grant of exclusive possession might be referable and which would or might negative the grant of an estate or interest in the land include occupancy under a contract for the sale of the land, occupancy pursuant to a contract of employment or occupancy referable to the holding of an office. But where as in the present case the only circumstances are that residential accommodation is offered and accepted with exclusive possession for a term at a rent, the result is a tenancy.

The position was well summarised by Windeyer J sitting in the High Court of Australia in *Radaich v Smith* (1959) 101 CLR 209, 222, where he said:

> 'What then is the fundamental right which a tenant has that distinguishes his position from that of a licensee? It is an interest in land as distinct from a personal permission to enter the land and use it for some stipulated purpose or purposes. And how is it to be ascertained whether such an interest in land has been given? By seeing whether the grantee was given a legal right of exclusive possession of the land for a term or from year to year or for a life or lives. If he was, he is a tenant. And he cannot be other than a tenant, because a legal right of exclusive possession is a tenancy and the creation of such a right is a demise. To say that a man who has, by agreement with a landlord, a right of exclusive possession of land for a term is not a tenant is simply to contradict the first proposition by the second. A right of exclusive possession is secured by the right of a lessee to maintain ejectment and, after his entry, trespass. A reservation to the landlord, either by contract or statute, of a limited right of entry, as for example to view or repair, is, of course, not inconsistent with the grant of exclusive possession. Subject to such reservations, a tenant for a term or from year to year or for a life or lives can exclude his landlord as well as strangers from the demised premises. All this is long-established law: see Cole on Ejectment (1857) pp 72, 73, 287, 458.'

My Lords, I gratefully adopt the logic and the language of Windeyer J. Henceforth the courts which deal with these problems will, save in exceptional circumstances, only be concerned to inquire whether as a result of an agreement relating to residential accommodation the occupier is a lodger or a tenant. In the present case I am satisfied that Mrs Mountford is a tenant, that the appeal should be allowed ...

The effect of this decision has been to provide a starting point from which to begin to resolve the lease/licence problem. The House of Lords explained earlier authorities, in which the intention of the parties had been considered as important, by suggesting that the arrangements in some of those cases lacked any intention to create legal relations, a prerequisite for any contractual relationship. Many of the earlier cases, it was said, could be explained on the basis that the arrangement was either a 'family' one or one where the landowner was acting out of generosity.

The House of Lords, however, did not resolve all future problems in *Street v Mountford*. There is still a volume of case law, some of which has had to address the problem of granting accommodation to two or more persons by means of separate agreements, each described as a licence. It is not uncommon for this to happen and for each occupant to be denied, either jointly or separately, exclusive possession of the accommodation concerned. Are such agreements to be taken at face value, or are they in reality sham devices intended to hide what is a joint tenancy between all the occupants? It was noted in *Booker Settled Estates Ltd v Ayres* (1987) 19 HLR 246, for example, that the decision in *Street v Mountford* did not create a presumption of a joint tenancy in such cases. This issue can therefore only be addressed on a case by case basis.

It is instructive to look at the three criteria identified in *Street v Mountford* in the light of the subsequent case-law, before being able to draw any conclusions.

Exclusive possession

In *Street v Mountford*, Lord Templeman identified 'exclusive possession' as the single most important factor which distinguishes a lease from a licence. Without exclusive possession, there cannot be a tenancy. It has been said that in the absence of some other legal relationship to which it can be attributed, the grant of a legal right to exclusive possession by a body with power to grant it to a body with power to take it, creates the relationship of landlord and tenant: see *London Borough of Camden v Shortlife Community Housing et al* [1993] 25 HLR 330.

Exclusive possession is often contrasted with exclusive occupation. The former means that an occupant is legally entitled to exclude all persons from the accommodation, including the landlord, unless those persons are exercising rights of access; the latter, as a description of the factual situation, refers to the fact that the occupant does not share the living accommodation with others, but does not mean that he has the right to exclude all comers from the premises. The importance of exclusive possession is illustrated in the joined cases of *AG Securities v Vaughan; Antoniades v Villiers* [1988] 3 All ER 1058.

In the former case, as a response to the extension of protection (in 1974, by the Rent Act of that year) to furnished lettings, the owner of a large four bedroom flat entered into separate agreements with four occupants. Each agreement was described as a licence and none of the occupants was entitled to exclusive possession of the whole flat.

Each occupant paid a different rent from the others and each agreement had started on a different date. The four occupants did not have any prior acquaintanceship with each other but came to the flat as individuals. The House of Lords had to decide whether in these circumstances the four occupants were licensees or joint tenants. A joint tenancy requires the presence of the 'four unities' of time, title, possession and interest. Here, these were not all present. The House of Lords therefore concluded that the occupants were contractual licensees. Lord Oliver considered that the agreements did accurately reflect the true bargain between the respective parties. The fact that each occupant had arrived independently of the others at a different time and paid a different rent showed that the agreements were not sham transactions.

In *Antoniades v Villiers*, two people, who wanted to live together as a couple in a one bedroom flat, had each signed separate but identical agreements. Each agreement was labelled 'Licence', and stated that the occupant did not have exclusive possession and gave the owner the right to use the rooms together with the licensee. The House of Lords held that these agreements were interdependent, since neither would have been entered into without the other. The two agreements were therefore to be read together as constituting a single transaction, the nature of which was to create a joint tenancy.

Certain parts of each agreement were clearly a sham, included with the sole object of denying to the couple the protection of the Rent Act 1977. When these parts were put to one side and ignored, the couple were left with an agreement which gave to them joint exclusive possession (exclusive possession having been granted jointly to the two cohabitees), for a term, at a rent and hence there was a joint tenancy.

AG Securities v Vaughan; Antoniades v Villiers

Lord Templeman: My Lords, in each of the two appeals now under consideration, the question is whether the owner of residential accommodation granted a tenancy or granted licences.

In the first appeal, the appellant company, AG Securities, owned a block of flats, Linden Mansions, Hornsey Lane, London. Flat 25 consists of six living rooms in addition to a kitchen and bathroom. The company furnished four living rooms as bedrooms, a fifth as a lounge and a sixth as a sitting room. In 1974 furnished lettings became subject to the Rent Acts. If the company granted exclusive possession of the flat to one single occupier or to two or more occupiers jointly in consideration of periodical payments, the grant would create a tenancy of the flat. If the company granted exclusive possession of one bedroom to four different occupiers with joint use of the lounge, sitting room, kitchen and bathroom, each of the four grants would create a tenancy of one bedroom. Exclusive possession means either exclusive occupation or receipt of rents and profits. The company entered into separate agreements with four different applicants. Each agreement was in the same form, and was expressed to be made between the company as 'the owner' and the applicant as 'Licensee' ...

In the second appeal, the appellant, Mr Antoniades, is the owner of the house, 6 Whiteley Road, Upper Norwood. The attic was converted into furnished residential accommodation comprising a bedroom, a bed-sitting room, kitchen and bathroom. The furniture in the sitting room consisted of a bed-settee, a table-bed, a sideboard and a chair.

The appellants, Mr Villiers and Miss Bridger, spent three months looking for a flat where they could live together. In February 1985 they were shown the attic flat. The bedroom lacked a bed; the appellants expressed a preference for a double bed which Mr Antoniades agreed to provide. Mr Antoniades and Mr Villiers entered into an agreement dated 9 February 1985. The agreement was described as a licence, Mr Antoniades was described as 'the licensor' and Mr Villiers was described as 'the licensee'.

The agreement recited that 'the licensor is not willing to grant the licensee exclusive possession of any part of the rooms hereinafter referred to' and that 'the licensor is anxious to secure the use of the rooms notwithstanding that such use be in common with the licensor and such other licensees or invitees as the licensor may permit from time to time to use the said rooms' ...

Mr Antoniades entered into a separate agreement and a separate addendum with Miss Bridger. The agreement and the addendum were in the same form, bore the same date, were executed on the same day and were signed and witnessed in the same way as the agreement and addendum entered into by Mr Villiers.

Thereupon Mr Villiers and Miss Bridger entered into occupation of the rooms comprised in the agreement. Mr Antoniades has never attempted to use any of the rooms or authorised any other person to use the rooms.

The appellants, Mr Villiers and Miss Bridger, claim that they became tenants of the whole of the attic flat. Mr Antoniades contends that each appellant is a licensee.

My Lords, ever since 1915 the Rent Acts have protected some tenants of residential accommodation with security of tenure and maximum rents. The scope and effect of the Rent Acts have been altered from time to time and the current legislative protection is contained in the Rent Act 1977 ...

Parties to an agreement cannot contract out of the Rent Acts; if they were able to do so the Acts would be a dead letter because in a state of housing shortage a person seeking residential accommodation may agree to anything to obtain shelter. The Rent Acts protect a tenant but they do not protect a licensee. Since parties to an agreement cannot contract out of the Rent Acts, a document which expresses the intention, genuine or bogus, of both parties or of one party to create a licence will nevertheless create a tenancy if the rights and obligations enjoyed and imposed satisfy the legal requirements of a tenancy. A person seeking residential accommodation may concur in any expression of intention in order to obtain shelter. Since parties to an agreement cannot contract out of the Rent Acts, a document expressed in the language of a licence must nevertheless be examined and construed by the court in order to decide whether the rights and obligations enjoyed and imposed create a licence or a tenancy. A person seeking residential accommodation may sign a document couched in any language in order to obtain shelter. Since parties to an agreement cannot contract out of the Rent Acts, the grant of a tenancy to two persons jointly cannot be concealed, accidentally or by design, by the creation of two documents in the form of licences. Two persons seeking residential accommodation may sign any number of documents in order to obtain joint shelter. In considering one or more documents for the purpose of deciding whether a tenancy has been created, the court must consider the surrounding circumstances, including any relationship between the prospective occupiers, the course of negotiations and the nature and extent of the accommodation and the intended and actual mode of occupation of the accommodation ...

The enjoyment of exclusive occupation for a term in consideration of periodical payments creates a tenancy, save in exceptional circumstances not relevant to these appeals: see *Street v Mountford* [1985] 2 All ER 289 at 300, [1985] AC 809 at 826–827. The grant of one room with exclusive occupation in consideration of a periodic payment creates a tenancy, although if the room is not a dwelling the tenant is not protected by the Rent Acts: see *Curl v Angelo* [1948] 2 All ER 189. The grant of one room with exclusive occupation as a dwelling creates a tenancy, but, if a tenant shares some other essential living premises such as a kitchen with his landlord or other persons, the room is not let as a separate dwelling within the meaning of s 1 of the Rent Act 1977: see *Neale v Del Soto* [1945] 1 All ER 191, [1945] KB 144 and *Cole v Harris* [1945] 2 All ER 146, [1945] KB 474. Section 21 of the 1977 Act confers some rights on a tenant who shares essential living premises with his landlord, and s 22 confers protection on a tenant who shares some essential living premises with persons other than the landlord.

If, under an agreement, the owner of residential accommodation provides services or attendance and retains possession for that purpose the occupier is a lodger and the agreement creates a licence. Under an agreement for the exclusive occupation of a room or rooms consisting of a dwelling for periodic payments then, save in the exceptional circumstances mentioned in *Street v Mountford*, a single occupier, if he is not a lodger, must be a tenant. The agreement may provide, expressly or by implication, power for the owner to enter the dwelling to inspect or repair but if the occupier is entitled to the use and enjoyment of the dwelling and is not a lodger he is in exclusive occupation and the agreement creates a tenancy.

Where residential accommodation is occupied by two or more persons the occupiers may be licensees or tenants of the whole or each occupier may be a separate tenant of part. In the present appeals the only question raised is whether the occupiers are licensees or tenants of the whole.

In the first appeal under consideration the company entered into four separate agreements with four separate persons between 1982 and 1985. The agreements were in the same form save that the periodical sum payable under one agreement did not correspond to the sum payable pursuant to any other agreement. The company was not bound to make agreements in the same form or to require any payment. The agreement signed by Mr Vaughan in 1982 did not and could not entitle or compel Mr Vaughan to become a joint tenant of the whole of the flat with Mr Cook in 1985 on the terms of Mr Vaughan's agreement or on the terms of Mr Cook's agreement or on the terms of any other agreement either alone with Mr Cook or together with any other persons. In 1985 Mr Vaughan did not agree to become a joint tenant of the flat with Mr Cook or anybody else. In 1985, in the events which had happened, the company possessed the right reserved to the company by cl 2(3) of Mr Vaughan's agreement to authorise Mr Cook to share the use of the flat in common with Mr Vaughan. In 1985 Mr Vaughan orally agreed with Mr Cook that, if the company authorised Mr Cook to use the flat in common with Mr Vaughan, then Mr Vaughan would allow Mr Cook to occupy a specified bedroom in the flat and share the occupation of the other parts of the flat excluding the other three bedrooms. Mr Vaughan's agreement with the company did not prevent him from entering into this oral agreement with Mr Cook. Under the standard form agreement the company did not retain power to allocate the four bedrooms but delegated this power to the occupiers for the time being. If the occupiers had failed to allocate the bedrooms the company would have been obliged to terminate one or more of the agreements. The respondents claim that they are joint tenants of the flat. No single respondent claims to be a tenant of a bedroom. The Court of Appeal (Fox and Mustill LJJ, Sir George Waller dissenting) ([1988] 2 All ER 173, [1988] 2 WLR 689) concluded that the four respondents were jointly entitled to exclusive occupation of the flat. I am unable to agree. If a landlord who owns a three bedroom flat enters into three separate independent tenancies with three independent tenants each of whom is entitled to one bedroom and to share the common parts, then the three tenants, if they agree, can exclude anyone else from the flat. But they do not enjoy exclusive occupation of the flat jointly under the terms of their tenancies. In the present case, if the four respondents had been jointly entitled to exclusive occupation of the flat then, on the death of one of the respondents, the remaining three would be entitled to joint and exclusive occupation. But, in fact, on the death of one respondent the remaining three would not be entitled to joint and exclusive occupation of the flat. They could not exclude a fourth person nominated by the company. I would allow the appeal.

In the first appeal the four agreements were independent of one another. In the second appeal the two agreements were interdependent. Both would have been signed or neither. The two agreements must therefore be read together. Mr Villiers and Miss Bridger applied to rent the flat jointly and sought and enjoyed joint and exclusive occupation of the whole of the flat. They shared the rights and the obligations imposed by the terms of their occupation. They acquired joint and exclusive occupation of the flat in consideration of periodical payments and they therefore acquired a tenancy jointly.

Mr Antoniades required each of them, Mr Villiers and Miss Bridger, to agree to pay one half of each aggregate periodical payment, but this circumstance cannot convert a tenancy into a licence. A tenancy remains a tenancy even though the landlord may choose to require each of two joint tenants to agree expressly to pay one-half of the rent. The tenancy conferred on Mr Villiers and Miss Bridger the right to occupy the whole flat as their dwelling. Clause 16 reserved to Mr Antoniades the power at any time to go into occupation of the flat jointly with Mr Villiers and Miss Bridger. The exercise of that power would at common law put an end to the exclusive occupation of the flat by Mr Villiers and Miss Bridger, terminate the tenancy of Mr Villiers and Miss Bridger and convert Mr Villiers and Miss Bridger into licensees. But the powers reserved to Mr Antoniades by cl 16 cannot be lawfully exercised because they are inconsistent with the provisions of the Rent Acts.

When Mr Antoniades entered into the agreements dated 9 February 1985 with Mr Villiers and Miss Bridger and when Mr Antoniades allowed Mr Villiers and Miss Bridger to occupy the flat, it is clear from the negotiations which had taken place, from the surrounding circumstances and from subsequent events, that Mr Antoniades did not intend in February 1985, immediately or contemporaneously, to share occupation or to authorise another person to deprive Mr Villiers and Miss Bridger of exclusive occupation of the flat. Clause 16, if genuine, was a reservation by a landlord of a power at some time during the currency of the tenancy to share occupation with the tenant. The exclusive occupation of the tenant coupled with the payment of rent created a tenancy which at common law could be terminated and converted into a licence as soon as the landlord exercised his power to share occupation. But under the Rent Acts, if a contractual tenancy is terminated, the Acts protect the occupiers from eviction ...

In *Street v Mountford* [1985] 2 All ER 289 at 299, [1985] AC 809 at 825 I said:

> 'Although the Rent Acts must not be allowed to alter or influence the construction of an agreement the court should, in my opinion, be astute to detect and frustrate sham devices and artificial transactions whose only object is to disguise the grant of a tenancy and to evade the Rent Acts.'

It would have been more accurate and less liable to give rise to misunderstandings if I had substituted the word 'pretence' for the references to 'sham devices' and 'artificial transactions'. *Street v Mountford* was not a case which involved a pretence concerning exclusive possession. The agreement did not mention exclusive possession and the owner conceded that the occupier enjoyed exclusive possession. In *Somma v Hazelhurst* [1978] 2 All ER 1011, [1978] 1 WLR 1014 and other cases considered in *Street v Mountford* the owner wished to let residential accommodation but to avoid the Rent Acts. The occupiers wished to take a letting of residential accommodation. The owner stipulated for the execution of agreements which pretended that exclusive possession was not to be enjoyed by the occupiers. The occupiers were obliged to acquiesce with this pretence in order to obtain the accommodation. In my opinion the occupiers either did not understand the language of the agreements or assumed, justifiably, that in practice the owner would not violate their privacy. The owner's real intention was to rely on the language of the agreement to escape the Rent Acts. The owner allowed the occupiers to enjoy jointly exclusive occupation and accepted rent. A tenancy was created. *Street v Mountford* reasserted three principles. First, parties to an agreement cannot contract out of the Rent Acts. Second, in the absence of special circumstances, not here relevant, the enjoyment of exclusive occupation for a term in consideration of periodic payments creates a tenancy. Third, where the language of licence contradicts the reality of lease, the facts must prevail. The facts must prevail over the language in order that the parties may not contract out of the Rent Acts. In the present case cl 16 was a pretence.

The fact that Clause 16 was a pretence appears from its terms and from the negotiations. Clause 16 in terms conferred on Mr Antoniades and other persons the right to share the bedroom occupied by Mr Villiers and Miss Bridger. Clause 16 conferred power on Mr Antoniades to convert the sitting room occupied by Mr Villiers and Miss Bridger into a bedroom which could be jointly occupied by Mr Villiers, Miss Bridger, Mr Antoniades and any person or persons nominated by Mr Antoniades. The facilities in the flat were not suitable for sharing between strangers. The flat, situated in an attic with a sloping roof, was too small for sharing between strangers. If cl 16 had been genuine there would have been some discussion between Mr Antoniades, Mr Villiers and Miss Bridger as to how cl 16 might be operated in practice and in whose favour it was likely to be operated.

The addendum imposed on Mr Villiers and Miss Bridger sought to add plausibility to the pretence of sharing by forfeiting the right of Mr Villiers and Miss Bridger to continue to occupy the flat if their double-bedded romance blossomed into wedding bells. Finally and significantly, Mr Antoniades never made any attempt to obtain increased income from the flat by exercising the powers which cl 16 purported to reserve to him. Clause 16 was only designed to disguise the grant of a tenancy and to contract out of the Rent Acts. In this case in the Court of Appeal Bingham LJ said ([1988] 2 All ER 309 at 317, [1988] 3 WLR 139 at 148):

'The written agreements cannot possibly be construed as giving the occupants (jointly or severally) exclusive possession of the flat or any part of it. They stipulate with reiterated emphasis that the occupants shall not have exclusive possession.'

My Lords, in *Street v Mountford* [1985] 2 All ER 289, [1985] AC 809 this House stipulated with reiterated emphasis that an express statement of intention is not decisive and that the court must pay attention to the facts and surrounding circumstances and to what people do as well as to what people say.

In *Somma v Hazlehurst* [1978] 2 All ER 1011, [1978] 1 WLR 1014 a young unmarried couple applied to take a double bed-sitting room in order that they might live together. Each signed an agreement to pay £38.80 per month to share the use of the room with the owner and with not more than one other person at any one time. The couple moved into the bed-sitting room and enjoyed exclusive occupation. In terms the owner reserved the right to share living and sleeping quarters with the two applicants. If the couple parted and the youth moved out, the owner could require the damsel to share her living and sleeping quarters with the owner and with a stranger or with one of them or move out herself. The couple enjoyed exclusive occupation until the owner decided to live with them or until one of their agreements was terminated. The right reserved to the owner to require the applicants or one of the applicants to share with the owner or some other third party was contrary to the provisions of the Rent Acts and in addition was, in the circumstances, a pretence intended only to get round the Rent Acts ...

In *Hadjiloucas v Crean* [1987] 3 All ER 1008, [1988] 1 WLR 1006 two single ladies applied to take a two-roomed flat with kitchen and bathroom. Each signed an agreement to pay £260 per month to share the use of the flat with one other person. The two ladies moved into the flat and enjoyed exclusive occupation. In terms, if the agreement of one lady was terminated, the owner could require the other to share the flat with a stranger. The county court judge decided that the agreements only created licences. The Court of Appeal ordered a retrial in order that all the facts might be investigated. Since, however, the two ladies applied for and enjoyed exclusive occupation unless and until one of their agreements was terminated, the ladies acquired a tenancy protected by the Rent Acts. The reservation to the owner of the right at common law to require one of the ladies to share the flat with a stranger was a pretence.

My Lords, in each of the cases which were disapproved by this House in *Street v Mountford*, and in the second appeal now under consideration, there was, in my opinion, the grant of a joint tenancy for the following reasons. (1) The applicants for the flat applied to rent the flat jointly and to enjoy exclusive occupation. (2) The landlord allowed the applicants jointly to enjoy exclusive occupation and accepted rent. A tenancy was created. (3) The power reserved to the landlord to deprive the applicants of exclusive occupation was inconsistent with the provisions of the Rent Acts. (4) Moreover, in all the circumstances the power which the landlord insisted on to deprive the applicants of exclusive occupation was a pretence only intended to deprive the applicants of the protection of the Rent Acts.

The Court of Appeal (Bingham and Mann LJJ) ([1988] 2 All ER 309, [1988] 3 WLR 139) decided in the second appeal under consideration that Mr Villiers and Miss Bridger were licensees. I would restore the order of his Honour Judge MacNair, who declared that Mr Villiers and Miss Bridger were tenants protected by the Rent Acts.

Lord Oliver of Aylmerton: *Antoniades v Villiers and another*

The appellants in this appeal are a young couple who at all material times were living together as man and wife. In about November 1984 they learnt from a letting agency that a flat was available in a house at 6 Whiteley Road, London SE 19, owned by the respondent, Mr Antoniades. They inspected the flat together and were told that the rent would be £174 per month. They were given the choice of having the bedroom furnished with a double bed or two single beds and they chose a double bed. So, right from the inception, there was never any question but that the appellants were seeking to establish a joint home and they have, at all material times, been the sole occupants of the flat. There is equally no question but that the premises are not suitable for occupation by more than one couple, save on a very temporary basis. The small living room contains a sofa capable of being converted into a double bed and also a bed-table capable of being opened out to form a narrow single bed. The appellants did in fact have a friend to stay with them for a time in what the trial judge found to be cramped conditions, but the size of the accommodation and the facilities available clearly do not make the flat suitable for multiple occupation. When it came to drawing up the contractual arrangements under which the appellants were to be let into possession, each was asked to and did sign a separate licence agreement in the terms set out in the speech of my noble and learned friend under which each assumed an individual, but not a joint, responsibility for payment of one-half of the sum of £174 previously quoted as the rent.

There is an air of total unreality about these documents read as separate and individual licences in the light of the circumstance that the appellants were together seeking a flat as a quasi-matrimonial home. A separate licensee does not realistically assume responsibility for all repairs and all outgoings. Nor in the circumstances can any realistic significance be given to cll 16 and 17 of the document. It cannot realistically have been contemplated that the respondent would either himself use or occupy any part of the flat or put some other person

39

in to share accommodation specifically adapted for the occupation by a couple living together. These clauses cannot be considered as seriously intended to have any practical operation or to serve any purpose apart from the purely technical one of seeking to avoid the ordinary legal consequences attendant on letting the appellants into possession at a monthly rent. The unreality is enhanced by the reservation of the right of eviction without court order, which cannot seriously have been thought to be effective, and by the accompanying agreement not to get married, which can only have been designed to prevent a situation arising in which it would be quite impossible to argue that the 'licensees' were enjoying separate rights of occupation.

The conclusion seems to me irresistible that these two so-called licences, executed contemporaneously and entered into in the circumstances already outlined, have to be read together as constituting in reality one single transaction under which the appellants became joint occupiers. That of course does not conclude the case because the question still remains: what is the effect?

The document is clearly based on the form of document which was upheld by the Court of Appeal as an effective licence in *Somma v Hazlehurst* [1978] 2 All ER 1011, [1978] 1 WLR 1014. That case, which rested on what was said to be the impossibility of the two licensees having between them exclusive possession, was overruled in *Street v Mountford* [1985] 2 All ER 289, [1985] AC 809. It was, however, a case which related to a single room and it is suggested that a similar agreement relating to premises containing space which could, albeit uncomfortably, accommodate another person is not necessarily governed by the same principle. On the other hand, in this case the trial judge found that apart from the few visits by the respondent (who, on all but one occasion, sought admission by knocking on the door) no one shared with the appellants and that they had exclusive possession. He held that the licences were 'artificial transactions designed to evade the Rent Acts', that a tenancy was created and that the appellants occupied as joint tenants.

His decision was reversed by the Court of Appeal on, broadly, the grounds that he had erred in treating the subsequent conduct of the parties admissible as an aid to construction of the agreements and that, in so far as the holding above referred to constituted a finding that the licences were a sham, that was unsupported by the evidence inasmuch as the appellants intention that they should enjoy exclusive possession was not shared by the respondent (see [1988] 2 All ER 309, [1988] 3 WLR 139). The licences could not, therefore, be said to mask the real intention of the parties and fell to be construed by reference to what they said in terms.

If the documents fail to be taken seriously at their face value and to be construed according to their terms, I see, for my part, no escape from the conclusion at which the Court of Appeal arrived. If it is once accepted that the respondent enjoyed the right, whether he exercised it or not, to share the accommodation with the appellants, either himself or by introducing one or more other persons to use the flat with them, it is, as it seems to me, incontestable that the appellants cannot claim to have had exclusive possession. The appellants' case therefore rests, as counsel for the appellants frankly admits, on upholding the judge's approach that the true transaction contemplated was that the appellants should jointly enjoy exclusive possession and that the licences were mere sham or window-dressing to indicate legal incidents which were never seriously intended in fact, but which would be inconsistent with the application to that transaction of the Rent Acts. Now to begin with, I do not, for my part, read the notes of the judge's judgment as showing that he construed the agreement in the light of what the parties subsequently did. I agree entirely with the Court of Appeal that if he did that he was in error. But, though subsequent conduct is irrelevant as an aid to construction, it is certainly admissible as evidence on the question of whether the documents were or were not genuine documents giving effect to the parties' true intentions. Broadly what is said by counsel for the appellants is that nobody acquainted with the circumstances in which the parties had come together and with the physical layout and size of the premises could seriously have imagined that the clauses in the licence which, on the face of them, contemplate the respondent and an apparently limitless number of other persons moving in to share the whole of the available accommodation, including the bedroom, with what, to all intents and purposes, was a married couple committed to paying £174 a month in advance, were anything other than a smoke-screen; and the fact the respondent, who might be assumed to want to make the maximum profit out of the premises, never sought to introduce any one else is at least some indication that that is exactly what it was.

Adopting the definition of a sham formulated by Purchas LJ in *Hadjiloucas v Crean* [1987] 3 All ER 1008 at 1014, [1988] 1 WLR 1006 at 1013, counsel for the appellants submits that the licences clearly incorporate clauses by which neither party intended to be bound and which were obviously a smoke-screen to cover the real intentions of both contracting parties. In the Court of Appeal Bingham LJ tested the matter by asking two questions, viz ([1987] 3 All ER 1008 at 317, [1988] 3 WLR 139 at 149): (1) on what grounds, if one party had left the premises, could the remaining party have been made liable for anything other than the £87 which he or she had agreed to pay? (2) on what ground could they have resisted a demand by the respondent to introduce a further person into the premises? For my part, however, I do not see how this helps. The assumed negative answers prove nothing, for they rest on the assumption that the licences are not sham documents, which is the question in issue.

If the real transaction was, as the judge found, one under which the appellants became joint tenants with exclusive possession, on the footing that the two agreements are to be construed together, then it would follow that they were together jointly and severally responsible for the whole rent. It would equally follow that they could effectively exclude the respondent and his nominees.

Although the facts are not precisely on all fours with *Somma v Hazlehurst* [1978] 2 All ER 1011, [1978] I WLR 1014, they are strikingly similar and the judge was, in my judgment, entitled to conclude that the appellants had exclusive possession of the premises. I read his finding that 'the licences are artificial transactions designed to evade the Rent Acts' as a finding that they were sham documents designed to conceal the true nature of the transaction. There was, in my judgment, material on which he could properly reach this conclusion and I, too, would allow the appeal.

AG Securities v Vaughan and others

The facts in this appeal are startlingly different from those in the Antoniades case. To begin with the appeal concerns a substantial flat in a mansion block consisting of four bedrooms, a sitting room and usual offices. The trial judge found, as a fact, that the premises could without difficulty provide residential accommodation for four persons. There is no question but that the agreements with which the appeal is concerned reflect the true bargain between the parties. It is the purpose and intention of both parties to each agreement that it should confer an individual right on the licensee named that he should be liable only for the payment which he had undertaken and that his agreement should be capable of termination without reference to the agreements with the other persons occupying the flat. The judge found that the agreements were not shams and that each of the four occupants had arrived independently of one another and not as a group. His finding was that there was never a group of persons coming to the flat altogether. That has been challenged because, it is said, the evidence established that initially in 1977 and 1978 there was one occupant who was joined by three others who, although they came independently and not as a trio, moved in at about the same time. Central heating was then installed, so that the weekly payments fell to be increased and new agreements were signed by the four occupants contemporaneously. Speaking for myself, I cannot see how this can make any difference to the terms on which the individuals were in occupation.

If they were in as licensees in the first instance, the mere replacement of their agreements by new agreements in similar form cannot convert them into tenants, and the case has, in my judgment, to be approached on the footing that agreements with the occupiers were entered into separately and individually. The only questions are those of the effect of each agreement *vis-à-vis* the individual licensee and whether the agreements collectively had the effect of creating a joint tenancy among the occupants of the premises for the time being by virtue of their having between them exclusive possession of the premises.

Taking first, by way of example, the position of the first occupier to be let into the premises on the terms of one of these agreements, it is, in my judgment, quite unarguable, once any question of sham is out of the way, that he has an estate in the premises which entitles him to exclusive possession. His right, which is, by definition, a right to share use and occupation with such other persons not exceeding three in number as the licensor shall introduce from time to time, is clearly inconsistent with any exclusive possession in him alone even though he may be the only person in physical occupation at a particular time. He has no legal title which will permit him to exclude other persons to whom the licensor may choose to grant the privilege of entry. That must equally apply to the additional licensees who join him. None of them has individually nor have they collectively the right or power lawfully to exclude a further nominee of the licensor within the prescribed maximum.

I pause to note that it has never been contended that any individual occupier has a tenancy of a particular room in the flat with a right to use the remainder of the flat in common with the tenants of other rooms. I can envisage that as a possibility in cases of arrangements of this kind if the facts support the marking out with the landlord's concurrence of a particular room as the exclusive domain of a particular individual. But to support that there would, I think, have to be proved the grant of an identifiable part of the flat and that simply does not fit with the system described in the evidence of the instant case.

The real question, and it is this on which the respondents rely, is what is the position when the flat is occupied concurrently by all four licensees? What is said then is that, since the licensor has now exhausted, for the time being, his right of nomination, the four occupants collectively have exclusive possession of the premises because they can collectively exclude the licensor himself. Because, it is argued, (1) they have thus exclusive possession and (2) there is an ascertainable term during which all have the right to use and occupy and (3) they are occupying in consideration of the payment of periodic sums of money, *Street v Mountford* [1985] 2 All ER 289, [1985] AC 809 shows that they are collectively tenants of the premises. They are not lodgers. Therefore they must be tenants. And, because each is not individually a tenant, they must together be joint tenants.

My Lords, there appear to me to be a number of fallacies here. In the first place, the assertion of an exclusive possession rests, as it seems to me, on assuming what it is sought to prove. If, of course, each licence agreement creates a tenancy, each tenant will be sharing with other persons whose rights to be there rest on their own estates which, once they have been granted, they enjoy in their own right independently of the landlord. Collectively they have the right to exclude everyone other than those who have concurrent estates. But if the licence agreement is what it purports to be, that is to say merely an agreement for permissive enjoyment as the invitee of the landlord, then each shares the use of the premises with other invitees of the same landlord. The landlord is not excluded for he continues to enjoy the premises through his invitees, even though he may for the time being have precluded himself by contract with each from withdrawing the invitation. Second, the fact that under each agreement an individual has the privilege of user and occupation for a term which overlaps the term of user and occupation of other persons in the premises does not create a single indivisible term of occupation for all four consisting of an amalgam of the individual overlapping periods.

Third, there is no single sum of money payable in respect of use and occupation. Each person is individually liable for the amount which he has agreed, which may differ in practice from the amounts paid by all or some of the others.

The respondents are compelled to support their claims by a strange and unnatural theory that, as each occupant terminates his agreement, there is an implied surrender by the other three and an implied grant of a new joint tenancy to them together with the new incumbent when he enters under his individual agreement. With great respect to the majority in the Court of Appeal, this appears to me to be entirely unreal. For my part, I agree with the dissenting judgment of Sir George Waller in finding no unity of interest, no unity of title, certainly no unity of time and, as I think, no unity of possession. I find it impossible to say that the agreements entered into with the respondents created either individually or collectively a single tenancy either of the entire flat or of any part of it. I agree that the appeal should be allowed.

These two cases appear to fall at opposite ends of the lease/licence spectrum; subsequent cases have tended to fall somewhere in between.

In *Stribling v Wickham* (1989) 21 HLR 381, three people claimed to have a tenancy of a large four room flat. The flat had originally been occupied by three friends, A, B and C, who had each signed separate agreements described as licences. Each agreement stated that each occupant agreed to share the use of the premises with the licensor and anyone else to whom the licensor might give a licence to use the premises, terms which denied to A, B and C exclusive possession of the premises. The agreements could also be brought to an end by 28 days' notice. A and B moved out to be replaced by two other people, D and E. As the agreements came to an end, they were replaced by new agreements in identical terms, each occupant agreeing to pay £114 per month. At the end of these agreements, the owner sought possession of the property, claiming that C, D and E were no more than licensees.

The Court of Appeal agreed that the agreements created licences, since the obligation on each occupant to pay only a third of the total monthly consideration, together with the ability of each occupant to terminate his or her own agreement on the giving of 28 days' notice, were inconsistent with a joint tenancy. Such provisions denied the presence of any 'unity of interest', which is essential for the existence of a joint tenancy.

The Court of Appeal provided five guidelines which a court should follow when considering the status of a bunch of agreements purporting to be licences. These were as follows:

(1) The court must construe the agreements in the light of the surrounding circumstances. These will include the relationship between the occupants, the course of negotiations between the parties, the nature and extent of the accommodation and the intended and actual mode of its occupation.

(2) Whilst the nature of the accommodation cannot be used as a guide to the construction of the agreements, it may be used as an aid in determining whether certain parts of the agreement were never intended to be used, but had been included solely in order to disguise what was in reality a tenancy.

(3) The task of the court is to determine what is the true nature of the agreement. An agreement which is nothing but a sham (ie a smoke screen intended to disguise what is in reality a tenancy) should therefore be identified as such by the court.

(4) No exhaustive list of factors which might be of assistance to the court in construing an agreement could be drawn up; there would be many such factors.

(5) The mere fact that several agreements had been entered into at the same time in order to replace earlier agreements, would not be significant if those earlier agreements had themselves been entered into separately.

Where there is only one agreement and it purports to deny exclusive possession to the occupant, the court has had less of a problem in deciding whether that agreement creates a tenancy or a licence, although this has not been universally true.

In *Family Housing Association v Jones and another* [1990] 1 All ER 385, for example, an agreement stated that it gave rise to only a temporary arrangement and was a licence entered into without the grant of exclusive possession. The Court of Appeal found no difficulty in reaching the conclusion that Mrs Jones had been granted a tenancy (governed by the Housing Act 1985) even though the Association had retained a key to the flat. Retention of a key, which might be done for many reasons, did not of itself negative the grant of exclusive possession. This case, however, might be argued to turn on the point that a licence, even without exclusive possession, was thought to be within s 79 of the Housing Act 1985; it was therefore criticised by the House of Lords in *Westminster City Council v Clarke* (above; see later for discussion of this case) on the ground that s 79(3) of the Housing Act 1985 had not altered the law so as to confer the status of a secure licensee on someone who did not enjoy exclusive possession.

In the jointly heard cases of *Aslan v Murphy* and *Wynne v Duke* [1989] 3 All ER 130, the Court of Appeal was more easily able to identify a sham transaction in each case. In *Aslan v Murphy*, the occupant of a single room had entered into an agreement, called a licence, which denied the grant of exclusive possession and which purported to oblige the occupant to vacate the room between 10.30 am and noon each day. The owner retained the keys and reserved an absolute right of entry at all times. The Court considered that the provisions of the agreement for sharing the room and denying access for 90 minutes each day were clearly sham terms to conceal what was in essence a tenancy. As for the retention of the keys, exclusive possession of keys was not a prerequisite of a tenancy anyway.

In *Wynne v Duke*, a married couple occupied a house, owned by a person resident abroad, under an agreement called a licence which stated that the owner wished to recover vacant possession at short notice, that no tenancy was created and that there was no right of exclusive possession. The owner reserved to herself the right to move someone else into the third bedroom as a lodger and she retained a key to the house. The Court of Appeal was able to 'see through' this thin disguise by holding that the Wynnes did, in reality, have exclusive possession of the whole house. The Court of Appeal stated that a careful eye had to be kept open for such pretences, after taking due account of how the parties had in fact acted on the agreement. The identification and exposure of such pretences, however, does not necessarily mean that the whole of an agreement is a sham; it merely means that those particular parts do not reflect the true bargain between the parties.

In *Skipton Building Society v Clayton et al* (1993) 25 HLR 596, the Court of Appeal was again able to identify an agreement described as a 'licence', as a sham. It was clear that the agreement otherwise had all the hallmarks of a tenancy if one ignored the artfully contrived provisions of it. The owners of a flat had reached an agreement with the Mortgage Advice Centre, a business carried on by Clayton, whereby Clayton agreed to purchase the flat at a discount on terms that the former owners would be entitled to occupy the property rent free for the rest of their lives under a 'licence'. The 'licence' stated that exclusive possession was not granted to the former owners, that the relationship of landlord and tenant was not being created and that the 'licensors' were to have possession and were to be treated as the occupiers for the purpose of management and control of the premises, but that the former owners were to be responsible for payment of ground rent and service charges. The judge at first instance, with whom the Court of Appeal agreed, stated:

> '[T]he first defendants were dishonest, as shown by their subsequent behaviour. The licence agreement ... is artfully contrived in an endeavour to avoid the consequences of *Street v Mountford* ... The provision that the first defendants were to have possession, management and control of the flat was a sham. The first defendants had not the slightest intention of sharing the flat with the Brownes or exercising any of the supposed rights of shared possession and occupation except, no doubt, if matters of inspection or repair arose ... The idea that the first defendants might chose to sleep at the flat or take meals there or put their guests up there overnight is simply fanciful. The intentions of the parties and the reality of the situation were that the Brownes were to have the exclusive use, occupation and possession of the flat for the rest of their lives ...' (*per* Judge Hull QC, Kingston Upon Thames County Court at pp 9 and 10).

The Court of Appeal then had to proceed in this case on the basis that the agreement did operate to grant exclusive possession to the former owners. The remaining issues which arose in this case are discussed later.

Skipton Building Society v Clayton

Sir Christopher Slade: *Tenancy or Licence*

I now turn to the second of the society's main propositions. At the date of the grant of the mortgage to the society, were Mr and Mrs Browne mere licensees, as opposed to tenants, of the property?

The decision of the House of Lords in *Street v Mountford* [1985] 1 AC 809, clearly establishes that, whether the label which the parties choose to attach to their arrangement be a tenancy or a licence, an arrangement under which exclusive possession of residential property is granted for a term at a rent will normally be regarded by the law as the grant of a tenancy. Furthermore, as Lord Templeman recognised (at p 818E), the same legal result will ensue if the occupier is granted exclusive possession for a fixed or periodic term certain in consideration of a premium.

Mr Behrens accepted that it is possible to have a tenancy without any provision for the payment of rent; (see *Street v Mountford* at page 818E of the report *per* Lord Templeman; see also section 205(1)(xxvii) of the Law of Property Act 1925 and the decision of the Court of Appeal in *Ashburn Anstalt v Arnold* [1989] 1 Ch 1). In his submission, however, the absence of any provision for the payment of rent by Mr and Mrs Browne is at least one factor which points to the absence of any tenancy in the present case.

In general terms he reminded us that both sides to the arrangements had had legal advice, that the 1989 agreement called itself a licence and, according to its wording, granted no more than a licence. He drew our attention to the various subclauses of clause 5, which I have already quoted, and also to clause 4. All of them in his submission point strongly to a licence rather than a tenancy. In regard to the crucial question of exclusive possession he naturally attached particular weight to clause 5(b), which purported to reserve management, possession and control of the property to the so-called licensor and specifically not to give exclusive possession to the so-called licensees.

If clause 5(b) is to be read and taken at its face value, there could he no question of the 1989 agreement operating so as to give exclusive possession to Mr and Mrs Browne. However, as the judge rightly pointed out, the court, in the words of Lord Templeman in *Street v Mountford*, at p 825H of the report, should 'be astute to detect and frustrate sham devices and artificial transactions whose only object is to disguise the grant of a tenancy and to evade the Rent Acts'. In this context the judge's findings of fact were clear and unequivocal ...

In my judgment the nature of the documents presented by the first defendants to Mr Browne at the meeting of June 20, 1989, and of the document soon afterwards presented by them to the society, in support of their application for a mortgage, would by themselves have justified the judge in drawing these inferences of fact, which entirely accord with the balance of probabilities. The references were further supported by the uncontroverted oral evidence of Mr Browne, who, according to the judge's notes, testified that he and his wife used to lock the property when they were not there, that the first defendants had no key, and that the first defendants did not take possession and control of the property. In my judgment there is no possible basis on which this court would be justified in interfering with the findings of fact made by the judge ... or with his finding of a sham. We must therefore proceed on the basis that the 1989 agreement, notwithstanding its misleading provisions, did operate to grant exclusive possession of the property to Mr and Mrs Browne.

For a term certain

The second criterion of a tenancy identified by Lord Templeman in *Street v Mountford* was that the agreement must be 'for a fixed or periodic term certain'. This means that the agreement must have both a definite beginning and ending date. Most of the cases on this point relate to non-residential premises, but are probably applicable by analogy.

The above requirement caused a problem during the Second World War, when agreements lasting 'for the duration of the war' were not uncommon. In *Lace v Chantler* [1944] KB 368, such an agreement was said not to be capable of amounting to a tenancy. The Validation of Wartime Lease Act 1944 rescued such agreements made 'for the duration of the war', but the principle of certainty of duration still applies to other types of agreement (see *Prudential Assurance Co Ltd v London Residuary Body and Others* [1992] 3 All ER 504).

The requirement of certainty of duration does not mean that the period of occupation has itself to be continuous. A time-sharing agreement, for instance, by which a person is allowed to occupy a property on certain specified dates in the year, is still a tenancy (see *Cottage Holiday Associates Ltd v Customs and Excise Commissioners* [1983] QB 735).

Although periodic tenancies appear to be at odds with the requirement of certainty of duration, it has come to be accepted that such agreements are ordinary tenancies, because they can be brought to an end by an appropriate period of notice.

Leases which are expressed to last for the lessee's lifetime are converted into 90 year tenancies which can be brought to an end after the lessee's death by one month's written notice. This effect is brought about by the application of s 149(6) Law of Property Act 1925.

Law of Property Act 1925

149(6) Any lease or underlease, at a rent, or in consideration of a fine, for life or lives or for any term of years determinable with life or lives, or on the marriage of the lessee, or any contract therefor, made before or after the commencement of this Act or created by virtue of Part V of the Law of Property Act 1922, shall take effect as a lease, underlease or contract therefor, for a term of ninety years determinable after the death or marriage (as the case may be) of the original lessee, or of the survivor of the original lessees, by at least one month's notice in writing given to determine the same on one of the quarter days applicable to the tenancy, either by the lessor or the persons deriving title under him, to the person entitled to the leasehold interest, or if no such person is in existence by affixing the same to the premises, or by the lessee or other persons in whom the leasehold interest is vested to the lessor or the persons deriving title under him ...

See, on this section, *Skipton Building Society v Clayton et al* (above).

Perpetually renewable leases (ie those leases which contain an option to renew on identical terms) are converted into tenancies lasting for 2,000 years, by virtue of s 145 Law of Property Act 1922.

Law of Property Act 1922

145 For the purpose of converting perpetually renewable leases and underleases (not being an interest in perpetually renewable copyhold land enfranchised by Part V of this Act but including a perpetually renewable underlease derived out of an interest in perpetually renewable copyhold land) into long terms, for preventing the creation of perpetually renewable leasehold interests and for providing for the interests of the persons affected, the provisions contained in the Fifteenth Schedule to this Act shall have effect.

In *Charles Clay & Sons Ltd v British Railways Board* [1971] Ch 725, the court had to consider whether a periodic agreement which could be brought to an end by three months' written notice given by either party could be a tenancy when the landowner could only exercise that right if they required the premises for their undertaking, and for no other purpose. The Court of Appeal held that the agreement amounted to a tenancy and that *Lace v Chantler* had no application to a periodic tenancy. This case was taken a step further in *Ashburn Anstalt v WJ Arnold* [1988] 2 All ER 147, [1989] Ch 1, [1988] 2 WLR 706, in which the issue was whether an agreement relating to non-domestic premises could be a tenancy where no ending date had been specified or could be calculated, but where a specified period of notice could be given by the owner. The Court of Appeal considered that the agreement did create a tenancy, but this case and *Charles Clay & Sons Ltd v British Railways Board* have both been overruled by the House of Lords in *Prudential Assurance Co Ltd v London Residuary Body and others* [1992] 3 All ER 504. That case concerned non-domestic land and in which the agreement was to last until the land was required by the landlord for road widening purposes. The London Residuary Body and the others did not have road widening powers, as none of them was a highway authority. The House of Lords ruled that the agreement itself had not created a tenancy because it was for an uncertain duration; but there was still a periodic tenancy from the fact of entry into possession and the payment and acceptance of a yearly rent.

Prudential Assurance Co Ltd v London v London Residuary Body and others

Lord Templeman: ... By the agreement, the London County Council let to one Nathan a strip of land with a frontage of 36 feet to Walworth Road, a thoroughfare in Southwark, and a depth of 25 feet, at a rent of £30 per annum from 19 December 1930 'until the tenancy shall be determined as hereinafter provided'. The only relevant proviso for determination is contained in cl 6 which reads as follows:

> 'THE Tenancy shall continue until the said land is required by the Council for the purposes of the widening of Walworth Road and the street paving works rendered necessary thereby and the Council shall give two months' notice to the tenant at least prior to the day of determination when the said land is so required and thereupon the tenant shall give vacant possession to the Council of the said land ...'

By the agreement the tenant was authorised to erect 'temporary one-storey shops or buildings of one storey and for the retention of such shops or buildings as temporary structures' until the land was required for road widening and he was then bound to remove the temporary structures and clear the land. The council agreed to pay all the costs of road making and paving works. The agreement was clearly intended to be of short duration and could have been secured by a lease for a fixed term, say five or ten years, with power for the landlord to determine before the expiry of that period for the purposes of the road widening. Unfortunately the agreement was not so drafted. Over 60 years later Walworth Road has not been widened, the freehold is now vested in the appellant second to fourth defendants, who purchased the property from the first defendant, the London Residuary Body, after it had issued a notice to quit, the defendants have no road-making powers and it does not appear that the road will ever be widened. The benefit of the agreement is now vested in the respondent plaintiffs, Prudential Assurance Co Ltd. The agreement purported to grant a term of uncertain duration which, if valid, now entitles the tenant to stay there for ever and a day at the 1930 rent of £30; valuers acting for both parties have agreed that the annual current commercial rent exceeds £10,000.

A demise for years is a contract for the exclusive possession and profit of land for some determinate period. Such an estate is called a 'term'. Thus Coke on Littleton said (Co Litt (19th edn, 1832) para 45b):

'"Terminus" in the understanding of the law does not only signify the limits and limitation of time, but also the estate and interest that passes for that time.'

Blackstone in his Commentaries (2 Bl Com (1st edn, 1766) 143) said:

'EVERY estate which must expire at a period certain and prefixed, by whatever words created, is an estate for years. And therefore this estate is frequently called a term, terminus, because its duration or continuance is bounded, limited, and determined: for every such estate must have a certain beginning, and certain end.'

In *Say v Smith* (1530) 1 Plowd 269, 75 ER 410 a lease for a certain term purported to add a term which was uncertain; the lease was held valid only as to the certain term ...

The Law of Property Act 1925, taking up the same theme, provided: '1(1) The only estates in land which are capable of subsisting or of being conveyed or created at law are – (a) An estate in fee simple absolute in possession; (b) A term of years absolute ...'

Section 205(1)(xxvii) was in these terms:

'"Term of years absolute" means a term of years ... either certain or liable to determination by notice, re-entry, operation of law, or by a provision for cesser on redemption, or in any other event (other than the dropping of a life, or the determination of a determinable life interest) ... and in this definition the expression "term of years" includes a term for less than a year, or for a year or years and a fraction of a year or from year to year.'

The term expressed to be granted by the agreement in the present case does not fall within this definition.

Ancient authority, recognised by the 1925 Act was applied in *Lace v Chandler* [1944] 1 All ER 305, [1944] KB 368. A dwelling-house was let at the rent of 16s 5d per week. Lord Greene MR (no less) said ([1944] 1 All ER 305 at 306, [1944] KB 368 at 370–371):

'Apart from one circumstance, there could be no question that this was an ordinary weekly tenancy, duly determinable at a week's notice. But the parties in the rent-book agreed to a term which appears there expressed by the words 'furnished for duration' – which must mean the duration of the war. The question immediately arises whether a tenancy for the duration of the war creates a good leasehold interest. In my opinion, it does not. A term created by a leasehold tenancy agreement must be a term which is either expressed with certainty and specifically, or is expressed by reference to something which can, at the time when the lease takes effect, be looked to as a certain ascertainment of what the term is meant to be. In the present case, when this tenancy agreement took effect, the term was completely uncertain. It was impossible to say how long the tenancy would endure. Counsel for the tenant in his argument has maintained that such a lease would be a good lease; and that, even if the term is uncertain at the beginning of the term, when the lease takes effect, the fact that at some future time it will be made certain is sufficient to make it a good lease. In my opinion, that argument is not to be sustained. I do not propose to go into the authorities on the matter; but in FOA on Landlord and Tenant ((6th edn, 1924) p 115), the law is stated in this way and, in my opinion, correctly stated: "The habendum in a lease must point out the period during which the enjoyment of the premises is to be had; so that the duration, as well as the commencement of the term, must be stated. The certainty of a lease as to its continuance must be ascertainable either by the express limitation of the parties at the time the lease is made, or by reference to some collateral act which may, with equal certainty, measure the continuance of it, otherwise it is void ...'"

The legislature concluded that it was inconvenient for leases for the duration of the war to be void and therefore by the Validation of War-Time Leases Act 1944 Parliament ... granted the fixed and certain term which the agreements between the parties lacked in the case of tenancies for the duration of the war and which the present agreement lacks.

When the agreement in the present case was made, it failed to grant an estate in the land. The tenant however entered into possession and paid the yearly rent of £30 reserved by the agreement. The tenant entering under a void lease became by virtue of possession and the payment of a yearly rent, a yearly tenant holding on the terms of the agreement so far as those terms were consistent with the yearly tenancy. A yearly tenancy is determinable by the landlord or the tenant at the end of the first or any subsequent year of the tenancy by six months' notice unless the agreement between the parties provides otherwise ...

Now it is said that when in the present case the tenant entered pursuant to the agreement and paid a yearly rent he became a tenant from year to year on the terms of the agreement including cl 6 which prevents the landlord from giving notice to quit until the land is required for road widening. This submission would make a nonsense of the rule that a grant for an uncertain term does not create a lease and would make nonsense of the concept of a tenancy from year to year because it is of the essence of a tenancy from year to year that both the landlord and the tenant shall be entitled to give notice determining the tenancy ...

My Lords, I consider that the principle in *Lace v Chandler* [1944] 1 All ER 305, [1944] 1 KB 368 reaffirming 500 years of judicial acceptance of the requirement that a term must be certain applies to all leases and tenancy agreements. A tenancy from year to year is saved from being uncertain because each party has power by notice to determine at the end of any year. The term continues until determined as if both parties made a new agreement at the end of each year for a new term for the ensuing year. A power for nobody to determine or for one party only to be able to determine is inconsistent with the concept of a term from year to year: see *Doe d Warner v Browne* (1807) 8 East 165, 103 ER 305 and *Cheshire Lines Committee v Lewis & Co* (1880) 50 LJQB 121. In *Charles Clay & Sons Ltd v British Railways Board* [1971] 1 All ER 1007, [1971] Ch 725 there was no 'clearly expressed bargain' that the term should continue until the crack of doom if the demised land was not required for the landlord's undertaking or if the undertaking ceased to exist. In the present case there was no 'clearly expressed bargain' that the tenant shall be entitled to enjoy his 'temporary structures' in perpetuity if Walworth Road is never widened. In any event principle and precedent dictate that it is beyond the power of the landlord and the tenant to create a term which is uncertain.

A lease can be made for five years subject to the tenant's right to determine if the war ends before the expiry of five years. A lease can be made from year to year subject to a fetter on the right of the landlord to determine the lease before the expiry of five years unless the war ends. Both leases are valid because they create a determinable certain term of five years. A lease might purport to be made for the duration of the war subject to the tenant's right to determine before the end of the war. A lease might be made from year to year subject to a fetter on the right of the landlord to determine the lease before the war ends. Both leases would be invalid because each purported to create an uncertain term. A term must either be certain or uncertain. It cannot be partly certain because the tenant can determine it at any time and partly uncertain because the landlord cannot determine it for an uncertain period. If the landlord does not grant and the tenant does not take a certain term the grant does not create a lease.

The decision of the Court of Appeal in *Charles Clay & Sons Ltd v British Railways Board* [1971] 1 All ER 1007, [1971] Ch 725 was taken a little further in *Ashburn Anstalt v Arnold* [1988] 2 All ER 147, [1989] Ch 1. That case, if it was correct, would make it unnecessary for a lease to be of a certain duration. In an agreement for the sale of land the vendor reserved the right to remain at the property after completion as licensee and to trade therefrom without payment of rent–

> 'save that it can be required by Matlodge Ltd [the purchaser] to give possession on not less than one quarter's notice in writing upon Matlodge certifying that it is ready at the expiration of such notice forthwith to proceed with the development of the property and the neighbouring property involving *inter alia* the demolition of the property.'

The Court of Appeal held that this reservation created a tenancy. The tenancy was not from year to year but for a term which would continue until Matlodge Ltd certified that it was ready to proceed with the development of the property. The Court of Appeal held that the term was not uncertain because the vendor could either give a quarter's notice or vacate the property without giving notice. But of course the same could be said of the situation in *Lace v Chandler* [1944] 1 All ER 305, [1944] KB 368. The cumulative result of the two Court of Appeal authorities, *Charles Clay & Sons Ltd v British Railways Board* [1971] 1 All ER 1007, [1971] Ch 725 and the *Ashburn* case, would therefore destroy the need for any term to be certain.

In the present case the Court of Appeal was bound by the decisions in *Charles Clay & Sons Ltd v British Railways Board* and the *Ashburn* case. In my opinion both those cases were wrongly decided. A grant for an uncertain term does not create a lease. A grant for an uncertain term which takes the form of a yearly tenancy which cannot be determined by the landlord does not create a lease. I would allow the appeal. The trial judge, Millett J, reached the conclusion that the six months' notice was a good notice. He was of course bound by the Court of Appeal decisions but managed to construe the memorandum of agreement so as to render cl 6 ineffective in fettering the right of the landlord to serve a notice to quit after the landlord had ceased to be a road widening authority. In the circumstances this question of construction need not be considered. For the reasons which I have given the order made by Millett J must be restored ...

The House of Lords considered that the situation in *Ashburn Anstalt v WJ Arnold* was not dissimilar to that in *Lace v Chantler*, and that, if correct, would make it unnecessary for a lease to be for a certain duration. Their Lordships' decision makes it clear that *Lace v Chantler* continues to represent the law in this area.

The situation in the Prudential case may be distinguishable from that in *Canadian Imperial Bank of Commerce v Bello and others* (1992) 24 HLR 155. That case involved an agreement by which a builder, who was owed money by a house owner for refurbishment work which he had done on the house, was allowed to take over the house and use it as he liked until he got paid for his work. The Court of Appeal relied on *Ashburn Anstalt v WJ Arnold* (above) and held that, as the terminating event, ie payment of the bill, was in the control of the parties, the builder had a tenancy. This case was not mentioned in the *Prudential* case, which overruled *Ashburn Anstalt v WJ Arnold*, so it remains to be seen whether *Canadian Imperial Bank of Commerce v Bello and others* has survived the overruling of the *Ashburn Anstalt* case upon which it was based; the probability is that it has not.

It might be argued in favour of the decision in *Canadian Imperial Bank of Commerce* that although no definite ending date was agreed between the parties, and it could not be otherwise calculated in advance, neither party had restricted his ability to terminate the agreement; each had full control over when the agreement could be brought to an end. But the implication of the House of Lords' decision in the *Prudential* case is that the *Canadian Imperial Bank* was wrongly decided.

In *Skipton Building Society v Clayton* (see earlier) the Court of Appeal was faced with having to decide whether an agreement described as a 'licence' for the lives of the occupants was sufficiently certain in duration to qualify as a tenancy. This it could only do by the application of s 149(6) Law of Property Act 1925 (see earlier), which converts leases for lives into 90 year terms. Since no rent was payable, the issue arose of whether the former owners were paying a 'fine' in return for the agreement. The term 'fine' is defined in s 205(1)(xxiii) as 'a premium or foregift ... or benefit in the nature of a fine, premium or foregift'. The former owners had granted to Clayton an option to purchase the flat for less than one-third of its true value; they would not have done this had it not been for the agreement promising to them the right to live in the flat for the rest of their lives. The Court of Appeal then had to consider whether this amounted to a premium within the statutory definition of a 'fine' and concluded that the monetary discount on the price of the flat was a 'benefit in the nature of a premium', with the consequence that the Brownes had a tenancy to which s 149(6) Law of Property Act 1925 applied.

Skipton Building Society v Clayton

Sir Christopher Slade: The next important question is whether the term of years granted to them by that agreement was of sufficiently certain duration to give rise to a tenancy, as opposed to a licence. The recent decision of the House of Lords in *Prudential Assurance Company Limited v London Residuary Body* [1992] 3 WLR 275, has reaffirmed that it is a requirement of all leases and tenancy agreements that the term created must be of certain duration – in other words that the maximum duration of the term shall be ascertainable from the outset (see at p 287E *per* Lord Browne-Wilkinson).

Mr Behrens submitted that the only way in which the term granted to Mr and Mrs Browne by the 1989 agreement could satisfy this requirement would be through the application of section 149(6) of the Law of Property Act 1925, which in his submission does not in fact apply ...

Section 205(1)(xxiii) of that Act states that 'fine' includes 'a premium or foregift and any payment, consideration, or benefit in the nature of a fine, premium or foregift.' The 1989 agreement provided for no payment of rent nor, in Mr Behrens' submission, can it be said to have been entered into by the first defendants in consideration of a 'fine' within the statutory definition of that word, since no monetary payment was made by Mr and Mrs Browne for the rights granted to them. In this context he referred us to *Waite v Jennings* [1906] 2 KB 11, where the Court of Appeal considered the identical definition of a 'fine' contained in section 2(9) of the Conveyancing Act 1881. In that case Vaughan-Williams and Stirling LJJ, Fletcher Moulton LJ dissenting on this point, expressed the *obiter* opinion that a covenant which secured to a lessor no sum of money beyond the rent to which he was entitled under a lease was not in the nature of a 'fine'.

However, to consider the validity or otherwise of Mr Behrens' submissions in this context, it is necessary to look at the judge's findings as to the consideration given by Mr and Mrs Browne to the first defendants for the rights granted to them by the 1989 agreement. The judge said, at p 9E:

'In my judgment, the true view of the events which I have described is as follows. Mr Browne granted to the first defendants an option to purchase the flat for less than one-third of the flat's true value in return for a promise to enter into the licence agreement. It is inconceivable that he could have entered into such an arrangement except on the basis that the licence agreement was to guarantee him and Mrs Browne, so far as might be, the right to live in the flat for their joint lives and the life of the survivor. This indeed was the very reason that led to his rejecting Mr Rooney's advice to sell the flat and use the proceeds to pay his debts and to buy another home elsewhere.'

A little later, at pp 11H to 12A, the judge said:

'In my judgment, the true view of the licence agreement, when its sham provision for shared occupation and possession and its misleading title are ignored, is that it was the grant of a term of years by the first defendants to Mr and Mrs Browne for their joint lives and the life of the survivor. The premium for this grant is the discount of more than two-thirds of the value of the flat for which it was sold to the first defendants.'

This analysis of the facts is, in my judgment, unassailable. On the basis of this analysis, I think it likewise indisputable that in return for the rights granted by the 1989 agreement the first defendants received a 'benefit in the nature of a ... premium' within the statutory definition of a 'fine' – that benefit consisting of the discount referred to by the judge, which was a monetary discount. It follows that in my view the 1989 agreement operated to grant Mr and Mrs Browne exclusive possession of the residential property to which it related for a term and correspondingly, according to *Street v Mountford* principles, had the effect of granting them a tenancy; the absence of any provision for payment of rent cannot save it from being a tenancy. It has not been submitted that the letter dated June 20, 1989, addressed to the landlords by one only of the two tenants, Mr Browne, operated to determine that tenancy pursuant to clause 6 of the 1989 agreement and I think that any such submission would not have been sustainable.

It follows that, in my judgment, Mr and Mrs Browne have at all material times been entitled to a tenancy of the property by virtue of the 1989 agreement, a tenancy to which section 149(6) of the Law of Property Act 1925 applies.

At a rent

'Rent' is a technical term which refers to a payment in consideration of a tenancy. It can be distinguished from a payment for 'use and occupation', which a licensee or even a trespasser may be asked to pay (see later, *Westminster City Council v Basson* (1991) 23 HLR 225). Lord Templeman in *Street v Mountford* stated that the payment of rent was also one of the hallmarks of a tenancy, but it has since become apparent that an obligation to pay rent is not essential to a tenancy. In *Ashburn Anstalt v WJ Arnold* (above), the Court of Appeal held that an agreement under which no money was payable could still be a tenancy. Fox LJ stated (at p 154, paras f and g):

'We are unable to read Lord Templeman's speech in *Street v Mountford* as laying down a principle of 'no rent, no lease' ... that would be inconsistent with s 205(xxvii) of the Law of Property Act 1925, which defines "term of years absolute" ... '

Ashburn Anstalt v WJ Arnold has been overruled by the House of Lords on other grounds (see earlier), but it is likely that the principle which it identified concerning the payment of rent still survives. This much appears to be assumed in *Skipton Building Society v Clayton* (1993) 25 HLR 596, in which the Court of Appeal made reference to the *Ashburn* case as an authority for the proposition that there could be a tenancy without any provision for the payment of rent.

The definition of 'term of years absolute' mentioned by Fox LJ (see above) is contained in s 205(xxvii) Law of Property Act 1925.

Law of Property Act 1925

205(xxvii) 'Term of years absolute' means a term of years (taking effect either in possession or in reversion whether or not at a rent) with or without impeachment for waste, subject or not to another legal estate, and either certain or liable to determination by notice, re-entry, operation of law, or by a provision for cesser on redemption or in any other event (other than the dropping of a life, or the determination of a determinable life interest); but does not include any term of years determinable with life or lives or with the cesser of a determinable life interest, nor, if created after the commencement of this Act a term of years which is not expressed to take effect in possession within twenty-one years after the creation thereof where required by this Act to take effect within that period; and in this definition the expression 'term of years' includes a term for less than a year, or for a year or years and a fraction of a year or from year to year.

Although it appears that rent is not essential to a tenancy, if a rent is to be paid then it must be either certain or calculable at the date of payment. In *GLC v Connelly* [1970] QB 100, the council had tried to raise the rents of its residential tenants by simply serving notice on them to that effect, but the tenants objected. The rent books each contained a provision whereby the rent was 'liable to be increased on notice being given'. As the amount of rent could therefore be calculated when its payment became due, the court held that the rent was certain and had been validly increased. In *Brown v Gould* [1972] Ch 53, a non-residential case, the rent was to be fixed by reference to market values. The rent was held to be sufficiently certain, since the concept of 'market rental' was well known in the landlord and tenant relationship.

The payment of rent may have important consequences in other respects. For example, a fixed-term tenancy may be created without the use of a deed if it is to last for no longer than three years and is for the best rent obtainable and takes effect in possession.

Law of Property Act 1925

54(2) Nothing in the forgoing provisions of this Part of this Act shall affect the creation by parol of leases taking effect in possession for a term not exceeding three years (whether or not the lessee is given power to extend the term) at the best rent which can be reasonably obtained without taking a fine.

Certain statutes only apply if a 'low rent' is payable. For example, the Leasehold Reform Act 1967 allows a tenant who has a 'long tenancy' to purchase the freehold from the landlord if a 'low rent' is payable under the terms of the tenancy (see later).

One consequence of having a tenancy under which no rent is payable is that the tenant cannot claim the protection afforded by some statutes to certain types of residential tenant. The Rent Act 1977 security of tenure regime, for example, does not apply to a tenant who pays no rent or a low 'ground' rent (see s 5 Rent Act 1977). Likewise, the Housing Act 1988, does not confer assured tenancy status on a tenant who is not obliged to pay rent or who pays a low 'ground' rent (see Schedule 1, para 3(1) Housing Act 1988). A tenant who pays no rent is equally not entitled to the protection of s 3 Protection from Eviction Act 1977, a provision which requires that a court order be obtained before a landlord may recover possession of the premises (see s 3(7)(b)).

For what can amount to 'rent', see *Bostock v Bryant* (1990) 22 HLR 449.

One of the problems which has arisen in the lease/licence controversy has been the question of whether two or more persons occupying property together can be tenants when each is responsible for paying only his own share of the rent. In *Mikeover Ltd v Brady* [1989] 3 All ER 618, for instance, there were two unrelated occupants who were sharing a two room flat. Although the couple did have exclusive occupation of the flat, the identical agreements under which they occupied the flat were described as licences and each had agreed to pay half the monthly payment required. The court (relying on some dicta of Lord Oliver in *Antoniades v Villiers*, above) considered that there could be no joint tenancy, since the two occupants had placed themselves merely under individual obligations to pay half the required monthly payment and the lack of a joint obligation was fatal to a joint tenancy. Unity of interest, one of the four required 'unities', implied the existence of both joint rights and joint obligations; the two occupants could therefore be licensees only. This point had not been resolved in *Antoniades v Villiers* (above), in which the House of Lords had been mainly concerned with whether the agreements contained terms included solely for the purpose of escaping Rent Act protection. The point had not escaped the Court of Appeal, however, in *Stribling v Wickham* (see earlier), in which three occupants of a flat were each paying a third of the total payment required by the owner; this fact, together with a 28 day notice provision, was considered as being inconsistent with a joint tenancy between the three occupants.

OTHER PROBLEMATIC SITUATIONS

The three hallmarks of a tenancy identified in *Street v Mountford* have proved insufficient to solve all the problems associated with the lease/licence issue. Further problems have been encountered even where there has been an arrangement which has purported to confer exclusive possession, for a term and at a rent.

In *Norris v Checksfield* (1991) 23 HLR 425, [1991] 4 All ER 327, for example, an employee had been allowed into occupation under a document called a 'licence' of a bungalow on the basis that he would work as a coach driver at a future date; he did not disclose at the time that he had been banned from driving. He paid £5.00 per week, deducted from his wages and had exclusive occupation of the bungalow.

The agreement which he had would terminate at the same time as his employment ended. Although all the requirements of a periodic tenancy were present, the Court of Appeal held that the agreement amounted to no more than a service licence, but here the exclusive possession was probably attributable to his employment – one of the situations regarded as exceptional by Lord Templeman in *Street v Mountford*.

In *Westminster City Council v Basson* (1991) 23 HLR 225, the Court of Appeal had to consider whether the three hallmarks from *Street v Mountford* applied to a case in which one department of the local authority had tried to reserve its position by declaring a woman's occupation of its property to be unlawful at the same time as another department was accepting payment from her for its use and occupation. When she applied for a rent rebate, the authority unfortunately wrote to her in terms which described her arrangement as a tenancy; she also had a rent book, internal council forms made reference to 'rent' and suggested that the 'tenancy' had commenced in 1985. This was a case of two council offices being unaware of what the other was doing! The Court of Appeal, however, upheld the council's contention by holding that the council's letter referring to 'unlawful occupation' was clearly inconsistent with the view that the woman was in occupation with the council's consent. The administrative confusion which had occurred did not change the nature of the occupancy, which was as a trespasser as opposed to a licensee. This case was distinguished by the Court of Appeal in *London Borough of Tower Hamlets v Ayinde* (1994) 26 HLR 631, concerned with the question of whether Mrs Ayinde was a secure tenant of a council flat or had been in occupation as a trespasser.

Agreements with a family connection have also caused problems. Lord Templeman in *Street v Mountford* tried to explain some of the earlier licence cases on the basis that they involved a family arrangement, where there was no intention to create legal relations. In *Nunn v Dalrymple and another* (1989) 21 HLR 569 the Court of Appeal was faced with the situation in which members of a family had reached an oral agreement by which the defendants were to renovate a vacant and dilapidated cottage before living in it and paying rent. The arrangement had all the hallmarks of a tenancy, but the plaintiffs, as owners of the cottage, claimed that the arrangement was a family one and therefore gave rise to a licence. The Court of Appeal considered that whilst family arrangements might sometimes give rise to nothing more than a licence, the facts in this case showed that there was merely a family connection, the existence of which did not prevent the arrangement from being a tenancy. The defendants had not been homeless but had given up a council house tenancy in order to carry out extensive repairs on the cottage and to live in it. This showed that the relationship was 'commercial' and not a 'family arrangement'; it therefore gave rise to a tenancy.

One device that can be used to ensure the creation of no more than a licence is for a property owner to buy an 'off the peg' company whose Memorandum and Articles of Association prevent the company from granting tenancies over its properties. If the company were then to purport to create any tenancies, this would be *ultra vires* its powers. An alternative is for the legal title to the property to remain vested in the person who formed the company but for the company to make the agreement. Such a possibility was recognised as being effective in *Torbett v Faulkner* [1952] 2 TLR 659.

Another difficult problem which has only recently been resolved concerns the provision of temporary accommodation in a hostel. This issue arose in *Westminster City Council v Clarke* [1992] 1 All ER 695 in which the council, as part of its duties to the homeless, had placed Mr Clarke in temporary accommodation in a hostel for single men. The hostel had a resident warden and was supported by a resettlement team of social workers. Mr Clarke paid a weekly accommodation charge under an agreement which provided that he had a licence to occupy and that he had no right of exclusive occupation of any particular accommodation or room. The council wished to evict Mr Clarke because of his behavioural problems, but he claimed to have a tenancy. The House of Lords ruled that Mr Clarke had no more than a licence.

Westminster City Council v Clarke

Lord Templeman: ... From the point of view of the council the grant of exclusive possession would be inconsistent with the purposes for which the council provided the accommodation at Cambridge Street. It was in the interests of Mr Clarke and each of the occupiers of the hostel that the council should retain possession of each room. If one room became uninhabitable another room could be shared between two occupiers. If one room became unsuitable for an occupier he could be moved elsewhere. If the occupier of one room became a nuisance he could be compelled to move to another room where his actions might be less troublesome to his neighbours. If the occupier of a room had exclusive possession he could prevent the council from entering the room, save for the purpose of protecting the council's interests and not for the purpose of supervising and controlling the conduct of the occupier in his interests. If the occupier of a room had exclusive possession he could not be obliged to comply with the terms of the conditions of occupation. Mr Clarke could not, for example, be obliged to comply with the directions of the warden or to exclude visitors or to comply with any of the other conditions of occupation which are designed to help Mr Clarke and the other occupiers of the hostel and to enable the hostel to be conducted in an efficient and harmonious manner. The only remedy of the council for breaches of the conditions of occupation would be the lengthy and uncertain procedure required by the 1985 Act to be operated for the purpose of obtaining possession from a secure tenant. In the circumstances of the present case I consider that the council legitimately and effectively retained for themselves possession of room E and that Mr Clarke was only a licensee with rights corresponding to the rights of a lodger ...

This is a very special case which depends on the peculiar nature of the hostel maintained by the council, the use of the hostel by the council, the totality, immediacy and objectives of the powers exercisable by the council and the restrictions imposed on Mr Clarke. The decision in this case will not allow a landlord private or public to free himself from the Rent Acts or from the restrictions of a secure tenancy merely by adopting or adapting the language of the licence to occupy. The provisions of the licence to occupy and the circumstances in which that licence was granted and continued lead to the conclusion that Mr Clarke has never enjoyed that exclusive possession which he claims. I would therefore allow the appeal.

Although Lord Templeman was at pains to point out that this was an exceptional case and was not to be taken as enabling a property owner to escape the statutory protection regime, the case does leave a question mark once more over the importance to be attached to the intention of the parties as expressed in the agreement, an issue which it was thought that *Street v Mountford* had buried for good.

The case law since *Street v Mountford* illustrates the difficulties which the courts continue to face in this troublesome area. While exclusive possession remains essential to a tenancy, the fact that a residential occupant does enjoy such exclusive possession does not necessarily make that occupant a tenant. Lord Templeman himself noted that there were a number of situations in which a person may have been granted exclusive possession of residential accommodation and yet be a licensee. It was not difficult on the facts of *Street v Mountford* for the House of Lords to conclude that a tenancy had been granted, since there was only one occupant and it was conceded that exclusive possession had been granted. However, the sharing of accommodation poses difficulties for the court. So does the situation where there is a clause in an agreement with a sole occupant denying to that occupant exclusive possession by reserving to the owner the right to use the accommodation in common with the occupant. Some tentative conclusions, however, may be made.

It appears that where there is one agreement or there is only one occupant involved, the three hallmarks of a tenancy identified by Lord Templeman in *Street v Mountford prima facie* create the presumption of a tenancy. But this presumption may be rebutted in a number of ways.

(1) It may be rebutted by showing that the arrangement was really part and parcel of the occupant's employment, so as to amount to a 'service occupancy' (see *Norris v Checksfield*).

(2) It may equally be rebutted by showing that the agreement was a 'family' one, in which there was never any intention to enter into legal relations; although where there is merely a family connection, there may still be a tenancy (see *Nunn v Dalrymple and another*).

(3) If accommodation has been provided merely out of generosity or as an act of friendship, legal relations may not have been intended and therefore no tenancy can arise (see, for example, *Booker v Palmer* [1942] 2 All ER 674, *Errington v Errington and Woods* [1952] 1 KB 290 and *Marcroft Wagons Ltd v*

Smith [1951] 2 KB 496; and the discussion of these cases by Denning LJ, as he then was, in *Facchini v Bryson* [1952] 1 TLR 1386).

Agreements entered into by local authorities, however, do not fit neatly into any of these exceptions, but may involve difficult questions of policy (see *Westminster City Council v Clarke, Westminster City Council v Basson,* and *London Borough of Tower Hamlets v Ayinde* (1994) 26 HLR 631, see earlier).

It is apparent that the issue of the intention of the parties is no longer a decisive factor except to the extent to which it may be used as evidence in deciding whether legal relations were ever intended. But even this fails to explain adequately the decision of the House of Lords in *Westminster City Council v Clarke.*

Where accommodation is being provided for two or more persons, the court has to take into account the following factors in order to determine whether a joint tenancy has been created:

(1) whether the agreements with each of the occupants are to last for the same period of time and commence on the same date;

(2) whether the accommodation provided can realistically be treated as divisible into separate units of accommodation, each for use by an individual occupant, or whether that accommodation is really a single living unit;

(3) whether any terms which purport to deny to the occupants exclusive possession were included solely for the purpose of avoiding statutory protection given to tenants, and were never seriously intended to be acted upon;

(4) whether there was a previous relationship of some kind between the occupants, or whether they came to the accommodation separately; and

(5) whether there is in existence the 'four unities' required for a joint tenancy. Was there, for example, a joint obligation to pay the whole sum required to be paid or merely separate obligations to pay an equal share?

These factors by no means comprise an exhaustive list and no doubt others will be added as the lease/licence debate continues into the future.

CHAPTER 4

FITNESS FOR HABITATION AND REPAIRS

INTRODUCTION

This chapter is concerned with the law relating to fitness for habitation and state of repair of tenanted premises. There are two main aspects to this area: one relates to the private remedies of a tenant, the other to what may be called 'public' remedies, involving the local housing authority or Environmental Health Department. Private remedies can also be divided into two parts, one concerned with the state of the premises at the start of the tenancy, the other with dilapidations that may arise during the course of the tenancy.

Fit housing is an important aspect of social and physical well-being. Poor housing tends to be associated with poor health and economic and social deprivation. Decent housing can therefore be argued to be as much a social right as a right to a decent income or a decent health service. One of the functions of housing law should, therefore, be to ensure that every tenant is entitled to basic amenities and standards of accommodation which are decent and humane. At the same time, however, tenants should not be free from all responsibility for the condition of their accommodation. Housing law ought therefore to aim to balance the often opposed interests of the landlord and tenant, whilst recognising that there are many different types of residential property and that it is not always the landlord who has the upper hand.

Unfortunately, English housing law concerned with the landlord/tenant relationship lurks far behind that of its American counterpart. American jurisprudence regards the contract of tenancy in the same way as it regards a contract for the provision of goods or services ie as 'consumer' based. This has led to a recognition in the United States that tenants are entitled to accommodation which is reasonably fit for its intended purpose, namely, fit to live in. American courts have therefore developed housing law over the last 30 years so that it now recognises an implied warranty of habitability in all types of residential tenancies. English law, on the other hand, still to some extent regards the tenancy as a conveyance of a leasehold estate in land and therefore as a special branch of land law, rather than as part of consumer law. Consequently, it has failed to rid itself of its historical shackles, principally that of *caveat emptor*; and has developed in a piecemeal way as a set of common law and statutory rules developed to meet specific situations without having any overall thread or principle (see Landlord and Tenant: Responsibility for State and Condition of Property, Law Com No 238). This chapter will outline the way in which this has come about.

PART I
PRIVATE LAW REMEDIES RELATING TO STANDARDS OF ACCOMMODATION

Landlords' private law duties concerning the state of tenanted premises arise from three different sources:

(1) Duties arising from express contractual agreement;

(2) Duties imposed by the common law; and

(3) Duties implied by statute.

This Part will outline the law relating to each of these three sources.

DUTIES ARISING FROM EXPRESS CONTRACTUAL AGREEMENT

The landlord may have included a covenant by which the exterior and/or interior repairs are his responsibility. If a dispute arises, the resolution of that dispute will often hinge on the correct interpretation of the repairing covenant. One fundamental question which may arise here is whether 'repair' will extend to replacement or what is essentially improvement.

The tenant may also have some responsibility for repairs cast upon him under the terms of the tenancy and this too may lead to a dispute between the parties.

Landlord's express covenant for repair

'Repair' differs from improvement, but it is not always easy in practice to distinguish between them. In *Brew Brothers v Snax Ross Ltd* [1970] 1 QB 612, Lord Justice Sachs stated that, in order to decide whether a particular fault came within a repairing obligation, one had to look: 'at the particular building ... at the state which it is in at the date of the lease, and then to come to a conclusion as to whether, on a fair interpretation of those terms in relation to that state, the requisite work can fairly be termed repair ... '.

The question of whether repair extends to the curing of a design defect arose in *Ravenseft Properties v Davstone (Holdings) Ltd* [1980] QB 12. In that case, a block of flats had been constructed without the use of expansion joints to retain the stone cladding against the concrete frame. When settlement occurred, the stone cladding threatened to come away from the frame; the only way to cure this problem was to put in the missing expansion joints. It was argued, however, that this involved the curing of a design defect and therefore did not fall within the landlord's repairing obligation in the tenancy. The court disagreed and took into account the necessity for the work to be done, the cost of that work in comparison to the value of the block as a whole, and the fact that the work required was not that extensive. The court concluded that 'repair' could include the remedying of an inherent design defect if the repairs could only sensibly be done by removing that defect. This decision was approved by the Court of Appeal in *Quick v Taff Ely BC* [1986] QB 809 after *Wainwright v Leeds City Council*

[1984] 270 EG 1289 appeared to go back on it. Lord Justice Lawton in *Quick* expressed the opinion that nearly all repair work involved some degree of renewal, but that the landlord was not obliged to provide the tenant with a better property than he had to start with. On the facts of *Quick*, however, the court rejected the tenant's claim on the basis that disrepair related to the physical condition of the property and not to its lack of amenity or inefficiency, eg, lack of sufficient heating which leads to mould growth on furniture and furnishings. In *McDougall v Easington DC* (1989) 21 HLR 310 the Court of Appeal went further by setting out guidelines for determining whether particular works fell within the concept of repairs. It stated that the distinction between 'repairs' and 'improvement' was essentially one of fact and degree. Three tests, which might be applied separately or concurrently according to the particular facts, were set out:

(1) Whether the alterations went to the whole (or substantially the whole) of the structure, or only to a subsidiary part;

(2) Whether the effect of the alterations would be to provide a building of a wholly different character than that which had been let; and

(3) What would be the cost of the works in relation to the previous value of the building, and what would their effect be on the value and life span of the building?

However, these were to be approached in the light of the following three factors:

1. The nature and age of the premises;

2. Their condition at the beginning of the tenancy;

3. The other express terms of the tenancy.

More recently, in *Holding & Management Ltd v Property Holding & Investment Trust plc* [1990] 1 All ER 938, the court made some important comments on what constitutes 'repair'. According to Nicholls LJ:

> [The] exercise involves considering the context in which the word 'repair' appears in a particular lease and also the defect and remedial work proposed. Accordingly, the circumstances to be taken into account in a particular case under one or other of these heads will include some or all of the following: the nature of the building; the terms of the lease; the state of the building at the date of the lease, the nature and extent of the defect sought to be remedied; the nature, extent and cost of the proposed remedial works, at whose expense the proposed remedial works are to be done; the value of the building and its expected life span; the effect of the works on such value and life span; current building practice; the likelihood of a recurrence if one remedy rather than another is adopted; and the comparative cost of alternative remedial works and their impact on the use and enjoyment of the building by the occupants. The weight to be attached to these circumstances will vary from case to case.

> This is not a comprehensive list. In some cases there will be other matters properly to be taken into account. For example, as in the present case, where a design or construction fault has led to part of the building falling into a state of disrepair, and the proposed remedial works extend to other parts of the building, an important consideration will be the likelihood of similar disrepair arising in the other parts of the building if remedial work is not undertaken there also, and how soon such further disrepair is likely to arise.

Although the above decisions add some clarity to the issue, there is still a degree of uncertainty over what constitutes 'repair'. It would appear, however, that the principle set out in *Ravenseft* has survived and that the issue remains essentially one of fact and degree.

The tenant's express obligations for repair

Short-term tenants do not commonly have repairing obligations imposed on them by the express terms of their tenancy. Longer term tenancies (such as 99 year leases) may, however, contain more onerous repairing covenants. Examples include covenants:

(1) To put in repair,

(2) To keep in repair, or

(3) To leave in repair.

An exception for 'fair wear and tear' may also be included.

A covenant to put in repair may require the tenant to do work of a specified standard (such as 'tenantable repair') either when the tenancy begins or within a reasonable time thereafter; if no such standard is specified, the tenant is only obliged to render the premises fit for the purpose for which he took the tenancy, ie in the context of domestic accommodation, to make the house fit for human habitation.

A covenant to keep the premises in repair will logically necessitate the tenant putting the property into repair if in need of repair at the start of the tenancy; the tenant will also be obliged to deliver up the premises in a state of repair at the end of the tenancy.

A separate covenant to leave in repair will not oblige the tenant to carry out any repairs until the lease is about to come to an end.

If an exception for 'fair wear and tear' is included in a repairing covenant, then the tenant:

> ... is bound to keep the house in good repair and condition, but is not liable for what is due to reasonable wear and tear ... Reasonable wear and tear means the reasonable use of the house by the tenant and the ordinary operation of natural forces. The exception of want of repair due to wear and tear must be construed as limited to what is directly due to wear and tear, reasonable conduct on the part of the tenant being assumed ... (*per* Talbot J in *Haskell v Marlow* [1928] KB 45 at pp 58–59).

The tenant is, therefore, relieved of liability only for the direct damage which he can prove flowed from the reasonable usage of the property and from the ordinary operation of the elements; he will not be relieved of liability for further, indirect damage which can be causally traced back to damage falling within the 'fair wear and tear' exception: 'He is bound to do such repairs as may be required to prevent the consequences flowing originally from wear and tear producing others which wear and tear would not directly produce' (*per* Talbot J, above).

See also *Regis Property Co Ltd v Dudley* [1959] AC 370.

DUTIES IMPOSED BY THE COMMON LAW

The starting point for any discussion of the landlord's liability at common law is the aged principle of *caveat emptor*: tenant beware.

The general principle is that unless a landlord specifically undertakes responsibility for repairs, the tenant has no right to demand that the premises be put or kept in repair or in a condition suitable for human habitation. The tenant was expected to negotiate with the landlord about repairs and to have expressly included suitable terms in the tenancy; otherwise he took the premises as he found them. There are, however, limited exceptions to this general principle, where the common law does impose certain obligations on the landlord despite no provision having been made for them in the tenancy agreement.

The landlord's obligations at common law can be divided into those that relate to the condition of the premises at the start of the tenancy and those which relate to disrepair occurring during the course of the tenancy.

Landlord's liability at common law for defects existing at the start of the tenancy

English law relating to standards of accommodation at the start of a tenancy has never successfully been able to escape from its historical roots. The principle of *caveat emptor* has been the proverbial 'millstone around the neck' in this respect. Despite the social and economic changes brought about as a result of the Industrial Revolution, *caveat emptor* is as much with us today as it was in the times when England was largely a rural community. Inroads on the principle have been made, however, by the courts developing the laws of negligence and nuisance so as to cover specific situations where a landlord bears some moral responsibility in the sense of having created a situation of danger for his tenant. Further inroads have been made by the recognition, in limited circumstances, of an implied condition of fitness for human habitation.

Implied condition of fitness for human habitation

The first important exception to *caveat emptor* was developed in 1843 in the case of *Smith v Marrable* (1843) 11 M&W 5. In that case it was recognised that a landlord undertakes an implied obligation that furnished residential premises are in a state reasonably fit for human habitation at the commencement of the tenancy. The tenant had discovered bugs in the furnished property immediately after entering into possession; despite attempts to get rid of the bugs, the problem remained. The tenant purported to repudiate the tenancy by sending to the landlord a week's rent with the key and by vacating the property.

The Court of Exchequer, in a landlord's action to recover the remaining rent, held that since there was an implied obligation on the landlord's part that the premises should be reasonably fit for human habitation at the start of the tenancy, the tenant had been entitled to repudiate the tenancy for breach of contract.

Smith v Marrable

Parke B: This case involves the question whether, in point of law, a person who lets a
house must be taken to let it under the implied condition that it is in a state fit for
decent and comfortable habitation, and whether he is at liberty to throw it up,
when he makes the discovery that it is not so. The case of *Edwards v Hetherington*
(1825) (Ry&M 268: SC, 7 D&R 117) appears to me to be an authority very nearly
in point. There the defendant, who held a house as from year to year, quitted
without notice, on the ground that the walls were in so dilapidated a state that it
had become unsafe to reside in it; and Lord Tenterden, at Nisi Prius, held these
facts to be an answer to an action by the landlord for use and occupation: telling
the jury, that although slight circumstances would not suffice, such serious
reasons might exist as would justify a tenant's quitting at any time, and that it
was for them to say whether, in the case before them, such serious reasons
existed as would exempt the defendant from the plaintiff's demand, on the
ground of his having had no beneficial use and occupation of the premises. The
jury found for the defendant, and the Court of King's Bench was afterwards
moved for a new trial on the ground of misdirection, but they refused to disturb
the verdict. There is also another case of *Collins v Barrow* (1831) (1 M&Rob 112),
in which Bayley B held that a tenant was justified in quitting without notice
premises which were noxious and unwholesome for want of proper sewerage.
These authorities appear to me fully to warrant the position, that if the demised
premises are encumbered with a nuisance of so serious a nature that no person
can reasonably be expected to live in them, the tenant is at liberty to throw them
up. This is not the case of a contract on the part of the landlord that the premises
were free from this nuisance; it rather rests in an implied condition of law, that
he undertakes to let them in a habitable state ...

The weakness of the decision in *Smith v Marrable* is that it does not extend to
unfurnished lettings, nor does it impose a duty upon the landlord to maintain
the premises in a fit state throughout the course of the tenancy. The obligation
relates only to fitness for human habitation and not to the state of repair
generally; and there is no obligation relating to the fitness of any furniture or
appliances provided by the landlord. The standard of fitness is also a common
law standard and not that imposed by legislation in other contexts, such as
under the Housing Act 1985 or under s 8 Landlord and Tenant Act 1985.
Another weakness is that the only remedy available to the tenant is to repudiate
the tenancy and claim damages for breach of contract – he cannot compel the
landlord to put the premises into a state fit for human habitation. Liability is
confined to the tenant himself and does not extend to members of his family
who may suffer health problems as a result of the defects.

The result of the limitations imposed upon *Smith v Marrable* has been to
curtail the potential for the development of a comprehensive body of law aimed
at eradicating poor housing in the tenanted residential sector. This stands in
stark contrast to housing law in the United States, where a general warranty of
habitability for residential tenancies has emerged. In American housing law, the
residential tenancy is perceived as a consumer contract and is treated as
analogous to a contract for the provision of goods and services (see *Javins v First
National Realty Corporation* 428 F 2d 1071 (1970)).

See further *Sarsons v Roberts* [1895] 2 QB 395 and *Hart v Windsor* (1844) 12
M&W 68.

Liability arising in the tort of negligence

At one time, the principle of *caveat emptor* would have prevented a landlord from being liable to his tenant in respect of the dangerous state of the premises at the start of the tenancy. This immunity from suit, however, no longer applies if the landlord has designed or built the premises in question.

As part of his common law duties, a landlord who has designed or built the tenanted premises must now ensure that those premises are reasonably safe when let. It is a duty imposed by the tort of negligence which extends to any foreseeable victim of the landlord's breach of duty and is therefore not confined within the contractual nexus. This common law duty was recognised by the Court of Appeal in *Rimmer v Liverpool Corporation* [1985] QB 1, in which the tenant of a flat was injured when he fell through a thin glass panel which formed part of a dividing wall inside the flat. The tenant had complained to the local authority about the potential danger from the glass panel at the start of the tenancy, but had been told that it was a 'standard feature' and that nothing could be done about it. The local authority were nevertheless held liable to the tenant for its negligence in the design and construction of the flat.

It had been considered that this case might have been impliedly overruled by the House of Lords' decision in *Murphy v Brentwood District Council* [1990] 2 All ER 908, which denied liability to a house owner for financial loss involving damage to the house arising from a defective raft foundation. The decision of the Court of Appeal in *Targett v Torfaen Borough Council* [1992] 2 All ER 27, (1992) 24 HLR 164, however, has not only confirmed the decision in *Rimmer* but has also made it clear that prior knowledge of the defect on the tenant's part can at most be treated as contributory negligence if the tenant cannot avoid the risk completely and cannot reasonably be expected to remove it himself eg, where steps give access to the property but are not adequately lit and have no, or too short, a handrail. In *McNerny v Lambeth Borough Council* (1988) 21 HLR 188, on the other hand, the Court of Appeal refused to hold a landlord authority liable for a defect on the basis that the landlord was a 'bare landlord' ie a landlord who was not responsible for creating the danger, and who had not designed or built the house. The principle of *caveat emptor* stemming from *Cavalier v Pope* [1906] AC 428 therefore still holds good for those lettings in which the landlord did not create the danger and is nothing more than a 'bare landlord'.

The most likely beneficiary of the principle established in *Rimmer* and approved in *Targett* will be the public sector or Housing Association tenant, since few private sector landlords will have been responsible for the design or construction of the leased residential property.

Apart from the situations discussed above, the landlord will not be held responsible for the state of the premises at the start of the tenancy.

The landlord's obligations at common law during the tenancy

Implied duty to repair the exterior

Where a tenant has a duty imposed upon him by the terms of the tenancy to repair the interior of a dwelling, but neither party has expressly agreed to be responsible for exterior repairs, the court may impose the latter obligation upon the landlord as a matter of ordinary contract law as an implied term of the contract. Such a duty may be imposed upon the landlord in order to give 'business efficacy' to the contract of tenancy. In *Barrett v Lounova* (1982) Ltd [1990] 1 QB 348, [1989] 1 All ER 351, the Court of Appeal considered that if the tenant's obligation to repair the interior was to be carried out properly, this could only be done if someone was responsible for exterior repairs; the only workable solution was to make the landlord responsible for such repairs by implying a term into the contract to that effect.

Barrett v Lounova Ltd

Kerr LJ: I turn now to the more recent cases. They show that there is no rule of law against the implication of any repairing covenant against landlords and that the ordinary principles of construction concerning implied terms apply to leases in that context as they apply generally in the law of contract. That is illustrated, but in a very different context, by the decision of the House of Lords in *Liverpool City Council v Irwin* [1976] 2 All ER 39, [1977] AC 239. I need not refer to that case, but I should mention two other cases, both decisions of this court, which show that implication of a landlord's repairing covenant is a permissible approach if the terms of the agreement and circumstances justify it ...

(Lord Justice Kerr referred to *Sleafer v Lambeth Metropolitan BC* [1959] 3 All ER 378, [1960] 1 QB 43 and to *Duke of Westminster v Guild* [1984] 3 All ER 144, [1985] QB 688, before continuing:)

So it follows that a repairing obligation on the landlord can clearly arise as a matter of implication. But that leaves the question already mentioned, which I find difficult and on the borderline whether the terms and circumstances of this particular lease enable such an implication to be made. As to that, although I have not found this an easy case, I agree with the conclusion of the recorder. In my view the clue lies in what Slade LJ referred to as a 'correlative obligation', in this case one which is correlative to the express covenant by the tenant to keep the inside and fixtures in good repair, order and condition. The considerations which lead me to that conclusion are the following. It is obvious, as shown by this case itself, that sooner or later the covenant imposed on the tenant in respect of the inside can no longer be complied with unless the outside has been kept in repair. Moreover, it is also clear that the covenant imposed on the tenant was intended to be enforceable throughout the tenancy. For instance, it could not possibly be contended that it would cease to be enforceable if the outside fell into disrepair. In my view it is therefore, as a matter of business efficacy to make this agreement workable, that an obligation to keep the outside in repair must be imposed on someone. For myself, I would reject the persuasive submission of counsel for the landlord that both parties may have thought that in practice the landlord (or possibly the tenant) would do the necessary repairs, so that no problem would arise. In my view that is not a businesslike construction of a tenancy agreement. Accordingly, on the basis that an obligation to keep the outside in a proper state of repair must be imposed on someone, three answers are possible.

First, that the tenant is obliged to keep the outside in repair as well as the inside, at any rate to such extent as may be necessary to enable him to perform his covenant. I would reject that as being unbusinesslike and unrealistic. In the case of a tenancy of this nature, which was to become a monthly tenancy after one year, the rent being paid weekly, it is clearly unrealistic to conclude that this could have been the common intention. In that context it is to be noted that in *Warren v Keen* [1953] 1 All ER 1118, [1954] 1 QB 15 this court held that a weekly tenant was under no implied obligation to do any repairs to the structure of the premises due to wear and tear or lapse of time or otherwise and that it was doubtful whether he was even obliged to ensure that the premises remained wind and watertight. Any construction which casts on the tenant the obligation to keep the outside in proper repair must in my view be rejected for these reasons, and also because there is an express tenant's covenant relating to the inside so that it would be wrong, as a matter of elementary construction, to imply a covenant relating to the outside as well.

The second solution would be the implication of a joint obligation on both parties to keep the outside in good repair. I reject that as being obviously unworkable and I do not think that counsel for the landlord really suggested the contrary.

That leaves one with the third solution, an implied obligation on the landlord. In my view this is the only solution which makes business sense. The recorder reached the same conclusion by following much the same route, and I agree with him. Accordingly I would dismiss this appeal.

In *Barrett v Lounova* (1982) Ltd, the tenancy agreement pre-dated s 11 Landlord and Tenant Act 1985, which imposes on a landlord a statutory obligation to repair the exterior of a dwelling-house.

The *Barrett* principle is a clear development of the law but is apparently confined to situations where the tenant has undertaken some repairing obligations (see *Demetriou v Poolaction Ltd* [1991] EGLR 100). It will not apply if no correlative duty is imposed on the tenant.

Landlord's duties relating to retained parts of, or adjoining, premises

There are two distinct situations where a tenant might justifiably complain about the condition of premises retained by the landlord. The first is where the defects in retained neighbouring property may have an adverse effect on either the tenanted property or its occupation. The second is where the defects on adjoining property, or on parts over which the landlord retains control, interfere with the exercise of the tenant's rights of access or similar rights.

The first situation is the most difficult of the two. Several possibilities arise here. One is for the tenant to sue the landlord on the covenant for quiet enjoyment if the state of neighbouring property is such as to interfere with the tenant's peaceful enjoyment of the tenanted premises.

Another is for the tenant to sue the landlord in the tort of nuisance, or in negligence (see *Sharpe v Manchester City Council* (1977) 5 HLR 71), or under the Rule in *Rylands v Fletcher* (1868) LR 330 if the defect 'escapes' onto the tenant's property, eg water escaping from the landlord's neighbouring property onto the tenant's adjoining property. Yet another possibility is for the tenant to allege breach of the principle of non-derogation from grant against the landlord, although this possibility is unlikely to work in the residential premises context.

A final possibility is to argue for an implied term of the tenancy (see *Edmonton Corporation v WM Knowles & Son Ltd* (1961) 60 LGR 124 cf *Tennant Radiant Heat Ltd v Warrington Development Corporation* [1988] 1 EGLR 41). The latter possibility, however, remains the most difficult and elusive of all; a court will be reluctant to imply a term to the effect that the landlord must repair neighbouring property for the tenant's benefit unless this is clearly necessary in order to lend 'business efficacy' to the tenancy contract.

The second situation is far clearer. The typical situation is where the landlord of a block of flats has retained control over those parts common to all tenants, such as the lift and stairways, and over which the tenant exercises certain rights. Adequate repair of means of access retained by landlords but used by tenants is fundamental if tenants are to be able to use the tenanted premises properly. This has been duly recognised by the House of Lords in *Liverpool City Council v Irwin* [1977] AC 239. In that case, Haigh Heights, a tower block in Liverpool, had been erected as part of a slum clearance scheme. The block had been the subject of much vandalism such that the lifts were often out of working order and the stairs were littered with rubbish and were badly lit. Communal rubbish chutes were provided for use by tenants. Each tenant therefore had a right to use the stairs, lifts and rubbish chutes. The defendants, who were tenants on a high floor maisonette, refused to pay rent as a result of which possession proceedings were commenced against them by the council. The defendants counterclaimed, *inter alia*, that the council was in breach of a common law duty to keep the common parts of the block in repair. The House of Lords ruled that the council did have an implied contractual duty of care to maintain in a state of reasonable repair and usability the lifts, rubbish chutes, lighting and stairs which were 'common parts' of the tower block.

Liverpool City Council v Irwin

Lord Wilberforce: ... I consider first the tenants' claim in so far as it is based on contract. The first step must be to ascertain what the contract is. This may look elementary, even naive, but it seems to me to be the essential step and to involve, from the start, an approach different from, if simpler than, that taken by the members of the Court of Appeal. We look first at documentary material. As is common with council lettings there is no formal demise, or lease or tenancy agreement. There is a document headed 'Liverpool Corporation, Liverpool City Housing Dept' and described as 'Conditions of Tenancy'. This contains a list of obligations upon the tenant – he shall do this, he shall not do that, or he shall not do that without the corporation's consent. This is an amalgam of obligations added to from time to time, no doubt, to meet complaints, emerging situations, or problems as they appear to the council's officers. In particular there have been added special provisions relating to multi-storey flats which are supposed to make the conditions suitable to such dwellings. We may note under 'Further special notes' some obligations not to obstruct staircases and passages, and not to permit children under 10 to operate any lifts. I mention these as a recognition of the existence and relevance of these facilities. At the end there is a form for signature by the tenant stating that he accepts the tenancy. On the landlords' side there is nothing, no signature, no demise, no covenant: the contract takes effect as soon as the tenants sign the form and are let into possession.

We have then a contract which is partly, but not wholly, stated in writing. In order to complete it, in particular to give it a bilateral character, it is necessary to take account of the actions of the parties and the circumstances. As actions of the parties, we must note the granting of possession by the landlords and reservation by them of the 'common parts' – stairs, lifts, chutes, etc. As circumstances we must include the nature of the premises, viz, a maisonette for family use on the ninth floor of a high block, one which is occupied by a large number of other tenants, all using the common parts and dependent upon them, none of them having any expressed obligation to maintain or repair them.

To say that the construction of a complete contract out of these elements involves a process of 'implication' may be correct; it would be so if implication means the supplying of what is not expressed. But there are varieties of implications which the courts think fit to make and they do not necessarily involve the same process. Where there is, on the face of it, a complete, bilateral contract, the courts are sometimes willing to add terms to it, as implied terms: this is very common in mercantile contracts where there is an established usage: in that case the courts are spelling out what both parties know and would, if asked, unhesitatingly agree to be part of the bargain. In other cases, where there is an apparently complete bargain, the courts are willing to add a term on the ground that without it the contract will not work – this is the case, if not of *The Moorcock* (1889) 14 PD 64 itself on its facts, at least of the doctrine of *The Moorcock* as usually applied. This is, as was pointed out by the majority in the Court of Appeal, a strict test – though the degree of strictness seems to vary with the current legal trend – and I think that they were right not to accept it as applicable here. There is a third variety of implication, that which I think Lord Denning MR favours, or at least did favour in this case, and that is the implication of reasonable terms. But though I agree with many of his instances, which in fact fall under one or other of the preceding heads, I cannot go so far as to endorse his principle; indeed, it seems to me, with respect, to extend a long, and undesirable, way beyond sound authority.

The present case, in my opinion, represents I would rather say a fourth category, or I would rather say a fourth shade on a continuous spectrum. The court here is simply concerned to establish what the contract is, the parties not having themselves fully stated the terms. In this sense the court is searching for what must be implied.

What then should this contract be held to be? There must first be implied a letting, that is, a grant of the right of exclusive possession to the tenants. With this there must, I would suppose, be implied a covenant for quiet enjoyment, as a necessary incident of the letting. The difficulty begins when we consider the common parts. We start with the fact that the demise is useless unless access is obtained by the staircase; we can add that, having regard to the height of the block, and the family nature of the dwellings, the demise would be useless without a lift service; we can continue that, there being rubbish chutes built into the structures and no other means of disposing of light rubbish, there must be a right to use the chutes. The question to be answered – and it is the only question in this case – is what is to be the legal relationship between landlord and tenant as regards these matters.

There can be no doubt that there must be implied (i) an easement for the tenants and their licensees to use the stairs, (ii) a right in the nature of an easement to use the lifts, (iii) an easement to use the rubbish chutes.

But are these easements to be accompanied by any obligation upon the landlord, and what obligation? There seem to be two alternatives. The first, for which the council contends, is for an easement coupled with no legal obligation, except such as may arise under the Occupiers' Liability Act 1957 as regards the safety of those using the facilities, and possibly such other liability as might exist under the ordinary law of tort. The alternative is for easements coupled with some obligation on the part of the landlords as regards the maintenance of the subject of them, so that they are available for use.

My Lords, in order to be able to choose between these, it is necessary to define what test is to be applied, and I do not find this difficult. In my opinion such obligation should be read into the contract as the nature of the contract itself implicitly requires, no more, no less: a test, in other words, of necessity. The relationship accepted by the corporation is that of landlord and tenant: the tenant accepts obligations accordingly, in relation *inter alia* to the stairs, the lifts and the chutes. All these are not just facilities, or conveniences provided at discretion: they are essentials of the tenancy without which life in the dwellings, as a tenant, is not possible. To leave the landlord free of contractual obligation as regards these matters, and subject only to administrative or political pressure, is, in my opinion, inconsistent totally with the nature of this relationship. The subject-matter of the lease (high rise blocks) and the relationship created by the tenancy demand, of their nature, some contractual obligation on the landlord.

I do not think that this approach involves any innovation as regards the law of contract. The necessity to have regard to the inherent nature of a contract and of the relationship thereby established was stated in this House in *Lister v Romford Ice and Cold Storage Co Ltd* [1957] AC 555. That was a case between master and servant and of a search for an 'implied term'. Viscount Simonds, at p 579, makes a clear distinction between a search for an implied term such as might be necessary to give 'business efficacy' to the particular contract and a search, based on wider considerations, for such a term as the nature of the contract might call for, or as a legal incident of this kind of contract. If the search were for the former, he says, ' ... I should lose myself in the attempt to formulate it with the necessary precision' (p 576). We see an echo of this in the present case, when the majority in the Court of Appeal, considering a 'business efficacy term' – ie, a 'Moorcock' term (*The Moorcock*, 14 PD 64) – found themselves faced with five alternative terms and therefore rejected all of them. But that is not, in my opinion, the end, or indeed the object, of the search.

We have some guidance in authority for the kind of term which this typical relationship (of landlord and tenant in a multi-occupational dwelling) requires in *Miller v Hancock* [1893] 2 QB 177. There Bowen LJ said, at pp 180–181:

> 'The tenants could only use their flats by using the staircase. The defendant, therefore, when he let the flats, impliedly granted to the tenants an easement over the staircase, which he retained in his own occupation, for the purpose of the enjoyment of the flats so let.

Under those circumstances, what is the law as to the repairs of the staircase? It was contended by the defendant's counsel that according to the common law, the person in enjoyment of an easement is bound to do the necessary repairs himself. That may be true with regard to easements in general, but it is subject to the qualification that the grantor of the easement may undertake to do the repairs either in express terms or by necessary implication. This is not the mere case of a grant of an easement without special circumstances. It appears to me obvious, when one considers what a flat of this kind is, and the only way in which it can be enjoyed, that the parties to the demise of it must have intended by necessary implication, as a basis without which the whole transaction would be futile, that the landlord should maintain the staircase, which is essential to the enjoyment of the premises demised, and should keep it reasonably safe for the use of the tenants, and also of those persons who would necessarily go up and down the stairs in the ordinary course of business with the tenants: because, of course, a landlord must know when he lets a flat that tradesmen and other persons having business with the tenant must have access to it. It seems to me that it would render the whole transaction inefficacious and absurd if an implied undertaking were not assumed on the part of the landlord to maintain the staircase so far as might be necessary for the reasonable enjoyment of the demised premises.'

Certainly that case, as a decision concerning a claim by a visitor, has been overruled: *Fairman v Perpetual Investment Building Society* [1923] AC 74. But I cite the passage for its common sense as between landlord and tenant, and you cannot overrule common sense.

There are other passages in which the same thought has been expressed. *De Meza v Ve-Ri-Best Manufacturing Co Ltd* (1952) 160 EG 364 was a case of failure to maintain a lift in which Lord Evershed MR sitting with Denning and Romer LJJ held the landlords liable in damages for breach of an implied obligation to provide a working lift. The agreement was more explicit than the present agreement in that there was an express demise of the flat 'together with the use of the lift', but I think there is no doubt that the same demise or grant must be implied here, and if so can lead to the same result.

In *Penn v Gatenex Co Ltd* [1958] 2 QB 210, a case about a refrigerator in a flat, Sellers LJ said, at p 227:

> 'If an agreement gives a tenant the use of something wholly in the occupation and control of the landlord, for example, a lift, it would, I think, be accepted that the landlord would be required to maintain the lift, especially if it were the only means of access to the demised premises. I recognise that a lift might vary in age and efficiency, but in order to give meaning to the words 'the use of' and to fulfil them, it should at least be maintained so that it would take a tenant up and down, subject to temporary breakdown and reasonable stoppages for maintenance and repairs.'

That was a dissenting judgment, but Lord Evershed MR, at p 220, makes a similar observation as to lifts.

These are all reflections of what necessarily arises *whenever* a landlord portions off a building for multiple occupation, retaining essential means of access.

I accept, of course, the argument that a mere grant of an easement does not carry with it any obligation on the part of the servient owner to maintain the subject-matter. The dominant owner must spend the money, for example in repairing a drive leading to his house. And the same principle may apply when a landlord lets an upper floor with access by a staircase: responsibility for maintenance may well rest on the tenant. But there is a difference between that case and the case where there is an essential means of access, retained in the landlord's occupation, to units in a building of multi-occupation, for unless the obligation to maintain is, in a defined manner, placed upon the tenants, individually or collectively, the nature of the contract and the circumstances, require that it be placed on the landlord.

It remains to define the standard. My Lords, if, as I think, the test of the existence of the term is necessity the standard must surely not exceed what is necessary having regard to the circumstances. To imply an absolute obligation to repair would go beyond what is a necessary legal incident and would indeed be unreasonable. An obligation to take reasonable care to keep in reasonable repair and usability is what fits the requirements of the case. Such a definition involves – and I think rightly – recognition that the tenants themselves have their responsibilities. What it is reasonable to expect of a landlord has a clear relation to what a reasonable set of tenants should do for themselves ...

I would hold therefore that the landlords' obligation is as I have described. And in agreement, I believe, with your Lordships I would hold that it has not been shown in this case that there was any breach of that obligation. On the main point therefore I would hold that the appeal fails.

The tenants had alleged that an absolute duty should be imposed, but the House of Lords considered that it would be unreasonable to impose so high a duty on the council.

It may be possible to exclude liability under *Liverpool CC v Irwin* to a tenant, since the House of Lords recognised that the duty is an implied contractual duty of care. However, the Unfair Contract Terms Act 1977 (which applies in the 'business context') might affect a purported exclusion of either the duty or any resulting liability, such as either to prevent reliance on it at all or to allow reliance only to the extent that the exclusion is 'reasonable'.

It had been suggested that the principle from the *Liverpool* case might only apply to dwellings designed for multiple occupation (see *Duke of Westminster v Guild* [1985] QB 688). In *King v South Northamptonshire District Council* (1992) 24 HLR 284, however, the court applied the same principle to a council house rear access in favour of a tenant who needed to use it for wheelchair access to the house.

It might be questioned whether the court was here extending the *Liverpool* case merely because it felt sorry for the disabled tenant, rather than on the basis of any coherent strategy. The result, however, is to leave the ambit of the principle from *Liverpool CC v Irwin* uncertain.

IMPLIED DUTIES ARISING UNDER STATUTE

The piecemeal nature with which the common law has treated the landlord's implied obligations relating to fitness and repair has led to statutory intervention. The present law is contained in ss 8 and 11 Landlord and Tenant Act 1985.

Landlord and Tenant Act 1985

8. Implied terms as to fitness for human habitation

(1) In a contract to which this section applies for the letting of a house for human habitation there is implied, notwithstanding any stipulation to the contrary–

    (a) a condition that the house is fit for human habitation at the commencement of the tenancy, and

    (b) an undertaking that the house will be kept by the landlord fit for human habitation during the tenancy.

(2) The landlord, or a person authorised by him in writing, may at reasonable times of the day, on giving 24 hours' notice in writing to the tenant or occupier, enter premises to which this section applies for the purpose of viewing their state and condition.

(3) This section applies to a contract if–

    (a) the rent does not exceed the figure applicable in accordance with subsection (4), and

    (b) the letting is not on such terms as to the tenant's responsibility as are mentioned in subsection (5).

(4) The rent limit for the application of this section is shown by the following Table, by reference to the date of making of the contract and the situation of the premises:

Table

Date of making of contract	*Rent limit*
Before 31st July 1923	In London: £40 Elsewhere: £26 or £16
On or after 31st July 1923 and before 6th July 1957	In London: £40 Elsewhere: £26
On or after 6th July 1957	In London: £80 Elsewhere: £52

10. Fitness for human habitation

In determining for the purposes of this Act whether a house is unfit for human habitation, regard shall be had to its condition in respect of the following matters–

repair,
stability,
freedom from damp,
internal arrangement,
natural lighting,
ventilation,
water supply,
drainage and sanitary conveniences,
facilities for preparation and cooking of food and for the disposal of waste water

and the house shall be regarded as unfit for human habitation if, and only if, it is so defective in one or more of those matters that it is not reasonably suitable for occupation in that condition.

11. Repairing obligations in short leases

(1) In a lease to which this section applies (as to which, see sections 13 and 14) there is implied a covenant by the lessor–

(a) to keep in repair the structure and exterior of the dwelling-house (including drains, gutters and external pipes),

(b) to keep in repair and proper working order the installations in the dwelling-house for the supply of water, gas and electricity and for sanitation (including basins, sinks, baths and sanitary conveniences, but not other fixtures, fittings and appliances for making use of the supply of water, gas or electricity), and

(c) to keep in repair and proper working order the installations in the dwelling-house for space heating and heating water.

(2) The covenant implied by subsection (1) ('the lessor's repairing covenant') shall not be construed as requiring the lessor–

(a) to carry out works or repairs for which the lessee is liable by virtue of his duty to use the premises in a tenant-like manner, or would be so liable but for an express covenant on his part,

(b) to rebuild or reinstate the premises in the case of destruction or damage by fire, or by tempest, flood or other inevitable accident, or

(c) to keep in repair or maintain anything which the lessee is entitled to remove from the dwelling-house.

(3) In determining the standard of repair required by the lessor's repairing covenant, regard shall be had to the age, character and prospective life of the dwelling-house and the locality in which it is situated.

(4) A covenant by the lessee for the repair of the premises is of no effect so far as it relates to the matters mentioned in subsection (1)(a) to (c), except so far as it imposes on the lessor any of the requirements mentioned in subsection (2)(a) or (c).

(5) The reference in subsection (4) to a covenant by the lessee for the repair of the premises includes a covenant–

    (a) to put in repair or deliver up in repair,

    (b) to paint, point or render,

    (c) to pay money in lieu of repairs by the lessee, or

    (d) to pay money on account of repairs by the lessor.

(6) In a lease in which the lessor's repairing covenant is implied there is also implied a covenant by the lessee that the lessor, or any person authorised by him in writing, may at reasonable times of the day and on giving 24 hours' notice in writing to the occupier, enter the premises comprised in the lease for the purpose of viewing their condition and state of repair.

12. Restriction on contracting out of s 11

(1) A covenant or agreement, whether contained in a lease to which section 11 applies or in an agreement collateral to such a lease, is void in so far as it purports–

    (a) to exclude or limit the obligations of the lessor or the immunities of the lessee under that section, or

    (b) to authorise any forfeiture or impose on the lessee any penalty, disability or obligation in the event of his enforcing or relying upon those obligations or immunities, unless the inclusion of the provision was authorised by the county court.

(2) The county court may by order made with the consent of the parties, authorise the inclusion in a lease, or in an agreement collateral to a lease, of provisions excluding or modifying in relation to the lease, the provisions of section 11 with respect to the repairing obligations of the parties if it appears to the court that it is reasonable to do so, having regard to all the circumstances of the case, including the other terms and conditions of the lease.

13. Leases to which s 11 applies: general rule

(1) Section 11 (repairing obligations) applies to a lease of a dwelling-house granted on or after 24th October 1961 for a term of less than seven years.

(2) In determining whether a lease is one to which section 11 applies–

    (a) any part of the term which falls before the grant shall be left out of account and the lease shall be treated as a lease for a term commencing with the grant,

    (b) a lease which is determinable at the option of the lessor before the expiration of seven years from the commencement of the term shall be treated as a lease for a term of less than seven years, and

    (c) a lease (other than a lease to which paragraph (b) applies) shall not be treated as a lease for a term of less than seven years if it confers on the lessee an option for renewal for a term which, together with the original term, amounts to seven years or more.

(3) This section has effect subject to–

section 14 (leases to which section 11 applies: exceptions), and section 32(2) (provisions not applying to tenancies within Part II of the Landlord and Tenant Act 1954).

14. Leases to which s 11 applies: exceptions

(1) Section 11 (repairing obligations) does not apply to a new lease granted to an existing tenant, or to a former tenant still in possession, if the previous lease was not a lease to which section 11 applied (and, in the case of a lease granted before 24th October 1961, would not have been if it had been granted on or after that date).

(2) In subsection (l)–

'existing tenant' means a person who is when, or immediately before, the new lease is granted, the lessee under another lease of the dwelling-house;

'former tenant still in possession' means a person who–

(a) was the lessee under another lease of the dwelling-house which terminated at some time before the new lease was granted, and

(b) between the termination of that other lease and the grant of the new lease was continuously in possession of the dwelling-house or of the rents and profits the dwelling-house; and

'the previous lease' means the other lease referred to in the above definitions.

(3) Section 11 does not apply to a lease of a dwelling-house which is a tenancy of an agricultural holding within the meaning of the Agricultural Holdings Act 1986.

(4) Section 11 does not apply to a lease granted on or after 3rd October 1980 to–

a local authority,

a new town corporation,

an urban development corporation,

the Development Board for Rural Wales,

a registered housing association,

a co-operative housing association, or

an educational institution or other body specified, or of a class specified, by regulations under section 8 of the Rent Act 1977 or paragraph 8 of Schedule I the Housing Act 1988 (bodies making student lettings),

a housing action trust established under Part III of the Housing Act 1988.

(5) Section 11 does not apply to a lease granted on or after 3rd October 1980 to–

(a) Her Majesty in right of the Crown (unless the lease is under the management of the Crown Estate Commissioners), or

(b) a government department or a person holding in trust for Her Majesty for the purposes of a government department.

Section 8 Landlord and Tenant Act 1985 (derived from s 6 Housing Act 1957)

Section 8, above, provides that in lettings of houses for very modest rents, there is an implied obligation on the landlord's part that the house is fit for human habitation at the start of the tenancy and will be kept fit throughout the tenancy. There is no 'contracting out' of this provision, but it does not apply if, under a tenancy for three years or more which cannot be terminated before three years has elapsed, the tenant is obliged to put the property into a condition fit for human habitation. Statutory guidance on the standard of fitness to be applied is contained in s 10. A house is therefore unfit under s 8 only if not reasonably suitable for human occupation because of the presence of one or more of the stated defects, which include repair, freedom from damp, internal arrangement, ventilation, stability, etc. The limitations on the operation of s 8 are such that it hardly ever applies in practice (see criticism of the low rent levels in *Quick v Taff Ely BC* [1986] QB 809). The statutory limits (for lettings before 6 July 1957: London £40, elsewhere £26; for lettings thereafter: London £80, elsewhere £52 per annum) impose severe restraints on the usefulness of the section; but judicial interpretation has added even more limitations. The section does not apply, for example, if the property cannot be rendered fit at reasonable expense but is a 'total constructive loss' (see *Buswell v Goodwin* [1971] 1 WLR 92). Nor does the landlord incur any liability to repair until he has had notice of the defect (see *Morgan v Liverpool Corporation* [1927] 2 KB 131).

Even where the section has been held to be applicable, the court has construed the relevant standard very narrowly. In *Stanton v Southwick* [1920] 2 KB 646, for example, the court refused to hold a landlord liable for rats which were entering a house from the sewer; but perhaps the court may be forgiven here for not realising the potential serious health hazards from the presence of rats in a house. According to the Law Commission (Landlord and Tenant: Responsibility for State and Condition of Property, No 238), landlords should be obliged to keep rented residential premises fit for human habitation. Reform can therefore be expected in the future.

Section 11 Landlord and Tenant Act 1985, as amended by s 116 Housing Act 1988 (derived from s 32 Housing Act 1961)

A far more important provision from the tenant's point of view is s 11, above. This provision relates to houses which have been let since 25 October 1961 for a period of less than seven years. It thus includes periodic tenancies. Since the s 116 Housing Act 1988 came into force, the landlord's obligations to repair under s 11 above extend to any part of a building in which he has an interest, provided that the tenanted premises form part only of that building, eg, a boiler in the basement of a block of flats would now come within s 11 if the boiler provides heating and hot water to individual tenants' flats. This has removed the former limitations placed on the Section in *Campden Hill Towers v Gardner* [1977] QB 823 and in *Douglas-Scott v Scorgie* [1984] 1 WLR 716, as to what part of the structure of a block of flats could be considered an integral part of the tenant's own flat. It has also filled in the gap which formerly had to be filled by such cases as *Liverpool CC v Irwin*.

Certain tenancies of a 'public' nature, however, are excluded if the tenancy was granted on or after 3 October 1980 (see s 14(4) and (5)).

Any agreement limiting or excluding the landlord's obligation to repair is rendered void unless the county court has authorised it in advance. Equally, of no effect is a tenant's covenant to repair insofar as it relates to matters falling within the landlord's obligation under the section.

In practice, however, the section provides only limited protection for tenants against bad housing conditions. As with s 8, so with s 11: the landlord's liability to repair only arises when he has had notice of the need for repair, although such notice need not come directly from the tenant (see *O'Brien v Robinson* [1973] AC 912 and *McGreal v Wake* (1984) 13 HLR 107).

Judicial limitations have also watered down the effectiveness of the section. In *Quick v Taff Ely BC* [1986] QB 809, [1985] 3 All ER 321, the Court of Appeal held that the section did not assist a tenant whose accommodation suffered from severe condensation dampness as a result of lack of proper insulation and insufficient heating, resulting in mould growth on furniture, bedding and clothing. 'Repair' related to the physical condition of the property and not to its lack of amenity.

Quick v Taff-Ely BC

Dillon LJ: The case turns on the construction and effect of the repairing covenant in s 32 of the 1961 Act ...

The covenant implied under s 32 is an ordinary repairing covenant. It does not only apply to local authorities as landlords, and this court has held in *Wainwright v Leeds City Council* (1984) 270 EG 1289 that the fact that a landlord is a local authority, which is discharging a social purpose in providing housing for people who cannot afford it, does not make the burden of the covenant greater on that landlord than it would be an any other landlord. The construction of the covenant must be the same whether it is implied as a local authority's covenant in a tenancy of a council house or is expressly included as a tenant's or landlord's covenant in a private lease which is outside s 32. A tenant under such a lease who had entered into such a repairing covenant would, no doubt, realise, if he suffered from problems of condensation in his house, that he could not compel the landlord to do anything about those problems. But I apprehend that the tenant would be startled to be told, as must follow from judge Francis's decision, that the landlord has the right to compel him, the tenant, to put in new windows. If the reasoning is valid, where is the process to stop? The evidence of Mr Pryce Thomas was that changing the windows and insulating the lintels would 'alleviate' the problems, not that it would cure them. If there was evidence that double glazing would further alleviate the problems, would a landlord, or tenant, under a repairing covenant be obliged to put in double glazing? Mr Pryce Thomas said that a radiator system of heating to all rooms in the place of the warm air system was 'necessary'; if the judge's reasoning was correct, it would seem that, if the point had been properly pleaded early enough, the tenant might have compelled the local authority to put in a radiator system of heating.

In my judgment, the key factor in the present case is that disrepair is related to the physical condition of whatever has to be repaired, and not to questions of lack of amenity or inefficiency. I find helpful the observation of Atkin LJ in *Anstruther-Gough-Calthorpe v McOscar* [1924] 1 KB 716 at 734, [1923] All ER Rep 198 at 206 that repair 'connotes the idea of making good damage so as to leave the subject so far as possible as though it had not been damaged'. Where decorative repair is in question one must look for damage to the decorations but where, as here, the obligation is merely to keep the structure and exterior of the house in repair, the covenant will only come into operation where there has been damage to the structure and exterior which requires to be made good.

If there is such damage caused by an unsuspected inherent defect, then it may be necessary to cure the defect, and thus to some extent improve without wholly renewing the property as the only practicable way of making good the damage to the subject-matter of the repairing covenant. That, as I read the case, was the basis of the decision in *Ravenseft*. There there was an inherent defect when the building, a relatively new one, was built in that no expansion joints had been included because it had not been realised that the different coefficients of expansion of the stone of the cladding and the concrete of the structure made it necessary to include such joints. There was, however, also physical damage to the subject-matter of the covenant in that, because of the differing coefficients of expansion, the stones of the cladding had become bowed, detached from the structure, loose and in danger of falling. Forbes J in a very valuable judgment rejected the argument that no liability arose under a repairing covenant if it could be shown that the disrepair was due to an inherent defect in the building. He allowed in the damages under the repairing covenant the cost of putting in expansion joints, and in that respect improving the building, because, as he put it ([1979] 1 All ER 929 at 938, [1980] QB 12 at 22), on the evidence 'In no realistic sense ... could it be said that there was any other possible way of reinstating this cladding than by providing the expansion joints which were, in fact, provided'.

The *Elmcroft* case was very similar. There was physical damage from rising damp in the walls of a flat in a fashionable area of London. That was due to an inherent defect in that when the flat had been built in late Victorian times as a high-class residential flat, the slate damp proof course had been put in too low and was therefore ineffective. The remedial work necessary to eradicate the rising damp was, on the evidence, the installation of a horizontal damp-proof course by silicone injection and formation of vertical barriers by silicone injection. This was held to be within the landlord's repairing covenant. It was necessary in order to repair the walls and, although it involved improvement over the previous ineffective slate damp proof course, it was held that, as a matter of degree, having regard to the nature and locality of the property, this did not involve giving the tenant a different thing from that which was demised. The decision of this court in *Smedley v Chumley & Hawke Ltd* (1981) 44 P&CR 50 is to the same effect; the damage to a recently constructed restaurant built on a concrete raft on piles over a river could only be cured by putting in further piles so that the structure of the walls and roof of the restaurant were stable and safe on foundations made structurally stable.

The only other of the many cases cited to us which I would mention is *Pembery v Lamdin* [1940] 2 All ER 434. There the property demised was a ground-floor shop and basement, built 100 years or more before the demise. The landlord was liable to repair the external part of the premises and there was physical damage to the walls of the basement in that they were permeated with damp because there had never been any damp proof course. The works required by the tenant to waterproof the basement were very extensive, involving cleaning and asphalting the existing walls, building internal brick walls and laying a concrete floor. This would have involved improvement to such an extent as to give the tenant a different thing from what had been demised and it was therefore outside the repairing covenant. But Slesser LJ appears to recognise (at 438) that repointing of the existing basement walls where the mortar had partly perished would have been within the repairing covenant.

In the present case the liability of the local authority was to keep the structure and exterior of the house in repair, not the decorations. Though there is ample evidence of damage to the decorations and to bedding, clothing and other fabrics, evidence of damage to the subject-matter of the covenant, the structure and exterior of the house, is far to seek. Though the condensation comes about from the effect of the warm atmosphere in the rooms on the cold surfaces of the walls and windows, there is no evidence at all of physical damage to the walls, as opposed to the decorations, or the windows.

There is indeed evidence of physical damage in the way of rot in parts of the wooden surrounds of some of the windows but (a) that can be sufficiently cured by replacing the defective lengths of wood and (b) it was palpably not the rot in the wooden surrounds which caused damage to the bedding, clothes and fabrics in the house, and the rot in the wooden surrounds cannot have contributed very much to the general inconvenience of living in the house for which the judge awarded general damages.

There was also, as I have mentioned, evidence of nails sweating in bedroom ceilings, and of some plaster perishing in a bedroom. The judge mentions the sweating nails in his judgment, but I have not found any mention of the perishing of plaster. The judge did not ask himself, since on the overall view he took of the case it was not necessary, whether these two elements of structural disrepair (since the local authority accepts for the purposes of this case in this court that the plaster was part of the structure of the house) were of themselves enough to require the replacement of the windows etc. They seem, however, to have been very minor elements indeed in the context of the case which the tenant was putting forward and, in my judgment, they do not warrant an order for a new trial or a remission to the judge for further findings, save in respect of the reassessment of damages as mentioned below.

As I have already mentioned, Mr Pryce Thomas used the word 'alleviate' to describe the effect which the replacement of the windows and the facing of the lintels with insulation materials would have on the problems of condensation. At one point in his judgment the judge refers to 'the work propounded by Mr Pryce Thomas as necessary to cure the condensation problems'. This must be a slip because alleviation *prima facie* falls short of cure. However, as the extent of alleviation was not probed in the court below, it is inappropriate to make any further comment.

It does appear from Mr Pryce Thomas's report that the problems of condensation would have also been alleviated if the tenant had kept the central heating on more continuously and at higher temperatures. In that event the walls and windows would have remained warm or warmer and condensation would have been reduced. As to this, the judge appreciated that some people for financial reasons have to be sparing in their use of central heating, and he found that there was no evidence at all to suggest that the lifestyle of the tenant and his family was likely to give rise to condensation problems because it was outside the spectrum of life-styles which a local authority could reasonably expect its tenants to follow. In my judgment, that finding answers the argument that it would be anomalous or unreasonable that this house should be held to be in disrepair because the tenant cannot afford to keep the heating on at a high enough temperature, whereas an identical adjoining house would not be in disrepair because the tenant had a good job and so spent more on his heating. If there is disrepair which the local authority is by its implied covenant bound to make good, then it is no answer for the local authority to say that, if the tenant could have afforded to spend more on his central heating, there would have been no disrepair, or less disrepair.

But the crux of the matter is whether there has been disrepair in relation to the structure and exterior of the building and, for the reasons I have endeavoured to explain, in my judgment, there has not, quoad the case put forward by the tenant on condensation as opposed to the case on water penetration.

I would accordingly allow this appeal. I would consequently set aside the order of the judge, save in respect of the award of costs and legal aid taxation and I would remit the case to the judge to reassess the damages (which, as I have mentioned, he assessed globally to cover both heads of claim) in the light of the judgments of this court.

One could hardly imagine more appalling living conditions than existed in *Quick*; but the Court was adamant that the landlord's duty under s 11 related to damage to the structure or exterior, and mould growing on the tenant's walls was not 'damage' for this purpose. The Court also insisted that no higher duty was to be imposed on a local authority landlord under the section than would be imposed on a private landlord.

Much of the case law on s 11 or its predecessor has been concerned with the question of what amounts to the 'structure and exterior' of a dwelling-house. In *Brown v Liverpool Corporation* [1963] 3 All ER 1345, it was held that a flagstone path and steps at the front of the house and which gave access were not part of the 'structure' but were part of the 'exterior' of a dwelling-house. In *Hopwood v Cannock Chase* [1975] 1 WLR 373, however, a back yard consisting of a concrete patio was not part of the exterior, presumably on the grounds that it did not give access to the house. Lord Justice Cairns stated that: '... the section cannot be extended beyond what was held in Brown's case to include a yard of this kind'.

If the landlord, in breach of his statutory obligation, fails to carry out repairs, as a result of which damage occurs to internal decorations, then the landlord will equally be responsible for making good that consequential damage. Likewise, if in carrying out his repairing obligation, the landlord causes damage to the internal decorative order, he must make good the damage (see *Bradley v Chorley BC* (1985) 17 HLR 305 and *McGreal v Wake* (1984) 13 HLR 107).

Liability under the Health and Safety at Work Act 1974, s 4

A surprising effect of the Health and Safety at Work Act 1974, is that certain of its provisions may be beneficial to tenants in improving the standard of access which they enjoy.

Health and Safety at Work Act 1974

4. **General duties of persons concerned with premises to persons other than their employees.**

   (1) This section has effect for imposing on persons duties in relation to those who–

   (a) are not their employees; but

   (b) use non-domestic premises made available to them as a place of work or as a place where they may use plant or substances provided for their use there, and applies to premises so made available and other non-domestic premises used in connection with them.

   (2) It shall be the duty of each person who has, to any extent, control of premises to which this section applies or of the means of access thereto or egress therefrom or of any plant or substance in such premises to take such measures as it is reasonable for a person in his position to take to ensure, so far as is reasonably practicable, that the premises, all means of access thereto

or egress therefrom available for use by persons using the premises, and any plant or substance in the premises or, as the case may be, provided for use there, is or are safe and without risks to health.

(3) Where a person has, by virtue of any contract or tenancy, an obligation of any extent in relation to–

    (a) the maintenance or repair of any premises to which this section applies or any means of access thereto or egress therefrom; or

    (b) the safety of or the absence of risks to health arising from plant or substances in any such premises;

that person shall be treated, for the purposes of subsection (2) above, as being a person who has control of the matters to which his obligation extends.

(4) Any reference in this section to a person having control of any premises or matter is a reference to a person having control of the premises or matter in connection with the carrying on by him of a trade, business or other undertaking (whether for profit or not).

This section therefore imposes on anyone having control of premises on which he carries on a trade, business or other undertaking, a duty to take reasonable care to ensure that means of access and exit from those premises are safe and without risk to health. This duty extends to any plant or substance provided for use on the premises, including lifts, but is confined to non-domestic premises and applies only in favour of non-employees. The unusual effect of this became apparent in *Westminster City Council v Select Management Ltd* [1984] 1 WLR 1058. This case concerned a block of flats in which there were lifts. The defendant management company were served with improvement notices under s 21 of the 1974 Act in relation to these lifts. The Court ruled that the lifts were 'plant'; and as they were common parts of the block of flats, they were non-domestic premises within the meaning of s 4. A failure to comply with an improvement notice under s 21 may lead to criminal liability and is therefore a potent weapon in the hands of a tenant of a block of flats who complains about the state of the lifts; but the 1974 Act is unlikely to assist the tenant of other types of residential accommodation.

Liability under s 4 Defective Premises Act 1972

Section 4 Defective Premises Act 1972 enables a tenant, and anyone else who is a foreseeable victim of the landlord's failure to perform his repairing obligations, to sue the landlord and recover damages for consequential injuries. It is therefore an additional weapon in the fight against substandard housing.

Defective Premises Act 1972

4. Landlord's duty of care in virtue of obligation or right to repair premises demised

(1) Where premises are let under a tenancy which puts on the landlord an obligation to the tenant for the maintenance or repair of the premises the landlord owes to all who might reasonably be expected to be affected by defects in the state of the premises a duty to take such care as is reasonable in all the circumstances to see that they are reasonably safe from personal injury or from damage to their property caused by a relevant defect.

(2) The said duty is owed if the landlord knows (whether as the result of being notified by the tenant or otherwise) or if he ought in all the circumstances to have known of the relevant defect.

(3) In this section 'relevant defect' means a defect in the state of the premises existing at or after the material time and arising from, or continuing because of, an act or omission by the landlord which constituted or would if he had had notice of the defect, have constituted a failure by him to carry out his obligation to the tenant for the maintenance or repair of the premises; and for the purposes of the foregoing provision 'the material time' means–

(a) where the tenancy commenced before this Act the commencement of this Act; and

(b) in all other cases, the earliest following times, that is to say–

(i) the time when the tenancy commences;

(ii) the time when the tenancy agreement is entered into;

(iii) the time when possession is taken of the premises in contemplation of the letting.

(4) Where premises are let under a tenancy which expressly or impliedly gives the landlord the right to enter the premises to carry out any description of maintenance or repair of the premises, then, as from the time when he first is, or by notice or otherwise can put himself, in a position to exercise the right and so long as he is or can put himself in that position, he shall be treated for the purposes of subsections (1) to (3) above (but for no other purpose) as if he were under an obligation to the tenant for that description of maintenance or repair of the premises; but the landlord shall not owe the tenant any duty by virtue of this subsection in respect of any defect in the state of the premises arising from, or continuing because of, a failure to carry out an obligation expressly imposed on the tenant by the tenancy.

(5) For the purposes of this section obligations imposed or rights given by any enactment in virtue of a tenancy shall be treated as imposed or given by the tenancy.

(6) This section applies to a right of occupation given by contract or any enactment and not amounting to a tenancy as if the right were a tenancy, and 'tenancy' and cognate expressions shall be construed accordingly.

Two conditions must be fulfilled before liability can arise under the section:

(1) The landlord must have either an express or an implied repairing obligation, or a right of entry for repair purposes. For this purpose, obligations to repair imposed by the common law or by statute suffice.

The common practice for certain landlords, notably local authority landlords, to include rights of entry for maintenance and repair purposes or to reserve a right of entry on the tenant's failure to carry out his repairing obligations, carries with it the hidden trap that the landlord may thereby render himself potentially liable under s 4 of the 1972 Act (see, for example, *McAuley v Bristol City Council* [1992] 1 All ER 749, (1991) 23 HLR 586).

(2) The landlord must have actual or constructive notice of the want of repair which gives rise to the relevant defect. It is sufficient in this respect that the defect is one which would be obvious on any reasonable inspection (see *Clarke v Taff Ely BC* (1980) 10 HLR 44). It is not essential, therefore, for the tenant to inform the landlord of the want of repair.

The duty under the section extends to any foreseeable victim of the landlord's failure to repair; and in appropriate circumstances may be enforced by means of an injunction (see *Barrett v Lounova* (1982) Ltd, above, *per* Kerr LJ).

Although s 4 of the 1972 Act undoubtedly has a deterrent effect on landlords who might otherwise allow their houses to become dilapidated, its usefulness at promoting high standards of accommodation must be questioned. In *McDonagh v Kent Area Health Authority* [1984] NLJ 567, for example, the limits of the section were exposed. In that case, a women was injured when she fell down very steep stairs in an old house. The house would not have passed modern Building Regulations; but the Court considered that the tenant and his family could reasonably be expected to use sufficient care when negotiating the stairs and to cope with any risks they posed. The authority therefore escaped liability under s 4.

If the landlord carries out his repairing obligations, he thereby escapes liability under s 4. If, however, the repairs are done in a shoddy manner, the landlord remains potentially liable for any injury resulting from those repairs.

REMEDIES FOR BREACH OF A LANDLORD'S REPAIRING OBLIGATIONS

Effective remedies for the tenant are essential if standards of accommodation are to be maintained; otherwise a tenant might be tempted to take the law into his own hands by withholding rent. The respective obligations of landlord and tenant are not interdependent on one another; therefore, a tenant who withholds rent in protest at the fact that the landlord has not carried out his repairing obligations runs the risk of action being taken against him. The tenant must therefore seek a remedy through legitimate means whilst at the same time continuing to pay his rent.

Specific performance

A court may be prepared to order specific performance of the landlord's repairing obligation, but this remedy is unlikely to be given lightly and will normally only be granted in cases of an obvious breach and where the work required to remedy it is equally clear. Section 17 Landlord and Tenant Act 1985 gives a court discretion to award specific performance in favour of a tenant by providing that:

  (1) In proceedings in which a tenant of a dwelling alleges a breach on the part of his landlord of a repairing covenant relating to any part of the premises which the dwelling is comprised, the court may order specific performance of the covenant whether or not the breach relates to a part of the premises let to the tenant and notwithstanding any equitable rule restricting the scope of the remedy, whether on the basis of a lack of mutuality or otherwise.

Injunction

An injunction may be issued in appropriate circumstances to enforce the duty imposed upon a landlord under s 4 Defective Premises Act 1972 (see earlier).

Self-help

In limited circumstances, a tenant may be able to force the landlord's hand by withholding rent and by counterclaiming for equitable set-off in the landlord's action. In *Televantos v McCulloch* (1991) 23 HLR 412, a protected tenant withheld rent because of the landlord's breach of covenant implied by s 11 Landlord and Tenant Act 1985. The landlord commenced proceedings for possession but the tenant counterclaimed that, as the disrepair had been present throughout the tenancy and damages on the counterclaim would exceed the arrears of rent, possession should not be granted. The Court of Appeal held that the tenant had a valid defence. The counterclaim would have been equally effective if the landlord had instead brought an action to recover the arrears of rent. As the set-off is an equitable claim, the tenant must himself have acted equitably, since 'he who comes to equity must come with clean hands'.

An alternative to a set-off is for the tenant to execute the repairs himself and deduct the amount from future rent. There are, however, very stringent conditions surrounding this form of self-help. First, the tenant must have given notice to the landlord that the property is in need of repair. Second, the tenant may only deduct expenditure on repairs which was reasonable and proper in the circumstances. Third, the landlord must have been clearly in breach of his repairing obligations.

The right to exercise this form of self-help was recognised in *Lee-Parker v Izzet* [1971] 1 WLR 1688.

Lee-Parker v Izzet

Goff J: ... [T]he third and fourth defendants further claim a lien for the cost of the repairs or alternatively for the value of any permanent improvement effected thereby, and they also claim a set off against rent in their capacity as tenants.

First they say that in so far as the first defendant was, as landlord, liable to do the repairs by the express or implied terms of the tenancy agreement, including the covenants imported section 32(1) of the Housing Act 1961, they, having done them themselves, are entitled to treat the expenditure as a payment of rent, for which reliance is placed on *Taylor v Beal* (1591) Cro Eliz 222. That is dicta only and the actual decision must have been the other way, because one of the majority in opinion thought the point was not open on the pleadings. However, Woodfall's Landlord and Tenant says the case – that is the dicta – would still seem to be the law: see 27th ed (1968) vol 1 p 655, para 1490. The case is dealt with in FOA's General Law of Landlord & Tenant, 8th (1957), on the question of distress only, at p 559, citing also *Davies v Stacey* (1840) 12 Ad&EL 506 where the point was left open. FOA states at p 559:

'Where the lessor covenants to repair and neglects to do so, and the repairs are thereupon executed by the lessee, a payment made by the lessee for the cost of such repairs is not (it is submitted) equivalent to payment of rent so as to reduce the amount for which the landlord may distrain.'

Waters v Weigall (1795) 2 Anst 575 which is cited in the footnote to *Surplice v Farnsworth* (1844) 7 Man&G 576, 586 does, however, support *Taylor v Beal*. In *Waters v Weigall* 2 Anst. 575 it was a case of sudden emergency due to a tempest but Macdonald CB laid down a quite general proposition as follows, at p 576.

> 'I do not see how you entitle yourself to the interposition of this court. If the landlord is bound in law or equity to repair in consequence of the accident that has happened and you were right in expending sum in repairs for him, it is money paid to his use, and may be set off against the demand for rent. If you fail in making these points, your ground of relief is destroyed in equity, as well as at law.'

In *Taylor v Webb* [1937] 2 KB 283 the question which went to the Court of Appeal was the extent of the liability under a covenant to repair, fair wear and tear excepted, but du Parcq J had held that the covenants to repair and to pay rent being independent, the tenant could maintain his cross-claim for damages although he had not paid the rent. Conversely, the landlord can sue for rent although he has not repaired. But again that does not touch the point in *Taylor v Beal* (1591) Cro Eliz 222.

I do not think this is bound up with technical rules of set off. It is an ancient common law right. I therefore declare that so far as the repairs are within the express or implied covenants of the landlord, the third and fourth defendants are entitled to recoup themselves out of future rents and defend any action for payment thereof. It does not follow however that the full amount expended by the third and fourth defendants on such repairs can properly be treated as payment of rent. It is a question of fact in every case whether and to what extent the expenditure was proper.

For the sake of avoiding misunderstanding I must add that of course the *Taylor v Beal* right can only be exercised when and so far as the landlord is in breach and any necessary notice must have been given to him.

The right to self-help under *Lee-Parker v Izzet* (above) is a proprietary right which, in the case of registered land, is an overriding interest and in the case of unregistered land is subject to the traditional doctrine of notice. (For the limits on the *Lee-Parker* principle, see further *Haringey London Borough Council v Stewart* (1991) *The Times*, 3 July.)

DAMAGES

The basic principle here is to put the tenant in the same position as he would have been in had the landlord not been in breach of his repairing obligations; damages are therefore compensatory and not punitive.

A starting point is the difference between the value of the tenanted property without the repairs and the value the property would have if those repairs had been carried out. This, however, is only a starting point (see *Calabar Properties Ltd v Stitcher* [1983] 3 All ER 759). Each case has to be looked at in the light of its individual facts. If the tenant has to vacate the premises temporarily whilst the repairs are being carried out, then the tenant's real loss is the loss of a home during that period; damages may therefore include the reasonable cost of alternative accommodation. This award will be allowed only if the tenant has given the landlord notice that the premises are in need of repair, the landlord has failed to carry out the necessary repairs within a reasonable time thereafter and the property has consequently become uninhabitable, making it necessary for the tenant to leave. In addition, the cost of internal redecoration rendered necessary by the landlord's breach and an amount for discomfort and inconvenience may be awarded.

In certain circumstances, the tenant may recover damages for commercial losses resulting from the landlord's breach of covenant for quiet enjoyment. For example, the loss of rental from subletting may, in appropriate circumstances, be claimed as part of the damages against the landlord (see *Mira v Aylmer Square Investments* (1989) 21 HLR 284).

PART II
'PUBLIC' DUTIES RELATING TO STANDARDS OF ACCOMMODATION

The piecemeal manner in which the private remedies for substandard housing have been developed and applied has led to the 'public' enforcement of standards of accommodation through the Public Health Departments of local authorities and the Health and Safety Inspectorate.

Part II of this chapter will address the question whether such enforcement has substantially improved the standard of residential accommodation in England and Wales.

THE ENVIRONMENTAL PROTECTION ACT 1990 (REPLACING CERTAIN SECTIONS OF THE PUBLIC HEALTH ACT 1936 AND THE CONTROL OF POLLUTION ACT 1974)

Until 1 January 1991, when the Environmental Protection Act 1990 came into force, there were two sources of law which governed the public control of pollution. Part III Public Health Act 1936 governed statutory nuisances other than noise whilst s 58 Control of Pollution Act 1974 dealt with noise nuisance. Both types of pollution are now governed by the 1990 Act as amended by the Noise and Statutory Nuisance Act 1993, which has introduced a new but similar regime aimed at eradicating statutory nuisances. Decisions reached under the previous law will still be relevant insofar as they are not inconsistent with the specific terms of the relevant sections of the 1990 Act. The relevant provisions of that Act largely repeat the provisions of the previous legislation, although there are some distinct differences between the previous law and the present law. The relevant law is contained in Part III, ss 79–82 of the 1990 Act as amended by the Noise and Statutory Nuisance Act 1993.

PART III
STATUTORY NUISANCES AND CLEAN AIR

Statutory nuisances: England and Wales

79(1) Subject to subsections (2) to (6A) below, the following matters constitute 'statutory nuisances' for the purposes of this Part, that is to say–

(a) any premises in such a state as to be prejudicial to health or a nuisance;

(b) smoke emitted from premises so as to be prejudicial to health or a nuisance;

(c) fumes or gases emitted from premises so as to be prejudicial to health or a nuisance;

(d) any dust, steam smell or other effluvia arising on industrial trade or business premises and being prejudicial to health or a nuisance;

(e) any accumulation or deposit which is prejudicial to health or a nuisance;

(f) any animal kept in such a place or manner as to be prejudicial to health or a nuisance;

(g) noise emitted from premises so as to be prejudicial to health or a nuisance;

(ga) noise that is prejudicial to health or a nuisance and is emitted from or caused by a vehicle, machinery or equipment in a street, and

(h) any other matter declared by any enactment to be a statutory nuisance;

and it shall be the duty of every local authority to cause its area to be inspected from time to time to detect any statutory nuisances which ought to be dealt with under section 80 below or sections 80 and 80A below and, where a complaint of a statutory nuisance is made to it by a person living within its area, to take such steps as are reasonably practicable to investigate the complaint.

(2) Subsection (1)(b) and (g) above do not apply in relation to premises–

(a) occupied on behalf of the Crown for naval, military or air force purposes or for the purposes of the department of the Secretary of State having responsibility for defence, or

(b) occupied by or for the purposes of a visiting force;

and 'visiting force' means any such body, contingent or detachment of the forces of any country as is a visiting force for the purposes of any of the provisions of the Visiting Forces Act 1952.

(3) Subsection (1)(b) above does not apply to–

(i) smoke emitted from a chimney of a private dwelling within a smoke control area,

(ii) dark smoke emitted from a chimney of a building or a chimney serving the furnace of a boiler or industrial plant attached to a building or for the time being fixed to or installed on any land,

(iii) smoke emitted from a railway locomotive steam engine,

(iv) dark smoke emitted otherwise than as mentioned above from industrial or trade premises.

(4) Subsection (1)(c) above does not apply in relation to premises other than private dwellings.

(5) Subsection (1)(d) above does not apply to steam emitted from a railway locomotive engine.

(6) Subsection (1)(g) above does not apply to noise caused by aircraft other than model aircraft.

(6A) Subsection (1)(ga) above does not apply to noise made–

(a) by traffic,

(b) by any naval, military or air force of the Crown or by a visiting force (as defined in subsection (2) above), or

(c) by a political demonstration or a demonstration supporting or opposing a cause or campaign.

(7) In this Part–

'chimney' includes structures and openings of any kind from or through which smoke may be emitted;

'dust' does not include dust emitted from a chimney as an ingredient of smoke;

'equipment' includes a musical instrument;

'fumes' means any airborne solid matter smaller than dust;

'gas' includes vapour and moisture precipitate from vapour;

'industrial, trade or business premises' means premises used for any industrial, trade or business purposes or premises not so used on which matter is burnt in connection with any industrial, trade or business process, and premises are used for industrial purposes where they are used for the purposes of any treatment or process as well as where they are used for the purposes of manufacturing;

'local authority' means subject to subsection (8) below–

(a) in Greater London, a London borough council, the Common Council of the City of London and, as respects the Temples, the Sub-Treasurer of the Inner Temple and the Under-Treasurer of the Middle Temple respectively,

(b) outside Greater London, a district council, and

(c) the Council of the Isles of Scilly;

'noise' includes vibration;

'person responsible',

(a) in relation to a statutory nuisance, means the person to whose act default or sufferance the nuisance is attributable;

(b) in relation to a vehicle, includes the person in whose name the vehicle is for the time being registered under the Vehicles (Excise) Act 1971 and any other person who is for the time being the driver of the vehicle;

(c) in relation to machinery or equipment, includes any person who is for the time being the operator of the machinery or equipment;

'prejudicial to health' means injurious, or likely to cause injury to health;

'premises' includes land and, subject to subsection (12) below, any vessel;

'private dwelling' means any building or part of a building used or intended to be used, as a dwelling;

'smoke' includes soot, ash, grit and gritty particles emitted in smoke, 'street' means a highway and any other road, footway, square or court that is for the time being open to the public.

and any expressions used in this section and in the Clean Air Act 1956 or the Clean Air Act 1969 have the same meaning in this section as in that Act and section 34(2) of the Clean Air Act 1956 shall apply for the interpretation of the expression 'dark smoke' and operation of this Part in relation to it.

(8) Where, by an order under section 2 of the Public Health (Control of Disease) Act 1984, a port health authority has been constituted for any port health district, the port health authority shall have by virtue of this subsection, as respects its district, the functions conferred or imposed by this Part in relation to statutory nuisances other than a nuisance falling within paragraph (g) or (ga) of subsection (1) above and no such order shall be made assigning those functions; and 'local authority' and 'area' shall be construed accordingly.

(9) In this Part 'best practicable means' is to be interpreted by reference to the following provisions–

   (a) 'practicable' means reasonably practicable having regard among other things to local conditions and circumstances, to the current state of technical knowledge and to the financial implications;

   (b) the means to be employed include the design, installation, maintenance and manner and periods of operation of plant and machinery, and the design, construction and maintenance of buildings and structures;

   (c) the test is to apply only so far as compatible with any duty imposed by law;

   (d) the test is to apply only so far as compatible with safety and safe working conditions and with the exigencies of any emergency or unforeseeable circumstances;

and, in circumstances where a code of practice under section 71 of the Control of Pollution Act 1974 (noise minimisation) is applicable, regard shall also be had to guidance given in it.

(10) A local authority shall not without the consent of the Secretary of State institute summary proceedings under this Part in respect of a nuisance falling within paragraph (b), (d) or (c) of subsection (1) above if proceedings in respect thereof might be instituted under Part I of the Alkali & Works Regulation Act 1906 or section 5 of the Health and Safety at Work etc. Act 1974.

(11) The area of a local authority which includes part of the seashore shall also include for the purposes of this Part the territorial sea lying seawards from that part of the shore; and subject to subsection (12) and section 81A(9) below, this Part shall have effect, in relation to any area included in the area of a local authority by virtue of this subsection–

   (a) as if references to premises and the occupier of premises included respectively a vessel and the master of a vessel; and

   (b) with such other modifications, if any, as are prescribed in regulations made by the Secretary of State.

(12) A vessel powered by steam reciprocating machinery is not a vessel to which this Part of this Act applies.

80(1) Where a local authority is satisfied that a statutory nuisance exists, or is likely to occur or recur, in the area of the authority, the local authority shall serve a notice ('an abatement notice') imposing all or any of the following requirements–

(a) requiring the abatement of the nuisance or prohibiting or restricting its occurrence or recurrence;

(b) requiring the execution of such works, and the taking of such other steps, as may be necessary for any of those purposes,

and the notice shall specify the time or time within which the requirements of the notice are to be complied with.

(2) Subject to section 80A(1) below, the abatement notice shall be served–

(a) except in a case falling within paragraph (b) or (c) below, on the person responsible for the nuisance;

(b) where the nuisance arises from any defect of a structural character, on the owner of the premises;

(c) where the person responsible for the nuisance cannot be found or the nuisance has not yet occurred, on the owner or occupier of the premises.

(3) The person served with the notice may appeal against the notice to a court within the period of twenty-one days beginning with the date on which he was served with the notice.

(4) If a person on whom an abatement notice is served, without reasonable excuse, contravenes or fails to comply with any requirement or prohibition imposed by the notice, he shall be guilty of an offence.

(5) Except in a case falling within subsection (6) below, a person who commits an offence under subsection (4) above shall be liable on summary conviction to a fine not exceeding level 5 on the standard scale together with a further fine of an amount equal to one-tenth of that level for each day on which the offence continues after the conviction.

(6) ...

82(1) A magistrates' court may act under this section on a complaint made by any person on the ground that he is aggrieved by the existence of a statutory nuisance.

(2) If the magistrates' court is satisfied that the alleged nuisance exists, or that although abated it is likely to recur on the same premises, the court shall make an order for either or both of the following purposes or, in the case of a nuisance within section 79(1)(ga) above, in the same street,

(a) requiring the defendant to abate the nuisance, within a time specified in the order, and to execute any works necessary for that purpose;

(b) prohibiting a recurrence of the nuisance, and requiring the defendant within a time specified in the order, to execute any works necessary to prevent the recurrence;

and may also impose on the defendant a fine not exceeding level 5 on the standard scale.

(3) If the magistrates' court is satisfied that the alleged nuisance exists and is such as, in the opinion of the court, to render premises unfit for human habitation, an order under subsection (2) above may prohibit the use of the premises for human habitation until the premises are, to the satisfaction of the court, rendered fit for that purpose.

(4) Proceedings for an order under subsection (2) above shall be brought–

(a) except in a case falling within paragraph (b), (c) or (d) below, against the person responsible for the nuisance;

(b) where the nuisance arises from any defect of a structural character, against the owner of the premises;

(c) where the person responsible for the nuisance cannot be found, against the owner or occupier of the premises;

(d) in the case of a statutory nuisance within section 79(1)(ga) above caused by noise emitted from or caused by an unattended vehicle or unattended machinery or equipment, against the person responsible for the vehicle, machinery or equipment.

(5) Where more that one person is responsible for a statutory nuisance, subsections (1) to (4) above shall apply to each of those persons whether or not what any one of them is responsible for would by itself amount to a nuisance.

(5A) In relation to a statutory nuisance within section 79(1)(ga) above for which more than one person is responsible (whether or not what any one of those persons is responsible for would by itself amount to such a nuisance), subsection (4)(a) above shall apply with the substitution of 'each person responsible for the nuisance who can be found' for 'the person responsible for the nuisance'.

(5B) In relation to a statutory nuisance within section 79(1)(ga) above caused by noise emitted from or caused by an unattended vehicle or unattended machinery or equipment for which more than one person is responsible, subsection (4)(d) above shall apply with the substitution of 'any person' for 'the person'.

(6) Before instituting proceedings for an order under subsection (2) above against any person, the person aggrieved by the nuisance shall give to that person such notice in writing of his intention to bring the proceedings as is applicable to proceedings in respect of a nuisance of that description and the notice shall specify the matter complained of.

(7) The notice of the bringing of proceedings in respect of a statutory nuisance required by subsection (6) above which is applicable is–

(a) in the case of a nuisance falling within paragraph (g) or (ga) of section 79(1) above, not less than three days' notice; and

(b) in the case of a nuisance of any other description, not less than twenty-one days' notice;

but the Secretary of State may, by order, provide that this subsection shall have effect as if such period as is specified in the order were the minimum period of notice applicable to any description of statutory nuisance specified in the order.

(8) A person who, without reasonable excuse, contravenes any requirement or prohibition imposed by an order under subsection (2) above shall be guilty of an offence and liable on summary conviction to a fine not exceeding level 5 on the standard scale together with a further fine of an amount equal to one-tenth of that level for each day on which the offence continues after the conviction.

(9) ...

The main difference between the present and the previous law is that under s 82(6) of the 1990 Act an aggrieved individual must now notify the person against whom a statutory nuisance is alleged that he intends to bring proceedings against the latter. Under the previous law, this was not necessary (see *Sandwell Metropolitan BC v Bujok* [1987] 3 All ER 545).

The responsibility for dealing with statutory nuisances falls on the local authority. The Environmental Health Department of the local authority can either act on its own initiative or as a result of a complaint made to it by someone living within its area. If after investigations the authority is satisfied that a statutory nuisance exists, it must serve an abatement notice under s 80. A right of appeal to a magistrates' court against such a notice is provided, but failure to comply with the terms of the notice amounts to a criminal offence in the absence of a reasonable excuse. An individual may also complain direct to a magistrates' court that he is aggrieved by a statutory nuisance. The court may then make an order in terms similar to an abatement notice and fine the defendant.

The relevance of the Environmental Protection Act 1990 to the landlord and tenant relationship can be demonstrated by reference to cases decided under the previous law. In relation to noise, it has been held that noisy lifts in a block of flats managed by a landlord company were causing a noise nuisance and that the company, which had ignored an abatement notice, could be convicted of a criminal offence: see *A Lambert Flat Management Ltd v Lomas* [1981] 1 WLR 898, decided under s 58 Control of Pollution Act 1974.

Under Part III Public Health Act 1936, it has also been held that a statutory nuisance may exist where drains have become blocked, where there is banned asbestos on the property or where plaster is crumbling (see *Coventry City Council v Quinn* [1981] 1 WLR 1325). It has also been held in exceptional circumstances that mould growth and decay resulting from excessive condensation dampness may amount to a statutory nuisance as being 'prejudicial to health' (see *GLC v London Borough of Tower Hamlets* (1983) 15 HLR 54). (This contrasts with the private remedies for substandard conditions under s 11 Landlord and Tenant Act 1985, where it has been held that mould growth on furnishings did not amount to a breach of s 11 if the cause was condensation from lack of adequate heating. See *Quick v Taff-Ely BC* [1985] 3 All ER 321.)

These decisions would be decided no differently under the 1990 Act.

It is not uncommon for some of the worst housing conditions to exist in council-owned residential property. The provisions of the 1990 Act therefore provide one means whereby council tenants can force the council (as landlord) to carry out repairs to their homes. As will be seen later, the provisions of the Housing Act 1985 relating to repair notices do not apply to local authority accommodation as a result of the decision in *R v Cardiff City Council, ex p Cross* (1983) 81 LGR 105. The ability of a council tenant to utilise the 1990 Act is therefore to be welcomed; but the court has said on more than one occasion that magistrates should act with sense and discretion and bear in mind that the local housing authority has many responsibilities and burdens. In a time of recession and large scale homelessness, this is more acutely so (see *Salford City Council v McNally* [1976] AC 379 and *Birmingham District Council v Kelly* (1985) 17 HLR 572).

THE HOUSING ACT 1985

The Housing Act 1985 contains two main methods of dealing with situations which can have an adverse effect on the standard of accommodation enjoyed by tenants:

(a) Those provisions which enable repair notices to be served on a landlord by the local authority; and

(b) Those provisions which deal with overcrowding of a dwelling-house.

The repair notice procedure

The Housing Act 1985, as amended by the Local Government and Housing Act 1989, enables a local authority to control substandard housing in its area by the issuing of repair notices. There are two sections of the 1985 Act which enable a local authority to issue repair notices, namely ss 189 and 190. Section 189 deals with the powers of the authority in relation to a dwelling which is considered to be unfit for human habitation, while s 190 concerns repair notices in respect of dwellings which, whilst requiring substantial repairs, are not yet unfit for human habitation but may become so if work is not done on them.

Housing Act 1985
189. Repair notice in respect of unfit house

(1) Subject to subsection (1A) where the local housing authority are satisfied that a dwelling-house or house in multiple occupation is unfit for human habitation, they shall serve a repair notice on the person having control of the dwelling-house or house in multiple occupation, if they are satisfied, in accordance with section 604A, that serving a notice under this subsection is the most satisfactory course of action.

(1A) Where the local authority are satisfied that either a dwelling-house which is a flat or a flat in multiple occupation is unfit for human habitation by virtue of section 604(2) they shall serve a repair notice on the person having control of the part of the building in question if they are satisfied, in accordance with section 604A, that serving a notice under this subsection is the most satisfactory course of action.

(1B) In the case of a house in multiple occupation, a repair notice may be served on the person managing the house instead of on the person having control; and where a notice is so served, then, subject to section 191, the person managing the house shall be regarded as the person having control of it for the purposes of the provisions of this Part following that section.

(2) A repair notice under this section shall–

(a) require the person on whom it is served to execute the works specified in the notice (which may be works of repair or improvement or both) and to begin those works not later than such reasonable date, not being earlier than the twenty-eighth day after the notice is served, as specified in the notice, and to complete those works within such reasonable time as is so specified; and

(b) state that in the opinion of the authority the works specified in the notice will render the dwelling-house or, as the case may be, house in multiple occupation fit for human habitation.

(3) The authority, in addition to serving the notice (a) on the person having control of the dwelling-house, or part of the building concerned or (b) on the person having control of or as the case may be, on the person managing the house in multiple occupation which is concerned shall serve a copy of the notice on any other person having an interest in the dwelling-house, or part of the building or house concerned, whether as freeholder, mortgagee, or lessee.

(4) The notice becomes operative, if no appeal is brought, on the expiration of 21 days from the date of the service of the notice and is final and conclusive as to matters which could have been raised on an appeal.

(5) A repair notice under this section which has become operative is a local land charge.

(6) This subsection has effect subject to the provisions of section 190A.

190. Repair notice in respect of house in state of disrepair but not unfit

(1) Subject to subsection (1B), where the local housing authority–

  (a) are satisfied that a dwelling-house or house in multiple occupation is in such a state of disrepair that, although not unfit for human habitation, substantial repairs are necessary to bring it up to a reasonable standard, having regard to its age, character and locality; or

  (b) are satisfied whether on a representation made by an occupying tenant or otherwise that a dwelling-house or house in multiple occupation is in such a state of disrepair that, although not unfit for human habitation, its condition is such as to interfere materially with the personal comfort of the occupying tenant, or, in the case of a house in multiple occupation, the persons occupying it (whether as tenants or licensees);

they may serve a repair notice on the person having control of the dwelling-house.

(1A) Subject to subsection (1B), where the local housing authority–

  (a) are satisfied that a building containing a flat including a flat in multiple occupation is in such a state of disrepair that, although the flat is not unfit for human habitation, substantial repairs are necessary to a part of the building outside the flat to bring the flat up to a reasonable standard, having regard to its age, character and locality; or

  (b) are satisfied, whether on a representation made by an occupying tenant or otherwise, that a building containing a flat is in such a state of disrepair that, although the flat is not unfit for human habitation, the condition of a part of the building outside the flat is such as to interfere materially with the personal comfort of the occupying tenant, or, in the case of a flat in multiple occupation, the persons occupying it (whether as tenants or licensees),

they may serve a repair notice on the person having control of the part of the building concerned.

(1B) The authority may not serve a notice under subsection (1) or subsection (1A) unless–

  (a) there is an occupying tenant of the dwelling-house or flat concerned; or

  (b) the dwelling-house or building concerned falls within a renewal area within the meaning of Part VII of the Local Government and Housing Act 1989.

(1C) In the case of a house in multiple occupation, a notice under subsection (1) or subsection (1A) may be served on the person managing the house instead of on the person having control of it; and where a notice is so served, then, subject to section 191, the person managing the house shall be regarded as the person having control of it for the purposes of the provisions of this Part following that section

(2) A repair notice under this section shall require the person on whom is served to execute the works specified in the notice, not being works of internal decorative repair, and–

    (a) to begin those works not later than such reasonable date, being not earlier than the twenty-eighth day after the notice is served as is specified in the notice; and

    (b) to complete those works within such reasonable time as is specified.

(3) The authority, in addition to serving the notice (a) on the person having control of the dwelling-house or part of the building concerned or (b) on the person having control of or, as the case may be, on the person managing the house in multiple occupation which is concerned, shall serve a copy of the notice on any other person having an interest in the dwelling-house, part of the building or house concerned whether as freeholder, mortgagee, or lessee.

(4) The notice becomes operative, if no appeal is brought, on the expiry of 21 days from the date of service of the notice and is final and conclusive as to matters which could have been raised on an appeal.

(5) A repair notice under this section which has become operative is a local land charge.

190A(1) A local housing authority shall not be under a duty to serve a repair notice under subsection (1) or, as the case may be, subsection (1A) of section 189 if, at the same time as they satisfy themselves as mentioned in the subsection in question, they determine–

    (a) that the premises concerned form part of a building which would be a qualifying building in relation to a group repair scheme; and

    (b) that, within the period of twelve months beginning at that time, they expect to prepare a group repair scheme in respect of the qualifying building (in this section referred to as a 'relevant scheme');

but where, having so determined, the authority do serve such a notice, they may do so with respect only to those works which, in their opinion, will not be carried out to the premises concerned in pursuance of the relevant scheme.

(2) Subject to subsection (3), subsection (1) shall apply in relation to the premises concerned from the time referred to in subsection (1) until the date on which the works specified in a relevant scheme are completed to the authority's satisfaction (as certified under section 130(1) of the Local Government and Housing Act 1989).

(3) Subsection (1) shall cease to have effect in relation to the premises concerned on the day when the first of the following events occurs, that is to say,

    (a) the local housing authority determine not to submit a relevant scheme to the Secretary of State for approval; or

    (b) the expiry of the period referred to in subsection (1)(b) without either the approval of a relevant scheme within that period or the submission of a relevant scheme to the Secretary of State within that period; or

(c) the Secretary of State notifies the authority that he does not approve a relevant scheme; or

(d) the authority ascertain that a relevant scheme, as submitted or approved, will not, for whatever reason, involve the carrying out of any works to the premises concerned.

(4) In any case where, in accordance with subsection (1), the authority serve a repair notice under subsection (1) or, as the case may be, subsection (1A) of section 189 with respect only to certain of the works which would otherwise be specified in the notice, subsection (2)(b) of that section shall have effect with respect to the notice as if after the word 'notice' there were inserted the words 'when taken together with works proposed to be carried out under a group repair scheme'.

(5) ...

The s 189 repair notice procedure

If a local housing authority is satisfied that a particular dwelling-house or house in multiple occupation (see later on HMOs) within its area is already unfit for human habitation, that authority must serve either a repair notice under s 189, a closing order under s 264 or a demolition order under s 265. Alternatively, the authority can decide that the area in which the property is situated is to be designated a 'clearance area', so that all property within that area will eventually be demolished (see s 289). A s 189 notice must be served on the person having control of the property or, in the case of a house in multiple occupation, the manager, and a copy must also be served on anyone having an interest in the property.

Section 604 of the 1985 Act contains the factors which the local housing authority must take into account in deciding whether a particular dwelling is unfit for human habitation. These include, *inter alia*, such things as structural stability, freedom from serious disrepair, freedom from damp prejudicial to the occupants' health, satisfactory facilities for preparing and cooking food, a supply of wholesome water and adequate provision of lighting, heating and ventilation (note the similarity with s 10 Landlord and Tenant Act 1985). Once the authority have decided this question in the affirmative, that authority then has to decide whether the most satisfactory course of action is to serve a repair notice as opposed to, for example, a closing order, by taking into account the requirements of s 604A. Guidelines to help the authority resolve this particular question have been issued in a DOE Code of Guidance (see DOE Circular 6/90, March 1990); this includes financial considerations. In *R v Southwark, ex p Cordwell* (1994) 26 HLR 107, on an application for judicial review, Auld J in the Queen's Bench Divisional Court stated that the approach when comparing the cost of repair and closure under the former test of 'reasonable expense' was equally applicable to the economic assessment part of the appraisal required under the new regime of 'the most satisfactory course of action'; hence one had to take into account the net enhancement in the value of the property if it became vacant and fit for habitation as a result of a closure order, as against it becoming fit but with a statutory tenant under a repair notice. However, the local authority's appraisal of 'the most satisfactory course of action' was said to be 'an inherently imprecise exercise', which was primarily a matter of judgment for the authority to identify in the light of the guidance contained in Circular 6/90. On appeal, the Court of Appeal upheld the judgment of Auld J and dismissed the appeal (see (1995) 27 HLR 594).

If the authority decide to issue a repair notice under s 189, the notice must specify the work to be done and the period of time within which that work should be completed.

A right of appeal against a repair notice lies to the county court. One of the grounds of appeal is that serving either a closing order or demolition order would have been the most satisfactory course of action to take (see s 191).

The s 190 repair notice procedure

If a local housing authority consider that a dwelling-house or house in multiple occupation is fit for human habitation, but that it either requires substantial repairs or is in a condition such as to materially interfere with an occupying tenant's comfort, that authority may serve a repair notice under s 190. Unlike s 189, the s 190 notice procedure is discretionary. The notice, if it is decided to proceed, must be served on the person who has control of the property (or the manager of the HMO, as the case may be) and also on anyone who has an interest in it.

The power to serve a repair notice under s 190 is confined to situations where there is either a tenant in occupation of the property or the dwelling is in a renewal area covered by Part VII Local Government and Housing Act 1989.

The notice cannot require that works of internal decorative repair be done, but can require that any other specified works be carried out within a stated time schedule. If the person on whom the notice is served agrees to pay, the authority can itself carry out the work even before any default on the notice has occurred (see s 191A). (This also applies to a s 189 notice.) The authority is also entitled to do the work at the expense of the recipient of the notice if the repairs specified in it have not been completed within the timetable (see s 193, which equally applies to a s 189 notice).

The purpose of a s 190 notice is obviously to prevent a particular dwelling from getting to the stage where it is unfit for human habitation. There are, however, limits to the s 190 repair notice procedure.

First, the notice must be served on the correct person if it is to be valid ie on the person having control of the dwelling. This is defined in s 207 of the Act as the person who receives the rack rent (defined as a rent which is not less than two thirds of the full net annual value of the premises), or who would receive it if the property were let at a rack rent. This provision caused a problem in *White v London Borough of Barnet* (1989) 21 HLR 346, in which the authority served the notice on two tenants of flats in a house, as well as on the owner. The rent paid by the tenants of both flats, when added together, did not amount to a rack rent, but that paid by the plaintiff did amount to a rack rent of her flat. The Court of Appeal held that where only part of the property is let at a rack rent, one still had to look at who would have been entitled to receive the rack rent had the whole premises been let at such a rent. It could not have been the intention of Parliament that a statutory tenant of a flat should bear the cost of repairs in compliance with a s 190 notice. The authority had therefore served notice on the wrong person.

Secondly, case law decided before amendments brought about by the Local Government and Housing Act 1989, introduced a 'reasonable expense' limitation into the s 190 procedure. In *Hillbank Properties Ltd v Hackney London Borough Council* [1978] QB 998, for example, the court considered that the predecessor to s 206 of the 1985 Act (which itself was repealed by the 1989 Act above) applied equally to the s 190 procedure as it did to the s 189 procedure. Section 206 contained a reasonable expense criterion which took into account the cost of the works and the increased value of the property as a result of those works. A similar limitation for s 189 notices was introduced in 1989 in the form of s 604A of the 1985 Act under which an authority must now have regard to guidance issued by the Secretary of State, which may take into account financial considerations. A Code of Guidance has been issued (see earlier) under this provision which includes financial considerations and hence a re-emergence of a 'reasonable expense' criteria. Will the same apply to a s 190 notice through judicial intervention? It is quite likely that it will.

The s 190 procedure also enables an individual occupying tenant of a dwelling which is falling into disrepair to make representations to a local housing authority that the property is in such a condition as to materially interfere with his comfort. If the authority is satisfied that such a complaint is justified, it may serve a repair notice under s 190. A right of appeal against a repair notice lies to the county court (see s 191).

A local housing authority is under a duty to carry out periodic reviews of housing conditions in its area in order to decide whether and what action should be taken by it. It is also under a duty to take account of written reports made to it by its officer(s) concerned with unfit housing.

If the authority which is obliged to serve a repair notice and the person having control of the relevant dwelling are one and the same, the repair notice procedure does not apply (see *R v Cardiff City Council, ex p Cross* [1983] JPL 245). In these situations, tenants of council accommodation are forced to use either private remedies or to utilise the procedure for abatement of a statutory nuisance under the Environmental Protection Act 1990 (see earlier discussion).

Although local housing authorities have adequate legal powers and duties for dealing with substandard housing in their area, the utilisation of their powers depends to a large extent on the financial resources and goodwill of the particular authority. It is also not unknown for some of the worst conditions to be present in council-owned residential property and yet councils are immune from the repair notice procedure (see above). It may therefore be questioned whether the Housing Act 1985 has had any real impact on eradicating substandard housing in this country; perhaps it is more useful as a deterrent to private owners of dwellings than as a mechanism for removing bad housing conditions which already exist.

The requirements of the Housing Act 1985 and of the Environmental Protection Act 1990 are separate and distinct; satisfying the requirements under one of the statutes will therefore not necessarily amount to satisfying the requirements of the other. In general, the standards imposed by the Housing

Act 1985, are higher than those imposed by the Environmental Protection Act 1990. A nuisance order, for example, which requires the carrying out of remedial work to abate the nuisance would not normally require such extensive work as a repair notice served under the Housing Act 1985.

The overcrowding provisions of the Housing Act 1985

Overcrowding is a factor which can detract from the comfort of tenants and often leads to poor housing conditions. Overcrowding is controlled in two ways under the Housing Act 1985, and both methods apply equally to licensees and to tenants. The first is contained in Part X of the Housing Act 1985; the second relates to houses in multiple occupation, contained in Part XI of the 1985 Act.

Part X of the Housing Act 1985

Part X Housing Act 1985 contains the main source of control over the number of persons who may lawfully occupy residential accommodation.

Housing Act 1985

Definition of overcrowding

324 A dwelling is overcrowded for the purposes of this Part when the number of persons sleeping in the dwelling is such as to contravene–

(a) the standard specified in section 325 (the room standard), or

(b) the standard specified in section 326 (the space standard).

The room standard

325(1) The room standard is contravened when the number of persons sleeping in a dwelling and the number of rooms available as sleeping accommodation is such that two persons of opposite sexes who are not living together as husband and wife must sleep in the same room.

(2) For this purpose–

(a) children under the age of ten shall be left out of account, and

(b) a room is available as sleeping accommodation if it is of a type normally used in the locality either as a bedroom or as a living room.

The space standard

326(1) The space standard is contravened when the number of persons sleeping in a dwelling is in excess of the permitted number, having regard to the number and floor area of the rooms of the dwelling available as sleeping accommodation.

(2) For this purpose–

(a) no account shall be taken of a child under the age of one and a child aged one or over but under ten shall be reckoned as one-half of a unit, and

(b) a room is available as sleeping accommodation if it is of a type normally used in the locality either as a living room or as a bedroom.

(3) The permitted number of persons in relation to a dwelling is whichever is the less of–

(a) the number specified in Table I in relation to the number of rooms in the dwelling available as sleeping accommodation, and

(b) the aggregate for all such rooms in the dwelling of the numbers specified in column 2 of Table II in relation to each room of the floor area specified in column 1.

No account shall be taken for the purposes of either Table of a room having a floor area of less than 50 square feet.

TABLE I

Number of rooms	Number of persons
1	2
2	3
3	5
4	$7^{1}/_{2}$
5 or more	2 for each room

TABLE II

Floor area of room	Number of persons
110 sq ft or more	2
90 sq ft or more but less than 110 sq ft	$1^{1}/_{2}$
70 sq ft or more but less than 90 sq ft	1
50 sq ft or more but less than 70 sq ft	$^{1}/_{2}$

(4) ... (5) ...

(6) A certificate of the local housing authority stating the number and floor areas of the rooms in a dwelling, and that the floor areas have been ascertained in the prescribed manner, is *prima facie* evidence for the purpose of legal proceedings of the facts stated in it.

Responsibility of occupier

Penalty for occupier causing or permitting overcrowding

327(1) The occupier of a dwelling who causes or permits it to be overcrowded commits a summary offence, subject to subsection (2).

(2) The occupier is not guilty of an offence–

(a) if the overcrowding is within the exceptions specified in section 328 or 329 (children attaining age of 10 or visiting relatives), or

(b) by reason of anything done under the authority of, and in accordance with any conditions specified in, a licence granted by the local housing authority under section 330.

(3) A person committing an offence under this section is liable on conviction to a fine not exceeding level 2 of the standard scale and to a further fine not exceeding one-tenth of the amount corresponding to that level in respect of every day subsequent to the date on which he is convicted on which the offence continues.

Under the statutory definition of 'overcrowding', contained in s 324, a dwelling is overcrowded when the number of persons sleeping in the same dwelling contravenes either a room standard or a space standard.

The room standard

The room standard is contravened when the available sleeping accommodation is such that two people of opposite sex over the age of ten years and who are not living as man and wife have to share the same bedroom (see s 325).

The space standard

The space standard is contravened whenever the number of persons sleeping in the dwelling exceeds the 'permitted number'. This permitted number is arrived at by a formula set out in s 326(3) of the 1985 Act and depends on either the number of rooms or the floor area available as sleeping accommodation. In this calculation, no account is taken of children under the age of one year; and children between the ages of one and ten years each count as half a person.

If a particular dwelling is considered to be overcrowded within the meaning of Part X of the 1985 Act the local housing authority can serve a notice on the occupier and on the landlord, requiring that overcrowding to be abated. A failure to comply with an abatement notice amounts to a criminal offence.

An occupier who either causes or permits overcrowding commits a summary offence unless he has either acted under a 's 330 local authority licence' or the circumstances fall within the exception outlined in s 327 of the 1985 Act. This exception concerns the situation where a dwelling has become overcrowded by reason only of the fact that a child who is living there has attained either one or ten years of age. For this exception to apply, however, the occupier should have applied to the local housing authority for suitable alternative accommodation prior to the child reaching its first or tenth birthday. If this has been done, the occupier commits no offence, provided that all the people sleeping in the dwelling are the same persons who occupied it at the time of the relevant child's birthday.

A temporary visit and stay by members of the family who normally live elsewhere is allowed without amounting to overcrowding (see s 329). A child at boarding school, however, is regarded as permanently resident in the parents' house.

An owner/landlord commits an offence in relation to overcrowding in three situations:

(1) If he has failed to take reasonable steps to abate overcrowding following the service upon him of an abatement notice; or

(2) If he or his agent leased the house having reasonable cause to believe that it would be overcrowded; or

(3) If he or his agent failed to ascertain from the proposed occupier the number, ages and sex of those who would be sleeping there (see s 331).

Serious consequences may follow illegal overcrowding. Illegal overcrowding not only involves criminal penalties but also may involve the loss of statutory protection from eviction (see, for example, s 101 Rent Act 1977).

Permissible overcrowding, however, does not remove statutory protection. Permissible overcrowding may occur in the following situations:

(1) Where the occupier has obtained a licence under s 330, permitting overcrowding for a period not exceeding one year, due to the exceptional circumstances;

(2) Where the excess persons are members of the occupier's family but are staying with him for a temporary period only; or

(3) Where a child has reached a relevant age and the occupier has sought alternative accommodation from the local housing authority.

In the latter case, the overcrowding will only become illegal either when the offer of alternative accommodation has been unreasonably refused or when a member of the household who is not a member of the occupier's family has not been asked to leave in circumstances where it would be reasonable for them to leave.

The local housing authority has power to require from an occupier information about the number of people sleeping in the dwelling; it also has the power of entry to ascertain this number for itself.

Following the service of an abatement notice for illegal overcrowding and its non-compliance, the authority may apply for vacant possession of the property to be given to the landlord. If this occurs, the tenant and his family will be classed as homeless persons and can apply to the local housing authority to be housed under Part III Housing Act 1985 (see Chapter 15).

Part XI of the Housing Act 1985

A second method by which overcrowding may be controlled, and hence standards of accommodation indirectly improved, is under Part XI Housing Act 1985. This Part deals with houses in multiple occupation (HMOs). These are often privately owned, 'bed and breakfast' type hostels, offering accommodation to the socially disadvantaged and single people who cannot get accommodation elsewhere (see, for example, *R v Southwark London Borough, ex p Lewis Levy Ltd* (1983) 3 HLR 6).

These places are often 'death traps'. In 1989, for example, 181 people were killed and 3,306 were injured in such places as a result of fires alone. These figures do not include those who suffer injury as a result of accidents caused by substandard housing conditions or of deaths caused by electrocution and gas leaks (see National Consumer Council Report on HMOs, 'Deathtrap Housing'). There were approximately 290,000 HMOs in England and Wales in 1985, according to a DOE postal survey. Approximately half of these were in Greater London.

The relevant provisions of Part XI Housing Act 1985 are set out below.

Housing Act 1985

Meaning of Multiple Occupation

345(1) In this Part 'house in multiple occupation' means a house which is occupied by persons who do not form a single household.

(2) For the purposes of this section 'house', in the expression 'house in multiple occupation', includes any part of a building which–

(a) apart from this subsection would not be regarded as a house; and

(b) was originally constructed or subsequently adapted for occupation by a single household;

and any reference to this Part to a flat in multiple occupation is a reference to a part of a building which, whether by virtue of this subsection or with regard to it, constitutes a house in multiple occupation.

Registration schemes

346(1) The local housing authority may make and submit to the Secretary of State for confirmation by him a registration scheme authorising the authority to compile and maintain a register for their district of–

(a) houses in multiple occupation,

and the Secretary of State may if he thinks fit confirm the scheme, with or without modification.

(2) ... (3) ... (4) ... (5) ...

(6) Subject to section 347(4), a person who contravenes or fails to comply with a provision of a registration scheme commits a summary offence and is liable on conviction to a fine not exceeding level 3 on the standard scale and, if the contravention or failure continues, he commits a further summary offence and is liable on conviction to a fine not exceeding one-tenth of the amount corresponding to that level for every day or part of a day during which the contravention or failure continues.

Fitness for the number of occupants

Power to require execution of works to render premises fit for number of occupants

352(1) Subject to section 365, the local housing authority may serve a notice under this section where in the opinion of the authority, a house in multiple occupation fails to meet one or more of the requirements in paragraphs (a) to (e) of subsection (1A) and, having regard to the number of individuals or households or both for the time being accommodated on the premises, by reason of that failure the premises are not reasonably suitable for occupation by those individuals or households.

(1A) The requirements in respect of a house in multiple occupation referred to in subsection (1) are the following, that is to say,

(a) there are satisfactory facilities for the storage, preparation and cooking of food including an adequate number of sinks with a satisfactory supply of hot and cold water;

(b) it has an adequate number of suitably located water-closets for the exclusive use of the occupants;

(c) it has, for the exclusive use of the occupants, an adequate number of suitably located fixed baths or showers and wash hand basins each of which is provided with a satisfactory supply of hot and cold water;

(d) subject to section 365, there are adequate means of escape from fire; and

(e) there are adequate other precautions.

(2) Subject to subsection (2A) the notice shall specify the works which in the opinion of the authority are required for rendering the house reasonably suitable–

(a) for occupation by the individuals and households for the time being accommodated there; or

(b) for a smaller number of individuals or households and the number of individuals or households, or both, which, in the opinion of the authority, the house could reasonably accommodate if the works were carried out, but the notice shall not specify any works to any premises outside the house.

(2A) Where the authority have exercised or propose to exercise their powers under section 368 to secure that part of the house is not used for human habitation, they may specify in the notice such work only as in their opinion is required to meet such of the requirements in subsection (1A) as may be applicable if that part is not so used.

(3) The notice may be served–

(a) on the person having control of the house; or

(b) on the person managing the house;

and the authority shall inform any other person who is to their knowledge an owner, occupier or mortgagee of the house of the fact that the notice has been served.

(4) The notice shall require the person on whom it is served to execute the works specified in the notice as follows, namely–

(a) to begin those works not later than such reasonable date, being not earlier then the twenty-first day after the date of service of the notice, as is specified in the notice; and

(b) to complete those works within such reasonable period as is so specified.

(5) If the authority are satisfied that–

(a) after the service of a notice under this section the number of individuals living on the premises has been reduced to a level which will make the works specified in the notice unnecessary; and

(b) that number will be maintained at or below that level, whether in consequence of the exercise of the authority's powers under section 354 (power to limit number of occupants of house) or otherwise;

they may withdraw the notice by notifying that fact in writing to the person on whom the notice was served, but without prejudice to the issue of a further notice.

(5A) A notice served under this section is a local land charge.

(5B) Each local housing authority shall–

(a) maintain a register of notices served by the authority under subsection (1) after the coming into force of this subsection;

(b) ensure the register is open to inspection by the public free of charge at all reasonable hours; and

(c) on request, and on payment of any such reasonable fee as the authority may require, supply copies of entries in the register to any person.

Overcrowding

Service of overcrowding notice

358(1) Where it appears to the local housing authority in the case of a house in multiple occupation–

(a) that an excessive number of persons is being accommodated on the premises, having regard to the rooms available; or

(b) that it is likely that an excessive number of persons will be accommodated on the premises, having regard to the rooms available;

they may serve an overcrowding notice on the occupier of the premises or on the person managing the premises, or on both.

(2) At least seven days before serving an overcrowding notice, the local housing authority shall–

(a) inform the occupier of the premises and any person appearing to them to be managing the premises, in writing, of their intention to do so; and

(b) ensure that, so far as is reasonably possible, every person living in the premises is informed of that intention;

and they shall afford those persons an opportunity of making representations regarding their proposal to serve the notice.

(3) If no appeal is brought under section 362, the overcrowding notice becomes operative at the end of the period of 21 days from the date of service, and is final and conclusive as to matters which could have been raised on such an appeal.

(4) A person who contravenes an overcrowding notice commits a summary offence and is liable on conviction to a fine not exceeding level 4 on the standard scale.

Contents of overcrowding notice

359(1) An overcrowding notice shall state in relation to every room on the premises–

(a) what in the opinion of the local housing authority is the maximum number of persons by whom the room is suitable to be occupied as sleeping accommodation at any one time; or

(b) that the room is in their opinion unsuitable to be occupied as sleeping accommodation;

and the notice may specify special maxima applicable where some or all of the persons occupying the room are under such age as may be specified in the notice.

(2) An overcrowding notice shall contain either–

(a) the requirement set out in section 360 (not to permit excessive number of persons to sleep on premises); or

(b) the requirement set out in section 361 (not to admit new residents if number of persons is excessive);

and where the local housing authority have served on a person an overcrowding notice containing the latter requirement, they may at any time withdraw the notice and serve on him in its place an overcrowding notice containing the former requirement.

Requirement as to overcrowding generally

360(1) The first requirement referred to in section 359(2) is that the person on whom the notice is served must refrain from knowingly–

(a) permitting a room to be occupied as sleeping accommodation otherwise than in accordance with the notice, or

(b) permitting persons to occupy the premises as sleeping accommodation in such numbers that it is not possible to avoid persons of opposite sexes who are not living together as husband and wife sleeping in the same room.

(2) For the purposes of subsection (1)(b)–

(a) children under the age of 12 shall be left out of account, and

(b) it shall be assumed that the persons occupying the premises as sleeping accommodation sleep only in rooms for which a maximum is set by the notice and that the maximum set for each room is not exceeded.

Requirement as to new residents

361(1) The second requirement referred to in section 359(2) is that the person on whom the notice is served must refrain from knowingly–

(a) permitting a room to be occupied by a new resident as sleeping accommodation otherwise than in accordance with the notice; or

(b) permitting a new resident to occupy any part of the premises as sleeping accommodation if that is not possible without persons of opposite sexes who are not living together as husband and wife sleeping in the same room;

and for this purpose 'new resident' means a person who was not living in the premises immediately before the notice was served.

(2) For the purposes of subsection (1)(b)–

(a) children under the age of 12 shall be left out of account; and

(b) it shall be assumed that the persons occupying any part of the premises as sleeping accommodation sleep only in rooms for which a maximum is set by the notice and that the maximum set for each room is not exceeded.

Appeal against overcrowding notice

362(1) A person aggrieved by an overcrowding notice may, within 21 days after the date of service of the notice, appeal to the county court, which may make such order either confirming, quashing or varying the notice as it thinks fit.

(2) If an appeal is brought the notice does not become operative until–

(a) a decision on the appeal confirming the order (with or without variation) is given and the period within which an appeal to the Court of Appeal may be brought expires without any such appeal having been brought; or

(b) if a further appeal to the Court of Appeal is brought, a decision on that appeal is given confirming the order (with or without variation);

and for this purpose the withdrawal of an appeal has the same effect as a decision confirming the notice or decision appealed against.

A house in multiple occupation is defined in s 345 as one which is occupied by persons who do not form a single household. 'Household', however, is not defined for this purpose. In *Simmons v Pizzey* [1979] AC 37, the House of Lords stated that this is a question of fact and degree. The case concerned a property in London run by Mrs Pizzey as a Battered women's refuge. The local housing authority had fixed the maximum number of people allowed to live there at any one time, but this number had been exceeded. Mrs Pizzey pleaded in her defence that the women in the refuge formed a single household because they were living communally together. The House of Lords rejected this plea and laid down three tests for determining whether a group of people could be said to form a single household:

(1) The number of occupants and the location of the place of occupancy should be taken into account. A large number of people living in a suburban house could hardly be considered as a single household.

(2) The length of time for which each person occupies the property has also to be considered. If the population is a constantly shifting one, then the property is likely to be multi-occupied.

(3) The intention of the owner of the property has to be taken into account. The evidence suggested that Mrs Pizzey's intention was not to set up a permanent community, but to provide temporary refuge for victims of domestic violence until they found somewhere else to live.

Simmons v Pizzey

Lord Hailsham: The test of multiple occupation is whether the house was, at the material times 'occupied by persons who do not form a single household' ...

In this case I am driven by at least three factors to place what happened in 369, Chiswick High Road outside the limits of what can be conceivably called a single household. The first is the mere size. There comes a point at which all differences of degree become differences of kind. Neither 36 nor 75 is a number which in the suburbs of London as they exist at the present time can ordinarily and reasonably be regarded as a single household. The second factor is the fluctuating character of the resident population both as regards the fact of fluctuation and the extent of it. The residents were coming and going in the words of Lord Widgery CJ 'each day of the week'. The first of the Canadian cases cited above does attempt a definition which, I think rightly, implies something more durable and more intimate than the fortuitous relationship between the unhappy inmates of number 369 at the material times. The third consideration is the fact that I cannot regard a temporary place of refuge for fortuitous arrivals as ordinarily forming a household at all. These residents came from a variety of homes and may have gone to a variety of different places after leaving number 369. No doubt some would have gone back home. These would never have ceased to be members of their former household. Others will have gone to relatives. Others will have been found accommodation elsewhere. They never had the intention to use number 369 as more than a temporary harbour in a storm. Whilst they were in number 369 no doubt each looked after her own children where possible, and no doubt each conformed with the very reasonable communal organisation described in the stated case. I do not think that every community consisting of temporary migrants housed under a single roof reasonably organised constitutes or can constitute a single household. I do not think this is necessarily true of a hostel, a monastery, or a school, but certainly not of a temporary haven in a storm.

I think the magistrates would not have come to the conclusion they did had they not, apparently, been tempted by the way in which the case was presented on behalf of the authority to treat the alternatives as being either 'separate households' or 'single household'. They do not seem to have contemplated the possibility that this unhappy migrant and fluctuating body of residents did not form a household at all but an amorphous and fluctuating assembly of unfortunate human beings belonging to different households or to none. Had they directed their minds to this question I do not believe they could have come to the conclusion they did.

In *Hackney London Borough v Ezedinma* [1981] 3 All ER 438, a group of students, each of whom had a separate tenancy of individual rooms in a house but who shared kitchen facilities, were said to be capable of forming a single household if they 'grouped together' as such. Each group occupied a separate floor and shared a kitchen on their own floor; the magistrates were therefore entitled to hold that the property contained no more than three 'households'.

'Occupation' is not confined to tenant occupation, but includes occupation under a licence.

Local housing authorities have certain overcrowding controls over HMOs. A local housing authority has the power to serve an 'overcrowding notice' on the occupier of an HMO or on the person who is responsible for its management and control. The power to serve such a notice is confined to situations where it appears that the HMO is already accommodating, or is likely to accommodate, an excessive number of persons.

An overcrowding notice in respect of an HMO should specify the maximum number of people who are allowed to sleep in each room, and specify which rooms are considered as unsuitable for sleeping accommodation. Details of other required contents of the notice are set out in s 360 of the 1985 Act.

A right of appeal to a county court lies in favour of anyone who is aggrieved by an overcrowding notice (see s 362). Failure to comply with an overcrowding notice amounts to the commission of a criminal offence unless an appeal against it has already been lodged. The serving of an overcrowding notice gives the local housing authority certain additional powers to control HMOs. The authority has the power to make a control order under s 379, which will give it management powers and possession of the premises.

The authority also has powers of entry upon the premises of an HMO for the purpose of determining whether its multi-occupation powers should be exercised; 24 hours prior notice of entry, however, must first be served on the owner and the occupier of the HMO (see s 395(1)). There is the additional power to enter, without prior warning, for the purposes of ascertaining, *inter alia*, whether an overcrowding notice is being contravened or whether there has been a failure to comply with a notice requiring the execution of any works (see s 395(2)).

In addition to its overcrowding control powers and its power to make a control order, the authority also has the power to serve a repair notice under the general repair notice procedure (see earlier, on s 189 and s 190 repair notices).

The Secretary of State is also able to make regulations relating to standards of management of HMOs. These may require the manager of an HMO to ensure the repair and maintenance of certain facilities, including fire escapes, water closets, sinks and bathrooms in common use, staircases, corridors and passage ways (see s 369). Regulations were introduced in 1990 (see Housing (Management of Houses in Multiple Occupation) Regulations, SI 1990/830).

The various and wide powers that local housing authorities and the Secretary of State have under Parts X and XI Housing Act 1985 go a long way to alleviating the problems associated with overcrowding. Full utilisation of those powers would ensure that property available for occupation by tenants and licensees was reasonably fit for human occupation. Much, however, depends upon the extent to which a particular local housing authority is both willing and financially able to utilise its powers and to enforce them through the prosecution of offenders.

In 1990, the National Consumer Council carried out a survey of local housing authorities in respect of HMOs. Its findings and conclusions are somewhat worrying. It found that, out of the 207 authorities which replied to its survey, 140 did not inspect HMOs on a systematic three year cycle (The recommended standard adopted by the Association of District Councils, the Association of Metropolitan Authorities and the Institution of Environmental Health Officers). Most of the authorities who took part in the survey could not accurately estimate the number of HMOs in their area, and only a minority were making any attempts to establish that number. More worrying still was the finding that many local authorities depended on individuals complaining to them about HMOs.

The report concluded that, overall, local authorities do not use their statutory powers to enforce improvements to unsafe housing often enough. The most common explanation given for this was inadequate staff and resources. It recommended that mandatory inspection and licensing of HMOs should be introduced, since the changes brought about by the Local Government and Housing Act 1989, had done little to improve HMO's fire safety in the short term (see also ROOF Safe as Houses, January and February 1995 pp 34–35).

The future: the Housing Act 1996

Provisions contained in Part II of the Act will provide local housing authorities with powers to control standards in HMOs in the future. Sections 65–70 amend local authority powers regarding registration schemes. Section 73 imposes a duty on HMO landlords to make their properties fit for the number of occupants as regards both amenity and fire safety, whilst s 75 amends the statutory duty imposed on local authorities to ensure adequate means of escape, in case of fire in relation to certain types of HMO.

CHAPTER 5

PROTECTION FROM EVICTION

INTRODUCTION

The subject of the protection of occupiers from arbitrary eviction is a complex one, which has seen many vicissitudes over the years. Much of the current law is contained in the Protection from Eviction Act 1977, replacing earlier legislation, and which, as amended by the Housing Act 1988 provides a battery of civil and criminal remedies against arbitrary eviction. The policy of the law has long been to encourage the owners of property not to resort to self-help to evict an unwanted occupant, but to proceed by way of action in court.

The springs of the original protection from eviction legislation are to be found in the 1965 Report on Housing in Greater London (the Milner Holland Report, Cmnd 2605). That report drew attention to the evils of Rachmanism – a type of conduct which derived its name from a particularly brutal and aggressive landlord who had sought to take advantage of the provisions of the Rent Act 1957 (a Conservative decontrolling measure) by terrorising his tenants so that they fled in despair, thus enabling him to re-let the premises free of control. Emergency legislation to remedy this abuse was introduced by the incoming Labour Government in 1964. These provisions were subsequently incorporated in the codifying Protection from Eviction Act 1977, which remains the principal statutory provision in this area, though it has subsequently been substantially amended by the Housing Act 1988. The legislation is complex and there are heavy penalties, including the award of what are in effect punitive damages, for breaches of the requirements of the Act.

The codes creating certain types of tenancy contain their own protection, by providing that tenancies of a particular type can only be brought to an end by an order of the court. In the case of assured tenancies, there is a broad provision in the 1988 Act that an assured tenancy cannot be brought to an end except by an order of the court (s 5(1)).Thus, an attempt by the landlord to determine a periodic assured tenancy by notice to quit will not be effective, as s 5(1) further provides (see *Love & Lugg v Herity* (1990) 23 HLR 217). The section goes on to provide that if a landlord takes advantage of a provision in a fixed-term assured tenancy which empowers him to determine that tenancy in certain circumstances, the tenant may remain in possession of the dwelling-house under a periodic assured tenancy, which can then only be brought to an end by an order of the court.

A similar provision applies to secure tenancies under the public sector code. Section 82(1) Housing Act 1985 again provides that a secure tenancy can only be brought to an end by a court order. Curiously, there is no such specific provision for protected tenancies under the Rent Act; but the net effect of the statutory regime is the same, as a determination of the tenancy by the landlord, either under a forfeiture clause or by the service of a valid notice to quit, will result in the creation of a statutory tenancy in favour of the occupying tenant, which again can only be brought to an end by a court order (s 98).

Section 2 Protection from Eviction Act reinforces this protection. It provides that 'where any premises are let as a dwelling on a lease which is subject to a right of re-entry or forfeiture it shall not be lawful to enforce that right otherwise than by proceedings in court while any person is lawfully residing in the premises or part of them'. The presence of unlawful occupants, eg sublessees where the subletting of the premises was in breach of a covenant in the head lease, will not preclude re-entry. This protection is reinforced by s 3 of the Act.

Protection from Eviction Act 1977

3   ... where any premises have been let as a dwelling which is neither a statutorily protected tenancy nor an excluded tenancy and

(a) the tenancy ... has come to an end, but

(b) the occupier continues to reside in the premises or part of them

it shall not be lawful for the owner to enforce against the occupier, otherwise than by proceedings in court, his right to recover possession of the premises.

Even a tenant against whom a court order for possession has been made, but which has not been enforced, has been held to enjoy protection by this provision and thus to be entitled to substantial damages against a landlord who 'jumps the gun': *Haniff v Robinson* (1992) 26 HLR 386.

Haniff v Robinson

Woolf LJ: ... The facts so far as relevant are not in dispute ... The landlord owned No 36 Ferndale Road, London, N15. On December 6, 1988, he entered into a tenancy agreement with Miss Robinson under which she was entitled to occupy the premises for a period of six months. The contractual tenancy therefore came to an end by effluxion of time on June 6, 1989. After June 6, 1989, the tenant remained in possession. The landlord served an invalid notice to quit which does not affect the situation. In September 1989 the tenant visited the United States, returning in November 1989. Without her knowledge, in August 1989 the landlord had issued proceedings, wrongly contending that he was a resident landlord. The proceedings did not come to the defendant's notice until after she returned from the United States. In her absence a possession order was made on October 31, 1989, to take effect on November 28, 1989. The day before it was due to take effect, the tenant, having learnt of the order, made an application to set aside the order for possession and the judgment which had resulted in that order. The landlord was aware of the fact that she had made that application, but notwithstanding that, on December 4, 1989, he applied for execution. On December 24, 1989, he forcibly ejected the tenant. On January 22, 1990, the possession order which had been made was set aside.

For the purposes of this appeal, it is not necessary to take account of the implications which arise or could arise as a result of the possession order being set aside. However the facts of this case do illustrate the injustice which could arise if Miss Marshall is correct in the admirable submissions which she has advanced on behalf of the landlord, to the effect that in this case he was entitled to resort to self-help.

As regrettably is often the case where Rent Act issues are involved, the answer to the issue identified at the beginning of this judgment requires an undesirably tortuous journey through a number of statutory provisions. It is convenient to start at the end of that journey and work backwards from the provisions dealing with unlawful eviction which resulted in the order for damages being made in the court below. The starting point is section 27 of the Housing Act 1988.

(Woolf LJ referred to s 27(1) and continued:)

I emphasise the word 'unlawfully' in that subsection and the words 'residential occupier'. Subsection (2) contains a similar provision to that contained in subsection (1), which it is not necessary to cite. Subsection (3) is important ...

(Woolf LJ then referred to s 27(3) and continued:)

I draw attention to the words 'right to occupy'. Subsection (4) indicates that the liability for damages shall be in the nature of a liability in tort. Subsection (9)(a) contains a definition of residential occupier, the relevant words being:

> ' ... "residential occupier" in relation to any premises, has the same meaning as section 1 of the 1977 Act.'

Section 1 of that Act states that:

> ' ... "residential occupier" in relation to any premises, means a person occupying the premises as a residence, whether under a contract or by virtue of any enactment or rule of law giving him the right to remain in occupation or restricting the right of any other person to recover possession of the premises.'

The important words so far as this appeal is concerned are the words 'any enactment or rule of law ... restricting the right of any other person to recover possession of the premises'. Any other person in this context would apply to the landlord. Section 28 sets out the measure of damages. It is not necessary to refer to the terms of that section.

We can leave the 1988 Act and proceed to the 1977 Act, bearing in mind that the issue in this case was whether there was a person, namely, the landlord, who was restricted in his right to recover possession of the premises by virtue of an enactment or rule of law.

(Woolf LJ referred to ss 1 and 2 (1)(a) of the 1977 Rent Act, and, having reviewed the authorities, he concluded that a statutory tenant remains a statutory tenant so long as he occupies the dwelling-house as his residence. He then continued:)

However, I do accept that once an order for possession is made, the extent of his right as a statutory tenant can and will be curtailed. If that is the position, it is necessary to consider section 3 of the Protection from Eviction Act 1977 ...

Unless the tenant here was a statutorily protected tenant, as the premises were not let to her on an excluded tenancy she is entitled to the benefit of that protection. Section 8(1) of the same Act contains a definition of a statutorily protected tenancy. That definition makes it clear that a statutory tenant is not the holder of a statutorily protected tenancy. Accordingly, the tenant whom we are here considering was entitled to the protection of section 3. The reason that a protected tenancy, for example, does not fall within section 3 is because there is a separate regime of protection provided for such tenants.

Having come to the conclusion that the tenant is entitled to the protection of section 3, the next question is, when does that protection cease? The section provides that it was to continue and to prevent the owner from enforcing against the occupier a right to possession otherwise than by proceeding in court. The words 'otherwise than by proceedings in court' do not clearly indicate what is to be treated as being included in the proceedings. However, I have no doubt that, in the context of the statutory tenancies with which we are here concerned, that what is intended to be the effect of section 3 is that it should continue to provide protection until there has actually been execution in the ordinary way by the court's bailiff in accordance with the requirement of the County Court Rules. Ord 26, r 17 of those rules provides:

'A judgment or order for the recovery of land shall be enforceable by warrant of possession.'

The rules indicate no other way of enforcement. The table of procedures presupposes that after an order is made, that will be followed by a request for execution in due course by the person in whose favour the order has been made, followed by the execution by the court bailiff. The actual warrant for possession of land which is issued in consequence of the request under Ord 26, r 7 makes the position clear. It is addressed to the Registrar and bailiffs of the court, and it presupposes that the bailiff, having obtained possession, will deliver that possession to the plaintiff.

The position is clarified by the effect of section 100 of the Rent Act 1977. Section 100 deals with the extent of discretion of the courts in respect of claims for possession of residential dwellings where the Rent Act applies. Subsection (2) states:

'On making of an order for possession of such a dwelling-house, or at any time before the execution of such an order ... the court, subject to subsection (5) below, may–

(a) stay or suspend execution of the order, or

(b) postpone the date of possession,

for such period or periods as the court thinks fit.'

As that subsection gives the court a discretion to stay or suspend execution of the order, it cannot be in the position that it was intended that the landlord could take the matter into his own hands. When there is a stay or a suspension of execution, he cannot rely on the order for possession as giving him a right to possession. There is also the problem, if Miss Marshall is correct, that you would have a situation arising where, once a statutory tenancy had ceased to exist on an order for possession being made, it would be revived if the court were to exercise the powers which are contained in subsection (4) of section 100, subsection (4) providing:

'If any such conditions as are referred to in subsection (3) above are complied with, the court may, if it thinks fit, discharge or rescind any such order as is referred to in subsection (2) above.'

There is a passage in *Megarry on the Rent Acts* (11th edn), p.386 which leaves the position open. It says this:

'Again, a landlord who has obtained an order for possession may still be entitled to re-enter peaceably without invoking the assistance of the sheriff, even during a stay of execution; but this may now be confined to cases where nobody is lawfully in residence.'

The passage refers to two authorities, *Aglionby v Cohen* [1955] 1 QB 558 and *Clifton Securities Limited v Huntley* [1948] 2 All ER 283. We have been referred to those authorities. They dealt with cases which did not involve statutory tenants. They did not deal with situations where the Protection from Eviction Act 1977 could apply and, in my judgment, they are of no assistance here. Indeed, the passage in Megarry is wrong, in so far as it suggests that there may be a right in a landlord to re-enter peaceably, in the circumstances of this sort of case, between an order for possession and execution of the order by the bailiff. In that regard, the note in the Supreme Court Practice (1991), p 726 is correct, in so far as it states in relation to Ord 45, r 4:

'In relation to a dwelling-house, whether it is a protected tenancy or not, the plaintiff may not enter into possession himself, even peaceably, and he can only enter into possession under a writ of possession (Protection from Eviction Act 1977, s 3) negativing to this extent *Aglionby v Cohen*.'

It also follows that the county court decision in the case of *Kyriacou v Pandeli* (1980) Current Law Year Book 1648 was correctly decided.

The position here is that the landlord, although he had obtained an order of possession, had no right to resort to self-help to take possession of the premises in question. By doing so he was guilty of unlawful eviction and, accordingly, the judge in the court below was right to conclude that this was a case in which the tenant, on her counterclaim, was entitled to damages under section 28 of the Housing Act 1988. I would dismiss this appeal.

The importance of these provisions is that a tenant who apprehends that he has become, or is becoming, the victim of an unlawful eviction or attempts at unlawful evictions, can seek the assistance of the court by way of injunction against the unlawful conduct concerned. An injunction will normally be granted to restrain the unlawful conduct. If the tenant has actually left and the property has been re-let, it will generally be regarded as inappropriate for an injunction to be granted (see *Love & Lugg v Herity* (1990) 23 HLR 217).

NOTICES TO QUIT

It is in this context that the statutory rules concerning the formality of notices to quit acquire their importance. It is trite law that periodic tenancies may normally be determined by notices to quit; but it is equally clear that in the context of residential property a notice to quit does not, of itself, require the tenant to vacate the property. In the case of a periodic assured tenancy, the tenancy can only be brought to an end by an order of the court.

In the case of a Rent Act protected tenancy, although the contractual periodic tenancy may be brought to an end by a landlord's notice to quit, the tenant will still be protected, provided he continues to reside, by the creation of a statutory tenancy which will, again, continue unless and until it is brought to an end by a court. It is thus important to ensure that a notice to quit indicates to a tenant the nature of his rights, or at least contains enough information to enable him to go about ascertaining his rights. Section 5 Protection from Eviction Act 1977 is designed to secure this result.

Protection from Eviction Act 1977

5(1) Subject to subsection (1B) no notice by a landlord or a tenant to quit any premises let (whether before or after the commencement of this Act) as a dwelling shall be valid unless–

(a) it is in writing and contains such information as may be prescribed, and

(b) it is given not less than 4 weeks before the date on which it is to take effect.

(1A) Subject to subsection (1B) below, no notice by a licensor or a licensee to determine a periodic licence to occupy premises as a dwelling (whether the licence was granted before or after the passing of this Act) shall be valid unless–

(a) it is in writing and contains such information as may be prescribed, and

(b) it is given not less than 4 weeks before the date on which it is to take effect.

(1B) Nothing in subsection (1) or subsection (1A) above applies to–

(a) premises let on an excluded tenancy which is entered into on or after the date on which the Housing Act 1988 came into force unless it is entered into pursuant to a contract made before that date; or

(b) premises occupied under an excluded licence.

(2) ... (3) ...

A few points should be made about this section.

Period of notice

The standard period is four weeks, even if the tenancy might be of a nature where a lesser period of notice would suffice at common law. Weekly tenancies of dwelling-houses are still common, and at common law a week's notice would have sufficed to bring a periodic weekly tenancy to an end. This rule was, however, changed by the Rent Act 1957 and the four week rule has been maintained ever since.

Prescribed information

The notice, to be valid, must contain the prescribed information. The purpose of this is to make it clear to the tenant or licensee that it will be necessary for the landlord to obtain a court order before he can recover possession of the premises. It also suggests to the tenant the desirability of obtaining appropriate advice from a solicitor, Citizens Advice Bureau, Housing Aid Centre, or a rent officer.

Applicability to licenses of dwelling-houses

For the first time in 1988, the 'notice to quit' rules were made applicable to certain types of residential licenses. Section 5(1A) of the Act produces this result, but its interpretation has given rise to some difficulties because the new provision applies to what the Act calls 'a periodic licence to occupy premises as a dwelling'. A 'periodic licence' is nowhere defined, and this caused difficulties for the Court of Appeal in *Norris v Checksfield* (1991) 23 HLR 425.

Norris v Checksfield

The plaintiff, who was the defendant's employer, owned a bungalow occupied by the defendant. The purpose of the transaction was to provide the employee with 'on-site' accommodation so that he could be more readily available for driving the coaches of his employer. He signed a document, declared to be a 'license', which provided specifically for the termination of his license if he left the employ of the defendant. The document provided that he was to have £5 per week deducted from his salary in relation to the occupation. The plaintiff's potential career as a coach driver, however, was unlikely to come to fruition, as he had already been banned from driving. When this became known to the employer, he sought to terminate the defendant's right to occupy the bungalow, and gave him a notice which did not comply with the requirements of s 5. The issue then arose whether the occupant was a 'periodical licensee'.

Having rejected, initially, the defendant's contention that he was a tenant, a baffled Woolf LJ remarked:

> The draftsman's reference to a 'periodic licence' in subsection (1A) creates as far as I am aware a new animal. 'Periodic tenancies' referred to in subsection (1) are well known but I am not aware of any previous reference to 'a periodic licence to occupy premises'. Clearly the draftsman in subsection (1A) was creating a parallel situation to that in subsection (1) but wished to restrict it not only to licences which were required to be determined by notice but also to those licences which could properly be described as periodic ... There is no definition of a periodic licence in either the 1977 Act or the amending Housing Act of 1988 ... The fact that rent is payable with reference to a period of time such as a week would only be of significance if there was no other express or implied event which terminates the licence ...

In this case, the licence was terminable with cesser of employment; but the inference must be that if the licence was otherwise indefinite, but a regular weekly rent had been payable, it would have amounted to a 'periodic licence'. This was a licence for a single period, the period of employment. The subsection, in referring to a periodic licence, confined its operation to those licences which continue for a series of periods until terminated by a notice, by analogy with weekly, monthly, or quarterly tenancies.

EXCLUDED TENANCIES AND LICENCES

The rules set out above have no application to 'excluded tenancies' and 'excluded licences'. These concepts are further explored below.

Excluded tenancies and licences were new additions to the already complex vocabulary of landlord and tenant law made by the Housing Act 1988. Their main effect, when they apply, is to exclude the operation of the 'notice to quit' rules, set out above, and to disapply the 'due process' requirements of s 3, thus enabling a landlord to recover possession by peaceable re-entry. They presumably do not disapply the harassment provisions, so as to entitle the landlord to harass his excluded tenants or licensees. If the landlord seeks to determine the excluded tenancy or licence by way of the remedy of forfeiture, however, the constraints of s 2 will apparently continue to apply.

The concept of the 'excluded tenancy or licence' is derived from s 3A Protection from Eviction Act 1977, which was added to the Protection from Eviction Act 1977 and came into force on 15 January 1989. It appears that a tenancy entered into before 15 January 1989 cannot possibly be an 'excluded tenancy', even if all the conditions for exclusion are met. However, a licence granted before that date can be an 'excluded licence', if the necessary conditions (ie resident and sharing) are met and thus it will be exempted from the onerous provisions of s 5 relating to a notice to quit. Since, though, such a licence is likely to give rise to a restricted contract, the requirements of due process will still apply to it by virtue of s 3 Protection from Eviction Act 1977.

Protection from Eviction Act 1977

3A Excluded tenancies and licences

(1) Any reference in this Act to an excluded tenancy or an excluded licence is a reference to a tenancy or licence which is excluded by virtue of any of the following provisions of this section.

(2) A tenancy or licence is excluded if–

 (a) under its terms the occupier shares any accommodation with the landlord or licensor; and

 (b) immediately before the tenancy or licence was granted and also at the time it comes to an end, the landlord or licensor occupied as his only or principal home premises of which the whole or part of the shared accommodation formed part.

(3) A tenancy or licence is also excluded if–

 (a) under its terms the occupier shares any accommodation with a member of the family of the landlord or licensor;

 (b) immediately before the tenancy or licence was granted and also at the time it comes to an end, the member of the family of the landlord or licensor occupied as his only or principal home premises of which the whole or part of the shared accommodation formed part; and

 (c) immediately before the tenancy or licence was granted and also at the time it comes to an end, the landlord or licensor occupied as his only or principal home premises in the same building as the shared accommodation and that building is not a purpose-built block of flats.

(4) For the purposes of subsections (2) and (3) above, an occupier shares accommodation with another person if he has the use of it in common with that person (whether or not also in common with others) and any reference in those subsections to shared accommodation shall be construed accordingly, and if, in relation to any tenancy or licence, there is at any time more than one person who is the landlord or licensor, any reference in those subsections to the landlord or licensor shall be construed as a reference to any one of those persons.

(5) In subsections (2) to (4) above–

 (a) 'accommodation' includes neither an area used for storage nor a staircase, passage, corridor or other means of access;

 (b) 'occupier' means, in relation to a tenancy, the tenant and, in relation to a licence, the licensee; and

 (c) 'purpose-built block of flats' has the same meaning as in Part III of Schedule 1 to the Housing Act 1988;

 and in section 113 of the Housing Act shall apply to determine whether a person is for the purposes of subsection (3) above a member of another's family as it applies for the purposes of Part IV of that Act.

(6) A tenancy or licence is excluded if it was granted as temporary expedient to a person who entered the premises in question of any other premises as a trespasser (whether or not, before the beginning of that tenancy or licence, another tenancy or licence to occupy the premises or any other premises had been granted to him).

(7) A tenancy or licence is excluded if–

 (a) it confers on the tenant or licensee the right to occupy the premises for a holiday only, or

(b) it is granted otherwise than for money or money's worth.

(8) A licence is excluded if it confers rights of occupation in a hostel, within the meaning of the Housing Act 1985, which is provided by–

(a) the council of a county, district or London Borough, the Common Council of the City of London, the Council of the Isles of Scilly, the Inner London Education Authority, a joint authority within the meaning of the Local Government Act 1985 or a residuary body within the meaning of that Act;

(b) a development corporation within the meaning of the New Towns Act 1981;

(c) the Commission for the New Towns;

(d) an urban development corporation established by an order under section 135 of the Local Government, Planning and Land Act 1980;

(e) a housing action trust established under Part III of the Housing Act 1988;

(f) the Development Board for Rural Wales;

(g) the Housing Corporation or Housing for Wales;

(h) a housing trust which is a charity or a registered housing association, within the meaning of the Housing Associations Act 1985; or

(i) any other person who is, or who belongs to a class of person which is, specified in an order made by the Secretary of State.

(9) ...

The main categories involved are as follows:

Resident and sharing landlords

This is likely to be the most important and significant of the categories, and it must be examined with some care. It does not follow that any and every resident landlord under the Housing Act will have excluded tenants or licensees under his wing or roof; a landlord can be 'resident' for the purpose of the 'resident landlord' exception without necessarily sharing any accommodation with the tenant. The crux of the exception here is the fact that the landlord is not only resident, but is also sharing some accommodation with the tenant. The 'shared accommodation' will have to be more than a passage or stairway; but presumably the sharing of a bathroom or kitchen will suffice. The landlord has to be resident in the strict sense enjoined by the Housing Act 1988, ie occupying as his only or principal home (for the interpretation of this expression see pp 140). It suffices also if some accommodation is shared with a member of the landlord's family (borrowing for this purpose the definition of 'family' found, for public sector tenancies, in s 113 Housing Act 1985 (see pp 288)), the landlord also being resident.

Holiday lets

These also amount to excluded tenancies or licenses, by virtue of s 3A(7).

Temporary expedients to trespassers

These are excluded by virtue of s 3A(6).

Hostel accommodation

These are excluded by virtue of s 3A(8).

Gratuitous lettings or licenses

A tenancy or license is also excluded if it is granted otherwise than for money or money's worth.

Other exclusions

In *Mohamed v Manek & Royal Borough of Kensington and Chelsea* (1995) 27 HLR 439, it was also stated that s 3(2B) does not apply to an agreement which was clearly intended as a temporary arrangement pending the making of inquiries under s 62 Housing Act 1995 in relation to homelessness. Where, therefore, a local housing authority, pending such inquiries, provides temporary 'bed and breakfast' type accommodation, either from its own housing resources or through those of a third party, to an applicant claiming to be homeless, that accommodation is not 'occupied as a dwelling under a licence'.

CRIMINAL SANCTIONS

A series of criminal offences are assembled in s 1 Protection from Eviction Act 1977. They can broadly be subdivided as follows:

Illegal eviction

This offence is set out in s 1(2) and (4) in the following terms.

Protection from Eviction Act 1977

1   Unlawful eviction and harassment of occupier

   (2) If any person unlawfully deprives the residential occupier of any premises of his occupation of the premises or any part thereof, or attempts to do so, he shall be guilty of an offence unless he proves that he believed, and had reasonable cause to believe, that the residential occupier had ceased to reside in the premises.

   (4) A person guilty of an offence under this section shall be liable–

      (a) on summary conviction, to a fine not exceeding [the prescribed sum] or to imprisonment for a term not exceeding 6 months or to both;

      (b) on conviction on indictment, to a fine or to imprisonment for a term not exceeding 2 years or to both.

The 'premises' have here been held to extend to static caravans – see *Norton v Knowles* [1969] 1 QB 572, where the Divisional Court showed a disposition to interpret the legislation in case of ambiguity in favour of the occupier.

It will be noted that the accused will have a defence if (the burden of proof being on him) he can show that he believed, and had reasonable grounds to believe, that the residential occupier had ceased to occupy the premises. Likewise, a belief, on reasonable grounds, that the actual occupiers are not the lawful occupiers (ie that their occupation is trespassory in nature) will be a defence: see *R v Phekoo* [1981] 1 WLR 1117.

A temporary deprivation may suffice, but it was observed in *R v Yuthiwattana* (1984) 80 Cr App Rep 55 that such cases (for instance, the withholding of a replacement key to a tenant who had managed to lose his) could more appropriately be dealt with as an instance of a 'harassment' offence (see below).

Harassment

Here there are two applicable offences – those set out in s 1(3) and (3A):

Protection from Eviction Act 1977
1   Unlawful eviction and harassment of occupier

(3) If any person with intent to cause the residential occupier of any premises–

  (a) to give up the occupation of the premises or any part thereof; or

  (b) to refrain from exercising any right or pursuing any remedy in respect of the premises or part thereof;

  does acts [likely] to interfere with the peace or comfort of the residential occupier or members of his household, or persistently withdraws or withholds services reasonably required for the occupation of the premises as a residence, he shall be guilty of an offence.

(3A) Subject to subsection (3B) below, the landlord of a residential occupier or an agent of the landlord shall be guilty of an offence if–

  (a) he does acts likely to interfere with the peace or comfort of the residential occupier or member of his household, or

  (b) he persistently withdraws or withholds services reasonably required for the occupation of the premises in question as a residence,

  and (in either case) he knows, or has reasonable cause to believe, that that conduct is likely to cause the residential occupier to give up the occupation of the whole part of the premises or to refrain from exercising any right or pursuing any remedy in respect of the whole or part of the premises.

(3B) A person shall not be guilty of an offence under subsection (3A) above if he proves that he had reasonable grounds for doing the acts or withdrawing or withholding the services in question.

(3C) In subsection (3A) above 'landlord', in relation to a residential occupier of any premises, means the person who, but for–

  (a) the residential occupier's right to remain in occupation of the premises, or

  (b) a restriction on the person's right to recover possession of the premises,

  would be entitled to occupation of the premises and any superior landlord under whom that person derives title.

(5) Nothing in this section shall be taken to prejudice any liability or remedy to which a person guilty of an offence thereunder may be subject in civil proceedings.

(6) ...

The reason for the rather untidy appearance of these sections lies in the differentiation of the mental element required. The original s 1(3) offence required 'intention'. A lesser degree of *mens rea* is required in the new offence contained in s 1(3A), added to the Protection from Eviction Act by the Housing Act 1988.

Do the 'acts' need to be independently unlawful, ie tortious or a breach of contract? This matter was unclear, as there is no requirement in s 1(3) or (3A) of 'unlawfulness', as appears in s 1(2). The matter has now been authoritatively decided by the House of Lords in *R v Burke* [1991] 1 AC 135.

R v Burke

Lord Griffiths: ...The appellant purchased 43, Fitzroy Street, London, W1, in about April 1983. The indictment alleged harassment by the appellant against a number of tenants who had been living in the house at the time of his purchase. Mr and Mrs Esteban occupied a room on the third floor of the house, Mustafa Hassouni occupied a room in the basement and Mr and Mrs Gesto occupied a room on the first floor. The first and second counts in the indictment related to the Estebans. The first count alleged an offence contrary to s 1(3)(a) of the Act of 1977 namely that the appellant did acts calculated to interfere with the peace and comfort of the Estebans with the intent to cause them to give up occupation of the premises. The second count alleged an offence contrary to s 1(3)(b) of the Act namely that the appellant did acts calculated to interfere with the peace and comfort of the Estebans with intent to cause them to refrain from exercising their rights or pursuing their remedies in respect of the premises or part thereof. Counts three and four related to Mustafa Hassouni, counts five and six related to the Gestos and they were framed identically with counts one and two.

At the close of the prosecution case the judge upheld a submission that there was no case to answer on counts two, four and six which alleged offences contrary to s 1(3)(b) because it had not been established that the principal acts of harassment relied upon by the prosecution infringed any contractual rights of the tenants and the whole thrust of the prosecution case was directed to establishing an intent to oust the tenants from the premises rather than to cause them to refrain from exercising any right or remedy in respect of the premises. The judge therefore directed the jury to acquit the appellant on counts two, four and six. The judge left counts one, three and five to the jury. They acquitted on count one but convicted on counts three and five which concerned Mr Hassouni and Mr and Mrs Gesto.

The principal acts of harassment relied upon by the prosecution in the case of Mr Hassouni may be summarised as follows: Mr Hassouni had been a tenant in the premises since 1972 and until the appellant purchased the premises Mr Hassouni had used the lavatory and bathroom in the basement adjacent to his room. The appellant prevented Mr Hassouni from using that bathroom and lavatory by storing furniture in the bathroom and corridor. The appellant padlocked the door to the lavatory on the half landing between the ground and first floors. The appellant deliberately disconnected a front door bell which communicated with the basement floor. The appellant attempted to get Mr Hassouni to sign an application form for accommodation addressed to the local housing authority and treated him in a dictatorial way ordering him to go down to the basement when he was speaking to Mr Gesto on the first floor. When Mr Hassouni told the appellant to stop harassing him he replied: 'If you don't want to be harassed go to the council to be rehoused'.

The principal acts of harassment relied upon in the case of the Gestos were padlocking the lavatory between the ground and first floors and deliberately disconnecting the front door bell communicating with the first floor.

In relation to these counts the judge directed the jury that none of the principal matters complained of constituted a breach of contract on the part of the appellant because the tenants in question (a) although were entitled to have the use of the bathroom and lavatory somewhere within the building, were not contractually entitled to insist upon a particular bathroom or lavatory being kept available and (b) were not entitled to require the appellant to maintain a system of front door bells. He then continued:

'The fact that these tenants were not entitled, as a matter of law, to have a system of front door bells, does not end the matter. You will have to decide (if you accept this man cut off the system of bells) why did he do it? If he padlocked the lavatory on the half landing and was entitled to take that lavatory out of use as a matter of civil law between the two of them, then why did he do it? If you are sure he did these acts (whatever the civil law may be) with the purpose or the aim of getting the tenants to leave, then you will convict.'

In directing the jury in those terms the judge was applying the law as laid down by the Court of Appeal in *R v Yuthiwattana* (1984) 16 HLR 49. The Court of Appeal in the present case held itself bound to follow that decision and said that it agreed with it.

In *Yuthiwattana* the act of harassment relied upon by the prosecution was the refusal of the landlady to replace a missing front door key for the occupier of the bed-sitting room in her house. In the course of giving judgment Kerr LJ said, at pp 59–60:

'The second ground of appeal concerns the refusal to replace the lost key. I have already summarised the facts about that. Mr Stephenson submitted that there was no obligation on the appellant to replace the lost key; that she was not in breach of contract under the civil law in that regard, and that, since there was no breach of contract, a refusal to replace the key could not constitute anything in the nature of an offence under section 1(3) of the Act. Mr Stephenson's submission on this point would, if correct, give rise to strange results. Take the instance of the key. Mr Nelson was originally given one, and when it disappeared the appellant refused to replace it. For this purpose I assume that it had not been taken by the appellant, as the prosecution contended. Without being given a replacement, or having one on loan, he could not replace it by having another key cut. He had to depend for the result of his time there on someone being in the premises to let him in, and the state of affairs continued until May 2. In our view, all that the jury had to be satisfied about was that the continuing refusal of a replacement key was an act 'calculated to interfere with the peace and comfort' of Mr Nelson with the intent to cause him to give up the occupation of his room. It was on those lines that the assistant recorder directed the jury, and in our view he was entirely correct. On Mr Stephenson's argument he should have taken an entirely different course. He should have directed the jury as a matter of law whether in those circumstances there was an implied term of the contract between the appellant and Mr Nelson that he should be provided with a replacement key, presumably at his own expense, or possibly that he should have been given the opportunity to have new key cut. Then, having decided as a matter of law whether the conduct charged amounted to a breach of express or implied term of contract, the jury should have been directed to acquit or convict on that count on the basis of that decision. We reject that submission without hesitation. It is not supported by the wording of section 1(3).'

The appellant submits that that case was wrongly decided and that in order to constitute an offence contrary to section 1(3) the conduct complained of must amount to a breach of the civil law in that it is either a breach of contract or tort. As Glidewell LJ observed in the Court of Appeal, this submission involves reading into the section the word 'unlawful' before 'acts'.

The appellant argues that because section 1(3)(b) is dealing with an intent to interfere with what are clearly civil rights or remedies of an occupier such as dissuading him from seeking to have a fair rent fixed or to enlist the help of the local health authority to get something done about the state of the premises or to pursue a claim for repairs of the premises it must follow that the conduct aimed at evicting the occupier is likewise conduct that interferes with a civil right of the occupier which is actionable as a civil wrong. In support of this submission the appellant relies upon a passage in the judgment of Ormrod LJ in *McCall v Abelesz* [1976] QB 585. That case decided that a breach of section 30(2) of the Rent Act 1965, which is in identical terms to section 1(3) of the present Act, does not give rise to a civil cause of action. No doubt in many cases a landlord's acts of harassment against a tenant may also involve a breach of the tenant's civil rights and this was naturally a factor that influenced the Court of Appeal in their decision that a breach of the section was not intended to create a new civil case of action. Lord Denning MR after discussing various civil remedies between landlord and tenant said, at p 594: 'Those civil remedies are sufficient to deal with most cases of harassment. So it is unnecessary to give a civil remedy for a breach of section 30(2)'.

Ormrod LJ said, at p 597:

'Subsection (2) is even more clearly a penal provision. First, a specific intent or *mens rea* must be proved before the offence is complete; that is, the intent to cause the residential occupier either to give up the premises or to refrain from exercising some right in respect of the premises. Secondly, the *actus reus* of the subsection is the doing of acts calculated to interfere with the peace and comfort of the occupier or the persistent withholding or withdrawal of services reasonably required for the occupation of the premises. All such acts must in the existing state of the law give rise either to a remedy in trespass or for breach of contract or for breach of the covenant of quiet enjoyment. Again it is unnecessary to imply into the subsection an intention to create a new civil remedy for breach of statutory duty.'

In this passage, which appears to go further than the dictum of Lord Denning, Ormrod LJ was not considering the entirely different question that arises in the present case which is whether in order to establish the criminal offence it is also necessary to prove a civil offence. I am quite satisfied that the appellant's argument is not well founded. The Act of 1977 is a consolidating act which re-enacts *inter alia* Part III of the Act of 1965 which is headed 'Protection against Harassment and Eviction without due process of Law'. The Act of 1965 created the criminal offence of harassment as a response to the Report of the Committee on Housing in Greater London (1965) (Cmnd 2605), more familiarly known as the Milner Holland Report. That report revealed a shocking variety of abuses to which landlords were subjecting their tenants in order to obtain vacant possession of rent-restricted properties. Discussing these abuses the report said, at pp 162–163 and 176:

'We began our inquiry into this part of the field by attempting a classification of the different forms of malpractice under separate heads, categorising them all under the general head of "abuses". This gave rise to two difficulties. First, it was not easy to draw a line between those acts which were plainly illegal, either as breaches of the criminal or civil law, and those which, while we regarded them as wholly reprehensible abuses, might possibly involve no actual illegality; indeed, many cases reported to us were of such complexity that the dividing line between what was illegal and what was just lawful became so shadowy as to be impossible to determine ...

We have given much thought to the question how far the existing criminal or civil law gives effective protection to tenants who are subjected to abuses of the kinds we have found to exist. Few of them are breaches of the criminal code; rather more may perhaps be sufficient to support a claim in a civil court for an injunction or damages; many are manifestations of unconscionable and anti-social behaviour which cannot be brought squarely within the purview either of crime or civil wrong.'

The report abounds in examples of unconscionable harassment designed to make life intolerable for occupiers and thus to drive them out of the premises and cited, at p 177, a New York Police Statute as an example of a statute that made criminal this type of abuse, which at present fell short of a civil or criminal wrong. When section 30(2) of the 1965 Act was enacted it closely followed the form of the New York Police Statute.

The social evil is so clearly set out in the report that I am quite satisfied that Parliament deliberately chose the language of section 30(2) of the Act of 1965 to make any action likely to interfere with the peace or comfort of the occupier a criminal offence if it was performed with the evil intention of forcing the occupier to give up occupation of the premises, 'intention' in this context meaning with the purpose or motive of causing the occupier to give up occupation of the premises.

A further reason for rejecting the argument that the act must involve a civil wrong is that harassment is not confined to the landlord and tenant relationship. The protected class is the 'residential occupier' which as defined in section 1(1) is far wider than 'tenant'. Furthermore not only landlords but 'any person' may be guilty of harassment. Therefore there may be no contractual relationship of any kind between the victim and the harasser, an obvious example being fellow occupiers who have fallen out.

I would therefore hold that *R v Yuthiwattana* (1984) 16 HLR 49 and the present case were correctly decided. We were invited by counsel to expand the certified question beyond the relationship of landlord and tenant and I would rephrase it so that it reads: 'Whether it is necessary for an act by the defendant to be an actionable civil wrong in order to be an offence under section 1(3) of the Protection from Eviction Act 1977'. I would answer the question in the negative, dismiss this appeal and order the costs of the prosecution to be paid out of central funds.

Lords Ackner and Lowry concurred.

It will be noted that the withdrawal of services, eg gas or electricity, reasonably required for the occupation of the premises as a residence, will only be a criminal offence if the withdrawal is 'persistent'. Furthermore, the existence of grounds for doing the acts or withdrawing the services in question will be a defence to any proceedings under s 1(3A) (see s 1(3B)).

DAMAGES AND CIVIL ACTIONS

In this area the law has developed in a complex manner over many years. In many situations which are of the nature of an illegal eviction, the landlord's conduct may give rise to liability in either contract (as a breach of the covenant for quiet enjoyment) or tort, for example, trespass to goods or to the person (assault). It was however clear that conduct which was criminal as a result of a contravention of s 1 Protection from Eviction Act 1977 was not, of itself, tortious, so no action could be brought for breach of statutory duty in respect of conduct contravening s 1 (*McCall v Abelesz* [1976] QB 585).

The situation has been altered by the introduction of a new statutory tort with express provision for substantial damages in the Housing Act 1988. It should, however, be remembered that in certain circumstances liability under the new tort will be excluded (for instance, if the tenant is reinstated in the premises: see s 27(6)(a) Housing Act 1988).

The tort of eviction under the Housing Act 1988

The reason for the introduction of the new liability was the chaotic state of the law prior to 1988; cases such as *McCall v Abelesz* had shown that the existing law was confused and arbitrary in its application. Also, the introduction of the new-style 'assured tenancy' under the Housing Act, with its abandonment of the 'fair rent' protection and the diminution in the security of tenure given to the tenant in comparison with the old style Rent Act tenancy, afforded an incentive to unscrupulous landlords to try to get rid of their existing Rent Act tenants, by hook or by crook, and replace them with 'assured tenants' under the Housing Act. Accordingly, the government found itself constrained to introduce the new tort in the Housing Act.

Date of operation: There is one peculiar feature about these provisions of the Housing Act 1988. Although the Act, in the main, came into operation on 15 January 1989, the eviction provisions came into operation on 9 June 1988. The liability was thus in a sense retrospective, which led to a challenge to the validity of the provisions under the European Convention for the Protection of Human Rights and Fundamental Freedoms. The Court of Appeal, in *Jones v Miah* (1992) 24 HLR 578, rejected the argument on the ground that the European Convention struck at retrospective criminal liabilities, rather than civil wrongs.

Conduct giving rise to liability

The main elements of the tort are set out in s 27(1) and (2) of the Housing Act 1988.

Housing Act 1988

27. Damages for unlawful eviction

(1) This section applies if, at any time after 9th June 1988, a landlord (in this section referred to as "the landlord in default") or any person acting on behalf of the landlord in default unlawfully deprives the residential occupier of any premises of his occupation of the whole or part of the premises.

(2) This section also applies if, at any time after 9th June 1988, a landlord (in this section referred to as 'the landlord in default') or any person acting on behalf of the landlord in default–

(a) attempts unlawfully to deprive the residential occupier of any premises of his occupation of the whole or part of the premises, or

(b) knowing or having reasonable cause to believe that the conduct is likely to cause the residential occupier of any premises–

(i) to give up his occupation of the premises or any part thereof, or

(ii) to refrain from exercising any right or pursuing any remedy in respect of the premises or any part thereof,

does acts likely to interfere with the peace or comfort of the residential occupier or members of his household, or persistently withdraws or withholds services reasonably required for the occupation of the premises as a residence, and as a result, the residential occupier gives up his occupation or the premises as a residence.

The Act covers actual evictions, as well as what one commentator has dubbed 'constructive evictions' (see Bridge, *Residential Leases*, pp 276–77) where a landlord has by his conduct in attempting an eviction or by harassment, caused the tenant to leave the premises. In both cases, though, there must be a departure from the premises. If a thick-skinned tenant decides to defy the landlord and sits tight, no liability can arise under the section. Thus the advice to the harassed tenant might well be to yield to the pressure, rather than to seek to withstand it.

It may be opportune here to consider the early case of *Tagro v Cafane* [1991] 2 All ER 235, (1991) 23 HLR 250.

Tagro v Cafane and Patel

The Master of the Rolls: This appeal is a cautionary tale for landlords who are minded unlawfully to evict their tenants by harassment or other means.

The facts are these. Miss Tagro was the residential tenant of a first floor front room in premises at 116 Landor Road, Stockwell, London, SW9. That was a bedsitting room and she had the use of the kitchen, bathroom and toilet jointly with the occupier of another room on that floor. Mr Cafane was Miss Tagro's landlord. He was the tenant of the whole building, the ground floor of which was used for his second-hand furniture business. The first floor to which I have already referred was used to provide these two bedsitting rooms, and there was a second floor which was similar to the first floor. The freehold owner of the premises let to Mr Cafane on a tenancy which was determinable on one month's notice, subject always, of course, to the effect of the Landlord and Tenant Act 1954.

Mr Cafane appeals against a judgment of His Honour Judge Simpson, given in the Lambeth County Court on November 24, 1989, whereby he awarded £31,000 damages to Miss Tagro for unlawful eviction, those damages being claimed by her under sections 27 and 28 of the relatively new Housing Act of 1988. In addition, he awarded her £15,588.28 damages for trespass to her personal belongings which were on the premises. This latter judgment was also given against the second defendant, a Mr Patel, who was the agent of Mr Cafane. Mr Patel does not appeal in respect of that part of the judgment, nor does Mr Cafane. The appeal is limited to the judgment for £31,000 which was solely against Mr Cafane because he alone was the landlord.

The defendants were not represented below, but we have been greatly assisted by the fact that Mr Cafane has been represented in this court by Mr Robert Carnwath, QC and Mr William Geldart, who have put in an admirable skeleton argument which, of course, Mr Carnwath has supplemented orally.

The further facts are these. It was in August 1989 that war really broke out, but some mention should be made of the previous history because it obviously affected the reaction of the tenant. For example, on one occasion she had been woken up at 2 o'clock in the morning with a demand for rent. There was some dispute as to whether the rent was due, but it really does not matter because 2 o'clock in the morning is not a time at which any landlord is entitled to demand rent from his tenant or even remind the tenant that rent is due. On another occasion there was even more outrageous conduct. Miss Tagro was visiting the lavatory which was situated in the bathroom, and the landlord, or somebody on his behalf, came and kicked the door down. She complained previously of having been referred to as a black bastard and of loud music being used to disturb her enjoyment of the flat and so on. That was the background.

On August 3 she returned to the room to find herself locked out and the locks changed. There has been no challenge in this court, and there could not be any serious challenge, to the fact that the locks were changed with the intention of evicting her. There was some suggestion at one stage that a number of keys had been floating around and got into the possession of various other people and that the lock was changed for security purposes. The judge rejected that on his assessment of the evidence in view of the fact that it was some days later before Miss Tagro was even offered a key which actually fitted the lock.

Faced with that situation, on August 4, the next day, she obtained an *ex parte* injunction to re-admit her to the premises and allow her access to her belongings. That injunction was very properly for a limited period, being given *ex parte*, and it came up for renewal on August 7, when it was continued, Mr Cafane having taken no step whatever to comply with it in the meantime. The application to continue the injunction was coupled with an application to commit for contempt of court.

On August 8 or 9 – it matters not which – Mr Cafane relented to the extent that he offered Miss Tagro a key. Her evidence about this I can take from her affidavit:

'I collected the key late morning on Wednesday 9 August 1989 in the office of Messrs Mohabir and Co and went to the building. The lock to the front door was broken and, in fact, I did not need the key to enter. I went upstairs to the premises. Everything inside was in chaos. Many things were broken. A large amount of my belongings were stolen. On the advice of my solicitor I called the Police, who arrived, then had to leave on an emergency call. They said they would be back to take fingerprints and that I should not touch anything shiny or any door or wardrobe or handle until they were able to return which at the time of swearing this affidavit they have not done although I have been reminding them. In the late afternoon my solicitor's surveyor arrived to take photographs and draw up a schedule of broken items.'

Later in her affidavit, she stated:

'I did not sleep at the premises on the night of Wednesday 9th August 1989. This was partly because the Police told me not to touch any of the objects in the premises including everything which was shiny and partly because the lock to the front of the building was damaged and would not "lock", leaving me with greatly reduced security. The main reason however was that I had by then become too frightened of the Defendants. I have not returned to the premises to sleep and do not intend to do so. After the recent events outlined above I cannot conceive of returning to the premises.'

I would add that the state of the premises to which Miss Tagro swore in her affidavit was attributed by the landlord to the fact that there had been a burglary. The learned judge wholly rejected the suggestion that there had been a burglary. It is perhaps inherently unlikely that there was one, in that the damage done to the flat was not the sort of damage that one would expect from a burglar who was intent upon removing goods. Such an intruder does not smash the goods and the flat itself. Any judge would be entitled to take judicial notice that that was an unusual way of proceeding. At all events, the judge clearly formed the view that this so-called burglary never took place and that what had happened was that, having locked Miss Tagro out, Mr Cafane or those acting on his behalf were determined to make certain that under no circumstances would she be prepared to return even if they were eventually obliged to let her in again as a result of the court order; and, of course, they were brilliantly successful.

One other date needs to be mentioned because it is relevant to Mr Carnwath's arguments, and that is August 26, 1989. The proceedings originally were in support of the *ex parte* injunction and claimed an injunction ordering the defendants to re-admit the plaintiff to the building and premises forthwith and to deliver keys to the building to the plaintiff and further restraining the defendants, their servants or agents or otherwise from further interfering with the plaintiff's quiet enjoyment of the premises and from further interfering with the plaintiff and from further trespassing on the premises of the plaintiff's goods and for damages. There was no claim under, or for damages under, s 27 of the Housing Act 1988. That claim was introduced by fairly extensive amendment on August 25, 1989.

As I have already made clear, this is a claim under the Housing Act and the defences raised also arise under that Act. The principal defences arise under section 27(6)(b) and section 27(7)(b) of the Act. So let me turn to the wording of the Act itself. Section 27 is headed 'Damages for unlawful eviction' and provides:

'(1) This section applies if, at any time after 9th June 1988, a landlord (in this section referred to as "the landlord in default") or any person acting on behalf of the landlord in default unlawfully deprives the residential occupier of any premises of his occupation of the whole or part of the premises.'

I do not think I need refer to subsection (2) save to say that it provides for similar treatment where there is what might be described as constructive eviction of the residential occupier cannot reasonably be expected to remain, although physically he or she could remain, and the occupier accordingly gives up his occupation of the premises ...

(The Master of the Rolls referred to sections 27(3)–(6) and continued:)

I will come to subsection (7) in a moment. I would like first of all to deal with the argument on subsection (6).

Before doing so I ought to mention that in subsection (9) '"residential occupier", in relation to any premises, has the same meaning as in section 1 of the 1977 Act'; that is to say the Protection From Eviction Act 1977, which in subsection 1(1) provides:

'In this section "residential occupier", in relation to any premises, means a person occupying the premises as a residence, whether under a contract or by virtue of any enactment or rule of law giving him the right to remain in occupation or restricting the right of any person to recover possession of the premises.'

There is no dispute, of course, that Miss Tagro was a residential occupier, and immediately after August 2 she was a former residential occupier.

Mr Carnwath says in relation to subsection (6) that, in the case of Miss Tagro, the court made an order as a result of which she was reinstated in the premises in question in such circumstances that she again became the residential occupier of them. He says it cannot seriously be suggested that a tenant who has been unlawfully evicted and whom the landlord is able and willing to reinstate, simply has an option whether to accept reinstatement or not.

There are two quite separate questions there. As to the first – was Miss Tagro actually reinstated? – for my part, I have no doubt or hesitation in saying that she was not and could not be at that stage. Reinstatement does not consist in merely handing the tenant a key to a lock which does not work and inviting her to resume occupation of a room which has been totally wrecked. Therefore, on the facts of this case, that is an argument which simply does not run.

On the question of whether the tenant has a right to choose whether or not to accept the offer, subject to a point which arises under a later subsection, for my part, I think that the tenant has. Mr Carnwath says that cannot be right because it means to say that a tenant who is unlawfully evicted, perhaps for a relatively short period, is able to achieve some enormous financial reward which is only available to him if he does not accept the offer of reinstatement. There is, of course, a good deal to be said for Mr Carnwath's argument, as there always is for Mr Carnwath's arguments, but there is no indication in the statute that the tenant does not have that choice. It is difficult to see how you can reinstate a tenant who does not wish to be reinstated. The apparent intention of Parliament is not as unreasonable as it might appear at first when you take into account the fact that, under section 28 to which I will come in a moment, the damages are designed to be equal in amount to the benefit which the landlord gets by having had the tenant removed from the premises, namely, the increase in the value to him of the premises. It is therefore quite intelligible that Parliament should have said, 'Well, if the tenant does not choose to go back, at least the landlord shall not benefit by it', and to have proceeded on that basis. So, for my part, I think that the argument that there is any defence for Mr Cafane under subsection (6) is quite untenable.

I turn therefore to subsection (7), which provides as follows:

'If, in proceedings to enforce a liability arising by virtue of subsection (3) above, it appears to the court–

(a) that prior to the event which gave raise to the liability, the conduct of the former residential occupier or any person living with him in the premises concerned was such that it is reasonable to mitigate the damages for which the landlord in default would otherwise be liable,

or

(b) that, before the proceedings were begun, the landlord in default offered to reinstate the former residential occupier in the premises in question and either it was unreasonable of the former residential occupier to refuse that offer or, if he had obtained alternative accommodation before the offer was made, it would have been unreasonable of him to refuse that offer if he had not obtained that accommodation,

the court may reduce the amount of damages which would otherwise be payable to such amount as it thinks appropriate.'

Let me say straightaway that paragraph (a) has no application whatever to this case. No suggestion has ever been made that Miss Tagro's conduct was such that it could be criticised and would make it reasonable to mitigate the damage. The two paragraphs seem to me to involve two quite different concepts.

Sub-paragraph (a) is dealing with what one might describe a contributory negligence concept, although contributory negligence, in the context of an unlawful eviction, is clearly not a happy phrase. But it is the idea that in some measure, although not in such measure as in any way to excuse the conduct of the landlord, the tenant has brought the problem on his own head and the paragraph enables the court to mitigate the consequences for the landlord.

Sub-paragraph (b) seems to me to borrow something from the concept of the defence of tender in relation to a debt, a defence which is only available if tender takes place before the proceedings are begun. It is, therefore, necessary to consider what is meant by the phrase 'before the proceedings were begun' in paragraph (b). It will be remembered that subsection (7) begins with the words, 'If, in proceedings to enforce a liability by virtue of subsection (3) above ...'

Mr Neuberger would have argued, if he had been given the opportunity of doing so, that that meant the totality of the proceedings which were begun at the beginning of August with the claim for an injunction, and that, therefore, there is no question here of any offer of reinstatement before the proceedings were begun. Mr Carnwath argues strongly that these were not proceedings to enforce a liability until an amendment took place later in August, and that sub-paragraph (b) with its reference to 'before the proceedings were begun' cannot be referring to proceedings which had nothing whatever to do with the enforcement of a liability under subsection (3).

I am bound to say that, for my part, although I have to accept that it is an *obiter* expression of opinion on the facts of this case, I think Mr Carnwath is wholly correct in his argument. I say it is *obiter* because the question would only arise as a matter of decision if Mr Carnwath could make good his argument that there was an offer to reinstate the former residential occupier in the premises in question at any time, on the facts as I see them, there never was any such offer. All that was on offer was to give her the key and to re-admit her. Certainly, there was no suggestion that the room was put into proper order, the locks repaired or any offer made to Miss Tagro to allow her to resume occupation in any realistic sense of the word. But, had it arisen, as I say, and it may arise in other cases, my view would have been that the subsection is referring to a time before there is a claim in the proceedings under sections 27 and 28 of the Act.

A number of points arising from this case should be noted.

Reinstatement

Liability is extinguished in the event of reinstatement in the premises of the tenant. This may take the form of an actual reinstatement by the landlord (which is clearly not satisfied by the offer of a key which does not work to a wrecked room) or by the tenant accepting reinstatement pursuant to a court order – but the tenant has a choice whether to accept or reject the reinstatement. If the tenant is in fact reinstated, as in *Ramdath v Daley* (1993) 25 HLR 273, damages will not be available under the Act, but they may be recovered at common law for 'ordinary' torts such as trespass to goods.

Reduction of damages because of contributory conduct

The Act contains a provision (s 27(7)) for reduction of the very considerable damages available under the provisions of s 28 because of the tenant's contributory conduct or the unreasonable refusal of reinstatement.

The proper defendant

The definition of 'landlord' in the Act is a comprehensive one, and will include, for instance, a purchaser from the original landlord who has been let into possession of the premises as a licensee of the vendor/landlord (see *Jones & Lee v Miah & Miah* (1992) 24 HLR 578).

Landlords often choose to employ agents to act for them in these sorts of situations; but it is clear that the acts of the agent are attributable to the landlord, as the Act includes the conduct of a person 'acting on behalf of the landlord'. Though the Act seems to place the liability to pay substantial damages on the landlord himself, even in those cases where an agent has acted on his behalf, in *Sampson v Wilson* (1994) 26 HLR 486 liability was imposed on the agent also.

Measure of damages

The purpose of the new statutory tort is to make it clear to the wrongdoing landlord that 'tort does not pay' and the Act contains elaborate provisions to ensure that the damages recoverable are measured by the gain to the landlord rather than the loss to the tenant. The operation of these provisions is illustrated by the following extract from *Tagro v Cafane*.

Tagro v Cafane

Master of the Rolls: So much for the appeal in respect of liability. But Mr Carnwath, on behalf of Mr Cafane, has also addressed arguments to us on the subject of quantum. That is governed by section 28 ...

On the facts of this case, the learned judge was not concerned to consider the value of the room which had been let to Miss Tagro but the value of the whole building, including four bedsitting rooms and the business premises below.

Miss Tagro, or those acting on her behalf, called a surveyor, who was an associate member of the Chartered Institute of Surveyors, to give evidence ... He capitalised a profit rental and he considered the extent to which the value of Mr Cafane's interests would be reduced by the presence of Miss Tagro. He said this:

'I start with freehold with occupancy ie £89,000 then made deduction of £45,000 ie amount of rent x 10 being capital value of Mr Cafane's interest. This produces £44,000 which represents value of leasehold interest with Miss Tagro as sitting tenant. £75,000 [which was the figure that he had valued Mr Cafane's interest with vacant possession] minus £44,000 equals £31,000. This represents the difference in value of the leasehold interest with or without Miss Tagro. £31,000 is my final figure for damages.'

Mr Cafane called no evidence to dispute this figure. Mr Carnwath is therefore reduced to saying that the learned judge can be faulted on the footing that no reasonable judge could have accepted that evidence. That submission he made simply and with force and with slightly more difficulty when Russell LJ said,

'Well, what should he have done?' It is true, I suppose, that he could have adjourned the hearing and urged the landlord to call expert evidence. But it is difficult to see how he could have said, 'I am not satisfied that any damages are due on this evidence' and, if he is not to say that, then he would have in some way to reduce the surveyor's figure on the basis, I suppose, of what he [the judge] thought were proper values. Had he done so, this court would probably have quashed his decision on the grounds that he was acting not upon evidence and not upon something of which a judge should take judicial knowledge but upon some extraneous view as to a matter of fact.

But, essentially, what Mr Carnwath concentrates upon is his submission that there is no evidence that the judge fully appreciated that this was only a monthly tenancy as far as Mr Cafane was concerned, and that, had he appreciated, he could not have accepted this evidence. The difficulty about that argument – apart from any other difficulties and there are many – is that the surveyor was entitled to have regard to the realities of the situation and to have regard to the extent to which the Lambeth Council were likely to be minded to service any notice to quit and would be successful in any event, bearing in mind the provisions of the Landlord and Tenant Act 1954. If the surveyor, applying his local knowledge and professional expertise, came to the conclusion that, other things being equal, notwithstanding that the lease could theoretically, determinable on a months' notice, it would go on virtually for ever, there could be no possible faulting of that aspect of his valuation.

He also says that the surveyor should have approached the matter on the basis that the value of the property without Miss Tagro would have been virtually nil because the lease contains prohibitions against assignments and subletting and, says Mr Carnwath, if we were to decided what Mr Cafane could have got for premises without Miss Tagro, no-one would have bought it because, as soon as they took an assignment, they would be faced with an application for forfeiture by the Lambeth Borough Council.

There is the scintilla of a point of law there in that clearly the court would have to have regard to what was the interest of the landlord whose value had to be determined under section 28(1)(b), but they would have had some guidance from section 28(3) ...

I do not understand that section to contemplate, as Mr Carnwath's argument contemplates, that the premises will be treated as virtually inalienable and having no value in consequence. Subsection (3) clearly contemplates that there shall be no increase in the damages because the effect of the tenant being dispossessed is that it enables some very valuable development to take place. But the whole concept of the landlord in default selling his interest on the open market to a willing buyer assumes that he can sell it on the open market to a willing buyer and that involves the subsidiary proposition on the facts of this case that the willing buyer would take a lease from the Lambeth Borough Council on a monthly basis subject to the Landlord and Tenant Act with a covenant against subletting or assignment in exactly the same way as Mr Cafane had done. In my judgment, there is nothing in that point.

I accept that the damages do seem to be high, but I have to warn myself against using any knowledge that I may have gained in other ways to support that view, and I am quite unable to say that the judge was at fault. If we were to interfere on this ground, it could only be on the basis of sending it back for a re-hearing designed to enable Mr Cafane to call valuation evidence. It is not clear to me why he should have a second opportunity to call valuation evidence when he had the opportunity originally and did not choose to avail himself of it.

Accordingly, and for those reasons, I would dismiss the appeal.

It will be seen that in this case the tenant was awarded substantial damages of £31,000. It appears that Miss Tagro was probably a protected tenant under the Rent Act (although she might possibly have been an assured tenant under the Housing Act: the report does not make it clear). If the tenant's occupation is less secure – for example, he is a 'restricted contract' tenant because of the 'resident landlord' provisions in the Rent Act – his interest will be less valuable, and the damages awarded will be consequently reduced. Thus, in *Nwokorie v Mason* [1993] EGCS 161, decided within about six months of *Tagro v Cafane*, the tenant's interest was valued at £4,500 (see also *Melville v Bruton* [1996] *The Times*, 29 March (CA)).

Nwokorie v Mason also illustrates the point about the inability of a plaintiff to recover damages under other heads in addition to the Housing Act damages. The county court judge had awarded the plaintiff, who had been unlawfully evicted by the defendant landlord in a humiliating and distressing manner, Housing Act damages of £4,500, general damages of £500 for the illegal eviction (presumably for breach of the covenant for quiet enjoyment) and exemplary damages of £1,000, though the Court of Appeal thought that it would be more proper to characterise the award as one of aggravated damages. On appeal the Court of Appeal accepted the defendant's contention that these damages fell to be set off against the award of Housing Act damages; to allow the plaintiff to retain these damages would in effect have been to compensate him twice over for the same wrong.

If, however, the tenant is awarded Housing Act damages as well as damages for tortious conduct in the period before the actual eviction, there is no need to set the damages off against the Housing Act damages. It is only damages 'for the loss of the home', under the *Nwokorie v Mason* principles which have to be set off in this manner. Thus, in *Sampson v Wilson* (1994) 26 HLR 486, the plaintiff was able to recover damages separately for the conduct of the defendant in making his property uninhabitable in the weeks before his eviction.

Other causes of action

The landlord's conduct may give rise to other proceedings, which may be of importance if, for example, the tenant has been reinstated in the premises, as then no liability under the statutory Housing Act tort can arise. The liability may be contractual or tortious.

Contractual

Disturbance, harassment or eviction may give rise to liability under the covenant for quiet enjoyment which is implied in tenancy agreements. Older authorities suggest that threats of physical violence or the cutting-off of gas or electricity supplies may amount to a breach of the covenant (*Kenny v Preen* [1963] 1 QB 499, *Perera v Vandiyar* [1953] 1 WLR 672). But as the cause of action is contractual, it is limited by the rules of privity to a claim by the tenant himself, and cannot attract the award of aggravated or exemplary damages.

Tortious

In many cases, the landlord's act in evicting the tenant may give rise to a cause of action in trespass to land, trespass to the person or trespass to goods. In a case of trespass to goods, the plaintiff will have to prove the value of the goods alleged to have been lost or damaged. This can occasion difficulties in cases such as *Ayari v Jetha* (1991) 24 HLR 639, where the plaintiff was alleging damage to, or loss of, items such as belly-dancers costumes said to have gone astray during her illegal eviction from her flat.

In a case where a tort is found to have occurred, the court may award aggravated damages to compensate the plaintiff for injury to his proper feelings of dignity and pride; it may also award exemplary damages to punish the landlord who has sought to make a profit from the illegal activity (see *McMillan v Singh* (1984) 17 HLR 120). In *Ramdath v Daley* (1993) 25 HLR 273 the plaintiff was evicted from the property and was later reinstated by the landlord. The trial judge awarded exemplary damages against the landlord, the first defendant (upheld on appeal), and also against the second defendant, who was managing the premises on behalf of the landlord. The Court of Appeal held that the award of exemplary damages against the second defendant was erroneous, as he could not 'profit' from the wrong in the same way as the first defendant. This decision, however, is not at first sight easy to reconcile with the later case of *Sampson v Wilson* (1994) 26 HLR 486, where exemplary damages were awarded against the landlord's agent, as well as the landlord – but it may be that in this case he too was seeking to profit from the wrong.

CHAPTER 6

STATUTORY PROTECTION IN THE PRIVATE SECTOR

INTRODUCTION

The purpose of this chapter is to introduce the reader to the framework of statutory protection in the private sector. The question of the application of the statutory schemes is often a difficult and complex issue. However, once protection is shown to apply, and the tenancy in question found to fall under the protective legislation, the question of the form that protection is to take becomes relatively simple.

Before considering the nature of the protection afforded by the current legislation, a little might be said about the history of these enactments.

The original Rent Act legislation stemmed from a crisis in the First World War, when increased demand for housing led to the exploitation of tenants by landlords, who took advantage of the housing shortage in war-time and the relatively high wages enjoyed by many workers in critical war industries. So severe was the crisis, the government introduced legislation which was designed to protect tenants against arbitrary eviction and the imposition of excessive rents. The original Act, the Rent and Mortgage Interest (War Restrictions) Act 1915, was conceived as a short-term measure to deal with the crisis during the currency of the war. Housing shortages after the end of the war, however, were still very grave, and in 1920 the legislation was made permanent, as it had by now become clear that the 'Rent Acts' had come to stay. Ever since, there has been some legislation interfering with the basic contractual principles between residential landlords and tenants, though there have been continuing skirmishes between 'controllers' generally seeking the extension of the scope of the legislation, and 'free marketeers' committed to a policy of reducing the impact of the legislation on the operation of the housing market. In general, the 'controllers' have been in the ascendancy during Labour administrations, as can be seen from legislation such as the Rent Act 1965 and the extension of control to furnished lettings in 1974; 'free marketeers' have heavily influenced the policy of the law under Conservative administrations, as shown by the effect of enactments such as the Rent Act 1957 and the Housing Act 1988.

In some ways the most drastic innovation has been the Housing Act 1988. This Act will, in due time, lead to the phasing out of Rent Act tenancies, and their replacement by the 1988 'assured tenancy' model, which affords considerably less protection to the tenant. The private rented sector has declined dramatically during the 20th century, from about 90% in the early years of the century to about 7% today. Undoubtedly a major influence in bringing about this decline has been the Rent Act itself, which dramatically reduced the attractiveness of private letting as a form of investment for landlords.

Other factors, of course, are also at work, including the incentives given by successive governments to owner-occupation as a form of tenure by the provision of tax relief and other forms of incentive. Furthermore, other forms of investment are now more widely available to renters. The UK is unusual among modern industrialised economies in its stress on owner-occupation as a favoured form of tenure; the Conservative government of the 1980s played its own part in this process by the incentives it gave, such as the right to buy in the public sector and other incentives. At the same time the government saw a need to try to stimulate the revival of the private rented sector, and the Housing Act 1988 was designed to bring about this resurgence. The governmental diagnosis was that the Rent Act operated as a substantial disincentive to landlords, and that there could be no renaissance of the private rented sector until the shackles of the Rent Act were removed from landlords. At the same time, there was a recognition that it would be unfair and improper to remove from an established tenant the protection which he had become accustomed to enjoy, and so the general principle of the Housing Act is that its terms only normally apply to tenancies created on or after the implementation of the Housing Act, ie with effect from 15 January 1989. To this rule, however, there are a number of exceptions: there are a number of cases where a post 15 January 1989 tenancy will still fall to be protected by the 'old' Rent Act, and a few cases where a tenancy created before 15 January 1989 will be a Housing Act tenancy.

The statutory definitions in s 1 of the Rent Act 1977 and s 1 of the Housing Act 1988 are strikingly similar.

Rent Act 1977

1. Protected tenants and tenancies

Subject to this Part of this Act, a tenancy under which a dwelling-house (which may be a house or part of a house) is let as a separate dwelling is a protected tenancy for the purposes of this Act.

Housing Act 1988

1. Assured tenancies

(1) A tenancy under which a dwelling-house is let as a separate dwelling is for the purposes of this Act an assured tenancy if and so long as –

(a) the tenant or, as the case may be, each of the joint tenants is an individual; and

(b) the tenant or, as the case may be, at least one of the joint tenants occupies the dwelling-house as his only or principal home; and

(c) the tenancy is not one which, by virtue of subsection (2) or (6) below, cannot be an assured tenancy.

The factors common to these definitions are as follows:

(1) The subject-matter of the tenancy must be a 'house';

(2) The premises must be 'let';

(3) The premises must be let 'as a dwelling';

(4) The premises must be let as a 'separate' dwelling;

(5) The premises must not be excluded from protection by some other provision of the Act.

In addition, there are certain residential requirements, though these differ substantially in the two Acts. What is protected by the legislation is the tenant's home, and it is only occupying tenants who are protected. This feature is common to both Acts, but the test in the Housing Act is much more onerous than that in the Rent Act, which has been extended by generous judicial interpretation rather more than necessary for the simple protection of the tenant's home.

The critical issue is often the date of the creation of the tenancy, and this must not be overlooked. Tenancies created before 15 January 1989 are Rent Act protected tenancies; those created on or after that date are normally Housing Act 'assured tenancies'.

In view of the similarity in language used in the two Acts, it seems legitimate to assume that the draftsman of the Housing Act was well aware of the rich case law which has grown up around the interpretation of s 1 Rent Act 1977, and that in those cases where he has used the identical language it is reasonable to suppose that the language will be interpreted in the same way. This assumption will be made in the following discussion.

'HOUSE'

The first requirement is that the subject-matter of the agreement must be a 'house', but this expression includes 'part of a house' and thus comprehends flats and bed-sitters (see s 1 Rent Act 1977 and s 46 Housing Act 1988). There is no statutory definition of 'house' in either Act, presumably on the basis that the recognition of a 'house' is a matter of common sense. In practice, the most difficult issues have concerned immobilised 'mobile homes' and cases where parts of more than one building have been used as a kind of composite residence by the tenant.

Caravans

It has been stated that an immobilised 'mobile home' can amount to a house for the purposes of the Acts – though only, seemingly, if it has been so totally immobilised as to have become static. In *R v Rent Officer of the Nottinghamshire Registration Area ex p Allen* (1985) 52 P&CR 41 the Nottinghamshire Rent Officer had purported to fix a rent under the Rent Act 1977 in relation to a static caravan owned by Allen. This could only lawfully be done if the letting of the caravan was one which fell within the Act. The owner of the caravan contended that the Rent Officer had exceeded his powers, and sought judicial review of his action. Granting the application, Farquharson J observed:

> In my judgment, it is not possible to say that, because the subject-matter is the letting of a caravan, it cannot be within the Act. Plainly, it must depend on the circumstances of the letting. Where the caravan is let as a moveable chattel, there can be no question of it being properly described as a house. Where, on the other hand, it is rendered completely immobile, either by the removal of its wheels or by its being permanently blocked by some brick or concrete construction, then it is more likely to be regarded as a house in the same way as a bungalow or prefabricated dwelling would be. Difficulties will arise when the facts are somewhere between those two extremes. The rent officer or the county court judge, as the case may be, will have regard to the features of the caravan that may reveal elements of site permanence, on the one hand, or mobility on the

other. Are the wheels still on the vehicle? Are the stabilising struts of a permanent nature or of a kind ordinarily used by a caravan when moving from site to site? Are the services attached to the caravan? If so, are they of a fixed nature or readily detachable? Is the caravan ever moved? If so, for what purpose and with what facility? Plainly, rent officers will be on their guard against landlords who rent out caravans on their estates on a permanent or long-term basis and who seek to avoid the controls of the Rent Acts by making superficial arrangements tending to show some mobility in their caravans when the reality is that they are permanently based on the site.

If the occupancy of the caravan is such that it is plainly used by the tenant as his or her permanent home, then there is a greater likelihood of the caravan being permanently in place rather than of its being used as a temporary expedient.

The 'composite house'

There is a possibility that a tenant may occupy parts of more than one building as a 'composite house'. In *Hampstead Way Investments v Lewis-Weare*, the House of Lords adverted to *Kavanagh v Lyroudias* [1985] 1 All ER 560. In that case, the Court of Appeal had held the tenant Lyroudias to be outside the protection of the Rent Act, since he did not occupy the disputed premises, 23 Rutland Street 'as his residence'. The evidence was that he slept in 23 Rutland Street because there was a separate bedroom there, but lived most of his life next door, in 21 Rutland Street, as there was no hot water supply at number 23. In number 21 he spent much of his time caring for an elderly and sick friend who lived there. In cases such as this, the tenant has to show that he occupies the premises 'as his residence' to enjoy protection. Lord Brandon, being invited by counsel to overrule *Kavanagh v Lyroudias*, observed:

> Although the Court of Appeal considered that the proper question to be asked and answered was whether no 23 was occupied separately from no 21 as a complete home in itself, it seems to me that ... there was a further question which needed to be asked and answered. That further question was whether the defendant tenant occupied nos 21 and 23 as a combined or composite home of the kind contemplated in *Wimbush v Cibulia* [1949] 2 All ER 432, [1949] 2 QB 564, bearing in mind that the leases of both houses had originally been granted to the tenant by a person who was the owner of both ... the Court of Appeal in *Kavanagh v Lyroudias* reached their decision by asking and answering only one of the two relevant questions. It does not, however, follow that the decision itself was wrong, for the further question which I consider should have been asked and answered would obviously have been an extremely difficult one ... Numbers 21 and 23 ... were next door to each other, and were treated by the tenant, for all practical purposes, as one unit of living accommodation, in one half of which he carried out some of his living activities, and in the other half of which he carried out the rest of his activities ...

See further Pettit [1985] All ER Re pp 217–19.

'LET'

For protection to apply, the property must be 'let'; a mere licence does not suffice. This distinction has been the stimulus for the lengthy and complex litigation which is discussed elsewhere in this book. In the public sector, in contrast, certain types of licence do qualify for protection. This point is also discussed elsewhere.

'LET AS A DWELLING'

This expression has led to abundant litigation over the years. The cases can conveniently be divided into two groups: those concerned with the 'purpose' of the letting, and those concerned with the 'singular nature' of the dwelling which has been let.

The 'purpose' test

The Rent Act (and the Housing Act) confers residential security, and Parliament's purpose in enacting the legislation was to confer security on those occupying property for residential purposes. The courts have been properly concerned to ensure that the protective code is confined to those situations where Parliament intended it to apply: the *bona fide* residential letting. In most cases, it will be obvious whether protection applies or not, but there may be a complex situation where the existence of residential sector protection will be in doubt. The problem may arise at the time of the initial letting – where the premises may be let for a single use or multiple uses – or may come about because of a subsequent change of use.

Those occupying property for other reasons, such as commercial tenants, may be entitled to a form of security of tenure – in the case of commercial tenants under Part II of the Landlord and Tenant Act 1954 (as amended).

The initial letting: single use premises

The leading case is *Wolfe v Hogan* [1949] 2 KB 194. Premises originally let as a lock-up shop for the purposes of the tenant's business as an antique dealer, came to be occupied by the tenant for residential purposes, apparently because the tenant understandably was anxious about the dangers of going home during the air-raids to which London was exposed during the blitz. The Court of Appeal rejected the tenant's claim to be protected under the Rent Act.

Wolfe v Hogan

Denning LJ: In determining whether a house or part of a house is 'let as a dwelling' within the meaning of the Rent Restrictions Acts, it is necessary to look at the purpose of the letting. If the lease contains an express provision as to the purpose of the letting, it is not necessary to look further. But, if there is no express provision, it is open to the court to look at the circumstances of the letting. If the house is constructed for use as a dwellinghouse, it is reasonable to infer the purpose was to let it as a dwelling. But if, on the other hand, it is constructed as a lock-up shop, the reasonable inference is that it was let for business purposes. If the position were neutral, then it would be proper to look at the actual user. It is not a question of implied terms. It is a question of the purpose for which the premises were let.

These premises were let in 1939 by the head lessee to Miss Hogan. On the facts there was ample material on which the judge could find that the purpose of the letting was for use as a shop. At the beginning of the tenancy, therefore, the premises were not within the Act. But the point that has arisen in the course of the argument is this: What is the effect of the tenant changing the use she made of the premises? She changed its use from one for business purposes to one partly for business and partly for dwelling purposes. During the air-raids in 1940 she started to sleep on the premises and continued to sleep there. She has thereafter continued to use a part for dwelling purposes. Indeed, when the notice to quit was given in 1947, she was for all practical purposes permanently residing in the back part of the room. Moreover, there is ground for supposing that the landlord accepted rent, knowing of the change of user because, in 1942, after the original letting to the head lessee under the lease had come to an end, the head landlord became the immediate landlord of Miss Hogan and, knowing the position of affairs in the house, accepted rent from her.

What is the effect of that? In my opinion, it does not give the tenant the protection of the Act. A house or part of a house originally let for business purposes does not become let for dwelling purposes, unless it can be inferred from the acceptance of rent that the landlord has affirmatively consented to the change of user. Let me illustrate that from the common law doctrine as to waiver of forfeiture. A breach of covenant not to use the premises in a particular way is a continuing breach. Any acceptance of rent by the landlord, after knowledge, only waives breaches up to the time of the acceptance of rent. It does not waive the continuance of the breach thereafter and, notwithstanding his previous acceptance of rent, the landlord can still proceed for forfeiture on that account. Indeed in the case of a continuing breach, the acceptance of rent, after knowledge, is only a bar to a claim for forfeiture if it goes on for so long, or is accepted in such circumstances, that it can be inferred that the landlord has not merely waived the breach, but has affirmatively consented to the tenant continuing to use the premises as he has done.

(See notes to Dumpor's case in the Smith's Leading Cases (13th edn) vol 1, at pp 48 and 49.)

A breach of covenant not to sublet, however, is not a continuing breach, at all events so long as the under-lease cannot be determined. It is a single breach which can be waived by acceptance of rent with knowledge. Accordingly, it has been held that, if a contractual tenant sublets without consent in breach of covenant, it may become a lawful subletting by acceptance of rent with knowledge (see *Norman v Simpson* [1946] KB 158 and *Watson v Saunders-Roe Ltd* [1947] KB 437). But I would point out that in the later case of *Oak Property Company Ltd v Chapman* [1947] KB 886, where a statutory tenant sublet without consent, this court held that the mere acceptance of rent after knowledge was not by itself sufficient, and said that there must be conduct by the landlord which is equivalent to a consent by him to the continuance of the state of affairs created by the tenant in order that the subletting should become a lawful subletting.

By parity of reasoning in this case, the mere acceptance of rent by the landlord, although it went on for some time – indeed, for four or five years – was not itself any assent to the change of user. Even if he had made no protest, it would not itself be an assent, but, in fact, from the very earliest times in 1942 there were letters of protest which clearly negated any assent. The acceptance of rent has no effect in a case of this kind so as to alter the premise into controlled premises, unless it can properly be inferred, as a matter of fact, that the landlord has affirmatively assented to the change of user and to it becoming let in whole or in part as a dwelling-house. That cannot be inferred here.

The Court also rejected a claim by the tenant that it could be inferred that the landlord had consented to the change of user.

From this decision it will be seen that a number of factors fall to be considered:

(1) The terms of the lease itself – which may contain a statement about the purpose of the letting, or, as in *Ponder v Hillman* [1969] 3 All ER 694, covenants which would be appropriate only if a commercial letting was in contemplation. Clearly, after *Street v Mountford*, the courts will be vigilant to ensure that false statements about the purpose of lettings in the tenancy itself (eg this letting is for business purposes only) will not be allowed to be used as a subterfuge to escape the operations of the Act. A covenant against residential use by the tenant will also be strong evidence as to the purpose of the original demise. Equally, a covenant to use the premises 'as a private residence' will not be taken to confer protection if the circumstances are such that the covenanted use as a single dwelling is, in practical terms, impossible (see *Grosvenor (Mayfair) Estates v Amberton* (1983) 265 EG 293).

(2) The nature of the premises themselves – are they a dwellinghouse or a lock-up shop?

(3) The conduct of the parties – it may be possible, though unlikely, that this conduct shows that the nature of the tenancy was from the beginning contemplated as being residential in character, or that the landlord, in full knowledge of the facts, has consented to the creation of a new tenancy of a residential nature.

The initial letting: multiple use

If the premises were let for multiple purposes – for example, business and residential use – the normal principle will be that the letting will not qualify for protection under the Rent Act (see the second situation in *Cheryl Investments v Saldanha* [1978] 1 WLR 1329, as the premises were not let 'as a dwelling'). This conclusion may be avoided if the business use is so insignificant as to be merely incidental to the residential use, for instance the doctor in *Royal Life Saving Society v Page* [1979] 1 All ER 5 who saw the occasional patient at his flat, rather than in his surgery.

The premises, in the case of a multiple purpose letting, will not fall back into the ambit of the protective legislation if the non-domestic use ceases because the premises will still not have been 'let as a dwelling' (see *Pulleng v Curran* (1982) 44 P&CR 58: shop with residential accommodation; *Henry Smith's Charity Trustees v Wagle* [1989] 2 WLR 669: artist's studio with residential accommodation; and *Russell v Booker* (1982) 5 HLR 10). Lord Denning neatly summarised this situation in one of the instances – situation four – which he gave in *Cheryl Investments v Saldanha* [1978] 1 WLR 1329.

Change of use

If premises are let for non-residential purposes (such as business purposes) a change to residential use will not bring protection – see *Wolfe v Hogan*, above. Similarly, an abandonment of the non-domestic use in the case of premises originally let for dual purposes will not bring protection.

What if the premises were originally let for residential purposes, but then the tenant develops a substantial business use? In this case, *Cheryl Investments v Saldanha* suggests that protection, though originally available to the tenant, will cease to apply, as the premises now enjoy business code protection, which, under s 24 Rent Act precludes Rent Act application. There is a possibility, however, that if the tenant ceases the business use and resumes the domestic use for which the property was originally let, protection will re-apply, as the property was originally 'let as a dwelling', and the business code protection disappears with the cessation of business use (see Martin [1983] Conv 391).

Cheryl Investments Ltd v Saldanha

Lord Denning MR: Here we have a topsy-turvy situation. Two landlords contend that their tenants are 'business tenants' and entitled to have their tenancies continued under the statute in that behalf, whereas the tenants contend that they are not so entitled at all. The reason for this oddity is because, if the tenants are not 'business tenants', their tenancies are 'regulated tenancies' and they are protected by the Rent Acts. The protection under the Rent Acts is much better for the tenants than the protection under the business statute. So the landlords seek to chase them out of the Rent Acts and put them into the 'Business Acts' ...

If a house is let as a separate dwelling (without being occupied in whole or in part for business purposes) it is a 'regulated tenancy'. But, if it is occupied by the tenant 'for the purposes of a business carried on by him' or for those and other purpose it is a 'business tenancy': see s 23(1) of the Business Tenancy Act. It cannot be both.

It is of the first importance now to be able to place a tenancy into the correct category, because the two categories are very different animals.

Regulated tenancy

When a tenancy is a 'regulated tenancy' the tenant is protected by the Rent Acts. So long as the contractual tenancy continues, the tenant is a 'protected tenant'. He is protected in respect of the rent he can be charged. As soon as the contractual tenancy is determined by effluxion of time or expiry of notice to quit, he becomes a 'statutory tenant'. This is a privilege which is personal to him, and, after he dies, to his widow or a member of the family residing with him. He cannot assign it to anyone else. His residence there must be continuous. If he ceases to reside thus, he loses his right as statutory tenant; and he cannot revive it by going in again. It is so personal that, if the tenant is a limited company, it has no right to continue the tenancy after the contractual tenancy has come to an end.

Business tenancy

This is altogether different. During the contractual tenancy, the tenant is there under the terms of the contract. But, once the contractual tenancy comes to an end (by effluxion of time or notice to quit) there is automatically a continuation of the tenancy for an indefinite time in the future unless and until it is terminated in accordance with the statute. There has to be at least six months' notice, and not more than 12 months' notice. Until it is so terminated, the relations of the parties are governed by the terms of the contract of tenancy. This 'continuation tenancy' is nothing like a 'statutory tenancy'. It is not a personal privilege of the tenant. It is a piece of property which he can assign or dispose of to a third person, provided that it was not prohibited by the terms of the contract. And he can give it up on proffering notice to the landlord.

The application of the statute

There was much discussion before us as to the meaning of the Business Tenancy Act (I use those words because I think the Landlord and Tenant Act 1954, Part II is a little confusing), especially the word 'purposes' in s 23(1); and the time or times at which those 'purposes' had to exist; and the effect of a change by the tenant in the use to which he put the property. Could he take himself in or out of the Act at his option? I found all these matters so confusing that I do not propose to attempt a solution today. I am only going to take four simple illustrations to show how the statute works, for they will suffice for our present cases.

First, take the case where a professional man is the tenant of two premises: one his office where he works; the other his flat, conveniently near, where he has his home. He has then a 'business tenancy' of his office; and a 'regulated tenancy' of his home. This remains the situation even though he takes papers home and works on them at evenings or weekends and occasionally sees a client at home. He cannot in such a case be said to be occupying his flat 'for the purposes of' his profession. He is occupying it for the purpose of his home, even though he incidentally does some work there: see *Sweet v Parsley* [1970] AC 132, by Lord Morris of Borth-y-Gest.

Second, take the case where a professional man takes a tenancy of one house for the very purpose of carrying on his profession in one room and of residing in the rest of the house with his family, like the doctor who has a consulting room in his house. He has not then a 'regulated tenancy' at all. His tenancy is a 'business tenancy' and nothing else. He is clearly occupying part of the house 'for the purposes of' his profession, as one purpose; and the other part for the purpose of his dwelling as another purpose. Each purpose is significant. Neither is merely incidental to the other.

Third, suppose now that the first man decides to give up his office and to do all his work from his home, there being nothing in the tenancy of his home to prevent him doing it. In that case he becomes in the same position as the second man. He ceases to have a 'regulated tenancy' of his home. He has only a 'business tenancy' of it.

Fourth, suppose now that the second man decides to give up his office at home and to take a tenancy of an office elsewhere so as to carry on his profession elsewhere. He then has a 'business tenancy' of his new premises. But he does not get a 'regulated tenancy' of his original home, even though he occupies it now only as his home, because it was never let to him as a separate dwelling, unless the landlord agrees to the change.

Those illustrations point to the solution of the present two cases.

Royal Life Saving Society v Page

... In 1963 the tenant, Mr Gut, made arrangements to assign the lease to Dr Ernest Donald Page. He was a medical practitioner who had his consulting rooms at 52 Harley Street ... He took this maisonette in Devonshire Street so that he could live there as his home. But he thought that in the future he might possibly want to use it occasionally so as to see patients.

So, when he took the assignment, he asked for consent to do so. Such consent was readily given by the society (his immediate landlords) and by the Howard de Walden Estate (the head landlords). It was a consent to carry on his profession in the maisonette. After the assignment he moved in and occupied it as his home. He put both addresses (Harley Street and Devonshire Street) in the Medical Directory. He had separate notepaper for each address and put both telephone numbers on each. This was, of course, so that anyone who wished to telephone him could get him at one or other place. But he did very little professional work at the maisonette. Over the whole period of the tenancy, he had only seen about one patient a year there. The last patient was in distress 18 months ago. He summarised the position in one sentence: 'Harley Street is my professional address, and the other is my home'.

On those facts it is quite clear that 14 Devonshire Street was let as a separate dwelling and occupied by Dr Page as a separate dwelling. There was only one significant purpose to which he occupied it. It was for his home. He carried on his profession elsewhere in Harley Street. His purpose is evidenced by his actual use of it. Such user as he made in Devonshire Street for his profession was not a significant user. It was only incidental to his use of it as his home. He comes within my first illustration. He is, therefore, protected by the Rent Acts as a 'regulated tenancy'.

The society later on alleged that he was a business tenant and gave him notice to terminate under the Business Tenancy Act. He was quite right to ignore it. He is entitled to stay on as a statutory tenant under the Rent Acts. I agree with the judge, and would dismiss the appeal.

Cheryl Investments Ltd v Saldanha

... Mr Saldanha is an accountant by profession. He is a partner in a firm called Best Marine Enterprises. They carry on the business of importing sea foods from India and processing them in Scotland. The firm has no trade premises. The two partners carry on the business from their own homes. The other partner works at his home at Basildon. Mr Saldanha works at the flat in Beaufort Gardens, and goes from there out to visit clients. When he went into the flat, he had a telephone specially installed for his own use, with the number 589 0232. He put a table in the hall.

He had a typewriter there, files and lots of paper. 'The usual office equipment', said the manageress. He had frequent visitors carrying brief cases. He had notepaper printed: 'Best Marine Enterprises. Importers of Quality Sea-foods. Telephone 589 0232 [that is the number I have just mentioned]. PO BOX 211, Knightsbridge, London SW3.'

He issued business statements on that very notepaper. A copy of one was found by the maid in a wastepaper basket showing that the firm had imported goods at a total cost of £49,903.30 and sold them for £58,152.35. The maid (whose evidence the judge explicitly accepted in preference to his) said: 'I presumed Mr Saldanha conducted business there'. On that evidence I should have thought it plain that Mr Saldanha was occupying this flat, not only as his dwelling, but also for the purpose of a business carried on by him in partnership with another. When he took the flat it was, no doubt, let to him as a separate dwelling; it was obviously a residential flat with just one large room with twin beds in it. No one can doubt that it was constructed for use as a dwelling and let to him as such within *Wolfe v Hogan*. But as soon as he equipped it for the purposes of his business of importing sea foods, with telephone, table and printed notepaper, and afterwards used it by receiving business calls there, seeing customers there and issuing business statements from there, it is plain that he was occupying it 'for the purposes of a business carried on by him'. This was a significant purpose for which he was occupying the flat, as well as a dwelling. It was his only home, and he was carrying on his business from it. It comes within my second illustration ...

The judge took a different view. He said:

> 'I think he [Mr Saldanha] is carrying on some business on the premises, but of a nominal kind, and not worth even considering. It is, in my view, *de minimis*. It amounts to having a few files at home and making a few telephone calls from home.'

I take a different view from the judge. I think that at the expiry of the notice to quit Mr Saldanha was occupying this flat for the purposes of a business carried on by him. So the landlords are entitled to a declaration to that effect.

I would allow the appeal ...

The 'singularity' rule

The Act refers to 'a' dwelling. If that which is let contains more than one dwelling, *prima facie* protection is excluded. The leading case is *Horford Investments v Lambert* [1974] 1 All ER 131, where the Court of Appeal clearly had their suspicions of an entrepreneur who seemed to be trying to manipulate the provisions of the Rent Act to his economic advantage. The crucial point in *Horford* is that the property, as let, could not reasonably be described as 'a' dwelling, as it consisted of a number of separate units of habitation.

Horford Investments Ltd v Lambert

Russell LJ: The first question is whether the tenancy is one under which the house 'is let as a separate dwelling' and hereunder it was common ground that the word 'separate' was not relevant since it was directed only to exclude cases in which the letting of a dwelling involved a sharing with another of an essential feature of a dwelling such as a kitchen: was the house therefore let as 'a ... dwelling' having regard to the fact that it was constructed so as to consist of a number of units of habitation and to the manifest intention that it should be used as several sublet dwellings? The second question is whether in such cases in general, and in these cases in particular, in truth the letting was for business purposes and for that reason outside the protection of the Rent Acts as a protected tenancy.

It was agreed that the tenant had never resided in either house and that in each case the premises comprised a 19th century purpose-built dwelling-house which at a date not later than the beginning of the tenancy (as to no 35) was used as to the ground and upper floors for the purpose of letting off in rooms and as to the basement for the purpose of a separate and self-contained flat, and (as to no 37) had been converted into five self-contained flats: and that user in this manner had continued ever since ...

As to the first question, the point appears to me to be this: whether the phrase 'A tenancy under which a dwelling-house (which may be a house or part of a house) is let as a separate dwelling' embraces a case in which the tenancy includes when created a residential building containing more than one of what might be conveniently described as units of habitation. The question appears ultimately to be whether by force of the Interpretation Act 1889 'is let as a ... dwelling' is to be construed as 'is let as a ... dwelling or dwellings'. On this point it seems to me immaterial that the houses in question are physically adapted for a great number of units of habitation; the question really is the same as would arise for solution when on the granting of the tenancy of a house it consisted of two separate and self-contained flats. It is as well at this point to bear in mind that we are not concerned here with protection against eviction after a contractual tenancy has been determined, where the question of occupation and protection of that occupation arises.

In *Langford Property Co Ltd v Goldrich* [1949] 1 KB 511, two flats in the same building (which had in fact been previously separately let) were let to a tenant for use by him and his family as one home. The flats were not directly connected and each was a self-contained flat. The whole argument proceeded on the assumption that under the comparable statutory phrase ('a house let as a separate dwelling or a part of a house being a part so let ... ') *prima facie* would not include a case when the letting comprised more than one unit of habitation. This was, as I understand it, accepted by the court, which decided that on the particular facts of the case it was a letting of one dwelling-house only, that is to say, for use as one unit of habitation. Somervell LJ accepted the applicability of the Interpretation Act 1889 to 'a house' but I think implicitly rejected its applicability to 'let as a ... dwelling'. This approach was followed in *Whitty v Scott-Russell* [1950] 2 KB 32 in this court. There there was a tenancy of a residence and cottage joined to it but without internal communication. This court was able to find that there was a letting of a single dwelling-house primarily because of a covenant by the tenant to use the whole premises as 'a private dwelling-house only'. In both those cases it would have been a simple road to the same conclusion if 'let as a ... dwelling' could be construed as 'let as a ... dwelling or dwellings'. In the judgment of the court in the latter case this was said:

'If the Interpretation Act 1889, alone were concerned, this reasoning would be open to the comment that, if the inclusion of the plural in the singular permitted us to read 'house' as including houses, it would equally permit (or perhaps require) one to read 'let as a separate dwelling' as including 'let as two separate dwellings'. An impartial application of the Interpretation Act might lead to odd results.'

In *R&P Properties Ltd v Baldwin* [1939] 1 KB 461 Goddard LJ said: 'If they are let as two dwellings, it follows that they are not let as a separate dwelling.' But I do not think that he had this point in mind: he was referring to two separate lettings of two separate flats.

In *Lower v Porter* [1956] 1 QB 325 the question was whether a premium on assignment of a tenancy was illegal. The letting was of a house not then divided but intended to be and soon after converted by the tenant into two self-contained flats. It was argued that the date of the assignment was the material date, and that it was then outside the protection as being a tenancy not of a single dwelling-house but of two: it was held that the date of the tenancy was the material date, when it was a single dwelling-house, and so the premium was illegal. Again what I have referred to as the simple road was not followed, though there is some indication that Morris LJ thought that at the date of the assignment it was still a dwelling-house.

In *Theis v Muir* (1951) Judge Dale held that leasehold premises comprising two self-contained flats and a shop were not at the date of the assignment of the lease (for which a premium was paid) 'let as a separate dwelling', presumably on the same basis that the phrase does not include a letting of a plurality of units of habitation.

There are authorities which demonstrate that for present purposes it is immaterial that the tenant does not propose to occupy any part of the premises the subject of the letting; but they are cases in which at the time of the letting there was physically only one unit of habitation. In *Carter v SU Carburettor Co* [1942] 2 KB 288 a company took a tenancy of a house and subsequently as it always intended converted it into three self-contained flats and sublet to three employees. See also *Anspatch v Charlton Steam Shipping Co Ltd* [1955] 2 QB 21 which concerned a single unit of habitation: as also did *Ebner v Lascelles* [1928] 2 KB 486.

It appears to me somewhat anomalous that there should be this radical distinction between a case where at the time of the letting there are comprised more than one unit of habitation (save in exceptional cases such as *Langford Property Co Ltd v Goldrich* [1949] and *Whitty's case*) and a case where there is at the outset only one, though immediately to be converted into two or more. Similarly it seems somewhat anomalous to find that a letting of premises comprising a shop and one unit of habitation is within protection (see eg *British Land Co Ltd v Herbert Silver (Menswear) Ltd* [1958] 1 QB 530), while a letting of premises comprising two units of habitation is not. But it appears to me that the weight of authority makes it necessary to accept these anomalies. I should in this connection refer to *Murgatroyd v Tresarden* [1947] KB 316. It appears that in that case the letting was of a house already divided into two self-contained flats. The question was whether on the expiry of the contractual tenancy the landlord could claim possession of the flat not occupied by the tenant. It does not appear to have been argued that in the circumstances stated the whole letting, not being a letting of a single dwelling-house, was outside protection. The only contention advanced in favour of ouster of the tenant also from the flat occupied by him was that alternative accommodation was offered. That argument failed and possession was ordered only of the flat not occupied by the tenant.

Accordingly, in my judgment the tenancy of each of the two houses in this case is not within the definition of a protected tenancy because of the plurality of dwellings, or, as I have labelled them, units of habitation, comprised in the premises when let and obliged by the terms of the letting to be so maintained.

It is, as Russell LJ pointed out, anomalous that where the premises as let constitute only a single unit of habitation, the tenant will be protected even if he intends thereafter to subdivide the premises. However, this seems to be an inescapable result of the statutory language.

Horford Investments was a case where the tenant was endeavouring to maximise his profit from the transaction by seeking to invoke the 'fair rent' provisions so as to minimise the rent due to the head landlord; there is no suggestion that he was minded to 'pass on' any reduction he thus achieved for the benefit of his subtenants. But the rule catches the altruistic, as well as the profit-seeking tenant. Thus, in *St Catherine's College v Dorling* [1979] 3 All ER 250, a College which sought to solve the residential problem of its students in Oxford by taking a lease of a house in which it then allowed some students to reside, was held not to be entitled to apply for 'fair rent' protection against the landlord, even though the College's intention was to pass on the benefit of any reduction it received to its student subtenants. Here the crucial factor seemed to have been the intention of the College, as tenant, to let the house as a number of 'dwellings'.

There is a further twist to the 'singularity' rule. If the premises let are so small as to be intrinsically incapable of accommodating all the activities contained in the ordinary notion of 'dwelling' (at least, presumably, eating and sleeping) it will not pass the test of having been let 'as a dwelling'. Thus, in *Metropolitan Properties (FCG) Ltd v Barder* [1968] 1 All ER 536 a 'tiny room', originally a servant's room, across the corridor from the tenant's main flat, was let under a separate contract for the accommodation of the tenant's au pair. The room was furnished as sleeping accommodation, but the Court of Appeal held that it was incapable of being let as a separate dwelling on its own. Sleeping, while essential to the notion of the separateness of the dwelling, is probably not enough on its own – see for example, *Curl v Angelo* [1948] 2 All ER 189, where a hotelier rented extra rooms as supplementary sleeping accommodation for guests or employees. The rooms so rented were held not to amount to a 'separate dwelling'.

There may be elements of 'sharing': many lets of bed-sitting rooms will involve the sharing of kitchen or bathroom accommodation. The general principle is that such 'sharing' with other tenants does not stop the tenancy being protected by the Acts, so long as that which is let to the individual tenant can fairly be described as a 'separate dwelling' and the tenant has exclusive possession of this separate dwelling. It does not matter if some of the ordinary activities of everyday life, such as cooking or bathing, are done in 'shared accommodation'.

Sharing with the landlord, however, may mean that the tenant only enjoys 'restricted contract' protection if he is a Rent Act tenant. If he is a Housing Act tenant there will be no statutory protection at all. The cases show, however, that nothing short of a genuine contemplation of the possibility of actual sharing of some of the accommodation will suffice (see *Gray v Brown* (1992) 25 HLR 144); in the case of a Housing Act tenant, the landlord must also occupy the premises 'as his only or principal home'. If the sharing is with the landlord, the likelihood is that the landlord will be able to qualify as a 'resident landlord' – which, in the case of the Rent Act leads to diminished protection, and, in the case of the Housing Act 1988 leads to the exclusion of statutory protection altogether.

Where part of the accommodation is 'shared', the tenant's use of the shared accommodation is regulated and safeguarded by statutory provisions in s 22 Rent Act 1977 and s 3 Housing Act 1988.

Rent Act 1977

22. Tenant sharing accommodation with persons other than landlord

(1) Where a tenant has the exclusive occupation of any accommodation ('the separate accommodation') and–

    (a) the terms as between the tenant and his landlord on which he holds the separate accommodation include the use of other accommodation ('the shared accommodation') in common with another person or other persons, not being or including the landlord, and

    (b) by reason only of the circumstances mentioned in paragraph (a) above, the separate accommodation would not, apart from this section, be a dwelling-house let on or subject to a protected or statutory tenancy,

the separate accommodation shall be deemed to be a dwelling-house let on a protected tenancy or, as the case may be, subject to a statutory tenancy and the following provisions of this section shall have effect.

(2) ... (3) ... (4) ...

(5) Without prejudice to the enforcement of any order made under subsection (6) below, while the tenant is in possession of the separate accommodation, no

order shall be made for possession of any of the shared accommodation, whether on the application of the immediate landlord of the tenant or on the application of any person under whom that landlord derives title, unless a like order has been made, or is made at the same time, in respect of the separate accommodation; and the provisions of section 98(1) of this Act shall apply accordingly.

(6) ... (7) ... (8) ...

Housing Act 1988

3. Tenant sharing accommodation with persons other than landlord

(1) Where a tenant has the exclusive occupation of any accommodation (in this section referred to as 'the separate accommodation') and–

(a) the terms as between the tenant and his landlord on which he holds the separate accommodation include the use of other accommodation (in this section referred to as 'the shared accommodation') in common with another person or other persons, not being or including the landlord, and

(b) by reason only of the circumstances mentioned in paragraph (a) above, the separate accommodation would not, apart from this section, be a dwelling-house let on an assured tenancy,

the separate accommodation shall be deemed to be a dwelling-house let on an assured tenancy and the following provisions of this section shall have effect.

(2) ...

(3) While the tenant is in possession of the separate accommodation, any term of the tenancy terminating or modifying, or providing for the termination or modification of, his right to the use of any of the shared accommodation which is living accommodation shall be of no effect.

(4) ... (5) ...

Date of operation of the 1988 Act

The 1988 Housing Act introduced a new scheme for residential tenancies; 'assured tenancies' now replace the old 'protected tenancies' under the Rent Act 1977.

In broad, general terms, the assured tenancy regime is less favourable to tenants than the old 'protected tenancy' scheme. In particular:

(1) The 'assured tenant', save in exceptional cases, does not enjoy the protection of the 'fair rent' mechanism which applied to protected tenancies.

(2) The security of tenure which an assured tenant enjoys is less generous than that created under the 'protected tenancy' regime.

(3) The rights of succession to 'assured tenancies' are limited more drastically than those under the Rent Act 'protected tenancy' regime.

(4) The residential requirements for 'assured tenancies' are stricter than those for 'protected tenancies'.

For all these reasons, it is frequently a matter of prime importance to decide whether a particular letting falls within the 'assured tenancy' rules of the Housing Act 1988 or the 'protected tenancy' rules of the Rent Act 1977. Old tenancies, which before the implementation of the Housing Act (ie, created before 15 January 1989) were 'protected tenancies', remain as such, though there have been some modifications of the rules, especially respecting succession. New tenancies, coming into existence after the implementation of the Housing Act (ie, on or after 15 January 1989) fall within the 'assured tenancy' regime.

Thus, for the application of these rules, the primary and most important question is the date of the creation of the original tenancy. If it was created before 15 January 1989, it will be a protected tenancy and cannot be an assured tenancy; if created on or after that date, it will be an assured tenancy and cannot be a protected tenancy. There are, however, a number of exceptions to this primary rule.

Pre-1989 'assured tenancies'

The number of exceptions here is very limited, and in practice is confined to two cases:

(a) 'Old style' assured tenancies under the Housing Act 1980.

This initiative created a form of tenancy of new, or newly converted, dwellings let by 'approved landlords' (usually housing associations, pension funds, and the like). These were converted into 'new-style' assured tenancies by s 1(3) of the Housing Act 1988.

(b) Succession to Rent Act protected tenancies.

Complex rules had developed governing the succession to 'protected tenancies'. The Housing Act contains provisions whereby a succession, after 15 January 1989, of an existing protected tenancy to a successor other than a spouse will 'trigger' the automatic conversion of that tenancy into an 'assured tenancy', which may, in turn, render the successor liable to a dramatic increase in rent (see, for example, *N & D (London) Ltd v Gadson* (1991) 24 HLR 64).

Post 1989 'protected tenancies'

These exceptions are likely to be more important than those above. The main exceptions here are the following:

(a) Tenancies created on or after 15 January 1989 in pursuance of a contract made before that date.

(b) New tenancies granted to a tenant who was, immediately before the grant of that tenancy, a protected or statutory tenant of the same landlord. The purpose of this rule is to prevent a landlord from 'converting' all his existing protected tenants into 'assured tenants' by the wheeze of granting them all a new tenancy, or even, more ingeniously, shuffling them around the building.

(c) Grants of new tenancies under the 'suitable alternative accommodation' ground for possession for protected tenancies. In this case the court may (as a matter of discretion) order that the tenancy of the alternative accommodation shall be in the form of a protected tenancy, if it is of the view that an 'assured tenancy' would not give the tenant adequate security of tenure.

The tenancy must not be 'excluded'

Here, there are complex provisions in both Acts excluding certain tenancies from protection. In the case of the Rent Act, these exclusions are spelled out in ss 3–16A; in the Housing Act 1988 they are set out in the First Schedule.

The main exclusions will be discussed briefly.

Houses of high rateable value

This test was originally designed to exclude the homes of the affluent, though it did not entirely achieve that objective because of the quirks of the rating system. When domestic rates gave way to the community charge, this test ceased to be apposite for the future, and so a 'rent level' test of £25,000 per annum was introduced.

Tenancies at low rents

The main objective here was to exclude 'ground rent' lettings; it may also exclude certain other types of lettings where the financial arrangements between the parties are unusual. An example of a case falling with this provision is *Bostock v Bryant* (1990) 22 HLR 449.

Bostock v Bryant

Stuart-Smith LJ: ... The plaintiff is the executor of the Will of Owen Henry Jones, who died on October 27, 1987, and who was known to the parties as Uncle Joe. He was the registered owner of the house at 48 Berrymede Road, and in about September 1964 the deceased had agreed with a Mr Bryant, who was the husband of the first defendant and father of the second defendant, that the Bryant family, which then consisted of husband and wife and three children, should occupy all of the house except for one room which was occupied by Uncle Joe himself.

The arrangement appears to have been that Uncle Joe paid the general and water rates and the Bryants paid the gas and electricity bills, in each case in respect of the whole house ...

Mr Bryant died in 1973 and, as I have said, Uncle Joe died in October 1987. A notice terminating the defendant's right to remain in the premises, whether that was a licence or a tenancy, was served on April 21, 1989, expressed to expire a month later.

The judge decided to make no order for possession because he held that there was a periodic tenancy in favour of the defendants and that there had been payment of rent in as much as there was payment of the gas and electricity bills and, although he does not specifically deal with the point, the inference is, and it clearly must be the case on that finding, that it was a protected tenancy until the date of Uncle Joe's death, and thereafter it became a statutory tenancy, and that grounds did not exist under the Rent Acts to enable the court to make an order for possession.

The appellant has challenged the learned judge's findings that there was a periodic tenancy at a rent. Mr Hodgson, on behalf of the appellant, accepts that *prima facie*, where a residential accommodation has been granted for a term at a rent with exclusive possession, the grantor providing neither attendance nor services, the legal consequence is the creation of a tenancy. That derives from the House of Lords decision in *Street v Mountford* [1985] 1 AC at p 809 ...

Mr Hodgson accepts that the defendants here had exclusive possession of that part of the house which was not occupied by the deceased, but he submits that there was neither a periodic term nor a rent payable. I do not find it necessary to look at the learning on rent at common law to which we have been referred. The learned judge dealt with the matter in a short judgment in this way:

'I find that there was a periodic tenancy and that the only rent payable under that tenancy was the payment for gas and electricity, which included gas and electricity for Uncle Joe and so was of benefit to him, although of small benefit. I find that those payments were capable of amounting to rent.'

Now, if parties to an agreement describe a payment from the occupier to the owner as rent, the court will normally accept that it is properly so described, though it is not bound to accept the label put upon a payment by the parties. Thus, if there is a payment of money described in some other way, such as a licence fee, the court may nevertheless draw the inference that it is in fact rent if it is paid as consideration for use and occupation of the premises, and that occupation is exclusive. But there may be other explanations of the payment, an explanation which is a more likely one, in which case the court will not draw the inference that it is paid as rent.

In this case the Bryants occupied by far the greater part of the house. They consumed a far greater part of the gas and electricity. The explanation of those bills, in the absence of express agreement that they were to represent rent, is, as it seems to me, that they were paying for what they consumed. The bills, it is true, were in Uncle Joe's name because he was the householder but, since they were by far the larger of the two consumers, the inference I would draw from the fact that they paid those bills is that they were making good their obligation to reimburse him for the amount expended on themselves.

Where people share a house in this way they often share outgoings and expenses, and they do not necessarily do so pound for pound. In this case the deceased, Uncle Joe, paid the general rates and water rates to which the Bryants made no contribution, and it seems to me that the more natural inference to be drawn from the payments by the Bryants of the gas and electricity was that it was simply a payment of their part of the expenses incurred and a sharing of the expenses of the house in the way that I have described.

Moreover, Mr Hodgson has relied upon the case of *Barnes v Barratt* [1970] 2 QB at p 657 and he submits that the effect of that case is that, so far as the Rent Acts are concerned, and we are dealing here with a Rent Act case, rent has to be a payment in money terms and not in the satisfaction of bills, which may vary from time to time. In that case the defendants, who claimed to be tenants, performed services for the landlord in the form of cleaning his room, cooking and so on, and also paid the electricity, gas and fuel bills for the whole house ...

Now, it is apparent that, if the rent is to be determined by the amount of fuel bills, the fuel bills are liable to fluctuate. They are likely to be more in the winter than in the summer. Indeed, it appears to be the position in this case that, the appropriate day being March 23, 1965, if the rent is to be taken as the entire amount of the gas and electricity bills, that is to say for the whole house, then that is more than two-thirds of the rateable value. But, if it is to be apportioned, namely that proportion of the bills which were attributable to the deceased's consumption, the matter could go either way, probably depending on whether it was summer or winter. It would, in my judgment, be a most unsatisfactory arrangement whereby a tenancy could be a protected tenancy one moment and an unprotected tenancy the next, depending on whether it was summer or winter and depending on when the notice terminating it was served.

It is not clear in this case entirely whether the learned judge took the view that the entire payments were the rent or whether it was only that part which was of benefit to the deceased. I think that the learned judge took the latter view. Mr Edlin has submitted to us that, in fact, the proper view is that it was the payment of the whole amount of the fuel bills which amounted to the payment of rent and that it is immaterial that the deceased made no profit out of it.

He referred us to the case of *Mackworth v Hellard* [1921] 2 KB at p 755 where the rent payable was £30 a year, the rateable value of the premises was £40, but the landlord agreed and paid the rates and taxes which amounted to £31 18s a year. It was contended on behalf of the landlord that the rent was the net receivable amount, which in fact amounted to nothing after payment of those necessary outgoings. But the court held that that was not so and it was immaterial that the landlord made no profit on the transaction. The rent was that which was described by the parties as the rent, namely the £30 a year.

But, in my judgment, that case does not assist the defendants here. As I have already indicated, in my judgment, where the payment is not specifically designated as rent and does not appear to be the payment of a sum in respect of rent, then the court can only reach the conclusion that it is rent if that is the proper inference to draw from all the circumstances of the case and, in my judgment, that is not the proper inference to draw.

So, for those two reasons – that, in my judgment, the matter is covered by the decision in *Barnes v Barratt* and also because I do not think the proper inference to draw here is that this was a payment of rent at all-in my judgment, the learned judge came to the wrong conclusion on the question of rent.

Possible attempts to take advantage of loopholes – for instance by letting furnished premises at a nominal rent but including substantial payments for the hire of furniture – would probably be regarded by the court as a 'sham' within the doctrines explained elsewhere.

Shared ownership leases

These are tenancies created in certain circumstances under the 'right to buy' legislation. They were excluded from the Rent Act so as to stop the 'fair rent' provisions from coming into play. Since there are no applicable fair rent provisions under the Housing Act, they are not expressly excluded from the operation of that Act as such, but since in many cases the landlord will be a local authority, they will be excluded from the operation of the Housing Act by virtue of the nature of the landlord.

Dwellings let with other land

This covers matters such as the letting of smallholdings.

Tenancies with board and attendance

This was an important exception under the Rent Act, but the 'board and attendance' exception is not preserved for lettings under the Housing Act. The leading case was *Otter v Norman* [1988] 3 WLR 321, where a 'continental breakfast' provided by the landlord was held to amount to 'board', and thus took the letting out of the Rent Act. The case was clearly near the line; the House of Lords thought that the proviso, for example, of an early-morning cup of tea would not suffice (see (1988) 51 MLR 645 – Rodgers).

Lettings to students

This category covers lettings to students in institutional premises, such as halls of residence and the like. Clearly, the current student population would be ill-served if former students were able to claim security of tenure and thus refuse to move out of institutional accommodation at the end of their courses. Probably, most such accommodation falls within the category of licenses rather than 'lettings'. In any event, although lettings by private landlords direct to students are covered by the Acts, a landlord can in practice escape control by letting to an educational institution, which then sublets to students of the institution. Such an educational institution, not being an 'individual', could not in any event qualify for protection under the Housing Act 1988; also, under the Rent Act, an institution cannot 'reside' so as to qualify for protection as a statutory tenant. An example of such a scheme can be seen in *St Catherine's College v Dorling*.

If the accommodation is 'student letting' accommodation, the letting of the premises during vacations, for instance, to tenants who are not students will also fall outside the protective provisions of the Acts, as there is a mandatory ground for possession in such cases.

A letting to an institution might, in appropriate cases, fall within the business tenancy code (see for instance *Groveside Properties Ltd v Westminster Medical School* (1983) 47 P&CR 507, [1984] Conv 57 (Martin)).

Holiday lettings

Holiday lettings clearly fulfil a different social purpose from a letting as a home, and for that reason it is inappropriate that control should apply to them. Likewise, off-season lets of holiday accommodation attract a 'mandatory ground' for possession, as otherwise owners of holiday accommodation might find it impossible to get rid of their 'off-season' guests if they enjoyed security of tenure (for an example of the pitfalls of these provisions see *Killick v Roberts* (1991)). Many so-called holiday lettings are probably licenses in any event, but it is clearly right that, even where a tenancy is created, it should not give rise to statutory security of tenure. There is a danger, however, that the provisions in the Acts excluding protection for holiday lets might be abused, and landlords might seek to disguise as a 'holiday let' a tenancy which is essentially residential.

A case which comes near the margin is *Buchmann v May* [1978] 2 All ER 993.

Buchmann v May

Sir John Pennycuick: ... Mr Buchmann is the owner of 24 Avenue Road, which had been his own home until 1972. He or his company own a number of other properties in the district which that company lets. The defendant, Mrs Colleen May, is an Australian national. Her husband, Richard Ernest May, is a New Zealand national. He is by profession an entertainer; and Mrs May herself was until recently a professional dancer. They have a child, Shari, aged 7 or 8. They worked in England from time to time between 1972 and 1974 on a series of temporary residence permits but had not, at any rate at the date of the hearing, been successful in obtaining full residence permits.

In or about May 1972, Mr Buchmann let 24 Avenue Road to Mr May, the defendant's husband, on a six month furnished tenancy at £20 a week. There followed a succession of short furnished tenancies, at the same rent, up to and including a three month tenancy expiring on 31st July 1974. These were ordinary residential tenancies ...

In the middle of October 1974, Mrs May returned to England, to be followed shortly afterwards by Mr May. Before Mr May's return, Mrs May rang up Mr Garlant, an employee of Mr Buchmann, and enquired as to the possibility of a further short tenancy. Mrs May told Mr Garlant that she would be leaving England before Christmas, and in any event she had in fact only a six month residence permit, which would expire before then. On 16th October Mr Buchmann, accompanied by a Mr Von Conrat, went to see Mrs May at 24 Avenue Road, where she was already installed. They then agreed in principle on the grant of a tenancy to run until 31st December 1974.

The next day, 17th October, Mr Buchmann and Mr Von Conrat again called on Mrs May. Mr Buchmann then produced two documents, namely a tenancy agreement and a counterpart. This agreement bears date 1st October 1974. The counterpart was in evidence. Mr Buchmann and Mrs May signed the respective documents. The agreement is made between Mr Buchmann, called 'the landlord', and Mrs May, called 'the tenant' ... Clause 6 is of critical importance:

'It is mutually agreed and declared that the letting hereby made is solely for the purpose of the tenant's holiday in the London area.' ...

Mr Buchmann commenced the present action in February 1975. The pleadings are extremely short. The particulars of claim set out that the plaintiff is the owner of 24 Avenue Road and continued:

'(2) While the plaintiff was the owner of and in possession of the said premises [they were] let to the defendant on a furnished holiday letting by an agreement in writing dated 1st October, 1974 [setting out the terms of the agreement].'

He then sets out that in breach of the agreement the defendant has failed to deliver up vacant possession, and that the tenancy is not a protected furnished tenancy by reason of the provisions of s 2(1)(bbb); and possession is claimed on that ground, with mesne profits.

The defence 'does not admit that the said premises were let for the purpose of a holiday', denies that the plaintiff is entitled to possession, alternatively claims the protection of the Rent Acts, and says 'Save as hereinbefore expressly admitted the defendant denies each and every allegation' ...

The judge gave a full judgment. Unfortunately he was apparently not requested for a considerable time to supply notes of his judgment, which must have made it considerably more difficult for him to write up those notes. However, we have quite a full note of what he said. I will read certain passages from the judgment. At the outset, after stating the plaintiff's claim for possession and his allegation that the premises were let 'for a holiday' as provided in s 2(1)(bbb), the judge said this:

'The defendant claims the protection of the Rent Act, because she says that it was not a holiday letting. Really, that is the issue I have to decide. As counsel rightly said, one is not tied down to the terms of the agreement; one must look at the reality of the situation. Were the premises let conferring a right to use for the purposes of a holiday?'

That is an extremely important statement, and, with all respect to the learned judge it very considerably distorts the proper approach to this question ...

Then he said this:

> 'One must be careful in interpreting this Act to give it the meaning Parliament intended; if the purpose of the tenancy was to confer on the tenant a right to occupy as a "holiday letting", it is not protected as it is taken out of the Act by s 2(1)(bbb).'

The next paragraph deals with Case 10B of the Act. Then:

> 'So far as s 2(1)(bbb) is concerned, which excepts the position of a "holiday letting", one must constantly bear in mind its purpose. There is no doubt about it that this was a "short" letting. As Mr Garlant said, it had to be a "short" letting as the plaintiff's policy was either short lettings or holiday letting. One has to draw a distinction between a short letting and a holiday letting. This was a short letting granted to Mrs May. I conclude that she is entitled to the protection of the Rent Act. Accordingly the plaintiff's claim for possession is dismissed.' ...

The notice of appeal states these grounds, so far as now important:

> '(1) That there was no evidence on which the learned judge could find that the defendant was a statutory tenant of No 24 ... (3) That the learned judge misdirected himself in holding on the facts found by him that the tenancy agreement of the 1st October, 1974 was not for the purpose of a holiday within the terms of section 2(1)(bbb).'

It seems to me that that judgment contains a fundamental misdirection in that the judge treats the purpose of the tenancy as something to be determined at large on the evidence of the various parties concerned, altogether, or at any rate in great part, without regard to cl 6 of the agreement, to which he does not expressly refer at all in his judgment. Where parties to an instrument express their purpose in entering into the transaction effected by it, or the purposes for which, in the case of a tenancy agreement, the demised property is to be used, this expression of purpose is at least *prima facie* evidence of their true purpose and as such can only be displaced by evidence that the express purpose does not represent the true purpose. There is no claim here based on misrepresentation, and no claim for rectification. When I say the express purpose does not represent the true purpose, I mean that the express purpose does not correspond to the true purpose, whether the express purpose is a deliberate sham or merely a false label in the sense of a mistake in expression of intention.

In the present case, cl 6 of the agreement is perfectly unequivocal: 'the letting hereby made is solely for the purpose of the tenant's holiday in the London area'. It seems to me that that provision must stand as evidence of the purpose of the parties unless Mrs May can establish that the provision does not correspond to the true purpose of the parties. The burden lies on her to do so. I do not doubt that in a context such as the present the court would be astute to detect a sham where it appears that a provision has been inserted for the purpose of depriving the tenant of statutory protection under the Rent Acts. But it is for the tenant to establish this, and not for the landlord to establish affirmatively that the express purpose is the true purpose.

In argument, counsel for Mrs May used the words 'absence of *bona fides*'. But, as I understood him, he was not alleging that there had been any deliberate sham on the part of Mr Buchmann, so much as the attachment of a label to this transaction which did not correspond to the true purpose. At any rate, there was no evidence which would justify a finding of anything resembling fraud.

We were referred to a line of cases in this court on the expression contained in the Rent Acts, 'let as a dwelling or as a separate dwelling'. Those decisions, although given on different words in the Act, are directly in point on the present question, namely, what is the position of an express declaration in a tenancy agreement that the letting is for the purpose of a holiday? The three cases to which we were referred are as follows. First, *Wolfe v Hogan*, where the headnote says this:

'Where the terms of the tenancy provide for or contemplate the user of the premises for some particular purpose, that purpose will *prima facie* be the essential factor. Thus, if the premises are let for business purposes, the tenant cannot claim that they have been converted into a dwelling-house merely because someone lives on the premises. If, however, the tenancy agreement contemplates no specified user, then the actual user of the premises at the time when possession is sought by the landlord, must be considered.'

Denning LJ said:

'In determining whether a house or part of a house is "let as a dwelling" within the meaning of the Rent Restriction Acts, it is necessary to look at the purpose of the letting. If the lease contains an express provision as to the purpose of the letting, it is not necessary to look further.'

He was, of course, not concerned there with an allegation of sham.

In *British Land Co Ltd v Herbert Silver (Menswear) Ltd* Upjohn J said:

'A long line of authorities, for the most part in this court, has established that, on the issue whether the premises are let as a separate dwelling, one looks to the bargain made between the parties and see for what purpose the parties intended the premises would be used. The first place to ascertain their intentions is in the lease itself.'

Finally, in *Horford Investments Ltd v Lambert* Scarman LJ said:

'The section affords protection to the tenancy of a house only if the house is let as a separate dwelling. The section directs attention to the letting, that is to say, the terms of the tenancy. The courts have proceeded on the basis that the terms of the tenancy are the primary consideration: see *Wolfe v Hogan*. In my opinion there is here a principle of cardinal importance: whether a tenancy of a house (or a part of a house) is protected depends on the terms of the tenancy, not on subsequent events.'

In all those cases this court laid down the principle that, in considering whether a house is let as a separate dwelling, where there is a written lease you ascertain the purpose of the parties from the terms of the lease and you do not go beyond the terms of the lease to ascertain what is the purpose of the parties. That is always so apart from the case where the terms of the lease do not correspond to the true intention of the parties.

It seems to me that on that fundamental ground the learned judge was in error in treating this as a question to be determined by reference to the oral evidence of the parties and without regard to the terms of cl 6, which would stand unless it is shown to be something in the nature of a sham or of a false label, and that on that ground his judgment cannot be supported.

What, then, is to be done? It seems to me that there was no evidence before the judge on which he could have held that cl 6 did not truly represent the common intention of the parties. Mrs May is a Dominion national not resident in England except on a series of short residence permits, the current one of which was due to expire in December 1974. She had been out of England since the spring of 1974, leaving only some personal chattels in 24 Avenue Road. She informed Mr Buchmann that she wished to stay in England for two months only before going abroad with her husband, who was taking up an engagement abroad. Mr Buchmann had no reason to suspect that this was untrue. It seems to me that a stay of less than three months in such circumstances would constitute a 'holiday' within the ordinary meaning of that word; and I can find no ground on which it could be properly said that the statement of purpose in cl 6 was a sham or was, without intention to deceive, an untrue statement of the purpose of the letting.

Counsel for the defendant, who has said all there was to be said on her behalf, contended, truly, that one must look at the true relation contemplated by the parties and not merely at the label. In other words, if it can be shown that the terms of this agreement do not correspond with some label in the agreement, then one can look behind the label. Then he says that here the evidence as accepted by the judge established that a holiday was not the true relation, in other words, not the true purpose for which 24 Avenue Road was being let. He said that Mrs May's motive was to protect her right of occupation, in other words, to continue it for the benefit of Mrs May and Mr May together; and he said that Mrs May did not know her rights and thought it was just one of the usual agreements. There is no evidence that Mr Buchmann thought that was the motive of the provision as to a holiday; indeed it plainly was not his motive. Whatever Mrs May may or may not have had in mind when she signed the agreement cannot of itself displace the effect of the express provision within the agreement. Her mere ignorance of her rights certainly could not do so.

I conclude that there is nothing in the evidence which could displace the effect of cl 6 of the agreement, and so one is left with a tenancy for a holiday, and that tenancy is withdrawn from protection by s 2(1)(bbb). Accordingly, Mr Buchmann is now entitled to possession of the property. I would allow the appeal.

Stephenson and Megaw LJJ agreed.

The critical factor in *Buchmann v May* may have been the immigration status of the tenant; immigration officers had been informed that the purpose of the tenant's stay in the UK was that of a 'holiday'. There is evidence that the courts will not allow the use of the 'holiday' exemption where there is a sham; even before the encouragement given by the House of Lords in cases such as *Street v Mountford* and *Antoniades v Villiers*, Glidewell J refused to recognise a letting in North London to a number of student nurses as a 'holiday let'.

Other tenancies excluded for particular reasons

There are further examples of tenancies which are excluded from the operation of the Acts, such as tenancies of licensed premises, tenancies falling within the Agricultural Holdings Act, tenancies where the landlord is the Crown, a local authority, a housing association, or a housing co-operative.

The 'resident landlord' exception

The most important and controversial is the 'resident landlord' exception. This exception made its appearance in the legislation when furnished tenancies came into protection by virtue of the Rent Act 1974. Here a number of policy factors come into play.

(1) First, it has to be recognised that where a tenant is living cheek by jowl with a resident landlord, it will be likely to exacerbate, rather than diminish, any tensions which may arise between them if the tenant is accorded full

security of tenure. There may be a case, as exemplified in the Rent Act 1977 regime, for according to the tenant a kind of qualified security of tenure, so that he is given a 'breathing space' to find alternative accommodation; but even that safeguard for the tenant has been abandoned in the Housing Act 1988, where the tenant is given no security at all.

(2) There is some evidence that landlords with spare accommodation in their houses were inhibited from making it available to tenants because of apprehensions about the difficulty of getting rid of tenants if the tenants proved to be unsuitable, or if the landlord's circumstances changed so as to make it desirable that he should be able to recover possession of the let premises. To encourage the economic and effective use of available accommodation, it was thought desirable to offer landlords an incentive to let spare rooms in their houses.

(3) There was some suggestion, in the Rent Act case law, that the test of 'residence' by a landlord was becoming too easy to satisfy, and that a landlord might thus be able to deny his tenants full security of tenure because of a rather tenuous 'residence' by the landlord in the form of a room in the property which the landlord occupied on a part-time footing.

(4) Where a landlord is not just a 'resident' landlord, but a 'resident and sharing' landlord, further factors may come into play, at least in respect of tenancies created on or after 15 January 1989, and the tenancy will be an 'excluded' tenancy, which diminished the protection enjoyed by a tenant under the (amended) Protection from Eviction Act 1977.

These factors have led to a rich case law, since the introduction of the 'resident landlord' exception in the Rent Act 1974; there has also been a shift in emphasis from the Rent Act test to that of the Housing Act. In the case of a Housing Act assured tenancy, although the tenant is denied all statutory security, the law has been tightened to the extent that a more rigorous test is applied to the test of 'residence' by a landlord; for that reason, the applicability of some of the earlier Rent Act cases to 'resident landlord' problems arising in respect of tenancies created on or after 15 January 1989, should be treated with some caution. The test, under the 1977 Act, was whether the landlord was 'resident'; the test under the 1988 Act is whether the landlord occupies 'as his only or principal home', which is meant to apply a more stringent test.

Two issues arise:

(1) Do the landlord and tenant inhabit 'the same building' (other than a purpose-built block of flats)?

(2) Is the landlord 'resident' in the true sense, or, in the case of a tenancy arising under the Housing Act, does the landlord occupy 'as his only or principal home'?

The 'same building' issue

This is fundamentally a question of fact for the court; there are difficult borderline cases, and much may turn on the physical configuration of the premises. If the premises are such that the landlord and tenant can manage to lead their lives in such a way that they do not impinge on each other, for example, if they enjoy separate means of access, this will be a factor which might lead the court to consider that they are not within 'the same building' (see for instance *Bardrick v Haycock* (1976) 31 P&CR 420, though the contrary decision, on basically similar facts, in *Griffiths v English* (1982) 261 EG 257, should also be noted (see Martin [1983] Conv 147)).

The authorities were reviewed in *Wolff v Waddington* (1989) 22 HLR 72.

Wolff v Waddington

Lloyd LJ: This is the defendant's appeal from a decision of His Honour Judge Barker, sitting in the Kingston upon Hull County Court on December 15, 1988, whereby he ordered the defendant to give up possession of a dwelling-house known as Flat 1, 205b Cottingham Road, Kingston upon Hull ...

The plaintiff's mother occupied the ground floor flat, known as 205a. In February 1987 the plaintiff's mother became ill. The plaintiff, who was married to an American and had been living in the United States, came to live with her mother; that was on February 17, 1987. On February 28, 1987, the plaintiff's mother died. The plaintiff has been living at 205a ever since, except for two periods of one month each, when she returned to the United States in June 1987 and again in January 1988. In March 1988 the house was put up for sale.

On July 2, 1988, the plaintiff served a notice to quit on the defendant ... By his defence the defendant claims that he is a protected tenant.

The relevant legislation is to be found in section 12 of the Rent Act of 1977 as amended ...

It is thus apparent that there were two questions to be determined by the judge:

(1) Are 205a and 205b parts of the same building?

(2) Was the plaintiff occupying 205a as her residence at the material time?

The judge regarded both those questions as questions of fact; he decided both questions in favour of the plaintiff and made his order accordingly. There is now an appeal to this court by the defendant.

On the first of those two questions we have seen a plan and we have also seen some photographs. It is not altogether easy to visualise the layout. But putting it at its most favourable from the defendant's point of view it would appear that his flat is part of an extension, the roof line of the extension being somewhat lower than the roof line of the rest of the house. The defendant's kitchen, on the first floor, is above the plaintiff's bathroom; the defendant's bedroom is above the plaintiff's garage and the defendant's sitting-room is above the plaintiff's utility room. There is an alleyway between the two parts of the house, if that is the right way to describe it, that alleyway being at the ground floor level only.

Mr Genney on behalf of the defendant relies on various matters in support of his submission that the two flats were not part of the same building. In the first place he relies on the fact that the plaintiff and the defendant had separate entrances. Secondly he relies on the absence of any vertical party wall between that part occupied by the plaintiff and that part occupied by the defendant. Thirdly, he relies on the existence of the alleyway which, as I have said, was at ground floor level only.

In addition – and this would appear to be the main point of the appeal – he relied on the fact that the plaintiff and the defendant were able to live separate lives without embarrassment, to quote the language of Scarman LJ in the case of *Bardrick v Haycock*, (1976) 31 P&CR 420, and this even though they were physically in close proximity to each other. Mr Genney submits that the judge erred in law when he said that it was neither here nor there that the parties could lead separate lives.

But as against that, the two flats have all the appearance of being part of one and the same building, a fact which was regarded as being of importance by Eveleigh LJ in the case of *Griffiths v English*, to which we were referred by Mr de la Piquerie, (1981) 2 HLR 127. I note that in the Bardrick case Cairns LJ, giving an example of the sort of case in which a judge might be said to have erred in law, said at the commencement of his judgment:

'When an Act of Parliament uses the word 'building' without defining it there must be some structures or pairs of structures which as a matter of law could be said to be two buildings within the meaning of the Act and some which as a matter of law could be said to be one building. If a judge held, for example, that two quite separate houses constituted one building, he might be said to have erred in law. On the other hand, if a judge held that two floors in the same house constituted separate buildings that might be said to be erroneous in law.'

My own strong impression is that these two flats were part of one and the same building. It could not be suggested for one moment that what I have called the extension to the plaintiff's flat, on the other side of the alleyway, that is to say, the bathroom, utility room and garage, were part of a separate building. They were part of the same building. The defendant's flat in this case was over that part of the plaintiff's flat which was on the other side of the alleyway. So for myself I would regard this as a straightforward case in which these two flats form part of the same building. But if it were a borderline case, I would never interfere with the decision of the judge on what is essentially a question of fact ...

I then turn to the second of the two questions, which the judge regarded as the more difficult of the two. As I have already said, the facts are that the plaintiff had been living at 205a more or less continuously since February 1987. Mr Genney on behalf of the defendant relies on the plaintiff's evidence that she regards America as her home and that she intends to return there. So she may. But the question is whether 205a has also been her home in England since her mother died. It is settled law that a person may have more than one home which he occupies as his residence for the purpose of the Rent Acts. That was decided by the Court of Appeal in *Langford Property Co Ltd v Athanassoglou* [1948] 2 All ER at p 722. That decision was approved by the House of Lords in *Hampstead Way Investments Ltd v Lewis-Weare & another* [1985] 1 All ER 564, *per* Lord Brandon at p 568. So it is clear that a person may have two homes for the purposes of this part of the Rent Act; indeed, so much was conceded by Mr Genney.

But Mr Genney relies on the subsequent case of *Beck v Scholz* [1953] 1 All ER at p 814G. But the facts of that case, when one comes to look at them, are really quite different. There the dwelling was being occupied as a matter of convenience for occasional visits only. That could not possibly be said of the plaintiff's occupation of 205a. Mr Genney says that *Beck v Scholz* establishes that one can look at the purpose of the occupation. He argued that the plaintiff occupied 205a only as a matter of convenience while she disposed of the property before her return to the United States. But, as I have said, the plaintiff was at 205a for a period of 13 months before she ever put up the house for sale. To my mind, it is quite clear that she was occupying 205a not merely as a matter of convenience. As has been said, it is a question of fact and degree in every case whether a person occupies a house as his residence or not; that is the way in which the matter was put by Lord Brandon in the *Hampstead Way Investments Case*, to which

I have already referred. To my mind it is clear as a matter of fact that the plaintiff occupied 205a as her residence.

For the reasons that I have mentioned, it seems to me that the judge reached the right decision on both these issues of fact, and I would dismiss the appeal.

Stocker LJ: agreed.

It will be seen from this extract that absence of the 'embarrassment factor' will not conclusively point to full protection if the tenant's accommodation and the landlord's accommodation are part 'of the same building'. Though the 'embarrassment factor' may have been the motive for the legislation, its presence (or absence) does not conclude the matter.

The landlord's 'residence'

The test differs under the two Acts; the Rent Act merely requires the landlord to be 'resident'; the Housing Act requires him to occupy 'as his only or principal home'. Under both Acts there are also provisions for 'disregards' – ie periods of non-residence which do not count, such as periods after the death of the landlord, or after a sale of the property by a landlord.

Leaving aside these cases, however, there is still the issue of the nature of the landlord's residence. The Rent Act adopted the 'residence' test which applies to those claiming a statutory tenancy (see s 2(3) and Schedule 2, para 5, with the addition of the enigmatic words 'so far as the nature of the case allows').

The result of this incorporation by reference is to let in to the definition of resident landlords those who satisfy the 'residence test' for statutory tenants. This test has been applied by the courts in a generous way, so as to protect statutory tenants, and can include such characters as the 'two-home tenant' – see *Hampstead Way Investments Ltd v Lewis-Weare*. The result of the statutory language in Schedule 2 would seem to be that these authorities also apply to 'resident' landlords. A difficult issue of fact was seen by the Court of Appeal to arise in *Wolff v Waddington* (above); but even more difficult issues arose in the cases of *Jackson v Pekic* (1989) 22 HLR 9 and *Palmer v McNamara* (1991) 23 HLR 168.

Jackson v Pekic and O'Brien

Ralph Gibson LJ: This is an appeal from the decision of His Honour Judge Krikler made in Willesden County Court on September 6, 1988. By his order he directed that the plaintiff, Mrs Jackson, recover possession of the first floor back room of 34 Macfarlane Road, W12 from the defendant, Mr Joseph O'Brien.

Mrs Jackson sued as administratrix of the estate of her mother, Mrs Jovanka Stojsavljevic, deceased ...

There was, in effect, no dispute that from the end of 1978 Mrs Jovanka resided in the first floor front room. If the defendant's tenancy had been granted in 1979, as the plaintiff's pleaded case had asserted, there would have been a good claim under section 12 of the Act. But once it was clear that the defendant's tenancy was granted in 1973 the question arose whether Mrs Jovanka had been a resident landlord on August 14, 1974 when the relevant provisions of the statute took effect.

The problem for the plaintiff at the trial was that her case that Mrs Jovanka had at all times occupied the first floor front room was unsustainable. The defendant's evidence was that in 1973 Mrs Jovanka was not living in the house. He described various other people occupying the first floor front room until, in 1974, his brother, Cyril O'Brien, moved in with a cousin Mr Kinsella. Mr Kinsella left in April 1977. Cyril O'Brien was locked out by Mrs Jovanka in September 1977 ...

Before Judge Krikler it was submitted for the defendant that the onus lay upon the plaintiff to prove that Mrs Jovanka was a resident landlord at the material time, namely August 14, 1974. That was accepted by Judge Krikler and has not been questioned by Mr Gordon. It is, I think, clearly right.

It was common ground also that if Mrs Jovanka was not in actual occupation of any part of 34 Macfarlane Road at the material time the plaintiff could only prove that Mrs Jovanka is nevertheless to be treated in law as having been in occupation of a dwelling-house within 34 Macfarlane Road as her residence if she could show an intention on the part of Mrs Jovanka to return to reside in it and that her inward intention was clothed with some sufficient visible manifestation of it: see *Brown v Brash* [1948] 2 KB 247. It seems that Judge Krikler reached the conclusion that this test was satisfied. The steps in his reasoning can be summarised as follows:

(i) Mrs Jovanka's intention had to be deduced from the history and the surrounding circumstances.

(ii) There were periods of time when she was not physically in occupation of the first floor front room: as when she was in hospital, or other periods of ill-health, or when staying with her daughters and her son. But that was no abandonment of home.

(iii) A person can absent himself from his home without it ceasing to be his residence. It depends upon his intention and 'the interim arrangement made'.

(iv) The evidence of Mrs Jackson and of Mrs Zabavnik, a friend and close neighbour, was to the effect that throughout the years Mrs Jovanka's home was at 34 Macfarlane Road. That, in the judge's view, was 'strong evidence'. Most important was the evidence of Dr Marks. Mrs Jovanka had been his patient since 1958. He had visited her on isolated occasions before 1978. He was unable to give any dates because his documents had been returned to where they belonged within the recording system of the National Health Service. He had, after she was severely ill in 1978, visited her more frequently. He had never been told by Mrs Jovanka of any address other than 34 Macfarlane Road. In the judge's view, if she had changed her address the doctor would have been told.

(v) As to who occupied the first floor front room it was 'undoubtedly occupied by Mrs Jovanka but also used by others,' and 'No relinquishing of the first floor front room took place notwithstanding the parting with possession of that room and that others lived there.'

(vi) The arrangement under which Mr Cyril O'Brien and Mr Kinsella occupied the room was 'informal'. Mrs Jovanka never regarded Mr Cyril O'Brien as having any entitlement to the room because she changed the lock and turned him out. Since the local authority had prosecuted with reference to the exclusion of Mrs Budden and not with reference to the turning out of Mr Cyril O'Brien, they did not regard his occupation in the same light as that of Mrs Budden.

(vii) Mrs Jovanka never regarded Mr Cyril O'Brien as anything more than a licensee. She never abandoned her intention to reside at 34 Macfarlane Road from 1955 onwards and she was resident on August 14, 1974 for the purposes of the Act notwithstanding her absence.

Ms McAllister, in a careful and most well-sustained submission for the defendant, argued that the learned judge had misdirected himself in various respects. I shall concentrate on three of her submissions.

(i) That he failed to have regard to the fact that upon the evidence Mrs Jovanka's intention cannot have been to continue to reside in 34 Macfarlane Road during 1973 to 1977 when she let to others and to Mr Cyril O'Brien the only room in which she had there resided.

(ii) He wrongly had regard to matters of no probative force, namely Mrs Jovanka's supposed view that Cyril O'Brien was a licensee only; to the supposed informality of her arrangements with Cyril O'Brien, and to the supposed view of the local authority as to the nature of his occupation.

(iii) The learned judge failed to make any finding as to what could or did constitute the outward manifestation (sometimes called the *corpus possessiones*) of Mrs Jovanka's intention to return to reside in the first floor front room ...

Judge Krikler made no specific finding as to who was occupying the front room in 1974, but he did find that Mrs Jovanka was not in it. He did not expressly reject the evidence of the defendant who said that Mrs Jovanka was not living there in 1973; and that a Mr Murray lived there until Mrs Jovanka locked him out; and that Mrs Jovanka did not use the room before Mr Cyril O'Brien occupied it in 1975. There was, however, no reason, so far as I can see, to reject this evidence. The defendant's evidence was in several important matters corroborated by the evidence produced by the Tenancy Relations Officer. There was nothing to set against it, since the evidence of Mrs Jackson on this aspect of the case was clearly mistaken. The facts are, accordingly, that Mrs Jovanka was not living in any part of the property as her residence from a date before October 1973 until after September 1977, a period of some four years.

What is the principle of law which may permit a court to say that a landlord who is not actually residing in any part of the building when the tenancy is granted, and does not actually reside in any part for a period of some three years thereafter, is nevertheless to be treated in law as residing in the property throughout that time? The principle was developed with reference to tenants losing or retaining the status of statutory tenant. It has been applied by statute to a landlord losing or retaining the status of resident landlord. It is summarised in Halsbury's Laws, Vol 27, para 592 – subject, of course, to reference to the cases there cited – as follows:

> 'A statutory tenant will lose the benefit of the Rent Acts if he abandons the premises without any intention of returning or in circumstances such that the prospect of his returning is remote. The onus of proving that the tenant has gone out of residence is in the first place, on the landlord, but where the tenant's absence is sufficiently long or continuous to raise the inference that he has ceased to occupy the premises as his residence the onus shifts to the tenant to rebut this inference by showing both (1) that he had throughout an intention to return, and (2) some outward and visible sign of that intention, for example occupation by a caretaker or licensee or the presence of the tenant's furniture.'

In *Skinner v Geary* [1931] 2 KB 546 the defendant, who lived in another house, resisted a claim for possession on the ground that he was still a statutory tenant of the property in which he had permitted his sister to live. Scrutton LJ, at p 561 said:

> 'A non-occupying tenant was in my opinion never within the precincts of the Acts, which were dealing only with an occupying tenant who had a right to stay in and not be turned out. This case is to be decided on the principle that the Acts do not apply to a person who is not personally occupying the house and who has no intention of returning to it. I except, of course, such a case as that to which I have already referred – namely, of temporary absence, the best instance of which is that of a sea captain who may be away for months but who intends to return, and whose wife and family occupy the house during his absence.'

That case, as I understand the law, states the basic principle upon which the position of a statutory tenant has been based, namely, to secure to the tenant who for some reason is not in physical occupation that protection which, upon the true construction of the statute, Parliament must be taken to have intended the tenant to have. Scrutton LJ referred to the example of the sea captain absent for a while, while his wife and family occupy the house: but how far was that principle of necessary latitude to be carried?

In *Brown v Brash* [1948] 2 KB 247 the tenant was sentenced to a term of imprisonment and was thus perforce absent. He left his mistress in occupation but after a while she left. The County Court Judge in effect held that the defendant's persisting intention to return was sufficient to retain for him the protection of the Rent Acts. It was submitted on appeal to this court that it was not necessary to prove that a licensee or caretaker or furniture was left on the premises and that such matters were only relevant as evidence of the intention to return. That was rejected. Asquith LJ, giving the judgment of the court in a well-known passage, stated the principle to be applied. It is sufficient for the purposes of this case to read a short passage of it, starting at p 254, the paragraph numbered (3):

> '(3) But we are of opinion that neither in principle nor on the authorities can this "an intention on his part to return" be enough. To suppose that he can absent himself for five or ten years or more and retain possession and his protected status simply by proving an inward intention to return after so protracted an absence would be to frustrate the spirit and policy of the Acts, as affirmed in *Keeves v Dean* and *Skinner v Geary*. (4) Notwithstanding an absence so protracted the authorities suggest that its effect may be averted if he couples and clothes his inward intention with some formal, outward, and visible sign of it; that is, installs in the premises some caretaker or representative, be it a relative or not, with the status of a licensee and with the function of preserving the premises for his own ultimate homecoming. There will then, at all events, be someone to profit by the housing accommodation involved, which will not stand empty. It may be that the same result can be secured by leaving on the premises, as a deliberate symbol of continued occupation, furniture; though we are not clear that this was necessary to the decision in *Brown v Draper* [1944] KB 309. Apart from authority, in principle, possession in fact (for it is with possession in fact and not with possession in law that we are here concerned) requires not merely an 'animus possidendi' but a 'corpus possessiones', namely, some visible state of affairs in which the animus possidendi finds expression. (5) If the caretaker (to use that term for short) leaves or the furniture is removed from the premises, otherwise than quite temporarily, we are of opinion that the protection, artificially prolonged by their presence, ceases, whether the tenant wills or desires such removal or not.'

As Staughton LJ pointed out in argument, Asquith LJ said that the effect of protracted absence may be averted if he clothes his inward intention with some visible sign of it; not that it will thereby be averted. In every case, in my view, the question is whether the tenant has demonstrated such continuing occupation of the dwelling-house as his residence as satisfies that concept within the meaning and policy of the Act.

Reference should be made now to *Lyons v Caffery*, which is reported in Estates Gazette Law Reports for 1982, Vol 266 at p 213. There, before going abroad, the landlord had occupied the basement of his house, the basement consisting of a bed-sitting-room, a sun-room and a kitchen, bathroom and lavatory. In his absence his mother, who occupied a bed-sitting-room on the ground floor, let to the tenant the basement bed-sitting-room, with shared use of the kitchen, bathroom and lavatory. On his return, the landlord took over the ground floor bed-sitting-room from his mother, who went to live elsewhere. He claimed possession of the basement room occupied by the tenant, on the ground that he was a resident landlord. The learned judge held that there was sufficient animus possidendi and corpus possessiones in the plaintiff to make him fall within the definition of a person who occupied the whole basement as a residence when the tenancy was granted to the defendant. Templeman LJ, at p 214, said:

'By section 12(1)(c) of the Rent Act 1977 the plaintiff landlord was entitled to possession of the basement front room ... provided that the landlord showed that the landlord occupied as his residence another dwelling-house which also formed part of the premises ...'

Before the grant of the tenancy, the landlord occupied as his residence the basement front room, another basement room known as the sun-room and the kitchen, bathroom and wc in the basement. The landlord shared the use of the kitchen, bathroom and wc in the basement with his mother, who occupied a room on the ground floor of the premises as her bed-sitting-room. The tenant was granted a tenancy of the basement front room with the use of the basement bathroom' etc 'with the landlord's mother. The landlord thus had occupied the same dwelling-house as the tenant and not another dwelling-house, unless the landlord's occupation of the sun-room was occupation of another dwelling-house.'

The learned Lord Justice went on to hold that it could not be, and held therefore that the appeal should be allowed ...

It is clear, in my judgment, from the passages cited that the concept of a tenant not losing the protection of the Rent Acts for his occupation of the dwelling-house as his residence, although he is not himself in physical occupation, was designed to ensure protection notwithstanding those absences which are consistent with the tenant retaining, and intending to retain, the dwelling-house as his residence, and not where, for example, the tenant's absence is because he is merely making money by sub-letting: see Slesser LJ in *Skinner v Geary* at p 567.

It is also clear to my mind that the continuing intention to return to occupy the premises at some later date is not by itself sufficient to constitute occupation of the dwelling-house as his residence if the tenant has left no sufficient visible sign of that intention. It may be that in some circumstances furniture will serve as such a visible sign, particularly if the tenant leaves also those personal possessions such as books, pictures and ornaments, which are capable of indicating that a tenant is still treating the premises as his home. There is no principle of law which says that the mere presence of furniture, consistent with an ordinary furnished letting at market rent, could serve for that purpose.

I return now to the grounds for the decision of the learned judge. In my judgment, the conclusion that there was no abandonment by Mrs Jovanka of her intention to reside at 34 Macfarlane Road between 1973 and 1977 cannot be sustained. The reference to informality in the arrangement under which Mr Cyril O'Brien occupied the first floor front room for more than two years showed, I think, a misapprehension of the facts. There was nothing more informal about the arrangement than, I suspect, most oral lettings of a furnished room. It was submitted by Mr Gordon that we should regard the arrangement as not amounting to a tenancy but a licence. I cannot accept that submission. On the evidence it was, in my judgment, plainly a tenancy. The premises to be let and the rent were agreed. There was nothing more formal in the arrangement between Mrs Jovanka and the defendant, which constituted a valid letting.

Next the reference to Mrs Jovanka regarding Mr Cyril O'Brien as a licensee because she turned him out, also seems to me to be misconceived. She granted a tenancy, ie exclusive occupation of the first floor front room at a rent, to Mr Cyril O'Brien. She clearly had no understanding of the limits imposed by law upon the rights of a landlord, as was demonstrated by her conduct towards Mrs Giggs and Mrs Budden. Mr Giggs' right of occupation was in existence when Mrs Jovanka's husband bought the house. Her conduct in evicting Mr Cyril O'Brien showed nothing more than that she wished to get him out. Notwithstanding the evidence of the plaintiff, the neighbour and the doctor, viewing her conduct over the period from 1973 to 1977 seems to me to result in her conduct being more consistent with an intention during those years not to reside in the house than with a continuing intention to reside there. There was no hint of an explanation why she should for a period of three years or more let the only room which she had herself occupied other than the simple purpose to obtain the rent paid by those who occupied it.

Next, if she had a continuing intention to reside in that room, when Mrs Jovanka let the first floor front room, the rest of the house being let off to others, there was nothing whatever in the nature of a visible sign of that intention. There was furniture in the room and it belonged to her, but there is nothing to show that it was other than such furniture as is required for a room to be let at a furnished rent. There is no evidence of anything in the way of personal possessions left in any part of the building during that time. Nothing, of course, was said or agreed to constitute Mr Cyril O'Brien her caretaker or representative, or to show that he was anything other than a furnished tenant paying a market rent.

For these reasons I would hold that the plaintiff did not prove that at the material time Mrs Jovanka was a resident landlord within section 12 of the Act, but that the contrary was proved on the evidence. I would therefore allow the appeal and set aside the order for possession.

Palmer v McNamara

Dillon LJ: The question is whether the defendant is entitled in respect of that flat to the protection of the Rent Act 1977 and that depends on section 12 of that Act, the side note of which is 'Resident landlords'. The question is whether the plaintiff qualifies, for the purposes of that section, as a resident landlord ...

The factual position is that on the ground floor of 84 Drakefield Road there is a front room which is let by a tenancy to the defendant. It is a bedsit with a kitchen diner at the rear of it. Beside that, leading towards the rear there is a hall and an inner hall. Off the inner hall there is a bathroom and wc and the ultimate arrangement between the plaintiff and the defendant was that that was to be shared. That, at any rate, was the case until the defendant took it upon himself to put a padlock on the door. There is a door from the bathroom out to the garden and the defendant was to have the right to use the garden, and at the back there was a room retained by the plaintiff. The question is whether in the circumstances that room of the plaintiff's is a dwelling-house and whether it is occupied and has throughout the tenancy been occupied by the plaintiff as his residence.

It appears that the plaintiff occupied the whole of the ground floor of the house from about 1982, at which stage he separated from his wife. In around 1984 he granted a tenancy of the front room to a Miss Murray, who was an aunt of the defendant. Under the terms of that tenancy the plaintiff had shared use, if he wanted it, with Miss Murray not only of the bathroom and wc but also of the kitchen at the rear of the bed-sitting room let to Miss Murray. Miss Murray left towards the end of 1987 and the tenancy was then granted to the defendant with exclusive use of the kitchen at the back of the front room let to him, which indeed includes the kitchen-diner. The plaintiff continued to occupy, and I will come in a moment to his use of it, the back room on the ground floor, which he still occupies.

The plaintiff is a gentleman who is now 59 years old. He used to be engaged in advertising, but he retired from that several years ago. However he does some part-time writing and it seems he has had a book published and has an interest in poetry.

In the rear room on the ground floor he keeps practically all his possessions. There are his books and his typewriter, a table and chairs, television, video, a refrigerator, a kettle, a sink, a fold-up bed which he used to use, cutlery and saucepans and obviously, because of the fridge and kettle, electric points. But there is no cooker. There is no cooker because the plaintiff does not cook and has never learnt to cook. When he wants meals in his room at the back, he either buys food which he can eat without cooking or buys hot take-away meals which he brings home and eats in his room. It is said that the room by itself does not constitute a dwelling-house because it has no cooker. It has of course a point, as I have said, and it would be very easy to install a small portable cooker or hot plate if the plaintiff wanted one, but he does not.

The test suggested for whether the room constitutes a dwelling-house is whether it had such qualities and facilities as permitted use for the ordinary purposes of living. It has been submitted to us that it is essential, for there to be a dwelling-house, that it must have facilities for cooking, eating and sleeping. It is not enough if it merely provides facilities for any two of those three, without the third.

We have been referred by Mr Rowland to various authorities, but they all have to be taken as decisions on the particular facts with which the court is dealing, or as containing comments directed to the particular situation with which the court was dealing. It seems to me quite clear that in considering whether a room or a series of rooms is a dwelling-house one has to look not only at the physical surroundings, but at the purpose. Thus in section 1 of the 1977 Act it is stated that 'a tenancy under which a dwellinghouse ... is let as a separate dwelling is a protected tenancy for the purposes of this Act'. If a flat is let unfurnished, at the moment of letting it will probably not have a bed in it and, if the tenant is going to provide his own portable cooker, it will not have a cooker in it, but I cannot believe that the criterion of the Act is so stringent on the need for a dwelling-house to contain a bed and a cooker that unfurnished lettings are not protected. Using common sense, as is permissible, the room occupied by the plaintiff contains everything required to be his dwelling-house, except a cooker, which he does not want. There could be a cooker there and it would then be a complete dwelling-house. I cannot take the view that just because he does not want a cooker, the room he occupies cannot rank as a dwellinghouse. It is of course clear that a single room may be a dwelling-house. That is commonly the case in tenancies and it can apply equally well to the landlord's occupation when section 12 has to be considered. Therefore I take the view that Judge Sumner was correct in holding that what the plaintiff retained was indeed a dwelling-house.

Does he then occupy it as his residence? He used to beyond any question. Indeed in this field of law the terms used, which have now been part of the jurisprudence on the subject for 70 years, are very well understood – residence, dwelling-house, occupied as his residence – and so the cases that come before the courts tend to be cases where the facts are unusual. To that generality the present case is no exception. Apart from his inability to cook, which has had the result that he does not have a cooker in his room, the plaintiff suffers from ailments as a result of which he has not slept in the room since before the tenancy was granted to the defendant. The plaintiff's evidence is that he has diabetes, but more seriously he has a three-inch shortening of his left leg and osteo-arthritis in his left hip which has caused serious deterioration. That is supported by a doctor's certificate which refers to it as 'long-standing hip joint disease'. The effect of that, particularly if the climate is damp, is that he needs help to dress and undress himself. Therefore since 1987 he has spent his nights in the spare room of the house of a very old friend, a Miss Ducker, who lives about a mile or mile-and-a-half away from Drakefield Road. The plaintiff has a car and can travel between the two houses. He uses her spare room and keeps a change of clothes there. He probably now has baths there, because of the difficulty in dressing and undressing, and sometimes has his evening meal or Sunday lunch with Miss Ducker at her home. He may keep the odd book there, but he does not keep his other possessions there. The furniture in the spare room is Miss Ducker's furniture.

It is said that because he sleeps at Miss Ducker's home he does not use his room at 84 Drakefield Road as his residence. He does not use Miss Ducker's spare room as a residence either, and he is therefore in the position, which is not impossible but perhaps unusual, of a man with accommodation but no residence. He spends his days at 84 Drakefield Road. He does his writing and reading there. He watches television and video and has meals that he brings in. But it is said that because he does not sleep there he does not occupy it as his residence.

The question whether a dwelling-house is occupied as a residence is commonly paraphrased as 'does he occupy it as his home?' See the observations of Lord Brandon in *Hampstead Way Investments v Lewis-Weare* [1985] 1 All ER 564 at 568A. He said:

'My Lords, in order to determine this appeal, it is necessary to examine the more important cases decided between 1920 and 1968 on what is meant by the occupation of a dwelling-house by a person as his residence, or, as it is put in many of the cases (without, in my view, any difference of meaning), the occupation of a dwellinghouse by a person as his home.'

The word 'home' was used by Scrutton LJ in the leading case of *Skinner v Geary* [1931] 2 KB 546. It was also used by Lord Evershed MR in *Beck v Scholz* [1953] 1 QB 570 at 575 and by May LJ in *Regalian Securities v Sheuer* (1982) 5 HLR 48.

Applying that test, which raises a question of fact and degree to be determined by applying ordinary common sense, I have no doubt that the judge was entitled, and indeed right, to take the view that the plaintiff occupied his back room as his home. That is enough to determine this appeal.

Bingham LJ: agreed.

Under the Housing Act, the test is: 'Does the landlord occupy "as his only or principal home"?' This seems to subdivide into two questions:

(1) Is it the landlord's only home? If so, that is an end of the matter.

(2) If not the landlord's only home, is it his principal home?

Though the test is almost certainly intended to be more stringent, it should be noted that in one of the few cases where this expression has been subject to judicial scrutiny – the public sector case of *Crawley BC v Sawyer* (1988) 20 HLR 98 – the expression received a generous interpretation; it is to be hoped that this construction will not be extended to resident landlords under the Housing Act 1988.

Joint entitlement gives rise to a problem; the Rent Act's approach to joint entitlement is to treat it as if it does not exist – and so some heroic construction was needed in *Cooper v Tait* (1984) 271 EG 195 to enable the Court of Appeal to hold that residence by one of two (or more) joint landlords was enough to fulfil the test. The Housing Act 1988, Schedule 1, para 10(2) applies the same rule to joint resident landlords under that Act.

Authority seems to suggest that the courts will not take too technical a view of the timing of the landlord's fulfilment of the residence requirements of the Acts. In *O'Sullivan v Barnett* [1994] 1 WLR 166, in a case where the hitherto resident landlord moved 'with' his tenant, but rather carelessly timed his arrival to the new premises in such a way that he arrived after the tenant, the court was willing to confer on him the status of 'resident landlord' throughout.

'Residence tests'

Both the Rent Act and the Housing Act have what might loosely be described as a 'residence requirement', but the tests differ substantially, and the way in which they apply is totally different. This residence requirement is sometimes strict, and sometimes relatively lax – but it is generally present, in one form or another. It also manifests itself in the public sector.

Rent Act tenancies

Here, paradoxically, whilst the contractual tenancy is still on foot, there is no 'residence requirement'. All that is needed is that the dwelling-house should be 'let as a dwelling' (s 1 Rent Act 1977) – not necessarily for the tenant to 'dwell in' it – and there is no requirement of residence by the tenant or anybody else. When a statutory tenancy has arisen under s 2 Rent Act 1977, after the determination of the contractual tenancy, the position changes, and residence becomes all important.

The story has often been told how the judges invented, in *Skinner v Geary* [1931] 2 KB 546, a 'residence requirement'. There was no such requirement in the original wartime Rent Act, but the judges justified its creation by the argument that the original wartime legislation was passed in haste, and Parliament had failed to express its real intention because of the constraints under which the legislation was passed.

Skinner v Geary

Scrutton LJ: ... The Acts were passed in a hurry, the language used was often extremely vague, and so it was always possible to say in any particular case that there were no clear words in the Acts which dealt with the point. That was the argument advanced in one of the earliest cases, *Remon v City of London Real Property Co.* There the contractual tenancy had expired on a given date. A day or two afterwards the landlords, without the tenant's knowledge, entered on the premises, saying that they did so in exercise of their right of re-entry. Mr Romer in the course of his argument for the landlords contended with vigour that there were no words in the Act which provided for such a case, and that the landlords were entitled to remain in. I there said this:

> 'Mr Romer argued very forcibly to us that though the policy were clear yet the Courts ought not to give effect to it unless they could find words apt in their ordinary meaning to justify them in so doing, and that the case of a landlord getting into possession of premises which under the agreement of tenancy he had a right to enter had not been dealt with by Parliament.'

The argument of Mr Safford may be called the twin brother of that just quoted, put the other way, for he says that s 4 of the Act of 1923 provides that an order for possession shall not be made except in certain specified circumstances, and where, he asks, are there any words in the section dealing with a tenant who is not in possession of the premises but is living somewhere else? Parliament, says Mr Safford, has not dealt with that case. In my opinion it has not done so because it never contemplated the possibility of the tenant living somewhere else. A non-occupying tenant was in my opinion never within the precincts of the Acts, which were dealing only with an occupying tenant who had a right to stay in and not be turned out. This case is to be decided on the principle that the Acts do not apply to a person who is not personally occupying the house and who has no intention of returning to it. I except, of course, such a case as that to which I have already referred – namely, of temporary absence, the best instance of which is that of a sea captain who may be away for months but who intends to return, and whose wife and family occupy the house during his absence ...

For the reasons I have given the Act does not in my opinion apply to protect a tenant who is not in occupation of a house in the sense that the house is his home and to which, although he may be absent for a time, he intends to return. If it were to be held otherwise odd consequences would follow. The appellant in this case has contented himself with living in one house and claiming another. Suppose he had a number of houses. One object of the Acts was to provide as many houses as possible at a moderate rent. A man who does not live in a house and never intends to do so, is, if I may use the expression, withdrawing from circulation that house which was intended for occupation by other people. To treat a man in the position of the appellant as a person entitled to be protected, is completely to misunderstand and misapply the policy of the Acts.

The importance of the test thus enunciated cannot be over-stressed; later cases have done much to explain its operation. For instance, it is now reasonably well established that a 'conditional intention' to reside will not suffice, at any rate if the condition is one which has no real chance of being fulfilled (*Robert Thackray's Estate v Kaye* (1989) 21 HLR 160). This two-fold test (*corpus* and *animus*) has subsequently been refined in later cases, such as in *Brown v Brash and Ambrose* [1948] 2 KB 247.

Brown v Brash and Ambrose

Asquith LJ: The appellants, the defendant landlords, on the appeal rely now on only two of the points set out in a voluminous notice of appeal. (a) The first is that from and after March 9, 1946, when Miss Mould left, the plaintiff had, as a legal result of her action, abandoned possession of the premises and was no longer a statutory tenant. His contractual tenancy having terminated at Christmas, 1945, he no longer had any rights at common law after that date; while the statutory tenancy which then succeeded his contractual one had, it was contended, ended in March, 1946. Hence he had no right to possession or to sue for a trespass committed in January, 1947, the material time. This point relates to the claim in the action. (b)The second, and only other point, relates to the counterclaim, and only arises if contrary to the defendants' first contention the plaintiff still enjoys the protection of the Rent Restriction Acts ...

(Having reviewed the relevant authorities, Asquith LJ continued:)

We are of opinion that a 'non-occupying' tenant *prima facie* forfeits his status as a statutory tenant. But what is meant by 'non-occupying'? The term clearly cannot cover every tenant who, for however short a time, or however necessary a purpose, or with whatever intention as regards returning, absents himself from the demised premises. To retain possession or occupation for the purpose of retaining protection the tenant cannot be compelled to spend twenty-four hours in all weathers under his own roof for three hundred and sixty-five days in the year. Clearly, for instance, the tenant of a London house who spends his week-ends in the country or his long vacation in Scotland does not necessarily cease to be in occupation. Nevertheless, absence may be sufficiently prolonged or unintermittent to compel the inference, *prima facie*, of a cesser of possession or occupation. The question is one of fact and of degree. Assume an absence sufficiently prolonged to have this effect: the legal result seems to us to be as follows:

(1) The onus is then on the tenant to repel the presumption that his possession has ceased.

(2) In order to repel it he must at all events establish a *de facto* intention on his part to return after his absence.

(3) But we are of opinion that neither in principle nor on the authorities can this be enough. To suppose that he can absent himself for five or ten years or more and retain possession and his protected status simply by proving an inward intention to return after so protracted an absence would be to frustrate the spirit and policy of the Acts, as affirmed in *Keeves v Dean* and *Skinner v Geary*.

(4) Notwithstanding an absence so protracted the authorities suggest that its effect may be averted if he couples and clothes his inward intention with some formal, outward, and visible sign of it; that is, installs in the premises some caretaker or representative, be it a relative or not, with the status of a licensee and with the function of preserving the premises for his own ultimate home-coming. There will then, at all-events, be someone to profit by the housing accommodation involved, which will not stand empty. It may be that the same result can be secured by leaving on the premises, as a deliberate symbol of continued occupation, furniture; though we are not clear that this was necessary to the decision in *Brown v Draper* [1944]. Apart from authority, in principle, possession in fact (for it is with possession in fact and not with possession in law that we are here concerned) requires not

merely an 'animus possidendi' but a 'corpus possessionis', namely, some visible state of affairs in which the animus possidendi finds expression.

(5) If the caretaker (to use that term for short) leaves or the furniture is removed from the premises, otherwise than quite temporarily, we are of opinion that the protection, artificially prolonged by their presence, ceases, whether the tenant wills or desires such removal or not. A man's possession of a wild bird, which he keeps in a cage, ceases if it escapes, notwithstanding that his desire to retain possession of it continues and that its escape is contrary thereto. We do not think in this connection that it is open to the plaintiff to rely on the fact of his imprisonment as preventing him from taking steps to assert possession by visible action. The plaintiff, it is true, had not intended to go to prison; he committed intentionally the felonious act which in the events which have happened, landed him there; and thereby put it out of his power to assert possession by visible acts after March 9, 1946. He cannot, in these circumstances, we feel, be in a better position than if his absence and inaction had been voluntary.

Applying these general propositions to the facts of the present case, we hold that the plaintiff ceased to possess the premises or to enjoy the protection of the Acts when Miss Mould and the children left in March, 1946; and that nothing which happened after this date (for instance, his resistance to the Metters and Plant action brought in July, 1946, or the visits of the Mulhollands starting in September of that year) could restore his possession or statutory status. As regards the three items of domestic furniture which on the evidence Miss Mould left behind (apart from questions of *de minimis*) there is no evidence that either the plaintiff or Miss Mould, or indeed anyone, intended these to remain on the premises as symbols of continued possession by the plaintiff. Nor was it either pleaded or argued that the judgment of the county court judge in the previous proceedings (amounting to a decision in September 1946 that the plaintiff had not abandoned possession) was res judicata or created an estoppel in the present case. From March, 1946, on, in our view, the plaintiff lost the protection of the Acts and with it his only rights in respect of the premises. The order for possession and the award of damages for trespass in his favour cannot stand. As regards the counterclaim the defendants, in substance, succeed. It is true that their claim for an order for possession of premises of which they were already in physical occupation is anomalous, but the question in substance is which of these parties is entitled in law to possession, and it follows from our decision on the claim that on this issue the defendants have prevailed. Questions of relative hardship and the reasonableness of making an order for possession for the defendants cannot arise where the tenant by abandoning possession has entirely removed himself from the protective orbit of the Acts. The appeal must be allowed.

The test has now been enshrined in statute (see s 2(3) Rent Act 1977), and Parliament has in effect directed the courts to apply the case law as it has developed since *Skinner v Geary*. The statutory expression is 'occupies the dwellinghouse as his residence'; subletting of the whole of the dwellinghouse will clearly involve a loss of protection for the original tenant, and any unlawful sublessees of his (see *RC Glaze Properties Ltd v Alabdinboni* (1992) 25 HLR 150). The statutory expression, 'occupies as his residence', however, would seem to allow for temporary absences for holidays, hospitalisation, imprisonment, education, and so forth – though some such reasons for absence may be regarded as more meritorious than others.

Indeed, it has been held by the House of Lords that it can cover the residential position of the 'two-home' tenant (see *Hampstead Way Investments v Lewis-Weare* [1985] 1 WLR 164), although the test of 'residence' was held not to be made out on the facts. Thus, the spectre of the sailor with a 'statutory tenancy in every port' (*per* Sir Raymond Evershed MR in *Hallwood Estates v Flack* (1950) 66 TLR (Part 2) 368, 370 remains a possibility (see also [1985] Conv 224, PF Smith)).

Hampstead Way Ltd v Lewis-Weare

Lord Brandon of Oakbrook: ... The material facts, as found by Judge Hill-Smith or appearing from uncontradicted evidence, are these. The flat had two living rooms, two bedrooms and a small boxroom. At some previous date the tenant had been granted by the landlords or their predecessors in title, a lease of the flat for three years from 1 May 1970 to 1 May 1973. In July 1970 the tenant married and his wife came to live with him at the flat. She already had two children by a previous marriage, a girl called Cheha and the stepson. In November 1971 the tenant's wife had a further child by the tenant, a girl called Naomi.

At all material times the tenant was employed as director and general manager of a night-club in the West End of London. In this employment he was required to work during the night five times a week from Tuesday to Saturday. He finished that work at 4 am.

From the time of the marriage until 1978 the tenant, his wife and first the two older children and later Naomi, occupied the flat as their home. In that year the tenant and his wife bought jointly, with the assistance of a mortgage, a house, 113 Erskine Hill, NW11 ('the house'). The house had two living rooms and three bedrooms, one of which was very small and inconvenient. It was situated about half a mile from the flat. A certain amount of furniture was moved from the flat to the house, but the rest remained there, and the family then moved to the house and occupied it as their home. By then Cheha had left and gone to America, so that the persons to be housed were the tenant, his wife, the stepson and Naomi.

After the move the wife and Naomi lived entirely at the house. The tenant on the other hand retained a room in the flat for limited use by him. His routine following the nights on which he worked was to sleep in the one room retained by him in the flat from about 5 am, when he got back to it from his work, until well into the afternoon. He then went to the house and had a light meal there prepared for him by his wife. After that, except on Sundays and Mondays, he went to the night-club and later ate his principal meal of the 24 hours there. The purpose of his sleeping at the flat, rather than at the house, was to avoid disturbing his wife and Naomi when he returned from work at about 5 am. The tenant kept his clothes in his room at the flat and had his mail addressed to him there. He never had any meals at the flat, nor did he entertain any of his friends there.

On Sunday and Monday, when the tenant was off work, he spent his time at the house, sleeping and eating there. In so far as he received and entertained friends, he did so at the house.

While the tenant retained the limited use of one room at the flat as described above, the stepson, who was a self-employed computer programmer and engineer, occupied the rest of the flat for all usual living activities.

The tenant paid all outgoings relating to the house. He also paid the outgoings relating to the flat, including the rent, but excluding the cost of gas, which was paid by the stepson. The telephones at both the house and the flat were rented by the tenant, the telephone accounts were paid by him, and both numbers were shown in the telephone directory as his.

It is not in dispute that the right of the tenant to remain in possession of the flat depends on the application to the particular circumstances of the case of the provisions contained in sections 1 and 2 of the Rent Act 1977 ...

It is common ground in the present case that the flat, when it was first let to the tenant, was let as a separate dwelling-house within the meaning of section 1 of the Rent Act 1977. The result of that is that when the lease for three years expired on 1 May 1973, the tenant became, and remained, so long as he occupied the flat as his residence, the statutory tenant of it within the meaning of section 2(1)(a) of the Rent Act 1977. The question in dispute between the parties is whether, after the move from the flat to the house in 1978, the tenant continued to occupy the flat as his residence. The tenant contends that he did; the landlords contend that he did not.

My Lords, the result of section 2(1)(a) of the Rent Act 1977, together with section 3(2) of the Rent Act 1968, is that the question, whether the tenant continued to occupy the flat as his residence after the move, has to be decided by reference to the case law on the subject which grew up during the period after the coming into force of the Increase of Rent and Mortgage Interest (Restrictions) Act 1920 and before the coming into force of the Rent Act 1968. It follows that, in order to decide the question in dispute, it is necessary to consider some of the relevant authorities forming part of that case law.

My Lords, the case which the tenant sought to make at the trial in the county court was that he occupied two dwelling houses as his residences: one was the house and the other was the flat. As will appear when I come to examine the authorities, there is no principle of law to prevent a person occupying two dwelling houses as his residences at the same time, and being a statutory tenant of either or both. Judge Hill-Smith, however, did not accept the tenant's contention in this respect ...

My Lords, in order to determine this appeal, it is necessary to examine the more important cases decided between 1920 and 1968 on what is meant by the occupation of a dwelling-house by a person as his residence, or, as it is put in many of the cases (without, in my view, any difference of meaning) the occupation of a dwelling-house by a person as his home. It will further be necessary to consider the nature and scope of the Court of Appeal's decision in *Kavanagh v Lyroudias*, and whether it was rightly regarded by the Court of Appeal as applying to, and governing their decision in, the present case.

Until the coming into force of the Rent Act 1968 the principle, that a person could only be a protected tenant of a dwelling-house so long as he occupied it as his home, was one which was not expressly laid down in any of the earlier Rent Acts. It was, rather, one which had been developed by judges as a matter of case law. The leading case on the existence of such a requirement is *Skinner v Geary* [1931] 2 KB 546.

That requirement having been laid down in *Skinner v Geary*, there followed a series of decisions on what was meant by occupation of a dwelling-house by a person as his home. Those decisions all depended on the particular facts of each case, and, as might be expected, are not always easy to reconcile. That being so, I do not consider that it would serve any useful purpose to examine each of such decisions in detail. In view of the terms of section 3(2) of the Rent Act 1968, it seems to me that the only useful course to take is to see to what extent it is possible to derive, from the decisions concerned, any propositions of general application with regard to the qualifications which have to be fulfilled, as to residence or otherwise, in order to create a situation in which a person is occupying a dwelling-house as his home.

Approaching the matter on that basis, it seems to me that the following propositions of general application, relevant to the present case, can be derived from the decisions concerned.

(1) A person may have two dwelling houses, each of which he occupies as his home, so that, if either of them is let to him, his tenancy of it is protected by the Rent Act 1977: *Langford Property Co Ltd v Tureman* [1949] 1 KB 29.

(2) Where a person is a tenant of two different parts of the same house under different lettings by the same landlord, and carries on some of his living activities in one part of the house and the rest of them in the other part, neither tenancy will normally be protected. If, however, the true view of the facts is that there is, in substance, a single combined or composite letting of the two parts of the house as a whole, then the tenancies of both parts together will, or anyhow may, be protected: *Wimbush v Cibulia* [1949] 2 KB 564.

(3) Where a person owns one dwelling-house which he occupies as his home for most of his time, and is at the same time the tenant of another dwelling-house which he only occupies rarely or for limited purposes, it is a question of fact and degree whether he occupies the latter dwelling-house as his second home: *Langford Property Co Ltd v Tureman* [1949] 1 KB 29; *Beck v Scholz* [1953] 1 QB 570. That principle has been followed and applied in cases since 1968: see *Roland House Gardens Ltd v Cravitz* (1974) 29 P&CR 432 and *Regalian Securities Ltd v Sheuer* (1982) 263 EG 973.

I turn now to examine the case of *Kavanagh v Lyroudias* (1984) 269 EG 629, on the authority of which both members of the Court of Appeal in the present case considered themselves bound to give judgment for the landlords. The facts of that case, which were somewhat unusual, were these. The landlord of a dwelling-house, 23 Rutland Street, London SW7, brought an action for possession of it in the West London County Court. His main case was that the tenant of it could not claim the protection of the Rent Acts because he no longer occupied the dwelling-house as his home. The tenant had occupied the next-door house, no 21, from about 1955, and until 1971 that was the only relevant property which he had. He shared it for the most part with a friend, C, although the latter was from time to time away living in the country. C retired from work in about 1973 and took up full-time residence at no 21. C was at that time sufficiently ill to impose on the tenant some responsibility for looking after him. The tenant himself was also anxious to have a bedroom of his own, which he did not have in no 21. In 1973 the landlord of no 21 offered the tenant a lease of no 23, which he also owned, and the tenant accepted the offer gladly. Subsequently the reversions of no 21 and no 23 passed into the hands of different landlords.

The accommodation in no 21 and no 23 was basically the same. Each house had a basement, a ground floor and a first floor. At no 21 the basement was used as a combined kitchen and dining room, the ground floor was used as a living room, and the first floor had a double bedroom and a bathroom. At no 23 the basement contained a gas cooker in working condition, the ground floor was used as a study with a telephone extension from no 21, and the first floor had a bedroom and a bathroom, the latter without any hot water supply. Each house was physically entirely separate. Each house had a garden, but the two gardens were used as one single garden. In this connection the garden gate of no 23 had been blocked-up, but the blocking-up was readily removable if it should be desired to remove it.

During the material period before the action for possession was brought, the tenant had been sleeping for the most part in no 23. He had been keeping his clothes for the most part in no 21, but had some clothes also in no 23. He had been using the bathroom at no 21 to bathe, because of the absence of hot water in the bathroom at no 23. The tenant had been using the living room at no 21 and also the combined kitchen and dining room there, where all his meals were prepared and eaten. He had been using the study at no 23 on occasions when he brought work home from his business at the Greek Embassy. He had never used no 23 for cooking or eating. On one occasion his sister, who was staying for a short time in no 23, baked some cakes there, and on two other occasions she or another member of the tenant's family had stayed at no 23.

On these facts the judge in the county court concluded that the tenant was in occupation of no 23 sufficiently to afford him the protection of the Rent Acts. On an appeal by the landlords the Court of Appeal (Sir John Arnold P and Hollings J) took the view that the judge in the county court had not given any consideration to the question whether no 23 was occupied separately from no 21 as a complete home in itself, and that, if he had done so, he would have found it impossible to answer the question otherwise than in the negative. In these circumstances the Court of Appeal held that the tenant's tenancy of no 23 was not protected, and that the landlords were accordingly entitled to possession of that house.

Your Lordships were invited by counsel for the appellants in the present case to hold that *Kavanagh v Lyroudias*, 269 EG 629 had been wrongly decided. In my opinion it is not necessary for your Lordships to decide that question, because the facts in *Kavanagh v Lyroudias* differ materially from those in the present case. Although the Court of Appeal in *Kavanagh v Lyroudias* considered that the proper question to be asked and answered was whether no 23 was occupied separately from no 21 as a complete home in itself, it seems to me that, on the authorities referred to earlier, there was a further question which needed to be asked and answered. That further question was whether the defendant tenant occupied no. 21 and no 23 as a combined or composite home of the kind contemplated in *Wimbush v Cibulia* [1949] 2 KB 564, bearing in mind that the leases of both houses had originally been granted to the tenant by a person who was the owner of both, and that it was only subsequently that the reversions of the two houses had passed into different hands. If I am right about this, the Court of Appeal in *Kavanagh v Lyroudias* reached their decision by asking and answering only one of the two relevant questions. It does not, however, follow that the decision itself was wrong, for the further question which I consider should have been asked and answered would obviously have been an extremely difficult one, on which it would be wrong to express an opinion without having first heard full argument on it. In fact the point was hardly raised before your Lordships at all.

It is, in my view, essential to bear in mind that all these Rent Act cases turn on their particular facts, and it is seldom helpful to decide one case with one set of facts by reference to another case with a different set of facts. On the view which I have expressed with regard to *Kavanagh v Lyroudias*, 269 EG 629, there is no real parallel between the facts of that case and those of the present case. No 21 and no 23 in the former case were next-door to each other, and were treated by the tenant, for all practical purposes, as one unit of living accommodation, in one half of which he carried out some of his living activities, and in the other half of which he carried out the rest of those activities. By contrast, in the present case, since the house and the flat were half a mile away from each other, they could not possibly be regarded as constituting together a single unit of living accommodation.

That the house and flat together constituted together one unit of living accommodation was nevertheless the conclusion reached by Judge Hill-Smith in the present case. For the reason which I have just given, however, I do not consider that that conclusion can be supported. In my opinion, on the facts of the present case, there is one, and only one, question to be asked and answered in relation to it. That question is whether the tenant occupied the flat as a second home.

My Lords, I set out earlier in detail the very limited use made of the flat by the tenant, and it is unnecessary to rehearse these matters again. If one treats the question as one of fact and degree, as the authorities require that a court should do, it is, in my opinion, impossible to conclude that that limited use of the flat made by the tenant was sufficient to make the flat his second home. The flat was in truth the home, not of the tenant, who slept there on five nights a week and kept his clothes there, but that of the adult stepson, who carried out all an ordinary person's living activities there.

Such cases of genuine 'two-home' tenants are probably rare, but from time to time cases where the 'two-home' test is satisfied arise. For instance, in *Blanway Investments Ltd v Lynch* (1993) 25 HLR 378 the court was prepared to find the residence test fulfilled in the case of a tenant who originally had a home in Chingford, and, at a later stage, near the Essex coast, but occupied the disputed premises as a pied à terre for his business activities in East London.

The 'residence requirement' may be fulfilled by occupation by the tenant's spouse (s 1(6) Matrimonial Homes Act 1983), mistress (*Brown v Brash* (above)), or children (see *Brickfield Properties v Hughes* (1988) 20 HLR 108, criticised at [1988] Conv 300), and may be satisfied by continuing residence of one of two or more joint tenants (see *Lloyd v Sadler* [1978] QB 774). It should be noted that a similar test applies to 'resident landlords' (s 12), and some of the cases under this heading have shown considerable generosity in its interpretation (see for instance *Palmer v McNamara* (1991) 23 HLR 168).

If, however, the tenant ceases to 'reside' in the sense indicated above, the statutory tenancy comes to an end and the landlord can recover possession of the property.

Housing Act 1988 tenancies

Again there is a 'residence requirement', but it is much more stringent than that in the Rent Act 1977. The key section is s 1(1) of the Act which provides:

A tenancy under which a dwellinghouse is let as a separate dwelling is for the purposes of this Act an assured tenancy if and so long as ... (b) the tenant, or as the case may be, at least one of the joint tenants occupies the dwellinghouse as his only or principal home.

There are several important points to note here:

(a) A contractual tenancy, to enjoy assured status, has a residence requirement (a marked distinction from the Rent Act).

(b) The 'only or principal home' test clearly excludes the possibility of statutory protection in both houses of the 'two-home tenant'. If he has two homes, neither will be his 'only home'; the question will be which is his 'principal' home and to that home, to the exclusion of the other, the statutory protection will attach.

(c) Protection is held to attach only 'if and so long as' the residence requirement is satisfied. Cesser of residence will involve forfeiture of statutory protection, and a resumption will probably not revive it (see Martin, Residential Security, p 182).

(d) It will be noted that there is a specific provision for joint tenancy.

Occupation by a spouse of a tenant will still satisfy the residence requirement (see Schedule 17, para 33 amending s 1(6) Matrimonial Homes Act 1983).

If the tenant ceases to 'occupy as his only or principal home', the tenancy forfeits assured status, and can be brought to an end by a notice to quit in the ordinary way. The landlord can then regain possession. Although the courts have accorded a generous interpretation to the expression 'only or principal home' in the public sector (see *Crawley BC v Sawyer*), it does not necessarily mean that this interpretation will be followed in the private sector.

Housing Act 1985 tenancies

Here again there is a residence requirement. The key provision is the 'tenant condition' in s 81. It is only 'at any time when' this condition (*inter alia*) is satisfied that protection will arise:

> The tenant condition is that the tenant is an individual and occupies the dwellinghouse as his only or principal home; or, where the tenancy is a joint tenancy, that each of the joint tenants is an individual and at least one of them occupies the dwellinghouse as his only or principal home.

This provision has been considered by the courts in *Crawley BC v Sawyer* (1988) 20 HLR 98. In that case S, a weekly tenant of a flat owned by Crawley Borough Council, moved out of the flat to cohabit with his girlfriend. His absence seemed so conclusive that the gas and electricity supplies to the flat were cut off, though he seems to have visited the flat occasionally for old times' sake. The Council, believing the premises to have been vacated, served a notice to quit, the object being to determine the periodic tenancy, which the Council now believed to have become insecure. Shortly after that, romance having failed to flourish, S sought to re-occupy the flat claiming that he was still a weekly secure tenant thereof. The Court of Appeal found in his favour, and held that the flat had remained his only or principal home throughout.

This decision has rightly been criticised as over-generous (see [1988] Conv 300 S Bridge).The court seemed to accept the possibility that a tenancy could move in and out of secure status as the tenant occupied or ceased to occupy. Cesser of occupation would cause the tenancy to become insecure, but if the landlord failed to determine the contractual tenancy at that (insecure) stage, full protection would re-attach if the tenant resumed occupation – though not if he had sublet or parted with possession of the entire property: s 93(2). This possibility of the re-emergence of secure status differs from the position in the private sector.

A possible explanation for the bizarre decision in *Crawley v Sawyer* is that, at the time when the notice was served, S's liaison with his girlfriend was more or less at an end, and thus it might be that at that stage, the tenancy had become secure again. However, this rationalisation of the decision is hard to square with the opinion of the court that the tenancy had remained secure throughout.

This case also illustrates the point that if the periodic tenancy becomes insecure by reason of non-occupation, it will still be necessary for the landlord to bring the tenancy to an end by a notice to quit in proper form, as the contractual tenancy will still be continuing.

CHAPTER 7

SECURITY OF TENURE IN THE PRIVATE SECTOR AND SUCCESSION

INTRODUCTION

In this chapter we shall be considering the scheme for security of tenure in the private sector. Both the Rent Act and the Housing Act confer a degree of security of tenure on the tenant, but the extent differs. In general, the security of tenure available to a tenant under the Rent Act is markedly greater than that under the Housing Act 1988. It is thus an essential preliminary to decide whether the tenancy in question is a protected (or statutory) tenancy under the Rent Act – which will generally be the case if the tenancy was created before 15 January 1989 – or is an assured tenancy under the Housing Act 1988 – which will generally be the case if the tenancy was created on or after 15 January 1989.

OUTLINE OF THE PROTECTIVE SCHEMES

The way in which security of tenure is conferred under both statutes is by suspending the landlord's normal right to determine the tenant's tenancy (for instance, by notice to quit in the case of a periodic tenancy, or by expiry in the case of a fixed-term tenancy) and recover possession. In general terms, the landlord's right to determine the contractual tenancy under the Rent Act is rendered irrelevant by a provision that the contractual tenancy is replaced by a 'statutory tenancy' (so long, at any rate, as the tenant remains in residence). The statutory tenancy arises where, immediately before the termination of the tenancy, the tenant was 'the protected tenant of the dwelling-house' (in the case of Rent Act tenancies), or on the coming to an end of a fixed-term assured tenancy, under the Housing Act.

It might be wondered why periodic assured tenancies, if brought to an end by a landlord's notice to quit, do not give rise to a statutory tenancy. The reason is that the Housing Act 1988 operates a rather different mechanism in these cases to the Rent Act, though the end result is broadly similar. The periodic tenancy is an assured tenancy from the outset – but s 5 Housing Act 1988 deprives a landlord's notice to quit of its usual effect of determining the periodic tenancy, and makes it clear that the assured tenancy can only be brought to an end by a court order granted under procedures laid down in the Act itself, which make the existence of certain grounds an essential preliminary to the granting of such an order.

If the tenant is not prepared to give up possession voluntarily, the statutory tenancy arising under either Act can only be brought to an end by the court on the establishment by the landlord of grounds for such a decision. Sometimes these grounds are mandatory; sometimes they are discretionary – that is to say, if the landlord can establish the necessary grounds, the court may (but not must) order possession, taking into account the 'reasonableness' of the possible order of possession in the landlord's favour. (As will be seen, one of the features of the Housing Act 1988 is a shift in emphasis from discretionary to mandatory grounds, so as to reduce the tenant's security of tenure.)

Some of the 'grounds' are common to both the Rent Act and the Housing Act; some are confined to one statutory scheme only.

It should be noted that a statutory tenancy can, in some instances, come to an end without a court order – for instance, if the tenant dies without a qualified successor, or if the tenant gives up the premises voluntarily (though a mere undertaking not to enforce his rights is insufficient – see *Appleton v Aspin* [1988] 1 WLR 410) or if there is a change of use of the premises so as to take the premises out of protection, for example, under the Housing Act, by the tenant ceasing to occupy the dwelling-house as his only or principal home.

The key provisions in the statutes are as follows.

Rent Act 1977

98(1) Subject to this Part of this Act, a court shall not make an order for possession of a dwelling-house which is for the time being let on a protected tenancy or subject to a statutory tenancy unless the court considers it reasonable to make such an order and either–

(a) the court is satisfied that suitable alternative accommodation is available for the tenant or will be available for him when the order in question takes effect; or

(b) the circumstances are as specified in any of the Cases in Part I of Schedule 15 to this Act (Discretionary Grounds).

(2) If, apart from subsection (1) above, the landlord would be entitled to recover possession of a dwelling-house which is for the time being let on or subject to a regulated tenancy, the court shall make an order for possession if the circumstances of the case are as specified in any of the Cases in Part II of Schedule 15 (Mandatory Grounds).

Housing Act 1988

7(1) The court shall not make an order for possession of a dwelling-house let on an assured tenancy except on one or more of the grounds set out in Schedule 2 to this Act ...

(2) ...

(3) If the court is satisfied that any of the grounds in Part I of Schedule 2 to this Act is established, then, subject to subsection (6) below, the court shall make an order for possession (Mandatory grounds).

(4) If the court is satisfied that any of the grounds in Part II of Schedule 2 to this Act is established, then, subject to subsection (6) below, the court shall make an order for possession if it considers it reasonable to do so (Discretionary grounds).

(5) ...

(6) [Provision related to assured fixed-term tenancies]

In the remainder of this chapter, the grounds and procedure for possession under both the Rent Act and the Housing Act will be considered together. There is, however, a preliminary issue which deserves close consideration. The key to protection is the 'statutory tenancy' – which springs from, and arises on the determination of the contractual tenancy. What is the position if that contractual tenancy was itself subject to some vitiating factor, such as mistake or misrepresentation?

As a general principle of the law of contract, a contract induced by misrepresentation is voidable, that is to say, liable to be set aside at the suit of the innocent party. Clearly, if the tenant procures a tenancy by misrepresentation, and the landlord 'avoids' the voidable tenancy thus created, no statutory tenancy can arise on the determination of the contractual tenancy.

But suppose the landlord has not taken steps to 'avoid' the voidable contractual tenancy? One might have thought, on general principles that a voidable tenancy where no steps have been taken to avoid it is a valid tenancy, capable of giving birth to a statutory tenancy. This is not the case, however, as appears from the important decision in *Killick v Roberts* (1991) 23 HLR 564.

Killick v Roberts

Nourse LJ: ... it is clear that the plaintiff, having been induced to enter into the tenancy agreement by the fraud of the defendant, was entitled to have it rescinded. Although it may be unusual, and in a sense contradictory, for a tenancy to be rescinded after it has expired by effluxion of time, I do not doubt that the remedy remains available. The effect of rescission is, so far as practicable, to restore the parties to the position they would have been in had the contract not been made. Moreover, being an equitable remedy, it is sometimes granted only on terms. On either count it may be appropriate for the rights of the parties to be adjusted even though the contract no longer subsists.

What effect did the order for rescission have in this case? In order to answer that question, I must start by supposing, contrary to the true facts, that the order was made at a time when the tenancy was still subsisting. It appears clear that in that state of affairs the right to a statutory tenancy would have perished with the protected tenancy: see *Solle v Butcher* [1950] 1 KB 671, where a subsisting lease of rent-protected premises was rescinded on the ground of a common mistake of fact, the landlord being put on terms to grant the tenant a licence and then a lease of the premises at the full permitted rent. At p 697 Denning LJ said:

'If the plaintiff does not choose to accept the licence or the new lease, he must go out. He will not be entitled to the protection of the Rent Restriction Acts because, the lease being set aside, there will be no initial contractual tenancy from which a statutory tenancy can spring.'

The observations of Asquith LJ in *Haberman v Westminster Permanent Building Society* [1950] 2 KB 294, 301–302, are to much the same effect. It seems probable that a similar view was taken by yet another division of this court in *Peters v Batchelor* (1950) 100 LJ 718. However, the report is very brief and it does not specifically state that the rescission of the lease would necessarily bring to an end the tenant's statutory right to remain in occupation.

Accordingly, where a protected tenancy is rescinded while it is still subsisting the tenant does not become a statutory tenant of the dwelling-house because there is no longer any contractual tenancy from which it can spring. However, Mr Naish submitted that the position is different where the contractual tenancy has expired before it is rescinded. He pointed to the fact that here the plaintiff did not issue her proceedings until about a week after the tenancy agreement had expired, so that the defendant had already become the statutory tenant of the bungalow. He relied on section 2(1)(a) of the Rent Act 1977 ...

Mr Naish then relied on section 98, which provides that the court shall not make an order for possession of a dwelling-house which is for the time being subject to a statutory tenancy, except on familiar grounds which would only have been available to the plaintiff here if she had served a written notice under Case 13. Mr Naish emphasised that a statutory tenant's right of occupation is personal to himself and incapable of transmission to a third party except in the special cases provided for by the Act: see eg, *Keeves v Dean* [1924] 1 KB 685.

Mr Lowry, for the plaintiff, pointed out that on facts such as we have here the defendant's fraud could not have been discovered until after the tenancy had expired. It was only then that the plaintiff could know that the defendant was not going to give up possession and that what he had told her about having another house built for him elsewhere was false. Mr Lowry submitted that it would be an unjustifiable exception to the rule that fraud unravels everything if the statutory tenancy could survive when the protected tenancy could not.

In my judgment the submissions of Mr Lowry are to be preferred. A statutory tenancy cannot arise unless there is a protected tenancy from which it can spring. If the effect of the rescission of the protected tenancy is, so far as practicable, to restore the parties to the position they would have been in had the tenancy not been granted, it would seem to follow that the statutory tenancy ought to come to an end on the rescission of the protected tenancy. Admittedly, the extinction of a statutory right is different from the extinction of a contractual right. In deciding whether there can be an extinction in the first category we must look at the policy of the statute under which the right arises. The policy of the Rent Act 1977 is to protect those who have been contractual tenants. It is not to protect someone who, having been deprived of his contractual tenancy, is adjudged not to have been entitled to occupy the premises in the first place. I therefore see no reason in principle why a statutory tenancy should survive the rescission of a protected tenancy which has already expired. On this approach no distinction is to be made between a rescission ordered on the ground of a fraudulent misrepresentation by the tenant and one ordered, for example, on the ground of a common mistake of fact. But if I was wrong in thinking that no such distinction ought to be made, I would nevertheless hold that it cannot on any footing be the policy of the 1977 Act that a statutory tenancy which has sprung from a protected tenancy obtained by fraud could survive the rescission of the protected tenancy. For these reasons I would decide the first question in favour of the plaintiff ...

I would dismiss this appeal accordingly.

Mustill and Neill LJJ agreed.

It might be thought that the tenant in *Killick v Roberts* was not particularly deserving; he had, as the court pointed out, been guilty of fraud, and in such a case an appeal to the underlying policy of the Act would seem appropriate. But a tenancy might be voidable for misrepresentation in circumstances falling far short of fraud; it is an established principle of the general law of contract that misrepresentations which are negligent or even totally innocent are voidable. It would be a serious step to extend the reasoning in *Killick v Roberts* to such situations. Perhaps it may be that in the case of non-fraudulent misrepresentations, the bar to the creation of a statutory tenancy will only apply if the landlord has taken steps to avoid the voidable contract before the event allegedly giving rise to the tenancy has occurred. *Solle v Butcher* – the case referred to in *Killick v Roberts* – was a case where the tenancy was held voidable for mistake, rather than misrepresentation – but the mistake in that case came to light before the expiry of the contractual tenancy.

Interestingly, s 102 of the Housing Act 1996, has introduced a new ground to the Housing Act 1988 (ground 17) enabling recovery of possession where the grant of the tenancy was induced by a false statement, made knowingly or recklessly.

AVAILABILITY OF SUITABLE ALTERNATIVE ACCOMMODATION

This is a discretionary ground for possession under both the Rent Act and the Housing Act, and thus it is subject to a 'reasonableness' test under both statutes. The relevant provision in the Rent Act is quoted earlier. In the Housing Act it is one of the discretionary grounds for possession (Part II, Schedule 2, ground 9).

Separate criterion of reasonableness

In cases falling under this heading, the court has to be satisfied of the suitability of the proposed alternative accommodation; but the court must also consider the reasonableness of the proposed possession order. If this matter is not considered, the case will be remitted to the county court judge for the issue of reasonableness to be addressed (see *Minchburn v Fernandez* (1986) 19 HLR 29). Though the provision of accommodation by the local housing authority may relieve the judge of the necessity of considering the question of the suitability of the proposed accommodation, the issue of 'reasonableness' of the order still has to be addressed (see *The Trustees of the Dame Margaret Hungerford Charity v Beazeley* (1993) 26 HLR 26). Under this heading, it seems that the court can take into account not only the landlord's motives in seeking the possession order, but also the understandable reluctance of a tenant to leave premises which have been his home for years and to which he may be sentimentally attached. In *Battlespring v Gates* (1993) 11 HLR 15 the tenant, an elderly widow, was offered by her landlord alternative nearby accommodation (at a lower rent) which was in many respects superior to the tenanted accommodation which had been her home for 35 years, and which had very tender and sentimental memories for her. The landlord sought possession to facilitate a profitable sale with vacant possession.

In accordance with precedent, the Court of Appeal declined to interfere with the finding of the county court judge on the issue of reasonableness, which would only be done if it was clear that the judge had misdirected himself.

Another factor which may fall to be considered under this heading is that of the circumstances of the original letting. In *Gladyric v Collinson* (1983) 11 HLR 14 the tenant took a letting of a cottage in the knowledge that the landlord had a planning application pending before the local planning authority. It was known to the tenant that the letting was to be for a short period only. The Court of Appeal took the view that this factor could be taken into account when considering the issue of 'reasonableness' when the landlord sought to regain possession by offering the tenant alternative accommodation. A further factor which might exceptionally bear on the issue of reasonableness is the landlord's inability to undertake necessary repairs, as in the exceptional case of a listed building in *The Trustees of the Dame Margaret Hungerford Charity v Beazeley* (1993) 26 HLR 269.

'Alternative' can be part of the same premises

In *Mykolshyn v Noah* [1971] 1 All ER 48, the Court of Appeal decided that an offer of part of the demised premises (at a reduced rent) can constitute suitable alternative accommodation. In that case the tenant occupied the top floor of a dwelling-house. The tenant was of advanced years and used one of the rooms (which had no gas, no heating, and no electric power) purely for the storage of furniture. The landlord lived on the ground floor and wanted to recover possession of this room for the use as a bedroom for one of his children. Accordingly, he sought (and obtained) possession of it by offering the tenant (at a reduced rent) the tenancy of the remaining rooms on the top floor.

The situation has been described as surprising by Evershed MR in *Wright v Walford* [1955] 1 QB 363, but seems now too well established to be shaken.

The 'suitability' of the proposed accommodation

The statutory provision is that 'the accommodation is reasonably suitable to the needs of the tenant and his family as regards proximity to place of work, and either –

(a) similar as regards rental and extent to the accommodation afforded by dwelling-houses provided in the neighbourhood by any local housing authority for persons whose needs as regards extent are, in the opinion of the court, similar to those of the tenant and of his family; or

(b) reasonably suitable to the means of the tenant and to the needs of the tenant as regards extent and character; and that if any furniture was provided for use under the [previous] tenancy in question, furniture is provided for use in the accommodation which is either similar to that so provided or is reasonably suitable to the needs of the tenant and his family' (Schedule 15 Rent Act 1977; Schedule 2 Housing Act 1988).

In addition, there is a requirement as to the suitability of the proposed alternative accommodation in terms of the security of tenure provided, which will be further considered below.

Relevance of the tenant's life style

In general terms it is the tenant's housing needs which fall to be considered under this heading. In *Hill v Rochard* [1983] 2 All ER 21 the tenants occupied a large period country house with extensive outbuildings. They were offered, as alternative accommodation, a modern detached house in a nearby village. The tenants objected to the proffered accommodation because they liked living in a large country house, where there was room for their numerous pets. Rejecting the tenants' argument, Dunn LJ in the Court of Appeal held that 'needs' meant 'needs for housing', and the question was 'whether the accommodation offered is reasonably suitable for the tenant's housing needs as regards extent and character'.

Relevance of environmental factors

It is clear from the cases that the court should have regard not only to the nature of the property itself, but also the environment of the proposed alternative accommodation. In *Redspring v Francis* [1973] 1 All ER 640 the tenant had for some years occupied a small flat in a house in a quiet residential road. The landlord offered superior alternative accommodation on a main road nearby, next door to a fish and chip shop and adjoining a transport depot. Buckley LJ held that environmental factors could properly be taken into account. (The decision in *Redspring v Francis* was followed in *Dawncar Investments v Plews* (1993) 25 HLR 639.)

The later case of *Siddiqui and another v Rashid* [1980] 3 All ER 184 makes it clear that it is the physical rather than the social environment which has to be considered in this context. In that case the tenant occupied premises in London, though he worked in Luton. The landlord offered him accommodation in Luton, but the tenant argued that the alternative accommodation offered would take him away from his friends, his local mosque and Islamic cultural centre in Regent's Park. Holding the offered alternative accommodation to be suitable, Stephenson LJ said:

> In *Redspring v Francis* ... noise and smell were matters which would directly affect the tenant in the enjoyment of her property, so they could well be said to relate to the character of the property. I cannot think that Parliament intended to include such matters as the society of friends, or cultural interest, in using the language that it did in the particular word 'character' ... To extend the character of the property to cover the two matters on which the defendant relies, namely his friends in London and his mosque and cultural centre, would, in my judgment, be unwarranted.

The court accordingly held that the alternative accommodation offered was suitable.

Needs of the tenant's family

The suitability of the accommodation for the needs of the tenant's family must also be considered. In the public sector case of *Wandsworth LBC v Fadayomi* [1987] 3 All ER 474 the Court of Appeal set aside a possession order granted in favour of the council on the ground that they had not taken into account the suitability of the proposed alternative accommodation to the needs of Mrs Fadayomi, the separated (but co-resident) wife of the tenant.

It is only family members, in the sense in which that term is generally understood within the legislation, whose needs have to be taken into account in this way. In *Kavanagh v Lyroudias* [1985] 1 All ER 560, the court refused to take into account the accommodation needs of the tenant's ailing friend, whom the court declined to regard as a member of the 'family' of the tenant, by analogy with the interpretation of 'family' adopted by the House of Lords in the succession case of *Carega Properties SA* (see later p248).

Proximity to place of work

In assessing 'suitability', proximity to place of work for the tenant and his family has to be considered. In *Yewbright Properties Ltd v Stone* (1980) 40 P&CR 402, the tenant was a freelance dress designer. She was the statutory tenant of a maisonette in London SW6. The landlords offered her alternative accommodation in East Dulwich, but the tenant contended that this was unsuitable on the ground of a lack of proximity to her place of work. She carried out some of her work on the premises of her customers, most of whom were in the London SW6 area. Rejecting counsel for the landlords' contention that a 'place of work' could not be an area such as London SW6, the court also rejected the contention that the only matter to be considered was the linear distance from the proposed accommodation to the place of work.

Suitability with regard to security of tenure

It will be noted from the language of Part IV Schedule 15 to the Rent Act that the degree of security of tenure to be enjoyed by the tenant in the proposed alternative accommodation is also relevant. Particular note should be taken in this context of the provision in s 34(1)(c) Housing Act 1988; if the court considers that a new style assured tenancy would not give the tenant adequate security of tenure, the court can direct that the tenancy shall take effect as a protected tenancy, notwithstanding the usual rule that, being created after 15 January 1989, it would normally be a Housing Act assured tenancy.

Payment of removal expenses

Where an order is made on the ground of suitable alternative accommodation under the Housing Act, provision is made for the payment of the tenant's removal expenses (s 11).

GROUNDS

As explained above, both the Rent Act and the Housing Act make use of the concept of 'grounds' which must be established before the bringing to an end by the court of a tenancy which is covered by the Acts. Some of these grounds are discretionary whilst others are mandatory. Many of these grounds are common to both Acts, and it seems a reasonable inference that where Parliament has re-enacted a 'ground' in unchanged language, it assumes that the case law decided concerning that 'ground' in the earlier legislation will continue to apply to cases decided under the new regime.

Rent Act 1977

SCHEDULE 15

SECTION 98

GROUNDS FOR POSSESSION OF DWELLING-HOUSES LET ON OR SUBJECT TO PROTECTED OR STATUTORY TENANCIES

PART I
Cases in which court may order possession

Case 1

Where any rent lawfully due from the tenant has not been paid, or any obligation of the protected or statutory tenancy which arises under this Act, or–

(a) in the case of a protected tenancy, any other obligation of the tenancy, in so far as is consistent with the provisions of Part VII of this Act, or

(b) in the case of a statutory tenancy, any other obligation of the previous protected tenancy which is applicable to the statutory tenancy,

has been broken or not performed.

Case 2

Where the tenant or any person residing or lodging with him or any sub-tenant of his has been guilty of conduct which is a nuisance or annoyance to adjoining occupiers, or has been convicted of using the dwelling-house or allowing the dwelling-house to be used for immoral or illegal purposes.

Case 3

Where the condition of the dwelling-house has, in the opinion of the court, deteriorated owing to acts of waste by, or the neglect or default of, the tenant or any person residing or lodging with him or any sub-tenant of his and, in the case of any act of waste by, or the neglect or default of, a person lodging with the tenant or a sub-tenant of his, where the court is satisfied that the tenant has not, before the making of the order in question, taken such steps as he ought reasonably to have taken for the removal of the lodger or sub-tenant, as the case may be.

Case 4

Where the condition of any furniture provided for use under the tenancy has, in the opinion of the court, deteriorated owing to ill-treatment by the tenant or any person residing or lodging with him or any sub-tenant of his and, in the case of any ill-treatment by a person lodging with the tenant or a sub-tenant of his, where the court is satisfied that the tenant has not, before the making of the order in question, taken such steps as he ought reasonably to have taken for the removal of the lodger or sub-tenant, as the case may be.

Case 5

Where the tenant has given notice to quit and, in consequence of that notice, the landlord has contracted to sell or let the dwelling-house or has taken any other steps as the result of which he would, in the opinion of the court, be seriously prejudiced if he could not obtain possession.

Case 6

Where, without the consent of the landlord, the tenant has, at any time after–

(a) ...

(b) 22nd March 1973, in the case of a tenancy which became a regulated tenancy by virtue of section 14 of the Counter-Inflation Act 1973;

(bb) the commencement of section 73 of the Housing Act 1980, in the case of a tenancy which became a regulated tenancy by virtue of that section;

(c) 14th August 1974, in the case of a regulated furnished tenancy; or

(d) 8th December 1965, in the case of any other tenancy,

assigned or sublet the whole of the dwelling-house or sublet part of the dwelling-house, the remainder being already sublet.

Case 8

Where the dwelling-house is reasonably required by the landlord for occupation as a residence for some person engaged in his whole-time employment, or in the whole-time employment of some tenant from him or with whom, conditional on housing being provided, a contract for such employment has been entered into, and the tenant was in the employment of the landlord or a former landlord, and the dwelling-house was let to him in consequence of that employment and he has ceased to be in that employment.

Case 9

Where the dwelling-house is reasonably required by the landlord for occupation as a residence for–

(a) himself, or

(b) any son or daughter of his over 18 years of age, or

(c) his father or mother, or

(d) if the dwelling-house is let on or subject to a regulated tenancy, the father or mother of his wife or husband,

and the landlord did not become landlord by purchasing the dwelling-house or any interest therein after–

(i) 7th November 1956, in the case of a tenancy which was then a controlled tenancy;

(ii) 8th March 1973, in the case of tenancy which became a regulated tenant by virtue of section 14 of the Counter-Inflation Act 1973;

(iii) 24th May 1974, in the case of a regulated furnished tenancy; or

(iv) 23rd March 1965, in the case of any other tenancy.

Case 10

Where the court is satisfied that the rent charged by the tenant–

(a) for any sublet part of the dwelling-house which is a dwelling-house let on a protected tenancy or subject to a statutory tenancy is or was in excess of the maximum rent for the time being recoverable for that part, having regard to Part III of this Act, or

(b) for any sublet part of the dwelling-house which is subject to a restricted contract is or was in excess of the maximum (if any) which it is lawful for the lessor, within the meaning of Part V of this Act to require or receive having regard to the provisions of that Part.

PART II
Cases in which court must order possession where dwelling-house subject to regulated tenancy

Case 11

Where a person (in this Case referred to as 'the owner-occupier') who let the dwelling-house on a regulated tenancy had, at any time before the letting, occupied it as his residence and–

(a) not later than the relevant date the landlord gave notice in writing to the tenant that possession might be recovered under this Case, and

(b) the dwelling-house has not, since–

    (i) 22nd March 1973, in the case of a tenancy which became a regulated tenancy by virtue of section 14 of the Counter-Inflation Act 1973;

    (ii) 14th August 1974, in the case of a regulated furnished tenancy; or

    (iii) 8th December 1965, in the case of any other tenancy,

    been let by the owner-occupier on a protected tenancy with respect to which the condition mentioned in paragraph (a) above was not satisfied, and

(c) the court is of the opinion that of the conditions set out in Part V of this Schedule one of those in paragraphs (a) and (c) to (f) is satisfied.

If the court is of the opinion that, notwithstanding that the condition in paragraph (a) or (b) above is not complied with, it is just and equitable to make an order for possession of the dwelling-house, the court may dispense with the requirements of either or both of those paragraphs, as the case may require.

The giving of a notice before 14th August 1974 under section 79 of the Rent Act 1968 shall be treated, in the case of a regulated furnished tenancy, as compliance with paragraph (a) of this Case.

Where the dwelling-house has been let by the owner-occupier on a protected tenancy (in this paragraph referred to as 'the earlier tenancy') granted on or after 16th November 1984 but not later than the end of the period of two months beginning with the commencement of the Rent (Amendment) Act 1985 and either–

(i) the earlier tenancy was granted for a term certain (whether or not to be followed by a further term or to continue thereafter from year to year or some other period) and was during that term a protected shorthold tenancy as defined in section 52 of the Housing Act 1980, or

(ii) the conditions mentioned in paragraphs (a) to (c) of Case 20 were satisfied with respect to the dwelling-house and the earlier tenancy,

then for the purposes of paragraph (b) above the condition in paragraph (a) above is to be treated as having been satisfied with respect to the earlier tenancy.

Case 12

Where the landlord (in this Case referred to as 'the owner') intends to occupy the dwelling-house as his residence at such time as he might retire from regular employment and has let it on a regulated tenancy before he has so retired and–

(a) not later than the relevant date the landlord gave notice in writing to the tenant that possession might be recovered under this Case; and

(b) the dwelling-house has not, since 14th August 1974, been let by the owner on a protected tenancy with respect to which the condition mentioned in paragraph (a) above was not satisfied; and

(c) the court is of the opinion that of the conditions set out in Part V of this Schedule one of those in paragraphs (b) to (e) is satisfied.

If the court is of the opinion that, notwithstanding that the condition in paragraph (a) or (b) above is not complied with, it is just and equitable to make an order for possession of the dwelling-house, the court may dispense with the requirements of either or both of those paragraphs, as the case may require.

Case 13

Where the dwelling-house is let under a tenancy for a term of years certain not exceeding 8 months and–

(a) not later than the relevant date the landlord gave notice in writing to the tenant that possession might be recovered under this Case; and

(b) the dwelling-house was, at some time within the period of 12 months ending on the relevant date, occupied under a right to occupy it for a holiday.

For the purposes of this Case a tenancy shall be treated as being for a term of years certain notwithstanding that it is liable to determination by re-entry or on the happening of any event other than the giving of notice by the landlord to determine the term.

Case 14

Where the dwelling-house is let under a tenancy for a term of years certain not exceeding 12 months and–

(a) not later than the relevant date the landlord gave notice in writing to the tenant that possession might be recovered under this Case; and

(b) at some time within the period of 12 months ending on the relevant date, the dwelling-house was subject to such a tenancy as is referred to in section 8(1) of this Act.

For the purposes of this Case a tenancy shall be treated as being for a term of years certain notwithstanding that it is liable to determination by re-entry or on the happening of any event other than the giving of notice by the landlord to determine the term.

Case 15

Where the dwelling-house is held for the purpose of being available for occupation by a minister of religion as a residence from which to perform the duties of his office and–

(a) not later than the relevant date the tenant was given notice in writing that possession might be recovered under this Case, and

(b) the court is satisfied that the dwelling-house is required for occupation by a minister of religion as such a residence.

Case 16

Where the dwelling-house was at any time occupied by a person under the terms of his employment as a person employed in agriculture, and–

(a) the tenant neither is nor at any time was so employed by the landlord and is not the widow of a person who was so employed, and

(b) not later than the relevant date, the tenant was given notice in writing that possession might be recovered under this Case, and

(c) the court is satisfied that the dwelling-house is required for occupation by a person employed, or to be employed, by the landlord in agriculture.

For the purposes of this Case 'employed', 'employment' and 'agriculture' have the same meanings as in the Agricultural Wages Act 1948.

Case 17

Where proposals for amalgamation, approved for the purposes of a scheme under section 26 of the Agriculture Act 1967, have been carried out and, at the time when the proposals were submitted, the dwelling-house was occupied by a person responsible (whether as owner, tenant, or servant or agent of another) for the control of the farming of any part of the land comprised in the amalgamation and–

(a) after the carrying out of the proposals, the dwelling-house was let on a regulated tenancy otherwise than to, or to the widow of, either a person ceasing to be so responsible as part of the amalgamation or a person who is, or at any time was, employed by the landlord in agriculture, and

(b) not later than the relevant date the tenant was given notice in writing that possession might be recovered under this Case, and

(c) the court is satisfied that the dwelling-house is required for occupation by a person employed, or to be employed, by the landlord in agriculture, and

(d) the proceedings for possession are commenced by the landlord at any time during the period of 5 years beginning with the date on which the proposals for the amalgamation were approved or, if occupation of the dwelling-house after the amalgamation continued in, or was first taken by, a person ceasing to be responsible as mentioned in paragraph (a) above or his widow, during a period expiring 3 years after the date on which the dwelling-house next became unoccupied.

For the purposes of this Case 'employed' and 'agriculture' have the same meanings as in the Agricultural Wages Act 1948 and 'amalgamation' has the same meaning as in Part II of the Agriculture Act 1967.

Case 18

Where–

(a) the last occupier of the dwelling-house before the relevant date was a person, or the widow of a person, who was at some time during his occupation responsible (whether as owner, tenant, or servant or agent of another) for the control of the farming of land which formed, together with the dwelling-house, an agricultural unit within the meaning of the Agriculture Act 1947, and

(b) the tenant is neither–

   (i) a person, or the widow of a person who is or has at any time been responsible for the control of the farming of any part of the said land, nor

   (ii) a person, or the widow of a person, who is or at any time was employed by the landlord in agriculture, and

(c) the creation of the tenancy was not preceded by the carrying out in connection with any of the said land of an amalgamation approved for the purposes of a scheme under section 26 of the Agriculture Act 1967, and

(d) not later than the relevant date the tenant was given notice in writing that possession might be recovered under this Case, and

(e) the court is satisfied that the dwelling-house is required for occupation either by a person responsible or to be responsible (whether as owner, tenant, or servant or agent of another) for the control of the farming of any part of the said land or by a person employed or to be employed by the landlord in agriculture, and

(f) in a case where the relevant date was before 9th August 1972, the proceedings for possession are commenced by the landlord before the expiry of 5 years from the date on which the occupier referred to in paragraph (a) above went out of occupation.

For the purposes of this Case 'employed' and 'agriculture' have the same meanings as in the Agricultural Wages Act 1948 and 'amalgamation' has the same meaning as in Part II of the Agriculture Act 1967.

Case 19

Where the dwelling-house was let under a protected shorthold tenancy (or is treated under section 55 of the Housing Act 1980 as having been so let) and–

(a) there either has been no grant of a further tenancy of the dwelling-house since the end of the protected shorthold tenancy or, if there was such a grant, it was to a person who immediately before the grant was in possession of the dwelling-house as a protected or statutory tenant, and

(b) the proceedings for possession were commenced after appropriate notice by the landlord to the tenant and not later than 3 months after the expiry of the notice.

A notice is appropriate for this Case if–

(i) it is in writing and states that proceedings for possession under this Case may be brought after its expiry, and

(ii) it expires not earlier than 3 months after it is served nor, if, when it is served, the tenancy is a periodic tenancy, before that periodic tenancy could be brought to an end by a notice to quit served by the landlord on the same day,

(iii) it is served–

   (a) in the period of 3 months immediately preceding the date on which the protected shorthold tenancy comes to an end, or

   (b) if that date has passed, in the period of 3 months immediately preceding any anniversary of that date, and

(iv) in a case where a previous notice has been served by the landlord on the tenant in respect of the dwelling-house, and that notice was an appropriate notice, it is served not earlier than 3 months after the expiry of the previous notice.

Case 20

Where the dwelling-house was let by a person (in this Case referred to as 'the owner') at any time after the commencement of section 67 of the Housing Act 1980 and–

(a) at the time when the owner acquired the dwelling-house he was a member of the regular armed forces of the Crown,

(b) at the relevant date the owner was a member of the regular armed forces of the Crown,

(c) not later than the relevant date the owner gave notice in writing to the tenant that possession might be recovered under this Case,

(d) the dwelling-house has not, since the commencement of section 67 of the Act of 1980 been let by the owner on a protected tenancy with respect to which the condition mentioned in paragraph (c) above was not satisfied, and

(e) the court is of the opinion that–

   (i) the dwelling-house is required as a residence for the owner, or

(ii) of the conditions set out in Part V of this Schedule one of those in paragraphs (c) to (f) is satisfied.

If the court is of the opinion that, notwithstanding that the condition in paragraph (c) or (d) above is not complied with, it is just and equitable to make an order for possession of the dwelling-house, the court may dispense with the requirements of either or both of these paragraphs, as the case may require.

For the purposes of this Case 'regular armed forces of the Crown' has the same meaning as in section 1 of the House of Commons Disqualification Act 1975.

PART III
Provisions applicable to case 9 and Part II of this schedule

Provision for Case 9

1 A court shall not make an order for possession of a dwelling-house by reason only that the circumstances of the case fall within Case 9 in Part I of this Schedule if the court is satisfied that, having regard to all the circumstances of the case, including the question whether other accommodation is available for the landlord or the tenant, greater hardship would be caused by granting the order than by refusing to grant it.

2 ...

PART IV
Suitable alternative accommodation

3 For the purposes of section 98(1)(a) of this Act, a certificate of the local housing authority for the district in which the dwelling-house in question is situated, certifying that the authority will provide suitable alternative accommodation for the tenant by a date specified in the certificate, shall be conclusive evidence that suitable alternative accommodation will be available for him by that date.

4(1) Where no such certificate as is mentioned in paragraph 3 above is produced to the court, accommodation shall be deemed to be suitable for the purposes of section 98(1)(a) of this Act if it consists of either–

(a) premises which are to be let as a separate dwelling such that they will then be let on a protected tenancy [(other than one under which the landlord might recover possession of the dwelling-house under one of the Cases in Part II of this Schedule)], or

(b) premises to be let as a separate dwelling on terms which will, in the opinion of the court, afford to the tenant security of tenure reasonably equivalent to the security afforded by Part VII of this Act in the case of a protected tenancy of a kind mentioned in paragraph (a) above,

and, in the opinion of the court, the accommodation fulfils the relevant conditions as defined in paragraph 5 below.

(2) ...

5(1) For the purposes of paragraph 4 above, the relevant conditions are that the accommodation is reasonably suitable to the needs of the tenant and his family as regards proximity to place of work, and either–

(a) similar as regards rental and extent to the accommodation afforded by dwelling-houses provided in the neighbourhood by any local housing authority for persons whose needs as regards extent are, in the opinion of the court, similar to those of the tenant and of his family; or

(b) reasonably suitable to the means of the tenant and to the needs of the tenant and his family as regards extent and character; and that if any furniture was provided for use under the protected or statutory tenancy in question, furniture is provided for use in the accommodation which is either similar to that so provided or is reasonably suitable to the needs of the tenant and his family.

(2) For the purposes of sub-paragraph (1)(a) above, a certificate of a local housing authority stating–

(a) the extent of the accommodation afforded by dwelling-houses provided by the authority to meet the needs of tenants with families of such number as may be specified in the certificate, and

(b) the amount of the rent charged by the authority for dwelling-houses affording accommodation of that extent,

shall be conclusive evidence of the facts so stated.

6   Accommodation shall not be deemed to be suitable to the needs of the tenant and his family if the result of their occupation of the accommodation would be that it would be an overcrowded dwelling-house for the purposes of Part X of the Housing Act 1985.

7 ... 8 ...

PART V
Provisions applying to Cases 11, 12 and 20

1   In this Part of this Schedule–

'mortgage' includes a charge and 'mortgagee' shall be construed accordingly;

'owner' means, in relation to Case 11, the owner-occupier; and

'successor in title' means any person deriving title from the owner, other than a purchaser for value or a person deriving title from a purchaser for value.

2   The conditions referred to in paragraph (c) in each of Cases 11 and 12 and in paragraph (e) (ii) of Case 20 are that–

(a) the dwelling-house is required as a residence for the owner or any member of his family who resided with the owner when he last occupied the dwelling-house as a residence;

(b) the owner has retired from regular employment and requires the dwelling-house as a residence;

(c) the owner has died and the dwelling-house is required as a residence for a member of his family who was residing with him at the time of his death;

(d) the owner has died and the dwelling-house is required by a successor in title as his residence or for the purpose of disposing of it with vacant possession;

(e) the dwelling-house is subject to a mortgage, made by deed and granted before the tenancy, and the mortgagee–

(i) is entitled to exercise a power of sale conferred on him by the mortgage or by section 101 of the Law of Property Act 1925, and

(ii) requires the dwelling-house for the purposes of disposing of it with vacant possession in exercise of that power; and

(f) the dwelling-house is not reasonably suitable to the needs of the owner, having regard to his place of work, and he requires it for the purpose of disposing of it with vacant possession and of using the proceeds of that disposal in acquiring as his residence, a dwelling-house which is more suitable to those needs.

Housing Act 1988

SCHEDULE 2

GROUNDS FOR POSSESSION OF DWELLING-HOUSES
LET ON ASSURED TENANCIES

PART I
Grounds on which court must order possession

Ground 1

Not later than the beginning of the tenancy the landlord gave notice in writing to the tenant that possession might be recovered on this ground or the court is of the opinion that it is just and equitable to dispense with the requirement of notice and (in either case)–

(a) at some time before the beginning of the tenancy, the landlord who is seeking possession or, in the case of joint landlords seeking possession, at least one of them occupied the dwelling-house as his only or principal home; or

(b) the landlord who is seeking possession or, in the case of joint landlords seeking possession, at least one of them requires the dwelling-house as his or his spouse's only or principal home and neither the landlord (or, in the case of joint landlords, any one of them) nor any other person who, as landlord, derived title under the landlord who gave the notice mentioned above acquired the reversion on the tenancy for money or money's worth.

Ground 2

The dwelling-house is subject to a mortgage granted before the beginning of the tenancy and–

(a) the mortgagee is entitled to exercise a power of sale conferred on him by the mortgage or by section 101 of the Law of Property Act 1925; and

(b) the mortgagee requires possession of the dwelling-house for the purpose of disposing of it with vacant possession in exercise of that power; and

(c) either notice was given as mentioned in Ground 1 above or the court is satisfied that it is just and equitable to dispense with the requirement of notice;

and for the purposes of this ground 'Mortgage' includes a charge and 'mortgagee' shall be construed accordingly.

Ground 3

The tenancy is a fixed term tenancy for a term not exceeding eight months and–

(a) not later than the beginning of the tenancy the landlord gave notice in writing to the tenant that possession might be recovered on this ground; and

(b) at some time within the period of twelve months ending with the beginning of the tenancy, the dwelling-house was occupied under a right to occupy it for a holiday.

Ground 4

The tenancy is a fixed term tenancy for a term not exceeding twelve months and–

(a) not later than the beginning of the tenancy the landlord gave notice in writing to the tenant that possession might be recovered on this ground; and

(b) at some time within the period of twelve months ending with the beginning of the tenancy, the dwelling-house was let on a tenancy falling within paragraph 8 of Schedule 1 to this Act.

Ground 5

The dwelling-house is held for the purpose of being available for occupation by a minister of religion as a residence from which to perform the duties of his office and–

(a) not later than the beginning of the tenancy the landlord gave notice in writing to the tenant that possession might be recovered on this ground; and

(b) the court is satisfied that the dwelling-house is required for occupation by a minister of religion as such a residence.

Ground 6

The landlord who is seeking possession or, if that landlord is a registered housing association or charitable housing trust, a superior landlord intends to demolish or reconstruct the whole or a substantial part of the dwelling-house or to carry out substantial works on the dwelling-house or any part thereof or any building of which it forms part and the following conditions are fulfilled–

(1A) the intended work cannot reasonably be carried out without the tenant giving up possession of the dwelling-house because–

    (i) the tenant is not willing to agree to such a variation of the terms of the tenancy as would give such access and other facilities as would permit the intended work to be carried out, or

    (ii) the nature of the intended work is such that no such variation is practicable, or

    (iii) the tenant is not willing to accept an assured tenancy of such part only of the dwelling-house (in this sub-paragraph referred to as 'the reduced part') as would leave in the possession of his landlord so much of the dwelling-house as would be reasonable to enable the intended work to be carried out and, where appropriate, as would give such access and other facilities over the reduced part as would permit the intended work to be carried out, or

    (iv) the nature of the intended work is such that such a tenancy is not practicable; and

(b) either the landlord seeking possession acquired his interest in the dwelling-house before the grant of the tenancy or that interest was in existence at the time of that grant and neither that landlord (or, in the case of joint landlords, any of them) nor any other person who, alone or jointly with others, has acquired that interest since that time acquired it for money or money's worth; and

(c) the assured tenancy on which the dwelling-house is let did not come into being by virtue of any provision of Schedule 1 to the Rent Act 1977, as amended by Part I of Schedule 4 to this Act or, as the case may be, section 4 of the Rent (Agriculture) Act 1976, as amended by Part II of that Schedule.

For the purposes of this ground, if, immediately before the grant of the tenancy, the tenant to whom it was granted or, if it was granted to joint tenants, any of them was the tenant or one of the joint tenants of the dwelling-house concerned under an earlier assured tenancy or, as the case may be, under a tenancy to which Schedule 10 to the Local Government and Housing Act 1989 applied, any reference in paragraph (b) above to the grant of the tenancy is a reference to the grant of that earlier assured tenancy or, as the case may be, the grant of the tenancy to which the said Schedule 10 applied.

For the purposes of this ground 'registered housing association' has the same meaning as in the Housing Associations Act 1985 and 'charitable housing trust' means a housing trust, within the meaning of that Act, which is a charity, within the meaning of the Charities Act 1960.

For the purposes of this ground, every acquisition under Part IV of this Act shall be taken to be an acquisition for money or money's worth; and in any case where–

(i) the tenancy (in this paragraph referred to as 'the current tenancy') was granted to a person (alone or jointly with others) who, immediately before it was granted, was a tenant under a tenancy of a different dwelling-house (in this paragraph referred to as 'the earlier tenancy'), and

(ii) the landlord under the current tenancy is the person who, immediately before that tenancy was granted, was the landlord under the earlier tenancy, and

(iii) the condition in paragraph (b) above could not have been fulfilled with respect to the earlier tenancy by virtue of an acquisition under Part IV of this Act (including one taken to be such an acquisition by virtue of the previous operation of this paragraph),

the acquisition of the landlord's interest under the current tenancy shall be taken to have been under that Part and the landlord shall be taken to have acquired that interest after the grant of the current tenancy.

Ground 7

The tenancy is a periodic tenancy (including a statutory periodic tenancy) which has devolved under the will or intestacy of the former tenant and the proceedings for the recovery of possession are begun not later than twelve months after the death of the former tenant or, if the court so directs, after the date on which, in the opinion of the court, the landlord or, in the case of joint landlords, any one of them became aware of the former tenant's death.

For the purposes of this ground, the acceptance by the landlord of rent from a new tenant after the death of the former tenant shall not be regarded as creating a new periodic tenancy, unless the landlord agrees in writing to a change (as compared with the tenancy before the death) in the amount of the rent, the period of the tenancy, the premises which are let or any other term of the tenancy.

Ground 8

Both at the date of the service of the notice under section 8 of this Act relating to the proceedings for possession and at the date of the hearing–

(a) if rent is payable weekly or fortnightly, at least eight weeks' rent is unpaid;

(b) if rent is payable monthly, at least three months' rent is unpaid;

(c) if rent is payable quarterly, at least one quarter's rent is more than two months in arrears; and

(d) if rent is payable yearly, at least three months' rent is more than three months in arrears;

and for the purpose of this ground 'rent' means rent lawfully due from the tenant.

PART II
Grounds on which court may order possession

Ground 9

Suitable alternative accommodation is available for the tenant or will be available for him when the order for possession takes effect.

Ground 10

Some rent lawfully due from the tenant–

(a) is unpaid on the date on which the proceedings for possession are begun; and

(b) except where subsection (1)(b) of section 8 of this Act applies, was in arrears at the date of the service of the notice under that section relating to those proceedings.

Ground 11

Whether or not any rent is in arrears on the date on which proceedings for possession are begun, the tenant has persistently delayed paying rent which has become lawfully due.

Ground 12

Any obligation of the tenancy (other than one related to the payment of rent) has been broken or not performed.

Ground 13

The condition of the dwelling-house or any of the common parts has deteriorated owing to acts of waste by, or the neglect or default of, the tenant or any other person residing in the dwelling-house and, in the case of an act of waste by, or the neglect or default of, a person lodging with the tenant or a sub-tenant of his, the tenant has not taken such steps as he ought reasonably to have taken for the removal of the lodger or sub-tenant.

For the purposes of this ground, 'common parts' means any part of a building comprising the dwelling-house and any other premises which the tenant is entitled under the terms of the tenancy to use in common with the occupiers of other dwelling-houses in which the landlord has an estate or interest.

Ground 14

The tenant or a person residing in or visiting the dwelling-house–

(a) has been guilty of conduct causing or likely to cause a nuisance or annoyance to a person residing, visiting or otherwise engaging in a lawful activity in the locality, or

(b) has been convicted of–

    (i) using the dwelling-house or allowing it to be used for immoral or illegal purposes, or

    (ii) an arrestable offence committed in, or in the locality of, the dwelling-house.

Ground 14A

The dwelling-house was occupied (whether alone or with others) by a married couple or a couple living together as husband and wife and–

(a) one or both of the partners is a tenant of the dwelling-house,

(b) the landlord who is seeking possession is a registered social landlord or a charitable housing trust,

(c) one partner has left the dwelling-house because of violence or threats of violence by the other towards–

(i) that partner, or

(ii) a member of the family of that partner who was residing with that partner immediately before the partner left, and

(d) the court is satisfied that the partner who has left is unlikely to return.

For the purposes of this ground 'registered social landlord' and 'member of the family' have the same meaning as in Part I of the Housing Act 1996 and 'charitable housing trust' means a housing trust, within the meaning of the Housing Associations Act 1985, which is a charity within the meaning of the Charities Act 1993.

Ground 15

The condition of any furniture provided for use under the tenancy has, in the opinion of the court, deteriorated owing to ill-treatment by the tenant or any other person residing in the dwelling-house and, in the case of ill-treatment by a person lodging with the tenant or by a sub-tenant of his, the tenant has not taken such steps as he ought reasonably to have taken for the removal of the lodger or sub-tenant.

Ground 16

The dwelling-house was let to the tenant in consequence of his employment by the landlord seeking possession or a previous landlord under the tenancy and the tenant has ceased to be in that employment.

Ground 17

The tenant is the person, or one of the persons, to whom the tenancy was granted, and the landlord was induced to grant the tenancy by a false statement made knowingly or recklessly by–

(a) the tenant, or

(b) a person acting at the tenant's instigation.

PART III
Suitable Alternative Accommodation

1 For the purposes of Ground 9 above, a certificate of the local housing authority for the district in which the dwelling-house in question is situated, certifying that the authority will provide suitable alternative accommodation for the tenant by a date specified in the certificate, shall be conclusive evidence that suitable alternative accommodation will be available for him by that date.

2 Where no such certificate as is mentioned in paragraph 1 above is produced to the court, accommodation shall be deemed to be suitable for the purposes of Ground 9 above if it consists of either–

(a) premises which are to be let as a separate dwelling such that they will then be let on an assured tenancy, other than–

(i) a tenancy in respect of which notice is given not later than the beginning of the tenancy that possession might be recovered on any of Grounds 1 to 5 above, or

(ii) an assured shorthold tenancy, within the meaning of Chapter II of Part I of this Act, or

(b) premises to be let as a separate dwelling on terms which will, in the opinion of the court, afford to the tenant security of tenure reasonably equivalent to the security afforded by Chapter I of Part I of this Act in the case of an assured tenancy of a kind mentioned in sub-paragraph (a) above,

and in the opinion of the court, the accommodation fulfils the relevant conditions as defined in paragraph 3 below.

3(1) For the purposes of paragraph 2 above, the relevant conditions are that the accommodation is reasonably suitable to the needs of the tenant and his family as regards proximity to place of work and either–

(a) similar as regards rental and extent to the accommodation afforded in the neighbourhood by any local housing authority for persons whose needs as regards extent are, in the opinion of the court, similar to those of the tenant and of his family; or

(b) reasonably suitable to the means of the tenant and to the needs of the tenant and his family as regards extent and character; and that if any furniture was provided for use under the assured tenancy in question, furniture is provided for use in the accommodation which is either similar to that so provided or is reasonably suitable to the needs of the tenant and his family.

(2) For the purposes of sub-paragraph (1)(a) above, a certificate of a local housing authority stating–

(a) the extent of the accommodation afforded by dwelling-houses provided by the authority to meet the needs of tenants with families or such number as may be specified in the certificate, and

(b) the amount of the rent charged by the authority for dwelling-houses affording accommodation of that extent,

shall be conclusive evidence of the facts so stated.

4 Accommodation shall not be deemed to be suitable to the needs of the tenant and his family if the result of their occupation of the accommodation would be that it would be an overcrowded dwelling-house for the purpose of Part X of the Housing Act 1985.

5 Any document purporting to be a certificate of a local housing authority named therein issued for the purposes of this Part of this Schedule and to be signed by the proper officer of that authority shall be received in evidence and, unless the contrary is shown, shall be deemed to be such a certificate without further proof.

6 In this Part of this Schedule 'local housing authority' and 'district', in relation to such an authority, have the same meaning as in the Housing Act 1985.

PART IV
Notices Relating to Recovery of Possession

7 Any reference in Grounds 1 to 5 in Part I of this Schedule or in the following provisions of this Part to the landlord giving a notice in writing to the tenant is, in the case of joint landlords, a reference to at least one of the joint landlords giving such a notice.

8(1) If, not later than the beginning of a tenancy (in this paragraph referred to as 'the earlier tenancy'), the landlord gives such a notice in writing to the tenant as is mentioned in any of Grounds 1 to 5 in Part I of this Schedule, then, for the purposes of the ground in question and any further application of this paragraph, that notice shall also have effect as if it had been given immediately before the beginning of any later tenancy falling within sub-paragraph (2) below.

(2) Subject to sub-paragraph (3) below, sub-paragraph (1) above applies to a later tenancy–

    (a) which takes effect immediately on the coming to an end of the earlier tenancy, and

    (b) which is granted (or deemed to be granted) to the person who was the tenant under the earlier tenancy immediately before it came to an end; and

    (c) which is of substantially the same dwelling-house as the earlier tenancy.

(3) Sub-paragraph (1) above does not apply in relation to a tenancy if, not later than the beginning of the tenancy, the landlord gave notice in writing to the tenant that the tenancy is not one in respect of which possession can be recovered on the ground in question.

9   Where paragraph 8(1) above has effect in relation to a notice given as mentioned in Ground 1 in Part I of this Schedule, the reference in paragraph (b) of that ground to the reversion on the tenancy is a reference to the reversion on the earlier tenancy and on any later tenancy falling within paragraph 8(2) above.

10   Where paragraph 8(1) above has effect in relation to a notice given as mentioned in Ground 3 or Ground 4 in Part I of this Schedule, any second or subsequent tenancy in relation to which the notice has effect shall be treated for the purpose of that ground as beginning at the beginning of the tenancy in respect of which the notice was actually given.

11   Any reference in Grounds 1 to 5 in Part I of this Schedule to a notice given not later than the beginning of the tenancy is a reference to its being given not later than the day on which the tenancy is entered into and, accordingly, section 45(2) of this Act shall not apply to any such reference.

In the following discussion the various possible grounds as they might arise in particular factual contexts will be set out.

Rent arrears

This is the most common ground alleged. Generally speaking, arrears of rent give rise to only a discretionary ground for possession, but there are circumstances under the Housing Act where substantial arrears of rent give rise to a mandatory ground. This principle, though, applies only to assured tenancies under the Housing Act 1988, and never applies to Rent Act protected or statutory tenancies.

The key provision for the Rent Act is Case 1 (a discretionary ground); under the Housing Act there are interlocking provisions in ground 10 (a discretionary ground relating to straightforward arrears), ground 11, (for persistent late payers – another discretionary ground), and ground 8 (two months arrears – a mandatory ground).

The Rent Act has no provision corresponding to ground 11 to deal with the persistent late payer; thus, if the tenant, though tardy, manages to get his act together so that no rent is unpaid at the time of the issue of proceedings, a Rent Act possession claim will fail. Being a discretionary ground, it is usually concerned with the tenant with a 'bad record' and an isolated breach is unlikely to lead to an immediate order for possession. Indeed, even in the case of substantial arrears, the practice has been for the court to grant a 'suspended order' for possession, conditional on the payment of arrears, under the broad discretion contained in s 100 Rent Act. A parallel provision is contained in s 9 Housing Act 1988.

Ground 8 of the Housing Act opens up a new vista: if the circumstances therein set out arise, the landlord, in the case of an assured tenancy, can point to a mandatory ground for possession. The courts, however, have shown a strict attitude to landlords seeking to rely on this ground. It involves arrears of the requisite amount both at the date of the service of the notice and at the date of the hearing. A landlord who is claiming possession on this ground might be well advised to specify, in his notice seeking possession, other relevant grounds such as grounds 10 and 11, even if they are discretionary in nature; the contents of this notice are regulated by the Housing Act itself.

Housing Act 1988

8(1) The court shall not entertain proceedings for possession of a dwelling-house let on an assured tenancy unless–

    (a) the landlord, or, in the case of joint landlords, at least one of them has served on the tenant a notice in accordance with this section and the proceedings are begun within the time limits stated in the notice in accordance with subsections (3) to (4B) below; or

    (b) the court considers it just and equitable to dispose with the requirement of such a notice.

(2) The court shall not make an order for possession on any of the grounds in Schedule 2 to this Act unless that ground and particulars of it are specified in the notice under this section; but the grounds specified in such a notice may be altered or added to with the leave of the court.

(3) A notice under this section is one in the prescribed form informing the tenant that–

    (a) the landlord intends to begin proceedings for possession of the dwelling-house on one more of the grounds specified in the notice; and

    (b) those proceedings will not begin earlier than a date specified in the notice in accordance with subsections (4) to (4B) below;

    (c) those proceedings will not begin later than twelve months from the date of the service of the notice.

(4) If a notice under this section specifies, in accordance with subsection (3)(a) above, Grounds 14 in Schedule 2 to this Act (whether with or without other grounds), the date specified in the notice as mentioned in subsection (3)(b) above shall not be earlier than the date of service of the notice.

(4A) If a notice under this section specifies in accordance with subsection (3)(a) above, any of Grounds 1, 2, 5 to 7, 9 and 16 in Schedule 2 to this Act (whether without other grounds or with any ground other than Ground 14), the date specified in the notice as mentioned in subsection (3)(b) above shall not be earlier than–

    (a) two months from the date of service of the notice; and

    (b) if the tenancy is a periodic tenancy, the earliest date on which, apart from section 5(1) above, the tenancy could be brought to an end by a notice to quit given by the landlord on the same date as the date of service of the notice under this section.

(4B) In any other case, the date specified in the notice as mentioned in subsection (3)(b) above shall not be earlier than the expiry of the period of two weeks from the date of the service of the notice.

(5) The court may not exercise the power conferred by subsection (1)(b) above if the landlord seeks to recover possession on Ground 8 in Schedule 2 to this Act.

(6) ...

8A (1) Where the ground specified in a notice under section 8 (whether with or without other grounds) is Ground 14A in Schedule 2 to this Act and the partner who has left the dwelling-house as mentioned in that ground is not a tenant of the dwelling-house, the court shall not entertain proceedings for possession of the dwelling-house unless–

(a) the landlord or, in the case of joint landlords, at least one of them has served on the partner who has left a copy of the notice or has taken all reasonable steps to serve a copy of the notice on that partner, or

(b) the court considers it just and equitable to dispense with such requirements as to service.

(2) Where Ground 14A in Schedule 2 to this Act is added to a notice under section 8 with the leave of the court after proceedings for possession are begun and the partner who has left the dwelling-house as mentioned in that ground is not a party to the proceedings, the court shall not continue to entertain the proceedings unless–

(a) the landlord or, in the case of joint landlords, at least one of them has served a notice under subsection (3) below on the partner who has left or has taken all reasonable steps to serve such a notice on that partner, or

(b) the court considers it just and equitable to dispense with the requirement of such a notice.

(3) A notice under this subsection shall–

(a) state that proceedings for the possession of the dwelling-house have begun,

(b) specify the ground or grounds on which possession is being sought, and

(c) give particulars of the ground or grounds.

The operation of this section was neatly illustrated in the important case of *Mountain v Hastings* (1993) 25 HLR 427.

Mountain v Hastings

Ralph Gibson LJ: I would allow this appeal on the ground that the notice was bad. I will consider first the arguments directed to the validity of the notice. I will give my reasons later for holding that the defendant must be permitted to raise that point in this court.

As to the submission that the notice was defective because ground 8 was not specified by the full text of that ground as set out in Schedule 2, I do not decide this issue upon that basis. I prefer the view that the ground in Schedule 2 may validly be 'specified in the notice' as required by Parliament, in words different from those in which the ground is set out in the Schedule, provided that the words used set out fully the substance of the ground so that the notice is adequate to achieve the legislative purpose of the provision. That purpose, in my judgment, is to give to the tenant the information which the provision requires to be given in the notice to enable the tenant to consider what she should do and, with or without advice, to do that which is in her power and which will best protect her against the loss of her home ...

If, with reference to the specification of the ground upon which the landlord intends to begin proceedings for possession, the ground is specified in words which give to the tenant every piece of information which Parliament has said that he shall have and in words which are clear, then, as it seems to me, the legislative purpose of the provision would be satisfied and there would be no effective requirement for the ground to be specified in the very words set out in Schedule 2 unless Parliament has made that requirement.

The word 'specified' takes its particular meaning from the context in which it is used and from the matter to which it is applied. The Shorter Oxford Dictionary gives the first meaning of the word as: 'to speak or make relation of some matter fully or in detail.'

The requirement in section 8(2) is to specify the ground: it is not that the ground be set out as in Schedule 2. I would add that it is also not merely to identify the ground. If the ground is specified in the notice in terms which set out all the necessary information, ie the substance of the ground, it seems to me that the requirement that the ground be specified would be met. I would add that it is difficult to think of any good reason why a person, given the task of settling a form of notice, should choose to use words different from those in which the ground is stated in the Schedule.

The notice must also be in the prescribed form. The regulation by which the form is prescribed requires the form used to be in the form there set out or 'substantially to the same effect'. If the form served is to be completed fully in accordance with the form, it will set out the text of the ground as it appears in Schedule 2 because the form in paragraph 3 says: 'the landlord intends to seek possession on ground(s) ... in Schedule 2 which reads' and Note (3) in the margin says: 'give the full text of each ground which is being relied on.'

The regulation, however, expressly permits the notice to be effective in the prescribed form if it is 'substantially to the same effect', which I take to mean to be showing no difference in substance having regard to the legislative purpose of the provisions as a whole. I, therefore, am not persuaded that there is a statutory requirement that the ground be set out verbatim from the Schedule. I am troubled by the risk that, if the tenant is faced with a set of words which effectively set out the substance of a ground but in markedly different words, the tenant may, if he has access to the words of Schedule 2, be puzzled and troubled by the difference. There is something to be said in favour of the use of the words in which the ground was enacted by Parliament. I do not decide this point, however, because the case can be, and I think should be, decided on the ground that the plaintiff's notice was not 'substantially to the same effect' as that required by the Act and regulations.

Further, on the question of any requirement to state the words of the ground in full as in Schedule 2, it is to be noted that this case does not raise any question as to parts of the text of a particular ground which could properly be considered surplus to the ground upon which the landlord will rely. Examples are one of the alternatives in ground 1 and one or more of the alternatives in ground 6. The point has not been argued. It seems that, if the omitted material can be regarded as irrelevant in the circumstances of the particular case, the omission may not invalidate the notice: see *Tegerdine v Brooks* [1978] 36 P&CR 261. If the omission or inaccuracy was inadvertent, and if it was obvious such a mistake had been made, and what was intended, again the error may not invalidate the notice: see *Morrow v Nadeem* [1986] 1 WLR 1381, *per* Nicholls LJ.

I would hold this notice to be defective because, in my judgment, it did not specify ground 8 by the words: 'at least three months rent is unpaid'. The omitted information is that the ground which must be proved includes the requirement that 'both at the date of the service of the notice ... and the date of the hearing ... at least ... three months rent is unpaid and ... 'rent' means rent lawfully due from the tenant...'

Mr Nance submitted that the description of ground 8 was substantially to the like effect as that required by the prescribed form because the omitted words with reference to rent unpaid at the hearing related to the future and the tenant in fact had all that she needed to know in order to decide what to do. That submission is, I think, unacceptable because the tenant who is three months in arrears might suppose from the plaintiff's notice that the mandatory ground of possession, upon which the court must make an order, was thereby established although he or she might be able, if aware of the significance of it, to pay all or part of the arrears before the date of the hearing and therefore prevent proof of such a mandatory ground. It was not submitted, rightly as I think, that for this purpose it matters whether or not the particular tenant could or would have paid before the hearing so as to be able to prove any specific detriment caused by the deficiency in the notice: see *per* Roskill LJ in *Tegerdine v Brooks* (above) at p 266. The provision of full information as to the terms in which ground 8 is expressed in the Schedule, and in which it must be proved, is, therefore, in my judgment part of that which must be stated if the ground is to be specified and if the notice is to be substantially to the like effect as the notice in the prescribed form.

If I am right so far, the notice upon which the Recorder assumed that the court had jurisdiction under section 8(1) to entertain the proceedings for possession in respect of the ground 8 claim, or that the court could under section 8(2) make an order for possession on ground 8, was in fact not such a notice ...

Mann and Nolan LJJ agreed.

Section 101 of the Housing Act 1996 amended ground 8 of the 1988 Act by the substitution of eight weeks' for 13 weeks' arrears (para (a)) and two months' for three months' (para (b)) arrears.

Other breaches of tenancy obligations

Under both statutes, such breaches give rise to discretionary grounds for possession, under case 1 (Rent Act) or ground 12 (Housing Act). Again, this is a case where a suspended order might be thought appropriate by the court.

Waste or damage to furniture

These are discretionary grounds for possession, set out in cases 3 and 4 of the Rent Act 1977 and in grounds 13 and 15 of the Housing Act 1988. It can apparently include such misconduct as allowing the garden to return to a state of nature (*Holloway v Povey* (1984) 15 HLR 104).

Nuisance or annoyance to neighbours

This is a discretionary ground for possession, set out in Case 2 of the Rent Act 1977 and in Ground 14 of the Housing Act 1988. It will suffice if the 'neighbours' occupy premises which are not physically adjacent, so long as they are affected by the tenant's conduct (see *Cobstone Investments Ltd v Maxim* [1985] QB 14; [1985] Conv 168 (Lyons)).

Sections 148–149 of the Housing Act, 1996, extend ground 14 of the 1988 Act and add a new ground: ground 14A, concerned with domestic violence.

Tied houses

This concerns the situation where a dwelling-house has been let to the tenant in consequence of his employment. Under the Rent Act 1977 (case 8) the landlord had to show, in addition, that he required the dwelling-house for occupation by a new employee. Under the Housing Act (ground 16) it is enough if the landlord can show that the tenant has ceased to be in his employment. In either case, it is a discretionary ground only.

Tenant's notice to quit

Here the position has become extremely complicated, largely as a result of the recent public sector decision of the House of Lords in *London Borough of Hammersmith v Monk* (1992).

At common law, any periodic tenancy can be determined by a written or oral notice to quit, emanating from either the landlord or the tenant. The normal common law rule was that (in the absence of a contrary agreement) the period of notice had to be commensurate with the 'period' of the periodic tenancy (a quarter for a quarterly tenancy, a month for a monthly tenancy, a week for a weekly tenancy). The only exception to this rule was the yearly tenancy, where half a year's notice would suffice.

So far as residential premises are concerned, this rule has now been radically modified by statute; with certain exceptions (not relevant here), a notice to quit any premises let as a dwelling (even for a weekly tenancy) must now be in writing and give a minimum of four weeks. This applies to both a notice by a landlord and a notice by a tenant (s 5 Protection from Eviction Act 1977). We are not concerned here with notices by a landlord; suffice to say that under the Rent Act, although a landlord's notice to quit may terminate a contractual periodic tenancy, the tenant, if remaining in residence, will be safeguarded by the emergence of a statutory tenancy, which can only be brought to an end by a court on 'grounds', the service of a notice to quit by the landlord being unnecessary (s 3(4) Rent Act 1977); a similar rule applies to assured tenancies in the private sector, where it is expressly provided that 'the service by a landlord of a notice to quit shall be of no effect in relation to a periodic assured tenancy' (s 5(1) Housing Act 1988). (If, however, the tenancy ceases to be governed by the appropriate Act, the normal rule applies so that a notice to quit will become effective again to determine the contractual tenancy.)

What we are concerned with here is the effect of a tenant's notice.

The Rent Act 1977

Under this Act, if a contractual tenant gives notice to quit, that will determine his contractual tenancy; but if he remains in occupation, a statutory tenancy will automatically arise. However, the tenant's notice will trigger one of the discretionary grounds for possession. One of the cases in which the court may make an order for possession (if satisfied as to reasonableness) is case 5:

> Where the tenant has given notice to quit, and, in consequence of that notice, the landlord has contracted to sell or let the dwelling-house or has taken any other steps as the result of which he would, in the opinion of the court, be seriously prejudiced if he could not obtain possession.

The obvious purpose of this provision is to protect a landlord against a shilly-shallying tenant; a mere intention to sell on the landlord's part will not suffice (see *Barton v Fincham* [1921] 2 KB 291). The statutory tenancy itself may be determined by a tenant's notice (see s 3(3)) and this may be significant in bringing to an end liabilities for future rent.

There may be a complication in the case of joint tenants. It was noted in *Lloyd v Sadler* [1973] QB 774 that the Rent Act did not deal effectively with issues of joint entitlement. The courts therefore have had to cobble together a set of principles to deal with joint landlords and joint tenants (see eg *Lloyd v Sadler* (above), *Tilling v Whiteman* [1980] AC 1, *Cooper v Tait* (1984) 15 HLR 98).

What is the position if there is a notice to quit by one of two or more joint contractual tenants? Suppose a house is let by L to T1 and T2 as joint tenants, and T1 gives notice to quit? It would seem, by application of the principles developed in *LB of Hammersmith & Fulham v Monk* (see earlier) that the notice (even if T2 knows nothing of it) will be effective to determine the contractual tenancy for both T1 and T2. If, however, T2 remains in residence, then that is enough to give rise to a statutory tenancy (see *Lloyd v Sadler* (above)). The landlord could seek to invoke ground 5 against T2; but this would be subject to the overriding requirement of reasonableness (it is a discretionary ground), and it is probable that a court would be reluctant to grant a possession order against T2 if T2 had not been a party to T1's notice.

The Housing Act 1988

Here, there is no counterpart to the Rent Act statutory tenancy springing up on determination of the contractual periodic tenancy. There is a provision for the creation of a creature called a 'statutory periodic tenancy', but this springs up in the event of the termination of a fixed-term assured tenancy. The Act, in the case of a contractual periodic tenancy, prolongs that tenancy, despite attempts to bring it to an end by the landlord until a court order is obtained.

This means that if the periodic tenancy is terminated in some other way – eg by a valid notice to quit by the tenant – the landlord will be entitled to possession. The provision of the Act rendering ineffective a notice to quit (s 5(1)) is clearly confined in its operation to a landlord's notice.

It also appears that a notice to quit by one of two or more joint tenants will be effective to end the tenancy, as the rule in *LB of Hammersmith & Fulham v*

Monk (infra) is one of general application to all forms of joint tenancies. Probably, s 45(3) does not affect the matter. That subsection provides:

> Where two or more persons jointly constitute either the landlord or the tenant in relation to a tenancy, then, except where this Part of this Act otherwise provides, any reference to the landlord or the tenant is a reference to all the persons who jointly constitute the landlord or the tenant, as the case may require.

The point here is that tenants' notices do not depend for their effectiveness on any provision of the Housing Act, but rather upon the common law principles as enunciated in *LB of Hammersmith and Fulham v Monk*. Thus, there is no statutory 'reference' in this context to a tenant which could bring s 45(3) into play. Even a statutory periodic tenancy is thought by commentators to be terminable by notice by one of the joint tenants (see Arden & Hunter Housing Act 1988 notes to s 5(7)).

There is only one provision of the Act which deals with a tenant's notice – ie s 5(5). This provides that a tenant's notice to quit, if given before the creation (or deemed creation, under s 5(3)(b), for statutory periodic tenancies) of a tenancy shall be of no effect. This is designed to prevent a landlord from making a pre-emptive strike by persuading the tenant to give a notice to quit before his tenancy commences. The object is to ensure that only voluntary notices to quit are effective.

Assignment or sub-letting without consent

Under the Rent Act, this was a discretionary ground for possession (case 6). There is no parallel provision in the Housing Act, since a tenant who sublet the whole of the property would no longer fulfil the residence requirement: a subletting of part, if in breach of covenant, would fall within ground 12.

Desire by landlord to occupy the premises himself

This sort of issue gives rise to a complex series of situations, which fall to be treated differently under the Rent Act and the Housing Act.

The Rent Act

Let us take first of all the case where a landlord wishes to recover possession of the property for occupation by himself or a member of his family. If the landlord has not occupied the property himself at an earlier stage (in which case different issues, discussed below, come into play), the only case available to him is case 9. This applies where the landlord, not being a landlord by purchase, requires the property for occupation by himself or a member of his family (closely defined, and limited to child, parent, or parent-in-law); possession will also only be granted if the 'greater hardship' test can be satisfied. Broadly this test requires the court to undertake a 'balance of hardship test' – ie to consider whether, in the light of the availability of other accommodation for landlord and tenant, greater hardship would be caused by granting the order than by refusing to grant it. The issue of greater hardship is basically one for the trial judge; higher courts are unlikely to interfere with his assessment of hardship unless it is manifestly based on the wrong grounds (as for example, in *Baker v*

McIver (1990) 22 HLR 328 (below). The onus of proving greater hardship would seem to be on the tenant (*Sims v Wilson* [1946] 2 All ER 261). The operation of case 9 (though at the time of these proceedings it was listed in the Act as case 8) can be illustrated from *Thomas v Fryer* [1970] 2 All ER 1.

Thomas v Fryer

Lord Donovan: The tenant, Alice Fryer, a widow aged 60 or 61, has lived in the house with members of her family for over 30 years. She has a controlled tenancy. Possession of the house is now sought by the landlord, Mildred Elizabeth Thomas. She does so pursuant to case 8 of Sch 3 to the Rent Act 1968, which, read with s 10 of the Act allows a court to make a possession order if the, landlord inter alia, reasonably requires the dwelling-house for occupation as a residence for himself, and did not become a landlord by purchasing the dwelling-house or any interest therein after one of two specified dates. In this case the specified date which is applicable is 7th November 1956.

Mrs Thomas became the landlord of this house in the following circumstances. It was owned by her mother, who died on 26th June 1961. In her will she disposed of the house by a residuary gift in these words 'The residue of my Estate I give and bequeath in equal shares unto my four children Barbara, Owen, Geoffrey and Mildred if living at my death ...'

Mildred is the landlord to whom I have already referred. All four children survived their mother. All four were named as executors. The eldest child alone, however, ie Mr Owen Thomas, proved the will on 5th October 1962. Besides the house the Testator left some £4,500 in stocks and shares. After making specific bequests of chattels, and leaving some pecuniary legacies to others, she disposed of the residue in the terms I have already quoted. The residuary gift therefore comprised the house and such of the investments as were not required to meet the legacies ...

Before her mother died, the landlord had told her mother that she would like to have the house. After the mother's funeral the question what should be done with the house arose, and there was a discussion among the four children ...

The landlord said:

> 'Owen asked us what should be done about the house and asked others if they wanted it – they said NO, he asked me; I said YES. Certain amount of effort to persuade me not to have it. But I wanted my own home in this country. Owen was strongest trying to persuade me not to have it; he said it would be better for me to have securities. Eventually all agreed that house should be mine. Nothing said about money on this occasion. Later Owen gave me deeds of house and said I had better see about getting the house transferred. I took deeds to a solicitor. Owen said I should probably have to pay money to make an adjustment, because he wanted to give me securities as well as the house, and we did not know whether this would be more than my share of the estate. Eventually he told me to make out a cheque for £500 to him – I assumed for him and other brother. On another occasion he told me to let my sister have £250, which in course of time I did. I had earlier been to an estate agent at Owen's request and asked him to value house. I obtained valuation – £900. After this Owen gave me the deeds. I took it to a solicitor, told him the house was to belong to me and asked him to do the necessary work. Eventually I also received stocks and shares from mother's estate. Never entered my head that I was "buying" the house from Owen or the family.' ...

The landlord had made an unsuccessful attempt to get possession of the house in 1968. The county court judge who tried that case decided no more than this, that greater hardship would be caused by granting the order than by refusing it. As to this, see the Rent Act 1968, Sch 3, Part III, para 1. He decided no other question.

The present proceedings represent a second attempt by the landlord. The case was heard by his Honour Judge Moylan, sitting at Edmonton County Court, and on 5th June 1969 he made an order for possession in the landlord's favour but postponing its operation for six months. Counsel on behalf of the tenant in the county court took a preliminary objection which the judge disposed of first. It was that the circumstances in which the landlord acquired the house involved the consequence that she could not discharge the onus which was on her of proving that she had become landlord otherwise than by purchasing the house or an interest therein after 7th November 1956. Accordingly, she could not bring herself within case 8 and her application for possession must therefore fail. The judge rejected this contention. His broad reason was this. This was a family arrangement between beneficiaries under the will by which the landlord was allowed to have the house as part of the residue, whilst at the same time making compensatory payments to her fellow residuary legatees in order to achieve equality of benefit. Such a family arrangement was not, he decided, equivalent to becoming a 'landlord by purchasing the dwelling-house or any interest therein' within the meaning of case 8.

In this appeal from that decision, counsel for the tenant, in a strenuous argument, insisted that it was wrong. A family arrangement and a purchase are not, he said, mutually exclusive terms. So much may be conceded. The motive for a transaction does not determine its legal character. Again, no one would dispute that Counsel then went on to say, in effect: 'Here is the house. The landlord was left by will an undivided fourth share in it. She wanted, however, the whole. Her fellow residuary legatees let her have it. She agreed to pay compensatory payments to them, and indeed paid them £750. That was equivalent to the three-quarters interest which they had in it. What is that except the purchase of an interest in the dwelling-house?' Despite the attraction of the argument, I find myself after due consideration unable to accept it. One has to decide what is meant by 'purchasing the dwelling-house' in the context of the Rent Act 1968, and particularly in the context of case 8. This particular provision has a history going back at least to the Rent and Mortgage Interest Restrictions (Amendment) Act 1933, the 1968 Act being a consolidating measure ...

One returns to what the county court judge said was the root question: Would the ordinary and reasonable person call this transaction a purchase and sale of the house? I think he would not. He would call it a domestic arrangement between members of a family for the division of their mother's estate in a manner which did justice to all of them. The landlord, if asked how she got the house would, I think, instinctively reply: 'I got it as my share under my mother's will, although I had to get my brothers and sister to agree, and I made adjusting payments so as to achieve fairness'. I think that is the true view, and that the learned county court judge was therefore entitled to rule as he did on the preliminary point ...

Counsel for the tenant then contended that greater hardship would be caused by granting the order than by refusing the order. On this point the judge went with great care into the relevant circumstances of both parties and decided against the contention This is a finding of fact against which there would ordinarily be no appeal. But it has been argued that it is vitiated because the judge took into account in favour of the landlord evidence which he should have ignored. This was evidence given on her behalf by Dr William Gooddy, a well-known neurologist. He said that the landlord's failure to obtain possession of the house in the proceedings which she brought in 1968 had worried and depressed her ever since; that in consequence she has not been able to keep up with her teaching work, despite her high qualifications. He gave an instance of her failure to complete the marking of certain Cambridge University examination papers; and eventually expressed his opinion thus:

'I am quite sure that her preoccupation with the situation which I have outlined is having an adverse effect on her health. I do not say that the situation is necessarily entirely responsible for her present state of health; but in a person of her age and background, who might anyway suffer from severe depression, her housing problem is damaging her to a serious medical degree. For these reasons, I am quite sure that the landlord is undergoing great hardship on medical grounds. Her general health will, in my opinion, deteriorate quite rapidly, if she is unable to obtain possession of her property. I feel it is most important for the future welfare of this conscientious and valuable teacher that, if her case is reconsidered in a county court, this medical point should be considered when assessing the degrees of hardship likely to be experienced when assessing the degrees of hardship likely to be experienced by the contending parties.'

Counsel for the tenant then said that, if this sort of evidence is to be admitted, where is the line to be drawn? Is it to be contended, for example, that a bad loser will suffer hardship whereas a good loser will not? Is a party to be allowed to say: 'If I lose this case all sorts of things may happen to my state of mind which will cause me hardship?' I recognise the danger that evidence may be given on these lines which could be without real weight, or even be spurious; but the trial judge will normally, I think, be able to recognise truth as distinct from falsehood or exaggeration. In the present case, where it was proved that the health of one of the parties was already suffering, and that her health was likely to deteriorate rapidly if possession were refused, I can see no reason whatever why the judge should not have taken this evidence into account, even though such deterioration had its origin in mental suffering.

In my opinion, therefore, this appeal fails and should be dismissed.

Russell and Megaw LJJ agreed that the appeal should be dismissed.

There is a second possibility under the Rent Act – the ground which might be termed, for convenience, the 'owner-occupiers ground'. It is a common feature that an owner-occupier of a dwelling-house might wish to let it for a period, for instance, during which the owner plans to work abroad. Clearly, if a house can be made available during the owner's absence it makes a modest contribution to the alleviation of the housing shortage, and the presence of a tenant may help to preserve the property. However, to an owner-occupier the situation will only be acceptable if he has the assurance that he will be able to recover possession, either for himself or for a member of his family, on his return. It is this situation which case 11 of the Rent Act seeks to address by providing the owner-occupier with a mandatory ground for possession. There is no issue of greater hardship here (thus distinguishing the situation from that encountered in case 9 above); but in distinction to case 9, the plaintiff landlord has to establish that he has previously been an owner-occupier (not essential for case 9), and there are requirements about the giving of written notice to the tenant, so that at least the tenant has taken the letting with his eyes open.

Prior occupation by the owner-occupier

Much concern was caused by the decision of the Court of Appeal in *Pocock v Steel* [1985] 1 WLR 229 which held that the case was only available to the landlord if he had occupied the dwelling-house immediately before the grant of the tenancy in respect of which possession was sought; thus, if O, an owner-occupier, let a house to T1 and subsequently re-let to T2 without, in the meantime, re-assuming occupation himself, the case would not be available to O who would have to proceed against T2 under the discretionary case 9, where issues of 'greater hardship' would come to play. The situation was rectified by the Rent (Amendment) Act 1985, making it clear that prior occupation at any time was enough to bring the case into play. Further litigation established that the amendment is retrospective (see *Hewitt v Lewis* [1986] 1 WLR 444).

That does not exhaust, however, the complexities of the residence requirements of Case 11. It will be noted that the statutory phrase is occupied as his residence – which presumably means that the authorities on this phrase as applied to statutory tenants (see eg *Skinner v Geary* and *Brown v Brash & Ambrose*) may apply – but this might be thought dubious in view of some of the remarks of Slade LJ in *Mistry v Isidore*; also the possibility of the two-home landlord, by analogy with *Hampstead Way Investments Ltd v Lewis-Weare* will have to be considered.

On the other hand, the test of the landlord's intention as to future residence will appear to be met by an intention to occupy from time to time; the test in the Rent Act does not require the landlord to intend to occupy as his permanent home. This seems clear from *Lipton v Whitworth* (1993) 26 HLR 293.

Lipton v Whitworth

Ralph Gibson LJ: ... The nature of the proceedings appear from the particulars of claim. The plaintiffs claimed possession of a house at Great Totham, Essex, which was let to the defendants for a term of six months from December 18, 1987, thereafter from month to month at £320 per month. The plaintiffs asserted that all things had been done to entitle them to recover possession of the house under Case 11 in Part II of Schedule 15 to the Rent Act 1977, in particular, on the grounds that the house was required as a residence for Mrs Whitworth, one of the plaintiffs (who are joint owners of the property) together with the daughter, Victoria, who was to live with her in the house. There was an alternative claim under Case 9 of Schedule 15 to the Rent Act. The judge ordered that the plaintiffs should recover possession of the house on June 21, 1992 ...

At the hearing, the plaintiffs' case was put on Case 11, paragraph A of Part V of the Schedule, and not upon Case 9. Case 9, which is in Part I of Schedule 15, is governed by section 98(1) of the Act. The relevant circumstances for the purposes of Case 9, are, of course, that the plaintiffs reasonably require the dwelling-house for occupation as a residence for the landlord.

By section 98(3), that case was to be read with paragraph 1, Part III of Schedule 15 which introduces the requirement of proof of greater hardship. By contrast, Case 11 is controlled by section 98(2). That provides that if the landlord would be entitled to recover possession of the dwelling-house, which is for the time being let on or subject to a regulated tenancy, the court shall make an order for possession if the circumstances of the case are as specified in any of the cases in Part II of Schedule 15, which includes Case 11.

The controlling words for the purposes of these proceedings in Case 11 are that the house 'is required as a residence' for the landlord or, putting it shortly, a member of his family.

The judge held that the necessary notice for paragraph (a) of Case 11 had not been served at the correct time, namely before the commencement of the regulated tenancy (see paragraph 2(d) of Part III of Schedule 15) but the defendants were aware of the then stated intention of the plaintiffs to return to the house, and, under Case 11, the judge held that it was just and equitable to dispense with that requirement. Nothing now turns on that matter ...

The judge, as to the question whether the plaintiffs had made out their case under paragraph 2(a) of Part IV of Schedule 15, namely, that 'the dwelling-house is required as a residence for the owner or any member of his family' proceeded as follows:

'That leads me to the fourth point. I am of the view that Mrs Whitworth genuinely has the immediate intention to return and occupy the premises. As I understand it, there is no requirement that she should hold the premises as a permanent residence. Therefore, the fact that she has honestly indicated her ultimate intention to sell does not disqualify her under sub-paragraph (a). Those requirements are therefore satisfied.'

I come now to the sequence of events after judgment. The defendants waited to see whether Mrs Whitworth did return to occupy the house as her residence. According to them, it appeared that after some 20 weeks she had not done so. The house had at once been advertised for sale ...

The applications by the defendants for leave to appeal out of time and to adduce additional evidence were referred by the Registrar to this court. They were listed on October 8, 1993. By that date, it appeared that the plaintiffs had completed the sale of the house. The defendants acknowledged that they could not obtain an order to be put back into occupation; they accepted that they could recover no compensation from the plaintiffs in this court if they succeeded in their appeal; but they sought the setting aside of the order for costs made against them.

At the prompting of the court, and in particular by me, the defendants applied for leave to amend the notice of appeal so as to make it clear that they questioned the judge's decision not only on the basis that Mrs Whitworth had at the time misrepresented her intention, but at the trial misrepresented her intention, but also on the ground that the judge had not directed himself correctly in law as to the meaning of the words 'required as a residence'. Leave was granted. Counsel for the plaintiffs asked for time to consider the point and the applications were adjourned ...

I shall consider first the question whether the judge correctly applied the law and, if he did or did not, whether the evidence for the plaintiffs can properly be held to have made out a case for possession against the defendants under Case 11. The full words in paragraph 2(a) of Part V of Schedule 15 to the 1977 Act are: 'The dwelling-house is required as a residence for the owner and any member of his family who resided with the owner when he last occupied the dwelling-house as a residence.'

These words were previously contained in Case 10 of Part II of Schedule 3 to the Rent Act 1968 and were considered by this court in *Kennealy v Dunne* [1977] 1 QB 837. The decision, for the reasons set out in the judgment of Stephenson LJ, was that the word 'required' in Case 10 could not be construed as importing any objective standard of reasonableness; that it imposed a burden on the landlord to prove no more than that he had a genuine desire and a genuine immediate intention to use the dwelling-house as his residence, or as a residence for members of his family. Accordingly, the judge, in applying a standard of reasonableness, had come to a wrong conclusion and an order for possession should be made.

That case was not primarily concerned with the question as to what is contained in the provision that the landlord must prove not merely that he requires to occupy the dwelling-house, but that he requires it as a residence for himself, etc. That point but in a different context, was considered in *Rowe v Truelove* (1977) 241 EG 533 (CA). It there arose under Case 8 of Schedule 3 to the 1968 Act which is now Case 9 under Schedule 15 to the 1977 Act, and contains the words 'reasonably required by the landlord for occupation as a residence', etc.

Cairns LJ in a judgment with which Scarman LJ and Sir Gordon Willner agreed, said at 537:

> 'What [the county court judge] did mean is quite clearly indicated by the following sentence, where he said:
>
> > "In my judgment if all he establishes is an intention to realise his interest in the premises as soon as he can and to live in the premises temporarily until he is able to do so, he is not entitled to succeed under case 8."
>
> That is the test which the learned judge applied in the latter part of his judgment, and it is one which to my mind is a perfectly apt test. The intention of Case 8 is to enable a landlord to get possession of a dwelling-house when his purpose in doing so is not with a view to a sale of the house, but is with a view to his living there for some reasonable period, definite or indefinite.'

Later, in his judgment (at 537), Cairns LJ said:

> 'Then the [county court] judge said:
>
> > "I have therefore come to the conclusion that although the plaintiffs reasonably and indeed desperately require the flat, they require it to relieve the serious financial difficulties of Mr Rowe, and I cannot find that it is reasonably required by them for occupation as a residence for themselves."
>
> That is a finding of fact which, to my mind, it is quite impossible for this court to say that the learned judge was not entitled to arrive at. It is said by [counsel] that the judge wrongly took into account the element of time in relation to the residence in that flat. That, I think, in the circumstances of this case, was an element which it was proper to take into account. If the learned judge was right in saying that the aim was to get possession of the flat with a view to residing there only up to the time when a sale of it could be brought about, then I do not think that that amounts to requiring the flat for residence within the meaning of the case in the Schedule.'

For the plaintiffs, Mr Lane has pointed out that whether the house is 'required' is to be judged at the time of the hearing: *Kennealy v Dunne* at 850B and *Alexander v Mohamadzadmeh* (1986) 51 P&CR 41. The evidence, therefore, which the defendants adduced to show what Mrs Whitworth did or did not do after the hearing was, he said, irrelevant. Further, on the evidence, the judge was entitled to hold that the plaintiffs had proved that they required the house as a residence for Mrs Whitworth and her daughter and the judge cannot fairly be taken to have misdirected himself as to what the plaintiffs were required to prove.

Mr Lane referred to the decision of this court in *Naish v Curzon* (1984) 17 HLR 220, CA, Oliver and Purchas LJJ, in support of his contention that Case 11 imposes no requirement of permanence or lack of intermittency in the residence by the landlord, and that the intention of Mrs Whitworth accepted by the judge constituted proof that the plaintiffs required the house for occupation as a residence, notwithstanding that the intended period of occupation as a residence might be short.

It is, I think, not surprising that Mr and Mrs Lipton were unable to accept the genuineness of the asserted intention and requirement of the plaintiffs. It was their belief that the plaintiffs required nothing more than to sell the house with vacant possession and to continue to live in their new home in the United States. That, in effect, is what in the end the plaintiffs have achieved. However, for the reasons which follow, it is not possible for this court to uphold the contentions of the defendants either that the evidence of Mrs Whitworth, which the judge accepted, should be rejected as incredible by this court in the light of the new evidence; or that, upon the basis of the evidence which the judge did accept, he was wrong in law to make the order for possession under Case 11.

As to the plaintiff's evidence, she asserted her intention to return to England to live in the house with her daughter. She planned to find work in the north and to sell the house in order to buy another near her family in Manchester. She could not afford to live in the house on her own. She could not say how long she would keep the house. She accepted in cross-examination that the logic of her position pointed to a sale forthwith and the purchase of a house in the north. If the house was vacant, she wanted to live in it.

After the order for possession was made, the plaintiff did move back into the house and she lived in it for some three weeks. The house was put on the market. She says that she was miserable in the house and moved out before it was sold instead of waiting until it was sold. The circumstances reasonably give rise to suspicion in the minds of the defendants. The new evidence in particular raises issues as to the state of the house when possession was given up. The lease contained a detailed covenant as to keeping the interior of the house and the fixtures and fittings, etc, in good clean and tenantable repair and condition. In fairness to Mr and Mrs Lipton, it is right to say that the allegations as to the dirty state of the house and the impact of that state upon Mrs Whitworth, are, in my judgment, unimpressive, having regard to the fact that the plaintiffs, who had professional agents and lawyers acting for them, pursued a claim against the defendants over the condition of the garden. They were awarded £40 out of a claim of £380, but no claim was advanced with reference to the state of the interior of the house. The new evidence, however, does not in my judgment demonstrate that the plaintiff did not at the hearing have the intentions which the judge held that she had. The difference between what she said she intended to do and what she did, can be explained by the simple fact that she changed her mind when she got back into the house because of the circumstances in which she was.

Did the plaintiffs prove that they required the house as a residence for Mrs Whitworth and her daughter? There appeared to me at first to be force in the argument that the plaintiffs could not be held to require the house as a residence for Mrs Whitworth if she only intended to occupy the house until it could be sold. Cairns LJ in *Rowe v Truelove* (at 537) in the passage to which I have referred, said that if the county court judge was right in saying that the aim was to get possession of the flat with a view to residing there only up to the time when a sale of it could be brought about, he did not think that that amounted to requiring the flat for a residence within the meaning of Case 8 under Schedule 3 to the 1968 Act. Although the issue there was as to reasonable requirement, it was not at once obvious that there could be any significant difference between the concept of residence under the present Case 9 and that under Case 11.

I am, however, driven to the conclusion that my first view of this case was wrong and that, on the facts found by the judge, the plaintiffs did prove that they required the house as a residence for Mrs Whitworth and for Victoria and that the judge did not misdirect himself. The purpose of the provisions in Case 11 (as now amended) was to enable a landlord who is living in his own house to be free to take up a post in another part of the country or abroad, and let his home to a tenant secure in the knowledge that, when the job is finished and he wants to return home, he can, on giving the proper notice, come back and resume life in his own home without being confronted with all the difficulties which a landlord who seeks possession under what is now Case 9 has to overcome (see *per* Stephenson LJ in *Kennealy v Dunne* cited by Oliver LJ in *Naish v Curzon*). Since that was the purpose of Case 11, then, as was pointed out in that passage by Stephenson LJ, it explains the apparently deliberate omission of the qualifying adverb 'reasonably'.

It was at the trial only Mrs Whitworth who wanted to return home and resume life in the house: the fact that it was one only of two joint owners who required the house as a residence does not matter (see *Tilling v Whiteman* [1980] AC 1). If such a landlord intends to return home and resume life in his own house he requires the house as a residence. The fact that he does not intend to live there all the time but intermittently only, does not cause him in law not to require the house as his residence (see *Naish v Curzon*). If such a landlord intends to return home and resume life in his own house, he, in my judgment, does not, by reason of the fact that he intends to sell the house as and when he can, thereby cease to require the house as a residence. Such a landlord, on returning from abroad, may plan to move to another part of the country. If he had not let his house, he could move back into occupation, reside there, and sell his house when he has found a new home and, unless he is unusually rich, manage to sell the present house. Such conduct is entirely consistent with occupying his present house as his residence. People usually do reside in their home until they sell it ...

In the present case, Mrs Whitworth's intention was to return to England and to live in the house which was her home before she left it with her husband to go abroad. Her intention was to live there with her daughter while both of them looked for work and another house. The judge was, I think, right to hold that the plaintiffs required the house as a residence for Mrs Whitworth.

For those reasons, the appeal, in my judgment, is rightly dismissed.

Hirst LJ agreed.

The relatively transitory nature of the residence required during the landlord's previous period of occupation, in some of the cases can be seen from the decisions in *Davies v Peterson* (1988) 21 HLR 63, and *Mistry v Isidore* (1990) 22 HLR 221 applying the earlier Court of Appeal decision in *Naish v Curzon* (1984) 17 HLR 220.

Davies v Peterson

Russell LJ: This is an appeal by the defendant/tenant from orders made by His Honour Judge Lipfriend sitting at Westminster County Court on February 19, last. The judge granted to the plaintiff, Mr John Washington Davies, possession of his dwelling-house tenanted by the defendant, Mrs Barbara Peterson, No 12 Tottenhall Road, London N13 ...

In the particulars of claim before the latter judge possession was claimed on three grounds. I can dispose of two of them very readily. Possession was sought on the ground of arrears of rent; the judge considered that that ground was inappropriate for reasons upon which I need not digress. In the alternative possession was sought pursuant to Case 9, to be found in Schedule 15 of the Rent Act 1977, and in the further alternative pursuant to Case 11.

The starting point, as referred to by the judge in his judgment, is section 98 of the 1977 ...

Case 9 under Part I of Schedule 15 is concerned with applications for possession where the dwelling-house is reasonably required by the landlord for occupation as a residence for himself. However, that case is subject to the overriding proviso to be found in Part III, Provisions Applicable to Case 9 ...

In his judgment the learned judge, having disposed of Case 1, considered the position under Case 9. He found under Case 9 that this plaintiff did require to occupy this dwelling-house himself, but he concluded, citing from p 7 of his judgment:

'So far as the question of greater hardship is concerned, I am satisfied that there would be a greater hardship on the tenant if I were to make an order for possession under Case 9 than there would be on the landlord if I were to refuse to do so and accordingly I do not make an order for possession under Case 9.'

There is no cross-appeal in this case and that finding properly remains undisturbed.

The ground upon which the order for possession was made was under Case 11. That is to be distinguished from Case 9 in at least two respects. First, it is not necessary for the court to make a finding that the dwelling is reasonably required as a residence for the owner; secondly, there is no overriding proviso, as there is in Case 9, involving greater hardship.

Case 11 is headed 'Cases in which Court must order possession ...

Case 11 continues in these terms:

'If the court is of the opinion that notwithstanding that the condition in paragraph (a) above' – which related to the requirement that there should be a notice in writing to the tenant that possession might be required – 'is not complied with, it is just and equitable to make an order for possession of the dwelling-house, the court may dispense with the requirements of either or both of those paragraphs as the case may require'.

What happened in this case in relation to the requirement that there should be a notice in writing to the tenant is that when the matter was before the County Court Judge in 1978 there was a specific finding that this landlord had orally told the tenant that he might want to recover possession at the conclusion of the contractual tenancy. That finding was binding upon the parties when the matter came before Judge Lipfriend.

To return to Case 11, it is necessary to look at the paragraphs giving the landlord the right to possession; they are to be found in Part V of Schedule 15. Paragraph 2 of Part V reads:

'The conditions referred to in paragraph (c) in each of Cases 11 and 12 and in paragraph (e) of Case 20, are that–

(a) the dwelling-house is required as a residence for the owner or any member of his family who resided with the owner when he last occupied the dwelling as a residence ...'

It is under that paragraph that the order here was made, the judge having found that the landlord had satisfied him that this dwelling-house was required by the plaintiff as a residence for himself. He rejected the proposition that the plaintiff required it as a residence for any member of his family, in particular his daughter, Miranda, who was a student living in London at the material time.

The point taken here on behalf of the tenant by Miss Lang – and, if I may say so, it was taken with skill, clarity and economy of language – was that on the evidence the judge should not have found that this plaintiff required this house as a residence for himself. The plaintiff's home is in Sierra Leone: he is a lawyer, is a member of Gray's Inn and he has a law practice in Sierra Leone. He told the judge that over the years he had been a frequent visitor to this country. The finding of the judge on this aspect of the case is to be found on p 6 of his judgment.

He said:

'In the case before me the Plaintiff/Landlord said he visited this country every year for the past three years; he came on holiday every summer. He is interested in his property and he wanted occupation of the house in order to stay in this country. He stays a minimum of more than three months. If that be right, there is no doubt that the landlord in this case certainly came and stayed in this country for periods far longer than the periods that the landlord lived in this country in the case of Naish v Curzon.'

That was an authority to which we were referred by Miss Lang; it is reported in (1984) 17 HLR 220, and it was a decision of this court. It is unnecessary to rehearse the facts of that case, because each of these cases, as is pointed out by the leading judgment of Oliver LJ, depend very much on their own facts. Oliver LJ, in the course of his judgment, cited a number of cases in which the courts have decided that tenants remained in occupation of controlled premises regarding them as a residence, even though the residence, in point of time, was not for a substantial period. For example, holiday homes occupied at weekends have been held to be protected. In this appeal, of course, the situation is reversed and we are concerned with whether this plaintiff, as a landlord, has established that the quality of his residence when he was seeking possession was such that he was entitled to possession pursuant to the Act. At the conclusion of his judgment in Naish v Curzon Oliver LJ said this:

'It seems to me that there is nothing in the Schedule which imposes any sort of requirement of permanence or lack of intermittency in the residence which is required by the landlord. The question is whether such residence was intended by this landlord, which is of course a question of fact and upon which the learned judge was entitled to form his own conclusion – as he did, accepting the respondent's evidence in toto.

For my part, it seems to me quite clear that the learned judge was entitled to take the view which he did. In my judgment, he was right in the conclusion at which he arrived on the evidence before him. I think the evidence was sufficient to establish the necessary requirement of residence for the landlord, albeit it was no doubt residence which was intermittent, or at times when the landlord was able to take advantage of it by reason of his presence here.'

Miss Lang criticises the finding of the learned judge by submitting that he did not, in terms in his judgment, spell out all the circumstances of this case before arriving at the conclusion that the landlord had satisfied the test required by the provisions to which I have made reference. There was, however, no suggestion which found favour with the judge that this plaintiff wanted the premises for any commercial purposes. He said he wanted it – and the judge seems to have accepted his evidence on this point – so that from time to time he could use it himself, particularly having regard to the presence of his daughter in this city. Unless that finding could be regarded in this court as a perverse finding which had no warrant from the facts as disclosed in the case, in my judgment this court should be very slow indeed to interfere with the finding made by the judge. In this case, over a period of three or four days, the judge must have had the flavour of this case and decided, as he was entitled to decide, in favour of the plaintiff that there was a genuine requirement on his part to live in this house as his residence. Once that requirement was satisfied, and once the judge was prepared to find that it was not necessary that there should have been a written communication to the tenant indicating an intention, or a possible intention, to seek possession, the order was inevitable ...

Accordingly, in all these circumstances I would dismiss the tenant's appeal against the order for possession, but I would allow her appeal in relation to her counterclaim and set-off to the extent that I have indicated, by increasing it in the sum of £750. There will therefore have to be an adjustment of the set-off procedure.

Kerr LJ: agreed.

Mistry v Isidore

Slade LJ: ... The plaintiff and his brother, Mr Naresh Mistry, are the assignees of a lease of the building in which the flat is situated. This building has four floors. The ground floor comprises a shop from which the plaintiff and his brother run their business as newsagents and confectioners, and where they also take in clothes for dry cleaning. The three upstairs floors are flats, together known as 188A Lavender Hill.

By a tenancy agreement of May 25, 1987, the first floor flat (which I shall henceforth call 'the flat') was let by the plaintiff to the defendant for three months from May 25, 1987. The agreement described the flat as partly furnished and consisting of two rooms, kitchen, shower unit and shared use of toilet (that is to say, shared with the shop).

Clause 5(8) of this agreement provided as follows:

'The Landlord hereby notifies the Tenant under the Rent Act 1977 that the Landlord is the owner/occupier of the property within the meaning of Case 11 of Part II of Schedule 15 of that Act and that possession of the property may be recovered by the Landlord under the said Case 11 and by virtue of Section 98(2) of the Rent Act 1977 as amended by the Housing Act 1980.'

After the expiration of the three-month period provided for by the tenancy agreement the defendant continued to occupy the flat. It is common ground, however, that any continuing contractual tenancy was determined by a notice to quit served by the plaintiff on the defendant which expired on December 31, 1988, and that thereafter a statutory tenancy subsisted.

In February 1989 the plaintiff issued proceedings seeking an order for recovery of possession of the flat under Case 11. The defendant in due course filed a defence and counterclaim. By his counterclaim he claimed damages for failure on the part of the landlord to keep the flat in repair. The judge at the trial awarded him £250 damages under that claim and there is no cross-appeal in that regard.

In the court below it was common ground that the plaintiff would be entitled to recover possession if and so far as Case 11, set out in Schedule 15 to the Rent Act 1977 (as amended), read together with section 98(2) of that Act, applied ...

The plaintiff in the present case, as I have indicated, relies on Case 11. If a landlord is successfully able to rely on Case 11, he has to satisfy a number of conditions specified in the Case ...

[I]n order to qualify for the benefit of the case the plaintiff had to satisfy the judge that 'at any time before the letting' he had occupied the flat 'as his residence'.

Secondly, the landlord relying on Case 11, has to satisfy the court that one or other of the conditions set out in paragraphs (a) and (c) to (f) of Part V of Schedule 15 is satisfied. In the present case the plaintiff relied on the condition set out in paragraph (a) ...

None of the other conditions of Case 11 being in issue, the judge rightly identified the two questions calling for his consideration as being:

'1. Is the Court satisfied that the flat was occupied by the Plaintiff as his residence at any time before the letting?;

and if so,

2. Is the Court satisfied that the Plaintiff requires the flat for his own use and has a genuine present intention so to occupy it within a reasonable time?'

As to the second question, the defendant's counsel at the trial submitted that the plaintiff's plans for the future, as stated, were at best incomplete, and at worst a sham. However, the judge having summarised the relevant evidence in this context and made his findings, said that he was quite satisfied that the flat was required by the plaintiff as a residence for himself and that he had a genuine present intention so to occupy it within a reasonable time.

There is no appeal from that finding. We are therefore concerned only with the first question falling for the judge's consideration, and decided by him in favour of the plaintiff.

On this appeal, as in the court below, much reliance has been placed by counsel for the defendant on the decision of the House of Lords in *Hampstead Way Investments Ltd v Lewis-Weare & another*, reported in [1985] 1 WLR 164, (1985) 17 HLR 269 ...

As was pointed out in the *Hampstead Way* case by Lord Brandon of Oakbrook, with whose speech all their lordships concurred, the statutory direction to construe the phrase 'if and so long as he occupies the dwelling-house as his residence' appearing in section 2(1)(a) of the 1977 Act, in accordance with section 3(2) of the Rent Act 1968, meant that a tenant could only qualify for protection by virtue of section 2(1)(a) if and so long as he continued to occupy the dwelling-house in question as his home.

Lord Brandon put the matter thus at p 169:

'My Lords, in order to determine this appeal, it is necessary to examine the more important cases decided between 1920 and 1968 on what is meant by the occupation of a dwelling-house by a person as his residence, or, as it is put in many of the cases (without, in my view, any difference of meaning) the occupation of a dwelling-house by a person as his home. It will further be necessary to consider the nature and scope of the Court of Appeal's decision in *Kavanagh v Lyroudias*, and whether it was rightly regarded by the Court of Appeal as applying to, and governing their decision in, the present case.

Until the coming into force of the Rent Act 1968 the principle, that a person could only be a protected tenant of a dwelling-house so long as he occupied it as his home, was one which was not expressly laid down in any of the earlier Rent Acts. It was, rather, one which had been developed by judges as a matter of case law. The leading case on the existence of such a requirement is *Skinner v Geary* [1931] 2 KB 546. That requirement having been laid down in *Skinner v Geary*, there follows a series of decisions on what was meant by occupation of a dwelling-house by a person as his home. Those decisions all depended on the particular facts of each case, and, as might be expected, are not always easy to reconcile. That being so, I do not consider that it would serve any useful purpose to examine each of such decisions in detail. In view of the terms of section 3(2) of the Rent Act 1968, it seems to me that the only useful course to take is to see to what extent it is possible to derive, from the decisions concerned, any propositions of general application with regard to the qualifications which have to be fulfilled, as to residence or otherwise, in order to create a situation in which a person is occupying a dwelling-house as his home.'

As to the qualifications which have to be fulfilled in order to create a situation in which a person is occupying a dwelling-house as his home Lord Brandon, (at p 169) stated the following three propositions (I omit his reference to the authorities):

'(1) A person may have two dwelling houses, each of which he occupies as his home, so that, if either of them is let to him, his tenancy of it is protected by the Rent Act 1977 ...

(2) Where a person is a tenant of two different parts of the same house under different lettings by the same landlord, and carries on some of his living activities in one part of the house and the rest of them in the other part, neither tenancy will normally be protected. If, however, the true view of the facts is that there is, in substance, a single combined or composite letting of the two parts of the house as a whole, then the tenancies of both parts together will, or anyhow may, be protected ...

(3) Where a person owns one dwelling-house which he occupies as his home for most of his time, and is at the same time the tenant of another dwelling-house which he only occupies rarely or for limited purposes, it is a question of fact and degree whether he occupies the latter dwelling-house as his second home ...'

In the court below, as in this court, counsel for the defendant placed strong reliance on the Hampstead Way decision, submitting that the same construction should be applied to the words: 'where a person had at any time before the letting occupied it as his residence' in Case 11 as was applied by the House of Lords to the construction of the words 'if and so long as he occupies the dwelling-house as his residence' in section 2(1)(a). The relevance of this submission, if correct, would be that for Case 11 purposes, as for section 2(1)(a) purposes, the occupation of the dwelling-house would have to be as a home ...

Mr Cakebread's principal submission on this appeal on behalf of the defendant has been that the judge, in dealing with this issue, applied the wrong test. The wording of Case 11, insofar as it relates to occupation as a residence, it is said, is virtually identical to that section 2(1)(a).

'Thus, it is argued, the test to be applied in determining whether a landlord has been resident for Case 11 purposes should be the same as that applicable in determining whether a tenant is resident so as to satisfy the requirements of section 2(1)(a); that is to say, in view of the *Hampstead Way* decision, whether he has been occupying the dwelling-house as his home.'

This being the correct test in Mr Cakebread's submission, it was not open to the judge as a matter of law to hold that the Plaintiff had occupied the flat as his residence during the period February–May 1987, because it was not open to him to hold that the plaintiff during this period had occupied it as his home. A person can be properly said to occupy premises as his home, it was argued only if he performs the usual functions of living in those premises, such as washing, cooking and eating. The judge was bound to look at the quality of the plaintiff's occupation to see whether he occupied the flat as his home. On such examination, it transpires that the plaintiff used it for no more than the limited purpose of sleeping. On an application of the correct test that, it was submitted, was not enough.

We have had the benefit of admirable argument from counsel on both sides, but Mr Cakebread's cogent submissions on this point have not persuaded me that the judge applied the wrong test. As the judge himself said, section 2 refers to a tenant, while Case 11 refers to a landlord. More important still, section 2 refers to a continuous occupation, while Case 11 does not; it merely refers to occupation 'at any time'. Mr Cakebread's submissions are in my judgment inconsistent both with the pattern of the 1977 Act and the decision of this court in *Naish v Curzon*, now reported in (1984) 17 HLR 220. (It appears that the learned judge did not have the full report before him.)

As to the pattern of the Act, Mr Williams, on behalf of the plaintiff, drew our attention to section 12 of the 1977 Act, which removes from protection of the Act certain tenancies where there is a resident landlord. Section 12(4) provides that Schedule 2 to the Act shall have effect for the purpose of supplementing the section. Paragraph 5 of Schedule 2 provides:

'For the purposes of section 12, a person shall be treated as occupying a dwelling-house as his residence if, so far as the nature of the case allows, he fulfils the same conditions as, by virtue of section 2(3) of this Act, are required to be fulfilled by a statutory tenant of a dwelling-house.'

Authority apart, the plain inference seems to me to be that where the legislature intended the line of authority relevant to the construction of section 3(2) of the 1968 Act to be applicable to specific provisions of the 1977 Act, it expressly said so. Significantly, no reference whatever to section 3(2) of the 1968 Act was made either in section 98(2) of the 1977 Act or in Case 11 itself.

Naish v Curzon, unlike *Hampstead Way*, was a case in which the plaintiff was seeking possession of the premises from a tenant in reliance on Case 11. In that case, as in this, the tenant sought to argue that on the facts it was not permissible for the judge to conclude that the quality of the occupation was such as to entitle him to say that it was residence 'as a home'.

Counsel for the landlord however, submitted that Case 11 was not referring to residence 'as a home', but simply to residence. Oliver LJ (with whom Purchas LJ, the only other member of the court, agreed) summarised the argument of the plaintiff's Counsel as follows (at p 1226):

'Nothing there imports, says Mr Hall, the necessity for any degree of permanence or residence 'as a home' and, as a second string to the argument, he points to the 1968 Act (to which I have referred) where one finds, in connection with section 3 of that Act (now section 2 of the 1977 Act) there was specific legislative provision bringing in the construction of the words 'he occupies the dwelling-house as his residence', the connotation which has been accorded to these words by the cases. That is brought in specifically in relation to occupation by the tenant – under section 2 of the present Act, section 3 of the 1968 Act as it then was.

Mr Hall suggests there is nothing in the provisions of section 98 and the Schedule to which we were referred which would import any similar necessity in the case of a landlord. Indeed, the whole purpose of the provision was to enable persons who had premises which might otherwise be let to put them on the market for letting in the safe knowledge that they would be able to recover them if they wanted them for their own occupation. It is nihil ad rem that the occupation for which they wanted them might only be a temporary or intermittent occupation.

He also submits that it is essentially (and this is I think borne out by the cases) a jury question whether the occupation required his occupation 'as a residence' and he submits (and again I think this is right) it all depends upon the circumstances of the case and the 'colour' of the occupation, which necessarily varies according to the property and the use of that property which is available for the particular landlord in the particular circumstances.

As he puts it, the burden, as it were, becomes smaller in inverse ratio to the distance separating the properties.'

Oliver LJ accepted these arguments, saying:

'These are no doubt sound arguments. There is no authority which binds this court one way or another, but to my mind I think it is tolerably clear that the purpose of this legislation was indeed to permit letting to take place without conferring security of tenure in circumstances such as these. It seems to me that there is nothing in the Schedule which imposes any sort of requirement of permanence or lack of intermittency in the residence which is required by the landlord. The question is whether such residence was intended by this landlord, which is of course a question of fact and upon which the learned judge was entitled to form his own conclusion – as he did, accepting the respondent's evidence in toto.

For my part, it seems to me quite clear that the learned judge was entitled to take the view which he did. In my judgment, he was right in the conclusion at which he arrived on the evidence before him. I think the evidence was sufficient to establish the necessary requirement of residence for the landlord, albeit it was no doubt residence which was intermittent, or at times when the landlord was able to take advantage of it by reason of his presence here. Nevertheless, in my judgment, it was "residence" within the terms of the Schedule, and for these reasons, therefore, I would dismiss the appeal.'

In the light of the decision of this court in *Naish v Curzon*, and of the pattern of the 1977 Act to which I have referred, I do not think that the judge can be said to have misdirected himself in any way in the present case in declining to apply precisely the same test to the construction of Case 11 as would be applied in a section 2(1)(a) situation.

In the passage from his speech in the *Hampstead Way* case, which I have already quoted, Lord Brandon, referring to the cases dealing with the protection of a protected tenant of a dwelling-house, indicated that he could see no difference of meaning between the occupation of a dwelling-house by a person as his residence and the occupation of a dwelling-house by a person as his home. However, this was said in the very different context of a continuing occupation by a tenant. As *Naish v Curzon* shows, very different considerations apply where the question at issue is whether a landlord has at any time occupied premises as his residence within the meaning of Case 11. Temporary, or intermittent, residence, which may suffice for the purpose of Case 11, by no means necessarily involves occupation as a home.

The passage in Oliver LJ's judgment in *Naish v Curzon*, in which he said that there was nothing in the Schedule which imposes any sort of requirement of permanency, or lack of intermittency, which is required by the landlord, was recently cited with approval by Russell LJ in *Davies v Peterson* (1988) 21 HLR 63. Mr Cakebread accepted that his primary submission on this appeal is not supported by any authority, and I for my part would reject it.

In the alternative he submitted that, even accepting that occupation as a home is not an essential feature for Case 11 purposes, the learned judge's finding that the plaintiff had occupied the flat as his residence within the meaning of Case 11 was against the weight of the evidence having regard to his findings that:

(1) the plaintiff only slept in the premises five or six nights a week, spending the other night at his brother's home where most of his things were;

(2) he had with him only such clothes as he needed for day-to-day living;

(3) there were no facilities in the flat for washing (which he did at his cousin's premises);

(4) there were no facilities for cooking at the flat.

The learned judge was, I think, entitled, and indeed bound, to consider this issue of residence, both without the constraint of the decisions relating to section 3(2) of the 1968 Act and (in view of *Naish v Curzon*) without the need to satisfy himself that the quality of the residence had been either permanent or non-intermittent. This was perhaps a case which, on its facts, was somewhat near the borderline. If he had decided as a matter of fact that over the relevant period the plaintiff had not occupied the flat as his residence, it may be that this court could not have interfered with his decision. Nevertheless, as Oliver LJ said in *Naish v Curzon*, it is essentially a jury question whether the occupation required is occupation as a residence, and it all depends on the circumstances of the case ...

Having heard and seen all the witnesses, he concluded without doubt that as a matter of fact the flat was, during the period in question, occupied by the plaintiff as his residence. In my judgment, in reaching this conclusion he did not misdirect himself in law and it was a conclusion of fact which he was entitled to reach.

In so concluding, I think it is particularly significant that, as the judge found, during the relevant period the plaintiff had no other home ...

I would accordingly dismiss the appeal.

Glidewell LJ agreed.

Sometimes, however, a more stringent test is applied, as in *Ibie v Trubshaw* (1990) 22 HLR 191, which was not referred to in *Mistry v Isidore*.

Ibie v Trubshaw

Staughton LJ: ... The ground floor is occupied by Mr Sean Brennan, the second defendant, and his sub-tenants. The first floor is occupied by Miss Patricia Cleland and her brother, Mr Stephen Cleland (and, I think a third person), those two being the third and fourth defendants. All of them moved into the house late in 1985 ... Mr Cleland and Miss Cleland were not licensees, they were tenants.

Notices to quit were served on behalf of Mr Ibie on March 8, 1988, so as to expire on April 5, 1988. The tenants have remained in possession, relying on their statutory rights, and this action was brought for possession of the premises by Mr Ibie ...

Mr Ibie relied on Case 11. He pleaded that he had occupied the house as his residence between September 1980 and April 1984 before any part of it was let to any of the present tenants. He said that he wishes now to occupy the house as his residence; and, for purposes of Case 11, he does not have to show that that is reasonable. He had not given notice before the letting to any of the tenants, as required by Case 11, that he was an owner/occupier and would seek to recover on that ground, or might do so. However, before the county court, he invoked the power of the court to make an order for possession on the ground that it was just and equitable to do so, notwithstanding the absence of such a notice at the appropriate time. The judge, on this aspect of the case, was not prepared to find that Mr Ibie had occupied the house as his residence. If he had reached the opposite conclusion, the judge would have had to decide whether he should waive the requirement (as it was put) of a notice ...

I take the point upon which the judge decided the case first. Was it made out that Mr Ibie had occupied the house as his residence? The meaning of those words is dealt with in Hill & Redman's Law of Landlord and Tenant, 18th edition, Volume 2, p C123. That is in the context of section 2 of the Rent Act, but it has not been suggested that the words have any different meaning in the context of the 15th Schedule, Case 11. It is established that, in order to occupy premises as one's residence, one does not have to be there daily throughout the year, to quote from the preface of the 'Service of Matins' in the Book of Common Prayer. One can be absent from time to time. It is a question of fact and degree whether the absence is sufficiently long or continuous as to raise the inference that occupation as a residence has ceased. One can perhaps put it the other way round and say: the question is whether the presence is sufficiently long and continuous as to show that there is genuine occupation as a residence.

Against that view of the law I turn to the evidence ...

The judge dealt with the matter in his judgment, of which we have an excellent note compiled by Mr Sears, although I do not doubt that it is only partially complete because it is virtually impossible to write down everything that judges say. The judge dealt with it in this way:

'The first question is whether Mr Ibie is within Case 11. It is for him to prove that he occupied the house as his residence. I accept that he does not have to have been in occupation immediately before the grant of the tenancy. It is sufficient that he was in occupation for some period prior to those tenancies.

I have heard a considerable amount of evidence about the background to Mr Ibie. Page 84 of the bundle is a document showing that during the period January 1986 to July 1987 Mr Ibie spent more than £12,000 on hotel bills. He was coming to the United Kingdom as a businessman. No one can criticise him for staying at that hotel if it would generate business. However it does give some indication of what he viewed as right and proper before the collapse of the Nigerian economy. It is an indication that Mr Ibie was accustomed to high standards and, of course, he had reached the highest ranks in the Civil Service.

At about the same time as he retired he acquired the place in London with an eye on the longer term, either for occupation by his children as students or in order to generate some income.

He says that he stayed here between 1980 and 1983 but not subsequently. That is by no means fatal to his case. He tells me that Paula Ewensoh was there in the house against his will. She did eventually go. However, having fallen out with her there was no great inducement for him to go and spend any time at this place and at that time Mr Ibie was a man of some standards. I find it difficult to accept that he regarded it as a residence. I do not exclude the possibility that he might have stayed there overnight.

It is not uncommon in cases of this sort for neighbours to give evidence of how they knew the Plaintiff as a former neighbour. I have not had such evidence in this case. It is for Mr Ibie to establish residence. I find that he has failed to do so.'

Then the judge deals with the Case 11 notice. He continues:

'I am considering the position between 1980 and 1983 and in that period his girlfriend had gone in and remained against his will. There is no evidence before me on which I can place any reliance that he used this place as his residence. Therefore Case 11 does not get off the ground.'

It is not wholly clear from that passage in the judgment which of two things the judge was saying. It may be that he took the view that Mr Ibie's evidence was thoroughly unreliable and that he could give no credence to it. There were other grounds upon which he might have reached that conclusion in that Mr Ibie, in his evidence-in-chief, denied that he had any assets here and, in re-examination, said that he had £50,000. Alternatively, the judge may have been saying that the nature and quality of the occupation of the premises described by Mr Ibie could not amount to occupation as his residence.

For my part, I think that the judge was, to some extent, saying each of those things: first, that he did not wholly give credence to Mr Ibie's evidence and, secondly, even if he did accept it, it did not amount, as a matter of fact and degree, to occupation of the house as his residence. I consider that the judge was fully entitled to reach either of those conclusions or, indeed, to decide the case (as I think he did) on both of them in part together. So I do not consider that it is in any way open to this court to arrive at a different conclusion on the point whether Mr Ibie had occupied the house as his residence.

Russell LJ agreed.

(ii) The 'notice' rule

The rationale of this requirement is obvious; the tenant knows from the start that he enjoys minimal security, and cannot claim therefore to be taken by surprise when the landlord re-asserts his right to possession. The court has a discretion to dispense with the exact requirements of the notice provision – if the tenant 'knows the score' from the start, the courts have shown a disinclination to punish the landlord for a failure to comply fully with the notice requirements. Oral communication has sometimes been held to be sufficient, as in *Davies v Peterson* (earlier).

Although some of the cases, such as *Davies v Peterson*, adopt a relatively generous attitude to the landlord in relation to his obligation to give written notice of his intention to rely on this ground, recent authorities suggest that the courts may be taking a more stringent attitude. In *White v Jones* (1993) 26 HLR 477 the Court of Appeal declined to allow a landlord to rely on Case 11 in the absence of written notice, holding that the notion of what was 'just and equitable' allowed the court to take into account a wide range of matters which might be relevant to the issue of hardship to the tenants.

White v Jones

Balcombe LJ: The defendants, Mr and Mrs White, appeal from an order made by His Honour Judge Shawcross in the Portsmouth County Court on August 2, 1993, granting as against them possession of the property 17 Kings Road, Fareham, Hampshire in favour of the plaintiffs, Mr and Mrs Jones ...

(Having reviewed the facts and the relevant authorities and the judgment below, Balcombe LJ continued:)

[I]t is clear that the judge concentrated his attention on the question of the effect of the oral notice, and gave little, if any, attention to the other circumstances of the case, and particularly to the issues of relative hardship. Clearly the question of notice is a relevant factor, but in my judgment it should have been approached in the following manner:

(1) At the time the tenancy was granted in 1972, no notice could have given it the full protection of the Rent Acts.

(2) If at the time a written notice had been given under section 79 of the 1968 Act, the tenancy might have had the very limited protection afforded by sections 77 and 78, viz up to six months' security of tenure if notice to quit had been given after the tenancy had been referred to a rent tribunal to register the rent.

(3) There was no suggestion that either side had any of these provisions in mind in 1972. Both sides then believed that the tenancy was unprotected.

(4) In 1974 Parliament changed the law so as to give full Rent Act protection to the tenancy. To call this a 'statutory windfall' is to use somewhat emotive language to describe a considered act of policy on the part of the legislature.

(5) At the same time Parliament gave the 'owner-occupier' landlord, who had not given a section 79 notice, a six months breathing space in which to give a written notice under Case 11. Mrs Jones, apparently because of her ignorance of the change in the law, did not take advantage of that opportunity. That was not the fault of Mrs White.

In my judgment this case differs significantly from *Fernandes v Parvadin* (1982) *264 EG 49* and *Davies v Peterson* (above). In both those cases the tenancy was granted at a time when the giving of written notice under Case 11 would have told the tenant that he was not obtaining a secure tenure. If the court was satisfied that the same knowledge had been acquired by notice given orally, then it could well be just and equitable to make an order for possession under Case 11. In the present case, at the time of the grant of the tenancy, when the oral notice was given, neither side believed that there was security of tenure and consequently the oral notice was of much less significance.

Accordingly, although I accept that the oral notice given in the present case was a relevant factor, in my judgment it was not entitled to the priority which the judge gave it, outweighing (as he put it) the relatively limited residential requirement of Mrs Jones, the balance of hardship and the balance of '[in]'convenience.

The length of time in which the Whites had lived in this property as their home – 20 years at the date of the hearing, 15 years at the time when they were first warned that possession would be required – and the severe hardship which would be inflicted upon the Whites if they were evicted, as compared to the lesser hardship to the Jones of being unable to use their English property as a pied-à-terre for a maximum of three months of the year, were all relevant factors which had to be taken into account in deciding what was just and equitable. In my judgment these factors clearly outweigh the significance of the 1972 oral notice in the circumstances of the present case.

I would therefore allow the appeal ...

Butler-Sloss and Mann LJJ agreed.

Housing Act 1988

Here, as far as the landlord is concerned, the position is much simpler. What has happened is that a new mandatory ground has been put in place (ground 1) which, in effect embraces the issues covered under the old legislation by cases 9 and 11.

In effect, assuming that the necessary written notice has been given (as to which, see below), the landlord can recover possession on either of the alternative grounds provided for the Rent Act in cases 9 or 11 – that is to say, either on the ground of a desire to occupy himself (even without any prior occupation), or on the ground of a prior occupation (even though the landlord's motive in recovering possession is not owner-occupation, but, for instance, sale). There are, however, some important changes.

First, where the landlord is seeking to rely on the 'prior occupation' leg of ground 1, it would seem a mere transitory occupation will no longer suffice; the statutory expression is 'occupied the dwelling-house as his only or principal home'. Second, at long last, the complexities of joint landlordism are recognised and covered by the statutory wording. Third, when the landlord is seeking possession for occupation by a relative, the extended range of relatives who may benefit is not reproduced from the Rent Act; it is the landlord himself or his spouse alone who may benefit from this provision. If the claimant does however fall within the provision, the issue of 'greater hardship' does not arise under the new ground.

The new Act, like its predecessor in the Rent Act, contains a requirement of written notice; there is also a discretion in the court to dispense with the provision of notice where it is just and equitable so to do and it seems reasonable to infer that the Rent Act cases on this issue will be applicable.

Holiday premises

Holiday lettings fall outside the scope of the protective legislation altogether. Similarly, an off-season holiday let gives rise to a mandatory ground for possession, providing that the tenancy is a fixed-term tenancy for a period not exceeding eight months, and providing that written notice is given that this ground might be relied on by the landlord. In this case there is no discretion in the court to dispense with the requirement of notice. For the consequences of a failure to take the necessary procedural steps to invoke this ground, see *Killick v Roberts*.

Student lettings

Student lettings by educational institutions to their own students fall outside the protective legislation. Similarly, an 'off-season' or 'vacation' fixed term letting of accommodation which is normally student-occupied yields a mandatory ground for possession, both under the Rent Act and the Housing Act (case 14, Rent Act 1977; and ground 4, Housing Act 1988). Again, there is a non-dispensable requirement of written notice.

Reconstruction

This is a new mandatory ground, appearing for the first time in the Housing Act 1988 and thus only applicable to assured tenancies arising under that Act. It is obviously modelled on, and derived from the corresponding provision relating to business tenancies under Part II Landlord and Tenant Act 1954, where a similar ground is available for a landlord seeking to resist a tenant's claim to a new lease of business premises. It may be assumed that the cases decided under the business tenancy code will be applicable by analogy. These authorities insist that more than an idle contemplation of reconstruction must be in the landlord's mind (see *Cunliffe v Goodman* [1950] 2 KB 237, and *Fisher v Taylor's Furnishing Stores* [1956] 2 QB 78). The court will also have to explore whether the landlord's objective can be met in a less drastic way – for instance by granting the tenant an assured tenancy of part only of the premises affected. The tenant, if evicted under this ground, is entitled to be paid his reasonable removal expenses.

Devolution on death of an assured periodic tenancy

This, a new mandatory ground under the Housing Act 1988, deals with a rather complex situation.

As we have seen, there may be a single statutory succession to a spouse or a quasi-spouse to an assured tenancy under the Housing Act. It is not that tenancy arising by succession which we are concerned with here: what this ground is concerned with is the devolution, by the ordinary rules of testator intestate succession of the periodic assured tenancy formerly enjoyed by the deceased tenant. The landlord may have formed an unfavourable view of the financial standing of the person (not the spouse) to whom the tenancy may have devolved by the operation of the rules of succession, and this ground gives him a right to bring the tenancy to an end by giving notice, provided that the landlord acts speedily after the death of the tenant.

SHORTHOLD TENANCIES

For a long time there has been a call, particularly from landlords, for a form of residential tenancy which would escape the shackles of the Rent Act (or more recently, the Housing Act) and which would guarantee the landlord the right to regain possession. The search for this 'untrammelled' tenancy has taken two forms, both of which can be conveniently accommodated under the term 'shorthold'. In many cases of residential tenancies, a landlord may be able to point to the availability of a mandatory ground for possession; but it is not always possible (though nowadays, under the regime of assured tenancies under the Housing Act 1988, it is much easier).

There are basically two types of shortholds: those created under the Rent Act 1977, (as amended) which might conveniently be called 'protected shortholds'; and those under the Housing Act 1988, which are called 'assured shortholds'. After the commencement of the Housing Act 1988 (on 15 January 1989) no further creations of 'protected shortholds' are possible, but those in existence at that date remain. The only type of shorthold which can be created today is the 'assured shorthold'.

These two types of special tenancy will be considered separately – but they share this characteristic, that the landlord is given, in both cases, a cast-iron ground for possession.

Protected shortholds

These did not exist under the Rent Act as consolidated in 1977; their existence was only sanctioned by the Housing Act 1980. The main objective of this statute was to create a level of security of tenure in the public sector; but opportunity was taken to amend the Rent Act 1977 so as to create a new species of tenancy in the private sector, which, it was hoped, would serve the function of satisfying the long-felt yearning for the untrammelled tenant mentioned above, and which might thus lead to a revival of the private rented sector. Landlords, it was thought, able to resort to a form of tenancy which denied security of tenure to their tenants would be more willing to put their property into the private rented market.

The way in which the creation of the protected shorthold was engineered was by the addition of a new 'mandatory' ground for possession (case 19, added by s 55 Housing Act 1980).

There are two issues here:

(a) what type of tenancy qualified as a 'protected shorthold'?

(b) what are the requirements as to service of notices for a protected shorthold?

(a) Type of tenancy

The tenancy had to be for a term certain (ie not a periodic tenancy), and the term certain had to be for at least one year (which was probably too long a period to appeal to many landlords) and not exceeding five years. The tenancy had to be one which could not be terminated by the landlord before the expiry of the fixed term, except in pursuance of a proviso for re-entry in the event of non-payment of rent.

The tenancy had to be one which would qualify for protection under the Rent Act – that is to say it had to be a tenancy 'of a dwelling-house' which is let as a dwelling' in accordance with the usual rules under s 1 Rent Act 1977. To defeat attempts by landlords to deprive existing tenants of their security of tenure, the Act provided that a tenancy could not be a shorthold if it was granted to a tenant who, immediately before the grant, was a protected or statutory tenant of that self-same dwelling-house – but this safeguard could be outflanked if the tenant could be prevailed upon to surrender his existing tenancy, and then, after a short interval, a new 'shorthold' was created in favour of the tenant (see [1989] Conv 98, Bridge, commenting on the rather unusual case of *Dibbs v Campbell* (1988) 20 HLR 374). Also, the tenancy was one which was not capable of assignment.

In the original scheme, the tenancy had to be one which had a 'fair rent' registered in respect of it; this requirement was eventually abolished by statutory instrument in 1987.

(b) The notice requirements

Here the position was rather complex. There was a requirement for 'pre-grant' notice, which had to be in the prescribed form, though the court could dispense with this requirement if it deemed it just and equitable so to do. Further, the possession proceedings had to be launched after service of a further notice, which had to be served within the strict time limits set out in Case 19. The effect of these notice requirements was that pitfalls abounded to trap the unwary, who might (wrongly) suppose that a shorthold tenancy had been created when there had been some slip-up; this would mean that the tenancy, though supposed to be a shorthold, would become a fully protected tenancy, with all the attendant difficulties of recovery of possession thereby involved. The rules as to the timing of the landlord's notice were particularly complicated (see [1982] Conv 29 at pp 41–42 (Smith) and *Ridehalgh v Horsefield & Isherwood* (1992) 24 HLR 453). The landlord was liable to find his proceedings dismissed, and be compelled to wait for a considerable period before he could commence proceedings again.

No new 'old-style' protected shortholds can be created; as they were all by definition, fixed-term tenancies, it is unlikely that there are many of them still around.

Assured shortholds

These are the shortholds which are much more likely to be encountered today. The draftsman, in the provisions relating to assured shortholds, has made a conscious attempt to get away from the complexities which bedevilled the 1980 scheme, and has tried to produce a regime which contains much less in the way of pitfalls for the unwary.

In this case too, there is a price to be paid by the landlord in the shape of a greater degree of rent control than would be the case if the tenancy was an 'ordinary' assured tenancy, without the addition of the 'shorthold' label.

The key provisions of the Act relating to the 'assured shorthold' are s 19A and s 20 Housing Act 1988, and the procedure for the recovery of possession in the case of an assured shorthold is set forth in s 21, as amended by the Housing Act 1996.

Housing Act 1988
19A. Assured shorthold tenancies, post-Housing Act 1996 tenancies

An assured tenancy which–

- (a) is entered into on or after the day on which section 96 of the Housing Act 1996 comes into force (otherwise than pursuant to a contract made before that day), or
- (b) comes into being by virtue of section 5 above on the coming to an end of an assured tenancy within paragraph (a) above,

is an assured shorthold tenancy unless it falls within any paragraph in Schedule 2A to this Act.

Schedule 2A

Assured Tenancies Non-Shorthold

Tenancies excluded by notice

1(1) An assured tenancy in respect of which a notice is served as mentioned in sub-paragraph (2) below.

(2) The notice referred to in sub-paragraph (1) above is one which–

   (a) is served before the assured tenancy is entered into,

   (b) is served by the person who is to be the landlord under the assured tenancy on the person who is to be the tenant under that tenancy, and

   (c) states that the assured tenancy to which it relates is not to be an assured shorthold tenancy.

2(1) An assured tenancy in respect of which a notice is served as mentioned in sub-paragraph (2) below.

(2) The notice referred to in sub-paragraph (2) above is one which–

   (a) is served after the assured tenancy has been entered into,

   (b) is served by the landlord under the assured tenancy on the tenant under that tenancy, and

   (c) states that the assured tenancy to which it relates is no longer an assured shorthold tenancy.

Tenancies containing exclusionary provision

3. An assured tenancy which contains a provision to the effect that the tenancy is not an assured shorthold tenancy.

Tenancies under section 39

4. An assured tenancy arising by virtue of section 39 above, other than one to which subsection (7) of that section applies.

Former secure tenancies

5. An assured tenancy which became an assured tenancy on ceasing to be a secure tenancy.

Tenancies under Schedule 10 to the Local Government and Housing Act 1989

6. An assured tenancy arising by virtue of Schedule 10 to the Local Government and Housing Act 1989 (security of tenure on ending of long residential tenancies).

Tenancies replacing non-shortholds

7(1) An assured tenancy which–

   (a) is granted to a person (alone or jointly with others) who, immediately before the tenancy was granted, was the tenant (or, in the case of joint tenants, one of the tenants) under an assured tenancy other than a shorthold tenancy ('the old tenancy').

   (b) is granted (alone or jointly with others) by a person who was at that time the landlord (or one of the joint landlords) under the old tenancy, and

   (c) is not one in respect of which a notice is served as mentioned in sub-paragraph (2) below.

(2) The notice referred to in sub-paragraph (1)(c) above is one which–

   (a) is in such form as may be prescribed,

   (b) is served before the assured tenancy is entered into,

    (c) is served by the person who is to be the tenant under the assured tenancy on the person who is to be the landlord under that tenancy (or, in the case of joint landlords, on at least one of the persons who are to be joint landlords), and

    (d) states that the assured tenancy to which is relates is to be a shorthold tenancy.

8.   An assured tenancy which comes into being by virtue of section 5 above on the coming to an end of an assured tenancy which is not a shorthold tenancy.

Assured agricultural occupancies

9(1) An assured tenancy–

    (a) in the case of which the agricultural worker condition is, by virtue of any provision of Schedule 3 to this Act, for the time being fulfilled with respect to the dwelling-house subject to the tenancy, and

    (b) which does not fall within sub-paragraph (2) or (4) below.

(2) An assured tenancy falls within this sub-paragraph if–

    (a) before it is entered into, a notice–

        (i) in such form as may be prescribed, and

        (ii) stating that the tenancy is to be a shorthold tenancy,

    is served by the person who is to be the landlord under the tenancy on the person who is to be the tenant under it, and

    (b) it is not an excepted tenancy.

(3) For the purposes of sub-paragraph (2)(b) above, an assured tenancy is an excepted tenancy if–

    (a) the person to whom it is granted or, as the case may be, at least one of the persons to whom it is granted was, immediately before it is granted, a tenant or licensee under an assured agricultural occupancy, and

    (b) the person by whom it is granted or, as the case may be, at least one of the persons by whom it is granted was, immediately before it is granted, a landlord or licensor under the assured agricultural occupancy referred to in paragraph (a) above.

(4) An assured tenancy falls within this sub-paragraph if it comes into being by virtue of section 5 above on the coming to an end of a tenancy falling within sub-paragraph (2) above.

20. Assured shorthold tenancies

(1) Subject to subsection (3) below, an assured tenancy which is not one to which section 19A above applies is an assured shorthold tenancy if–

    (a) it is a fixed term tenancy granted for a term certain of not less than six months; and

    (b) there is no power for the landlord to determine the tenancy at any time earlier than six months from the beginning of the tenancy; and

    (c) a notice in respect of it is served as mentioned in subsection (2) below.

(2) The notice referred to in subsection (1)(c) above is one which–

    (a) is in such form as may be prescribed;

    (b) is served before the assured tenancy is entered into;

    (c) is served by the person who is to be the landlord under the assured tenancy on the person who is to be the tenant under that tenancy; and

(d) states that the assured tenancy to which it relates is to be a shorthold tenancy.

(3) Notwithstanding anything in subsection (1) above, where–

(a) immediately before a tenancy (in this subsection referred to as 'the new tenancy') is granted, the person to whom it is granted or, as the case may be, at least one of the persons to whom it is granted was a tenant under an assured tenancy which was not a shorthold tenancy, and

(b) the new tenancy is granted by the person who, immediately before the beginning of the tenancy, was the landlord under the assured tenancy referred to in paragraph (a) above,

the new tenancy cannot be an assured shorthold tenancy.

(4) Subject to subsection (5) below, if, on the coming to an end of an assured shorthold tenancy (including a tenancy which was an assured shorthold but ceased to be assured before it came to an end), a new tenancy of the same or substantially the same premises comes into being under which the landlord and the tenant are the same as at the coming to an end of the earlier tenancy, then, if and so long as the new tenancy is an assured tenancy, it shall be an assured shorthold tenancy, whether or not it fulfils the conditions in paragraphs (a) to (c) of subsection (1) above.

(5) Subsection (4) above does not apply if, before the new tenancy is entered into (or, in the case of a statutory periodic tenancy, takes effect in possession), the landlord serves notice on the tenant that the new tenancy is not to be a shorthold tenancy.

(5A) Subsections (3) and (4) above do not apply where the new tenancy is one to which section 19A above applies.

(6) In the case of joint landlords–

(a) the reference in subsection (2)(c) above to the person who is to be the landlord is a reference to at least one of the persons who are to be joint landlords; and

(b) the reference in subsection (5) above to the landlord is a reference to at least one of the joint landlords.

(7) ...

20A Post-Housing Act 1996 tenancies: duty of landlord to provide statement as to terms of tenancy

(1) Subject to subsection (3) below, a tenant under an assured shorthold tenancy to which section 19A above applies may, by notice in writing, require the landlord under the tenancy to provide him with a written statement of any term of the tenancy which–

(a) falls within subsection (2) below, and

(b) is not evidenced in writing.

(2) The following terms of a tenancy fall within this subsection, namely–

(a) the date on which the tenancy began or, if it is a statutory periodic tenancy or a tenancy to which section 39(7) below applies, the date on which the tenancy came into being,

(b) the rent payable under the tenancy and the dates on which that rent is payable,

(c) any term providing for a review of the rent payable under the tenancy, and

(d) in the case of a fixed term tenancy, the length of the fixed term.

(3) No notice may be given under subjection (1) above in relation to a term of the tenancy if–

    (a) the landlord under the tenancy has provided a statement of that term in response to an earlier notice under that subsection given by the tenant under the tenancy, and

    (b) the term has not been varied since the provision of the statement referred to in paragraph (a) above.

(4) A landlord who fails, without reasonable excuse, to comply with a notice under subsection (1) above within the period of 28 days beginning with the date on which he received the notice is liable on summary conviction to a fine not exceeding level 4 on the standard scale.

(5) A statement provided for the purposes of subsection (1) above shall not be regarded as conclusive evidence of what was agreed by the parties to the tenancy in question.

(6) Where–

    (a) a term of a statutory periodic tenancy is one which has effect by virtue of section 5(3)(e) above, or

    (b) a term of a tenancy to which subsection (7) of section 39 below applies is one which has effect by virtue of subsection (6)(e) of that section,

subsection (1) above shall have effect in relation to it as if paragraph (b) related to the term of the tenancy from which it derives.

(7) In subsections (1) and (3) above–

    (a) references to the tenant under the tenancy shall, in the case of joint tenants, be taken to be references to any of the tenants, and

    (b) references to the landlord under the tenancy shall, in the case of joint landlords, be taken to be references to any of the landlords.

21. Recovery of possession on expiry or termination of assured shorthold tenancy

(1) Without prejudice to any right of the landlord under an assured shorthold tenancy to recover possession of the dwelling-house let on the tenancy in accordance with Chapter I above, on or after the coming to an end of an assured shorthold tenancy which was a fixed term tenancy, a court shall make an order for possession of the dwelling-house if it is satisfied–

    (a) that the assured shorthold tenancy has come to an end and no further assured tenancy (whether shorthold or not) is for the time being in existence, other than an assured shorthold periodic tenancy (whether statutory or not); and

    (b) the landlord or, in the case of joint landlords, at least one of them has given to the tenant not less than two months' notice in writing stating that he requires possession of the dwelling-house.

(2) A notice under paragraph (b) of subsection (1) above may be given before or on the day on which the tenancy comes to an end; and that subsection shall have effect notwithstanding that on the coming to an end of the fixed term tenancy a statutory periodic tenancy arises.

(3) ...

(4) Without prejudice to any such right as is referred to in subsection (1) above, a court shall make an order for possession of a dwelling let on an assured shorthold tenancy which is a periodic tenancy if the court is satisfied–

(a) that the landlord or, in the case of joint landlords, at least one of them has given to the tenant a notice in writing stating that, after a date specified in the notice, being the last day of a period of the tenancy and not earlier than two months after the date the notice was given, possession of the dwelling-house is required by virtue of this section; and

(b) that the date specified in the notice under paragraph (a) above is not earlier than the earliest day on which, apart from section 5(1) above, the tenancy could be brought to an end by a notice to quit given by the landlord on the same date as the notice under paragraph (a) above.

(5) Where an order for possession under subsection (1) or (4) above is made in relation to a dwelling-house let on a tenancy to which section 19A above applies, the order may not be made so as to take effect earlier than–

(a) in the case of a tenancy which is not a replacement tenancy, six months after the beginning of the tenancy, and

(b) in the case of a replacement tenancy, six months after the beginning of the original tenancy.

(6) In subsection (5)(b) above, the reference to the original tenancy is–

(a) where the replacement tenancy came into being on the coming to an end of a tenancy which was not a replacement tenancy, to the immediately preceding tenancy, and

(b) where there have been successive replacement tenancies, to the tenancy immediately preceding the first in the succession of replacement tenancies.

(7) For the purposes of this section, a replacement tenancy is a tenancy–

(a) which comes into being on the coming to an end of an assured shorthold tenancy, and

(b) under which, on its coming into being–

(i) the landlord and tenant are the same as under the earlier tenancy as at its coming to an end, and

(ii) the premises let are the same or substantially the same as those let under the earlier tenancy as at that time.

There are a number of points to observe about these provisions:

(a) the normal principle that the tenancy has first to be 'an assured tenancy' – ie a letting of a dwelling-house as a separate dwelling – applies.

(b) As in the case of the old style shorthold, the tenancy has to be a 'fixed-term' tenancy, though the minimum 'fixed term' has been reduced from a year to six months, and there is now no maximum period for the fixed term. There must be no power for the landlord to determine the tenancy prematurely – though a forfeiture clause for breach would not seem to fall under this stricture.

(c) Again, there is a 'preliminary notice' requirement – which must be punctiliously observed, as the court has no power to dispense from it – and the recent case of *Panayi & Pyrkos v Roberts* (1993) 25 HLR 421 illustrates the stringency of these requirements.

(d) As an anti-avoidance measure, there is a provision that a tenancy granted to a tenant by a landlord who was, immediately prior to the grant, the tenant's landlord under an assured non-shorthold tenancy will not be an assured shorthold; in contrast, a new tenancy of substantially the same premises, granted by a landlord to the same tenant who was previously an assured shorthold tenant shall be an assured shorthold even though the s 20 conditions are not fully satisfied (eg if the new tenancy is a periodic, as opposed to fixed-term tenancy).

(e) The price to be paid by the landlord, for the enhanced right to recover possession, is a modest degree of rent control.

The Housing Act 1996

Part II, Chapter I of the 1996 Act contains provisions making it possible to create an assured shorthold tenancy without serving a prior notice; it also imposes restrictions on recovery of possession on expiry or termination of an assured shorthold tenancy and amends s 22 of the 1988 Act concerning applications for determination of rent (see ss 96–100).

SUCCESSION IN THE PRIVATE SECTOR

THE NATURE OF THE SUCCESSION RULES

The scheme of the protective legislation is that security is provided in respect of the tenant's home. It would frustrate the purpose of the protective legislation if that security was to be arbitrarily brought to an end, and his elderly widow or widower evicted on the tenant's death; the protection he enjoyed in his lifetime was a protection also available to the members of his family, and the policy of the various legislative enactments is to extend that security after his death, at least to members of his immediate family, so long as the claimant can show the necessary residential connection with the property. To that extent, the policy of the Acts is to protect the rights of the family as a whole, and not just the original tenant.

Against that, however, it must be recognised that the succession rules represent a substantial inroad into a landlord's property rights. In an extreme case, he may find himself unable to regain possession of the property for up to three generations of tenants. Of course, it could be argued that the whole scheme of the Rent Act legislation is an interference with property rights – but in the area of succession it has, over the years, proved to be a particular bone of contention, where landlords have, with some justification, argued that the protection conferred upon the tenant's extended family goes beyond what is justifiable in terms of residential security.

The nature of the succession rights granted to tenants has long been controversial, and for that reason the more recent legislation does mark a substantial cutting back of these rights. It has long been thought that the existence of these succession rights operates as a considerable disincentive to lettings by private landlords, and it is with a view to diminishing the deterrent effect of these provisions that the Housing Act 1988 marks a new departure, restricting abruptly the succession rights in the case of new style assured tenancies, as well as curtailing them drastically in the case of Rent Act protected tenancies existing before the Housing Act 1988, at least in those cases where the death of the tenant occurs on or after the commencement of the Housing Act on 15 January 1989.

This situation is one of the few instances in the Act where the rights of existing – ie pre-Act tenancies are severely and adversely affected.

There are thus at least three regimes which need to be discussed:

(1) Rent Act succession before 1989;

(2) Rent Act succession after 1989;

(3) Housing Act succession.

Traditional (pre-1989) Rent Act succession

These rules, now diminishing in importance, will be discussed relatively briefly – though it should not be forgotten that these issues have the knack of surfacing after a long interlude. For example, in *Dyson Holdings Ltd v Fox* (see later) the male tenant died in 1961, and it was only in 1973 that the landlord became aware of the status of the 'widow' and commenced proceedings for possession.

The Rent Act gave primacy of succession rights to a spouse of a deceased tenant; other members of the household were less favoured, and could only succeed normally in the absence of a qualifying spouse as successor. In addition, a non-spouse successor had (and to some extent still has) to satisfy a more stringent residence test than a spouse. A second succession (but not a third) was also possible in certain restricted circumstances, subject, again, to the establishment of the necessary residence requirement and the necessary kinship with the deceased first successor.

Spousal (first) succession

Originally, the Rent Act rules allowed primacy of succession in favour only of a widow of a deceased male protected or statutory tenant, so long as she was living with the deceased tenant at the time of his death; widowers claiming by succession from a deceased female tenant were less generously treated (though it was recognised at an early stage that a widower was a member of his wife's family (see *Salter v Lask* [1925] 1 KB 584)) and might have to compete for the succession with other members of the family. This odd rule only applied in favour of a widow strictly so called; *de facto* relationships did not suffice for the operation of this rule, though it might be enough to confer 'membership of the family'. (The rule has now been changed with respect to deaths occurring after the commencement of the Housing Act on 15 January 1989.)

Although the original rule applied only in favour of a widow, the situation was changed with effect from 26 November 1980 by s 76(1) Housing Act 1980, so that a widower was given equivalent rights of succession. Also, by the same provision in the Housing Act 1980, the requirement that the claimant had to be 'living with' the deceased tenant at the time of the death was relaxed to the extent that the claimant had only to be 'residing in the dwelling-house immediately before the death of the original tenant' – thus making a succession possible in favour of a widow or a widower, in the case of spouses who were separated but living under the same roof, but not living together. A decree nisi of divorce will not be enough to terminate the entitlement, as the parties remain validly married until decree absolute.

Family (first) succession where no surviving spouse

Where there was no qualifying spouse, the Act allowed a succession to a member of the original tenant's family, providing that the necessary residence qualification could be established. Two issues fall to be considered here:

(1) What is meant by a member of the 'family'?

(2) What residence requirements need to be satisfied?

Establishment of a 'family' relationship

There have been few issues which have been so productive of litigation under the Rent Act as the establishment of a 'family relationship' between the deceased protected or statutory tenant and a postulated successor. Many of the difficulties have been caused by the unfortunate absence of a definition in the Rent Act – an omission which Parliament has remedied in later codes applying in different circumstances, such as the public sector code now enshrined in the Housing Act 1985.

Broadly speaking, the issue has arisen in three contexts:

(a) Kinship;

(b) Cohabitation;

(c) Platonic relationships.

Kinship and family

Lacking a statutory definition, the courts have rightly approached the matter in a broad sense, asking whether, in common parlance, the postulant could be said to be within the 'family' of the deceased. The general approach can be discerned from the judgment of Russell LJ in *Ross v Collins* [1964] 1 All ER 861, which was subsequently approved by the House of Lords in *Joram Developments v Sharratt* [1979] 1 WLR 928. Russell LJ said:

> Granted that 'family' is not limited to cases of a strict legal familial nexus, I cannot agree that it extends to a case such as this (a platonic liaison). It still requires, it seems to me, at least a broadly recognisable *de facto* familial nexus. This may be capable of being found and recognised as such by the ordinary man – where the link would be strictly familial had there been a marriage, or where the link is through the adoption of a minor, de jure or *de facto*, or where the link is 'step-', or where the link is 'in-law' or by marriage. But two strangers cannot, it seems to me ever establish artificially for the purposes of this section a familial nexus by acting as brothers or as sisters, even if they call each other such and consider their relationship to be tantamount to that. Nor, in my view, can an adult man and woman who establish a platonic relationship establish a familial nexus by acting as a devoted brother and sister or father and daughter would act, even if they address each other as such and even if they refer to each other as such and regard their association as tantamount to such. Nor, in my view, would they indeed be recognised as familial links by the ordinary man.

Thus, protection has rightly been extended to a child (including an informally adopted child: *Brock v Wollams* [1949] 2 KB 388). Informal adoption of an adult as a kind of quasi-daughter would seem to be insufficient, following *Sefton Holdings Ltd v Cairns* [1988] 2 FLR 109. It also includes, a grandchild (*Collier v Stoneman* [1957] 1 WLR 1108), a sibling (*Price v Gould* (1930) 143 LT 333 (though not *de facto* sisterhood: *Sefton Holdings Ltd v Cairns* (above)), and relations by marriage (*Jones v Whitehill* [1950] 2 KB 204, *Stewart v Higgins* [1951] EGD 353).

The difficulties implicit in these distinctions were illustrated in *Sefton Holdings Ltd v Cairns* [1988] 2 FLR 109. In that case T was the original tenant. The claimant, then aged 23, came to live with T and his wife in 1941. She was a single woman, whose parents were already dead, and who had lost her boy friend in the war. She had come to live with T and his family at the suggestion of T's only daughter Ada. T treated the claimant as a daughter, and she and Ada regarded each other as sisters. Ada succeeded to the statutory tenancy on T's death in 1965, but the Court of Appeal felt unable to accede to the suggestion that the claimant was a *de facto* sister to Ada, able to succeed to the tenancy on Ada's death. The Court of Appeal held that it could not extend the meaning of family to cover what might appear to be a hard case.

Mere consanguinity, though, is not of itself enough. The conduct of the postulant is also relevant. In *Ross v Collins* [1964] 1 All ER 861 (where on the facts the necessary familial nexus was held not to be established), Pearson LJ said: 'the existence of a family relationship is not always in itself enough to make the surviving person a member of the deceased tenant's family. The way in which the parties acted is also to be taken into account.'

In that case the claimant, who was unrelated to the deceased, had looked after him in his last illness and had nursed him with care and affection. Such conduct will apparently have to be established in all such cases, though the assumption seems to be that the proof of such conduct is more necessary, the more remote the degree of kinship involved. This factor may explain the decision denying succession in favour of a cousin in *Langdon v Horton* [1951] KB 666, where the parties seem to have lived together for motives of convenience rather than for reasons of consanguinity.

The cohabitation cases

Here again there is a rich tapestry of cases, almost impossible to reconcile with each other. The earlier cases are heavily overlaid with the moralistic outpourings of the judiciary, and these atavistic sentiments occasionally return.

Succession rights of 'spouses' were traditionally not available to cohabitees. If a cohabitee seeks to establish a succession, it must be by way of membership of the 'family' of the deceased tenant. In *Gammans v Ekins* [1950] 2 KB 328, the Court of Appeal was outraged by a claim of a male cohabitee to succeed, as a member of her 'family', to his deceased partner's tenancy. An affronted Asquith LJ declared:

> [It is] anomalous that a person can acquire a 'status of irremovability' by living or having lived in sin even if the liaison has not been a mere casual encounter but protracted in time and conclusive in character ... To say of two people masquerading, as these two were, as husband and wife, there being no children to complicate the picture, that they were members of the same family, seems to me an abuse of the English language.

A mild amelioration was achieved in *Hawes v Evendon* [1953] 1 WLR 1169, in a case where the long-standing union was blessed with children. This was thought to create a crucial distinction, so that the female cohabitee (where there were children) could succeed as a member of the tenant's family to the tenancy on the death of the male tenant.

A later Court of Appeal, however, achieved a complete volte-face in *Dyson Holdings Ltd v Fox* [1976] QB 503. In that case Mr Wright, a bachelor, lived together with Olive Fox, a spinster, for 40 years. She was known in the neighbourhood as Mrs Wright. There were no children. For the last 21 years of his life Mr Wright was the tenant of a house, and Olive remained in occupation after his death. Some 12 years after his death the landlords discovered the true state of affairs, and claimed possession of the house from Olive. Denouncing the distinction between *Gammans v Ekins* and *Hawes v Evendon* as 'ridiculous', Denning MR was prepared to permit a succession to Olive Fox, holding for his part that the decision in *Gammans v Ekins* was wrongly decided, and not in accord with modern thinking.

The uneasy relationship between the two Court of Appeal decisions in *Gammans v Ekins* and *Dyson Holdings Ltd v Fox* had to be confronted again in *Helby v Rafferty* [1978] 3 All ER 1016. Holding that a male cohabitee, after a relationship of some five years with Miss Taylor, the female tenant, was not a member of her 'family', the Court seized on the question of the supposed impermanence of the relationship as a ground for distinguishing the decision in *Dyson Holdings v Fox*.

Miss Taylor, in *Helby v Rafferty*, had resolutely preserved her independence. The union was childless, and the woman was determined to maintain her freedom, and kept her maiden name so far as the outside world was concerned. The Court obviously had doubts about the process which had been employed by the Court of Appeal in *Dyson Holdings Ltd v Fox* to dispose of the prior decision in *Gammans v Ekins*. The decision culminated in a cri de coeur to the House of Lords to sort the whole thing out – an invitation which the House of Lords declined to accept in *Carega Properties SA v Sharratt* [1979] 2 All ER 1084.

Later developments, however, suggest that *Helby v Rafferty* is to be regarded as a particular decision on its own facts, and not a revival of the rule in *Gammans v Ekins*. In *Watson v Lucas* [1980] 3 All ER 647 a majority of the Court of Appeal was prepared to regard *Helby v Rafferty* as anomalous, and declined to reinstate *Gammans v Ekins*, holding that such a course was open only to the House of Lords (to whom an appeal was not pursued). In *Watson v Lucas* the parties had cohabited for 19 years, their association commencing a few years after Mr Lucas and his wife had separated; they did not marry, as Mr Lucas's wife was a Roman Catholic, and unwilling to petition for a divorce. The County Court judge had declined to regard Mr Lucas as a member of the family of the female tenant because both parties to the relationship had kept their own names and also because Mr Lucas was already married to another lady, thus precluding the creation of another 'family' relationship with the cohabitee. Stephenson LJ regarded the County Court judge's decision, declining to accept a succession, based on these criteria as erroneous.

Oliver LJ dissented, but all members of the Court of Appeal were united in an intention not to extend *Dyson Holdings Ltd v Fox*, Oliver LJ going so far as to say that he regarded the case as one which rested on its own peculiar facts and as standing at the very limit of any ordinarily accepted or acceptable definition of a family relationship. Notwithstanding the reluctance expressed here to extend *Dyson Holdings v Fox*, the Court of Appeal managed to do just that in *Chios Property Investment Co v Lopez* (1987) 20 HLR 120, when a female cohabitee was held to be entitled to succeed to a tenancy as a member of the male cohabitee's family, after two years cohabitation. The parties had intended to marry if their financial position improved. The union was childless and the parties retained their original names. The case was regarded as exceptional and not as a precedent for other short relationships unless they were also similarly exceptional.

The platonic relationship cases

The question whether persons in a close but platonic relationship could count as 'family' was authoritatively considered by the House of Lords in *Carega Properties SA (formerly Joram Developments Ltd) v Sharratt* [1979] 2 All ER 1084. Here the association was between a young man of 24 and an elderly widow of 75 at the time of its commencement. The couple lived together in amicable terms for over 18 years in a flat of which the widow was the tenant until the widow died in 1976 at the age of 94. As Lord Diplock said:

> The relationship between them throughout was platonic and filial. He behaved towards her as a dutiful and affectionate son and looked after her during her declining years. She would have liked to speak of him as her son, but this was not acceptable to Mr Sharratt, whose mother was still alive; so that they decided that he would call her Aunt Norah and she addressed him by an affectionate nickname ('Bunny').

The House of Lords held that the young man could not claim to be a member of the widow's family, also approving the earlier case of *Ross v Collins* [1964] 1 All ER 861 where a younger woman devotedly nursed an elderly male tenant during his declining years, and the familial nexus was found to be lacking.

It is surely right that the valuable rights inherent in succession to a protected or statutory tenancy cannot be claimed, as Asquith LJ put it in *Gammans v Ekins* between 'two old cronies of the same sex innocently sharing a flat'.

Residence requirements for 'family' succession

In the case of a spouse all that the claimant has to establish is that he or she 'was residing in the dwelling-house immediately before the death of the original tenant'. There is no requirement that the postulant should be 'living with' the deceased.

For members of a family (including, where they are so entitled, cohabitees) claiming to take by succession, a more onerous test is required, and the claimant has to show that he was residing with the original tenant at the time of and for the period of six months immediately before his death ... It is not clear whether this had to be in the dwelling-house in respect of which a succession is claimed (see *South Northamptonshire District Council v Power*). Although *South Northants v*

Power declared this to be a requirement for the private sector, the case has since been disapproved by the House of Lords in *Waltham Forest LBC v Thomas*, and the general approach of the House of Lords in Thomas' case was that restrictions of this kind should not be imposed without clear authority in the statute. Under the pre-1988 scheme, there was no such express requirement for members of the family claiming a succession, and the House of Lords seems to discourage the implication of such a requirement.

At one time the notion of 'residing with' was thought to involve a requirement of the sharing of the whole premises in respect of which the succession was claimed. This requirement was derived from *Edmunds v Jones* [1957] 1 WLR 1108, 1120; it was subsequently relaxed by the later decision of the Court of Appeal in *Collier v Stoneman* [1957] 1 WLR 1108.

It should be noted that for deaths occurring after 15 January 1989 the qualifying period has been extended to two years; and now residence in the dwelling-house is clearly part of the requirement. The purpose of this rule is to prevent a family member claiming the valuable rights involved in a succession to a statutory or protected tenancy merely by moving in a short period before the death of the original tenant.

The concept of 'residence' is one which appears elsewhere in the legislation-for instance, in dealing with the rights of a statutory tenant under s 2 Rent Act 1977. The same test applies here, so that residence is not defeated by a temporary absence, whether for business or pleasure.

It would seem that there has to be some community of living with the deceased tenant, as the Act refers to 'residing with' the deceased. Thus, in *Foreman v Beagley* [1969] 3 All ER 838, the defendant's mother until her death on 7 June 1968 was the statutory tenant of a flat. For the last three years of her life she was in hospital, but the court was prepared to regard her residence as continuing so as to keep the statutory tenancy on foot. In October 1967, during her stay in hospital the defendant, who was the son of the deceased tenant, began to live in the flat. He had left his wife, who was a council tenant. The defendant's purpose in occupying the flat was to keep it aired in order to keep the damp at bay and to prepare it for renewed occupation by his mother if she were discharged from hospital. He had clearly occupied the flat for the qualifying six month period, but it could not be said that he was residing 'with' his mother. The evidence did not show any arrangement or understanding between mother and the defendant that his residence was to consist of or even be a preliminary to a membership of the mother's household, or a residing together or 'with' the mother.

A more generous attitude was displayed in *Hedgedale Ltd v Hards* (1990) 23 HLR 158, where a grandson moved in with his grandmother, a statutory tenant. Soon after his arrival his grandmother, having broken her arm, went to stay with her daughter to recuperate. Although grandmother, having recovered from her injuries, moved back into the property in December, she died the following May, and so the period from December to May did not yield the necessary six months qualifying period of residence. The Court was prepared to hold, however, that the grandson was 'living with' grandmother, in the sense of forming a common household with her, notwithstanding her absence for recuperation. The intentions of the parties, where there is no contemporaneous residence, may be significant, though not decisive (see *Hildebrand v Moon*).

By analogy with the 'two-home' cases arising under the residence test for statutory tenancies, it would appear that a successor can be residing with the original tenant while retaining some residential status elsewhere. *Morgan v Murch* [1970] 1 WLR 778, where a son deserted his wife to move in with his mother may be such a case (as he retained the tenancy of the matrimonial home), but this case can perhaps be best understood as a case where the claimant had only one residence – with his mother. It was said in *Swanbrae Ltd v Elliott* [1987] 1 EGLR 99, 19 HLR 86 that the fact that the claimant had a permanent home of her own was not conclusive against any claim to succession, but the court thought that cases where the necessary residence could be established in such circumstances were necessarily rare.

One of the rare cases where such residence has been held to be established is *Hildebrand v Moon* (1989) 22 HLR 1. In that case the claimant, who had a flat of her own, moved in to nurse her mother, a statutory tenant, when the mother fell ill with cancer. The period of occupation of the mother's flat was well over six months, but the claimant kept all her furniture and her papers at her old flat. It seemed that her intention was not clearly established to be resident with, rather than merely looking after, her mother. The trial judge found against the claimant, largely on the issue of intention, saying that there was no contemporaneous evidence of an intention to reside with the mother. Reversing the decision, Mann LJ said that all the objective indicia were that the claimant had made her home with the mother; intention was relevant and can make the difference between a visitor and a resident, but the judge had erred in law in giving this factor of intention excessive weight; there was evidence that she had intended to remain in her mother's house, at least for the foreseeable future.

It should be noted that there is also a requirement of continuing residence on the part of a successor, as in any other case of a statutory tenancy (see p 251).

More than one family claimant qualified to succeed

It may be that more than one claimant will qualify for a succession. In such cases, *prima facie*, the matter is to be settled by agreement between the parties; if no agreement can be reached the matter can be decided by the court. A joint succession is not possible: *Dealex Properties Ltd v Brooks* [1966] 1 QB 542. In adjudicating between rival claimants, the court will have regard to need and the wishes of the deceased tenant as well as the behaviour of the claimants. In *Williams v Williams* [1970] 3 All ER 988 the two rival claimants on the death of a female tenant were her husband (who as the law then stood had no primacy in succession rights) and her son. Both fulfilled the necessary residence qualification. The husband had treated the tenant badly, whereas the son had treated the tenant kindly and largely supported her in her last years. The judge found that on the facts the mother would have preferred the tenancy to go to the son. Lord Denning MR said:

> From the point of view of conduct, the son was the more meritorious; but, from the point of view of necessity, the father was the more in need; and the need of the father outweighed the merits of the son ... the son, being a single man earning a very good living, would easily be able to get accommodation elsewhere.

Need for continuing residence by the successor

The statutory tenancy will only be prolonged in favour of the successor 'if and so long as he or she occupies the dwelling-house as his or her residence'. This is similar to the test in s 2 Rent Act 1977 to establish a statutory tenancy, and the authorities under that section will be equally relevant here.

Second succession possible

Under the Rent Act, a second succession was possible. If the first successor died leaving a spouse, that spouse was entitled to succeed to the statutory tenancy in like manner to the spouse of the original tenant. In the absence of such a spouse, a member of the first successor's family may succeed, providing that the necessary residence qualification (which is the same as that for a first succession) can be established.

What is the position if the landlord grants a new tenancy to the 'successor'? Does this mean that the clock starts again, so that a further two successions are possible? Schedule 1, para 10 Rent Act 1977 provides that the 'successor' remains a 'first successor', so as to make only one further succession available after his death.

Interrelation with the ordinary rules of succession

A particular problem may arise if someone other than the 'Rent Act successor' is entitled to the estate of the deceased tenant under the terms of his will or the rules of intestacy. A statutory tenancy cannot be disposed of by will, but a contractual tenancy is a 'term of years absolute', and thus, *prima facie*, is capable of passing on death. In *Moodie v Hosegood* [1952] AC 61, the House of Lords in effect held that in a situation of this kind the 'successor' will still be protected, and the person taking the estate by succession will have to endure a suspension of his rights until the death of the Rent Act successor. If the same person is entitled under the will and by the rules of statutory succession to tenancies, it has been held that the taker acquires the tenancy as a contractual tenant (see *Whitmore v Lambert* [1955] 1 WLR 495), but this case must be regarded as dubious in authority since *Moodie v Hosegood* was not cited.

THE 1988 AMENDMENTS TO THE RENT ACT SUCCESSION SCHEME

As mentioned earlier, there is evidence that the Rent Act succession rules have come to represent a substantial disincentive to private sector letting. Their effect, in broad terms, is that a landlord may be kept out of vacant possession of his property for up to three generations of tenants. To promote the private letting sector, the decision was taken to restrict the succession rules applying to Rent Act tenancies after the coming into force of the 1988 Act. The critical date is 15 January 1989. The old rules apply to deaths before that date, and the new, stricter regime will apply to deaths on or after that date. There are complex transitional arrangements to cater for those cases where there could be said to be an 'acquired right' by the accumulation of the necessary residence period before the coming into force of the 1988 Act. In this section, we will consider first the rules which apply on a death on or after 15 January 1989. The transitional provisions will be considered later.

The assimilation of spouse and cohabitee succession rules

Much judicial time had been spent in deciding whether, in the absence of a surviving spouse (who was accorded primacy of succession rights), a cohabitee can succeed to the statutory tenancy under the umbrella of membership of the 'family' of the original tenant. Having initially set their faces sternly against such novelties (in *Gammans v Ekins* (see earlier)), the courts have relaxed their rules through such cases as *Dyson Holdings Ltd v Fox* and *Watson v Lucas*, though not without an occasional nostalgic glance towards the old ways in such cases as *Helby v Rafferty*.

This debate, now, seems to be consigned to the oubliette it richly deserved, because a new subparagraph has been inserted into Schedule 1 Rent Act 1977: 'For the purposes of this paragraph, a person who was living with the original tenant as his or her wife or husband shall be treated as the spouse of the original tenant.'

The expression 'living together as husband and wife', which also appears in the public sector code, was considered by the Court of Appeal in the public sector case of *Westminster City Council v Peart* (1991) 24 HLR 389, presumably applicable by analogy in the private sector cases. In that case it was held that the retention by one of the parties of accommodation elsewhere justified a finding by the court that they were not living together as husband and wife, even though they had lived together in the same household.

As a supplement to this new paragraph, Parliament added:

> If, immediately after the death of the original tenant, there is ... more than one person who fulfils the conditions ... above, such one of them as may be decided by agreement, or in default of agreement, by the county court shall be treated as the surviving spouse for the purposes of this paragraph.

Such a successor, who takes as a spouse or a quasi-spouse, will succeed to a Rent Act statutory tenancy in the old way.

Non-spousal (ie family) succession

Here the rules have been changed more abruptly, and family members will be treated much less generously after 15 January 1989. There is still no statutory definition of 'family', so the old cases decided under the original Rent Act (and discussed above at pp 244) must be examined to discover who might be entitled to succeed under this heading. Changes have been made, however, to the residence rules, the period of qualifying residence, and the nature of the tenancy which a successful claimant in this category will acquire. These changes will now be considered in turn.

The place of the qualifying residence

Oddly, the Rent Act contained no stipulation that the residence with the deceased tenant had to be 'in' the dwelling-house in question. It was, however, observed in *South Northamptonshire District Council v Power* [1987] 3 All ER 831 that this requirement was implicit in the Rent Act (quoting *Edmunds v Jones* [1957] 3 All ER 23, *Collier v Stoneman* [1957] 3 All ER 20, and the Malaysian case of *Wee Ban Yan v Eyun Eng Lowi* (1962) 29 MLJ 62). In *South Northamptonshire District Council v Power*, Kerr LJ said: 'Everybody's understanding has always been that the connection which is required to establish a succession is a double one, both a family one and a residential one in the premises in question to which the succession is claimed.' This dictum was probably affected by the subsequent overruling of *South Northamptonshire District Council v Power* by the House of Lords in *London Borough of Waltham Forest v Thomas* (1992) 24 HLR 622.

What was probably once (though erroneously) thought to be implicit has now been made explicit by Parliament: the words 'in the dwelling-house' are now added to the section containing the residential requirement for family members.

Presumably, the test for 'residence' remains as it was under the former provisions (see p 243); the authorities referred to in those paragraphs will presumably be used to test the question of whether a particular 'residence' entitles a claimant to take by succession.

The qualifying period for succession

The qualifying period of residence has been extended from six months to two years. There are transitional provisions in respect of deaths before 15 July 1990. The purpose of this provision is clearly to discourage adventitious 'moving in' to the property of an aged tenant, so as to secure succession rights. Where more than one person is entitled under these provisions, the usual rules for the settlement of the issue by agreement, or in default of agreement by the county court will apply.

Change in nature of the tenancy on succession

This may prove to be one of the most important features of the change in the rules made by the 1988 Act. Under the 1977 Act, the tenancy, on succession, always remained a Rent Act statutory tenancy. This is no longer so; a succession to a spouse (or a person treated as a spouse under the cohabitee extension) results in the continuation of the Rent Act statutory tenancy as before; but a succession to a member of the family with the necessary residence qualification will lead to the automatic conversion of the tenancy into an assured tenancy within the Housing Act. This will have important (and adverse) consequences to the tenant in the following ways, which will be considered separately:

(1) Diminution of security of tenure;

(2) Exposure to market rents, instead of the former 'fair rent' regime.

Diminution of security of tenure

In general terms, although an assured tenancy provides some security of tenure, it is not as all-embracing as the security of tenure provided under the Rent Act. In particular, rent arrears (if substantial) can provide a mandatory ground for possession, and also certain 'grounds for possession', which had no counterpart in the Rent Act, will become available to the landlord.

Exposure to market rents

Under the Rent Act, a tenant was entitled to the benefit of the 'fair rent' provisions. These 'fair rents' were lower than market rents, as the scarcity element was disregarded in their calculation. The rent payable under an assured tenancy is a market rent. Though the terms of the assured tenancy, initially at least, are similar to the terms of the previous statutory tenancy, the landlord can invoke the procedure contained in s 13 of the Housing Act to raise the rent. An illustration of the operation of these provisions can be discerned in *N & D (London) Ltd v Gadson* (1991) 24 HLR 64.

Restriction on opportunities for a second succession

It will be recalled that under the Rent Act a second succession was possible. It remains possible under the Housing Act, but the circumstances under which such a second succession can take place are very strictly controlled.

First of all, there can only be a second succession where the first succession has been a spousal (or quasi-spousal) succession. To qualify as a second successor, the postulant must be:

(1) a member of the original tenant's family; and

(2) a member of the first successor's family; and

(3) resident in the dwelling-house with the first successor at the time of, and for the period of two years immediately before the first successor's death (Schedule 4 para 6).

The rules would seem to be designed to secure a succession to a child of the original tenant and the first successor. A (second) spouse of the first successor will not qualify, as he or she will be unlikely to be establish a familial connection with the original tenant. If more than one person is qualified to succeed under this rule, there is the usual provision for deciding the succession by agreement, or in default of agreement, by the county court. Any such second succession will result in an assured periodic tenancy, with the consequences outlined above in the case of a first succession by a member of the family.

TRANSITIONAL PROVISIONS

Death of original tenant

In the case of a member of the family (though not a spouse) taking an assured tenancy by succession from the original tenant, the residence requirement is raised from the original six month period to two years. In the case of a death between 15 January 1989 and 15 July 1990, however, the family member will be qualified to succeed so long as the claimant was resident from 15 July 1988 until the death of the original tenant.

Residence for second succession

Here again, the Housing Act imposes a two year residence requirement in the normal way. But where the second successor dies before 15 July 1990, the requirement is deemed to be satisfied so long as the claimant was resident from 15 July 1988 until the time of the second successor's death. If the first successor became the tenant by succession before 15 January 1989, the claimant will not have to establish a familial connection with the original tenant, but only with the successor.

HOUSING ACT 1988 SUCCESSION

The scheme under the Housing Act is short and, in the view of some commentators, nasty and brutish as well. It was clearly the intention of the legislature to cut down abruptly succession rights under the new system, as the existence of the wide-ranging succession rights under the Rent Act was believed to be one of the 'disincentives' discouraging private landlordism. Hence the system adopted by the Housing Act allows only one succession, in favour of a spouse, or quasi-spouse. In addition there are significant changes in the residence requirements for the claimant; these have been drastically simplified to accommodate the exclusion of the 'family' successor.

Spousal succession under the Housing Act

The basic rule is contained in s 17 Housing Act 1988, which provides that on the death of an 'assured periodic tenant', the tenancy vests in the 'spouse', which expression is taken to include a cohabitee. The Act seems to contemplate the possibility of more than one claimant falling within the section, and provides the usual machinery for resolving the difficulty by agreement or (in default of agreement) by the county court (s 17(5)).

Residence requirements

Here there are some significant changes. Since there is no succession to 'family' members, there is thus no need to prescribe a qualifying 'residential period'. The essence of the new scheme is that the claimant must be occupying the dwelling-house as 'his or her only or principal home'. This expression marks a clear and deliberate departure from the 'residence' concept which has prevailed formerly. One clear impact of the change must be to remove from the succession scheme the 'two-home' tenant, with a succession in the case of both properties; if two dwelling-houses are involved, the claimant will have to show (since it cannot be shown that the dwelling-house is the only home) that it is the principal home.

There may be difficulties if the parties are living separately but under the same roof; in the case of a spouse correctly so called, there should still be a succession in such a case, because the statute does not demand that the spouse must have been 'living with' the deceased tenant. But in the case of cohabitees, it may be difficult to show that they are living as man and wife if they are leading separate existences, though under the same roof, at the time of the tenant's death. Though the statute does not specify when the cohabitation condition must be satisfied, it seems reasonable to suppose that the claimant must establish that this state of affairs existed at the time of the tenant's death, and not at some previous and possibly remote juncture.

Exclusion of ordinary rules of succession

In the past, difficulties have been caused by an attempt to reconcile the succession scheme of the Rent Act with the ordinary rules relating to the devolution of property rights under the will or intestacy of the deceased tenant (see *Moodie v Hosegood* [1952] AC 61, HL). The Housing Act ejects the normal rules of succession by will or intestacy, and provides that the statutory succession under the Act prevails over any devolution under the tenant's will or intestacy.

Cases where succession excluded: joint tenants

If a joint tenant dies, there will normally be a survivorship by *jus accrescendi* in favour of the co-tenant. This is not a 'succession' under the Act, as the statutory succession scheme under s 17 only applies where the deceased tenant was a 'sole tenant' at his death, and the survivorship operates by force of the original limitation rather than by a succession under the Act. It is also provided, however, that the surviving tenant is deemed to be a 'successor' himself, so that on the death of the survivor any further succession is precluded (see s 17(1)(c) and s 17(2)(b)).

Exclusion of a second succession

There is only one succession under the Act; if the deceased has already become a tenant by succession there can be no further succession (see s 17(2)(a)). This rule also applies if the assured tenancy came into being as a result of a 'family' succession under the amendments to the Rent Act (s 39(5)).

CHAPTER 8

SECURITY OF TENURE IN THE PUBLIC SECTOR AND SUCCESSION

INTRODUCTION

The key concept in any understanding of the public sector regime is that of the 'secure tenancy'. This is the central concept in the Housing Act and it is from the status of the 'secure tenant' that many of the rights enshrined in the public sector Housing Act flow. A 'secure tenant' enjoys the benefit of certain implied terms in the regulation of the landlord–tenant relationship, and the security of tenure which is modelled on that enjoyed by private sector tenants under the Rent Act 1977 and the Housing Act 1988. In addition, the 'secure tenant' enjoys a 'right to buy', which has no parallel in the private sector.

The first task is to analyse the sections of the legislation which define the status of the secure tenant. The key sections are ss 79–81 Housing Act 1985, reproducing the corresponding provisions in the 1980 Act.

Housing Act 1985

79(1) A tenancy under which a dwelling-house is let as a separate dwelling is a secure tenancy at any time when the conditions described in sections 80 and 81 as the landlord condition and the tenant condition are satisfied.

(2) Subsection (1) has effect subject to–

(a) the exceptions in Schedule 1 (tenancies which are not secure tenancies);

(b) sections 89(3) and (4) and 90(3) and (4) (tenancies ceasing to be secure after death of tenant); and

(c) sections 91(2) and 93(2) (tenancies ceasing to be secure in consequence of assigning or subletting) ...

(3) The provisions of this Part apply in relation to a licence to occupy a dwelling-house (whether or not granted for a consideration) as they apply in relation to a tenancy.

(4) Subsection (3) does not apply to a licence granted as a temporary expedient to a person who entered the dwelling-house or any other land as a trespasser (whether or not, before the grant of that licence, another licence to occupy that or another dwelling-house had been granted to him).

80(1) The landlord condition is that the interest of the landlord belongs to one of the following authorities or bodies–

a local authority,
a new town corporation,
a housing action trust,
an urban development corporation,
the Development Board for Rural Wales,
the housing corporation,
a housing trust which is a charity, or
a housing association or housing co-operative to which this section applies.

(2) ... (3) ... (4) ...

81 The tenant condition is that the tenant is an individual and occupies the dwelling-house as his only or principal home; or, where the tenancy is a joint

tenancy, that each of the joint tenants is an individual and at least one of them occupies the dwelling-house as his only or principal home.

These provisions cover a number of points:

(1) The status of the landlord;

(2) The status of the tenant;

(3) The nature of the arrangement between landlord and tenant;

(4) A residence requirement;

(5) The tenancy must not be excluded.

Each of these will now be explained.

The status of the landlord

Broadly speaking, the landlord must be a 'public sector' landlord of the type set out in s 80.

The status of the tenant

The tenant must be an individual. Lettings to limited companies, for example, will not enjoy protection under the legislation.

The nature of the arrangement between landlord and tenant

This is rather more complex. The legislation uses the expression about a dwelling-house (which includes a part of a house: s 112(1)) 'let as a separate dwelling', which has been enshrined in the private sector legislation since the very beginning. Accordingly, at first sight, it might look as if all the case law from the private sector will be incorporated into the public sector definition. Things are not what they seem, however, and there are a number of important differences.

Inclusion of certain licences

Here there is a fundamental change. One of the critical questions which needs to be tackled in the private sector is the issue of whether the arrangement between grantor and grantee is one of lease or of licence. Broadly, for private sector purposes, a lease confers protection, and a licence does not.

In the public sector, however, it is clear that some licences are protected, as s 79(3) makes clear. The fundamental issue, however, is whether s 79(3) applies to any licence, other than those temporary licences specifically excluded under s 79(4), or only a licence conferring exclusive occupation. The issue seems now to have been authoritatively settled, so as to confine protection to licences conferring exclusive occupation, by the decision of the House of Lords in *Westminster City Council v Clarke* [1992] 1 All ER 695. In that case Mr Clarke applied to Westminster City Council claiming to be homeless. Forming the view that his homelessness was not unintentional, the Council provided accommodation for him in a hostel. The document under which the right to occupy was granted made it clear that he was not to enjoy exclusive occupation of any particular accommodation which might be allocated to him. The council sought to evict Mr Clarke because of his conduct in causing nuisance, annoyance, and noise. The House of Lords concurred with the speech of Lord Templeman.

Westminster City Council v Clarke

Lord Templeman: Section 112 of the 1985 Act provides that for the purposes of Pt IV a dwelling-house may be a house or part of a house. Under the Rent Acts, in order to create a letting of part of a house as a separate dwelling there must be an agreement by which the occupier has exclusive possession of essential living rooms of a separate dwelling-house. Essential living rooms provide the necessary facilities for living, sleeping and cooking. Thus a bed-sitting room with cooking facilities may be a separate dwelling-house even though bathroom and lavatory facilities might be elsewhere and shared with other people: see *Neale v Del Soto* [1945] 1 All ER 191, [1945] KB 144, *Cole v Harris* [1945] 2 All ER 146, [1945] KB 474 and *Goodrich v Paisner* [1956] 2 All ER 176 at 179–180 [1957] AC 65 at 79. Room E provides facilities for living, sleeping and cooking. Room E is occupied by Mr Clarke as his only home. Section 79(1) of the 1985 Act employs the language of the Rent Acts. Accordingly, Mr Clarke is a secure tenant of room E if he enjoys exclusive possession of room E. In order to determine whether Mr Clarke enjoys exclusive possession of room E, the rights conferred on Mr Clarke and the rights reserved to the council by the licence to occupy must be considered and evaluated.

Mr Sedley QC, who appeared on behalf of Mr Clarke, submitted that Mr Clarke was a secure tenant even if he was not granted exclusive possession of room E. Section 79(3), he said, applies to any licence to occupy a dwelling-house. This submission would confer security of tenure on a lodger and on a variety of licensees and is contrary to the language of s 79(3), which applies the provisions of Pt IV of the Act to a licence 'as they apply in relation to a tenancy'. Part IV only applies to a tenancy of a dwelling-house let as a separate dwelling, namely with exclusive possession. Part IV therefore applies to a licence which has the same characteristics. A tenant or licensee can only claim to be a secure tenant if he has been granted exclusive possession of a separate dwelling-house.

The predecessor of s 79(3) of the 1985 Act was s 48 of the Housing Act 1980, which provided that where under a licence 'the circumstances are such that, if the licence were a tenancy, it would be a secure tenancy, then ... this Part of this Act applies to the licence as it applies to a secure tenancy'. The result of s 48 of the 1980 Act was that, whether the occupier was a tenant or a licensee, he must be granted exclusive possession in order to become a secure tenant. The Court of Appeal so held in *Family Housing Association v Miah* (1982) 5 HLR 94 and *Kensington and Chelsea Royal Borough v Hayden* (1984) 17 HLR 114.

The Rent Acts do not apply to a licence and s 48 of the 1980 Act was enacted at the time when some private landlords were granting exclusive possession of residential accommodation at a rent but in the form of a licence. Section 48 of the 1980 Act made clear that such a licence created a secure tenancy. Subsequently, in *Street v Mountford* [1985] 2 All ER 289, [1985] AC 809 this House reaffirmed the general principle that a grant of exclusive possession of residential accommodation at a rent created a tenancy protected by the Rent Acts notwithstanding that the parties intended to grant and expressed themselves as having granted a licence and not a tenancy. The decision of this House in *Street v Mountford* was published on 2 May 1985. The 1985 Act received the royal assent on 30 October 1985. In *Family Housing Association v Jones* [1990] 1 All ER 385 at 393, [1990] 1 WLR 779 at 790 Balcombe LJ held that in these circumstances s 79(3) of the 1985 Act must have been intended to alter the law and to confer the status of a secure tenant on a licensee who did not enjoy exclusive possession. The Court of Appeal in the instant case felt bound to follow its decision in *Family Housing Association v Jones*, though Dillon LJ doubted the soundness of that decision so far as it construed s 79(3) and Balcombe LJ to some extent resiled from his earlier views. In my opinion s 79(3) did not alter the law. The 1985 Act was an enactment which consolidated various statutes including the 1980 Act and gave effect to certain recommendations of the Law Commission (Report on the consolidation of the Housing Acts (Law Com no 144)). Those recommendations did not relate to s 48 of the 1980 Act. Therefore s 79(3) was a consolidating measure and in redrafting s 48 of the 1980 Act in the form of s 79(3) of the 1985 Act the draftsman had no power to alter the law. In my opinion, on the true construction of s 48 of the 1980 Act and on the true construction of s 79(3) of the 1985 Act, whether those sections be considered together or separately, a licence can only create a secure tenancy if it confers exclusive possession of a dwelling-house.

So the question is whether the 'licence to occupy' followed by the allocation of room E and the Mountford payment of rent conferred on Mr Clarke exclusive possession of room E. In *Street v Mountford* [1985] 2 All ER 289, [1985] AC 809 the landlord agreed to grant a licence of residential accommodation for a weekly fee. The agreement was designated a licence and contained a declaration that the licence did not create and was not intended to create a tenancy protected by the Rent Acts. Nevertheless the licensee enjoyed exclusive possession; a third party could not lawfully interfere with that possession and the landlord only reserved limited power to enter to protect his own interests as a landlord. The licence created a tenancy.

In *AG Securities v Vaughan* [1988] 3 All ER 1058, [1990] 1 AC 417 four separate bedrooms in a house were occupied by four separate individuals under four separate and independent agreements, all four occupiers being entitled to share the house in common. But they did not enjoy exclusive possession of the house jointly. Each had exclusive possession of one bedroom but shared possession of the other parts of the house. The bedroom was not a dwelling-house and the house was shared. In these circumstances each occupier was a licensee. In *Antoniades v Villiers* [1988] 3 All ER 1058, [1990] 1 AC 417 a one-bedroomed flat was occupied by a couple on the terms of licences which expressly reserved to the owner the right to share and permit other persons to share the flat. The reservation, which was not and could not reasonably be acted upon, was a pretence designed to disguise the fact that the couple were granted exclusive possession at a rent and were therefore tenants. In the present case no pretence is involved. The question is whether upon the true construction of the licence to occupy and in the circumstances in which Mr Clarke was allowed to occupy room E, there was a grant by the council to Mr Clarke of exclusive possession of room E.

From the point of view of the council the grant of exclusive possession would be inconsistent with the purposes for which the council provided the accommodation at Cambridge Street. It was in the interests of Mr Clarke and each of the occupiers of the hostel that the council should retain possession of each room. If one room became uninhabitable another room could be shared between two occupiers. If one room became unsuitable for an occupier he could be moved elsewhere. If the occupier of one room became a nuisance he could be compelled to move to another room where his actions might be less troublesome to his neighbours. If the occupier of a room had exclusive possession he could prevent the council from entering the room save for the purpose of protecting the council's interests and not for the purpose of supervising and controlling the conduct of the occupier in his interests. If the occupier of a room had exclusive possession he could not be obliged to comply with the terms of the conditions of occupation. Mr Clarke could not, for example, be obliged to comply with the directions of the warden or to exclude visitors or to comply with any of the other conditions of occupation which are designed to help Mr Clarke and the other occupiers of the hostel and to enable the hostel to be conducted in an efficient and harmonious manner. The only remedy of the council for breaches of the conditions of occupation would be the lengthy and uncertain procedure required by the 1985 Act to be operated for the purpose of obtaining possession from a secure tenant. In the circumstances of the present case I consider that the council legitimately and effectively retained for themselves possession of room E and that Mr Clarke was only a licensee with rights corresponding to the rights of a lodger.

In reaching this conclusion I take into account the object of the council, namely the provision of temporary accommodation for vulnerable homeless persons, the necessity for the council to retain possession of all the rooms in order to make and administer arrangements for the suitable accommodation of all the occupiers and the need for the council to retain possession of every room not only in the interests of the council as the owners of the hostel but also for the purpose of providing for the occupier supervision and assistance. For many obvious reasons it was highly undesirable for the council to grant to any occupier of a room exclusive possession which obstructed the use by the council of all the rooms of the hostel in the interests of every occupier ...

This is a very special case which depends on the peculiar nature of the hostel maintained by the council, the use of the hostel by the council, the totality, immediacy and objectives of the powers exercisable by the council and the restrictions imposed on Mr Clarke. The decision in this case will not allow a landlord private or public to free himself from the Rent Acts or from the restrictions of a secure tenancy merely by adopting or adapting the language of the licence to occupy. The provisions of the licence to occupy and the circumstances in which that licence was granted and continued lead to the conclusion that Mr Clarke has never enjoyed that exclusive possession which he claims. I would therefore allow the appeal and restore the order for possession made by the trial judge.

Of course, even an exclusive occupation licence to an ex-squatter will be denied protection in view of s 79(4).

Need for a separate dwelling

Sharing arrangements give rise to trouble in both private and public sectors. In the private sector, so long as the tenant has exclusive possession of some living accommodation (such as a bed-sitter), even though he shares some facilities, such as a kitchen or bathroom, he may still be protected (see s 22 Rent Act 1977 and s 3 Housing Act 1988). There is no parallel provision for public sector tenancies; thus an occupant of a bed-sitter with shared kitchen facilities will not be a secure tenant (see *Central YMCA Housing Association Ltd v Saunders* (1990) 23 HLR 212). There is, of course, no parallel right to buy in the private sector, where the issue is only one of security of tenure.

Similarly, in *Tyler v Royal Borough of Kensington & Chelsea* (1990) 23 HLR 380, a tenant of a ground floor flat was permitted to occupy a first floor flat while building works were carried out on the ground floor premises. He was held not to be a secure tenant of the first floor flat, since his licence to occupy it was only a licence to occupy the first floor in conjunction with the ground floor, and so it was not a 'separate dwelling'.

Not only must the premises be a 'separate dwelling', they must be let 'as' a separate dwelling. In *Webb and Barrett v LB of Barnet* (1988) 21 HLR 228, Webb claimed the 'right to buy' – only of course, available to a secure tenant – in respect of premises which had been let to him by Barnet Council for residential and business purposes, where the business of car body repair was carried on. This business had ceased at the time when the tenant sought to exercise his right to buy, but the Court of Appeal held that the premises had not been let 'as' a dwelling in the first place.

The residence requirement

Section 81 requires the dwelling-house to be occupied as the tenant's 'only or principal home' or, in the case of a joint tenancy, to be the 'only or principal home' of one of the joint tenants. This expression has received a generous interpretation in some of the cases. It is understandable that a tenant who spends the major part of his time on the premises can still claim it is his 'principal' home, as in *Peabody Donation Fund Governors v Grant* (1982) 6 HLR 41, but the decision in *Crawley BC v Sawyer* (1988) 20 HLR 98 strains credulity.

Crawley Borough Council v Sawyer

Parker LJ: The plaintiffs appeal from a decision of His Honour Judge Macmanus in the Horsham County Court on March 16, 1987, whereby he dismissed their claim for possession of premises known as 22 Cobnor Close, Gossops Green, Crawley. The defendant was granted the tenancy of those premises on September 6, 1982, but had in fact been occupying them for some years before. He first went into occupation in 1978.

On May 20, 1986 it was reported to the plaintiffs that the premises were vacant, and on enquiry they discovered that the electricity had been cut off in June 1985 and the gas some time in 1986. It is common ground that what happened was that in 1985 the defendant had gone to live with his girlfriend at 26 Drakes Close, Horsham.

In July 1986 there was a conversation between the defendant and the plaintiffs' representative, during which the defendant said that he was living with his girlfriend at Drakes Close and was purchasing it with her. He enquired, apparently, whether he could purchase the premises the subject of the action. That meeting was followed by some correspondence, which is referred to in the notes of evidence. The letters were produced, but apparently they were not read by the learned judge and they are not before us. During the period when he was absent the defendant had paid the rent of the premises including the rates, he had visited them about once per month, and at some time had spent a week there.

On August 29, the plaintiffs gave notice to quit, expiring on September 30. By that time the defendant and his girlfriend had broken up, and the defendant had apparently ceased to make mortgage payments. He returned to the premises, according to his evidence, on October 10 and has been there ever since ...

The plaintiffs duly brought proceedings in the county court ...

The issue before the learned judge, on facts which to a very large extent were not disputed, was simply whether the tenant was or was not a secure tenant within the meaning of section 81 of the Housing Act, and I must now refer briefly to certain sections of that Act.

(Parker LJ referred to s 79 and continued:)

It would therefore appear that a tenancy can at one time be a secure tenancy, cease to be a secure tenancy and become a secure tenancy again if in the interim period it has not been determined. The landlord condition is set out in section 80. It is unnecessary to refer to it. It is common ground that the landlord condition was satisfied in the present case.

(Parker LJ referred to s 81 and continued:)

The judge, therefore, had to determine, and only to determine, whether the defendant satisfied the provisions of section 81.

It is quite plain that it is possible to occupy as a home two places at the same time, and indeed that is inherent in the wording of section 81. It is therefore plain that, if you can occupy two houses at the same time as a home, actual physical occupation cannot be necessary, because one cannot be physically in two places at the same time.

So far as the two cases relied upon by the learned judge are concerned, they do not appear to me to be open to criticism as cases to which he was entitled to refer. Going through the whole thread of these matters is the common principle that in order to occupy premises as a home, first, there must be signs of occupation – that is to say, there must be furniture and so forth so that the house can be occupied as a home-and, secondly, there must be an intention, if not physically present, to return to it. That is the situation envisaged in the examples given by the Master of the Rolls of, for example, the sea captain who is away for a while. His house is left fully furnished, ready for occupation, no doubt the rent paid in his absence, but he is not physically there and may not be for a very long period indeed.

In the present case the learned judge was, on the evidence, in my view well entitled to hold that throughout the period the premises the subject of the action were occupied by the defendant as a home. The only question which really arose is whether it was occupied as a principal home. The learned judge considered the question. He came to the conclusion which he did on the basis that the defendant had left to live with his girlfriend but with no intention of giving up permanent residence of Cobnor Close.

Some criticism is made of that wording, but we are not analysing a judgment which was carefully prepared and delivered after reservation. It is in my view unjustified to latch on to sentences in a short extempore judgment and try to find on them an argument that the learned judge misdirected himself in law. The situation, which the judge was entitled to take into account, was that he had before him the evidence of the defendant, who asserted throughout that he had every intention of returning and not merely that he had not abandoned the flat. He said in his evidence-in-chief: 'I accept I was not there but I had every intention to return'. He again said he had every intention to return somewhat later on and that he did not intend to give up the flat. He was staying with his girlfriend helping her to buy a house. I fail myself to understand how he could have been a tenant in common, and the matter was not investigated. The learned judge was entitled to take the view that he was there on a temporary basis and that his principal home throughout remained the premises the subject of the action.

The position as at the time the notice to quit was served was that the girlfriend had already told him that he had to get out. He did not in fact move back into Cobnor Close until after the expiry of the notice, but in my view it was well open to the learned judge to have come to the conclusion that, both when the notice to quit was served and when it expired and indeed throughout the whole period, Cobnor Close remained his principal home. That the matter was a matter for the learned judge to conclude on the facts appears clearly from the decision of this court in *Peabody Donation Fund Governors v Grant* (1982) 6 HLR 41. The learned judge reached his conclusion here on evidence on which he was, in my view, entitled to reach that conclusion. I am unable to accept that in reaching it he misdirected himself in any way as to the law.

Accordingly I would dismiss this appeal.

O'Connor LJ agreed.

It is difficult not to agree with a learned commentator who has pointed out that the evidence of the occupation of the flat as the tenant's 'only or principal home' seems far too weak, and that the decision gives insufficient weight to the change in the statutory formula from 'occupation as a residence' (the Rent Act test) to 'occupation as the only or principal home' (Bridge 1988 Conv 3030–5). Rather, it is suggested that the problem should be approached in two stages:

(1) Is the property in question the tenant's only home?

(2) If not, is it his principal home?

The decision relies heavily on Rent Act authorities, which are not really in point.

A possible way of mitigating the effect of the decision, which may also affect the interpretation of the same phrase 'only or principal home' in the private sector (Housing Act 1988) is to say that the court was concentrating on the situation at the time when the landlord served notice to quit on Sawyer. At that stage, having split up with his girlfriend, arguably the flat had again become Sawyer's 'only or principal home'. This suggestion, however, is not easy to reconcile with the finding of the trial judge, apparently accepted by the Court of Appeal, that the flat remained 'his only or principal home' throughout.

It seems clear from the decision that the premises may move in (or out) of protection depending on the state of affairs at any given time.

Further problems can arise in the case of breakdown of a domestic relationship. If spouses are joint tenants the residence requirement will clearly be satisfied so long as either of them continues to occupy the house as his or her 'only or principal home'. If the husband is the sole tenant, and leaves his wife occupying the home, her presence will suffice to keep the tenancy alive (see s 1(6) Matrimonial Homes Act 1983). This provision, however, does not apply to a cohabitee (who is not a joint tenant), and it will be more difficult in these cases to suggest that the tenancy continues as a secure tenancy, as the courts are less willing to treat residence by a family member in such circumstances as satisfying the test. (See *Colin Smith (Music) Ltd v Ridge* [1975] 1 WLR 463 (private sector), and *London Borough of Sutton v Swann* (1985) 18 HLR 140, where it was assumed that a tenant who had vacated his council house but had allowed his daughter and her family to move in ceased to be a secure tenant. This decision was subsequently followed in the housing association tenancy case of *Muir*

Group Housing Association Ltd v Thornley & Thornley (1992) 25 HLR 89, and in *Jennings & Jennings v Epping Forest DC* (1992) 25 HLR 241.)

Problems can arise if a cohabitee is excluded from a matrimonial home under a Court Order made under the Domestic Violence and Matrimonial Proceedings Act 1976. In *Fairweather v Kolosine* (1982) 11 HLR 61 the Court of Appeal declined to decide whether the excluded cohabitee would remain a secure tenant in these circumstances; it is possible that, in order to protect the partner, a court might have recourse to some form of constructive occupation by the excluded absentee in a case like this.

Clearly, occupation of the whole house is not required, as a secure tenant has certain rights to sublet and take in lodgers (see p 4). Subletting of the whole house, though, terminates the secure tenancy irrevocably (see p 264).

The tenancy must not be excluded

Schedule 1 Housing Act 1985 contains a series of exclusions. Some of these relate to the nature of the tenancy itself (long tenancies, para 1), some to the employment of the tenant (local authority employees and other public sector workers, eg police and fire-fighters, para 2), some to the nature of the land (development land, para 3; agricultural holdings, para 8; licensed premises; para 9; business premises, para 11; almshouses, para 12), some to the nature of the tenant (homeless persons, para 4; persons taking up employment, para 5; students, para 10). A brief explanation of some of these provisions may help.

Employment cases: para 2

This exemption applies where accommodation is provided for an employee in circumstances where his contract of employment requires him to occupy the dwelling-house for the better performance of his duties. This provision has been considered in two cases, both of which turn on the issue of whether such a term can be implied in the absence of an express stipulation. In *South Glamorgan County Council v Griffiths* (1982) 24 HLR 334 it was held that a retired school caretaker was not, and had never been, a secure tenant, as he was impliedly required to live in a house adjacent to the school for the better performance of his duties. This 'insecure' status remained notwithstanding his retirement. On the other hand, in *Hughes & Hughes v London Borough of Greenwich* (1992) 24 HLR 605 (followed in the House of Lords – see p 372) a different division of the Court of Appeal refused to imply a term into the contract of employment of a headmaster of a special school requiring him to reside in a dwelling-house in the school grounds, but not within the curtilage of the school. The result was that he was a secure tenant, with the right to buy. The court seems to have felt that he could have carried out his scholastic duties adequately whilst living in other nearby property. *South Glamorgan* does not appear to have been cited in *Hughes*.

Development Land: para 3

Tenancies on land acquired for development – and used as temporary housing accommodation – are not secure. It appears that the non-secure exception will apply even if the local authority's development aspirations change (see *Attley v*

Cherwell District Council (1989) 21 HLR 613 where the land in question was originally acquired for overspill residential development, but was subsequently intended for industrial development). Nor is it essential that the landlord be the person who acquired the land for development. In *Hyde Housing Association v Harrison* (1990) 23 HLR 57 the Department of Transport, having acquired land for a road widening scheme, made an arrangement with the plaintiff housing association under which they were to use the land for temporary housing provision. Harrison, permitted to occupy the premises pending implementation of the scheme, claimed to be a secure tenant. This claim was rejected, as the premises had been acquired by the Department of Transport for development. They were subsequently granted by the housing association to Harrison, but the court held that there was no requirement in para 3 that the landlord had to be the person who had 'acquired' the land for development.

If the development project for which the land is acquired is abandoned, then the land can no longer be said to be being used 'pending development', and so any tenancy created thereon will normally be secure (see *Lillieshall Road Housing Co-operative v Brennan* (1991) 24 HLR 195).

If, of course, the tenancy is secure, a redeveloping landlord may be able to rely on a ground for possession: ground 10 (see later p 273). However, this ground can only be relied on if suitable alternative accommodation is available.

The homeless: para 4

Local authorities have a variety of duties in respect of homelessness (see Chapter 15). In some cases, they have a duty to provide accommodation, which will normally be secure. In other cases (eg intentional homelessness) their duty is only to provide temporary accommodation. Tenancies thus granted will not be secure in the first instance, but they may become so. The nature of the trap which this provision posed for local housing authorities was illustrated in *Eastleigh Borough Council v Walsh* [1985] 2 All ER 112. Here Walsh, claiming to be homeless and in priority need, was let into possession of certain council accommodation by Eastleigh. He was clearly a tenant, and the tenancy was on the basis of a temporary letting pending further enquiries. Shortly thereafter, Walsh's wife and children left him to go to Darlington: thus he could no longer be said to be in priority need and so no housing obligation was owed to him. The local authority, having discovered this, sent him an invalid notice to quit, but then took no further action until the 12 month period specified in para 4 had elapsed. Thus, they found themselves confronted by a secure tenant, Walsh. Having failed to determine Walsh's tenancy during the initial year, the local authority had 'allowed [Walsh] to acquire a secure tenancy, which he certainly did not deserve ... due to nothing but their own ineptitude'. The solution, of course, was for the local authority to serve a valid notice to quit during the initial 12 month period (see *Swansea City Council v Hearn* (1990) 23 HLR 284). The Housing Act 1996 has now replaced paragraph 4 with one which states that a tenancy granted in pursuance of any function under Part VII of the 1996 Act (Homelessness) is not a secure tenancy unless the local housing authority concerned have notified the tenant that the tenancy is to be regarded as a secure tenancy.

Short term arrangements: 'North Wiltshire' schemes

These schemes, originally developed in North Wiltshire, are essentially arrangements made with private landlords whereby the private landlord makes available to the council residential property for subletting on a temporary basis. These schemes do not depend upon the arrangement between the private landlord and the local authority creating a tenancy as such. It seems that a licence will suffice (see *London Borough of Tower Hamlets v Miah* (1991) 24 HLR 199).

SECURITY OF TENURE

The purpose of this part of the chapter is to examine the principles of security of tenure established in the public sector under the Housing Act 1988. Public sector tenants did not enjoy any systematic security of tenure before the introduction of the Housing Act 1980, though they did enjoy a modicum of protection from the public law principles. These principles remain of significance for non-secure tenants, but secure tenants now have the advantage of a comprehensive code of protection. The scheme owes something to the analogy of the Rent Act in the private sector, though there are necessarily many modifications because of the differing nature of the landlord.

The nature of the relationship between the private and the public sector codes was discussed by the Court of Appeal in the leading case of *LB of Hammersmith & Fulham v Harrison* [1981] 2 All ER 588. The essential point in that case was whether security of tenure extended to tenants whose tenancies had been validly determined by a landlord's notice to quit before the coming into force of the Housing Act 1980. The Court of Appeal decided this issue against the tenants, but also made some general remarks about the nature of the security enjoyed.

LB of Hammersmith & Fulham v Harrison

Brandon LJ: It is true that there are certain important similarities between the relevant provisions of the earlier Rent Acts and those of Chapter II of Part I of the 1980 Act. The first such similarity is that both pieces of legislation have as their purpose the provision of security of tenure for tenants of rented homes. The second similarity is that the legislature has in both cases achieved this purpose by (a) preventing a landlord from obtaining possession of the premises which he has let except in pursuance of an order of a court, and (b) prohibiting a court from making such an order for possession unless and until it is satisfied by the landlord that certain circumstances exist or certain conditions are fulfilled. Against these two important similarities, however, there must be set what appear to me to be two even more important differences. The first difference is between the housing situation in which, and the social background against which, the two pieces of legislation were passed. The 1920 Act, in relation to which Remon's case was decided, was passed to deal with the critical housing shortage which followed the demobilisation of immense numbers of the armed forces after the end of the 1914-18 war. It was necessary that legislation to meet that situation should be passed, and that its remedial qualities should take effect, as quickly as possible.

By contrast, Chapter II of Part I of the 1980 Act was not enacted in order to meet any immediate or urgent crisis in housing accommodation. Its purpose was rather the social one of giving to tenants in the public housing sector, so far as reasonably practicable, the same kind of protection from being evicted from their homes without good and sufficient cause as had been enjoyed by tenants in the private housing sector for many decades under the Rent Acts. This assimilation of rights as between public and private sector tenants, though no doubt regarded as desirable in the general interests of social equality and non-discrimination, was not an urgent matter, and no special reason for setting the earliest possible deadline for such assimilation existed. In this connection it is to be observed that, for numerous years past, it had been thought safe and proper to give to local authority landlords a complete discretion with regard to the eviction of public sector tenants, and to rely on them to exercise such discretion fairly and wisely.

The second difference is between the method used by the legislature in order to effect its purpose in the Rent Acts, particularly the earlier Acts prior to 1965, on the one hand, and that used by it to effect its purposes in Chapter II of Part I of the 1980 Act on the other hand.

In the earlier Rent Acts the legislature did not seek to interfere with the common law principles on which contractual tenancies, whether periodical or for a term certain, could be brought to an end. In the case of periodical tenancies, the legislature left landlords free to bring them to an end by the service and expiry of valid notices to quit.

In the case of tenancies for a term certain, the legislature left such tenancies to come to an end automatically by effluxion of time. What the legislature did, however, in order to protect the person who had been a contractual tenant before his contractual tenancy came to an end, was to create a new relationship between that person and his former contractual landlord which Scrutton LJ described, in the second passage from his judgment in *Remon's* case [1921] 1 KB 49 at 58 which I quoted earlier, as a 'statutory tenancy', the parties to which were the former contractual tenant, from then on described as a 'statutory tenant', and the former contractual landlord or his successor in title. The concept of a statutory, as distinct from a contractual, tenancy, having been formulated initially by the court, as a matter of necessary implication, from such provisions as s 15(1) of the 1920 Act, and accepted for many years thereafter as a convenient description of the relationship concerned, was in the end formally recognised by the legislature in s 1(4)(b) of the Rent Act 1965, and still remains, despite subsequent developments with regard to 'controlled' and 'regulated' tenancies, ingrained in the Rent Acts legislation as a whole.

By contrast, in the 1980 Act the legislature went about the matter in quite a different way. It abolished altogether the common law principles on which contractual tenancies, both periodical and for a term certain, could be brought or come to an end. It did this by providing, first, that on the expiry of a contractual tenancy for a term certain, there should come into existence a periodic tenancy in its place, unless a further contractual tenancy for a term certain should be granted (s 29(1)(2)); and, second, that a periodic tenancy, whether having that character originally, or coming into being on the expiry of a term certain, should not be capable of being brought to an end by a landlord except by the latter obtaining an order of the court for possession (s 32(1)), or, in cases where provisions for re-entry or forfeiture are relied on, an order terminating the secure tenancy (s 32(2)).

The significance of the first difference between the two pieces of legislation to which I have referred above is that, in a situation where the legislature, having passed the 1980 Act as a whole on 8th August 1980, has then seen fit not to bring Chapter II of Part I into operation until eight weeks later, namely on 3rd October 1980, there is no policy reason of any kind why the court should seek, by giving a strained and unnatural meaning to certain expressions in the Act, to give retrospective effect to the provisions of that chapter.

The significance of the second difference between the two pieces of legislation to which I have referred is this. Whereas a court interpreting the earlier Rent Acts, such as the 1920 Act in *Remon's* case, felt obliged to fill gaps in the express provisions of the Acts on the basis of necessary implication from their manifest purpose, the 1980 Act deals much more fully and explicitly with the methods by which the purpose of providing security of tenure for public sector tenants is to be achieved. The result is that gaps in the express provisions of the kind which existed in the earlier Rent Acts do not exist in the 1980 Act, and do not therefore require to be filled up by the kind of process of strained and unnatural construction to which the Court of Appeal was admittedly driven in Remon's case.

In my view, when one looks at the differences, as well as the similarities, between the Rent Acts legislation on the one hand and Chapter II of Part I of the 1980 Act on the other, it is impossible to say that the two pieces of legislation are *in pari materia*, so that a decision on the retrospective effect of certain provisions in the first of these two pieces of legislation should be regarded as binding this court to reach a similar decision with regard to the retrospective effect of what are, to some extent at least, comparable provisions in the second of the two pieces of legislation.

In *Remon's* case the Court of Appeal felt bound to give strained and unnatural meanings to perfectly ordinary words, such as 'tenant', 'tenancy', 'letting' and 'let'. It did so for one reason, and one reason only, namely that unless those words were given strained and unnatural meanings, the manifest purpose of the 1920 Act (to protect from eviction persons whose contractual tenancies had been brought or come to an end) would be defeated.

In the three cases with which these appeals are concerned, I do not see any compelling reason why the court should follow its predecessor in *Remon's* case by giving a strained and unnatural meaning to the expression 'let under a secure tenancy' as used in ss 33(1) and 34(1) of the 1980 Act.

The ordinary and natural meaning of the expression is 'let under a secure tenancy at the date to which each subsection concerned relates', that is to say the date of commencement of an action for possession in the case of s 33(1) and the date of deciding whether an order for possession should be made in such an action in the case of s 34(1).

To adopt that ordinary and natural meaning of the expression concerned will not, so far as I can see, in any way defeat the purposes of Chapter II of Part I of the 1980 Act. It will only mean that, since under s 153(2) of the Act Chapter II of Part I did not come into operation, by the decision of the legislature and the Secretary of State, until eight weeks after the passing of the Act, namely on 3rd October 1980, only those public sector tenants whose tenancies were not lawfully brought to an end before that date will benefit from the provisions of that chapter.

It will be seen from these remarks that the cumbersome concept of the 'statutory tenancy' has no corresponding role to play in the public sector. The way the public sector works is to abolish altogether the common law principles about termination of tenancies, both periodical and for a term certain (though as will be seen later, the effect of a notice to quit by the tenant may be to bring the security of tenure to an end). Most local authority tenancies are periodic; but if there is a fixed-term tenancy, on the expiry of the fixed-term tenancy, it is replaced by a periodic tenancy, the 'period' being related to the frequency of rent payments under the former fixed-term tenancy. This periodic tenancy, whether arising by force of the original grant or arising automatically on the expiry of a fixed-term tenancy, can only then be brought to an end in certain defined circumstances, and by following defined procedures. This gives rise to two questions:

(a) What is the procedure to be followed by the landlord?

(b) What are the circumstances in which a court may order possession?

Procedure

In the case of a periodic secure tenancy, the landlord must comply with the procedure laid down in s 83 Housing Act 1988, and serve a notice on the tenant. The object of this is clearly to let the tenant know that he is in peril, and to give him a chance to put matters right. The notice must also specify the date after which possession proceedings may be begun, and this must amount to at least four weeks (by analogy with the Protection from Eviction Act 1977). Proceedings, if begun, must then be commenced within 12 months of the date specified in the notice. If the proceedings are not commenced within that period, the landlord has to start the process anew by service of a fresh notice. If the tenancy is a fixed-term secure tenancy, then again a notice must be served, specifying the ground relied on, but there is no need to specify a date after which possession proceedings may be commenced. It may be, in the case of a fixed-term tenancy, that there is a possibility of forfeiture; but the court cannot, for that reason alone, bring the tenant's occupation to an end, as an order terminating by forfeiture the fixed-term tenancy will then cause a periodic tenancy to spring up, under s 82(3).

Since the service of a valid notice (which must specify the ground on which possession is to be sought) is an essential preliminary to possession proceedings, it is not surprising that there has sometimes been an issue as to whether a particular notice is valid. Although the ground specified in the notice may be added to, or amended, at the hearing with the leave of the court, it is clear that such leave will not be automatically granted. If a particular notice is invalid, the proceedings must be halted then and there, as the landlord cannot proceed with his claim for possession in the absence of a valid notice. In general, the notice must spell out with sufficient clarity the alleged breach or breaches of the tenancy agreement in those cases where the landlord is relying on a breach. A general allegation of 'non-payment of rent' will not suffice (see *Torridge DC v Jones* (1985) 18 HLR 107), though an error in calculating the alleged arrears will not, in itself, necessarily invalidate the notice (see *Dudley MBC v Bailey* (1990) 22 HLR 424. Compare, in the interpretation of the similar section in the private sector (s 8 Housing Act 1988) *Mountain v Roberts* (1993) 25 HLR 427.

The circumstances in which an order may be made

The concept of 'grounds' for an order for possession is one which is familiar in the private sector; both the Rent Act 1977 and the Housing Act 1988 depend for their operation on the idea of termination of a tenancy only where 'grounds' for such termination can be shown to exist. There is however one marked difference; in both the private sector schemes there exist certain 'mandatory' grounds. There is no direct parallel in the public sector; mandatory grounds, as such, do not arise (though in a sense grounds 9-11 are quasi-mandatory) and, in general, in many situations the issue of reasonableness must be considered by the court. In a few cases the issue of 'reasonableness' as such does not arise, but the court has to be satisfied as to the availability of suitable alternative accommodation.

The grounds can most conveniently be grouped under three headings:

(a) Those which depend upon 'reasonableness' alone (grounds 1-8).

(b) Those which depend upon the availability of suitable alternative accommodation (grounds 9–11).

(c) Those which depend upon 'reasonableness' and the availability of suitable alternative accommodation (grounds 12–16).

These grounds are set out in Schedule 2 Housing Act 1985.

Housing Act 1985

SCHEDULE 2

PART 1
Grounds on which court may order possession if it considers it reasonable

Ground 1

Rent lawfully due from the tenant has not been paid or an obligation of the tenancy has been broken or not performed.

Ground 2

The tenant or a person residing in the dwelling-house has been guilty of conduct which is a nuisance or annoyance to neighbours, or has been convicted of using the dwelling-house or allowing it to be used for immoral or illegal purposes.

Ground 3

The condition of the dwelling-house or of any of the common parts has deteriorated owing to acts of waste by, or the neglect or default of, the tenant or a person residing in the dwelling-house and, in the case of an act of waste by, or the neglect or default of, a person lodging with the tenant or a sub-tenant of his, the tenant has not taken such steps as he ought reasonably to have taken for the removal of the lodger or sub-tenant.

Ground 4

The condition of furniture provided by the landlord for use under the tenancy, or for use in the common parts, has deteriorated owing to ill-treatment by the tenant or a person residing in the dwelling-house and, in the case of ill-treatment by a person lodging with the tenant or a sub-tenant of his, the tenant has not taken such steps as he ought reasonably to have taken for the removal of the lodger or sub-tenant.

Ground 5

The tenant is the person, or one of the persons, to whom the tenancy was granted and the landlord was induced to grant the tenancy by a false statement made knowingly or recklessly by the tenant.

Ground 6

The tenancy was assigned to the tenant, or to a predecessor in title of his who is a member of his family and is residing in the dwelling-house, by an assignment made by virtue of section 92 (assignments by way of exchange) and a premium was paid either in connection with that assignment or the assignment which the tenant or predecessor made by virtue of that section.

In this paragraph 'premium' means any fine or other like sum and any other pecuniary consideration in addition to rent.

Ground 7

The dwelling-house forms part of, or is within the curtilage of, a building which, or so much of it as is held by the landlord, is held mainly for purposes other than housing purposes and consists mainly of accommodation other than housing accommodation, and–

(a) the dwelling-house was let to the tenant or a predecessor in title of his in consequence of the tenant or a predecessor being in the employment of the landlord, or of–

a local authority,
a new town corporation
[a housing action trust]
an urban develop development corporation,
the Development Board for Rural Wales, or
the governors of an aided school,
and

(b) the tenant or a person residing in the dwelling-house has been guilty of conduct such that, having regard to the purpose for which the building is used, it would not be right for him to continue in occupation of the dwelling-house.

Ground 8

The dwelling-house was made available for occupation by the tenant (or a predecessor in title of his) while works were carried out on the dwelling-house which he previously occupied as his only or principal home and–

(a) the tenant (or predecessor) was a secure tenant of the other dwelling-house at the time when he ceased to occupy it as his home;

(b) the tenant (or predecessor) accepted the tenancy of the dwelling-house of which possession is sought when, on completion of the works, the other dwelling-house was again available for occupation by him under a secure tenancy; and

(c) the works have been completed and the other dwelling-house is so available.

PART II
Grounds on which the court may order possession if suitable alternative accommodation is available

Ground 9

The dwelling-house is overcrowded, within the meaning of Part X, in such circumstances as to render the occupier guilty of an offence.

Ground 10

The landlord intends, within a reasonable time of obtaining possession of the dwelling-house–

(a) to demolish or reconstruct the building or part of the building comprising the dwelling-house; or

(b) to carry out work on that building or on land let together with, and thus treated as part of, the dwelling-house,

and cannot reasonably do so without obtaining possession of the dwelling-house.

Ground 10A

The dwelling-house is in an area which is the subject of a redevelopment scheme approved by the Secretary of State or the [Corporation] in accordance with Part V of this Schedule and the landlord intends within a reasonable time of obtaining possession to dispose of the dwelling-house in accordance with the scheme,

or

part of the dwelling-house is in such an area and the landlord intends within a reasonable time of obtaining possession to dispose of that part in accordance with the scheme and for that purpose reasonably requires possession of the dwelling-house.

Ground 11

The landlord is a charity and the tenant's continued occupation of the dwelling-house would conflict with the objects of the charity.

PART III
Grounds on which the court may order possession if it considers it reasonable and suitable alternative accommodation is available

Ground 12

The dwelling-house forms part of, or is within the curtilage of, a building which, or so much of it as is held by the landlord, is held mainly for purposes other than housing purposes and consists mainly of accommodation other than housing accommodation, or is situated in a cemetery, and–

(a) the dwelling-house was let to the tenant or a predecessor in title of his in consequence of the tenant or predecessor being in the employment of the landlord or of–

a local authority,
a new town corporation,
[a housing action trust],
an urban development corporation,
the Development Board for Rural Wales, or
the governors of an aided school
and that employment has ceased, and

(b) the landlord reasonably requires the dwelling-house for occupation as a residence for some person either engaged in the employment of the landlord, or of such a body, or with whom a contract for such employment has been entered into conditional on housing being provided.

Ground 13

The dwelling-house has features which are substantially different from those of ordinary dwelling-houses and which are physically designed to make it suitable

273

for occupation by a physically disabled person who requires accommodation of a kind provided by the dwelling-house and–

(a) there is no longer such a person residing in the dwelling-house, and

(b) the landlord requires it for occupation (whether alone or with members of his family) by such a person.

Ground 14

The landlord is a housing association or housing trust which lets dwelling-houses only for occupation (whether alone or with others) by persons whose circumstances (other than merely financial circumstances) make it especially difficult for them to satisfy their need for housing, and–

(a) either there is no longer such a person residing in the dwelling-house or the tenant has received from a local housing authority an offer of accommodation in premises which are to be let as a separate dwelling under a secure tenancy,

and

(b) the landlord requires the dwelling-house for occupation (whether alone or with members of his family) by such a person.

Ground 15

The dwelling-house is one of a group of dwelling-houses which it is the practice of the landlord to let for occupation by persons with special needs and–

(a) a social service or special facility is provided in close proximity to the group of dwelling-houses in order to assist persons with those special needs,

(b) there is no longer a person with those special needs residing in the dwelling-house, and

(c) the landlord requires the dwelling-house for occupation (whether alone or with members of his family) by a person who has those special needs.

Ground 16

The accommodation afforded by the dwelling-house is more extensive than is reasonably required by the tenant and–

(a) the tenancy vested in the tenant by virtue of section 89 (succession to periodic tenancy), the tenant being qualified to succeed by virtue of section 87(b) (members of family other than spouse), and

(b) notice of the proceedings for possession was served under section 83 more than six months but less than twelve months after the date of the previous tenant's death.

The matters to be taken into account by the court in determining whether it is reasonable to make an order on this ground include–

(a) the age of the tenant,

(b) the period during which the tenant has occupied the dwelling-house as his only or principal home, and

(c) any financial or other support given by the tenant to the previous tenant.

PART IV
Suitability of accommodation

1   For the purposes of section 84(2)(b) and (c) (case in which court is not to make an order for possession unless satisfied that suitable alternative accommodation will be available) accommodation is suitable if it consists of premises–

(a) which are to be let as a separate dwelling under a secure tenancy, or

(b) which are to be let as a separate dwelling under a protected tenancy, not being a tenancy under which the landlord might recover possession under one of the Cases in Part II of Schedule 15 to the Rent Act 1977 (cases where court must order possession), or

(c) which are to be let as a separate dwelling under an assured tenancy which is neither an assured shorthold tenancy, within the meaning of Part I of the Housing Act 1988, nor a tenancy under which the landlord might recover possession under any of grounds 1 to 5 in Schedule 2 to that Act,

and, in the opinion of the court, the accommodation is reasonably suitable to the needs of the tenant and his family.

2   In determining whether the accommodation is reasonably suitable to the needs of the tenant and his family, regard shall be had to–

(a) the nature of the accommodation which it is the practice of the landlord to allocate to persons with similar needs;

(b) the distance of the accommodation available from the place of work or education of the tenant and of any members of his family;

(c) its distance from the home of any member of the tenant's family if proximity to it is essential to that member's or the tenant's well-being;

(d) the needs (as regards extent of accommodation) and means of the tenant and his family;

(e) the terms on which the accommodation is available and the terms of the secure tenancy;

(f) if furniture was provided by the landlord for use under the secure tenancy, whether furniture is to be provided for use in the other accommodation, and if so the nature of the furniture to be provided.

3   Where possession of a dwelling is sought on ground 9 (overcrowding such as to render occupier guilty of offence), other accommodation may be reasonably suitable to the needs of the tenant and his family notwithstanding that the permitted number of persons for that accommodation, as defined in section 326(3) (overcrowding: the space standard), is less than the number of persons living in the dwelling-house of which possession is sought.

4(1) A certificate of the appropriate local housing authority that they will provide suitable accommodation for the tenant by a date specified in the certificate is conclusive evidence that suitable accommodation will be available for him by that date.

(2)   ... (3) ...

Some of these grounds, for instance grounds 1–4, are obviously modelled on the parallel grounds in the private sector, and presumably any authorities decided under the private sector provisions will be relevant; others, such as ground 16, have no counterpart in the private sector. As in the private sector, where reasonableness is in issue, the courts normally regard this as an issue for the trial judge; the Court of Appeal will only rarely interfere with a trial judge's finding on reasonableness – for instance, where the view is taken that the judge has misdirected himself on the issue (see, for example, *Sheffield City Council v Jepson* (1993) 25 HLR 299).

A few more detailed comments on some of the grounds may be helpful.

The first group of grounds: the 'reasonableness' cases

Ground 1 (rent arrears or breach of some other provision)

In the public sector there is no counterpart to the private sector mandatory ground for rent arrears introduced in the Housing Act 1988 (see p 204). In all cases, reasonableness will be in issue, and thus it will be relevant for the court to consider such matters as the tenant's record of payment. For instance, in *Woodspring DC v Taylor* (1982) 4 HLR 95, where possession was sought on the ground of rent arrears, it was regarded as relevant to the issue of reasonableness that the tenants had been satisfactory tenants for almost 20 years and had fallen into arrears only because of illness and unemployment. Those with a persistent record of late payment will find it harder to convince a court that it is not reasonable to make a possession order (see *Dellenty v Pellow* [1951] 2 KB 858, *Lal v Nakum* (1981) 1 HLR 50, and *Lee-Steere v Jennings* (1986) 20 HLR 1). Rent will not be 'due' if it has been lawfully withheld, for instance, because the tenant is claiming a right of set-off on account of the landlord's breach of repairing obligations (see *Haringey LB v Stewart* (1991) 23 HLR 557, where the tenant failed to sustain his contention that the landlord was in breach).

This ground also covers other breaches by the tenant, for instance, relating to such matters as the keeping of a dog in breach of the tenancy agreement (see *Sheffield City Council v Jepson* (1993) 25 HLR 299 (followed in *Green v Sheffield City Council* (1993) 26 HLR 349)). In *Jepson's* case the county court judge had refused (on the ground of reasonableness) the plaintiff's application for possession, but the Court of Appeal stressed that it was in the public interest that necessary and reasonable conditions in the tenancy agreements of occupiers of public housing be enforced fairly and effectively.

Ground 2 (nuisance or annoyance)

This is similar to the corresponding provisions in the private sector code and can be used in circumstances, for instance, of racial harassment.

Ground 5 (false statement by the tenant)

There is no counterpart to this provision in the private sector (though it might be useful if there was – see *Killick v Roberts* (above p 187). In any event, the local authority seeking to rely on this ground has to show that the grant of the tenancy was 'induced' by the misrepresentation of the tenant, and that the said misrepresentation was made knowingly or recklessly.

The second group of grounds: the 'suitable alternative accommodation' grounds

These are grounds where the court does not, as such, have to investigate the issue of reasonableness, but where the court has to be satisfied as to the availability of suitable alternative accommodation. Unlike in the private sector (see p 204) the availability of suitable alternative accommodation is not, in itself, a ground for possession.

In general, these grounds give rise to two issues:

(a) When do they arise?

(b) What is meant by suitable alternative accommodation?

When do the grounds arise?

The two most important situations in which these grounds arise are overcrowding (ground 9) and redevelopment (grounds 10 and 10A).

If the dwelling is overcrowded in circumstances making the occupier guilty of an offence (as to which, see Chapter 4, Part II), the landlord can recover possession. It should be noted that in this case the alternative accommodation, by virtue of a special provision in the Act, does not, in order to pass the test of 'suitability' have to be large enough to accommodate all the occupants of the 'overcrowded' dwelling – only the tenant and his family.

So far as ground 10 is concerned, the leading authority is the case of *Wansbeck DC v Marley* (1987) 20 HLR 247. In that case the defendant tenant and her husband had for many years occupied a cottage adjacent to a swimming pool, both owned by the plaintiff authority. On the husband's death, Mrs Marley succeeded to the tenancy, though the swimming pool was no longer in use. The council claimed possession of the cottage on ground 10 (offering alternative accommodation to Mrs Marley), as it was anxious to use the cottage for the installation of a warden to supervise a projected countryside park. Rejecting the council's application, the Court of Appeal stressed that it was necessary for a landlord seeking to rely on this ground to show that it had formed the necessary intention, at the date of the hearing, to carry out the necessary works, and that the works in question could not be carried out without securing possession of the holding. In giving judgment for the tenant, Purchas LJ said:

> I have come to the conclusion that there was no evidence upon which the judge could reasonably have held that the council had established a settled and clearly defined intention to carry out the construction ... No doubt there had been an idea that such facilities might well be provided in due course as part of the rolling plan of development of the leisure park. However, in my judgment, this fell far short of the settled intention necessary to satisfy the test outlined by Asquith LJ (in *Cunliffe v Goodman* [1950] 2 KB 237) and adopted in *Betty's Cafes Ltd v Phillips Furnishing Stores* [1959] AC 20 ... [E]ven if the evidence ... was capable of supporting such an intention the council must also establish that the work could not reasonably be done without obtaining possession of the cottage ... In my judgment there was simply no evidence to support this.

It will be noted that in this case the Court of Appeal relied upon authorities under the equivalent provision in the business tenancy code, namely s 30(1)(f) Landlord and Tenant Act 1954.

Ground 10A (added by s 9(1) Housing and Planning Act 1986, as amended by s 140(1), Schedule 17, Part II, para 106 Housing Act 1988, is designed to cover the situation where the housing authority intends to dispose of the dwelling to a private developer so that he may carry out development work under a redevelopment scheme approved by the Minister, and where there has been notification to, and consultation with, the affected tenants.

What is meant by suitable alternative accommodation?

There is a rich case law on the meaning of this expression in the Rent Act, but the definition in the Housing Act 1985 (for the public sector) is more restrictive, and for that reason the authorities discussed in relation to the private sector will need to be regarded with some caution.

In particular, in the case of the 'overcrowding' ground (ground 9) there is no requirement that the proffered alternative accommodation be large enough to accommodate all those who were in the overcrowded accommodation. Thus, if a tenant causes the dwelling-house to become overcrowded by the addition of lodgers or subtenants, the proffered alternative accommodation will be suitable if there is space enough for the tenant's family.

The issue of suitability needs to be addressed with respect to all the members of the tenant's family living with him at the date of the proceedings. Thus, in *Wandsworth LBC v Fadayomi* [1987] 3 All ER 474, the council claimed possession of a flat under ground 10. The flat was occupied by Mr and Mrs Fadayomi and their two younger daughters, the older two daughters having left. The tenancy was in the name of Mr Fadayomi alone. The marriage was on the point of breaking down, and the court held that the wishes of Mrs Fadayomi should be considered in assessing the suitability of the proposed alternative accommodation.

The private sector provisions direct the court to have regard to the character of the proposed alternative accommodation, and this enables the court to take into account environmental factors. The public sector provision makes no reference to character, and this may enable tenants to be decanted to environmentally inferior accommodation. Though the list of factors in the schedule is not exhaustive (so that the court can take into account, for instance, the tenant's hobbies, such as the need for a garden – though rejected on the facts – see *Enfield LB v French* (1984) 17 HLR 211) the court expressed the view in *Wansbeck DC v Marley* (see earlier) that environmental factors did not come into consideration.

The third group: reasonableness plus alternative accommodation

In this group of cases, the features of groups (a) and (b) are combined, so that the landlord has to demonstrate both the reasonableness of a possession order and the availability of alternative accommodation. These grounds are what might be called 'good administration' grounds, directed to ensure, as far as possible, that the council's housing stock is used to maximum efficiency. The list of grounds thus covers matters such as tied housing (ground 12), housing for physically disabled persons (ground 13, though the physical characteristics must involve substantial modifications – *Freeman v Wansbeck DC* [1984] 2 All ER 746 – a right to buy case), sheltered housing for people with special needs (ground 15), and under-occupation by a successor (ground 16). The last instance needs further explanation.

It may be that after the death of the original tenant a statutory successor will be found to be occupying a house which is far too large for his or her housing needs. It might well be that the house in question could advantageously be used for the accommodation of a family, with the 'successor' being found suitable alternative accommodation. This ground is not available against a spousal successor, but it will apply to other members of the original tenant's family, including a cohabitee, taking by succession. There are strict time limits for the invocation of this ground; the notice of intended proceedings must be served with a 'window' of between six and 12 months after the original tenant's death.

Orders

The procedure for recovery of possession by a landlord under the Housing Act 1985 contains provisions, parallel to those in the private sector, for the granting of a suspended possession order conditional (for instance) on the payment of rent arrears. The governing provision is s 85.

Housing Act 1985

85. Extended discretion of court in certain proceedings for possession

(1) Where proceedings are brought for possession of a dwelling-house let under a secure tenancy on any of the grounds set out in Part I or Part III of Schedule 2 (grounds 1-8 and 12-16: cases in which the court must be satisfied that it is reasonable to make a possession order), the court may adjourn the proceedings for such period or periods as it thinks fit.

(2) On the making of an order for possession of such a dwelling-house on any of those grounds, or at any time before the execution of the order, the court may–

   (a) stay or suspend the execution of the order, or

   (b) postpone the date of possession,

   for such period or periods as the court thinks fit.

(3) ... (5) ...

The operation of a suspended order under this section should be carefully noted; a breach by the tenant of the terms of the suspended order will generally cause his secure tenancy to terminate, and enable the landlord to issue a warrant for possession without any further court order (see *Thompson v Elmbridge BC* (1987) 19 HLR 526). This decision seems to be inconsistent with decisions on corresponding provisions in the private sector Rent Act (see for instance *Sherrin v Brand* [1956] QB 103).

Besides termination by an order of the court, there are other ways in which a tenancy may terminate. These are generally matters which are covered by the ordinary law of landlord and tenant, though they may require modification in view of the terms of the Housing Act, which provides that a secure periodic tenancy can only be brought to an end by the landlord 'obtaining an order of the court for the possession of the dwelling-house' – see s 82.

Two matters in particular require more detailed consideration: surrender and notice to quit by the tenant. In considering these issues, however, it is well to bear in mind that a statutorily safeguarded tenancy is a valuable thing and that it would be wrong for the courts to infer too easily that such a right had been lost. The courts seem generally to have kept this point in mind with regard to issues of surrender, but they seem to be more willing to sacrifice the victim on the issue of legal principle when notice to quit is in issue.

Surrender

Any tenancy will normally come to an end by surrender, which may be express or implied. Just as in the private sector, the courts are unwilling to imply a surrender of an asset as valuable as a protected or statutory tenancy, something which is not to be regarded lightly as 'given away', the courts have shown a similar reluctance to infer the surrender of a secure tenancy. In *Preston BC v Fairclough* (1983) 8 HLR 70 the court declined to find there had been a surrender of the tenancy when the tenants, having 'invited' Mrs Fairclough and her five children to move in with them, then decamped (leaving the Faircloughs in occupation) owing a considerable sum in rent. This decision was followed, in the private sector, in *Chamberlain v Scalley* (1992) 26 HLR 26.

Only a distinct and unequivocal act, as in *R v Croydon ex p Toth* (1986) 18 HLR 493, 20 HLR 576 (clear absence and very substantial arrears of rent) would justify the inference of a surrender. It will also be noted that for a surrender (unlike a notice to quit) all joint tenants must concur (see *Leek and Moorlands Building Society v Clark* [1952] 2 All ER 492, [1952] 2 QB 788).

Surrender is basically bilateral; there must be an intention on the tenant's part to yield up his tenancy, and an intention on the part of the landlord to accept the surrender. In some cases, the court has managed to spell out an intention to accept a surrender from a landlord's conduct which *prima facie* looks equivocal. In the case of *LB of Brent v Sharma and Vyas* (1992) 25 HLR 257 a secure tenancy was granted by Brent Council originally to S, the first defendant, who validly surrendered the tenancy which was then granted to V, the second defendant. V then left the premises, and went to live some distance away, sending a letter to the council indicating an intention to relinquish the tenancy, though adding that she would have no objection to the transfer of the flat to S! The council then sent a notice to quit to V, though it was not validly served, and would, in any event, have been inappropriate to terminate a secure tenancy, as a secure tenancy can only be brought to an end by a court order. The Court of Appeal held that the tenancy had been surrendered, though this must be dubious in view of the council's conduct in sending the notice to quit, which would only make some sense on the footing that there was a continuing relationship of landlord and tenant.

Even if there has been an effective surrender, it may be necessary to consider whether the subsequent conduct of the parties has given rise to a new tenancy. In *LB of Tower Hamlets v Ayinde* (1994) 26 HLR 631 the Court of Appeal distinguished the earlier decision in *Westminster City Council v Basson* (1990) 23 HLR 225 and held that the conduct of the parties had been sufficient to create a new tenancy.

LB Tower Hamlets v Ayinde

Nourse LJ: The sole question on this appeal is whether the defendant, Mrs Julie Ayinde, is the secure tenant under the Housing Act 1985 of a flat known as 4 Panama House, Beaumont Square, London E1, or whether she has lived there for the last eight years as a trespasser ...

On November 30, 1981 the GLC granted to Mr and Mrs Joseph Obajulawa a tenancy of 4 Panama House. It is a purpose built flat on the first floor comprising three bedrooms, living room kitchen and bathroom. It was a secure tenancy, then under the Housing Act 1980. In about 1984 the defendant, her husband and three children were homeless and were offered accommodation at the flat. The defendant is a cousin of Mrs Obajulawa and she and her family moved into the flat. The precise date of the move is uncertain, either December 1984 or March 1985.

On April 19, 1985 Mr Ayinde made an application to the plaintiffs for accommodation for himself and his family. At about this time the Obajulawas returned to Nigeria, and on May 1, 1985 Mr and Mrs Ayinde applied to the GLC for succession to their tenancy. On June 17, 1985 the Obajulawas wrote to the GLC Housing Department as follows:

'I am writing to inform you that I will no longer be returning to London, as I am now in full-time employment in Nigeria. I agree that my cousin Mr and Mrs Ayinde who have been living in my flat since December 1984, take over my tenancy and have it transferred into their name. I hope now you have received this information from me you will be able to put the tenancy in Mr and Mrs Ayinde's name as soon as possible.'

In a further letter to the GLC dated July 21, 1985 the Obajulawas purported to transfer the tenancy to the Ayindes and declared that all former agreements remained void ...

On July 1, 1985, as a result of the dissolution of the GLC, the plaintiffs succeeded to the ownership of the property. Thereafter there was a succession of visits by their officers to 4 Panama House. On May 29, 1986 came one of their visiting officers in the lettings section, Mr Abdul Razzaque. That was an important event in the history of the case to which I will return in due course.

On October 28, 1986 Mr Ayinde died. Until his death he had dealt with the problem of accommodation. Thereafter the task fell on the defendant. She said in evidence that she wrote more than 20 letters asking for a rent book in her name. She also attended the plaintiffs' offices about twice a week between October 1986 and August 1988 making the same requests and on those occasions she was told that they would deal with it ...

The judge's findings as to the payments made by the Ayindes to the plaintiffs were to the following effect. The rent books and the accounts maintained by the plaintiffs were at all material times in the names of the Obajulawas. From July 24 1985 until July 2, 1990 the full amount of the rent was paid to the plaintiffs, first, by Mr Ayinde from the housing benefit received by him and, after his death, by the defendant from her own resources. All those payments were accepted by the plaintiffs. At all times after Mr Ayinde's death the plaintiffs were aware that the rent was being paid by the defendant on her own behalf.

In his reserved judgment the judge identified the questions for his decision as being twofold. First, was the tenancy of the Obajulawas terminated? Secondly was a new tenancy, necessarily a secure tenancy, granted in favour of the defendant? In answering those questions, he held that there was a surrender of the Obajulawas' tenancy by operation of law by means, first, of an unambiguous statement by them that their tenancy was at an end, ie an offer to surrender, and secondly the acceptance of that offer by the grant of a new tenancy to the defendant. He held that that tenancy was granted on May 29, 1986 when Mr Razzaque visited the flat.

Even if there had been no such visit, the judge would have concluded that a new tenancy had been granted from the following facts: first, the plaintiffs had had express notice that the Obajulawas had permanently vacated the flat in the summer of 1985 and had expressed an unequivocal intention to terminate the tenancy; secondly, the plaintiffs well knew that the defendant and her family had exclusive occupation of the flat from that date; thirdly, the plaintiffs knew that the defendant and her husband were paying rent on their own behalf from that date. The judge added a fourth fact which has been treated, I think correctly, by Mr Rutledge, for the plaintiffs, as a third ground for his decision. Since I am entirely satisfied that the second ground, if not the first, was entirely correct I need not refer to the third ...

In my view this case falls to be decided in accordance with well-established principles of the law of landlord and tenant. Mr Rutledge has sought to persuade us that the Obajulawas' tenancy was never determined, so that a new tenancy could never have been granted to anyone else; that the plaintiffs and the Ayindes never intended to enter into legal relations; that the Ayindes were at all times in occupation as trespassers on sufferance; and that the sums they have paid to the plaintiffs for nearly five years were not paid as rent but as *mesne* profits or damages for trespass.

These submissions must be viewed against the basic facts, first, that from July 24, 1985, if not before, the Ayindes or the defendant alone were in exclusive occupation of the flat and were paying the rent out of their own resources and on their own account; secondly, that those facts were known to the plaintiffs from May 29, 1986, if not before; thirdly, that the plaintiffs continued to accept the payments; fourthly, that they never communicated to the Ayindes in any effective way their view that they were unlawful occupants of the flat.

So viewed, Mr Rutledge's submissions are bound to fail. On an objective view of the facts, no court could come to any conclusion other than that at some time after May 29, 1986 the plaintiffs accepted the Ayindes or the defendant alone as the tenants or tenant of the flat. It is well possible that that happened before the plaintiffs' receipt of the letter the defendant wrote in February or March 1987, but it must have happened, at the latest, within a reasonable time thereafter. How could a landlord who had received a letter in such terms and had continued, without protest, to accept payments from its author deny that he had accepted her as a tenant? That question, being unanswerable, has not been answered.

We were referred to a number of authorities of which it is only necessary to mention the decisions of this court in *Marcroft Wagons Ltd v Smith* [1951] 2 KB 496 and *Westminster City Council v Basson* (1990) 23 HLR 255. The first of those decisions demonstrates that even where, as here, the implications of a tenancy will give the tenant a status of irremovability, the court will be slow to withhold the implication where all the badges of a tenancy are there, especially when the situation is allowed to linger on for more than a short period. The second, by its reliance on the clear and prompt assertion by the landlords of the unlawfulness of the occupation and their acceptance of payments effectively as mesne profits and not as rent, well demonstrates the sort of conduct needed in order to preclude the implication of a tenancy, conduct of which there was a notable absence here.

Both cases strongly support the correctness of Judge Graham's decision. I would affirm it and dismiss the plaintiffs' appeal accordingly.

Wall J: agreed.

Notice to quit

It is in the nature of a periodic tenancy that it can be brought to an end by a notice to quit by either party – though this rule does not apply in the case of secure periodic tenancies, which can only be brought to an end on the application of a landlord by an order of the court. True, in the case of residential tenancies, there is a minimum period of notice prescribed by the Protection from Eviction Act 1977 of four weeks – so in the case of a weekly tenancy, no notice, whether by a landlord or a tenant, is valid unless it is given not less than four weeks before the date on which it is to take effect.

It is thus clear that a notice to quit by a sole tenant, if it complies with the provisions of the Protection from Eviction Act, will terminate his tenancy; but there are major problems in the case of joint tenants.

It must now be taken to have been authoritatively decided that a valid notice to quit by one of two or more joint tenants will be effective to bring the tenancy to an end, with effect for both or all of the tenants: see *Hammersmith and Fulham LBC v Monk* [1992] 1 AC 478, [1992] 1 All ER 1.

Hammersmith and Fulham LBC v Monk

Lord Bridge of Harwich: My Lords, the issue in this appeal is whether a periodic tenancy held by two or more tenants jointly can be brought to an end by a notice to quit by one of the joint tenants without the consent of the others ...

As a matter of principle I see no reason why this question should receive any different answer in the context of the contractual relationship of landlord and tenant than that which it would receive in any other contractual context. If A and B contract with C on terms which are to continue in operation for one year in the first place and thereafter from year to year unless determined by notice at the end of the first or any subsequent year, neither A nor B has bound himself contractually for longer than one year. To hold that A could not determine the contract at the end of any year without the concurrence of B and vice versa would presuppose that each had assumed a potentially irrevocable contractual obligation for the duration of their joint lives, which, whatever the nature of the contractual obligations undertaken, would be such an improbable intention to impute to the parties that nothing less than the clearest express contractual language would suffice to manifest it. Hence, in any ordinary agreement for an initial term which is to continue for successive terms unless determined by notice, the obvious inference is that the agreement is intended to continue beyond the initial term only if so long as all parties to the agreement are willing that it should do so. In a common law situation, where parties are free to contract as they wish and are bound only so far as they have agreed to be bound, this leads to the only sensible result.

Thus the application of ordinary contractual principles leads me to expect that a periodic tenancy granted to two or more joint tenants must be terminable at common law by an appropriate notice to quit given by any one of them whether or not the others are prepared to concur ...

(Having reviewed the relevant authorities, Lord Bridge continued:)

In *Greenwich London BC v McGrady* (1982) 46 P&CR 223 the point at issue was precisely the same as in the present appeal. After citing the judgment of the court in *Leek and Moorlands Building Society v Clark*, Sir John Donaldson MR said (at 224):

'In my judgment, it is clear law that, if there is to be a surrender of a joint tenancy – that is, a surrender before its natural termination – then all must agree to the surrender. If there is to be a renewal, which is the position at the end of each period of a periodic tenancy, then again all must concur. In this case, Mrs McGrady made it quite clear by her notice to quit that she was not content to renew the joint tenancy on and after June 15, 1981. That left Mr McGrady without any tenancy at all, although it was faintly argued by (counsel for Mr McGrady) that on, as he put it, the severance of a joint tenancy the joint tenant who did not concur was left with a sole tenancy. That cannot be the law, and no authority has been cited in support of it. The only point that remains is whether Mr McGrady is entitled to the protection of the

Act of 1980 on the ground that what was a secure contractual tenancy has been brought to an end. The short answer to that is that the Act of 1980 operates to give security where landlords give notice to quit; it does not give security where tenants give notice to quit.'

In the instant case it has not been suggested either that the notice to quit given by Mrs Powell could have had the effect of 'severing' the joint tenancy leaving Mr Monk in possession as sole tenant or that, if Mrs Powell's notice was effective, Mr Monk was entitled to any statutory protection.

To this formidable body of English authority which supports the conclusion reached by the Court of Appeal there must be added the decision of the Court of Session in *Smith v Grayton Estates Ltd* 1960 SC 349, which shows that Scottish law, although using different terminology, applies essentially the same principle to give the same answer to the same question. The issue in that case was whether a tenancy continuing from year to year after the expiry of a fixed term by virtue of the Agricultural Holdings (Scotland) Act 1949 was determined by notice given by one of two joint tenants. The Lord President (Clyde) said (at 354–355):

'In considering this matter, it is of importance to realise that in the present case the tenants were occupying under tacit relocation, in other words, that the tenancy was being prolonged from year to year beyond the stipulated term in the lease, but that otherwise the conditions in the lease continued to operate – see Rankine, Law of Leases (p 601); *Cowe v Millar* (3 March 1922), reported only in Connell on The Agricultural Holdings (Scotland) Act, 1923 (2nd edn, 1928, p 346 at p 355) *per* Lord President Clyde. The question comes to be whether, in that situation, a timeous notice by one of the two joint tenants is invalid to bring the tenancy to an end. The argument for the appellant was that a valid notice must be from both the joint tenants, and this notice, not being a joint one, consequently is bad. But, as I see it, this argument overlooks the meaning and effect of tacit relocation. Tacit relocation is not an indefinite prolongation of a lease. It is the prolongation each year of the tenancy for a further one year, if the actings of the parties to the lease show that they are consenting to this prolongation. For, as in all contracts, a tacit relocation or re-letting must be based on consent. In the case of tacit relocation the law implies that consent if all the parties are silent on the matter. Hence, where there are joint tenants, tacit consent by both of them is necessary to secure the prolongation and to enable tacit relocation to operate. Silence by both is necessary to presume that both the tenants wish the tenancy to continue for another year. On the other hand, if both are not silent, and if one gives due notice of termination, the consent necessary for tacit relocation to operate is demonstrably not present, and tacit relocation will not operate beyond the date of termination in the notice. Clearly, in the present case, there is not such tacit consent, and, in my view, a notice by one of the two joint tenants is enough to exclude the further operation of tacit relocation.'

Lord Sorn is to the like effect (at 356).

These then are the principles and the authorities which the appellant seeks to controvert. In the light of the careful analysis of *Howson v Buxton* in the judgment of Slade LJ (see 61 P&CR 414), which I gratefully adopt and need not repeat, it is now rightly accepted that the case affords no greater support for the appellant than can be derived from the obiter dictum of Scrutton LJ, who said with reference to a notice to determine a yearly tenancy (97 LJKB 749 at 752, [1928] All ER Rep 434 at 436):

'I personally take the view that one joint tenant cannot give a notice to terminate the tenancy unless he does so with the authority of the other joint tenant ... '

Despite the eminence of the author of this observation, I do not feel able to give any weight to it in the absence of any indication of the reasoning on which it is based.

There are three principal strands in the argument advanced for the appellant. First, reliance is placed on the judgment in *Gandy v Jubber* (1865) 9 B&S 15, 122 ER 914 for the proposition that a tenancy from year to year, however long it continues, is a single term, not a series of separate lettings. The case arose out of an action for damages by a plaintiff who had been injured by a defective iron grating which was out of repair so as to amount to a nuisance. The property was occupied by a yearly tenant but the claim was brought against the reversioner, who was held liable by the Court of Queen's Bench (see 5 B&S 78, 122 ER 762). The defendant appealed to the Court of Exchequer Chamber on the ground that it was not alleged that the defendant knew of the nuisance, nor that it had existed prior to the commencement of the yearly tenancy. The argument is reported (see 5 B&S 485, 122 ER 911). Judgment was reserved but before it was delivered the case was settled and Erle CJ announced (5 B&S 485 at 494, 122 ER 911 at 914): 'it will not be necessary to deliver the judgment we have prepared'. The undelivered judgment in the defendant's favour is nevertheless reported and has always been regarded as authoritative. The passage relied on reads (9 B&S 15 at 18, 122 ER 914 at 916):

> 'There frequently is an actual demise from year to year so long as both parties please. The nature of this tenancy is discussed in 4 Bac Abr tit Leases and Terms for Years ((7th edn, 1832) 838-839) and this article has always been deemed to be the highest authority being said to be the work of Chief Baron Gilbert. It seems clear that the learned author considered that the true nature of such a tenancy is that it is a lease for two years certain, and that every year after it is a springing interest arising upon the first contract and parcel of it, so that if the lessee occupies for a number of years, these years, by computation from time past, make an entire lease for so many years, and that after the commencement of each new year it becomes an entire lease certain for the years past and also for the years entered on, and that it is not a re-letting at the commencement of the third and subsequent years. We think this is the true nature of a tenancy from year to year created by express words, and that there is not in contemplation of law a recommencing or re-letting at the beginning of each year.'

It must follow from this principle, Mr Reid submits, that the determination of a periodic tenancy by notice is in all respects analogous to the determination of a lease for a fixed term in the exercise of a break clause which in the case of joint lessees clearly requires the concurrence of all. But reference to the passage from Bacon's Abridgment (4 Bac Abr (7th edn, 1832) p 839) on which the reasoning is founded shows that his analogy is not valid. The relevant passage reads:

> 'A parol lease was made *de anno in annum, quamdiu ambabus partibus placuerit*; it was adjudged that this was but a lease for a year certain, and that every year after it was a springing interest, arising upon the first contract and parcel of it; so that if the lessee had occupied eight or ten years, or more, these years, by computation from the time past, made an entire lease for so many years; and if rent was in arrears for part of one of those years, and part of another, the lessor might distrain and avow as for so much rent arrear upon one entire lease, and need not avow as for several rents due upon several leases, accounting each year a new lease. It was also adjudged, that after the commencement of each new year, this was become an entire lease certain for the years past, and also for the year so entered upon; so that

neither party could determine their wills till that year was run out, according to the opinion of the two judges in the last case. And this seems no way impeached by the statute of frauds and perjuries, which enacts, that no parol lease for above three years shall be accounted to have any other force or effect than of a lease only at will: for at first, this being a lease certain only for one year, and each accruing year after being a springing interest for that year, it is not a lease for any three years to come, though by a computation backwards, when five or six or more years are past, this may be said a parol lease for so many years; but with this the statute has nothing to do, but only looks forward to parol leases for above three years to come.'

Thus the fact that the law regards a tenancy from year to year which has continued for a number of years, considered retrospectively, as a single term in no way affects the principle that continuation beyond the end of each year depends on the will of the parties that it should continue or that, considered prospectively, the tenancy continues no further than the parties have already impliedly agreed upon by their omission to serve notice to quit.

The second submission for the appellant is that, whatever the law may have been before the enactment of the Law of Property Act 1925, the effect of that statute, whereby a legal estate in land vested in joint tenants is held on trust for sale for the parties beneficially entitled, coupled with the principle that trustees must act unanimously in dealing with trust property, is to reverse the decision in Summersett's case and to prevent one of two joint tenants determining a periodic tenancy without the concurrence of the other. It is unnecessary to consider the position where the parties beneficially entitled are different from those who hold the legal interest. But where, as here, two joint tenants of a periodic tenancy hold both the legal and the beneficial interest, the existence of a trust for sale can make no difference to the principles applicable to the termination of the tenancy. At any given moment the extent of the interest to which the trust relates extends no further than the end of the period of the tenancy which will next expire on a date for which it is still possible to give notice to quit. If before 1925 the implied consent of both joint tenants, signified by the omission to give notice to quit, was necessary to extend the tenancy from one period to the next, precisely the same applies since 1925 to the extension by the joint trustee beneficiaries of the periodic tenancy which is the subject of the trust.

Finally, it is said that all positive dealings with a joint tenancy require the concurrence of all joint tenants if they are to be effective. Thus, a single joint tenant cannot exercise a break clause in a lease, surrender the term, make a disclaimer, exercise an option to renew the term or apply for relief from forfeiture.

All these positive acts which joint tenants must concur in performing are said to afford analogies with the service of notice to determine a periodic tenancy which is likewise a positive act. But this is to confuse the form with the substance. The action of giving notice to determine a periodic tenancy is in form positive; but both on authority and on the principle so aptly summed up in the pithy Scottish phrase 'tacit relocation' the substance of the matter is that it is by his omission to give notice of termination that each party signifies the necessary positive assent to the extension of the term for a further period.

For all these reasons I agree with the Court of Appeal that, unless the terms of the tenancy agreement otherwise provide, notice to quit given by one joint tenant without the concurrence of any other joint tenant is effective to determine a periodic tenancy.

Lords Brandon of Oakbrook, Ackner and Jauncey of Tullichettle agreed.

In *Crawley Borough Council v Ure* (1995) 27 HLR 524, it was held, following *Monk*, that s 26(3) Law of Property Act 1925 (concerning consultation between joint tenants where there is a trust for sale) does not apply to a joint secure tenancy of a council house; *Monk* applies to terminate that joint tenancy when either party, without consulting the other gives, notice to quit.

The effect of *Monk's* case is drastic; it means that a disgruntled joint tenant can deprive his or her former partner of a secure home by giving notice to quit. There might be relief in the terms of the tenancy; if, for instance, the tenancy agreement were to provide that a notice to quit by the tenant should only be valid if concurred in by all joint tenants, this might have protected Mr Monk, but the House of Lords and the Court of Appeal declined to construe the tenancy agreement in this way.

It must be stressed, however, that it is only a valid notice to quit by one of several joint tenants which will have this effect. In the later case of *LB of Hounslow v Pilling* (1993) 25 HLR 305, two cohabitees, Mr Pilling and Miss Doubtfire were joint weekly tenants of the plaintiff council. After alleged incidents of domestic violence, Miss Doubtfire left the property. It was the council's policy to re-house victims of domestic violence, provided that the victim surrendered his or her tenancy. At the behest of the council, Miss Doubtfire wrote a letter to the council in which she purported to terminate her tenancy 'with immediate effect'. In the Court of Appeal, after considering *Monk*, Nourse LJ stressed that the House of Lords had made it clear that 'a joint tenant cannot unilaterally determine the tenancy by giving an inappropriate notice, for example one which does not give the period of notice required at common law or by the terms of the tenancy'. This, said the court, was not a valid notice to quit at all; if anything, it purported to be the exercise of a 'break' clause in the tenancy agreement (by clause 14, the tenant was obliged 'to give the council four weeks' written notice or such lesser period as the council may accept when the tenant wishes to end the tenancy), which would in any event require the concurrence of both or all of the tenants.

The court also held that in any event the notice could not be a valid notice as it failed to give the four week period of notice required by the Protection from Eviction Act 1977.

SUCCESSION IN THE PUBLIC SECTOR

Prior to the introduction of the 'Tenants' Charter' in the Housing Act 1980, the rules about succession to tenancies in the public sector were virtually non-existent, though local authorities, as a matter of discretion and good housing practice, were commonly willing to allow a tenancy to be transferred to a resident relative of a deceased tenant in the event of the tenant's death. The situation has now been transformed, so far as secure tenancies are concerned, by the provisions of the Housing Act 1980 (now replaced by corresponding provisions in the consolidating Housing Act 1985). The scheme contained in the Act has resemblances to the Rent Act succession scheme, in that it allows a succession to a spouse or a member of the family; it differs from the Rent Act regime, however, in allowing only one succession.

Need for a secure tenancy

The key concept in the understanding of the succession rules is that there must, first of all, be a 'secure tenancy' as defined in ss 79–81 Housing Act 1985.

General principle of succession in the public sector

The general rule is that the primacy of succession rights is given to a spouse (in the strict sense), who has to fulfil a (fairly minimal) residence requirement. Other members of the family enjoy secondary succession rights, and, in their case, the residence requirement is more onerous.

Spousal succession

The tenant's spouse is accorded a preferential right of succession to the secure tenancy (s 89(2)(b)). The term 'spouse' here is restricted to the lawfully married; a cohabitee will have to claim as a member of the 'family', where more onerous residential conditions are prescribed (see below).

Residential requirement: spouses

The Act requires that a spouse seeking to succeed under this provision must occupy the dwelling-house at the time of the secure tenant's death. The claimant must also occupy the dwelling-house 'as his only or principal home'. The significance of this expression is examined elsewhere. In the case of a spouse, there is no requirement of a qualifying residence period.

Other members of the family

Unlike the Rent Act, the Housing Act provides a definition of this concept. The relevant section of the Act is s 113.

Housing Act 1985

> 113(1) A person is a member of another's family ... if–
>
> > (a) he is the spouse of that person, or he and that person live together as husband and wife; or
> >
> > (b) he is that person's parent, grandparent, child, grandchild, brother, sister, uncle, aunt, nephew or niece.
>
> (2) For the purpose of subsection 1 (b)–
>
> > (a) a relationship by marriage shall be treated as a relationship by blood;
> >
> > (b) a relationship of the half-blood shall be treated as a relationship of the full-blood;
> >
> > (c) the stepchild of a person shall be treated as his child;
> >
> > (d) an illegitimate child shall be treated as the legitimate child of his mother and reputed father.

In *Harrogate Borough Council v Simpson* [1986] 2 FLR 91, the Court of Appeal considered these provisions in their application to a lesbian couple (fulfilling the necessary residence requirements) who, it was said, could not be taken to be living together 'as man and wife'. The Court of Appeal noted that, in recent years, some recognition had been given to heterosexual cohabitation 'which the public had come to accept as being a perfectly proper and normal association'.

But it was thought that if Parliament had wished homosexual relationships to be brought into the realm of the lawfully recognised state of the living together of man and wife for the purposes of the legislation it would plainly have stated so in the legislation, and it had not done so.

Watkins LJ added: 'I am also firmly of the view that it would be surprising in the extreme to learn that public opinion is such today that it would recognise a homosexual union as being akin to a state of living as husband and wife.'

Family succession: residence requirements

The basic rule is that laid down in s 87(b) Housing Act 1985, which requires the family member to have resided with the tenant throughout the period of 12 months ending with the tenant's death.

The section is silent as to whether the residence has to have taken place in the dwelling-house in question. This issue was considered by the Court of Appeal in *South Northamptonshire District Council v Power* [1987] 3 All ER 831. In that case the defendant claimed to be entitled to a secure tenancy by succession on the death of the original tenant, Mrs Tulloch. The defendant and Mrs Tulloch had begun to live together as husband and wife in 1982. At the commencement of their relationship they lived together in Mrs Tulloch's former matrimonial home, of which she appears to have been the owner-occupier. In 1985 she moved into accommodation provided by the plaintiff council. The accommodation in question was senior citizen's accommodation for a single person. The defendant moved in with her, though the parties seem to have been at some pains to conceal the fact of his presence from the council. Mrs Tulloch died on 31 October 1985, when she had been a secure tenant for some nine months, and when she and the defendant had been living together in the Council's property for about five months.

Kerr LJ summarised the issue as follows:

> [T]he question, of course, is whether the fact that they had previously lived together as husband and wife in other premises ... entitles Mr Power to say that he falls within the provisions of [s 87(b)]. Being 'another member of Mrs Tulloch's family' the question is; has he resided with the tenant 'throughout the period of twelve months ending with the tenant's death'? ... What is said, not surprisingly on behalf of the local authority is that these words connote a requirement of residence, not only with the person who, until his or her death, had been the tenant, but at the premises in question with that particular person for twelve months, during which he or she was the tenant.

He continued:

> The reference in [the section] is to the requirement that the member of the family 'has resided with the tenant'. This suggests a connection with the premises of which he claims to be a successor to the tenant. The words 'resided with' are to be contrasted with the words 'live together' as husband and wife. Of course, the expression 'living together as husband and wife' is a colloquial phrase, and one cannot place too much emphasis on it. But the word 'resides' connotes a connection with the property and not merely a close connection with the person who was the tenant of it.

The Court in *South Northamptonshire v Power* left open the position of a putative successor who had resided with the tenant in other secure council property (including, possibly, the property of another local housing authority) before the occupation (as a secure tenant) of the property in respect of which the succession was claimed. In such cases, by analogy with the 'right to buy' provisions, the successor might be regarded as satisfying, by such residence, the necessary qualifications for succession.

This decision of the Court of Appeal, however, was discarded by the House of Lords in the later case of *Waltham Forest LBC v Thomas* [1992] 2 AC 98. Overruling *South Northamptonshire v Power* so far as the public sector was concerned, Lord Templeman declined to construe s 87 in such a way as to 'produce unwelcome and unjustifiable distress and hardship in the event of an untimely death'.

Waltham Forest v Thomas

Lord Templeman: ... The plaintiffs claim that the defendant did not succeed to the secure tenancy of 336, Stocksfield Road because he had not resided at 336. Stocksfield Road for 12 months before his brother died.

My Lords, section 87 does not stipulate that the successor must have resided at a particular house for 12 months but only that he should have resided with the deceased tenant for that period. The effect of section 87 is to ensure that a qualified member of the tenant's family who has made his home with the tenant shall not lose his home when the tenant dies but shall succeed to that home and to the secure tenancy which protected both the tenant and the successor while the tenant was alive and which shall continue to protect the successor after the death of the tenant. In order to qualify, a successor must have resided with the tenant during the period of 12 months ending with the tenant's death. This restriction ensures that section 87 cannot be exploited, that there will be no difficulty in identifying a genuine successor and that only bona fide claims to have been residing with the tenant shall succeed. This protection for the local authority does not require the residence to have taken place for the whole 12 months in the house to which succession is claimed. The section only requires residence with the tenant for the period of 12 months and I see no justification for implying any other requirement.

When a tenant and a potential successor move from one council house to another the tenant does not lose the protection of a secure tenancy and there is no good reason why the potential successor should lose the protection which he has obtained or is in the course of obtaining under section 87. When a tenant who is not already a council tenant applies for a council house, the local authority, before granting a secure tenancy finds out whether the council house will be occupied by the tenant alone or whether the council house will become the joint home of the tenant and a member of the tenant's family who has been residing with the tenant. The local authority will know whether if they let the council house to the tenant the house will also be occupied by a potential successor who has made his home with the tenant. If the tenant's death is untimely, that is to say within one year of the date of the letting, there is no reason why the potential successor should lose his home if he has in fact resided with the tenant for 12 months. In the present case the plaintiffs have been unable to suggest why the defendant should lose his home as well as his brother by reason of the death of his brother. It frequently happens that a daughter lives with a widowed parent for 20 years or more; if the parent changes council houses or moves from the private sector to a council house within one year of the death of the parent then on the death of the parent the council house will be the home which contains all the furniture and other articles which form part of the home and have been fitted into the council house by the parent and the daughter. It would he cruel if the daughter could be evicted and left to find another home for herself and for her belongings simply because of the accident of the untimely death of the parent within one year. In the absence of express language, section 87 should not be construed in a manner which can only, as in the present case, produce unwelcome and unjustifiable distress and hardship in the event of an untimely death.

In the present case the Court of Appeal (Nourse and Stuart Smith LJJ) (1991) 89 LGR 729, upholding Judge Butter QC were reluctantly constrained to order the defendant to give up possession of 336, Stocksfield Road to the plaintiffs because of the earlier decision of the Court of Appeal (Kerr and Woolf LJJ) in *South Northamptonshire District Council v Power* [1987] 1 WLR 1433. In that case the defendant had made her home with a tenant of a private sector house for three years and continued to make her home with the tenant when he was granted a secure tenancy of a council house. The tenant died within nine months after the grant of the council house tenancy and it was held that section 87 did not protect the defendant. Kerr LJ relied on *Collier v Stoneman* [1957] 1 WLR 1108. In that case, it was held that the sub-tenant of part of a house was not 'residing with' her mother in the whole house just because her sub-tenancy entitled her to share the kitchen with her mother. In *Edmunds v Jones* (Note) [1957] 1 WLR 1118, also cited by Kerr LJ, a grand-daughter was allowed to occupy one room in the house of her grandmother and it was held that the grand-daughter was entitled to succeed to the tenancy of the whole house. Those cases only decided that the successor must live with the tenant in the whole of the premises. They do not approach the present problem which arises when the successor lived with the tenant in different premises during the qualifying period. Kerr LJ also relied on the reluctance of Viscount Simonds expressed in *In re 'Wonderland', Cleethorpes* [1965] AC 58, 70–71, to construe an ambiguity in a statute in a manner which derogated from common law rights. But this principle does not constrain the courts to invent an ambiguity or to construe an ambiguity in a way which does not make good sense.

In the *Power* case Woolf LJ agreed with Kerr LJ but left open the question whether there is any difference under section 87 if the successor has resided for 12 months with the deceased tenant in two or more council houses or has resided partly in a council house and partly in private sector accommodation: [1987] WLR 1433, 1441H. I can see no logical distinction. Section 87 requires that the successor shall occupy the council house as his home at the death of the tenant and shall have resided with the tenant during 'the period of 12 months ending with the tenant's death'. It does not matter whether the successor and the tenant resided together in one or more houses or whether the residences were all council houses provided they resided together in a council house at the moment of death and provided that the successor and the tenant resided together during the period of 12 months prior to the death of the tenant. In my opinion *South Northamptonshire District Council v Power* [1987] 1 WLR 1433 was wrongly decided ...

I would allow the appeal.

Family succession: competing claimants

It might occur that more than one person is qualified to succeed to the tenancy under the above provisions. In such a case, the matter would be settled, *prima facie*, by agreement; in default of agreement, the landlord may select the successor from amongst those qualified (s 89(2)(b)).

Single succession only

In the public sector, only one succession, either to a spouse or a 'family member' is permitted. The situation must be examined carefully, however, as what might appear to be a succession might, in effect, be the commencement of a new tenancy. Thus, in *Epping Forest DC v Pomphrett* (1990) 22 HLR 475 what appeared, at first blush, to be a succession transpired to have been the grant of a new tenancy, thus making available the possibility of a succession on the death of the apparent 'successor'.

Epping Forest DC v Pomphrett

Beldam LJ: ... The defendants are the son and daughter of Mr Percy William Pomphrett. They are unmarried and have lived virtually all their lives at the premises. Their father moved with his wife Mrs Dorothy Pomphrett and his family to 14 Frampton Road, Epping in 1948 or 1949. He was granted by the plaintiff's predecessors a periodic tenancy of the property from week to week terminable by four weeks' notice. The rent was to be payable on Mondays fortnightly and the letting contained the usual terms of such a tenancy.

Mr Pomphrett remained the plaintiff's tenant until his death in January 1978. He died intestate. No letters of administration have ever been applied for on behalf of his estate.

On January 29, 1978 Mrs Dorothy Pomphrett, his widow, wrote to the plaintiffs asking to have the tenancy transferred to her name, sending the rent book to be altered accordingly. The plaintiffs replied on February 3 1978, agreeing that they would formally transfer the tenancy to Mrs Pomphrett on the same terms at a fortnightly rent of £20.54.

On October 3, 1980 Chapter II of Part I of the Housing Act 1980 came into force. That Act created rights of security of tenure for a tenant of a local authority, to which he had not previously been entitled.

Mrs Dorothy Pomphrett paid rent, as the tenant of the council, until her death on December 8, 1985. She too died intestate. No letters of administration were ever applied for for her estate.

On December 10, 1985 the defendants applied to take over the tenancy of the house. The plaintiff wrote saying that regrettably they had no right in law to succeed to the tenancy of 14 Frampton Road: however, the council would offer them alternative accommodation, but until that could be arranged they agreed that the defendants could remain in occupation as licensees, the charges now having increased to £45.68 per fortnight. The defendants were anxious to remain in their home. They had tended the garden, which they enjoyed, they had a dog and they had lived there for all their lives. However, the plaintiff had a policy that, as this was a three bedroomed house, it should not be occupied by persons in the defendants' position, but should be made available to families with children. That was a strict policy based on housing need which had been resolved upon by the council.

By March 3, 1986, because there had been no agreement, the defendants had consulted solicitors, who claimed on their behalf that on the death of their mother in 1985 the defendants had a right to succeed to the tenancy and accordingly were entitled to a secure tenancy.

The learned judge held, first, that he could not draw the inference that there had been an unequivocal acceptance by both parties that the tenancy of the father had been terminated. He held therefore that there had been no surrender by operation of law of the father's interest. He also held that the father's tenancy had become vested in the mother by virtue of the mother's authority to vest it in herself, in conjunction with the local authority, and he therefore held that the tenancy of the mother at the date of her death was a tenancy which had vested in her on the death of her husband the previous tenant under the provisions of section 31 of the Act of 1980. Accordingly, as Mrs Pomphrett herself was a successor within the meaning of section 31(1)(d), the defendants could not succeed to her tenancy under the provisions of section 30(1) of that Act. He thus made the orders for possession and dismissed the counterclaim

Before us it has been argued that on the death of the father in 1978 his tenancy, which was a periodic tenancy, vested in the President of the Family Division, and as to that there could be no dispute. His wife, Mrs Pomphrett, when she applied to take over the tenancy, was in effect acting either as agent for the President of the Family Division, or on her own behalf, and so in conjunction with the plaintiff succeeded in transferring her husband's legal estate in the weekly periodic tenancy to herself. In that way Mr Hockman, who argued the case on behalf of the plaintiff concisely and with ability, said that the learned judge's judgment could be upheld.

For my part I cannot agree with that submission. On the death of the father the legal estate in his periodic tenancy passed to the President of the Family Division, but as no administrators were ever appointed to the estate of Mr Pomphrett the legal estate in that tenancy remained in the President. What then was the effect of the exchange of letters and the acceptance by the plaintiff of Mrs Pomphrett, as their tenant, in 1978 very shortly after the death of Mr Pomphrett?

It seems to me clear that the plaintiff and Mrs Pomphrett intended the relationship of landlord and tenant to be created between them. The language of the letters is only consistent with that interpretation. The plaintiff could not at that stage, or at any time, convey to Mrs Pomphrett the legal estate in the periodic tenancy which was then vested in the President of the Family Division, but they could not in equity deny that she was their tenant. Accordingly, it seems to me that the effect in law of what the plaintiff and Mrs Pomphrett agreed was to create a new tenancy for Mrs Pomphrett which became a secure tenancy when Part I, Chap 2 of the Housing Act came into force and which subsisted until the date of her death. On her death, by section 31 of the Housing Act 1980 the defendants, or one of them, became entitled to succeed to that periodic tenancy, and for that reason I would have allowed the appeal. At Mr Hockman's request I have expressed my view on the issue raised, although it was unnecessary to do so because in the course of argument the plaintiff reached an agreement with the defendants and that agreement will in due course be incorporated into an agreed draft minute.

For those reasons I would set aside the order of the learned judge and substitute the agreed order of the parties.

Balcombe and Dillon LJJ agreed.

293

It should be noted that if facts such as *Pomphrett* occurred in the private sector, the grant of a new tenancy to the statutory 'successor' would not create a further possibility of succession; the effect of Schedule 1, para 10 Rent Act 1977 is to leave the grantee of the new tenancy in the position of a 'first successor'.

If the tenant is himself a successor (which includes the survivor of joint tenants), no further succession is possible (s 88). It is clear, however, that only a passing by 'survivorship' brings this rule into play. If the (previously joint) tenancy has become vested in one of the previous tenants by, in effect, a renunciation of the tenancy by one of the tenants and a recognition of the other as the sole tenant, there is still scope for a succession to take place. Thus, in *Bassetlaw DC v Renshaw* [1992] 1 All ER 925, a succession was held to be possible; the postulant's mother, once a joint tenant with his father, had been held to have become a sole tenant by the grant of a new tenancy to her after the father left, terminating his tenancy.

Bassetlaw DC v Renshaw & Renshaw

Fox LJ: This is an appeal by the defendant, Mr Christopher Renshaw, from a decision of Judge Heald at the Worksop County Court that he give possession to Bassetlaw District Council of a house at 33 Ramsden Avenue, Worksop ('the house').

On June 6, 1982, the house was let by the Council to Graham and Freda Renshaw (the appellant's parents) on a weekly tenancy as joint tenants. By a notice dated March 20, 1989, and received by the Council on March 31, 1989, Graham Renshaw gave notice in the following terms: 'I wish to give one month's notice terminating my part of the tenancy of 33 Ramsden Avenue on 1.5.89.'

On May 1, 1989, a new tenancy agreement was entered into whereby the Council let the house to Freda Renshaw. It was signed by, or on behalf of, those parties.

Freda Renshaw died on July 6, 1989.

The house is property which falls within the provisions of Part IV of the Housing Act 1985. Sections 87 and 88 of the Act deal with succession on the death of the tenant ...

Any material tenancy of the house was a secure tenancy for the purposes of the Act.

The appellant claims that on the death of Freda Renshaw he became entitled to succeed her as a secure tenant of the house because it was his principal home at the time of her death and he was a member of her family who had resided with her throughout the period of 12 months ending with her death. The facts which he so asserts were accepted by the judge as established.

If, however, Freda Renshaw was herself a 'successor' as defined in section 88 the successor provisions of section 87 are excluded (see the concluding words of section 87).

The judge held that the case came within section 88(1)(b) in that Freda Renshaw was a joint tenant who had become the sole tenant. Accordingly, he made an order for possession against the appellant.

The first question is whether the joint tenancy of the house was determined. One joint tenant can determine a short periodic tenancy of the sort with which we are concerned in this case (*Greenwich LBC v McGrady* (1982) 6 HLR 36). The judge found that it was determined. He said that Mrs Renshaw's tenancy 'succeeded immediately upon the termination of the joint tenancy'. There is no respondent's notice as to that. So the point is concluded for the purpose of this appeal. I only add that if the notice given by Graham Renshaw on March 20, 1989, did not operate as a determination as from May 1, it would seem that (as against the Council for the purposes of this appeal) the tenancy must have been determined by grant and acceptance of the new tenancy to Freda Renshaw on May 1.

The joint tenancy having been determined the next question is whether the case comes within section 88(1)(b). In my view, it does not. It is said that the literal meaning of paragraph (b) is satisfied. Freda Renshaw, it is said, was a joint tenant and became the sole tenant. I do not think that is correct. Section 87 is concerned with succession to a tenancy. It provides that 'A person is entitled to succeed the tenant under a secure tenancy ... '

Thus, the statute is dealing with succession to a single tenancy ... The language and structure of sections 87 and 88 all indicate that Parliament was dealing with a single tenancy ...

Approaching the case, therefore, on the basis that the sections are concerned with a single tenancy, the position is as follows. Freda Renshaw was a joint tenant under the 1982 tenancy but she was never a sole tenant under that tenancy. She could only have become so if Graham Renshaw had pre-deceased her or had released his joint interest. Neither event happened. The Notice of March 1989 did not purport to be a release (even assuming that release could be achieved by a document not under seal).

So far as the 1989 tenancy is concerned, Freda Renshaw was never a joint tenant of that tenancy. Thus, while she was a joint tenant of the 1982 tenancy she was never the sole tenant and while she was the sole tenant of the 1985 tenancy she was never a joint tenant of it.

In construing paragraph (b) it is important not to confuse the property with the tenancy. Freda Renshaw was successively a joint tenant and then a single tenant of the property. But she was never both a joint tenant and a single tenant under one tenancy.

I should add that the Council accepts that section 88(4) is not applicable to this case.

The result, in my opinion, is that the appeal succeeds and that the order for possession should be discharged.

Beldam and Leggatt LJJ agreed.

If the tenancy was, however, assigned in accordance with an order under s 24 Matrimonial Causes Act 1973, the assignee will only be treated as a successor if the assignor was already a successor at the time of the assignment.

Deemed succession in the case of a grant of a new tenancy to a successor

There is a complex provision to deal with the situation where a successor becomes the grantee of a new periodic secure tenancy, either of the same premises or from the same landlord, after the determination of his previous periodic secure tenancy. This may be of particular importance in the case where a local authority regains possession from a successor on the ground of 'under-occupation'. The result of s 88(4) Housing Act 1985 is to deem the tenant to be a 'successor' in relation to his new tenancy (thus precluding further succession rights), unless the tenancy agreement relating to his new tenancy otherwise provides.

Implications of change of landlord for succession rights

If, under the change of landlord provisions contained in the Housing Act 1988, a tenancy leaves the public sector and enters the private sector, this may have serious consequences on the succession regime. Such a tenancy will enter the category of an assured tenancy; in such a case there may still be only a single succession, but this may only be to a spouse or quasi-spouse; family successions are excluded. The situation may, however, be alleviated if the new landlord agrees to the insertion, in his tenancy agreement, of 'secure tenancy' style succession rights. The 'Tenant's Guarantee', a code drawn up by the Housing Corporation which lays down the standards of management required of tenants' choice landlords, recommends that landlords consider extending succession rights to 'carers'.

The Housing Act 1996 and amendments

Part V of the Act includes provisions to enable local authorities to offer 'introductory tenancies' to new tenants which are to last for one year but which can be terminated by a court order for possession obtained by the end of that year. Failing such an order, a secure tenancy will then arise (see ss 124, 125, 127 and 130).

The Act also contains provisions that will introduce a new ground for possession in domestic violence cases (s 145), extend ground 2 (nuisance or annoyance to neighbours, etc) (s 144) and amend s 83 of the 1995 Act (proceedings for possession or termination: notice requirements) (s 147).

Section 146 also extends Ground 5 in Schedule 2 to The Housing Act 1985 (ground that the grant of the tenancy was induced by a false statement). Schedule 14, paragraph 1, adds a new paragraph to s 88(1) of the Housing Act 1985 (cases where the secure tenant is a successor) by inserting a provision relating to an 'introductory tenancy'. Further amendments are contained in Schedule 18, Part III of the 1996 Act.

CHAPTER 9

RENT

INTRODUCTION

The purpose of this chapter is to outline the ways in which the level of rent payable by a tenant is sometimes limited by law. The original Rent Act legislation was designed to confer upon tenants a measure of protection against both arbitrary eviction and excessive rents, and until recently these twin objectives featured as the parallel objectives of any rent control system. However, the Housing Act 1988 marks a clear departure from the pattern of earlier legislation: whilst it affords a degree of protection against arbitrary eviction to tenants, it diminishes markedly the attempts to control rent, so that tenants are now, in general, expected to pay 'market rents'. In this chapter, we will consider first of all the 'fair rent' provisions of the Rent Act 1977. These are probably diminishing in importance and, in any event, today show less departure from market rents as supply and demand are brought into equilibrium. We will then consider the minimal level of rent control for tenancies falling within the Housing Act 1988. Finally we will set out briefly the factors affecting rent in the public sector.

CONTROL UNDER THE RENT ACT 1977

In many ways, one of the most significant features of the system of control imposed by the Rent Act 1977 was the 'fair rent' machinery. In simple terms, the system worked by fixing a 'fair rent' for any property falling within the Act. The fixing of a 'fair rent' was a matter for the initiative of the parties, or, originally, of the local authority. (The power of a local authority to make a 'fair rent' reference was abolished in 1989.)

As it was a matter for the initiative of the parties, in many cases no 'fair rent' was actually fixed; in only about one third of the cases of regulated tenancies (ie protected and statutory tenancies) was the procedure actually invoked. This is despite the fact that statute required landlords to provide their tenant with a rent book, in which 'fair rent' principles were explained.

Once a 'fair rent' was fixed the landlord could not lawfully extract more than that 'fair rent' from his tenant. The 'fair rent' thus fixed became an obligation binding *in rem* on future landlords and tenants of the property.

The background to the 1965 'fair rent' legislation

Under the early versions of the Rent Act, the process of rent control operated by reference to a series of strict formulae related to the rateable value of the premises. These schemes were mechanistic in their operation and frequently unfair in their results, and so a determination was made in 1965 to abandon these schemes and apply a 'fair rent' scheme throughout the protected sector.

The scheme of the 1965 'fair rent' legislation

The general scheme was that it was possible for either landlord or tenant (or, originally, a local authority) to apply to a Rent Officer for the registration of a 'fair rent'. A 'fair rent' was often considerably below a 'market rent', as the value arising from 'scarcity' was to be disregarded. The idea was that a 'fair rent' should be 'fair' to both landlord and tenant.

Applications for a fair rent

The general procedure is that application is made to the Rent Officer, from whom there is an appeal to a rent assessment committee, and thereafter on a point of law to the High Court. The register of rents is a public document (s 66 Rent Act) and the procedure for registration is laid down in s 67 of the Act.

Rent Act 1977

67. Application for registration of rent

(1) An application for the registration of a rent for a dwelling-house may be made to the rent officer by the landlord or the tenant, or jointly by the landlord and the tenant, under a regulated tenancy of the dwelling-house.

(2) Any such application must be in the prescribed form and must–

(a) specify the rent which it is sought to register;

(b) where the rent includes any sum payable by the tenant to the landlord for services and the application is made by the landlord, specify that sum and be accompanied by details of the expenditure incurred by the landlord in providing those services; and

(c) contain such other particulars as may be prescribed.

(3) Subject to subsection (4) below, where a rent for a dwelling-house has been registered under this Part of this Act, no application by the tenant alone or by the landlord alone for the registration of a different rent for that dwelling-house shall be entertained before the expiry of 2 years from the relevant date (as defined in subsection (5) below) except on the ground that, since that date, there has been such a change in–

(a) the condition of the dwelling-house (including the making of any improvement therein);

(b) the terms of the tenancy;

(c) the quantity, quality or condition of any furniture provided for use under the tenancy (deterioration by fair wear and tear excluded); or

(d) any other circumstances taken into consideration when the rent was registered or confirmed;

as to make the registered rent no longer a fair rent.

(4) Notwithstanding anything in subsection (3) above, an application such as is mentioned in that subsection which is made by the landlord alone and is so made within the last 3 months of the period of 2 years referred to in that subsection may be entertained notwithstanding that that period has not expired.

(5) In this section ... 'relevant date', in relation to a rent which has been registered under this Part of this Act, means the date from which the registration took effect or, in the case of a registered rent which has been

confirmed, the date from which the confirmation (or, where there have been two or more successive confirmations, the last of them) took effect.

(6) ...

(7) Subject to section 69(4) of this Act, the provisions of Part I of Schedule 11 to this Act [as modified by the Regulated Tenancies (Procedure) Regulations 1980] shall have effect with respect to the procedure to be followed on applications for the registration of rents.

The general effect of the registration of a rent is that the rent stands for two years, though under s 67(3) an application can be made to vary the registered rent in defined circumstances, including, for instance, the improvement of the property.

The setting of the 'fair rent'

The factors which are to be taken into account in the setting of a 'fair rent' are enumerated in s 70. As can be seen, personal factors are excluded, and, as will be seen, any 'scarcity factor' is excluded.

Rent Act 1977

70. Determination of fair rent

(1) In determining, for the purposes of this Part of this Act, what rent is or would be a fair rent under a regulated tenancy of a dwelling-house, regard shall be had to all the circumstances (other than personal circumstances) and in particular to–

(a) the age, character, locality and state of repair of the dwelling-house ...

(b) if any furniture is provided for use under the tenancy, the quantity, quality and condition of the furniture; and

(c) any premium, or sum in the nature of a premium, which has been or may be lawfully required or received on the grant, renewal, continuance or assignment of the tenancy.

(2) For the purposes of the determination it shall be assumed that the number of persons seeking to become tenants of similar dwelling-houses in the locality on the terms (other than those relating to rent) of the regulated tenancy is not substantially greater than the number of such dwelling-houses in the locality which are available for letting on such terms.

(3) There shall be disregarded–

(a) any disrepair or other defect attributable to a failure by the tenant under the regulated tenancy or any predecessor in title of his to comply with any terms thereof;

(b) any improvement carried out, otherwise than in pursuance of the terms of the tenancy, by the tenant under the regulated tenancy or any predecessor in title of his;

(c) ... (d) ...

(e) if any furniture is provided for use under the regulated tenancy, any improvement to the furniture by the tenant under the regulated tenancy or any predecessor in title of his or, as the case may be, any deterioration in the condition of the furniture due to any ill-treatment by the tenant, any person residing or lodging with him, or any subtenant of his.

(4) In this section 'improvement' includes the replacement of any fixture or fitting.

[(4A) In this section 'premium' has the same meaning as in Part IX of this Act, and 'sum in the nature of a premium' means–

   (a) any such loan as is mentioned in section 119 or 120 of this Act,

   (b) any such excess over the reasonable price of furniture as is mentioned in section 123 of this Act, and

   (c) any such advance payment of rent as is mentioned in section 126 of this Act.]

For an example of the way in which the courts have approached these issues, reference may be made to *Metropolitan Properties v Finegold* [1975] 1 WLR 349. Here the presence in the locality of an American School in St John's Wood made the area attractive to American families, resulting in a shortage of accommodation.

Metropolitan Properties v Finegold

Lord Widgery: This is an appeal by Metropolitan Property Holdings Ltd. brought under the Tribunals and Inquiries Act 1958 against the decision of a committee of the London Rent Assessment Panel given on July 23, 1973, and affecting a large number of flats belonging to the company in a block known as South Lodge in St John's Wood. The company complains that in reaching its conclusions as to the fair rents of each of these several flats the committee misdirected itself in its application of section 46 of the Rent Act 1968 ...

The flats in question, as I have said, are in St John's Wood, and there was recently built in St John's Wood a substantial school restricted in its entry to the children of American families in London. The result of that school being built has undoubtedly rendered this part of St John's Wood far more attractive to American families than it might otherwise have been because of the facility of the education of their children which this school provides. Although there is no specific finding to this effect on the part of the committee, it is a reasonable inference, I think, from the material which has been put before us that the presence of this school has almost certainly put up the market rental values of flats and houses in the neighbourhood. And it may be, although again there is no specific finding to this effect, that this has produced locally an element of scarcity in the sense that more Americans want to come and live in St John's Wood and have the facility of having their children educated at this school than the accommodation vacant and to let in St John's Wood would permit. I think it only right to approach the problem on the footing that both those assumptions are good, namely, that the school in its own immediate surroundings has produced an increase in the number of Americans, and, secondly, that it may well have produced an element of scarcity, or accentuated an element of scarcity which previously existed.

The bone of contention between the parties is this: that applying their minds to section 46 of the Rent Act of 1968 the rent assessment committee has reached the conclusion that the presence of the school has produced an element of scarcity of the kind mentioned in section 46(2) and has thought it right, in fixing the fair rents of these flats, to make a deduction, and one can go no further than that, on account of that scarcity.

To see why this contention is put forward and what the answer to it might be, one has to look at the section itself.

(His Lordship referred to s 46(1) and continued:)

I would observe on that straightaway that it seems to be saying in parliamentary language that one must have regard to the sort of factors which tend to push rents up or down on the market. One must have regard to the age of the premises, and that may have an effect up or down according to whether the premises are old or modern. One must have regard to their character and their locality. Their locality is important because a house situate in pleasant surroundings, and with the advantage of local amenities, may very well command a higher rent than an identical house in a less attractive setting.

Looking for a moment at the American school to which I have referred, if the committee took the view that the presence of that school made the houses in the surrounding area, and in particular these flats, more attractive, and thus likely to command more rent, then so far as section 46(1) is concerned the fair rent ought to reflect that factor. In other words, looking for the moment only at subsection (1), any amenity (as the word has been used frequently in this argument), any advantage which the premises inherently have, in their construction, their nature, their scale, their situation, their proximity to a school, a zoo or a theatre, whatever it may be, all those factors which would tend in the market to increase the rental, are factors to be taken into account by the committee in fixing the fair rent. To what extent they are taken into account is, of course, the duty of the committee to decide, but that these are matters which are eligible for consideration is beyond doubt.

At this point, as I have already said, the presence of the American school would, on the face of it, tend to put up the fair rent because it would be an amenity making the premises more attractive.

Then one comes to section 46 (2) of the Act of 1968:

> 'For the purposes of the determination it shall be assumed that the number of persons seeking to become tenants of similar dwelling-houses in the locality on the terms (other than those relating to rent) of the regulated tenancy is not substantially greater than the number of such dwelling-houses in the locality which are available for letting on such terms.'

This is the provision which is intended to eliminate what is popularly called 'scarcity value' from the fair rent fixed by the committee, and it is a provision which has given rise to a great deal of difficulty in practice.

I think that before one begins to consider the difficulties, and before one begins to consider the section in detail, one must have clearly in mind what Parliament's obvious intention was in including this provision in the Act. It seems to me that what Parliament is saying is this. If the house has inherent amenities and advantages, by all means let them be reflected in the rent, under subsection (1); but if the market rent would be influenced simply by the fact that in the locality there is a shortage, and in the locality rents are being forced up beyond the market figure, then that element of market rent must not be included when the fair rent is being considered.

Parliament, I am sure, is not seeking to deprive the landlord of a proper return on the inherent value and quality of his investment in the house, but Parliament is undoubtedly seeking to deprive a landlord of a wholly unmeritorious increase in rent which has come about simply because there is a scarcity of houses in the district and thus an excess of demand over supply.

Bearing that in mind, one turns to the point in the committee's decision which is under attack in this appeal and indeed the point upon which Mr Woolf has usefully made submissions on their behalf. The committee have come to the conclusion, and expressed it in more than one way, that the presence of the

American school has created a local scarcity of premises. When I say 'local', I deliberately do not attempt at this stage to define it further. But what was in the committee's mind undoubtedly was that the attraction of the school has produced a local scarcity of houses, and that there are consequently in the premises now under review all the elements contained in section 46(2) of the Act of 1968 of a scarcity which ought to be eliminated when the fair rent is assessed ...

I find the committee's views on this somewhat difficult to follow, I must confess ...

It seems to me, with all deference to the committee, that they have somewhat lost sight of the fact that the sort of scarcity we are concerned with is a broad, overall, general scarcity affecting a really substantial area, and they wrongly focused their attention on the extremely limited area which would not, I think, qualify as a 'locality' for the purposes of section 46(2) of the Act of 1968.

What should be done? What can we add which may be of some assistance in the future? I think that committees will find their consideration of section 46 of the Act of 1968 somewhat easier if they start with the propositions clearly in mind that amenity advantages which can increase the fair rent under section 46(1) do not result in a set off under section 46(2) merely because the amenity advantages of a particular house or district attract more people than can live there. The test on scarcity is to be taken over the locality as a whole, and that, as I emphasised, is a broad area.

What area? We have been referred to *Palmer v Peabody Trust* [1974] 3 WLR 575 where, dealing with the word, 'locality' in section 46(1), I said, at p 581, that the exact extent of the locality was something which was primarily for the committee to fix. I would repeat that with regard to the fixing of the locality under section 46(2), but, at the risk of repetition, I do emphasise that when the committee fix their locality for the purpose of deciding whether there is an overall scarcity or not they must pick a really large area, an area that really gives them a fair appreciation of the trends of scarcity and their consequences.

It may be, although I would not for a moment attempt to define the limits of the area precisely, that when operating section 46(2) committees will be well advised to draw their inspiration from the area with which they are familiar in their work. Of course different parts of the country require different considerations, but there will be many instances in practice where the most reliable area for the committee to choose on which they are likely to achieve the most accurate result is the area from which their work regularly and normally comes.

However, to return to this case, it seems to me that the committee have erred in, I say at once, the one relatively small respect which I have tried to describe, and I think that the matter must be re-considered in the light of that error ...

I think that, when one has regard to all the work which has been done in this case, the inspections by the committee and all the other matters, the proper thing to do here would be to allow the appeal and send the case back to the committee to review their approach to section 46(2) of the Act of 1968 in the light of the judgment of this court.

In general, the approach of the courts has been to decline to interfere with the decisions of Rent Officers (or an appeal, rent assessment committees) unless their approach has been manifestly erroneous. In *Mason v Skilling* [1974] 1 WLR 1437 the House of Lords endorsed this approach.

Mason v Skilling

Lord Reid: My Lords, the Rent (Scotland) Act 1971 makes provision for the registration of rents under regulated tenancies. The rent officer for an area prepares a register and he has to determine a fair rent. The appellants are the landlord and the respondent is tenant of a dwelling-house at 83, Inglefield Street, Glasgow, under a regulated tenancy. The former rent was £17.70 per annum. The rent officer determined the fair rent to be £82. The landlord was dissatisfied and the matter was referred to the rent assessment committee. They inspected the premises and heard the case. They confirmed the rent officer's decision ...

The tenant then appealed to the Court of Session, his grounds of appeal being:

'1. In arriving at their decision the rent assessment committee erred in law by having regard to the capital value of the subjects in question with vacant possession rather than their capital value with a sitting tenant ...'

In answer the landlord pleaded:

'1. Insofar as the committee in arriving at its decision had regard to the capital value of the subjects in question with vacant possession, it was correct in having regard thereto rather than to the capital value of the subjects with a sitting tenant ...'

The Second Division upheld the tenant's contention and remitted the case to the rent assessment committee for further consideration in the light of their opinion. The landlord now appeals to this House.

Section 42 of the Act provides:

'(1) In determining for the purposes of this Part of this Act what rent is or would be a fair rent under a regulated tenancy of a dwelling-house, regard shall be had, subject to the following provisions of this section, to all the circumstances (other than personal circumstances) and in particular to the age, character and locality of the dwelling-house and to its state of repair.

(2) For the purposes of the determination it shall be assumed that the number of persons seeking to become tenants of similar dwelling-houses in the locality on the terms (other than those relating to rent) of the regulated tenancy is not substantially greater than the number of such dwelling-houses in the locality which are available for letting on such terms.

(3) There shall be disregarded–

(a) any disrepair or other defect attributable to a failure by the tenant under the regulated tenancy or any predecessor in title of his to comply with any terms thereof; and

(b) any improvement, or the replacement of any fixture or fitting, carried out, otherwise than in pursuance of the terms of the tenancy, by the tenant under the regulated tenancy or any predecessor in title of his.'

In my view, this section leaves it open to the rent officer or committee to adopt any method or methods of ascertaining a fair rent provided that they do not use any method which is unlawful or unreasonable. The most obvious and direct method is to have regard to registered rents of comparable houses in the area. In the initial stages this method may not be available but as the number of comparable registered rents increases the more likely it will be that it will lead to a correct result. Of course it must be open to either party to show that those comparable rents have been determined on a wrong basis but until that is shown it must be assumed that rents already determined have been rightly ascertained.

In the present case the committee did consider comparable rents and it is not said that they acted wrongly in this respect. Criticism is limited to the manner in which they dealt with the capital value of the house.

The committee were quite entitled and may have been well advised to use other methods in addition to considering comparable rents. In particular they were entitled to have regard to the capital value. A fair rent should be fair to the landlord as well as fair to the tenant and it can be regarded as fair to the landlord that he should receive a fair return on his capital. We are not concerned in this case with the percentage which in present circumstances can be regarded as a fair return.

It is notorious that in existing circumstances the price which a house will fetch in the market is much higher if the buyer can get possession immediately, than if there is a sitting tenant with a statutory right to remain in possession. Admittedly the committee had regard to the capital value with vacant possession but the respondent argues that the only relevant capital value is the price which the appellants could get for the house today: as the respondent is a sitting tenant that would be much lower than if the appellants could give vacant possession. Their argument was accepted by the Second Division. Lord Milligan said, 1973 SLT 139, 142:

'Counsel for the tenant founded on section 42 of the Act, in which it was provided that regard should, subject to certain exceptions, be had to "all the circumstances". One of the "circumstances" in the present case was that there was a sitting tenant. This was not one of the circumstances which were excluded from the consideration of the committee and it must accordingly be taken into consideration.'

It is quite true that the fact that there is a sitting tenant is a 'circumstance' but, in my opinion, it is excluded by the Act. Section 42(1) directs that regard shall be had to 'all the circumstances (other than personal circumstances)'. In my view the tenant's right to remain in possession is a personal circumstance. A right to possess a house (or anything else) appears to me to pertain to the person who has the right, whether the right is statutory or contractual. The house itself remains the same whoever is entitled to possess it. Moreover, under the Act the tenant's right to possess lasts so long, but only so long, as he complies with certain obligations. I am confirmed in this view by the fact that all the circumstances specified at the end of the subsection relate entirely to the house itself.

If this were not so it would lead to strange results. Suppose two identical adjacent houses one of which is vacant and the other occupied by a tenant with a regulated tenancy. If the respondent's argument is right then the fair rents would be different. No reasons have been suggested why two such houses should have different fair rents. Moreover the Act appears to aim at uniformity but if the respondent is right there would be no uniformity and it would be difficult to find comparable cases. Of two similar houses one might be occupied by a tenant in the prime of life who has a wife and family who could succeed him in the event of his death. Then the selling price of the house would be low; it would be improbable that the purchaser could obtain vacant possession for a very long time to come. But the other house might be occupied by an aged infirm tenant with no wife or family, or a tenant who was likely soon to leave. Then the selling price would be higher because the purchaser was likely to be able to get vacant possession quite soon. I find it impossible to believe that the statute contemplates different fair rents in these two cases.

Section 41 entitles a landlord intending to let on a regulated tenancy to have a fair rent fixed. There, in so far as the committee relied on capital value, they would have to take selling price with vacant possession. Then when under section 40 the rent had to be reviewed there would be a sitting tenant. Is the fair rent, then, to be diminished because the capital value is diminished by reason of the tenant's statutory right to retain possession?

And there is another difficulty if the respondent is right and the committee must take the capital value subject to the rights of the sitting tenant. How can that capital value be ascertained until one knows what rent the tenant is going to pay in future? It would be quite wrong to take the price which could have been obtained if there were no provision in the Act to alter the old rent. So you could not fix the capital value until you knew the fair rent and you could not fix the fair rent until you knew the capital value.

All these difficulties reinforce my opinion that the respondents' contention is wrong, and that the proper construction of section 42(1) is that the circumstance that a sitting tenant has a right to possess the house is a personal circumstance to which regard must not be had.

I would therefore allow this appeal and hold that the determination of the rent assessment committee is valid.

Lords Diplock and Cross agreed.

Lords Morris and Kilbrandon delivered concurring judgments.

Deduction for scarcity habitually posed a problem. The figure usually employed for this deduction was between 10% and 25%, but in *Western Heritable Investment Co Ltd v Husband* [1983] 2 AC 849, decided under the parallel provisions of the Scottish legislation, the House of Lords declined to interfere when the deduction for scarcity was fixed at 40%.

Modern conditions, however, and the increase in the availability of assured tenancies as a direct result of the Housing Act 1988, have led to a change. The effect of the greater availability of properties for letting will gradually eliminate the scarcity element, as the important decision of Hutchison J in *BTE Ltd v Merseyside and Cheshire Rent Assessment Committee and Jones* (1991) 24 HLR 514 makes clear. The natural result of these developments is that, as time goes by, the rents of regulated tenancies will come to be equated with those for assured tenancies.

BTE Ltd v Merseyside and Cheshire RAC

Hutchison J: This appeal is brought pursuant to the provisions of the Tribunals and Inquiries Act 1971, which permits an appeal on a point of law from an assessment of a fair rent by a Rent Tribunal acting within the scope of Part IV of the Rent Act 1977. It relates to property in Liverpool at 11, Cronton Road. In my judgment, it is possible to deal with the appeal quite shortly ...

The position is this. Under the scheme embodied in that part of the Act it is possible to obtain registration of a fair rent on application to the Rent Officer, and if dissatisfaction is felt with his determination, there is provision for a reference to the Rent Assessment Committee who hear evidence and determine what should be the fair rent.

In this case, the landlord was contending for a rent in the order of £30 a week. The rent officer had fixed a rent of some £13.

Looking ahead to the conclusion at which the Rent Assessment Committee arrived, they determined the fair rent at a slightly higher figure, £16.50 a week ...

I go straight to the relevant provisions of the 1977 Act so far as this case is concerned. They are to be found in section 70 of the Act (as amended) ...

The effect of those two subsections [ie s 70(1),(2)] is most conveniently summarised in a passage in the judgment of Lord Widgery CJ in *Metropolitan Property Holdings v Finegold* (1975) 1 WLR 349. At p 352 Lord Widgery, having set out the provisions of a predecessor Act, which were in the same terms as those of section 70, said this:

> 'This is the provision which is intended to eliminate what is popularly called "scarcity value" from the fair rent fixed by the committee, and it is a provision which has given rise to a great deal of difficulty in practice. I think that before one begins to consider the difficulties' – they were difficulties which arose in that case but do not arise in this case – 'and before one begins to consider the section in detail, one must have clearly in mind what Parliament's obvious intention was in including this provision in the Act. It seems to me that what Parliament is saying is this. If the house has inherent amenities and advantages, by all means let them be reflected in the rent under subsection (1); but if the market rent would be influenced simply by the fact that in the locality there is a shortage, and in the locality rents are being forced up beyond the market figure, then that element of market rent must not be included when the fair rent is being considered. Parliament, I am sure, is not seeking to deprive the landlord of a proper return on the inherent value and quality of his investment in the house, but Parliament is undoubtedly seeking to deprive a landlord of a wholly unmeritorious increase in rent which has come about simply because there is a scarcity of houses in the district and thus an excess of demand over supply.'

That passage summarises the object of the two parts of the sections, and also, by implication, makes it clear that, subject to adjustment in appropriate cases to reflect the scarcity element, the fair rent is to be equated with the market rent. It is said in other authorities that a fair rent must be fair to the landlord as well as the tenant. That supports the view that scarcity value apart, the fair and proper market rent is the criterion which ordinarily should guide the Rent Officer and the Rent Assessment Committee. That is not to say that the only way of arriving at a fair rent is by considering comparable lettings, because there are other possible ways of going about it but it seems to me it is clearly established that in general and subject to the scarcity value qualification, the object must be to try to arrive at what is the fair market rent of the property.

With those preliminary observations and with that citation of authority, I turn to the facts of the case and the decision appealed against. The property is a three-bedroomed terraced house with an upstairs bath and lavatory, though no washbasin, two living rooms and a kitchen below. The living rooms are heated by two gas fires which had been installed by the tenants. There was evidence, the Committee said, of considerable damp ...

I ... come to the crucial passage on which this appeal is based. It reads as follows: 'Mr Bennett addressed the Committee on the effects of recent legislation, adding that scarcity of accommodation no longer applied.'

I interpolate that that is not a submission that the law had been changed to eliminate the necessity to have regard to scarcity of accommodation. It is meant to encapsulate Mr Bennett's submission, that in current conditions and given the liberalisation achieved by recent legislation, there was no longer a shortage of property of a comparable nature for letting.

The decision letter continues:

'As a result he contended that market rents should be the appropriate level. The Rent Assessment Committee took careful note of Mr Bennett's comments, but felt that despite more housing becoming available for rental, there was still a paucity of accommodation available at reasonable rents. The properties which Mr Bennett's firm had recently let at market rents were likely to be those with the benefit of vacant possession, some, at least, of which would have been refurbished by the landlord prior to letting. This situation was clearly not the same as accommodation which in some cases was in need of repair and which was occupied by tenants on statutory tenancies.'

It seems to me it is a reasonable construction of those words that the Committee were accepting the evidence they had from Mr Bennett to the effect that there was an abundance of comparable properties for letting. They appear to have accepted that the lettings which he achieved recently (of which he had given evidence) had been at market rent, because they used those words. But what they are saying is that they do not regard market rents as being appropriate because there is a paucity of accommodation available at what they regard as reasonable rents. As I ventured to suggest in the course of argument, that seems to be begging the question, since the issue which the Committee had to address was, what was a fair rent? The test of that in a climate where there was no scarcity of comparable rented accommodation, was, what was the fair market rent? It is nothing to the point, having made a finding about the level of fair market rents, to go on to say that fair market rents do not represent reasonable rents.

Of course, tenants will always wish to have as low a rent as they can. From one point of view, if one applies absolute or arbitrary standards, it may be possible to say that the market rates do not represent a reasonable rent but that is not the approach which, it seems to me, the statute enjoins.

Secondly, the Committee seem to be saying that it is illegitimate to use as the test of the comparable, as the means of determining the market, lettings with the benefit of vacant possession, and that regard should be had to a different type of property; that is to say, property occupied by tenants with statutory tenancies. That plainly, on the basis of the wording of subsection (1), is illegitimate. I refer to the case of *Mason et al v Skilling* (1974) 1 WLR 1437, to which Mr Nugee drew my attention. It is contrary to authority.

The other thing they seem to be saying, and this is, it seems to me, a legitimate comment, is that there may be a distinction between the properties let by Mr Bennett (of which he gave evidence) which may have been in an apple pie state of repair, and the instant property, the state of repair of which, though fair to good in their assessment, suffered from the problem of damp. That is, as Mr Nugee conceded, a legitimate distinction, if the evidence supported it, because, plainly, property in bad repair, on the wording of the section, should command a lower rent than comparable property in good repair.

Allowing for that legitimate consideration, it does seem to me that in two important respects the Committee have approached the matter in an incorrect manner. The way in which Mr Nugee put it was to submit first of all, that having in effect found that there was not any scarcity of comparable properties for letting purposes and having found that such properties were being let at the market rate, the Committee found that those lettings did not afford a guidance because they were not at a reasonable rent. They took some arbitrary standards, the basis of which does not appear, as their measure of a reasonable rent.

Secondly, Mr Nugee submits that the Committee discounted the comparison which was put forward to show what the market rent was, and the reasons they gave, apart, possibly, from the point about the state of repair, were invalid reasons. Of course, a current letting is a letting with vacant possession. That is a statement of the obvious. The consideration of cases where there was a sitting statutory tenant was illegitimate for the reasons I have indicated.

Accordingly, it seems to me that the decision of the Committee discloses an error of law in the approach which they adopted. Assuming, as I think their finding indicates, that they accepted the evidence of Mr Bennett and they accepted that the lettings of which he gave evidence were of comparable value, they should have taken account of those when arriving at the fair rent. In so far as there was evidence on which they could find that the state of repair of those properties was better than the state of repair of the property they were considering, that is a factor which they could have reflected when fixing the fair rent. But they could not arrive at a fair rent simply by applying their own notions of what was reasonable or by the decision that the lettings adverted to by Mr Bennett were lettings with vacant possession and were to be contrasted with lettings to tenants on statutory tenancies.

That is sufficient in my judgment to compel me to allow this appeal. The appropriate course, in my judgment is to allow the appeal, which will involve quashing the decision of the Committee and to remit the matter to be reheard by a Committee ...

The consequences of the setting of a 'fair rent'

The 'fair rent' thus set may be higher, or lower, than the existing rent. Generally, it today takes effect from the date of registration, and the landlord may not lawfully charge a higher rent than the registered rent from that date. If the tenant has, prior to registration, been paying a higher rent, he cannot now recover the amount overpaid, though he could do so under the original legislation when the fair rent was backdated to the date of the tenant's application. The landlord similarly may not recover any 'shortfall' if the registered rent turns out to be higher than the tenant was previously paying. Indeed, in this case he will normally have to go through the process of serving a statutory notice of increase of rent in accordance with the provisions of s 49 of the Act. Such a 'notice of increase' is in effect subjected to the validity rules of a 'notice to quit', which, under s 5 Protection from Eviction Act 1977, will have to be of at least four weeks duration even in the case of a weekly tenancy (s 45(3)).

Rent Act 1977

49. Notices of increase

(1) Any reference in this section to a notice of increase is a reference to a notice of increase under section 45(2), [or 46] of this Act.

(2) A notice of increase must be in the prescribed form.

(3) Notwithstanding that a notice of increase relates to statutory periods, it may be served during a contractual period.

(4) Where a notice of increase is served during a contractual period and the protected tenancy could, by a notice to quit served by the landlord at the same time, be brought to an end before the date specified in the notice of increase, the notice of increase shall operate to convert the protected tenancy into a statutory tenancy as from that date.

(5) ... (6) ... (7) ...

Once fixed, the rent is normally in force for two years; there is a limited right to apply for variation of a registered rent if one of the factors mentioned in s 67(3) is present. The serious consequence of failure to have regard to a registered 'fair rent', and to make any necessary application for a re-assessment of the 'fair rent' can be seen from *Rakhit v Carty* [1990] 2 QB 315.

Rakkit v Carty

Russell LJ: (giving the first judgment at the invitation of Lord Donaldson MR) No 24 Burnham Court, Brent Street, London NW4, is a third-floor flat. On 30 September 1986 the plaintiff, Mr Sunil Rakhit (the landlord), granted a lease of the flat to four tenants for a period of one year at a rent of £433.33 per calendar month. At the time of the letting the flat had been substantially furnished by the landlord. On 10 December 1986 the plaintiff, Mrs Carty (the tenant), joined the other tenants in occupation of the flat and on 1 October 1987 she entered into a tenancy agreement with the landlord for a term of 364 days from 1 October 1987 at the rent of £450 per month. Unknown to any of the parties to these tenancy agreements a rent officer had, much earlier, determined a fair rent for the flat effective from 19 November 1973 of £550 per annum, that rent being registered in the rent register for the London borough of Barnet on 12 March 1974. At that date the flat was unfurnished and was so recorded in the rent register. The landlord had no interest in the premises at that time.

The tenant's tenancy came to an end by effluxion of time, but she remained in occupation as a statutory tenant entitled to the protection of the Rent Act 1977. However, within a matter of days, on 9 October 1988, the landlord commenced proceedings in the Willesden County Court seeking possession of the flat on, inter alia, the ground that he reasonably required possession of the demised premises as a residence for himself under Case 9 of Sch 15 to the Rent Act 1977. The claim was resisted by the tenant on the grounds that it was not reasonable to make the order and that, pursuant to Pt III of Sch 15, greater hardship would be caused to the tenant by granting the order than would be caused to the landlord by refusing to grant it.

On 12 June 1989 at the Willesden County Court his Honour Judge Rountree made an order for possession of the flat in favour of the landlord, and the tenant appeals against that order ...

I turn to those submissions of counsel that occupied the court for most of this hearing. The landlord claimed arrears of rent and the judge awarded him £2,710.58 together with mesne profits of £380 per month until possession. The arrears were based on the rent payable under the tenancy agreement of 1 October 1987 up to 8 December 1988 when, on an application lodged by the tenant, the rent officer had determined and registered a fair rent of £180 per month. The entry in the register on 9 December 1988 recorded the flat as furnished.

The submission made to the judge and repeated before this court can be shortly stated. Counsel for the tenant contends that the rent registration on 12 March 1974 limited the rent payable by the tenant under the agreement dated 1 October 1987 and that, far from there being arrears of rental, the tenant had overpaid £3,069.82 from 1 October 1987 to the date of the hearing. There was a counterclaim in respect of overpaid rent.

The judge rejected this submission, regarding himself as bound by *Kent v Millmead Properties Ltd* (1982) 44 P&CR 353 and *Cheniston Investments Ltd v Waddock* [1988] 46 EG 88. The landlord's claim for arrears and mesne profits was therefore upheld, and the tenant's counterclaim dismissed.

It is now convenient to look at the relevant statutory provisions which bear on this appeal. The starting point is s 44(1) of the Rent Act 1977 ...

Part IV of the Act contains detailed provisions relating to the registration of rents under regulated tenancies. Section 67 deals with the machinery for making an application for the registration of a rent. Section 70 is concerned with the circumstances to which regard must be paid by the rent officer in fixing a fair rent under a regulated tenancy. Both the application for registration and the assessment must deal with details of any furniture provided for use under the tenancy ...

(Russell LJ referred to s 66 and continued:)

Section 72 (as substituted by s 61(1) of the Housing Act 1980) is concerned with the effect of a registration of rent ...

Section 73 makes provision for the cancellation of the registration of a fair rent by the landlord and tenant jointly. However, in the context of this appeal, s 67(3) (as amended by s 60(1) of the 1980 Act is of greater importance. It provides:

'Subject to subsection (4) below, where a rent for a dwelling-house has been registered under this Part of this Act, no application by the tenant alone or by the landlord alone for the registration of a different rent for that dwelling-house shall be entertained before the expiry of 2 years from the relevant date (as defined in subsection (5) below) except on the ground that, since that date, there has been such a change in–

(a) the condition of the dwelling-house (including the making of an improvement therein);

(b) the terms of the tenancy;

(c) the quantity, quality or condition of any furniture provided for use under the tenancy (deterioration by fair wear and tear excluded); or

(d) any other circumstances taken into consideration when the rent was registered or confirmed as to make the registered rent no longer a fair rent.'

Subsection (4) enables a landlord alone to make an application within the last three months of the period referred to in sub-s (3), and sub-s (5), for the purposes of this appeal, defines the relevant date as the date when the registration took effect, ie when entered in the register.

In my judgment, the scheme of Pts III and IV of the 1977 Act is plain. Once a fair rent is registered, it remains the recoverable rent for the dwelling-house in respect of which the rent is payable until either the demised premises undergo such a change in their structure as to render them no longer the dwelling-house referred to in s 44 or there is a cancellation of the registration under s 73 or there is a new registration consequent on a fresh application pursuant to s 67(3) or s 68(4). This last subsection (which has since been repealed) is in similar terms to s 67(3) and deals with applications by a local authority.

Section 67(3) deals specifically with a change in the terms of the tenancy or in the quantity of any furniture provided as preconditions without which no application for registration of a different rent 'for that dwelling-house shall be entertained'. In other words, provided the dwelling-house remains as the same demised property, the provision of furniture as a term of the tenancy does not affect the recoverable rent until the registered rent is increased and that rent is registered. So much, to my mind, is clear from the terms of s 44(1), which does not refer to any change in the terms of the tenancy of the dwelling-house, but expressly provides that the rent recoverable 'for any contractual period of a regulated tenancy of the dwelling-house shall be limited to the rent so registered'.

The authority which led the judge to the conclusion at which he arrived in relation to rent and mesne profits was, as earlier indicated, *Kent v Millmead Properties Ltd* (1982) 44 P&CR 353. I take the facts from the headnote. In all material respects they cannot be distinguished from the facts in the instant case. In 1974 a registration of a fair rent of a flat was determined as £5 a week. The register kept under the Rent Act showed that the tenancy was a weekly tenancy and that it was an unfurnished tenancy. In May 1977 the flat became vacant and was fully furnished, extensively redecorated and improved by the defendant landlords. It was let in August 1978 to the plaintiff tenants at a weekly rent of £28.50. In June 1980 a fair rent of £17.50 per week for the premises and £5 for furniture was registered. The tenants discovered that there was a registered rent of £5 per week for the premises. They withheld the excess rent. They brought proceedings in the county court claiming the excess rent paid by them. The landlords counterclaimed for arrears of rent on the ground that, as in March 1974, before the commencement of the Rent Act 1974, the premises were unfurnished, the rent then registered did not apply to the premises re-let furnished and improved. The county court judge gave judgment for the landlords. The tenants appealed. Giving the leading judgment, Ormrod LJ said (at 357):

> 'One should start from this position that, anybody looking at the rent register in order to discover what the registered rent of these premises was, would see immediately that the registered rent of some £260 per annum was the rent registered in respect of an unfurnished tenancy and so it could not possibly be said that anyone inspecting the register, who was intending to take a furnished tenancy of this flat, could be misled in any way. Going back to the 1977 Act which, as I have said, is the operative Act for our purposes, I think section 44(1) must be read in the light of section 66(2) and that the reference to a 'rent for a dwelling-house registered under Part IV of this Act' means the rent for a dwelling-house registered under Part IV of this Act as set out in the register, that is for the premises, and for the type of tenancy described in the register for which the rent was fixed and not otherwise, so that, if there is a material change either in the specification of the dwelling-house, by either adding or subtracting a room or rooms, or a material change in the particulars with regard to the tenancy, then the rent registered in respect of a different tenancy, different in the sense of different in character and incidence, is not the registered rent for the purposes of section 44(1) and so does not operate to enable the tenants in this case to enjoy for the price of £5 a week the tenancy of a furnished flat for which, in 1980, the fair rent was considered to be £22.50.'

Kent v Millmead Properties Ltd was followed in *Cheniston Investments v Waddock* [1988] 46 EG 88 with obvious reluctance (see, in particular, the judgments of Lloyd and Ralph Gibson LJJ (at 141)). However, it was not argued in *Cheniston's* case that the *Kent* decision was *per incuriam*.

Counsel for the tenant has now submitted to this court that the *Kent* decision was indeed *per incuriam*, in that she submits that the judgment of Ormrod LJ, with which Dunn LJ and Sir Sebag Shaw agreed, made no reference to s 67(3), that if the Court of Appeal had been referred to that subsection and had had regard to its terms the decision would plainly have been different and that, consequently, this court should not follow *Kent's* case. I have already expressed my own views as to the proper construction of s 44(1) and the impact of s 67(3).

In *Rickards v Rickards* [1989] 3 All ER 193 at 198–199, [1989] 3 WLR 748 at 755 Lord Donaldson MR said:

> 'The importance of the rule of stare decisis in relation to the Court of Appeal's own decisions can hardly be overstated. We now sometimes sit in eight divisions and, in the absence of such a rule, the law would quickly become wholly uncertain. However, the rule is not without exceptions, albeit very limited. These exceptions were considered in *Young v Bristol Aeroplane Co Ltd* [1944] 2 All ER 293, [1944] KB 718, *Morelle Ltd v Wakeling* [1955] 1 All ER 708, [1955] 2 QB 379 and, more recently, in *Williams v Fawcett* [1985] 1 All ER 787 at 794-795, [1986] QB 604 at 615-616, where relevant extracts from the two earlier decisions are set out. These decisions show that this court is justified in refusing to follow one of its own previous decisions not only where that decision is given in ignorance or forgetfulness of some inconsistent statutory provision or some authority binding on it, but also, in rare and exceptional cases, if it is satisfied that the decision involved a manifest slip or error. In previous cases the judges of this court have always refrained from defining this exceptional category and I have no intention of departing from that approach save to echo the words of Lord Greene MR (in *Young's* case [1944] 2 All ER 293 at 300, [1944] 1 KB 718 at 729) and Evershed MR (in *Morelle's* case [1955] 1 All ER 708 at 718, [1955] 2 QB 379 at 406) and to say that they will be of the rarest occurrence.'

In my judgment, the effect of allowing this appeal will produce no injustice to the landlord, for the 1977 Act provided him and his advisers with ample opportunity to protect his interests by the simple process of inspecting the public register of rents before letting the flat to the tenant. A fresh application for registration of a fair rent could then have been made enabling that fair rent to be recoverable from the commencement of the tenant's tenancy.

For my part, I am satisfied that this court erred in *Kent v Millmead Properties Ltd* and that, following the observations of Lord Donaldson MR in *Rickards's* case, this court is justified in declining to follow *Kent v Millmead Properties Ltd*.

Accordingly, I would allow the tenant's appeal and hold that the landlord's monetary claim should be dismissed and that judgment should be entered in favour of the tenant on her counterclaim.

Sir Roualeyn Cumming-Bruce and Lord Donaldson of Lymington MR delivered concurring judgments.

Restricted contracts

A similar procedure applied to 'restricted contracts' (usually resident landlord lettings), under which either party may refer the rent to a rent tribunal (which nowadays is the same body as a rent assessment committee). This body was charged with a duty similar to that involved in the Rent Officer's jurisdiction, though the rent they set was dubbed a 'reasonable rent' rather than a 'fair rent'. As a result of s 36(2) Housing Act 1988, this procedure is now virtually obsolete. The general procedure is set out in ss 77–81A Rent Act 1977.

Rent Act 1977

77. Reference of contracts to rent tribunals and obtaining by them of information

(1) Either the lessor or the lessee under a restricted contract ... may refer the contract to the rent tribunal ...

(2) Where a restricted contract is referred to a rent tribunal under subsection (1) above they may, by notice in writing served on the lessor, require him to give to them, within such period (not less than 7 days from the date of the service of the notice) as may be specified in the notice, such information as they may reasonably require regarding such of the prescribed particulars relating to the contract as are specified in the notice.

(3) If, within the period specified in a notice under subsection (2) above, the lessor fails without reasonable cause to comply with the provisions of the notice he shall be liable to a fine not exceeding level 3 on the standard scale.

(4) Proceedings for an offence under this section shall not be instituted otherwise than by the local authority.

78. Powers of rent tribunals on reference of contracts

(1) Where a restricted contract is referred to a rent tribunal and the reference is not, before the tribunal have entered upon consideration of it, withdrawn by the party or authority who made it, the tribunal shall consider it.

(2) After making such inquiry as they think fit and giving to–

   (a) each party to the contract; and

   (b) if the general management of the dwelling is vested in and exercisable by a housing authority, that authority;

   an opportunity of being heard or, at his or their option, of submitting representations in writing, the tribunal, subject to subsections (3) and (4) below–

   (i) shall approve the rent payable under the contract, or

   (ii) shall reduce or increase the rent to such sum as they may, in all the circumstances, think reasonable, or

   (iii) may, if they think fit in all the circumstances, dismiss the reference, and shall notify the parties ... of their decision.

(3) On the reference of a restricted contract relating to a dwelling for which a rent is registered under Part IV of this Act, the rent tribunal may not reduce the rent payable under the contract below the amount which would be recoverable from the tenant under a regulated tenancy of the dwelling.

(4) An approval, reduction or increase under this section may be limited to rent payable in respect of a particular period.

(5) In subsection (2) above, 'housing authority' means a local housing authority within the meaning of the Housing Act 1985.

79. Register of rents under restricted contracts

(1) The president of every rent assessment panel shall prepare and keep up to date a register for the purposes of this Part of this Act and shall make the register available for inspection in such place or places and in such manner as the Secretary of State may direct.

(2) The register shall be so prepared and kept up to date as to contain, with regard to any contract relating to a dwelling situated in the area of the rent assessment panel and under which a rent is payable which has been approved, reduced or increased under section 78 of this Act, entries of–

   (a) the prescribed particulars with regard to the contract;

   (b) a specification of the dwelling to which the contract relates; and

   (c) the rent as approved, reduced or increased by the rent tribunal, and in a case in which the approval, reduction or increase is limited to rent payable in respect of a particular period, a specification of that period.

(3) Where any rates in respect of a dwelling are borne by the lessor or any person having any title superior to that of the lessor, the amount to be entered in the register under this section as the rent payable for the dwelling shall be the same as if the rates were not so borne; but the fact that they are so borne shall be noted in the register.

(4) ...

(5) A copy of an entry in the register certified under the hand of an officer duly authorised in that behalf by the president of the rent assessment panel concerned shall be receivable in evidence in any court and in any proceedings.

(6) A person requiring such a certified copy shall be entitled to obtain it on payment of the prescribed fee.

(6A) Every local authority shall, before the expiry of the period of three months beginning with the commencement of paragraph 44 of Schedule 25 to the Housing Act 1980, send to the president of the appropriate rent assessment panel the register previously kept by the authority under this section.

80. Reconsideration of rent after registration

(1) Where the rent payable for any dwelling has been entered in the register under section 79 of this Act the lessor or the lessee ... may refer the case to the rent tribunal for reconsideration of the rent so entered.

(2) Where the rent under a restricted contract has been registered under section 79 of this Act, a rent tribunal shall not be required to entertain a reference, made otherwise than by the lessor and the lessee jointly, for the registration of a different rent for the dwelling concerned before the expiry of the period of 2 years beginning on the date on which the rent was last considered by the tribunal, except on the ground that, since that date, there has been such a change in–

(a) the condition of the dwelling;

(b) the furniture or services provided;

(c) the terms of the contract; or

(d) any other circumstances taken into consideration when the rent was last considered;

as to make the registered rent no longer a reasonable rent.

81. Effect of registration of rent

(1) Where the rent payable for any dwelling is entered in the register under section 79 of this Act, it shall not be lawful to require or receive on account of rent for that dwelling under a restricted contract payment of any amount in excess of the rent so registered–

(a) in respect of any period subsequent to the date of the entry; or

(b) where a particular period is specified in the register, in respect of that period.

(2) Where subsection (3) of section 79 applies, the amount entered in the register under that section shall be treated for the purposes of this section as increased for any rental period by the amount of the rates for that period, ascertained in accordance with Schedule 5 to this Act.

(3) Where any payment has been made or received in contravention of this section, the amount of the excess shall be recoverable by the person by whom it was paid.

(4) Any person who requires or receives any payment in contravention of this section shall be liable to a fine not exceeding level 3 on the standard scale or to imprisonment for a term not exceeding 6 months or both, and, without prejudice to any other method of recovery, the court by which a person is found guilty of an offence under this subsection may order the amount paid in excess to be repaid to the person by whom the payment was made.

(5) ...

81A. Cancellation of registration of rent

(1) Where the rent payable for any dwelling is entered in the register under section 79 of this Act, the rent tribunal shall cancel the entry, on an application made under this section, if–

(a) ...

(b) the dwelling is not for the time being subject to a restricted contract; and

(c) the application is made by the person who would be the lessor if the dwelling were subject to a restricted contract.

(2) An application under this section must be in the prescribed form, and contain the prescribed particulars.

(3) Cancellation of the registration shall be without prejudice to a further registration of a rent at any time after the cancellation.

(4) The rent tribunal shall notify the applicant of their decision to grant, or to refuse, any application under this section.

HOUSING ACT RENTS

In comparison with the procedures under the Rent Act, the Housing Act 1988 makes little provision for the control of rent levels. The general philosophy underlying the new legislation is to let market forces prevail, and the circumstances in which there can be any external intervention in the prevailing level of rents are very few.

Fixed-term tenancies

The general principle is that under an assured tenancy the parties are free to fix the amount of rent for themselves in the light of market conditions. If the parties agree to a fixed rent for the entire duration of the lease, they are bound by their agreement. Equally, if the parties elect to include a rent review clause in the terms of the lease, they are equally bound by its terms. The landlord can use the rent review clause to increase the rent payable, but only in the circumstances, and in accordance with the procedure, laid down by that rent review clause. If, however, the parties can agree on a variation of the rent laid down by the lease, even in the absence of a rent review clause, there would appear to be no obstacle to their 'agreed' rent taking effect from the moment of their choosing (s 13(5) below).

Statutory periodic tenancies consequent upon fixed-term tenancies

The next possibility to consider is that an assured tenancy, originally fixed term, has expired and the tenant remains in possession. This 'periodic tenancy' arises under s 5(2) of the Act, and initially the rent payable thereunder remains the same as the rent which was payable under the previous fixed-term tenancy. There is, though, an important difference in that the landlord can now seek an increase in rent under s 13 of the Act.

Housing Act 1988

13. Increases of rent under assured periodic tenancies

(1) This section applies to–

    (a) a statutory periodic tenancy other than one which, by virtue paragraph 11 or paragraph 12 in Part I of Schedule I to this Act, cannot for the time being be an assured tenancy; and

    (b) any other periodic tenancy which is an assured tenancy, other than one in relation to which there is a provision, for the time being binding on the tenant, under which the rent for a particular period of the tenancy will or may be greater than the rent for an earlier period.

(2) For the purpose of securing an increase in the rent under a tenancy to which this section applies, the landlord may serve on the tenant a notice in the prescribed form proposing a new rent to take effect at the beginning of a new period of the tenancy specified in the notice, being a period beginning no earlier than–

    (a) the minimum period after the date of the service of the notice; and

    (b) except in the case of a statutory periodic tenancy, the first anniversary of the date on which the first period of the tenancy began; and

    (c) if the rent under the tenancy has previously been increased by virtue of a notice under this subsection or a determination under section 14 below, the first anniversary of the date on which the increased rent took effect.

(3) The minimum period referred to in subsection (2) above is–

    (a) in the case of a yearly tenancy, six months;

    (b) in the case of a tenancy where the period is less than a month, one month; and

    (c) in any other case, a period equal to the period of the tenancy.

(4) Where a notice is served under subsection (2) above, a new rent specified in the notice shall take effect as mentioned in the notice unless, before the beginning of the new period specified in the notice–

    (a) the tenant by an application in the prescribed form refers the notice to a rent assessment committee; or

    (b) the landlord and the tenant agree on a variation of the rent which is different from that proposed in the notice or agree that the rent should not be varied.

(5) Nothing in this section (or in section 14 below) affects the right of the landlord and the tenant under an assured tenancy to vary by agreement any term of the tenancy (including a term relating to rent).

The general assumption is that the initiative will be taken by the landlord, who will serve on the tenant a notice in the form required by s 6. On the receipt of such a notice, if the tenant takes no action, the proposed increase in rent will come into force on the date proposed by the landlord. If the tenant wishes, he may refer the proposal to a rent assessment committee. The rent assessment committee is required to consider the 'market rent' in accordance with s 14 of the Act.

Housing Act 1988

14. Determination of rent by rent assessment committee

(1) Where, under subsection (4)(a) of section 13 above, a tenant refers to a rent assessment committee a notice under subsection (2) of that section, the committee shall determine the rent at which, subject to subsections (2) and (4) below, the committee consider that the dwelling-house concerned might reasonably be expected to be let in the open market by a willing landlord under an assured tenancy–

    (a) which is a periodic tenancy having the same periods as those of the tenancy to which the notice relates;

    (b) which begins at the beginning of the new period specified in the notice;

    (c) the terms of which (other than relating to the amount of the rent) are the same as those of the tenancy to which the notice relates; and

    (d) in respect of which the same notices, if any, have been given under any of Grounds 1 to 5 of Schedule 2 to this Act, as have been given (or have effect as if given) in relation to the tenancy to which the notice relates.

(2) In making a determination under this section, there shall be disregarded–

    (a) any effect on the rent attributable to the granting of a tenancy to a sitting tenant;

    (b) any increase in the value of the dwelling-house attributable to a relevant improvement carried out by a person who at the time it was carried out was the tenant, if the improvement–

        (i) was carried out otherwise than in pursuance of an obligation to his immediate landlord; or

        (ii) was carried out pursuant to an obligation to his immediate landlord being an obligation which did not relate to the specific improvement concerned but arose by reference to consent given to the carrying out of that improvement; and

    (c) any reduction in the value of the dwelling-house attributable to a failure by the tenant to comply with any terms of the tenancy.

(3) For the purposes of subsection (2)(b) above, in relation to a notice which is referred by a tenant as mentioned in subsection (1) above, an improvement is a relevant improvement if either it was carried out during the tenancy to which the notice relates or the following conditions are satisfied, namely–

    (a) that it was carried out not more than twenty-one years before the date of service of the notice; and

    (b) that, at all times during the period beginning when the improvement was carried out and ending on the date of service of the notice, the dwelling-house has been let under an assured tenancy; and

(c) that, on the coming to an end of an assured tenancy at any time during that period, the tenant (or, in the case of joint tenants, at least one of them) did not quit.

(4) In this section 'rent' does not include any service charge, within the meaning of section 18 of the Landlord and Tenant Act 1985, but, subject to that, includes any sums payable by the tenant to the landlord on account of the use of furniture or for any of the matters referred to in subsection (1)(a) of that section, whether or not those sums are separate from the sums payable for the occupation of the dwelling-house concerned or are payable under separate agreements.

(5) Where any rates in respect of the dwelling-house concerned are borne by the landlord or a superior landlord, the rent assessment committee shall make their determination under this section as if the rates were not so borne.

(6) In any case where–

(a) a rent assessment committee have before them at the same time the reference of a notice under section 6(2) above relating to a tenancy (in this subsection referred to as 'the section 6 reference') and the reference of a notice under section 13(2) above relating to the same tenancy (in this subsection referred to as 'the section 13 reference'), and

(b) the date specified in the notice under section 6(2) above is not later than the first day of the new period specified in the notice under section 13(2) above, and

(c) the committee propose to hear the two references together,

the committee shall make a determination in relation to the section 6 reference before making their determination in relation to the section 13 reference and, accordingly, in such a case the reference in subsection (1)(c) above to the terms of the tenancy to which the notice relates shall be construed as a reference to those terms as varied by virtue of the determination made in relation to the section 6 reference.

(7) Where a notice under section 13(2) above has been referred to a rent assessment committee, then, unless the landlord and the tenant otherwise agree, the rent determined by the committee (subject, in a case where subsection (5) above applies, to the addition of the appropriate amount in respect of rates) shall be the rent under the tenancy with effect from the beginning of the new period specified in the notice or, if it appears to the rent assessment committee that that would cause undue hardship to the tenant, with effect from such later date (not being later than the date the rent is determined) as the committee may direct.

(8) Nothing in this section requires a rent assessment committee to continue with their determination of a rent for a dwelling-house if the landlord and tenant give notice in writing that they no longer require such a determination or if the tenancy has come to an end.

Contractual periodic assured tenancies

A similar procedure applies to an assured tenancy which was, from the outset, periodic. It is subject to one caveat, however. If the terms of the original periodic tenancy are such that the landlord may increase the rent for a later period, the landlord can increase the rent as specified in the express terms of the periodic tenancy, but not otherwise – for instance by reference to the statutory procedure contained in s 13. The theory is that the landlord, by inserting a provision for variation of rent in the terms of the contractual tenancy itself, has put it out of his own power to invoke the s 13 procedure. Thus, the s 13 rent raising procedure is only apposite in those cases where the tenancy agreement itself contains no 'rent review' terms. Also, in any event, the rent increase procedure cannot be invoked until the first anniversary of the contractual periodic tenancy (s 13(2)(a)). Subsequent increases are subject to another 'yearly' cycle as a result of s 13(2)(c).

Assured tenancies by succession

One of the ways in which an assured tenancy can arise is by succession from a protected or statutory tenancy in favour of a member of a family other than a spouse under the amended rules for succession to protected and statutory tenancies introduced by the Housing Act 1988. One result of such a transformation on succession will be to expose the successor to market rents under the Housing Act 1988, and to deprive the successor of the benefit of the fair rent procedure which his predecessor in title enjoyed as a result of the Rent Act. The operation of these provisions can be seen in *N & D Ltd v Gadson* (1991) 24 HLR 64.

Assured shortholds

This is one of the rare instances in the Housing Act where there is some interference with the free operation of market forces during the initial stage of a tenancy. Although the general policy of the Act is to encourage the untrammelled operation of market forces in the private rented sector, assured shortholds form an exception. Here, by virtue of s 22 of the Act, an assured shorthold tenant can apply to a rent assessment committee for a reduction in his rent. Unlike registration of rent under the Rent Act, however, the determination, even if favourable to the tenant, does not apply in rem, and thus a landlord who has 'lost' on a reference of this kind will be able to charge his next tenant whatever he likes. Furthermore, the circumstances in which the rent assessment committee can intervene are severely circumscribed by s 22; the rent payable has to be 'significantly higher' than a market rent. One assumes that the landlord who lets by an assured shorthold will recover a lower rent than that payable under an assured 'non-shorthold' tenancy, as the non-shorthold tenant enjoys a greater measure of security of tenure for which it is not unreasonable to pay by way of higher rent. In addition, the Secretary of State has power to order that the procedure shall not apply in certain areas or in certain circumstances (s 23).

If an assured shorthold tenant holds over after the expiry of his original assured shorthold (which must be a fixed-term tenancy) the tenant will hold over as an assured periodic tenant, and thus hold subject to the s 13 procedure outlined above, under which the landlord can apply for an increase in the rent. This power is, however, restricted if the tenant has already successfully applied for a reduction under s 22 until 12 months after that determination. If the landlord does invoke the s 13 procedure, one would expect the rent assessment committee's determination to reflect the fact that the tenant had the inferior security afforded by an assured shorthold tenancy.

PUBLIC SECTOR

There has traditionally been little legal control over the levels of rent charged by local housing authorities for their public sector accommodation, and the Housing Act 1985 baldly provides in s 24 that a housing authority 'may make such reasonable charges as they may determine for the tenancy or the occupation of their houses'. Occasionally challenges have been made, by way of applications for judicial review, of such determinations, but they have only rarely succeeded. There was, until 1989, no requirement that the rents so fixed should approximate to market rents, but s 162 Local Government and Housing Act 1989 added two new subsections to s 24.

Local Government and Housing Act 1989

162(3) In exercising their functions under this section, a local housing authority shall have regard in particular to the principle that the rents of houses of any class or description should bear broadly the same proportion to private sector rents as the rents of houses of any other class or description.

(4) In subsection (3) 'private sector rents' in relation to houses of any class or description, means the rents which would be recoverable if they were let on assured tenancies within the meaning of the Housing Act 1988 by a person other than the authority.

CHAPTER 10

THE RIGHT TO BUY IN THE PRIVATE SECTOR

INTRODUCTION

This chapter is concerned with the right of certain tenants to purchase the freehold from their private landlord under the Leasehold Reform Act 1967 and under the Leasehold Reform, Housing and Urban Development Act 1993. The right to buy in the private sector of the rented housing market has met with controversy and fierce opposition in the past. The tenant's ability to purchase the landlord's reversionary interest has proved about as popular with landlords as the local authority's rights of compulsory purchase. The Leasehold Reform Act 1967 and the Leasehold Reform, Housing and Urban Development Act 1993, seem to run counter to all traditional thinking about property rights and ownership of land; and, not surprisingly, the right to buy in the private rented sector has led to a challenge before the European Court of Human Rights by the Duke of Westminster. This challenge will be dealt with later in this chapter.

The motivation for the enactment of the 1967 Act lies in the historical background. Apart from isolated situations where a tenant of a private landlord might have acquired a right of enfranchisement (such as under s 153 Law of Property Act 1925), a tenant, prior to the 1967 Act, would have had to contract specifically for a right to buy through an option to purchase the freehold. Historically, however, many leases took the form of a building lease, under which a developer agreed to develop an area of land for housing purposes in return for a long lease, often for 999 years, at a ground rent (usually a small amount). Other leases often took the form of long leases at a premium, whereby the tenant paid a large sum to acquire the tenancy. The typical length of such leases was 99 years and they tended to be popular in certain urban areas of the country, particularly London, South Wales and the Midlands. Whether the long lease took the form of the building lease or the premium lease, the landlord had a valuable asset, whilst the tenant had a diminishing asset as the years went by. The tenant often found it difficult to transfer the lease, at least in its later years, to anyone else because most financial institutions were not prepared to lend on the security of what was a diminishing asset to the tenant. The difficulties, however, did not really become apparent until after the Second World War, when a number of these leases were about to expire. Such tenancies had been excluded from the protection of the older Rent Acts as a result of their low rents and so the problems of eviction loomed large for many of the tenants.

The government's response in 1950 was to review the whole area by appointing a committee (see Leasehold Committee Final Report, 1950, Cmnd 7982 – the Jenkins Report). As a result of the Jenkins Committee Report, Rent Act-type protection was extended to tenants holding under long leases at low rents in the form of Part I Landlord and Tenant Act 1954. Pressure, however, increased for there to be something more done to help those tenants holding under long leases; and in 1966, the Wilson Labour Government published a White Paper (CMND 2916, 1966, Leasehold Reform in England and Wales), which led directly to the passing of the Leasehold Reform Act 1967. The White

Paper recognised that the leaseholder usually got the worst deal out of the bargain; it was usually the leaseholder who had either built the dwelling on the landlord's land or who had expended vast sums of money over the years in maintaining and improving the property. In a sense, the long leaseholder had already paid for the house, even though the land on which it stood belonged to the landlord. The Wilson government therefore gave effect to the reality of the situation by enabling the tenant compulsorily to purchase the freehold from the landlord if certain conditions were satisfied in the tenant's favour.

The Leasehold Reform, Housing and Urban Development Act 1993 takes this policy a stage further by not only amending the 1967 Act, but extending the right to buy to tenants of flats as a collective group (collective enfranchisement) (see Chapter 1, Part 1) and giving to individual tenants of flats the right to acquire a new lease (see Chapter 2, Part 1). The Housing Act 1996 amends the 1967 Act and Part I 1993 Act. These matters are dealt with later in this chapter.

The Leasehold Reform Act 1967

1. Tenants entitled to enfranchisement or extension

(1) This Part of this Act shall have effect to confer on a tenant of a leasehold house, occupying the house as his residence, a right to acquire on fair terms the freehold or an extended lease of the house and premises where–

(a) his tenancy is a long tenancy at a low rent and–

(i) if the tenancy was entered into before 1st April 1990 or on or after 1st April 1990 in pursuance of a contract made before that date, and the house and premises had a rateable value at the date of commencement of the tenancy or else at any time before 1st April 1990, subject to subsections (5) and (6) below, the rateable value of the house and premises on the appropriate day was not more than £200 or, if it is in Greater London, more than £400; and

(ii) if the tenancy does not fall within sub-paragraph (i) above, on the date the contract for the grant of the tenancy was made or, if there was no such contract, on the date the tenancy was entered into R did not exceed £25,000 under the formula–

$R = (P \times I) / (1 - (1 + I)$ to the power of $-T)$

where–

P is the premium payable as a condition of the grant of the tenancy (and includes a payment of money's worth) or, where no premium is so payable, zero;

I is 0.06; and

T is the term, expressed in years, granted by the tenancy (disregarding any right to terminate the tenancy before the end of the term or to extend the tenancy); and

(b) at the relevant time (that is to say, at the time when he gives notice in accordance with this Act of his desire to have the freehold or to have an extended lease, as the case may be) he has been tenant of the house under a long tenancy at a low rent, and occupying it as his residence, for the last [three years] or for periods amounting to [three years] in the last ten years;

and to confer the like right in the other cases for which provision is made in this Part of this Act.

(1A) The references in subsection (1)(a) and (b) to a long tenancy at a low rent do not include a tenancy excluded from the operation of this Part by section 33A of and Schedule 4A to this Act.

(2) In this Part of this Act references, in relation to any tenancy, to the tenant occupying a house as his residence shall be construed as applying where, but only where, the tenant is, in right of the tenancy, occupying it as his only or main residence (whether or not he uses it also for other purposes); but–

    (a) references to a person occupying a house shall apply where he occupies it in part only; and

    (b) in determining in what right the tenant occupies, there shall be disregarded any mortgage term and any interest arising in favour of any person by his attorning tenant to a mortgagee or chargee.

(3) This Part of this Act shall not confer on the tenant of a house any right by reference to his occupation of it as his residence (but shall apply as if he were not so occupying it) at any time when–

    (a) it is let to and occupied by him with other land or premises to which it is ancillary; or

    (b) it is comprised in an agricultural holding within the meaning of the Agricultural Holdings Act 1986.

or, in the case of any right to which subsection (3A) below applies, at any time when the tenant's immediate landlord is a charitable housing trust and the house forms part of the housing accommodation provided by the trust in the pursuit of its charitable purposes.

(3A) For the purposes of subsection (3) above this subsection applies as follows–

    (a) where the tenancy was created after the commencement of Chapter III of Part I of the Leasehold Reform, Housing and Urban Development Act 1993, this subsection applies to any right to acquire the freehold of the house and premises; but

    (b) where the tenancy was created before that commencement, this subsection applies only to any such right exercisable by virtue of any one or more of the provisions of sections 1A and 1B below–

and in that subsection 'charitable housing trust' means a housing trust within the meaning of the Housing Act 1985 which is a charity within the meaning of the Charities Act 1993.

(4) In subsection (1)(a) above, 'the appropriate day', in relation to any house and premises, means the 23rd March 1965 or such later day as by virtue of [section 25(3) Rent Act 1977] would be the appropriate day for purposes of that Act in relation to a dwelling-house consisting of that house.

(4A) Schedule 8 to the Housing Act 1974 shall have effect to enable a tenant to have the rateable value of the house and premises reduced for purposes of this section in consequence of tenant's improvements.

(5) If, in relation to any house and premises, the appropriate day for the purposes of subsection (1)(a) above falls on or after 1st April 1973 that subsection shall have effect in relation to the house and premises–

    (a) in a case where the tenancy was created on or before 18th February 1966, as if for the sums of £200 and £400 specified in that subsection there were substituted respectively the sums of £750 and £1,500; and

    (b) in a case where the tenancy was created after 18th February 1966, as if for those sums of £200 and £400 there were substituted respectively the sums of £500 and £1,000.

(6) If, in relation to any house and premises–

  (a) the appropriate day for the purposes of subsection (1)(a) above falls before 1st April 1973; and

  (b) the rateable value of the house and premises on the appropriate day was more than £200 or, if it was then in Greater London, £400, and

  (c) the tenancy was created on or before 18th February 1966,

subsection (1)(a) above shall have effect in relation to the house and premises as if for the reference to the appropriate day there were substituted a reference to 1st April 1973 and as if for the sums of £200 and £400 specified in that subsection there were substituted respectively the sums of £500 and £1,500.

(7) The Secretary of State may by order replace the amount referred to in subsection (1)(a)(ii) above and the number in the definition of '1' in that subsection by such amount or number as is specified in the order; and such an order shall be made by statutory instrument which shall be subject to annulment in pursuance of a resolution of either House of Parliament.

1A(1) Where subsection (1) of section 1 above would apply in the case of the tenant of a house but for the fact that the applicable financial limit specified in subsection (1)(a)(i) or (ii) or (as the case may be) subsection (5) or (6) of that section is exceeded, this Part of this Act shall have effect to confer on the tenant the same right to acquire the freehold of the house and premises as would be conferred by subsection (1) of that section if that limit were not exceeded.

(2) Where a tenancy of any property is not a tenancy at a low rent in accordance with section 4(1) below but is a tenancy falling within section 4A(1) below, the tenancy shall nevertheless be treated as a tenancy at a low rent for the purposes of this Part of this Act so far as it has effect for conferring on any person a right to acquire the freehold of a house and premises.

Additional rights to enfranchisement only in case of houses whose rent exceeds applicable limit under section 4

1AA (1) Where–

  (a) section 1(1) above would apply in the case of the tenant of a house but for the fact that the tenancy is not a tenancy at a low rent, and

  (b) the tenancy falls within subsection (2) below and is not an excluded tenancy,

this Part of this Act shall have effect to confer on the tenant the same right to acquire the freehold of the house and premises as would be conferred by section 1(1) above if it were a tenancy at a low rent.

(2) A tenancy falls within this subsection if–

  (a) it is granted for a term of years certain exceeding thirty-five years, whether or not it is (or may become) terminable before the end of that term by notice given by or to the tenant or by re-entry, forfeiture or otherwise,

  (b) it is for a term fixed by law under a grant with a covenant or obligation for perpetual renewal, unless it is a tenancy by sub-demise from one which is not a tenancy which falls within this subsection.

  (c) it is a tenancy taking effect under section 149(6) of the Law of Property Act 1925 (leases terminable after a death or marriage), or

(d) it is a tenancy which–

    (i) is or has been granted for a term of years certain not exceeding thirty-five years, but with a covenant or obligation for renewal without payment of a premium (but not for perpetual renewal), and

    (ii) is or has been once or more renewed so as to bring to more than thirty-five years the total of the terms granted (including any interval between the end of a tenancy and the grant of a renewal).

(3) A tenancy is an excluded tenancy for the purposes of subsection (1) above if–

    (a) the house which the tenant occupies under the tenancy is in an area designated for the purposes of this provision as a rural area by order made by the Secretary of State,

    (b) the freehold of that house is owned together with adjoining land which is not occupied for residential purposes and has been owned together with such land since the coming into force of section 106 of the Housing Act 1996, and

    (c) the tenancy was granted on or before the day on which that section came into force.

(4) Where this Part of this Act applies as if there were a single tenancy of property comprised in two or more separate tenancies, then, if each of the separate tenancies falls within subsection (2) above, this section shall apply as if the single tenancy did so.

(5) The power to make an order under subsection (3) above shall be exercisable by statutory instrument which shall be subject to annulment in pursuance of a resolution of either House of Parliament.

1B(1) Where a tenancy granted so as to become terminable by notice after a death or marriage–

    (a) is (apart from this section) a long tenancy in accordance with section 3(1) below; but

    (b) was granted before 18th April 1980 or in pursuance of a contract entered into before that date;

then (notwithstanding section 3(1)) the tenancy shall be a long tenancy for the purposes of this Part of this Act only so far as this Part has effect for conferring on any person a right to acquire the freehold of a house and premises.

(2) For the purposes of subsection (1) above–

    (a) 'the initial year', in relation to any tenancy, means the period of one year beginning with the date of the commencement of the tenancy;

    (b) 'the relevant date' means the date of the commencement of the tenancy or, if the property did not have a rateable value on that date, the date on which it first had a rateable value; and

    (c) paragraphs (b) and (c) of section 4(1) above shall apply as they apply for the purposes of section 4(1);

and it is hereby declared that in subsection (1) above the reference to the letting value of any property is to be construed in like manner as the reference in similar terms which appears in the proviso to section 4(1) above.

(3) Section 1(7) above applies to any amount referred to in subsection (1)(c) above as it applies to the amount referred to in subsection (1)(a)(ii) of that section.

2(1) For purposes of this Part of this Act, 'house' includes any building designed or adapted for living in and reasonably so called, notwithstanding that the building is not structurally detached, or was or is not solely designed or adapted for living in, or is divided horizontally into flats or maisonettes; and–

(a) where a building is divided horizontally, the flats or other units into which it is so divided are not separate 'houses', though the building as a whole may be; and

(b) where a building is divided vertically the building as a whole is not a 'house' though any of the units into which it is divided may be.

(2) References in this Part of this Act to a house do not apply to a house which is not structurally detached and of which a material part lies above or below a part of the structure not comprised in the house.

(3) Subject to the following provisions of this section, where in relation to a house let to and occupied by a tenant reference is made in this Part of this Act to the house and premises, the reference to premises is to be taken as referring to any garage, outhouse, garden, yard and appurtenances which at the relevant time are let to him with the house and are occupied with and used for the purposes of the house or any part of it by him or by another occupant.

(4) In relation to the exercise by a tenant of any right conferred by this Part of this Act there shall be treated as included in the house and premises any other premises let with the house and premises but not at the relevant time occupied and used as mentioned in subsection (3) above (whether in consequence of an assignment of the term therein or a subletting or otherwise), if–

(a) the landlord at the relevant time has an interest in the other premises and, not later than two months after the relevant time, gives to the tenant written notice objecting to the further severance of them from the house and premises; and

(b) either the tenant agrees to their inclusion with the house and premises or the court is satisfied that it would be unreasonable to require the landlord to retain them without the house and premises.

(5) In relation to the exercise by a tenant of any right conferred by this Part of this Act there shall be treated as not included in the house and premises any part of them which lies above or below other premises (not consisting only of underlying mines or minerals), if–

(a) the landlord at the relevant time has an interest in the other premises and, not later than two months after the relevant time, gives to the tenant written notice objecting to the further severance from them of that part of the house and premises; and

(b) either the tenant agrees to the exclusion of that part of the house and premises or the court is satisfied that any hardship or inconvenience likely to result to the tenant from the exclusion, when account is taken of anything that can be done to mitigate its effects and of any undertaking of the landlord to take steps to mitigate them, is outweighed by the difficulties involved in the further severance from the other premises and any hardship or inconvenience likely to result from that severance to persons interested in those premises.

(6) The rights conferred on a tenant by this Part of this Act in relation to any house and premises shall not extend to underlying minerals comprised in the tenancy if the landlord requires that the minerals be excepted, and if proper provision is made for the support of the house and premises as they have been enjoyed during the tenancy and in accordance with its terms.

(7) Where by virtue of subsection (4) above a tenant of a house acquiring the freehold or an extended lease is required to include premises of which the tenancy is not vested in him, this Part of this Act shall apply for the purpose as if in the case of those premises a tenancy on identical terms were vested in him and the holder of the actual tenancy were a sub-tenant; and where by virtue of subsection (5) or (6) above a tenant of a house acquiring the freehold or an extended lease is required to exclude property of which the tenancy is vested in him, then unless the landlord and the tenant otherwise agree or the court for the protection of either of them from hardship or inconvenience otherwise orders, the grant to the tenant shall operate as a surrender of the tenancy in that property and the provision to be made by the grant shall be determined as if the surrender had taken place before the relevant time.

3. Meaning of 'long tenancy'

(1) In this Part of this Act 'long tenancy' means, subject to the provisions of this section, a tenancy granted for a term of years certain exceeding twenty-one years, whether or not the tenancy is (or may become) terminable before the end of that term by notice given by or to the tenant or by re-entry, forfeiture or otherwise, and includes both a tenancy taking effect under section 149(6) of the Law of Property Act 1925 (leases terminable after a death or marriage) and a tenancy for a term fixed by law under a grant with a covenant or obligation for perpetual renewal unless it is a tenancy by sub-demise from one which is not a long tenancy:

Provided that a tenancy granted so as to become terminable by notice after a death or marriage is not to be treated as a long tenancy), if–

(a) the notice is capable of being given at any time after the death or marriage of the tenant;

(b) the length of the notice is not more than three months; and

(c) the terms of the tenancy preclude both–

   (i) its assignment otherwise than by virtue of section 92 of the Housing Act 1985 (assignments by way of exchange), and

   (ii) the sub-letting of the whole of the premises comprised in it.

(2) Where the tenant of any property under a long tenancy at a low rent (other than a lease excluded from the operation of this Part by section 33A of and Schedule 4A to this Act), on the coming to an end of that tenancy, becomes or has become tenant of the property or part of it under another tenancy (whether by express grant or by implication of law), then the later tenancy shall be deemed for the purposes of this Part of this Act, including any further application of this subsection, to be a long tenancy irrespective of its terms.

(3) Where the tenant of any property under a long tenancy, on the coming to an end of that tenancy, becomes or has become tenant of the property or part of it under another long tenancy, then in relation to the property or that part of it this Part of this Act except section 1AA shall apply as if there had been a single tenancy granted for a term beginning at the same time as the term under the earlier tenancy and expiring at the same time as the term under the later tenancy.

(4) Where a tenancy is or has been granted for a term of years certain not exceeding twenty-one years, but with a covenant or obligation for renewal without payment of a premium (but not for perpetual renewal), and the tenancy is or has been once or more renewed so as to bring to more than twenty-one years the total of the terms granted (including any interval between the end of a tenancy and the grant of a renewal), then this Part of this Act shall apply as it would apply if the term originally granted had been one exceeding twenty-one years.

(5) References in this Part of this Act to a long tenancy include any period during which the tenancy is or was continued under Part I or II of the Landlord and Tenant Act 1954 or under the Leasehold Property (Temporary Provisions) Act 1951.

(6) Where at any time there are separate tenancies, with the same landlord and the same tenant, of two or more parts of a house, or of a house or part of it and land or other premises occupied therewith, then in relation to the property comprised in such of those tenancies as are long tenancies this Part of this Act shall apply as it would if at that time there were a single tenancy of that property and the tenancy were a long tenancy, and for that purpose references in this Part of this Act to the commencement of the term or to the term date shall, if the separate tenancies commenced at different dates or have different term dates, have effect as references to the commencement or term date, as the case may be, of the tenancy, comprising the house (or the earliest commencement or earliest term date of the tenancies comprising it):

Provided that this subsection shall have effect subject to the operation of subsections (2) to (5) above in relation to any of the separate tenancies.

4. (1) For purposes of this Part of this Act a tenancy of any property is a tenancy at a low rent at any time when rent is not payable under the tenancy in respect of the property at a yearly rate:

(i) if the tenancy was entered into before 1st April 1990 or on or after 1st April 1990 in pursuance of a contract made before that date, and the property had a rateable value other than nil at the date of the commencement of the tenancy or else at any time before 1st April 1990, equal to or more than two-thirds of the rateable value of the property on the appropriate day or, if later, the first day of the term;

(ii) if the tenancy does not fall within paragraph (i) above, more than £1,000 if the property is in Greater London and £250 if the property is elsewhere:

Provided that a tenancy granted between the end of August 1939 and the beginning of April 1963 otherwise than by way of building lease (whether or not it is, by virtue of section 3(3) above, to be treated for other purposes as forming a single tenancy with a previous tenancy) shall not be regarded as a tenancy at a low rent if at the commencement of the tenancy the rent payable under the tenancy exceeded two-thirds of the letting value of the property (on the same terms).

For the purposes of this subsection–

(a) 'appropriate day' means the 23rd March 1965 or such later day as by virtue of section 25(3) of the Rent Act 1977 would be the appropriate day for purposes of that Act in relation to a dwelling-house consisting of the house in question if the reference in paragraph (a) of that provision to a rateable value were to a rateable value other than nil; and

(b) 'rent' means rent reserved as such, and there shall be disregarded any part of the rent expressed to be payable in consideration of services to be provided, or of repairs, maintenance or insurance to be effected by the landlord, or to be payable in respect of the cost thereof to the landlord or a superior landlord; and

(c) there shall be disregarded any term of the tenancy providing for suspension or reduction of rent in the event of damage to property demised, or for any penal addition to the rent in the event of a contravention of or non-compliance with the terms of the tenancy or an agreement collateral thereto; and

(d) 'building lease' means a lease granted in pursuance or in consideration of an agreement for the erection or the substantial rebuilding or reconstruction of the whole or part of the house in question or a building comprising it.

(2) Where on a claim by the tenant of a house to exercise any right conferred by this Part of this Act a question arises under section 1(1) above whether his tenancy of the house is or was at any time a tenancy at a low rent, the question shall be determined by reference to the rent and rateable value of the house and premises as a whole, and in relation to a time before the relevant time shall be so determined whether or not the property then occupied with the house or any part of it was the same in all respects as that comprised in the house and premises for purposes of the claim; but, in a case where the tenancy derives (in accordance with section 3(6) above) from more than one separate tenancy, the proviso to subsection (1) above shall have effect if, but only if, it applies to one of the separate tenancies which comprises the house or part of it.

(3) Where on a claim by the tenant of a house to exercise any right conferred by this Part of this Act a question arises under section 3(2) above whether a tenancy is or was a long tenancy by reason of a previous tenancy having been a long tenancy at a low rent, the question whether the previous tenancy was one at a low rent shall be determined in accordance with subsection (2) above as if it were a question arising under section 1(1), and shall be so determined by reference to the rent and rateable value of the house and premises or the part included in the previous tenancy, exclusive of any other land or premises so included:

Provided that where an apportionment of rent or rateable value is required because the previous tenancy did not include the whole of the house and premises or included other property, the apportionment shall be made as at the end of the previous tenancy except in so far as, in the case of rent, an apportionment falls to be made at an earlier date under subsection (6) below.

(4) For purposes of subsection (2) or (3) above a house and premises shall be taken as not including any premises which are to be or may be included under section 2(4) above in giving effect to the tenant's claim, and as including any part which is to be or may be excluded under section 2(5) or (6).

(5) Where on a claim by the tenant of a house to exercise any right conferred by this Part of this Act a question arises whether a tenancy granted as mentioned in the proviso to subsection (1) above is or was at any time a tenancy at a low rent, it shall be presumed until the contrary is shown that the letting value referred to in that proviso was such that the proviso does not apply.

(6) Any entire rent payable at any time in respect of both a house and premises or part thereof and of property not included in the house and premises shall for purposes of this section be apportioned as may be just according to the circumstances existing at the date of the severance giving rise to the apportionment, and references in this section to the rent of a house and premises or of part thereof shall be construed accordingly.

(7) Section 1(7) above applies to any amount referred to in subsection (1)(ii) above as it applies to the amount referred to in subsection (1)(a)(ii) of that section.

4A(1) For the purposes of section 1A(2) above a tenancy of any property falls within this subsection if either no rent was payable under it in respect of the property during the initial year or the aggregate amount of rent so payable during that year did not exceed the following amount, namely–

   (a) where the tenancy was entered into before 1st April 1963, two-thirds of the letting value of the property (on the same terms) on the date of the commencement of the tenancy;

   (b) where–

      (i) the tenancy was entered into either on or after 1st April 1963 but before 1st April 1990, or on or after 1st April 1990 in pursuance of a contract made before that date, and

      (ii) the property had a rateable value other than nil at the date of the commencement of the tenancy or else at any time before 1st April 1990,

     two-thirds of the rateable value of the property on the relevant date; or

   (c) in any other case, £1,000 if the property is in Greater London or £250 if elsewhere.

8. Obligation to enfranchise

(1) Where a tenant of a house has under this Part of this Act a right to acquire the freehold, and gives to the landlord written notice of his desire to have the freehold, then except as provided by this Part of this Act the landlord shall be bound to make to the tenant and the tenant to accept (at the price and on the conditions so provided) a grant of the house and premises for an estate in fee simple absolute, subject to the tenancy and to tenant's incumbrances, but otherwise free of incumbrances.

(2) For purposes of this Part of this Act 'incumbrances' includes rentcharges and, subject to subsection (3) below, personal liabilities attaching in respect of the ownership of land or an interest in land though not charged on that land or interest; and 'tenant's incumbrances' includes any interest directly or indirectly derived out of the tenancy, and any incumbrance on the tenancy or any such interest (whether or not the same matter is an incumbrance also on any interest reversionary on the tenancy).

(3) Burdens originating in tenure and burdens in respect of the upkeep or regulation for the benefit of any locality of any land, building structure works, ways or watercourse shall not be treated as incumbrances for purposes of this Part of this Act, but any conveyance executed to give effect to this section shall be made subject thereto except as otherwise provided by section 11 below.

(4) A conveyance executed to give effect to this section–

   (a) shall have effect under section 2(1) of the Law of Property Act 1925 to overreach any incumbrance capable of being overreached under that section as if, where the interest conveyed is settled land, the conveyance were made under the powers of the Settled Land Act 1925 and as if the requirements of section 2(1) as to payment of the capital money allowed any part of the purchase price paid or applied in accordance with sections 11 to 13 below to be so paid or applied;

(b) shall not be made subject to any incumbrance capable of being overreached by the conveyance, but shall be made subject (where they are not capable of being overreached) to rentcharges [redeemable under sections 8 to 10 of the Rentcharges Act 1977 and those falling within paragraphs (c) and (d) of section 2(3) of that Act (estate rentcharges and rentcharges imposed under certain enactments)], except as otherwise provided by section 11 below.

(5) Notwithstanding that on a grant to a tenant of a house and premises under this section no payment or a nominal payment only is required from the tenant for the price of the house and premises, the tenant shall nevertheless be deemed for all purposes to be a purchaser for a valuable consideration in money or money's worth.

9. Purchase price and costs of enfranchisement, and tenant's right to withdraw

(1) Subject to subsection (2) below, the price payable for a house and premises on a conveyance under section 8 above shall be the amount which at the relevant time the house and premises, if sold in the open market by a willing seller [(with the tenant and members of his family who reside in the house not buying or seeking to buy)], might be expected to realise on the following assumptions:

(a) on the assumption that the vendor was selling for an estate in fee simple, subject to the tenancy but on the assumption that this Part of this Act conferred no right to acquire the freehold, and if the tenancy has not been extended under this Part of this Act, on the assumption that (subject to the landlord's rights under section 17 below) it was to be so extended;

(b) on the assumption that (subject to paragraph (a) above) the vendor was selling subject, in respect of rentcharges ... to which section 11(2) below applies, to the same annual charge as the conveyance to the tenant is to be subject to, but the purchaser would otherwise be effectively exonerated until termination of the tenancy from any liability or charge in respect of tenant's incumbrances; and

(c) on the assumption that (subject to paragraphs (a) and (b) above) the vendor was selling with and subject to the rights and burdens with and subject to which the conveyance to the tenant is to be made, and in particular with and subject to such permanent or extended rights and burdens as are to be created in order to give effect to section 10 below.

The reference in this subsection to members of the tenants family shall be construed in accordance with section 7(7) of this Act.

(1A) Notwithstanding the foregoing subsection, the price payable for a house and premises–

(i) the rateable value of which was above £1,000 in Greater London and £500 elsewhere on 31st March 1990; or

(ii) which had no rateable value on that date and R exceeded £16,333 under the formula in section 1(1)(a) above (and section 1(7) above shall apply to that amount as it applies to the amount referred to in subsection (1)(a)(ii) of that section);

shall be the amount which at the relevant time the house and premises, if sold in the open market by a willing seller, might be expected to realise on the following assumptions–

(a) on the assumption that the vendor was selling for an estate in fee simple, subject to the tenancy, but on the assumption that this Part of this Act conferred no right to acquire the freehold or an extended lease and, where the tenancy has been extended under this Part of this Act that the tenancy will terminate on the original term date;

(b) on the assumption that at the end of the tenancy the tenant has the right to remain in possession of the house and premises–

    (i) if the tenancy is such a tenancy as is mentioned in subsection (2) or subsection (3) of section 186 of the Local Government and Housing Act 1989, or is a tenancy which is a long tenancy at a low rent for the purposes of Part I of the Landlord and Tenant Act 1954 in respect of which the landlord is not able to serve a notice under section 4 of that Act specifying a date of termination earlier than 15th January 1999, under the provisions of Schedule 10 to the Local Government and Housing Act 1989; and

    (ii) in any other case under the provisions of Part I of the Landlord and Tenant Act 1954;

(c) on the assumption that the tenant has no liability to carry out any repairs, maintenance or redecorations under the terms of the tenancy or Part I of the Landlord and Tenant Act 1954;

(d) on the assumption that the price be diminished by the extent to which the value of the house and premises has been increased by any improvement carried out by the tenant or his predecessors in title at their own expense;

(e) on the assumption that (subject to paragraph (a) above) the vendor was selling subject, in respect of rentcharges ... to which section 11(2) below applies, to the same annual charge as the conveyance to the tenant is to be subject to, but the purchaser would otherwise be effectively exonerated until the termination of the tenancy from any liability or charge in respect of tenant's incumbrances; and

(f) on the assumption that (subject to paragraphs (a) and (b) above) the vendor was selling with and subject to the rights and burdens with and subject to which the conveyance to the tenant is to be made, and in particular with and subject to such permanent or extended rights and burdens as are to be created in order to give effect to section 10 below.

(1B) For the purpose of determining whether the rateable value of the house and premises is above £1,000 in Greater London, or £500 elsewhere the rateable value shall be adjusted to take into account any tenant's improvements in accordance with Schedule 8 to the Housing Act 1974.

(1C) Notwithstanding subsection (1) above, the price payable for a house and premises where the right to acquire the freehold arises by virtue of any one or more of the provisions of sections 1A, 1AA and 1B above shall be determined in accordance with subsection (1A) above; but in any such case–

(a) if in determining the price so payable there falls to be taken into account any marriage value arising by virtue of the coalescence of the freehold and leasehold interests, the share of the marriage value to which the tenant is to be regarded as being entitled shall not exceed one-half of it; and

(b) section 9A below has effect for determining whether any additional amount is payable by way of compensation under that section;

and in a case where the provision (or one of the provisions) by virtue of which the right to acquire the freehold arises is section 1A(1) above, subsection (1A) above shall apply with the omission of the assumption set out in paragraph (b) of that subsection.

(2) The price payable for the house and premises shall be subject to such deduction (if any) in respect of any defect in the title to be conveyed to the tenant as on a sale in the open market might be expected to be allowed between a willing seller and a willing buyer.

(3) On ascertaining the amount payable, or likely to be payable, as the price for a house and premises in accordance with this section (but not more than one month after the amount payable has been determined by agreement or otherwise), the tenant may give written notice to the landlord that he is unable or unwilling to acquire the house and premises at the price he must pay; and thereupon–

(a) the notice under section 8 above of his desire to have the freehold shall cease to have effect, and he shall be liable to make such compensation as may be just to the landlord in respect of the interference (if any) by the notice with the exercise by the landlord of his power to dispose of or deal with the house and premises or any neighbouring property; and

(b) any further notice given under that section with respect to the house or any part of it (with or without other property) shall be void if given within the following three years.

(4) Where a person gives notice of his desire to have the freehold of a house and premises under this Part of this Act, then unless the notice lapses under any provision of this Act excluding his liability, there shall be borne by him (so far as they are incurred in pursuance of the notice) the reasonable costs of or incidental to any of the following matters:

(a) any investigation by the landlord of that person's right to acquire the freehold;

(b) any conveyance or assurance of the house and premises or any part thereof or of any outstanding estate or interest therein;

(c) deducing, evidencing and verifying the title to the house and premises or any estate or interest therein;

(d) making out and furnishing such abstracts and copies as the person giving the notice may require;

(e) any valuation of the house and premises;

but so that this subsection shall not apply to any costs if on a sale made voluntarily a stipulation that they were to be borne by the purchaser would be void.

(5) The landlord's lien (as vendor) on the house and premises for the price payable shall extend–

(a) to any sums payable by way of rent or recoverable as rent in respect of the house and premises up to the date of the conveyance; and

(b) to any sums for which the tenant is liable under subsection (4) above; and

(c) to any other sums due and payable by him to the landlord under or in respect of the tenancy or any agreement collateral thereto.

9A(1) If, in a case where the right to acquire the freehold of a house and premises arises by virtue of any one or more of the provisions of sections 1A, 1AA and 1B above, the landlord will suffer any loss or damage to which this section applies, there shall be payable to him such amount as is reasonable to compensate him for that loss or damage.

(2) This section applies to–

    (a) any diminution in value of any interest of the landlord in other property resulting from the acquisition of his interest in the house and premises; and

    (b) any other loss or damage which results therefrom to the extent that it is referable to his ownership of any interest in other property,

(3) Without prejudice to the generality of paragraph (b) of subsection (2) above, the kinds of loss falling within that paragraph include loss of development value in relation to the house and premises to the extent that it is referable as mentioned in that paragraph.

(4) In subsection (3) above 'development value', in relation to the house and premises, means any increase in the value of the landlord's interest in the house and premises which is attributable to the possibility of demolishing, reconstructing, or carrying out substantial works of construction on, the whole or a substantial part of the house and premises.

(5) In relation to any case falling within subsection (1) above–

    (a) any reference (however expressed)–

        (i) in section 8 or 9(3) or (5) above; or

        (ii) in any of the following provisions of this Act,

    to the price payable under section 9 above shall be construed as including a reference to any amount payable to the landlord under this section; and

    (b) for the purpose of determining any such separate price as is mentioned in paragraph 7(1)(b) of Schedule I to this Act, this section shall accordingly apply (with any necessary modifications) to each of the superior interests in question.

WHAT PROPERTY IS COVERED BY THE 1967 ACT?

A house

The 1967 Act only applies to houses, and not to individual flats. Section 1 confers on a tenant of a leasehold house the right to purchase the freehold of that house if certain other conditions are satisfied. Flats were excluded from the right to buy because of problems of the enforceability of repairing covenants (see, for example, the discussion of 'flying freeholds' by Kevin Gray, *Elements of Land Law*, 1st edn, pp 18–19). Section 2 explains what is meant by 'house'; but the phrase 'reasonably so called' has caused some problems, especially in relation to mixed user property. One of the first cases to come before the Court of Appeal on this question was that of *Lake v Bennett* [1970] 1 QB 633, [1970] 1 All ER 457. This case was concerned with whether premises, which were in part let as a shop, could be 'reasonably ... called' a house. In concluding that the building was a house 'reasonably so called', the Court of Appeal stated that the question was really partly one of fact and partly one of law.

Lake v Bennett

Lord Denning MR: If the building is a 'house' within the meaning of the Act, the applicant is entitled to buy the freehold at a price to be fixed in accordance with the Act, which would be a very modest sum. But, if it is not a 'house' within the meaning of the Act, she is not entitled to buy it at all. The first respondent, on the assumption that she has no right, has already arranged to let it to the second respondent after the expiry of the lease.

The material definition is s 2(1) ...

Some things are clear. First, the subletting of the ground floor does not take the case out of the Act, see *Harris v Swick Securities Ltd*; secondly, the use of the ground floor for business purposes does not take it out of the Act. Several sections contemplate that part of a house may be used for business purposes. The only question is whether this is a 'house' within the definition of a 'building designed or adapted for living in and reasonably so called'?

I believe that this is the first Act in which Parliament has endeavoured to give a definition of a 'house'. There have been many statutes which have used the word 'house' without defining it. And the courts have given it a wide interpretation. The first case was the most extreme: *Richards v Swansea Improvement and Tramways Co* (1878) 9 CLD 425. It was under the Lands Clauses Consolidation Act 1845. It was held that a mass of buildings was a 'house', although part of it was residence, part cottages, and part manufactory. It was all held to be a 'house'. That is going a long way. It would not apply, I should think, to the present Act, because of the words 'reasonably so called'.

In the Rent Acts too there was no definition of a 'house'; but under them a hotel was held to be a 'house', see *Epsom Grand Stand Association Ltd v Clarke* (1919); and also a building which was part dwelling and part business premises, see *Ellen v Goldstein* (1920) ...

Quite recently in *Luganda v Services Hotels Ltd* [1969] 2 CL 209 this court held that a building (four houses knocked into one) with 88 rooms which were let off in furnished rooms, was a 'house'. I doubt whether the whole would be a 'house' within the Leasehold Reform Act 1967, because of the limitation 'reasonably so called', although each one of the four might be. In the Housing Acts there was no definition of a 'house', but we considered it in *Ashbridge Investments Ltd v Minister of Housing and Local Government* [1965] 1 WLR 1320. I ventured to suggest that 'a house' in the Act [ie the Housing Act 1957] means a building which is constructed or adapted for use as, or for the purposes of, a dwelling. It would appear that in the Leasehold Reform Act 1967 Parliament adopted these words, but added the limitation 'reasonably so called'.

It is quite plain that this building was a 'house' within all these earlier statutes. The point is: what is the limitation conveyed by the words 'reasonably so called'? I would not pretend on this occasion to attempt to define the limitation. But it may be useful to give an illustration. I do not think that a tower block of flats would reasonably be called a 'house'. But I think that a four-storied building like the present one is reasonably called a 'house'. Take it in stages. First, if the tenant occupied the building entirely by himself, using the ground floor for his shop premises, that would plainly be a 'house' reasonably so called. Secondly, if the tenant, instead of using the ground floor for himself for business purposes, sublets it, that does not alter the character of the building. It is still a 'house' reasonably so called. And that is this case.

But counsel for the respondents say: 'It depends on the nature of the business. If one has a business which is a bookmaker's office, financially very profitable, that gives a colour to the whole building. It is not a house but a bookmaker's office.' I am afraid that I do not agree. It seems to me that, even though the subletting is financially profitable for the tenant, the character of the building remains the same. It is a 'house' within the meaning of the Act.

Then counsel for the respondents says that it is a question of fact for the judge; and this court has no jurisdiction to interfere with his decision. He points out, quite rightly, that there is an appeal to this court only on a point of law. This is how the judge puts his finding:

' ... having regard to the appearance of the front elevation of the building in the present case, the proportion of it taken up by the shop front, and to the fact that the structure of the ground floor has been altered so that the shop takes up virtually the whole of it and forms a self-contained unit, and the fact that the rest of the building is clearly of much less value, I have come to the conclusion that the building in question is not reasonably called a house.'

I do not regard that as a finding of fact. It is an inference from primary facts. It depends in part at least on the true interpretation of the words 'reasonably so called'. In any case, even if it were a finding of fact, this court can interfere if it is a conclusion to which the county court could not reasonably come.

Viewing the whole case, I am quite satisfied that this building is a house reasonably so called. I can see that there may be difficult questions arising in regard to other buildings which may come before us. But this is a typical case. I have found no doubt that this was a 'house', and the applicant is entitled to buy the freehold on terms prescribed by the Act. I would allow the appeal accordingly.

Salmon LJ agreed.

Of more importance, however, is the House of Lords' decision in *Tandon v Trustees of Spurgeon's Homes* [1982] AC 755, [1982] 1 All ER 1086, again concerned with a mixed user unit. In that case, the House of Lords decided that premises which consisted of 75% shop space and 25% living accommodation could reasonably be called a house for the purposes of the 1967 Act.

Tandon v Trustees of Spurgeon's Homes

Lord Roskill: ... My Lords, the appellant is the tenant of premises at 116 Mitcham Lane, London SW16. His title originated in a building lease for 99 years from 25 March 1881 under which these premises, described as 'ALL THAT messuage or dwelling-house and shop', were on completion to be demised to the then lessee for the period just stated.

The primary facts regarding these premises were clearly stated by the county court judge and subject to the correction of one small error were accepted by both parties as having been properly found. For brevity I shall repeat the same passage of the county court judge's judgment as Griffiths LJ cited in his judgment ([1981] 2 All ER 960 at 961, [1981] 3 WLR 74 at 75) in the Court of Appeal, first mentioning that your Lordships have seen the same agreed plan, description and photographs as did the Court of Appeal:

'The property is clearly shown by the agreed plan, description and photographs which are before me. The site is a long narrow plot with a frontage of about 21 feet on Mitcham Lane. The ground floor is a shop front in the main road and is one of four identical shops with varying shop fronts. There is a first floor above containing three effective rooms in the main part of the building and a back addition. Behind this building there was originally a narrow open path running between the back addition and behind that an open space leading to a two-storey stable which in turn gave access to a rear service road. At some uncertain time but certainly before 1962 when Mr Kirkaldie inspected the premises, a roof, treated for London building consent as temporary, was erected over the whole of the yard except an outside water closet. This roof runs from and is attached to the rear of the main building and extends right back to the stable. The doors are arranged so that there is internal communication from the shop in front through the original open space to the stable and service road at the back. The interior layout is that at the rear of the main building there is an opening to the right which forms the access to the upper part of the building and also to the combined bathroom and water closet at ground level. The stairs rise by a right angle to the right and open on [to] the first floor. At present the whole of the ground floor, including the covered yard and stable, are used as a shop, and the first floor is residential. In 1962 the layout was the same but the first floor was used as offices.'

It was in the penultimate sentence that the county court judge made a slight error. The combined bathroom and water closet at ground level to which he referred do not form part of the shop but form part of the residential accommodation which is otherwise entirely on the first floor.

On those primary facts, is the appellant as tenant entitled to acquire the freehold interest in the premises from his landlords, the respondents? The county court judge, and Ormrod LJ thought he was. Griffiths and Watkins LJJ thought not. It was throughout common ground that the appellant could satisfy all the requirements of the 1967 Act save one. But the respondents contended that these premises were not a 'house' within the definition of that word in s 2(1) while the appellant contended that they were. This is the issue for decision by your Lords.

The relevant part of the definition [is] in s 2(1) ...

My Lords, looking only at the words of this subsection and regardless of any authority on its construction, two points seem to me clearly to emerge. First, though the definition of 'house' is expressed to be inclusive and not exhaustive, the words 'any building ... reasonably so called' are intended as words of limitation for clearly premises are not to treated as a 'house' within the subsection merely because they are a building designed or adapted for living in unless they can also in ordinary parlance be reasonably called 'a house'. Second, premises are not to be treated as without the definition merely because the building is not structurally detached or 'was *or is not solely designed or adapted for living in*'. Nothing in the present case turns on 'not structurally detached', for these premises were not structurally detached. But the words which I have italicised suggest to my mind that Parliament was intending in certain circumstances to extend the benefits and privileges of the 1967 Act to tenants of premises not exclusively designed or adapted for living in for residential purposes. If that approach be correct, the next question is: what are the circumstances in which the tenant of such premises can successfully assert a claim to those benefits and privileges?

My Lords, counsel for the respondents did not seek to argue that the mere fact that part of the premises were used as a shop constituted a complete bar to the successful assertion of such a claim. Counsel for the appellant did not seek to argue that such a claim could be successfully asserted in every case of mixed user, that part of the user which was non-residential being wholly ignored.

Each counsel therefore avoided the extreme argument possibly open to him and in my view one has only to look at the definition in s 2(1) to see that each was right to do so. The definition clearly contemplates some mixed user but leaves it to the courts to determine whether the particular premises fall within or without the definition, bearing in mind that it is the residential tenant of a 'house' as defined for whom the benefits and privileges of the statute are intended. I would add that I think it important in resolving the problems to which the definition gives rise that the court should hold the balance fairly between the conflicting interests. The 1967 Act operates to deprive a landlord of his rights as freeholder albeit in return for the payment of a sum of money, but the social purpose of the statute is to secure this result in favour of the tenant if, but only if, the tenant can satisfy the conditions precedent to acquiring for himself the landlord's antecedent freehold interest.

My Lords, counsel for the appellant advanced three propositions from which counsel for the respondents did not dissent. First, the question whether the particular premises were a 'house' within the definition was a mixed question of fact and law, so that if there were no evidence on which a particular conclusion one way or the other was reached that conclusion could be reviewed on appeal. Second, if the premises might also be called something other than a 'house within the definition, that fact alone did not prevent those premises from being 'a house ... reasonably so called'. Third, it was implicit from such previous decisions as there have been on this question that premises used for non-residential as well as for residential purposes could in law be a 'house' within the definition and that it depended on the character of the premises in question whether by reason of their mixed user they fell within or without the definition.

My Lords, in agreement with both counsel I accept these propositions as correct, but they restate the question rather than resolve it. How is the 'character' of the premises to be determined? It is tempting to look at the history of the premises and having regard to the language of the original demise which I have already quoted, counsel for the respondents naturally urged your Lordships so to do. As already stated these premises were built in 1881 as a 'dwelling-house and shop'. I think it clear, having regard to the definition of 'relevant time' in s 37(i)(d) of the 1967 Act, that the question must be resolved as at the time of the tenant's notice under the statute. The character of the premises at that time will usually, though not perhaps invariably, reflect its history. Accordingly the history will be relevant though certainly not conclusive. The terms of the lease will also be relevant, as will be the proportion of the premises respectively used for residential and non-residential purposes, and also the physical appearance of the premises.

My Lords, in the instant case the county court judge did not find it necessary to decide precisely the proportions devoted to the respective users for the reasons he gave. On the view most favourable to the respondents, the figures were 75% shop, 25% residential, but if the yard and stable be excluded as part of the premises the two figures would be approximately equal. On any view both users were substantial.

My Lords, the county court judge largely founded his conclusion on the decision of the Court of Appeal in *Lake v Bennett* [1970] 1 All ER 457, [1970] 1 QB 663. Ormrod LJ thought that decision indistinguishable, though he added that apart from it he might have agreed with the views of the majority. But the majority, though accepting that the county court judge applied the right test, held that he reached the wrong conclusion on the facts that he had found. This conclusion must, I think, involve that the Lords Justices in the majority thought that on those facts there was no evidence on which the county court judge could hold that these premises were 'a house' within the definition, the obverse of the conclusion in *Lake v Bennett*, where the Court of Appeal held, reversing the trial judge there concerned, that there was no evidence that the premises there in question were not such 'a house'.

My Lords, though the respondents in their printed case advanced the alternative contention that *Lake v Bennett* was wrongly decided, their counsel expressly refrained from so arguing and I think he was right, for in my view on the facts of that case it was correctly decided by the Court of Appeal. The weight of his able argument in support of the view taken by the majority of the Court of Appeal was that the county court judge had given wholly insufficient weight to what was described as the shop element. It was argued that, if one looked at these premises in their state as it existed at the date of the appellant's notice and as shown in the photographs and other documents, any description which did not give prime emphasis to the shop element (the first-floor accommodation being only ancillary to the shop beneath) was unreasonable and misleading.

The purpose of these words in the definition is clear. Tenants who live over a shop are not to be denied the right conferred by the 1967 Act, whether they themselves trade from the shop or not, merely because the building in which they work and live accommodates the two uses. Such a tenant occupies the house as his residence, even though it is also used for another purpose.

Small corner shops and terrace shops combined with living accommodation are to be found in almost every town and village in England and Wales. Parliament plainly intended that a tenant who occupied such premises as his residence should have the benefit of the 1967 Act if the building could reasonably be called a 'house'. It is imperative, if the law is to be evenly and justly administered, that there should not only be uniformity of principle in the approach of the courts to the question but a broad consistency in the conclusions reached. The question must not, save within narrow limits, be treated by the courts as a question of fact, for the variation of judicial response could well be such as to give rise to unacceptable, indeed unjust, differences between one case and another. This could lead to the statute being applied to two practically identical buildings, one way by one judge and another by another, an echo of equity and the length of the Chancellor's foot. For this reason, the Court of Appeal's decision in *Lake v Bennett* was welcome as stating a principle and confining the question of fact to a narrow area. I deduce from it the following propositions of law: (1) as long as a building of mixed use can reasonably be called a house, it is within the statutory meaning of 'house', even though it may also reasonably be called something else; (2) it is a question of law whether it is reasonable to call a building a 'house'; (3) if the building is designed or adapted for living in, by which, as is plain from s 1(1) of the 1967 Act, is meant designed or adapted for occupation as a residence, only exceptional circumstances, which I find hard to envisage, would justify a judge in holding that it could not reasonably be called a house. They would have to be such that nobody could reasonably call the building a house.

My Lords, reading the careful judgment of Griffiths LJ, I cannot but think that the majority of the Court of Appeal allowed themselves to be influenced by the consideration that the appellant would or might be entitled to protection under Part II of the Landlord and Tenant Act 1954. With respect, I think this is an irrelevant consideration. Schedule 3 to the 1967 Act shows that there is an overlap between the two statutes, and the fact that there may be different protection available to the appellant as a tenant is no reason why he should not be able to exercise his other rights also as a tenant under the 1967 Act if the premises in question possess the relevant qualifications.

My Lords, as I have already stated, the majority in the Court of Appeal accepted that the county court judge applied the right test. With all respect to those who take a different view, I think he came to the right conclusion. I would therefore allow the appeal, restore the decision of the county court judge and grant the appellant the declaration which he sought.

Another problem with which the courts have been faced concerns property which is either vertically or horizontally divided. Can the building as a whole be considered a 'house', even though the individual dwellings of which it is comprised may not? Section 2(1) (which is set out earlier in this chapter) provides that, in the case of a horizontal division, the building as a whole may be a 'house', although the individual parts will not be; but in the case of a vertical division, the building as a whole will not count as a 'house', although the individual units may be. In *Malpas v St Ermin's Property Co Ltd* [1992] *The Times* 21 February the Court of Appeal was faced with the situation of a building which was divided horizontally into two maisonettes with two front doors on the ground floor. The Court of Appeal decided that the whole building could reasonably be called a house as well as being a building divided into two flats. Following the decision in *Lake v Bennett* (earlier), the Court of Appeal found no difficulty in stating that a building could be described by two different labels and had not ceased to be a house 'properly so called' merely because it now had two front entrance doors.

The house must be let on a long tenancy

Section 1 of the 1967 Act applies the legislation to a house only if the tenancy is a 'long tenancy', which is then defined in s 3 as a tenancy for a term certain exceeding 21 years. The legislation has retrospective effect in that it applies to a tenancy which was entered into prior to the 1967 Act coming into force. A tenancy will also qualify even though it could be brought to an end before the 21 year minimum period has elapsed, either by a notice given by either party, re-entry, forfeiture or otherwise.

The rent must be a 'low rent'

The right to buy only applies to a tenant who is paying a low rent for the house. The definition of 'low rent' has undergone quite a few changes over the years and remains complicated. A 'low rent' is defined in s 4 as a rent which, at a yearly rate, is not more than two thirds of the rateable value on the appropriate day (or, if the tenancy was entered into on or after 1 April 1990, does not exceed £1,000 in Greater London or £250 elsewhere).

The Leasehold Reform, Housing and Urban Development Act 1993, through the introduction of ss 1A(2) and 4A, has included alternative rent limits where the tenancy would not be at a low rent in accordance with s 4. Under these complicated new provisions, a tenancy will still be regarded as at a low rent if, in the case of a tenancy entered into before 1 April 1963, the aggregate amount of rent payable during the initial year of the tenancy was less than two-thirds of the letting value of the property on the date of commencement of the tenancy. In the case of a tenancy entered into between 1 April 1963 and 1 April 1990, the tenancy will still be regarded as let at a low rent if the aggregate amount of rent payable during the initial year of the tenancy was less than two-thirds of the rateable value on the appropriate day; in any other case, the rent should not exceed £1,000 in Greater London or £250 elsewhere. It is declared in s 4A(2) that the reference to the letting value is to be construed 'in like manner as the reference in similar terms which appears in the proviso to s 4(1)'. This is a reference to the previous law on this phrase, which has caused the courts problems in the past, as will be discussed below.

By virtue of the new s 1A(1), the rateable value limits on the property itself and the complicated formula under s 1(1)(a) of the 1967 Act will no longer prevent a tenant from exercising the right to buy.

Another amendment introduced by the 1993 Act is the 'tenancies terminable after death or marriage' provision contained in s 64. Under this provision, applicable to long tenancies granted before 18 April 1980 (the date when the Housing Act of that year introduced the equivalent provision for long tenancies granted after that date), a tenancy expressed to be terminable on the death of a third party or on marriage is no longer taken outside of enfranchisement. This has thwarted those landlords who attempt to avoid the right to enfranchisement by such an artificial device. None of the amendments, however, have any application to the right to acquire an extended lease.

Since tenants covered by either the Rent Act 1977 or the Housing Act 1988 have to be paying a rent which is not less than two thirds of the rateable value (see s 5 of the 1977 Act and Schedule 1, para 3 of the 1988 Act), tenants with a right to buy under the 1967 Act were not usually protected or assured tenants under other legislation.

It might be thought that the requirement of a low rent would not cause much difficulty for the lawyer, but that has not in fact been the case. At least three cases have caused difficulty for the Court of Appeal. In *Gidlow-Jackson v Middlegate Properties Ltd* [1974] 1 All ER 830, the Court of Appeal was faced with the situation where a tenant was paying £70 per annum on a 28 year tenancy but had certain repairing obligations under the tenancy. The tenancy had originally been granted to another tenant for an annual rent of £90, but subject to a reduction of £20 per annum if certain repairs were carried out by the tenant. The tenant's right to acquire the freehold under the 1967 Act was disputed by the landlord on the alleged ground that the rent was not a low rent, since £70 exceeded two-thirds of the letting value of the house ie the £90 which had been the original rent. The Court of Appeal agreed with the landlord's submissions on this point, *per* Stamp LJ:

The principal question raised in this court was whether in relation to a tenancy in respect of which there was at the date of the commencement of the lease a standard rent, the standard rent is to be taken as the letting value or whether the letting value falls to be ascertained as if there were no standard rent. So one was left with the question what is meant by the phrase 'the letting value'.

In the context I think it means quite simply the rent which a landlord could have obtained in the market if he had offered the property for letting on the terms of the lease. Manifestly, he could not have obtained a rent in excess of the rent permitted by the Rent Acts and if, as was accepted as well before the county court judge as before this court, the rent so permitted was a standard rent of £90, the 'letting value', could not in my judgment exceed that figure. There was no evidence adduced to show that the landlords could have obtained a higher rent than the standard rent of £90 and the landlords' witnesses as to the letting value were not, as I understand it, cross-examined to show that they could. Indeed, as I understand, the question was not touched on in evidence.

However, in *Manson v Duke of Westminster* [1981] 2 All ER 40, the Court of Appeal criticised *Gidlow-Jackson v Middlegate Properties Ltd* (above). In *Manson v Duke of Westminster* (see below) the tenant paid £100 per annum, which was the maximum permitted under the Rent and Mortgage Interest Restrictions Act 1939, which was still in force when the lease was granted. The tenant, however, had also paid a premium of £500, upon which there was no restriction. The landlord disputed the tenant's right to acquire the freehold on the basis that the rent payable at the start of the tenancy was more than two thirds of the 'letting value' of the house. The Court of Appeal, however, took into account the premium which the tenant had paid in order to acquire the tenancy in calculating the 'letting value' and held that the tenant was entitled to buy the freehold from the landlord.

Manson v Duke of Westminster

Stephenson LJ: ... The rent of £100 a year was admitted to be the highest rent which the landlords could exact in 1945. Tenancies of dwelling-houses within the 1967 Act are not generally tenancies controlled by the Rent Acts because the rent of the former must not equal or exceed two-thirds of the rateable value whereas the rent of the latter must. But this house is subject to new control under the Rent and Mortgage Interest Restrictions Act 1939, £100 a year is the standard rent and there were no permitted increases entitling the landlords to recover more. It was also common ground that as the law stood in 1945 there was nothing to prevent the landlords charging and recovering a premium as the term of this lease was not less than 14 years. Furthermore, the landlords did not challenge, and the judge accepted, the evidence of an experienced valuer and chartered surveyor called by the tenant that 7% was the correct percentage to apply to a premium in order to obtain its annual equivalent by decapitalisation and that to produce by this means the £50 a year necessary to keep the £100 a year rent down to two-thirds of the sum of those two amounts the minimum amount required as capital premium was £581. Finally it was conceded by the landlords that they could not call evidence to discharge the burden imposed on them by s 4(5) of proving that less than £581 could be lawfully exacted from a tenant in the open market on 29th September 1945. So the tenant's right to acquire the freehold rests on the single question whether the court can take into account a premium in assessing 'the letting value of the property (on the same terms)'.

My first impression was that the court can and should take it into account as the judge did, because the natural and ordinary meaning of the words would not be limited to the rent but would include any other consideration, certainly any other consideration in cash, which the landlords would get for letting the house.

The expression is not defined in the 1967 Act. The industry of counsel has not found it in any other statute. The expression 'the lettable value of the premises' occurs in the Liabilities (War-Time Adjustment) Act 1944, s 6, where it was defined as–

'the rent at which in the opinion of the court the premises might reasonably be expected to let, or, as the case may be, might reasonably have been expected to let, under a tenancy for one year granted upon the same terms and conditions (so far as applicable) as those upon which the debtor is holding the premises.'

But 'the letting value' is not an expression of legal art, as Stamp LJ said in *Gidlow-Jackson v Middlegate Ltd* [1974] 1 All ER 830 at 840, [1974] QB 361 at 376; and, though he went on to use 'letting value' and 'lettable value' as apparently convertible terms, I derive no more help from the definition in the 1944 Act than from the absence of any definition in the 1967 Act.

In that case this court held that the letting value of the property could not exceed the amount of rent at which the property could lawfully be let and the standard rent was the letting value. But there was no premium for the lease granted in that case and no possibility of lawfully exacting it and so no question whether a premium could be included in that value was raised or considered, let alone decided. Unhelped and unhampered by any statutory definition or judicial authority I would have thought a landlord who had been paid a good-sized premium by the tenant of his property would be astonished if he were told by an estate agent or his legal adviser, or by a judge, that the letting value of the property was confined to the rent. That value is what the property would be worth to him if he let it; and I agree with counsel for the tenant that, if the landlord had asked an estate agent what it would be worth to him if he let it, the estate agent would surely reply: 'You can get a rent of no more than £100 a year, but you can charge a premium if you are prepared to give up possession of it for 14 years.' The letting value of a property is its value to the landlord in annual or perhaps other periodic terms. Its value to him as a landlord is what he is paid for it by his tenant, and all that he is paid, and until I heard the cogent submissions of counsel for the landlords I wondered, reacting as did Sir George Jeffreys CJ, three centuries ago to an attempt to introduce hearsay evidence (*R v Braddon and Speke* (1684) 9 State Tr 1127 at 1189) 'to hear any man that wears a gown, to make a doubt of it'. But a doubt of it counsel certainly has made.

His submissions in the form in which he recorded them for our assistance are these.

1. The natural meaning of 'letting value' is rental or annual value and that is the meaning of those words in s 4(1) of the 1967 Act.

2. If the natural meaning of 'letting value' is the total consideration for which a property can be let, nevertheless for the purposes of s 4(1) the meaning of the phrase 'letting value' is restricted to rental or annual value.

3. The conclusion in 2 above is based on the following reasons.

   (1) Parliament cannot have intended that rent should be compared with something other than rental value, for that would be to compare like with unlike. It would also be unfair to the landlord, for whose very benefit the proviso to s 4(1) was inserted, because the proviso requires the actual rent to be compared with 'the letting value'.

   (2) In the only other statutory provision in which the phrase 'letting value' appears, namely s 15(2) of the 1967 Act letting value means and can only mean the rental or annual value.

   (3) The 'building lease' exception in s 4(1)(d) of the 1967 Act is only explicable on the basis that a premium cannot be taken into account in ascertaining the 'letting value'.

   (4) The proviso to s 4(1) requires the rent to be compared with the letting value *on the same terms*. One of the terms of the letting is the payment of a premium, and that shows that 'letting value' in the section is something other than a premium. Further, to take into account the actual premium is inconsistent with the contention that 'letting value' means the best

consideration that could have been obtained and not the actual consideration obtained.

(5) If letting value meant total consideration, there would be great and possibly insuperable problems of valuation. It would mean reduction to an annual value of the best consideration that could have been obtained regardless of what was actually obtained, eg an infinite variety of combinations of premium and rent. It would also pose extraordinary problems of valuation where part of the consideration for the letting was or might have been the execution of works to the premises. Parliament cannot have intended these difficulties of valuation: see the simple treatment of premiums for income tax purposes. (We were referred to the Income and Corporation Taxes Act 1970, s 80.)

(6) When Parliament enacted the 1967 Act, it must be taken to have been aware that premiums had formerly been chargeable and had in fact been charged in respect of Rent Act premises, and Parliament would have dealt specifically with premiums if it had intended premiums to be taken into account in ascertaining the letting value.

(7) In the long history of rent restrictions and landlord and tenant legislation since 1914, the court has always drawn a sharp distinction between a genuine premium and a mere commuted rent. (We were referred to *Samrose Properties Ltd v Gibbard* [1958] 1 All ER 502, [1958] 1 WLR 225.) If Parliament had intended that in the 1967 Act a premium should be decapitalised for the purposes of s 4(1), it would have said so and provided how it should be done. Further, if it is proper to treat the premium as a commuted rent, then the commuted rent would exceed the standard rent under the Rent Act and would not be enforceable as rent.

(8) The intention of Parliament, as disclosed by the White Paper, Leasehold Reform in England and Wales (Cmnd 2916 (1966)), referred to in the judgment of Lord Denning MR in *Gidlow-Jackson v Middlegate Properties Ltd* [1974] 1 All ER 830 at 835, [1974] QB 361 at 370, was to distinguish between long tenancies at a low rent and long tenancies at a high rent; this is also borne out by the long title to the 1967 Act. The tenancy in the present case is a tenancy at a rack rent because it reserved the best rent obtainable at the grant of the tenancy.

(9) The 1967 Act is an expropriatory Act, and if there are genuine doubts as to the meaning of 'letting value' that phrase should be construed in favour of the landlord. Further the proviso to s 4(1) was inserted for the benefit of the landlord, and for that reason, if there is genuine doubt as to the meaning of 'letting value', the phrase should be construed in favour of the landlord. (We were referred to *Methuen-Campbell v Walters* [1979] 1 All ER 606 at 610, 615, 619, 620, [1979] QB 525 at 529, 536, 541, 542 and to *Jones v Wrotham Park Estates* [1979] 1 All ER 286 at 295, [1980] AC 74 at 113).

Counsel's argument has not altered my first impression and I do not accept his first submission. His second submission I find formidable, in particular the first two reasons which he has submitted for restricting the natural meaning of the words.

(1) I agree that the value to be compared with the rent must be in one sense an annual or rental value. It is not expressed as 'the full net annual value of the house', the phrase considered in *Rawlence v Croydon Corp* [1952] 2 All ER 335, [1952] 2 QB 803; but the 'yearly rate' expressed in sub-s (1) must, I think, be implied in the proviso.

It is however, in my judgment, fallacious to conclude that the value to be compared cannot include a lump sum capable of being decapitalised, or 'rentalised' (to use counsel's alternative). A premium is the capital value of the difference between the actual rent and the best rent that might otherwise be obtained: see *King v Cadogan* [1915] 3 KB 485 at 492. Decapitalisation is an exercise carried out whenever an annuity is bought or in reverse whenever judgment under Lord Campbell's Act (the Fatal Accidents Act 1846) is delivered. It is an exercise which these landlords carry out when they grant a lease for any term from 21 to 60 years at a standard rent: they require in addition to an undertaking to carry out tenant's repairs a 'cash payment (representing part of the annual value capitalised)'.

It was agreed that the tenant would have signed an acceptance of an offer of the 1945 lease in those terms (though the particular document had been destroyed); and the unchallenged evidence of the tenant's surveyor was that the annual equivalent of the premium was obtained by dividing it by the year's purchase figure in Parry's Valuation Tables for 40_ years at 7% (though the landlords used 6%) with a sinking fund of 2% (untaxed).

(2) The 1967 Act gives the tenant who qualifies for purchase of the freehold the alternative right to acquire a 50 years' extension of his lease. Section 15(2) provides:

> 'The new tenancy shall provide that as from the original term date the rent payable for the house and premises shall be a rent ascertained or to be ascertained as follows: (a) the rent shall be a ground rent in the sense that it shall represent the letting value of the site (without including anything for the value of buildings on the site) for the uses to which the house and premises have been put since the commencement of the existing tenancy, other than uses which by the terms of the new tenancy are not permitted or are permitted only with the landlord's consent; (b) the letting value for this purpose shall be in the first instance the letting value at the date from which the rent based on it is to commence ... (c) the betting value at either of the times mentioned shall be determined not earlier than twelve months before that time (the reasonable cost of obtaining a valuation for the purpose being borne by the tenant) ...'

It was rightly conceded by counsel for the tenant that the letting value there referred to is a hypothetical rent and nothing else. But that letting value is 'the letting value of the site', which would be the ground rent. No premium would be payable for the site in the circumstances postulated in s 15, and what we have to interpret is 'the letting value of the property', where payment of a premium for the lease of the property would often be payable, even when the property and the lease were controlled by the Rent Acts. Premiums could lawfully be exacted from the tenants of such properties from 1920 to 1949 if the term was 14 years or more and from 1957 to 1967 (and 1969 onwards) if the term was 21 years or more; but no premium was lawful between 1949 and 1957 or between 1967 and 1969: see the Rent Act 1920, s 8(3), the Landlord and Tenant (Rent Control) Act 1949, s 2, the Rent Act 1957, s 21, the Leasehold Reform Act 1967, s 39, and the Housing Act 1969, s 81. I am accordingly of the opinion that there is nothing in s 15(2) to restrict the meaning of the words used in the proviso to s 4(1), and to give 'the letting value of the property' in s 4 a wider meaning than the 'letting value of the site' in s 15 would not involve a difference of definition.

I find less force in the rest of counsel's reasons.

(3) His argument on the building lease exception is that if a premium is to be decapitalised then the cost of building the house must be treated in the same way. If this were done the rent under the building lease would almost always be under two-thirds of the rent plus the decapitalised value of the house so the exception is unnecessary. Counsel's answer for the tenant is that the value to be taken into account is not the cost to the tenant but the value to the landlord and that the value to him of the reversion will be far less than the cost of building the house (indeed with a 99-year lease it will be a very small sum) and there may well be cases where the rent would exceed two-thirds of the rent plus the decapitalised value of the reversion. Both arguments proceed on the basis that the hypothetical lease is a building lease. On that basis, which I think must be right, I find the answer for the tenant convincing.

(4) I understood counsel for the landlords to concede in his reply that the payment of a premium was not one of the 'terms' of the lease, but the consideration for the grant of the lease, as counsel for the tenant had argued in reliance on *Hill v Booth* [1930] 1 KB 381, [1929] All ER Rep 84. Though there are difficulties in either interpretation, I prefer the second thoughts of counsel for the landlord on this point. Since letting value is to be assessed on the basis of a hypothetical letting and since rent and premium are mutually dependent on each other, it seems right to consider a hypothetical premium as well as a hypothetical rent. If the premium is one of the 'terms' referred to in the parenthesis and if the hypothetical premium has to be the same as the actual premium, there will be hardly any tenancies granted in the years covered by the proviso in which the actual rent is less than two-thirds of the hypothetical rent.

(5) The problems of valuation which the judge's interpretation of letting value would create are not, in my opinion, great enough to drive me to the landlords' interpretation and are certainly not insuperable. The combinations of rent plus premium actually obtained are nothing like infinite; and I would confine the total consideration to the total consideration in cash and exclude from the letting value of the property any other part of the consideration such as the execution of works of repair undertaken as a condition of the grant of the 1945 tenancy.

(6) and (7) The history of premiums charged for Rent Act premises and the presumption that Parliament had them in mind when enacting this proviso do not lead to the conclusion that by not mentioning them or providing for their decapitalisation Parliament intended to exclude them from the letting value of such premises. It would indeed be odd if Parliament had lost sight not only of such an important factor as premiums in causing low rents to be charged but of all the enactments dealing with such premiums to which I have already referred. After all, for every tenancy granted in the 24 years to which the proviso applies, a premium could lawfully be charged except for tenancies controlled by the Rent Acts which were granted in eight of those years. But if Parliament had premiums in mind it is difficult to suppose that it would not have regarded them as an obvious part of the letting value of Rent Act premises requiring specific exclusion rather than specific inclusion. To have disregarded them would have produced an anomaly arising from Parliament's alternating intention to allow them, on which counsel for the tenant relied. The tendency would be for rents to be nearer the permitted rent during those years when premiums were forbidden than at other times. So if one house with a permitted rent of £100 a year were let in 1948 on a 30-year

lease at a rent of £20 a year with a premium of £2,000 and an exactly similar house with the same permitted rent were let in 1950 on a 30-year lease at a rent of £100 a year with no premium it might well be that if letting value is to be tested by rent alone the first tenant would be able to enfranchise and the second would not. I think there is some force in counsel's argument that this would be an unacceptable anomaly.

(8) and (9) It is plain that the 1967 Act is an expropriatory Act, that the proviso to s 4(1) was inserted for the benefit of landlords and, without recourse to the White Paper, that it expressed the intention of Parliament to distinguish between long tenancies at a low rent and long tenancies at a high rent (and, of course, to exclude short tenancies at any rent). The landlord is being required to submit to a compulsory purchase of his freehold property by a leaseholder who has a long tenancy at a low rent. The dividing line between low rents within the Act and high rents outside it is not fixed at any boundary between ground rents and rack rents but by the figure of two-thirds of the rateable value. But, as inflation operating on that figure between 1939 and 1963 would have 'enfranchised' leases at a rent which could not have been considered low at the commencement of the tenancy, the proviso introduced the letting value instead of the rateable value to prevent injustice which the landlords would have suffered without that substitution.

I would, however, respectfully follow the judgments in this court and in the House of Lords in the cases cited by counsel for the landlords and regard the expropriatory nature of the 1967 Act as of little weight in construing its provisions, and I would not regard the standard rent of £100 a year, to which the Rent Acts restricted the rent of this house, as a rack rent even in 1945. There is therefore nothing in those last reasons submitted by counsel for the landlords that weighs against the construction of counsel for the tenant which the judge accepted. I return therefore to Lord Wensleydale's golden rule cited by Lord Blackburn in *River Wear Comrs v Adamson* (1877) 2 App Cas 743 at 764-765, [1874-80] All ER Rep 1 at 12:

' ... that we are to take the whole statute together, and construe it all together, giving the words their ordinary signification, unless when so applied they produce an inconsistency, or an absurdity or inconvenience so great as to convince the Court that the intention could not have been to use them in their ordinary signification, and to justify the Court in putting on them some other signification, which, though less proper, is one which the Court thinks the words will bear.'

It may be that in inserting the proviso to s 4(1) and replacing the value to the tenant (rateable value) by the value to the landlord (letting value) as the basis of distinction between high and low rents Parliament gave inadequate consideration to that alternative basis and to an important class of tenancies within which this tenancy and (we are told) a number of others granted by these landlords fall, and, like this court in *Gidlow-Jackson v Middlegate Properties Ltd* did not have premiums in mind. In doubt whether it did or did not, the right course for the courts is to apply the golden rule. Its application leads to no inconsistency or absurdity or inconvenience so great as to be contrary to Parliament's intention. Not to apply it would have the absurd result of making a property which could be let at £100 a year with a premium of £2,000 of equal letting value to another similar property which could be let at £100 a year with no premium. Either construction may give rise to anomalies but to none greater than that. Balancing them as best I can I conclude that the judge was right to come down in favour of what I agree is the natural meaning of the proviso. I would accordingly dismiss the appeal.

Under the 1993 Act amendments, the 'letting value' is still used in respect of tenancies entered into before 1 April 1963; and, as mentioned previously, there is a specific reference to this phrase being construed in the same way as in the proviso to s 4(1) of the 1967 Act. This was the very cause of the complication in the *Manson* case.

The residence qualification

It is not enough for a tenant to show that he has a long tenancy of a house at a low rent – he must have occupied the house as his only or main residence for either the last three years or for periods totalling three years during the last 10 years (see ss 1(1) and (2) of the 1967 Act).

The purpose behind this requirement is to prevent speculators taking out long tenancies on houses, buying the freehold when the market suits and then selling when house prices boom. It is not essential that the tenant has occupied the whole of the house – occupying part will suffice, eg occupying accommodation above a shop and where the property as a whole is considered as a 'house' or living in part of a house and subletting the rest (see s 1(2)(a) and *Harris v Swick Securities Ltd* [1969] 1 WLR 1604). It is interesting to note in comparison that the Housing Acts 1988 and 1985 use the phrase 'only or principal home', which the tenant must occupy, as the requirement for protection as an assured or secure tenant. The Rent Act 1977, in comparison, talks of occupation as a residence as the qualifying factor for protection as a statutory tenant (see s 2(1)(a) Rent Act 1977). It is doubtful, however, whether there is any real difference in principle between the phrase used by the 1967 Act and that used in both of the Housing Acts, although the Court of Appeal has indicated that there is a difference between the requirements of the Rent Act and of the 1967 Act: See *Poland v Earl Cadogan* [1980] 3 All ER 544, which is discussed below.

Exactly what, however is meant by the phrase 'occupying it as his only or main residence' in Section 1(2)? The Court of Appeal has had to address this question in *Poland v Earl Cadogan*. In that case the tenant had gone abroad for a lengthy period and had made arrangements for the property to be sublet in his absence. The Court of Appeal considered that in these circumstances the tenant was not occupying the property as his only or main residence so as to be entitled to purchase the freehold.

Poland v Earl Cadogan

Waller LJ: ... I now consider the argument which the landlords regard as more important, namely, whether the applicants were or were not occupying the house as their residence from October 1973 until the time of the notice.

In argument before the county court judge it was submitted that, having regard to the terms of s 3(2) of the Rent Act 1968, cases decided under the Rent Act did not assist in deciding what was required to comply with s 1 of the Leasehold Reform Act 1967. Reference has also been made to *Brown v Brash* [1948] 1 All ER 922, [1948] 2 KB 247. I have found the analysis of occupation in the judgment of Asquith LJ extremely helpful. But in my opinion, it is also helpful to look at both ss, ie s 3(2) of the Rent Act 1968 as well as s 1 of the Leasehold Reform Act 1967, in order to ascertain the way in which s 1 of the Leasehold Reform Act should be interpreted. Section 1 requires the tenant to have been occupying the house as his residence for the last five years' and, by sub-s (2), that is to be construed as 'applying where, but only where, the tenant is in right of the tenancy occupying it as his only or main residence'. I emphasis the words 'only where' because it shows that the section should be applied strictly. Section 3(2) of Rent Act 1968 reads as follows:

'In paragraph (a) of subsection (1) above and in Schedule 1 to this Act, the phrase "if and so long as he occupies the dwelling-house as his residence" shall be construed as requiring the fulfilment of the same, and only the same, qualifications (whether as to residence or otherwise) as had to be fulfilled before the commencement of this Act to entitle a tenant, within the meaning of the Increase of Rent and Mortgage Interest (Restrictions) Act 1920 to retain possession, by virtue of that Act and not by virtue of a tenancy, of a dwelling-house to which that Act applied.'

It is important to notice the words 'the same and only the same qualifications'.

It seems to me that, comparing those two sections, they are each confining the definition strictly but strictly with different emphases. In the Rent Act the meaning of 'occupation' is to be construed for the purposes of the Rent Act as it had been up to that time. Were it not for s 3 there might be other qualifications to be included. The object of the Rent Act was to provide accommodation for persons, and, in cases under the Rent Act, occupation had been very much discussed and the law made clear. In the Leasehold Reform Act, which is concerned with conferring the right to acquire on fair terms a freehold or extended lease of the house, occupation is restricted to those cases where, and only where 'the tenant is, in right of the tenancy, occupying [the house] as his only or main residence'.

There is a further provision in the Leasehold Reform Act which enables a tenant to qualify if he has occupied the house as his residence 'for the last five years or for periods amounting to five years in the last ten years'. This clearly contemplates periods when the residential occupation is interrupted. But, if the interruptions were to be confined to sublettings, I would have expected the subsection to say so.

How should the test be applied in relation to the Leasehold Reform Act? Going away for a short holiday clearly does not involve a break, but, when asking whether the tenant is occupying it as his residence when he is not physically living in it, the court must look more critically than under the Rent Act. As in the case of the Rent Act it is a question of fact and degree; but to adopt precisely the same criteria does not give effect to the differences eg 'and only the same' in the Rent Act and the five years of ten which qualifies under the Leasehold Reform Act. The difference lies in the purposes of the two Acts. The Rent Acts are to provide accommodation and the court need only look at the qualifications established prior to 1968. The Leasehold Reform Act is to enable a tenant to acquire compulsorily a greater interest in his house. It confers a right on a tenant who can fulfil certain conditions to acquire compulsorily the freehold belonging to his landlord on terms prescribed in the Act. The terms are laid down in the Act to be fair terms but, nevertheless, the landlord has no choice. It is compulsory.

In my opinion, the words 'where, but only where' themselves imply a strict approach and, therefore, 'occupying it as his only or main residence' must be approached to see whether the occupation has been of a nature to entitle the tenants to the benefit of a compulsory freehold or extended lease. Furthermore, the phrase 'occupying as' implies an existing state of affairs. It is not 'for the purpose of' his only residence. It is 'as his only residence'. Once it becomes clear that the tenant is not physically in occupation the onus is firmly on him to show that the steps which he has taken to maintain occupation are clear. Going away for a short holiday is simple but the longer the period the more difficult it becomes to infer continued occupation. If the family (wife or children) are still in physical occupation then the position is clear, but to infer occupation because furniture is left in the house or because there is a caretaker requires closer examination. If the period is short the inference of continued occupation may be easy, but where many months are concerned, very much more doubtful. The tenant does not lose the benefit of his periods of genuine occupation because of the provisions of allowing aggregation.

I should be reluctant to upset the judgment of the county court judge on a question of primary fact but there is no dispute about primary facts. Here the question is one of mixed fact and law. It is the approach to these primary facts and inferences to be drawn.

In my judgment, bearing in mind the considerations that I have mentioned above as to the different emphasis and approach under the Leasehold Reform Act and accepting, as I do, the findings of primary fact by the learned judge, I am satisfied that Commander Poland's arrangements about subletting were such as to make him cease to occupy the house as his residence. He was physically abroad and had left it to his daughter and Harrods to sublet. It was not a mere intention. In my judgment, from the time he left the house having that intention he was no longer 'occupying it as his only or main residence'.

I would, therefore, allow the appeal.

Specific exclusions

The 1967 Act, as amended, contains specific exclusions from the right to buy. These include a house comprised in an agricultural holding and a house let as ancillary to other land or premises. Under the 1993 Act amendments, charitable housing trust property used for the charitable trust's accommodation purposes is now 'exempt' property; and any property designated by the Treasury under s 31 Inheritance Tax Act 1984 (houses of outstanding scenic, historic, architectural or scientific interest to which the public are granted access) is also excluded. Both of the two new exclusions apply to tenancies granted after the coming into force of the 1993 Act, except in cases where tenancies have been brought within the scope of the 1967 Act by ss 63–65 of the 1993 Act (see earlier), in which event the exempting provisions have retrospective effect.

THE TENANT'S RIGHTS

A qualifying tenant is given the option of exercising one of two statutory rights, but these alternatives do not apply to those tenants who have been brought into the right to buy only by virtue of ss 63–65 of the 1993 Act. Apart from these special situations, however, a tenant can either acquire the freehold (enfranchisement) or he can have an extended lease which will expire 50 years after the end of his present tenancy. If the latter option is chosen, the tenant will pay a ground rent for the first 25 years, but may have to pay a higher rent thereafter (see ss 14 and 15(2)(b) of the 1967 Act, as amended). In order to exercise either of the rights conferred on him, the tenant must serve a written notice on the landlord claiming the appropriate right. The serving of the notice contractually binds both parties; and whilst mutual withdrawal thereafter is allowed, a unilateral withdrawal is not, unless it amounts to an estoppel, even if purportedly made by the tenant himself. This was one of two issues which arose in *Collin v Duke of Westminster* [1985] QB 581, [1985] 1 All ER 463, the other being the correct period of limitation to apply under the Limitation Act 1980.

Collin v Duke of Westminster

Oliver J: The judge in a most helpful and detailed judgment, rejected all four of the respondents' claims.

As regards abandonment he held (and in my judgment he was clearly right in this) that in order to succeed the respondents had to show either some reliance and change of position amounting to an estoppel (of which there was no suggestion) or what amounted in effect to a contract for mutual release. Quite clearly there was no question of an express contract and what he had, therefore, to look for was whether there was material from which mutual promises could be implied. On the facts, he found himself unable to find any mutual release but, perhaps even more importantly, he held that the 1967 Act and the regulations provided, as it were, a complete statutory code which regulated exclusively how the statutory contract of sale was to be either completed or discharged and that there was no room for the application of the common law concept of inferred abandonment by mutual consent.

With respect to the judge, I doubt whether this latter conclusion can be right. In his judgment, the judge referred extensively to the speeches of Lord Brandon, Lord Diplock and Lord Brightman in *Paal Wilson & Co A/S v Partenreederei Hannah Blumenthal, The Hannah Blumenthal* [1983] 1 All ER 34, [1983] 1 AC 854, and to the principles to be deduced from that case. As he rightly pointed out there is, in the law of contract, no room for a concept of unilateral abandonment. What the court has to look for is either some representation or promise, whether express or by conduct, which has been relied on by the other party so as to ground an estoppel, or material from which there can be inferred mutual releases or mutual promises not to proceed. In other words, short of estoppel, and it is not contended that the facts in the instant case give rise to an estoppel, there has to be established, if only by inference, a fresh contract which has the effect of dissolving the relationship originally entered into by the parties and on which one party still seeks to rely. Now tenants who are entitled to enfranchise under the 1967 Act are not permitted to contract out of their entitlement, but there is nothing in the Act which prevents them, once their right of enfranchisement has accrued, from releasing contractually the immediate right of enfranchisement which they have acquired by serving a notice under the Act. Once such a notice has been served, there comes into being under s 8 of the 1967 Act (to which I will have to refer in a little more detail later) a statutory obligation on the landlord to transfer the freehold which, by s 5, is accorded incidents similar to those inherent in a contract freely entered into. Section 23(1) Of the 1967 Act avoids agreements so far as they purport to exclude or modify the right to acquire the freehold or an extended lease conferred by the Act, but sub-s (2) of s 23 specifically provides that this shall not–

> 'where the tenant has given notice of his desire to have the freehold or an extended lease under this Part of this Act, invalidate any agreement between the landlord and the tenant that that notice shall cease to be binding ...'

Nothing in this subsection carries, in my judgment, any necessary implication that the agreement there referred to has to be an express agreement and I can see no reason why, if the facts are such that the court is able to infer on both sides the necessary agreement to release the parties' respective rights arising from the service of a notice, that agreement should not be effective as an express agreement to that effect.

The principal ground for the judge's decision, however, was that on the facts there simply was no material from which he could infer the mutual release necessary to support a successful plea of abandonment. Although expressed in slightly different terms in the three speeches in the *Hannah Blumenthal* case to which the judge referred, the essential concept is contained in the following passage from the speech of Lord Diplock [1983] 1 All ER 34 at 48, [1983] 1 AC 854 at 915:

> 'To the formation of the contract of abandonment the ordinary principles of the English law of contract apply. To create a contract by exchange of promises between two parties where the promise of each party constitutes the consideration for the promise of the other what is necessary is that the intention of each *as it has been communicated to and understood by the other*, (even though that which has been communicated does not represent the actual state of mind of the communicator) should coincide.' (Lord Diplock's emphasis.)

In support of the respondents' contention that the applicant's notice under the Act and such rights as he had acquired under it had been abandoned the estate relied on two things, that is to say, first, the failure of the applicant to pursue the matter further after the initial landlord's notice of non-admission in March 1975 and, second, certain correspondence which passed between the applicant and Mr Lingren, the respondents' surveyor, in November 1976. As regards the former, following the landlord's notice and the covering letter on 11 March unequivocally declining to proceed and referring to the *Gidlow-Jackson* case, no further communication was received by them save for a letter from the applicant's solicitors saying that they were taking instructions. There the matter rested until 24 November 1976 when the applicant himself wrote to Mr Lingren inquiring whether the estate was 'selling freeholds to tenants who do not have the right to claim them' and 'whether the Estate is prepared ... to grant an extension to a lease'.

Mr Lingren's reply made it clear that the estate, while unwilling to sell the freehold, would contemplate the grant of an extension to the existing lease, and thereafter a negotiation, if such it can be called, ensued in the course of which the estate quoted terms for an extension which involved not only an immediate and substantial increase in rent but also a substantial premium. That proved wholly unacceptable to the applicant, who broke off the correspondence in March 1977, whereafter nothing further was heard from him until, on 6 July 1981, his agents sought to revive the 1975 notice. In his evidence, Mr Lingren (who was the only person on behalf of the estate who applied his mind to the matter at all) made it quite clear that at the material time, that is in 1975, he thought that the estate was undeniably right in its contention and that the applicant had no claim at all under the Act. At the time when he received the letter of 24 November 1976, which, when he gave his evidence, he thought impliedly amounted to the applicant's giving up his rights, his view was that the applicant did not have any rights. He said:

> 'I cannot put it any clearer. The claim was made and refused. I thought he was evincing a view that he accepted the position in 1975, the position was that claim had been made and properly refused. Our view was Estate had no obligations.'

Counsel for the respondents rightly recognised that, in the light of the estate's refusal to proceed, it was a matter of no little difficulty for him to rely simply on the applicant's inactivity, although, for what it is worth, he points out that the procedural provisions set out in Pt II of Sch 3 to the 1967 Act contemplate (in para 7) the possibility of a notice by the landlord not admitting a tenant's claim to enfranchisement, indeed, they impose an obligation on the landlord to give a notice saying whether or not he admits the claim, and lay down a minimum period before the expiry of which the tenant is disabled from applying to the court to enforce his right. But it would, I think, be very difficult to infer merely from the tenant's failure to pursue a claim which was plainly disputed and which, at the time, appeared to be disputed on sustainable grounds, a promise not to pursue it further. He couples this, however, with the subsequent correspondence in which the applicant clearly implies that he does not put himself in the category of tenants having a right to enfranchise and with the abortive negotiations for the grant of an extension of the existing lease, which, he submits, were clearly inconsistent with a continuing intention to proceed with the acquisition of the freehold under the 1975 notice.

This would, no doubt, be a formidable point if the estate had in some way altered its position in reliance on the negotiations. Nothing of that sort however, is or can be alleged and the judge found himself quite unable to spell out of the inactivity and the correspondence the necessary contract for abandonment. For my part, I entirely agree with him. Even granted, for the moment, that the applicant's conduct would justify the inference that he was, as it were, making an offer of a promise to release the estate from any rights which might have accrued from the notice (or, if one prefers it, a promise to release the estate from any obligation to enfranchise as a result of the notice) I find it quite impossible to find anything from which any counter-promise or release on the part of the estate can be inferred. If it is suggested (and there is a measure of justification in the assertion) that the inferences of mutual promises which the court can draw objectively from the conduct of parties are somewhat artificial, at least they must be inferences which do not fly in the face of the proved facts. It seems to me quite impossible to infer from Mr Lingren's conduct any sort of promise or release of any kind. Quite apart from his own evidence that he never for a moment thought that the applicant ever had any rights, nobody looking at the correspondence could, in my judgment, draw any inference beyond this that the estate had rejected the claim, that it thought throughout that it had rightly rejected the claim and that it never departed from that position. Essentially, the abandonment on which counsel for the respondent is compelled to rely is, by the very nature of the case, entirely unilateral and unsupported by any consideration in the form of any inferential counter-promise or release on the part of his clients.

We have been referred by counsel for the respondents to the judgment of Upjohn J in *Grice v Dudley Corp* [1957] 1 All ER 673 at 679, [1958] Ch 329 at 339 in which it might, at first sight, appear that he contemplated the possibility of an effective unilateral abandonment. Dealing, as he was there, with the position of a promoter under the Lands Clauses (Consolidation) Act 1845 he observed: '... the [promoter] may evince an intention to abandon [his] rights given to [him] by the notice to treat, in which case the owner is entitled to treat those rights as abandoned.'

It is, however, clear from *Simpsons Motor Sales (London) Ltd v Hendon Corp* [1962] 3 All ER 75 at 81–82, [1963] Ch 57, at 83–84, in this court, in which the same judge delivered the judgment of the court that the term 'abandonment' was being used by him to comprehend a number of different concepts. In the context of compulsory purchase orders it is used to express the special rule peculiar to such cases that unreasonable delay in proceedings with the purchase may bar the promoter from proceeding under a notice to treat. Secondly it is used as describing a proposal to proceed with the purchase for a purpose other than that for which it was originally authorised. Thirdly it is used in the sense of evincing an intention not to proceed at all, and in this latter context, Upjohn LJ made it clear that he had no different contemplation of the operation of the concept from that subsequently expressed by the House of Lords in the *Hannah Blumenthal* case, for he quoted from the judgment of Lord Bramwell in *Tiverton and North Devon Rly Co v Loosemore* (1884) 9 App Cas 480 at 506 where he said:

> 'I quite agree that they might abandon their notice to purchase. If they had said so in so many words, and the respondent had assented, no doubt the notice would have ceased to have any effect. It would have operated like an agreement to rescind a contract. And no doubt what can be done in words can be done by conduct; and further it can be done unintentionally by conduct such that those to be affected by it reasonably infer the intention.'

For the reasons which I have endeavoured to express I can find no conduct here which could, in my judgment, properly be treated as justifying any assumption of the mutual promises necessary to support an abandonment. But I question in any event whether it is permissible on the facts to infer even a unilateral promise on the part of the applicant. The position with which he was faced is the not unfamiliar one in which one claiming a right is met by a challenge to its existence which appears to be based on unassailable legal grounds. It is very difficult in those circumstances to see how the reasonable man, looking at the position objectively, could infer from a reluctant acquiescence in the validity of the objection any sort of promise not to proceed with the claim if in fact the objection turns out to be ill-founded. Counsel for the applicant has referred us to two cases in this court, *James v Heim Gallery (London) Ltd* (1980) 41 P&CR 269, and *Amherst v James Walker Goldsmith and Silversmith Ltd* [1983] 2 All ER 1067, [1983] 1 Ch 305, in which it has been sought unsuccessfully to rely on a grudging acceptance of what was thought on both sides to be the legal position as constituting an abandonment by a landlord of his right to seek a rent review.

The following passages from the judgment of Buckley LJ in *James v Heim Gallery* (London) Ltd (at 277) seems particularly appropriate to the facts of the instant case:

> 'It seems to me that the plaintiffs, although they formally reserved their position for a short time, accepted that the point taken by the defendants was a valid point, or at least was a point which the plaintiffs would be unwise to contest in the light of the law as then understood. That, in my view, would involve nothing in the nature of a promise. To bow to the inevitable, or the near inevitable, is quite different from agreeing to forgo a right. Even assuming that the plaintiffs did always regard the point as of doubtful validity, it seems to me that the mere fact that they did not pursue it imports no promise or representation that they would not do so at any later time. As the authorities then stood, it would have been very probable that no conclusive decision would have been short of the House of Lords. In these circumstances a potential plaintiff might very justifiably and reasonably choose to hold his hand in the hope that the point might be cleared up in litigation between other litigants before deciding whether to press his claim.'

All that seems equally applicable in the circumstances of the instant case and I cannot, for my part, attribute to the subsequent inquiry by the applicant as to the estate's willingness to treat with tenants not entitled to enfranchise any promissory quality. It shows, in my judgment, no more than the grudging acceptance of what everyone then thought was the legal position.

In my judgment, therefore, reliance on the concept of abandonment is of no assistance to the respondents and the judge was right in so holding.

The service of the notice also prevents the landlord exercising any right of re-entry without the court's leave, which will not be granted unless the court is satisfied that the tenant's claim under the Act is not being made in good faith. A tenant would not be considered as acting in good faith if the only reason that he had served notice was in order to prevent the landlord forfeiting the lease for breach of covenant in circumstances where equitable relief from forfeiture would not be granted. This was aptly illustrated in the case of *Central Estates (Belgravia) Ltd v Woolgar* [1972] 1 QB 48, [1971] 3 All ER 647, in which the tenant had been convicted of running a brothel.

Central Estates (Belgravia) Ltd v Woolgar

Phillimore LJ: This appeal raises the question of whether and, if so, in what circumstances, an application by a tenant to acquire the freehold can be said to be made otherwise than in good faith. The question depends on the true construction of para 4 of Sch 3 to the Leasehold Reform Act 1967 – an ill-designed piece of legislation which has caused endless litigation. It was designed to help a deserving class of tenants, namely those holding on long leases small and often terrace houses in Wales where the landlord had in effect been paid the value of the house over and over again.

In effect and certainly for the purposes of this appeal the tenant, if he applies to purchase the freehold, is to be granted what he asks, unless it can be said that his application is not made in good faith. Despite his plea of not guilty, the tenant was convicted on 22nd May 1970 of keeping a brothel on the premises. He asked the landlords for permission to assign his lease to a Mrs Anthony, but then applied to purchase the freehold in accordance with his rights under the Act. This application crossed in the post with a notice by the landlords claiming to forfeit on the ground of the conviction. Obviously the tenant had realised that the landlords were about to learn or had learned of the conviction.

Was the claim made otherwise than in good faith? Counsel could not help us very much. One said that a claim was not made in good faith when it was made in bad faith. Another said that a claim must be dishonest if it was to be described as made otherwise than in good faith. It was said that a claim would not be made in good faith if the facts stated in it were untrue to the knowledge of the tenant or if the claim was made for some ulterior motive. One counsel said it all depended on 'quo animo' the claim was made and another said that motive must be distinguished from intention. Further it is said that even if the tenant has so breached his covenants that his landlord has become entitled to forfeit his lease in circumstances where no court would grant relief, it is impossible to say that a claim to acquire the freehold is made in bad faith in the light of the provisions of Sch 3, para 4(2).

I have come to the conclusion that the only course that this court can follow is to deal with this matter on the facts of this case. So far as the tenant is concerned, he had breached his covenant and committed a criminal offence. He had exposed himself to forfeiture in circumstances where no court would grant relief. He sought agreement to assign, and then, having realised that the true facts were likely to emerge, he applied for the freehold. I think he acted otherwise than in good faith and that his application was plainly a dishonest manoeuvre to achieve a result which he did not really want and which he had forfeited his right to claim.

I would dismiss his appeal.

Once a tenant has served notice of his right to acquire either an extended lease or the freehold, he should protect his rights under the 1967 Act as against anyone to whom the landlord might transfer the property. This can be done by the entry of a Class C(iv) Land Charge (in the case of unregistered land) or by the entry of a minor interest (notice or caution in the case of registered land). The tenant's right to enfranchise cannot amount to an overriding interest within s 70 Land Registration Act 1925.

THE PURCHASE PRICE

The 1967 Act originally extended the right to buy to certain properties only, but in 1974 the Housing Act of that year brought many more properties within its scope. There were therefore two bases of assessing the price payable by the tenant for the purchase of the freehold:

(a) the 1967 basis of assessment, which applied to lower valued houses (ie to houses with a rateable value not exceeding £500 (or £1,000 in Greater London)); and

(b) the 1974 basis of assessment, which applies to houses of a higher rateable value (ie between £500 and £750 (or £1,000 and £1,500 in Greater London)). In 1990, the References to Rating (Housing) Regulations amended the wording of s 9 without making substantial changes of principle (see SI 1990/434).

The 1967 basis of assessment is very generous to the tenant in that it fixes the price at whatever the property could be expected to fetch on the open market if sold to someone other than a tenant but with a sitting tenant who has a 50 year tenancy on the property. This gives the tenant a considerable discount, but is justified in that the tenant has in effect already paid for the house, either through a combination of rent and a premium or by building the house and paying a ground rent thereafter.

The 1974 basis of assessment is less generous to the tenant, as it fixes the price nearer to current market value, although the tenant still receives a discount. The price is set at whatever the house would fetch on the open market if it had a sitting tenant with statutory protection under Part I Landlord and Tenant Act 1954, giving him a right to remain at the end of his tenancy but with no right to an extension of the lease.

Amendments introduced by the Leasehold Reform, Housing and Urban Development Act 1993 have now added a third basis of assessment. Under ss 9(1C) and 9A of the 1967 Act (added by s 66 of the 1993 Act), compensation may be payable to the landlord if the right to buy has arisen as a result of the application of ss 1A, 1AA or 1B. Equally under these provisions, the tenant is not entitled, in assessing the price payable, to more than one half of the marriage value (which refers to the difference between the value of all interests in the house before the tenant purchases the freehold and the aggregate value of the leasehold and freehold interests on merger) that may arise due to the merger of the leasehold with the freehold interest. It is not uncommon for the value of the leasehold and the freehold reversionary interest, when taken separately and then added together, to be worth less than the value of the two interests upon merger, so that the tenant, if entitled to all of this difference in the two values upon enfranchisement, would be getting the full benefit of merger at the landlord's expense; hence the equitable principle, recognised by the 1993 Act, that this should be split equally between the two.

If the parties cannot agree on the appropriate price, the matter is referred to a local Leasehold Valuation Tribunal, from whose determination a right of appeal lies to the Lands Tribunal.

THE EUROPEAN DIMENSION

Certain landlords, particularly the Duke of Westminster, have been badly affected by the 1967 Act. The Act's provisions are 'expropriatory' in their effect, giving the landlord no choice but to submit to compulsory purchase. In 1984, dissatisfaction with the Act led trustees for the Duke of Westminster to challenge its provisions before the European Court of Human Rights. Basing their case on Article 1 of the First Protocol to the European Convention on Human Rights (see below), the trustees argued in *The Case of James* (see later) that the 1967 Act contravened the provision in the Protocol that 'No one shall be deprived of his possessions except in the public interest ...'. The European Court of Human Rights rejected this claim by holding that a policy of allowing compulsory purchase of property for reasons of social justice could be said to be 'in the public interest'.

European Convention on Human Rights
Article I of Protocol No I

Every natural or legal person is entitled to the peaceful enjoyment of his possessions. No one shall be deprived of his possessions except in the public interest and subject to the conditions provided for by law and by the general principles of international law.

The preceding provisions shall not, however, in any way impair the right of a State to enforce such laws as it deems necessary to control the use of property in accordance with the general interest or to secure the payment of taxes or other contributions or penalties.

Case of James (3/1984/75/119)

Eliminating what are judged to be social injustices is an example of the functions of a democratic legislature. More especially, modern societies consider housing of the population to be a prime social need, the regulation of which cannot be left to the play of market forces. The margin of appreciation is wide enough to cover legislation aimed at securing greater social justice in the sphere of people's homes, even where such legislation interferes with existing contractual relations between private parties and confers no direct benefit on the State or the community at large. In principle, therefore, the aim pursued by the leasehold reform legislation is a legitimate one (para 47).

ENFRANCHISEMENT FOR TENANTS OF FLATS

The Landlord and Tenant Act 1987, as amended by The Housing Act 1996

In 1987 Part I of the Landlord and Tenant Act introduced a limited right for tenants of flats to acquire their landlord's interest. If the landlord chooses to sell his interest in the property, his tenants obtain a right of first refusal on the sale of that interest. This is achieved by the requirement that the landlord serve on his tenants who qualify under the 1987 Act a notice which states his intention to sell his interest and includes a price at which he intends to sell. The notice is then deemed to be an offer of sale which may be accepted by the required number of qualifying tenants. A tenant 'qualifies' under the Act if he is a tenant of a flat other than as a protected shorthold tenant, business tenant, or holds a tenancy terminable with the end of the tenant's employment or an assured tenancy/assured agricultural tenancy under the Housing Act 1988.

Qualifying tenants are allowed two months after receipt of the landlord's notice (deemed offer) to either accept or reject it, or to make a counter-offer. The requisite majority for the exercise of the rights given under the 1987 Act is a bare majority ie qualifying tenants of constituent flats with more than 50% of the available votes.

In the event of the qualifying tenants rejecting the offer, the landlord may dispose of his interest within 12 months subject to two restrictions, namely that the price is the same or more than was specified in the notice given to the tenants and that the terms of sale are no more generous than those offered to the qualifying tenants.

Part III of the 1987 Act, as originally enacted, enabled qualifying tenants of flats to buy out their landlord's interest by making an application to the court for an acquisition order. The rationale for this was to deal with the problems of bad management and where the appointment of a manager under Part II of the 1987 Act would not be an adequate means of dealing with the problem. The procedure began with the service of a notice under s 27 by more than 50% of the qualifying tenants. A court order would only be granted thereafter if the court was satisfied that the landlord was seriously in breach of his repairing, maintenance or management obligations and that this was likely to continue. A court acquisition order provided for a nominated person to acquire the landlord's interest. The unamended provisions of Part III were considered by the High Court in *Gray v Standard Home and Counties Ltd* (1994) 26 HLR 565. Part III, however, was amended by s 85 of the 1993 Act. A notice must now be served by not less than two-thirds of the qualifying tenants and the conditions for making an acquisition order have been amended so as to remove the former requirement that the appointment of a manager would not be an adequate remedy.

The problem with the 1987 Act is that it has not been used much by tenants. A study conducted in 1991 (*The Landlord and Tenant Act 1987: Awareness, Experience and Impact* (1991) HMSO) discovered that few tenants of flats who might qualify under the right of first refusal knew about the 1987 Act and its provisions. The Act was passed as a knee-jerk response to the criticisms levelled at the management of leasehold flats by the Nugee Committee in its report *The Management of Privately Owned Blocks of Flats* (1985). The report highlighted the problems faced by tenants in getting repairs done and the high level of service charges being levied by landlords. The government's response was therefore a measure to deal with bad management and not essentially a pro owner-occupation extension measure.

The Leasehold Reform, Housing and Urban Development Act 1993, as amended by the Housing Act 1996

As noted previously, the 1967 Act only applied to a 'house' and not to an individual flat. Although the Landlord and Tenant Act 1987 went some way towards removing this deficiency, that Act did not give qualifying tenants the right to buy the freehold unless the landlord owned the freehold and was proposing to sell his interest. The 1993 Act takes the next logical step by conferring a right of 'collective enfranchisement' on tenants in blocks of flats if certain conditions are satisfied. In addition, the 1993 Act confers on individual tenants the right to acquire a new lease on payment of a premium if they 'qualify' and have occupied the flat as their only or principal home for the last three years or for periods amounting to three years in the last 10.

Collective enfranchisement

The right to collective enfranchisement is given by the 1993 Act to qualifying tenants so as to enable tenants of a block of flats to have effective control over their residences. The Report of the Committee of Inquiry on the Management of Privately Owned Blocks of Flats under the chairmanship of EG Nugee QC in 1985 had expressed some concern about the protection of the interests of long leaseholders living in privately owned blocks of flats and the relevant provisions of the 1987 Act reflect this concern. But that Act did not go so far as to enable a group of tenants in a block of flats to purchase the freehold irrespective of the wishes of the landlord. The 1993 Act, however, which came into force in November 1993, does provide for compulsory acquisition by enabling the freehold to be acquired on behalf of qualifying tenants by a person (or persons) who they have nominated for that purpose.

Property covered by the 1993 Act

In order to qualify, the building must contain two or more flats held by qualifying tenants, and the total number of flats held by qualifying tenants must not be less than two-thirds of the number of flats in the premises. Certain premises are, however, excluded. The right of collective enfranchisement does not apply if there is a resident landlord and the premises do not contain more than four units nor if more than 10% of the internal floor area is allocated for non-residential purposes, such as office space.

Qualifying tenants

It is only tenants holding flats on 'long leases' at a low rent or for a particularly long term who qualify for the right to collective enfranchisement under the 1993 Act (see s 5(1)). 'Long lease' is defined in s 7 as basically a lease granted for a term of years certain exceeding 21 years and which is neither a business tenancy nor a tenancy granted by a charitable housing trust. 'Low rent' is then defined in s 8 as annual rent which does not exceed: two-thirds of the letting value (lease entered into before 1 April 1963), two-thirds of the rateable value (lease entered into between 1 April 1963 and 1 April 1990, and where the flat had a rateable value other than nil) or £1,000 in Greater London or £250 elsewhere (lease entered into after 1 April 1990). A particularly long term is defined in s 8A as, *inter alia*, a term exceeding 35 years. There is also a residence qualification which is dealt with in s 6 and requires the tenant to have occupied the flat as his 'only or principal home' for either the last 12 months or for periods amounting to three years in the last 10 years. Residence by a company or 'other artificial person' is not regarded as occupation for this purpose.

Although the qualification may appear to cause few problems in the case of an individual tenant, the exercise of collective enfranchisement requires a notice from a number of qualifying tenants which is not less than two-thirds of such tenants, nor less than half of the total number of flats in the premises, and of which at least half of their number satisfy the residence qualification. This means that the right to collective enfranchisement will be lost if a relatively small number of people in the block of flats fail to satisfy the residence requirement. It is therefore to be expected that there may be some problems associated with this requirement. The same phrase 'only or principal home' is to be found in the Housing Act 1988 in relation to an assured tenancy and in the Housing Act 1985 in relation to secure tenancies, ruling out the two-home tenant phenomenon experienced under the Rent Act 1977 where the qualification 'occupies as his residence' is used. In *Crawley BC v Sawyer* (1988) 20 HLR 98, decided under s 81 Housing Act 1985, Parker LJ gave a very generous interpretation to the phrase 'occupies ... as his only or principal home'. In that case a local authority tenant had gone to live with his girlfriend elsewhere, although he had continued to pay the rent, rates and visit the premises about once a month, and had also stayed there on at least one occasion.

Despite the fact that the gas and electricity had been cut off and it had been reported to the local authority that the premises were vacant, the Court took the view that the council property had remained the tenant's principal home.

It remains to be seen whether such a generous interpretation will be given to the similar phrase used by the 1993 Act, where the consequence for the landlord is more severe than an issue of security of tenure.

How is the right to collective enfranchisement to be exercised?

A claim to exercise the right to collective enfranchisement is made by the issuing of a notice to the reversioner of the premises (or, in certain circumstances, to the person specified in the notice as the recipient) by the requisite number of qualifying tenants. As mentioned earlier, the number of tenants putting their name to the notice must not be less than two-thirds of the qualifying tenants and must relate to not less than half the number of flats contained in the premises. The notice must specify certain matters, including the proposed purchase price, and state the name of the person(s) appointed as the nominee purchaser. After service of the initial notice, the nominee purchaser conducts all proceedings on behalf of the participating tenants. Following service of the initial notice on the part of the participating tenants, the recipient must reply with a counter-notice by the date specified in the initial notice, being a date not less than two months later. This counter-notice must state either that the recipient admits the claim to collective enfranchisement or does not admit it or, alternatively, add that the recipient will be seeking an order on the ground that he intends to redevelop the whole or a substantial part of the premises in question.

If certain conditions specified in s 23 are met, the tenants' claim to collective enfranchisement is liable to be defeated by the granting of a court order in favour of a reversioner who claims to have the above-mentioned intention. If the reversioner does not dispute the tenants' claim, completion goes ahead by a conveyance to the nominee purchaser at a price determined in accordance with Schedule 6 of the Act.

In order to buy the freehold, leaseholders who qualify will normally have to form a management company. One of the problems not envisaged by the 1993 Act, however, is that building societies, who are the most likely sources of funds for the purchase, are not keen to lend to a management company. Banks have also indicated that they are likely to regard such management companies as a commercial proposition, with the result that if they do lend at all it is likely to be at commercial rates, 3–6% above base rate, assuming that the block of flats is regarded as good enough security in the first place. It may well be that, unless the building societies change their apparent attitude towards management companies, the 1993 Act will become a dead letter except for those who can afford to purchase out of their own pocket.

The individual right of a tenant of a flat to acquire a new lease

Part I, Chapter II of the 1993 Act confers on a qualifying tenant who has occupied a flat as his only or principal home for either the last three years or for periods amounting to three years in the last 10, a right to acquire a new lease of that flat. The new term is to be for 90 years, commencing on the term date of the existing lease; and the terms on which it is to be granted are those of the existing lease with whatever modifications are necessary to take account of specified factors. The right to acquire a new lease of a flat is claimed by the giving of a notice, and is replied to by a landlord's counter-notice.

One of the reasons for a tenant being denied a new lease is that the landlord intends to redevelop the premises in which the flat is contained. A landlord who makes such a claim must then apply for a court order. The order will not be granted unless the lease is due to expire within five years and the court is satisfied that the landlord then intends to demolish, reconstruct or carry out substantial works of construction and could not reasonably do so unless he was granted vacant possession of the claimant tenant's flat. These are also grounds upon which a landlord can terminate a new lease once granted, with the proviso that such a claim can only be made by the landlord either within 12 months of the term date of the old lease or five years of the term date of the new one. The amount payable by the tenant for the new lease, in addition to a peppercorn ground rent, is a premium calculated in accordance with Schedule 13. This aggregates the diminution in value of the landlord's interest in the flat, the landlord's share of the marriage value (see Schedule 13, para 4(2)) and any compensation payable to the landlord under Schedule 13 for loss arising out of the grant of the new lease.

It is more likely that tenants of flats holding on long leases will chose to exercise the individual right of extension rather than utilise the complicated and expensive alternative of collective enfranchisement. In practice, therefore, all that the 1993 Act has achieved in this area is leasehold extension for tenants of flats who qualify.

CONCLUSIONS

Leasehold Reform has proved a political hot potato since its introduction in 1967. Its unpopularity with landlords has led to much heavily contested litigation, with the result that the area has become very technical. The 1993 Act has not improved on matters of simplicity and is likely to become a dead letter as far as 'collective enfranchisement' is concerned. Those determined landlords who wish to avoid the effects of the new legislation can easily do so, by, for example, letting to companies, which cannot satisfy the 'residence' requirement. It is relatively easy to purchase an 'off the peg' company and decisions in other areas of housing law have not always seen through such devices. In *Hilton v Plustitle* [1988] 1 WLR 149, for example, decided under the Rent Act 1977, the Court of Appeal was not astute enough to detect what looked like a sham in this respect.

Rents have also increased, particularly in London where the new legislation was likely to have most practical impact, and this is likely to take many recent lettings above the 'low rent' requirement. The introduction of the alternative 'particularly long term' provision by the Housing Act 1996 has gone some way to improving the situation. There is nothing, however, to prevent a landlord from letting a flat on a 20-year lease, taking the letting out of the 'long tenancy' definition. Far from being the most important change to housing law since 1925, the 1993 Act is a long way from being a significant piece of legislation when judged by its likely practical impact. As far as leasehold enfranchisement in the private sector is concerned, the 1967 Act is therefore likely to continue to be of more importance.

CHAPTER 11

THE RIGHT TO BUY IN THE PUBLIC SECTOR

INTRODUCTION

This chapter is concerned with the public sector tenant's right to buy under the Housing Act 1985. Until 1980, public sector tenants were not, as a class, able to purchase the freehold of their Council houses as of right, but certain local authorities did have a policy of allowing their tenants to purchase their council house.

The sale of council houses has been a big political issue for a number of years. Labour policy has tended to allow local authorities to sell off their houses to tenants on the condition that this did not adversely affect the rest of the local community by running down the council's housing stock in the area and providing that the Local Authority could still meet its general housing obligations. Conservative policy, however, has been to promote the sale of council houses to tenants. The consequence of this difference in policy had been to give local authorities the power to take the decision for themselves whether or not to sell to tenants. The exercise of this local authority discretion tended to benefit tenants of Conservative-run local authorities, since Labour-run councils were, on the whole reluctant to see council housing stock in their area diminish. Pre-1980 policy of local authorities fluctuated. In *Storer v Manchester City Council* [1974] 1 WLR 1403, for example, a contract was held to have been concluded when the tenant signed and returned the form of agreement. In *Gibson v Manchester City Council* [1979] 1 WLR 294, [1979] 1 All ER 972, however, the council was held not to have got beyond the stage of an invitation to treat when the tenant had completed the application form and returned it to the council; in the period before contracts were prepared and exchanged, there had been a change in control of the council following local government elections and the council had resolved to discontinue the policy of selling council houses except where there had already been an exchange of contracts.

In 1980, the Conservative government (in a bid to provide a 'Tenants' Charter', and true to its policy of promoting a 'property-owning democracy') introduced a general 'right to buy' via the Housing Act of that year. This right is now contained in the Housing Act 1985, as amended.

The result of the legislative right to buy has been fundamentally to alter the geographical distribution of home ownership throughout England and Wales as more and more people have become owner occupiers in the 'property-owning democracy' of the 20th century. About 15% of council housing stock has now been sold under these provisions.

The Housing Act 1985 is similar in approach to that of the Leasehold Reform Act 1967 which operates in the private sector. Provided that a tenant has the status of a 'secure' tenant (see Chapter 8), then he or she may purchase the freehold of the property if it constitutes a 'house'. If the property is a flat, then the secure tenant is entitled to be granted a long lease; likewise if the property (although eligible as a house) belongs to someone other than the landlord, the secure tenant may get an extended lease.

Where the tenancy is a joint secure tenancy, the right to buy belongs to all the joint tenants (see s 118 Housing Act 1985). The 1985 Act, however, applies to a wider category of tenants than just local authority tenants.

The relevant provisions of the Housing Act 1985 are set out below.

Housing Act 1985

118. The right to buy

(1) A secure tenant has the right to buy, that is to say, the right, in the circumstances and subject to the conditions and exceptions stated in the following provisions of this Part–

    (a) if the dwelling-house is a house and the landlord owns the freehold, to acquire the freehold of the dwelling-house;

    (b) if the landlord does not own the freehold or if the dwelling-house is a flat (whether or not the landlord owns the freehold), to be granted a lease of the dwelling-house.

(2) Where a secure tenancy is a joint tenancy then, whether or not each of the joint tenants occupies the dwelling-house as his only or principal home, the right to buy belongs jointly to all of them or to such one or more of them as may be agreed between them; but such an agreement is not valid unless the person or at least one of the persons to whom the right to buy is to belong occupies the dwelling-house as his only or principal home.

119. Qualifying period for right to buy

(1) The right to buy does not arise unless the period which, in accordance with Schedule 4, is to be taken into account for the purposes of this section is at least two years.

(2) Where the secure tenancy is a joint tenancy the condition in subsection (1) need be satisfied with respect to one only of the joint tenants.

120. Exceptions to the right to buy

The right to buy does not arise in the cases specified in Schedule 5 (exceptions to the right to buy).

121. Circumstances in which the right to buy cannot be exercised

(1) The right to buy cannot be exercised if the tenant is obliged to give up possession of the dwelling-house in pursuance of an order of the court or will be so obliged at a date specified in the order.

(2) The right to buy cannot be exercised if the person, or one of the persons, to whom the right to buy belongs–

    (a) has a bankruptcy petition pending against him,

    (b) ...

    (c) is an undischarged bankrupt; or

    (d) has made a composition or arrangement with his creditors the terms of which remain to be fulfilled.

122. Tenant's notice claiming to exercise right to buy

(1) A secure tenant claims to exercise the right to buy by written notice to that effect served on the landlord.

(2) In this Part 'the relevant time', in relation to an exercise of the right to buy, means the date on which that notice is served.

(3) The notice may be withdrawn at any time by notice in writing served on the landlord.

124. Landlord's notice admitting or denying right to buy

(1) Where a notice under section 122 (notice claiming to exercise right to buy) has been served by the tenant, the landlord shall, unless the notice is withdrawn, serve on the tenant within the period specified in subsection (2) a written notice either–

    (a) admitting his right, or

    (b) denying it and stating the reasons why, in the opinion of the landlord, the tenant does not have the right to buy.

(2) The period for serving a notice under this section is four weeks where the requirement of section 119 (qualifying period for the right to buy) is satisfied by a period or periods during which the landlord was the landlord on which the tenants notice under section 122 was served, and eight weeks in any other case.

(3) A landlord's notice under this section shall inform the tenant of any application for a determination under paragraph 11 of Schedule 5 (determination that right to buy not to be capable of exercise) and, in the case of a notice admitting the tenant's right to buy, is without prejudice to any determination made on such an application.

Discount

129(1) Subject to the following provisions of this Part, a person exercising the right to buy is entitled to a discount of a percentage calculated by reference to the period which is to be taken into account in accordance with Schedule 4 (qualifying period for right to buy and discount).

(2) The discount is, subject to any order under subsection (2A)–

    (a) in the case of a house, 32 per cent plus one per cent for each complete year by which the qualifying period exceeds two years, up to a maximum of 60 per cent;

    (b) in the case of a flat, 44 per cent plus two per cent for each complete year by which the qualifying period exceeds two years, up to a maximum of 70 per cent.

(2A) The Secretary of State may by order made with the consent of the Treasury provide that, in such cases as may be specified in the order–

    (a) the minimum percentage discount;

    (b) the percentage increase for each complete year of the qualifying period after the first two; or

    (c) the maximum percentage discount;

shall be such percentage, higher than that specified in subsection (2), as may be specified in the order.

(2B)...

(3) Where joint tenants exercise the right to buy, Schedule 4 shall be construed as if for the secure tenant there were substituted that one of the joint tenants whose substitution will produce the largest discount.

Right to acquire on rent to mortgage terms

143(1) Subject to subsection (2) and sections 143A and 143B, where–

    (a) a secure tenant has claimed to exercise the right to buy; and

(b) his right to buy has been established and his notice claiming to exercise it remains in force;

he also has the right to acquire on rent to mortgage terms in accordance with the following provisions of this Part.

(2) The right to acquire on rent to mortgage terms cannot be exercised if the exercise of the right to buy is precluded by section 121 (circumstances in which right to buy cannot be exercised).

(3) Where the right to buy belongs to two or more persons jointly, the right to acquire on rent to mortgage terms also belongs to them jointly.

143A(1) The right to acquire on rent to mortgage to terms cannot be exercised if–

(a) it has been determined that the tenant is or was entitled to housing benefit in respect of any part of the relevant period, or

(b) a claim for housing benefit in respect of any part of that period has been made (or is treated as having been made) by or on behalf of the tenant and has not been determined or withdrawn.

(2) In this section 'the relevant period' means the period–

(a) beginning twelve months before the day on which the tenant claims to exercise the right to acquire on rent to mortgage terms; and

(b) ending with the day on which the conveyance or grant is executed in pursuance of that right.

143B(1) The right to acquire on rent to mortgage terms cannot be exercised if the minimum initial payment in respect of the dwelling-house exceeds the maximum initial payment in respect of it.

(2) The maximum initial payment in respect of a dwelling-house is 80 per cent of the price which would be payable if the tenant were exercising the right to buy.

(3) Where, in the case of a dwelling-house which is a house, the weekly rent at the relevant time did not exceed the relevant amount, the minimum initial payment shall be determined by the formula–

$$P = R \times M$$

where–

P = the minimum initial payment;

R = the amount of the weekly rent at the relevant time;

M = the multiplier which at that time was for the time being declared by the Secretary of State for the purposes of this subsection.

(4) Where, in the case of a dwelling-house which is a house, the weekly rent at the relevant time éxceeded the relevant amount, the minimum initial payment shall be determined by the formula–

$$P = Q + (E \times M)$$

where –

P = the minimum initial payment;

Q = the qualifying maximum for the year of assessment which included the relevant time;

E = the amount by which the weekly rent at that time exceeded the relevant amount;

M = the multiplier which at that time was for the time being declared by the Secretary of State for the purposes of this subsection.

(5) The minimum initial payment in respect of a dwelling-house which is a flat is 80 per cent of the amount which would be the minimum initial payment in respect of the dwelling-house if it were a house.

(6) The relevant amount and multipliers for the time being declared for the purposes of this section shall be such that, in the case of a dwelling-house which is a house, they will produce a minimum initial payment equal to the capital sum which, in the opinion of the Secretary of State, could be raised on a 25 year repayment mortgage in the case of which the net amount of the monthly mortgage payments was equal to the rent at the relevant time calculated on a monthly basis.

(7) ...

(8) In this section–

'net amount', in relation to monthly mortgage payments, means the amount of such payments after deduction of tax under section 369 of the Income and Corporation Taxes Act 1988 (mortgage interest payable under deduction of tax);

'qualifying maximum' means the qualifying maximum defined in section 367(5) of that Act (limit on relief for interest on certain loans);

'relevant amount' means the amount which at the relevant time was for the time being declared by the Secretary of State for the purposes of this section;

'relevant time' means the time of the service of the landlord's notice under section 146 (landlord's notice admitting or denying right);

'rent' means rent payable under the secure tenancy, but excluding any element which is expressed to be payable for services, repairs, maintenance or insurance or the landlord's costs of management.

144(1) A secure tenant claims to exercise the right to acquire on rent to mortgage terms by written notice to that effect served on the landlord.

(2) The notice may be withdrawn at any time by notice in writing served on the landlord.

(3) On the service of a notice under this section, any notice served by the landlord under section 140 or 141 (landlord's notices to complete purchase in pursuance of right to buy) shall be deemed to have been withdrawn; and no such notice may be served by the landlord whilst a notice under this section remains in force.

(4) Where a notice under this section is withdrawn, the tenant may complete the transaction in accordance with the provisions of this Part relating to the right to buy.

QUALIFYING CONDITIONS

The property must be a 'house'

A secure tenant's right to buy the freehold is confined to property which falls within the definition of a 'house'. Under s 183 Housing Act 1985, a dwelling will only qualify as a 'house' if 'reasonably so called', and any dwelling which does not qualify under this definition will qualify as a flat, and therefore the tenant will, at most, have a right to an extended lease. A horizontal division of a dwelling will result in each unit of accommodation being a flat, whereas a vertical division makes each unit of accommodation a 'house' (eg terraced or semi-detached properties).

Exclusions

Certain properties are automatically excluded from the right to buy. These include houses which have been built or adapted for physically disabled persons (see Schedule 5, para 7). Also excluded are houses which are part of a group of dwellings especially suited to occupation by elderly persons and which it is the practice of the landlord to let for occupation either by a persons aged 60 years or more or for occupation by such persons and physically disabled persons, and which are provided with special facilities (such as a resident warden) in order to assist such persons (see Schedule 5, para 10, as amended by s 106 Leasehold Reform, Housing and Urban Development Act 1993). In addition, a house designed for occupation by an elderly person and which was let to the tenant or a predecessor in title for occupation by a person aged 60 years or more, are also excluded from the right to buy (see amendments introduced by s 106 of the 1993 Act). So also are mentally disabled persons' dwellings, dwellings let in connection with employment with the council or other prescribed public body, and properties where the council neither owns the freehold nor has a sufficient interest in the property to be able to grant an extended lease for the appropriate period (see Schedule 5 Housing Act 1985).

These exclusions have led to hard-fought litigation, particularly those concerned with dwellings let in connection with employment and physically disabled persons' accommodation.

In *Freeman v Wansbeck DC* (1983) 82 LGR 131, the downstairs toilet had been installed for use by a disabled child. The property already had two upstairs toilets and the provision of three toilets was unusual in the area. The Local Authority sought to resist the plaintiff's right to buy the house on the ground that the property had been especially adapted for a disabled person, but the Court of Appeal considered that much more drastic adaptation than this was needed in order to take the property out of the right to buy. The special features which would be required would include such things as ramps, specially widened doors for wheelchair access, stair lifts and cooking surfaces at heights suited to the physically disabled.

In *Dyer v Dorset County Council* [1989] QB 346, [1988] 3 WLR 213, the Court of Appeal was faced with the situation where the tenant was a college lecturer who was seeking to purchase a house in the college grounds. The Court of Appeal stated that, as a general principle, the right to buy would apply, provided that the house could be bought without doing damage to the college or school. On the facts, the house was so far from the other buildings as not to be within the 'curtilage' of the college and the tenant was therefore entitled to purchase it.

Dyer v Dorset CC

Lord Donaldson: ... It is accepted by both parties to the appeal that (a) Mr Dyer's house does not form part of any other building and (b) it was let to him by his landlords, the council. Mr Dyer therefore has a right to buy his house *unless* that house is within the curtilage of a building which is held by the council mainly for purposes other than housing purposes and consisting of accommodation other than housing accommodation. It is also common ground that none of the Kingston Maurward College are held for housing purposes as defined. Thus the sole issue is whether Mr Dyer's house is or is not within the curtilage of another building or, by the application of section 6 of the Interpretation Act 1978, of more than one other building. This is a question of fact and degree and thus primarily a matter for the trial judge, provided that he has correctly directed himself on the meaning of 'curtilage' in its statutory context.

The judge was familiar with Kingston Maurward College, but we can, I think, obtain a fairly accurate idea of the layout from the maps and plans with which we have been provided. There are a number of buildings clustered around and to the east of Kingston Maurward House, the great house of the old estate and the headquarters of the college. To the west lies the principal's house and six staff houses, all within 200 to 400 yards of Kingston Maurward House. A little further to the west there is Stinsford Dairy, which was one of Mr Dyer's principal responsibilities. The four lecturers' houses are about 450 yards to the north-west of Kingston Maurward House, forming an isolated close. The remainder of the estate is not built on and consists of a driveway from the public road fronting the lecturers' houses to Kingston Maurward House and fenced fields. Parliament has not seen fit to define the word 'curtilage' in this statutory context and we have to have regard to dictionaries and to such authorities as to its meaning as existed in 1980 and 1984.

The *Shorter Oxford English Dictionary* defines the word as 'a small court, yard, or piece of ground attached to a dwelling-house, and forming one enclosure with it'.

In *Jepson v Gribble* (1876) 1 TC 78 the issue was whether the house occupied by the medical superintendent of an asylum was part of the asylum. As in the present case, the house fronted on to a public road and had access from the back to the asylum itself, although it would appear that it was very much closer to the asylum than are the cottages to any other college buildings. Kelly CB said, at p 80:

'it is within the walls; it is part of the curtilage, in the language of the old law, and it is for the residence of a person whose attendance may be required at any moment, and who ought therefore to be at hand, and for that purpose it is put within the grounds; it is a part of the premises themselves, and with a ready, rapid and almost instantaneous communication with the building which contains the lunatics.'

Amphlett B, agreeing with him, referred to the judgment of Blackburn J in *Congreve v Overseers of Upton* (1864) 4 BS 857, 871, and said, at p 81:

'But with regard to the medical superintendent, Blackburn J says, "The statute expressly directs that he shall be resident in the asylum"; and then Blackburn J says, "Mr Welsby argued that the words 'in such asylum' must be construed to mean strictly within the curtilage of the building where the patients sleep at night, a place which might be so laid in an indictment for burglary. But that is not a reasonable meaning of those words. They mean that his residence must be in grounds appropriated to the asylum, so as to be reasonably within it. Now, looking at the position of the building as described in this case, we cannot say that it was not in the asylum, if we once assume that it need not be under the actual roof." For the same reason here, inasmuch as it is necessary for the proper conducting of the asylum that there should be a resident medical officer, whether that medical officer is accommodated by private rooms or by a house, and whether that house happens actually to form part of the building or not, it is a necessary adjunct to the asylum, and therefore it is a part of the asylum, and as the asylum is exempted, I think that this house must be exempted.'

In *Vestry of St Martin-in-the-Fields v Bird* [1895] 1 QB 428 this court had to decide whether a number of separate houses let to different people with an open space or passage running between the two rows of houses was either one building or could properly be called 'premises within the same curtilage'. It held that they could not.

There are also a number of ecclesiastical authorities to the effect that a curtilage must be near a house and must 'belong' to it: see *In re St John's Church, Bishops Hatfield* [1967] P 113; [1966] 2 WLR 705.

Finally there is *Methuen-Campbell v Walters* [1979] QB 525. It was a 'right to buy' case under the Leasehold Reform Act 1967, the issue being whether a paddock at the bottom of, and fenced off from, a garden was to be enfranchised with the house and garden. That Act did not use the word 'curtilage', but provided instead (section 2(3)): 'the reference to premises is to be taken as referring to any garage, outhouse, garden, yard and appurtenances which at the relevant time are let to [the tenant] with the house and are occupied with and used for the purposes of the house or any part of it by him or by another occupant.'

Goff LJ, at p 535, held that the decision of this court in *Trim v Sturminster Rural District Council* [1938] 2 QB 508 confined 'appurtances' to the curtilage of the house and in the following pages of his judgment expressed the view that the curtilage of a house is narrowly confined to the area surrounding it and did not extend to this paddock. Buckley LJ said, at pp 543–544:

'In my judgment, for one corporeal hereditament to fall within the curtilage of another, the former must be so intimately associated with the latter as to lead to the conclusion that the former in truth forms part and parcel of the latter. There can be very few houses indeed that do not have associated with them at least some few square yards of land, constituting a yard or a basement area or passageway or something of the kind, owned and enjoyed with the house, which on a reasonable view could only be regarded as part of the messuage and such small pieces of land would be held to fall within the curtilage of the messuage. This may extend to ancillary buildings, structures or areas such as outhouses, a garage, a driveway, a garden and so forth. How far it is appropriate to regard this identity as parts of one messuage or parcel of land as extending must depend on the character and the circumstances of the items under consideration. To the extent that it is reasonable to regard them as constituting one messuage or parcel of land, they will be properly regarded as all falling within one curtilage; they constitute an integral whole ... Thus a conveyance of The Gables without more, will pass everything within the curtilage to which that description applies, because every component part falls within the description.'

Mr Toulson rightly urges us to bear in mind that this is an Act which compulsorily transfers property from one person to another. It should therefore be so construed as to confine its effects to those clearly intended by the legislature. In this context he calls attention to the fact that under the Act of 1980, in its original form, where the exemption related to the existence of a secure tenancy rather than to the right to buy, Parliament, in referring to the dwelling-house being within curtilage of another building, had educational and social service institutions in mind: see Schedule 23, paragraph 3. In his submission 'curtilage' in that and in the present context must necessarily refer to a much larger area than would otherwise be the case.

Mr Toulson also referred us to *Paul Popper Ltd v Grimsey* [1963] 1 QB 44 where the issue was whether the whole of the defendant's premises were a factory for the purposes of the Factories Act 1937. Lord Parker CJ, reading the judgment of the Divisional Court, said, at p 52:

'We have come to the conclusion that the premises to be considered in this case are all the rooms occupied by the defendants, and not merely the glazing room and dark room. The definition of 'workshop' in the Factory and Workshop Act 1901, directed attention to individual rooms in a building, but the definition of 'factory' in both Acts seems to us, *prima facie*, to refer to the whole of the premises within the curtilage of which the manufacturing activity is carried on, and, although we have not been referred to any authority which in terms so decides, this seems to be implicit in many of the earlier cases.'

I do not think that this assists him. 'Curtilage' seems to involve some small and necessary extension to that to which the word is attached. In *Paul Popper Ltd v Grimsey* the court was concerned with the curtilage of a factory and it is not surprising that it was held to comprise the grounds of the factory. In *Jepson v Gribble* 1 TC 78 it was, in effect, the 'curtilage of the asylum'. Similarly, if the words with which we are concerned had been the 'curtilage of the college', I have little doubt that, despite the fact that Mr Dyer's house is on the edge of the college 'campus' and is divided from it by a fence, it would rightly have been held to have been within that curtilage. Certainly the judge would have so held. But these are not the words. We have to find that Mr Dyer's house lies within the curtilage of another college building or buildings. Giving the fullest effect to Mr Toulson's submissions and to the authority on which he relies, I am quite unable to find that Mr Dyer's house lies within the curtilage of any other college building or collection of college buildings. He therefore has a right to buy.

The tenancy must be a 'secure tenancy'

This requirement is discussed in more detail elsewhere in this book. One of the exclusions, however, concerns a tenancy where the tenant is an employee of the landlord and his contract of employment requires him to occupy the dwelling-house for the better performance of his duties (see Schedule 1, para 2(1)). This particular exception has caused its own difficulties, especially in relation to houses in or near to school grounds.

In *South Glamorgan County Council v Griffiths* (1992) 24 HLR 334, a caretaker of a school had lived for two years in accommodation owned by the county borough but unconnected with the school. He was then moved into a house adjacent to the school and owned by the same Borough, but in 1976 the plaintiffs replaced the County Borough as the education authority and became the caretaker's employer. The caretaker was provided by his new employers with a statement of his duties which included a paragraph that: 'It shall be a condition of employment that a caretaker must reside in school accommodation where such premises are available and a tenancy agreement must be entered into.' The caretaker was not asked to enter a formal tenancy agreement and in 1990 the school was closed. The caretaker wished to purchase the house in which he had been living adjacent to the school, but the plaintiffs took possession proceedings. The plaintiffs claimed that the caretaker was not a secure tenant, since his occupation fell within Schedule 1, para 2(1) Housing Act 1985. The Court of Appeal upheld the findings of the judge at first instance, who had ruled that, even though there was no express term in the caretaker's contract of employment requiring him to occupy the house for the better performance of his duties, at least not before the detailed statement of conditions of service in 1976, a term to the same effect was implied. The tenancy had therefore not been a secure tenancy and could be terminated when the caretaker's employment came to an end on retirement.

In *Hughes and another v Greenwich London Borough Council* [1993] 4 All ER 577, the House of Lords was faced with a situation where a person living in accommodation in school grounds wished to purchase the property from the local authority. In that case, a headmaster of a boarding school had accepted an offer of free accommodation in the headmaster's house which was situated on the campus of the school where he was employed. The accommodation had been provided by the local authority, but there was no express obligation in the headmaster's contract requiring him to occupy the headmaster's house, although he had lived there for the past four years. The House of Lords was not prepared to imply a term to the effect that the headmaster was required to occupy the house for the better performance of his duties, since it was not essential that he should live in the house in order to carry out his job as headmaster. He was therefore a secure tenant with the right to buy.

In *Elvidge v Coventry City Council* [1993] 4 All ER 903, (1994) 26 HLR 281, a person had been employed by the city council as a water bailiff in a countryside park managed by the council and had been granted a tenancy of a cottage in the park. The tenancy agreement which the employee had signed contained a clause that the right to occupy the cottage would cease if his employment with the council ceased. The contract of employment, however, did not expressly require the employee to live in the cottage, but when the employee was promoted to assistant ranger of the park, the conditions of employment were altered so as to require him to live in the park. The employee claimed to exercise the right to buy the cottage. The Court of Appeal ruled that Schedule 1, para 2 (1) Housing Act 1985 applied to remove a tenancy out of the category of 'secure tenancy' at any time when the tenant's contract of employment required him to occupy the premises for the better performance of his duties and accordingly it was irrelevant that the employee was not required to do so at the start of the tenancy – the crucial moment of time for this purpose was when the application for purchase of the property was made. This decision therefore means that a tenancy granted to a local authority employee can start out as a 'secure tenancy', with the right to buy, but cease to be so if the conditions of employment are subsequently changed so as to require that employee to reside in the property of which he is already the tenant.

The reasoning of the Court of Appeal in this case was based on the wording of Schedule 1, para 2(1) Housing Act 1985. This paragraph, in using the present tense, was not to be construed as laying down a once-and-for-all condition which had to be satisfied at the start of the tenancy, but applied at any time when the tenant's contract of employment required him to occupy the premises for the better performance of his duties, implying that a tenancy can move in and out of the category of 'secure tenancy' as conditions of employment change.

Mention should also be made here of the effect of family contributions to enable a secure tenant to purchase a house. This problem arose in acute form in

Burrows v Burrows & Sharp (1991) 23 HLR 213. In that case, the secure tenant could not afford to purchase the house without the aid of contributions from her granddaughter and the granddaughter's husband. The couple moved in with the grandmother on condition that if they paid the mortgage and undertook to look after the grandmother's handicapped daughter on the grandmother's death, then the house would be left to them in the grandmother's will. The various wills and a trust deed were executed by the parties, but the relationship between the grandmother and the couple broke down. The couple sought an order vesting the property in them in accordance with the terms of the trust deed, whilst the grandmother claimed a declaration that she was absolutely beneficially entitled to the house. This led to a complex discussion about constructive trusts and estoppel; but the Court of Appeal considered that the only workable solution was to make a clean break and ordered the couple to vacate the property whilst the grandmother was to refund their expenditure.

A further but more straight forward example is provided by *Saville v Goodall* (1993) 25 HLR 588. In that case the defendant had become the secure tenant of a council house and had then purchased it in the joint names of herself and her male partner. No mention was made as to how the beneficial interests in the property were to be divided between them, but the partner agreed to pay the mortgage and did so until the couple split up.

The Court of Appeal upheld the decision of the county court that the beneficial interests were held in equal shares, since there was no agreement as to the beneficial shares which then fell to be ascertained by reference to the parties' contributions. This decision follows the line of reasoning taken in *Lloyds Bank plc v Rosset* (1990) 22 HLR 349 and in *Springette v Defoe* (1992) 24 HLR 552 that where there is no expressed declaration of trust in the conveyance itself, there is a presumption of a resulting trust for the joint owners in the proportions in which they contributed to the purchase of the property unless there is evidence of a common intention that they should share in some other proportions. Such a common intention must involve a shared intention communicated between them rather than a mere coincidence of mind which was not disclosed to each other.

Cases like this demonstrate the complexities which can be encountered when members of the family, including cohabitees, join in to help purchase a public sector property.

Excluded tenants

Even though a tenant may be a secure tenant who has lived in the property for the qualifying period (see later), he may be prevented from exercising the right to buy if he (or she) falls into certain categories. For example, if the claimant has a bankruptcy petition pending against him, is an undischarged bankrupt, has made a composition agreement which has not been fulfilled or has a court order for possession against him, the right to buy cannot be exercised (see s 121 of the 1985 Act). See also *Enfield LBC v McKeon* [1986] 1 WLR 1007, discussed later.

Qualifying period

A secure tenant of qualifying property must have been a public sector tenant for a period of at least two years or for periods totalling not less than two years, though he need not have been residing in the same house or within the same local authority area during that qualifying period (see s 119 and Schedule 4 of the 1985 Act). A secure tenant can therefore add together periods spent moving from one local authority area to another or from one house to another within the same local authority area. It is prudent for a person who is moving around the country to obtain a statutory declaration as proof of his periods of residence in different local authority houses.

In the case of an application by joint tenants, the residence qualification will be satisfied if either of them qualifies (see s 119(2)).

Exercising the right to buy

A secure tenant may claim the right to buy simply by serving a written notice in the prescribed form on the landlord to that effect (see s 122 of the 1985 Act). The local authority is obliged to provide the appropriate form – Form RTB1 – if the tenant so requests. There is an intricate procedure to be followed after the tenant has served the relevant notice. The local authority first serves a response notice, which must be served within four weeks of the service of the tenant's notice. This response notice must state whether or not the local authority is prepared to admit the tenant's right to buy. Within eight weeks thereafter, if the right to buy has been established, a second response notice must be sent to the tenant, stating the price, terms and certain prescribed information about, *inter alia*, service charges, the right to have the property valued by the district valuer and the right to acquire the property on rent to mortgage terms.

The tenant must then respond to this notice within 12 weeks of either the service of the landlord's notice or of the notice stating the effect of the district valuer's valuation. The tenant's second notice must either amount to a statement of intention to pursue his claim or to withdraw it, or amount to a notice claiming to exercise the right to acquire on rent to mortgage terms (see s 125D). If the tenant fails to serve this second notice within the prescribed period, the landlord may serve on the tenant a further written notice requiring the tenant to serve the second tenant's notice referred to above within 28 days (or such period as extended by the landlord). The latter notice must inform the tenant that if he fails to respond, the original notice claiming to exercise the right to buy shall be deemed to be withdrawn at the end of the relevant period.

Where the council has obtained a possession order against the tenant, this can prevent the tenant's continued exercise of his right to buy. In *Enfield LBC v McKeon* [1986] 1 WLR 1007, the tenancy had originally been granted to the applicant's father, but passed to the applicant on the father's death. The council wanted to obtain possession on the grounds that the property was under-occupied, but the tenant then attempted to exercise the right to buy by serving the appropriate notice on the council. Whilst negotiations for the purchase were under way, the council sought possession on the basis of ground 16 (under-occupation by a non-spousal successor). The tenant was not allowed to purchase the property because the court considered that the council should not be deprived of its ordinary management powers during a protracted period of negotiations. Lord Justice Slade pointed out that such a ruling was necessary in order to prevent a tenant from frustrating a possession order made against him merely by serving the appropriate notice on the council.

Enfield Council v McKeon

Slade LJ: Before the judge there was argued on behalf of the defendant a point of law which had been foreshadowed by the first sentence of paragraph 5 of her defence and, if well founded, afforded by itself a complete answer to the proceedings. The gist of the argument submitted on her behalf was that, before the plaintiffs had served their notice of intent to seek possession, the defendant's right to buy the premises had been both exercised and established within the meaning of the Act of 1980. In those circumstances, it was submitted that by virtue of section 16 the plaintiffs were under a statutory obligation to convey the freehold of the house to her. This obligation, it was contended, overrode any right which they might otherwise have had to claim possession of the house. The plaintiffs countered this argument by relying on section 2(4)(b) and paragraph 1 of Part II of Schedule 1. If and when an order for possession had been made in their favour, they contended, this would mean that the defendant could no longer *exercise* her admitted right to buy by insisting on completion of the purchase.

The judge rejected the plaintiffs' submissions on the point of law and held that the defendant's submissions were well founded. She accordingly held that the plaintiffs' claim failed *in limine* and did not find it necessary to consider the further or alternative defences to the action respectively embodied in paragraph 6 of the defence (denying that ground 13 was satisfied), paragraph 7 of the defence (based on the alleged failure to satisfy the condition set out in section 34(3)(a) of the Act of 1980) and paragraph 8 (based on the alleged failure to comply with the condition set out in section 34(3)(b)). Her reasoning appears in the following passage from her short extempore judgment:

'I am concerned with the argument put forward by the plaintiffs that because of Part II of Schedule 1, the defendant cannot exercise her right to buy. In my judgment Part II of Schedule 1 is referring to an order already in existence at the time the right to buy is admitted. It is quite clear. I do not think that it is right to say that the right to buy cannot be exercised. Section 16 of the Act says that where the tenant has claimed the right to buy the landlord 'shall be bound' to sell the property to the tenant. In my view the plaintiffs' arguments are not correct. There would have to be in existence a possession order at the date of the death of the defendant's father. The plaintiffs' claim therefore fails. I do not therefore need to go on to consider the reasonableness test nor the matter of alternative accommodation. I grant the declaration sought by the defendant as prayed. The defendant is entitled to complete the purchase of the premises.'

It will have been seen that section 2 of the Act of 1980 draws a clear distinction between the case where a right to buy does not arise at all and the case where such right has arisen but cannot be exercised. Part II of Schedule 1 identifies the circumstances which give rise to the latter case. With all respect to the judge, I think there are at least two obvious fallacies in the passage which I have quoted from her judgment. First, on any possible construction of paragraph 1 of Part II of Schedule 1, I can see no grounds for saying that there would have had to be in existence a possession order at the date of the death of the defendant's father in order to prevent her from exercising her right to purchase. If a possession order had been made in favour of the plaintiff before she served her notice of claim to exercise her right to buy under section 5, her right to buy, on any possible footing, would never have become exercisable, because of paragraph 1 of Part II of Schedule 1. Secondly, and more importantly, I think that the judge erred in saying that paragraph 1 of Part II of Schedule 1 is referring to an order already in existence when the right to buy is 'admitted'. It is referring to an order in existence when the tenant seeks or purports to *'exercise'* the right to buy, which is quite a different matter.

I therefore think that on any footing the judge, with respect to her, erred in her approach to the relevant statutory provisions. However, this does not necessarily mean that her ultimate conclusion was wrong. The argument which Mr Pears has presented to this court on behalf of the defendant has been one of attractive simplicity. Essentially, it is to the following effect. When the defendant (who had an admitted 'right to buy' her house), on or about 30 August 1984, served on the plaintiffs her notice under section 5 claiming to exercise the right to buy, she 'exercised', once and for all, that right within the meaning of section 2(4)(b). That right was 'established' within the meaning of that word as used in sections 10 and 16, when in September 1984 the plaintiffs served on her a notice admitting her right to buy. After such right had been thus established, so it is submitted, the plaintiffs became subject to a statutory obligation under section 16 to convey the house to her, subject to the provisions of that section. Paragraph 1 of Part II of Schedule 1, in Mr Pears' submission, has no relevance to the present case, because at the time when the defendant 'exercised' her right to buy, there was no order for possession in existence.

Thus, if an order for possession were to be made now, he contends, it would not be capable of depriving her of her statutory right to complete the purchase in reliance on section 16. He pointed out that if, contrary to his submissions, the plaintiffs are still entitled to proceed with their claim for possession, it must follow that the court could wholly defeat her statutory right to purchase by making the order sought, provided only that it considered that ground 13 was established, that it was reasonable to make the order and that suitable accommodation would be available for her when the order took effect. Her right to buy would thus be attenuated and depend on what Mr Pears called 'a balancing act'. This, in his submission, could not have represented the intention of the legislature.

In answer to these submissions Mr Stephenson, on behalf of the plaintiffs, drew particular attention to the provisions of section 16(11) and 32(1) of the Act of 1980, which show that even where a secure tenant has claimed to exercise the right to buy, the tenancy continues until the purchase is actually completed by a grant, or a possession order is made in favour of the landlord. He pointed out that in view of the provisions of section 16, at least two years may elapse in many cases between the service of the tenant's notice under section 5, claiming the exercise of the right to buy and completion itself; and indeed that if the tenant ultimately fails to complete by producing the requisite money, completion may never take place. In his submission the Act of 1980 makes it clear that just as a secure tenancy itself continues during the interim period pending completion, so do the rights of the landlord continue during such period. He pointed out that while the Act imposes a number of express restrictions on the landlord's right to seek possession, it contains no explicit statutory bar on the landlord seeking an order for possession on any of the statutory grounds set out in Part I of Schedule 4 during this interim period. In his submission, having received the defendant's written notice claiming to exercise the right to buy under section 5, the plaintiffs had no alternative open to them but to serve on the defendant a section 5 notice admitting the tenant's right, which indubitably existed. Similarly, having admitted her right to buy, they were bound as soon as practicable, by virtue of section 10, to serve on her a notice of the nature described in that section. But the service of neither of these notices debarred them as landlords under the continuing secure tenancy from seeking an order for possession against the defendant in accordance with section 34. The judge, in his submission, should have dealt with the plaintiffs' claim not by dismissing it on the short point of law, but by considering all the several matters to which section 34 directs attention, or alternatively by adjourning the proceedings pursuant to the powers vested in her by section 87. There was, in Mr Stephenson's submission, no statutory basis upon which the judge could properly dismiss the plaintiffs' claim. Paragraph 1 of Part II of Schedule 1 is still capable of being invoked by the plaintiffs because, under the statute, the 'exercise' of the tenant's right to buy is a continuing process which begins when the tenant serves his notice claiming to exercise the right to buy and only ends when he finally pays the purchase price and takes his conveyance on completion. In Mr Stephenson's submission, if, during the interim period before completion, the court, with due regard to all the several facts mentioned in section 34 of the Act of 1980, makes an order for possession, paragraph 1 will cause the tenant's right to buy to cease to be exercisable, and thus to be abrogated.

There is only one link in the chain of Mr Stephenson's argument which I have had any difficulty in accepting. According to usual legal terminology, an ordinary option to purchase is, I think, commonly regarded as being exercised at the moment when notice is first given of the donee's intention to exercise the option. Correspondingly, on a first reading of section 2(4)(b), I was inclined to think that the tenant's right to buy must be 'exercised' for the purpose of that subsection at the moment when he serves his notice under section 5 (which is also the 'relevant time' for ascertaining the purchase price payable – see section 10(2)(a)) – and at no other time. Nevertheless, I am now satisfied that this is not the correct way to read the word 'exercised' in the particular context of section 2(4)(b) and Part II of Schedule 1. In my judgment, the right is 'exercised' each and every time when the tenant takes any step towards the implementation of his right to purchase ...

In my judgment, the short answer to the defendant's point of law is that, for the purpose of applying section 2(4)(b) and Part II of Schedule 1 (on the true construction of which her case depends) the Act of 1980 treats a tenant as purporting to exercise his right to buy at any time and from time to time when he takes steps towards implementation of that right, up to and including completion of the purchase. If, therefore, any of the circumstances set out in Part II of Schedule 1 subsist at any time between the time when he serves his section 5 notice and completion, his right to buy ceases to be exercisable.

However, in *Dance v Welwyn Hatfield DC* [1990] 1 WLR 1097, [1990] 3 All ER 572, the Court of Appeal distinguished *Enfield LBC v McKeon* (above) on the ground that in that case the parties had not reached the stage where all matters relating to the sale and the mortgage had been agreed. In *Dance v Welwyn Hatfield DC*, the council wanted to demolish the tenant's house, relying on ground 10, but the tenant wished to purchase the house and therefore served notice on the council. The court accepted that the tenant had a right to purchase the freehold in this case by treating the right to buy as akin to an option to purchase.

Dance v Welwyn Hatfield DC

Nourse LJ: *Enfield London BC v McKeon* was decided under the 1980 Act as amended by the Housing and Building Control Act 1984. For the sake of convenience, I will continue to refer to the corresponding provisions of the 1985 Act. The material facts of that case were these. The tenant served on the council a notice claiming to exercise the right to buy under s 122(1). The council then served a notice admitting the right to buy under s 124. The next thing which happened was that the council served on the tenant a notice indicating its intention to seek possession of the property, on ground 16 in Pt III of Sch 2 to the Act, namely that the accommodation was more extensive than was reasonably required by the tenant. Some seven weeks later the council, pursuant to the obligation imposed on it by s 25, served on the tenant a notice containing the particulars required by that section. Two months later the council issued proceedings, claiming possession on ground 16. Although it is not clear whether the price proposed by the council had been accepted by the tenant, it is, I think, clear that a stage had not been reached when, for the purposes of s 138(1), all matters relating to the grant and to the amount to be left outstanding or advanced on the security of the property had been agreed or determined.

The facts accordingly differed from those of the present case in an important respect.

It was argued on behalf of the tenant that the right to buy had been 'exercised' for the purposes of s 121(1) when she had served her notice under s 122(1). As to that, Slade LJ, with whose judgment the other member of the court, Eastham J, agreed, said ([1986] 2 All ER 730 at 736, [1986] 1 WLR 1007 at 1014):

'According to usual legal terminology, an ordinary option to purchase is, I think, commonly regarded as being exercised at the moment when notice is first given of the donee's intention to exercise the option. Correspondingly, on a first reading of s [121(1)], I was inclined to think that the tenant's right to buy must be "exercised" for the purpose of that subsection at the moment when he serves his notice under s [122(1)] (which is also the 'relevant time' for ascertaining the purchase price payable: see s [125(2)(a)]), and at no other time. Nevertheless, I am now satisfied that this is not the correct way to read the word "exercised" in the particular context of s [121]. In my judgment, the right is "exercised" each and every time when the tenant takes any step towards the implementation of his right to purchase.'

Counsel for the defendants submitted that the decision in *Enfield London BC v McKeon* is binding on this court and, moreover, that it is decisive of this case. He relied particularly on the view of Slade LJ that the Act treats a tenant as purporting to exercise his right to buy at any time and from time to time when he takes steps towards implementation of that right 'up to and including completion of the purchase'. Although others might have preferred the simple view of s 121(1) which had been urged on Slade LJ and Eastham J by the tenant, we must certainly accept that their decision is binding on us. I do not, however, think that it is decisive of this case. Although the words of Slade LJ on their face apply here, the decision is only a binding authority for a case where the facts are the same. As I have already pointed out, the facts of this case are different. Indeed, the facts of the McKeon case were such that it never became necessary to consider s 138, to whose effect on the facts of this case I now turn.

By his letter of 6 August 1987 the defendants' chief legal officer informed the plaintiffs' solicitors that he had received instructions to proceed with the sale of the property. Subject perhaps to a notification by the plaintiffs that the amount to be left outstanding on the mortgage was acceptable to them, that was effectively an acknowledgement that all matters relating to the grant and to the amount to be left outstanding or advanced on the security of the dwelling-house had been granted or determined as contemplated by s 138(1). Accordingly, as recognised by that letter, the defendants had already come under a duty to convey the freehold to the plaintiffs if and when they were requested to do so. No request was made at that time, because on 29 September 1987 the plaintiffs exercised their right to defer completion. But that deferment was brought to a premature end by their solicitors' letter of 1 September 1988 requesting completion on 26 September following. At that stage, by virtue of s 138(3), the defendants' duty to convey the freehold became enforceable by injunction.

What was the effect of the coming into operation of s 138(3)? There was some debate as to the intention of Parliament in making the duty to convey enforceable by injunction. It was suggested that it was in order to make good the inability of the county court to grant an order by way of mandamus. I do not think that the reason is important. What is important is that the tenant's remedy is an injunction, that is to say an order that the landlord shall convey to him the legal estate in the property. The right to an injunction in a case where there is no contract cannot be any different in its incidents from the right to an order for specific performance in a case where there is a contract, as to which I need only cite a passage from the well-known judgment of Jessel MR in *London and South Western Rly Co v Gomm* (1882) 20 Ch D 562 at 581, [1881–5] All ER Rep 1190 at 1193:

> 'The right to call for a conveyance of the land is an equitable interest or equitable estate. In the ordinary case of a contract for purchase there is no doubt about this, and an option for repurchase is not different in its nature. A person exercising the option has to do two things, he has to give notice of his intention to purchase and to pay the purchase money; but as far as the man who is liable to convey is concerned, his estate or interest is taken away from him without his consent, and the right to take it away being vested in another, the covenant giving the option must give that other interest in the land.'

Although that was a case of a contractual option to purchase, the principle is the same. Here the equitable interest in the property is acquired by the tenant directly the landlord's duty to convey arises and becomes exercisable by injunction under s 138. Subject to payment of the purchase price and execution of the mortgage, if there is one, by the tenant the landlord is bound to convey to him the legal estate in the property.

Although neither s 142 nor s 140(3)(c) contain any express provision bearing on the point, it was not suggested by council for the defendants that the three-year deferment period could not be prematurely determined by the tenant. I am in no doubt that that is a correct view of the matter. I therefore conclude that as from 2 September or, at the latest 26 September 1988 the plaintiffs, being entitled to enforce the defendants' duty by injunction, became the equitable owners of the freehold in the property. At that stage, if not beforehand, they must, on any natural use of language, have 'exercised' their right to buy for the purpose of s 121(1). At that stage there was no order of the court obliging them to give up possession of the property. Nor had any proceedings been commenced. Nor had the plaintiffs ever been served with a formal notice requiring them to give up possession. In the circumstances, I do not see how s 121(1) can be said to affect the matter ...

I fully recognise that to distinguish this case from the McKeon case will leave the law in a somewhat unsatisfactory state. It is perhaps inevitable that novel legislation of this kind will give rise to difficulties which can only be identified on a case-by-case process. Be that as it may, I am in no doubt that the distinction ought to be made and we in this court are in a better position to make it than was

Judge Hamilton in the court below.

I would allow the appeal and make an order for specific performance of an uncompleted contract.

If a secure tenant dies before the conveyance or grant of the freehold but after the terms of the sale have been agreed, and there is no-one who qualifies as his successor, the right to buy is lost and the representatives of the deceased's estate do not have the right to purchase the property. In *Bradford Metropolitan City Council v McMahon* [1993] 4 All ER 237, the Court of Appeal considered both *Enfield London BC v McKeon* (above) and *Dance v Welwyn Hatfield DC* (above) and outlined five events which are to take place in the process of purchase:

(1) A secure tenant gives written notice claiming to exercises the right to buy.

(2) The landlord, within the required period, must state whether it admits or denies the right to buy.

(3) If the right to buy is established, the landlord must then, within the stated period, state the price at which the house ought to be sold and the terms to be included in the conveyance.

(4) The terms stated are then either agreed by the tenant or any issue is agreed between the parties.

(5) The landlord then conveys the freehold to the tenant, a duty which the tenant may enforce by injunction.

Lord Justice Staughton considered that both the *Enfield* and *Dance* cases were concerned with s 121 Housing Act 1985, which could operate to ban the exercise of the right to buy up to and after the third event but not after the fourth event had occurred. He concluded that the 1985 Act contains the implicit requirement that the tenant must remain a secure tenant until the fifth event has taken place.

It should be noted that all the above cases were decided before the Leasehold Reform, Housing and Urban Development Act 1993, amended the procedure contained in s 125 of the 1985 Act for exercising the right to buy.

The purchase price

The price which a secure tenant has to pay is based on the market value of the property less a discount, which is set on a sliding scale according to length of residence. The minimum discount is 32%; and for each year of secure tenancy residence beyond the minimum qualifying period a further 1% is added to the discount, with a maximum 60% discount following 30 years of such residence (see s 129 of the 1985 Act, as amended). In the case of a flat the discount is 44% minimum and 70% maximum.

In order to prevent tenants from profiteering on the housing market, the tenant may be required to pay back some or all of this discount if he resells or disposes of the property within three years. A resale within one year attracts repayment of the entire discount, whilst a resale within two or three years attracts repayment of two-thirds or one-third of the discount respectively. In the case of an acquisition on rent to mortgage terms, the repayment following a disposal is either the initial payment, any interim payment made before the disposal or the final payment, if it has been made, and in each case reduced by one-third for each complete year which has elapsed since the initial payment was made. This obligation is enforced by means of a covenant to repay, which the tenant is obliged to enter, and which is registrable as a charge under the Land Registration Act 1925 (see ss 155 and 156 of the 1985 Act, as amended).

A property adjustment order in matrimonial proceedings does not attract an obligation to repay any discount (see s 160 of the 1985 Act). A sale, however, under a court order in matrimonial proceedings does attract an obligation to repay. In *R v Rushmoor Borough Council, ex parte Barrett and another* [1988] 2 All ER 268, the Court of Appeal ruled that an outright sale pursuant to an order made under s 24A of the Matrimonial Causes Act 1973 was not exempted by s 160 of the 1985 Act and therefore attracted an obligation to repay discount. If repossession occurs, that may also attract liability to repay the discount.

Mortgage entitlement?

A tenant who wished to exercise his right to buy was originally entitled to a mortgage from the local authority, but could have obtained a mortgage from any other lender if he so wished. The right to obtain a mortgage from the local authority was abolished by the Leasehold Reform, Housing and Urban Development Act 1993.

Local authority tenants wishing to exercise the right to buy are therefore now in the same position as any other freehold purchaser as regards obtaining a mortgage.

Rent to mortgage terms

A council tenant who was eligible to buy but who could not afford to buy the whole house in one go, was once able to chose the alternative of entering into shared ownership with the local authority under a shared ownership lease. This right was abolished by s 107 Leasehold Reform, Housing and Urban Development Act 1993. In place of the shared ownership lease, the 1993 Act introduced the right to acquire on rent to mortgage terms (see ss 108–120 of the 1993 Act). This had originally been an experiment carried out in Scotland, whereby a person could become part owner and part tenant of the property. The Conservative Government of the early 1990s was impressed with the Scottish experiment and decided to extend it to England and Wales.

A tenant acquiring on rent to mortgage terms now becomes a semi-purchaser, whilst at the same time remaining a tenant, with a proportion of their payments being allocated to rent and a proportion to mortgage instalments. This scheme is similar to the now abolished shared ownership lease scheme, but with the subtle difference that, instead of being a long leaseholder of part and a periodic tenant of the rest of the property, the tenant would now own part of the freehold.

The preserved right to buy

If the house is taken out of the public sector and 'privatised', the tenant's right to purchase the freehold is 'preserved' under the Housing and Planning Act 1986. Once registered, this right is as effective against the new landlord as it was against the old one.

The Housing Act 1996

The Housing Act introduces, *inter alia*, introducing the right to buy for housing association tenants whose properties are built or acquired after the Act becomes law.

CONCLUSIONS

There is no doubt that the 1980s and 1990s have seen an increase in the number of tenants purchasing their homes under the right to buy provisions of the Housing Act 1985. For some, however, this has proved to have been a major disaster as house prices have tumbled and interest rates have risen to 15%, before falling back into single figures. The number of home repossessions in recent years has dramatically increased; and for many the right to buy has meant them entering the 'property-owning democracy' for a relatively short period only. These people are then often thrown upon the mercy of the local authority under the homelessness legislation, sometimes to find that their action or inaction in relation to their previous housing situation is to be classified as 'intentional homelessness'. Such people would undoubtedly have been better off staying as secure tenants of the council in the first place. This has been particularly true of tenants of flats:

'It was supposed to be a dream come true: the chance for council flat tenants to own their own home and take their rightful place in the property-owning democracy. Instead it is becoming a living nightmare for thousands trapped in homes they cannot sell and facing bills they cannot pay.

More than 120,000 people – 70% of them in London and the south east – bought the leaseholds to their council flats confidently expecting to get just as good a deal as their neighbours who bought their houses. Many have benefited, but many of those who bought flats on estates, especially if they were high-rise or system-built, are now regretting the day the right to buy leaflet dropped through their letter box.' (*ROOF*, November and December, 1993, p 18.)

In addition, the inability of councils to use capital receipts from the sale of council houses (except in special circumstances) for the provision of new homes has prevented local authorities from maintaining their levels of housing stock for those who need it most, especially the homeless whose numbers have dramatically increased in recent years. It is therefore no wonder that the right to buy in the public sector has proved a political hot potato since the Conservative Party adopted it as a central part of its policy. Some may argue that the right to buy has been the cause of more misery for families who might have been better advised to remain public sector tenants. But it must not be forgotten that there are those whom the right to buy has given the opportunity to improve their standards of living. It remains to be seen, however, just how well the new rent to mortgage scheme works and how popular it turns out to be in England and Wales.

CHAPTER 12

OWNER OCCUPIERS, SURVEYORS AND THE MORTGAGE RELATIONSHIP

INTRODUCTION

The general approach of the law has been *caveat emptor*, or 'buyer beware', but in recent years the law has developed a degree of protection for owner occupiers. This chapter is concerned with the protection which the law gives to the owner occupier against the negligence of surveyors when purchasing a house with the aid of a mortgage. Much of housing law concentrates on the landlord and tenant relationship, but the majority of residential property is in fact owner occupied. During the course of this century the shift has been away from renting towards purchasing one's own home. Britain has become what has been described as a 'real-property-mortgaged-to-a-building-society-owning-democracy' (*per* Lord Diplock in *Pettitt v Pettitt* [1970] AC 777 at page 824, para b). This situation has come about partly as a result of better living standards, partly as a result of the greater availability and diversity of mortgage finance and partly as a result of government policy, which has encouraged home ownership in the public (as well as in the private) sector, through the 'right to buy' provisions of the Housing Act 1985. Purchasing a home, however, is a costly business. Not only are there the mortgage costs, conveyancing fees and removal expenses, but there is also the cost of a survey to take into account.

Many of the owner occupied properties in Britain are subject to a mortgage, mostly with a building society, although some mortgages are provided by banks, local authorities and fringe lending institutions. There are certain tax advantages to be gained from having a mortgage on residential property, since tax relief is given on the first £30,000 of money borrowed on any one property. This figure has remained constant over several Budgets, and is now too low compared to average house prices. One consequence of this, when added to fluctuating interest rates and the recession of recent years, has been that mortgages have at times become expensive to finance for many people; the number of possession actions by mortgagees has correspondingly increased when interest rates have been highest (see Chapter 13).

When a person purchases a house with the aid of a mortgage from a building society, that society is obliged by law to have a valuation placed on the property by an independent surveyor (see s 13 Building Societies Act 1986 which is dealt with later in this chapter). Often that valuation is the nearest that a purchaser gets to having the property surveyed before committing himself to buying it. In practice, it is the purchaser who pays the 'survey fee', but there is no contract between the purchaser and the surveyor, since the latter is engaged by the building society.

Many people do not get a separate survey carried out on the property, more through lack of finance than through indolence. This exclusive reliance on the valuation obtained for the building society's benefit does raise some interesting legal issues:

(1) Can the purchaser/mortgagor obtain any legal remedy if the valuation is conducted in a negligent fashion, and if so, against whom?

(2) Are there any ways in which this legal liability can be avoided?

(3) What is the basis of any damages payable to the purchaser/mortgagor when such liability exists?

This chapter will address these, among other, issues.

There are certain problems which legal actions against surveyors raise:

First, the surveyor's profession itself may not be agreed on what actually constitutes 'proper practice', so that it can be difficult to decide in some circumstances whether the defendant surveyor acted with the skill and competence to be expected of someone in that profession. Ask any two or three surveyors selected at random what they would do in a given situation and you might find that they each will give you a slightly different answer.

Second, the implications of a surveyor's negligence can be far more serious than that of a layman. If subsidence problems are not picked up, or damp is not detected, the result may be that the householder or his family suffer personal injury or health problems, not to mention expense, inconvenience and distress.

Third, the often high cost of successful legal actions against surveyors results in higher insurance claims and a consequent increase in insurance premiums and the cost of surveys. Legal actions against surveyors are therefore often vigorously defended by the surveyor with the backing of his insurers; and the result has been to take cases as high as the House of Lords itself. The cost of an unsuccessfully fought legal action on the part of a surveyor has to be borne ultimately by future consumers who use the surveyor's services, with the economic repercussions involved.

For these reasons, legal actions against surveyors have been far from being free of difficulty, as this chapter will demonstrate.

BUYER BEWARE

Buying a house can be a stressful as well as a costly business, as the National Consumers' Council has said in its report *Home Truths* (September, 1990). The main worry, apart from the expense of it all, is whether the house has any major or minor defects that could be expensive to cure and an inconvenience to the occupants.

When a person buys a house in a private sale, he does not normally receive any warranty of fitness for habitation or state of good order and repair of the house from the vendor. The maxim *caveat emptor* still applies to the purchase of a house, unless the purchaser is buying direct from the builder or obtains a specific warranty from the vendor. The sensible thing to do is to get a full structural survey oneself, or at least some sort of survey carried out on the property before contracts are exchanged, but not everybody who buys a house has the money to pay for such a survey and not everyone appreciates the need for a survey. In any event, if a building society mortgage is involved in the purchase the society will obtain its own valuation of the property at the buyer's expense. This valuation is a legal requirement under s 13 Building Societies Act 1986.

Building Societies Act 1986

13(1) It shall be the duty of every director of a building society to satisfy himself that the arrangements made for assessing the adequacy of the security for any advance to be fully secured on land which is to be made by the society are such as may reasonably be expected to ensure that–

(a) an assessment will be made on the occasion of each advance whether or not any previous assessment was made with a view to further advances or re-advances;

(b) each assessment will be made by a person holding office in or employed by the society who is competent to make the assessment and is not disqualified under this section from making it;

(c) each person making the assessment will have furnished to him a written report on the value of the land and any factors likely materially to affect its value made by a person who is competent to value, and is not disqualified under this section from making a report on, the land in question;

but the arrangements need not require each report to be made with a view to a particular assessment so long as it is adequate for the purpose of making the assessment.

This independent valuation is required solely for the protection of depositors with the building society and not for the protection of the mortgagor. (A similar duty to obtain a valuation is placed on a local authority which lends on the security of a former council house under the 'right to buy' provisions of the Housing Act 1985: see s 127 and related provisions.) The mortgagor, however, often relies on this valuation when purchasing the property and fails to get a separate survey carried out. A valuation may not involve such an extensive inspection of the property as a full survey would involve; nevertheless, a valuation should pick up the not-so-obvious as well as the obvious defects, since it involves a professional person from whom a professional job can reasonably be expected (see s 13 Supply of Goods and Services Act 1982).

If the valuation is negligently carried out by the independent surveyor, it is usually the mortgagor who suffers in the long run. He may find himself owning a property which has rising damp, rot or, worse still, subsidence. These are expensive problems to cure and cause a large degree of disruption in the property whilst remedial work is being carried out; they also greatly reduce the value and saleability of the property if left uncured. The question inevitably arises whether the mortgagor has any legal remedy against either the building society who provided the finance or the independent surveyor instructed by the building society who was negligent when preparing the valuation report.

THE LEGAL POSITION OF THE SURVEYOR

In the absence of a private survey commissioned by the purchaser, two separate contracts are involved in the survey preliminary to the purchase of a house with the aid of a mortgage. One of these is between the building society and the purchaser, the other is between the society and the surveyor, although the mortgagor pays the fee for the valuation. There is thus no direct contractual relationship between surveyor and purchaser and any liability on the part of the surveyor towards the purchaser necessarily lies in tort. Any such liability depends on the principle developed in *Hedley Byrne & Co Ltd v Heller & Partners Ltd* [1964] AC 465, [1963] 2 All ER 575.

The recognition of such liability on the surveyor's part came in the case of *Yianni v Edwin Evans & Sons* [1982] QB 438, [1981] 3 All ER 592. The case involved a buyer's claim in negligence against a surveyor instructed by the Halifax Building Society who had failed to discover serious faults with the foundations of a house in London which Mr Yianni purchased with a Halifax Building Society mortgage. The valuation report in that case was not shown to Mr Yianni, but he assumed, from the fact that the Building Society was prepared to lend him £12,000, that the report was favourable. The house became in danger of structural collapse. Mr Yianni's action against the surveyor was successful because the court (Park J) considered that a duty of care was owed by the surveyor to Mr Yianni and had been breached by the surveyor's failure to detect the problems with the foundations.

Yianni's case came under heavy criticism because it involved a novel recognition that liability may extend to A for advice given by B to C, but its legitimacy is now beyond doubt after the decision of the House of Lords in the joined cases of *Smith v Eric Bush; Harris v Wyre Forest DC* [1989] 2 WLR 790, in which Lord Griffiths stated that '*Yianni* [1982] QB 438 was correctly decided'.

The case of *Yianni* raised further questions concerning a surveyor's liability for a negligent valuation:

(1) Could damages be reduced on the basis of contributory negligence on the mortgagor's part, since a separate survey could have been obtained by him?

(2) Would the surveyor be liable for the negligent valuation to anyone other than the mortgagor, such as a subsequent cash purchaser who relied on the earlier valuation or an equitable owner?

(3) Could liability be avoided by means of a disclaimer of responsibility?

These three questions will now be addressed.

Contributory negligence

At a time when finances are already stretched, reliance exclusively on the valuation report prepared for the building society is a great temptation to many house buyers. Does such exclusive reliance amount to contributory negligence when a proper private survey could have been commissioned? After all, a valuation is not the same thing as a survey. The former merely indicates to the building society whether the house is worth the amount which it is being asked to lend, whereas a survey specifically looks for particular faults. Should not a purchaser therefore be expected to err on the side of caution and commission his own survey? This specific issue was pleaded unsuccessfully by the surveyor in Yianni. In that case the purchase price of the house was £15,000 – then towards the bottom end of the property market. The court refused to accept that a failure to obtain a separate survey report in these circumstances amounted to contributory negligence (Park J [1981] 3 All ER 592 at 606).

One can only speculate whether the court would have taken such a generous line had the price of the house been £150,000. At the bottom end of the market, however, it is apparent that a plea of contributory negligence is likely to fail.

How far does liability extend?

In *Smith v Eric Bush*, following *Yianni*, Lord Griffiths indicated that liability would extend to the mortgagor and no further.

Smith v E Bush

Lord Griffiths: It is just and reasonable that the duty should be imposed for the advice is given in a professional as opposed to social context and liability for breach of the duty will be limited to the purchaser of the house – I would not extend it to subsequent purchasers.

It would appear that liability will not extend to a future purchaser, whether cash or mortgage-based; but what is not so clear is whether a donee of the property would have a cause of action against the surveyor. Suppose, for example, that in *Yianni*, Mr Yianni had died but had left the house by will to a member of his family. Is it likely that liability could have extended to such a person? There is no direct authority on this point, but decisions in other areas based upon *Hedley Byrne* suggest that liability would not extend that far, since the movement now seems to be to confine liability within fairly narrow limits (see, for example, *Caparo Industries plc v Dickman* [1990] 1 All ER 568).

Can liability be avoided by means of a disclaimer of responsibility?

In *Yianni*, there was no disclaimer of responsibility, but following the decision of Park J in that case, building societies began to include disclaimers in their mortgage application forms and in the valuation report, which were increasingly shown to purchasers. The idea behind these disclaimers was to take advantage of the 'get-out' which had been recognised in *Hedley Byrne* itself. If no responsibility were to be accepted for the advice or information given, then no liability could arise in the first place – or so it was thought. What surveyors and building societies had not bargained for, however, was the effect of the Unfair Contract Terms Act 1977. It was not until the joined cases of *Smith v E Bush; Harris v Wyre Forest* (above) that the full impact of this legislation was realised. The relevant provisions of the Unfair Contract Terms Act 1977 are contained in ss 2, 11 and 13.

Two issues arose in *Smith v E Bush; Harris v Wyre Forest DC* (above) concerning the 1977 Act:

(a) Were the disclaimers in each case within the scope of the legislation?

(b) If they were, were they rendered invalid under that legislation?

Section 2 of the 1977 Act contains a general limit on excluding liability for negligence which occurs in the 'business liability' context; but sub-s 2 imposes a test of 'reasonableness' on a clause which purports to exclude liability for a loss other than death or personal injury (such as the economic loss which a house owner might suffer as a result of a negligent valuation). It was this particular provision which would therefore be relevant in most cases, if indeed the 1977 Act applied at all to the situation in *Smith v E Bush*; the Act would only apply if the disclaimer could be considered as equivalent to an exclusion clause. The difference between a disclaimer and an exclusion clause is that whilst the latter quite clearly purports to avoid a liability that is frankly admitted in principle, the former purports to deny that liability even arose. The Court of Appeal in *Harris v Wyre Forest DC* had concluded that the 1977 Act did not apply to the disclaimer since the effect of the disclaimer was to prevent any duty of care from arising. *Hedley Byrne & Co Ltd v Heller & Partners Ltd* admitted the possibility of disclaimers but was decided long before the 1977 Act. The Court of Appeal's approach in *Harris v Wyre Forest DC* failed to take adequate account of s 13 of the 1977 Act as the House of Lords recognised.

Were the disclaimers within the scope of the Unfair Contract Terms Act 1977?

At this point the facts of *Smith v E Bush; Harris v Wyre Forest DC* become relevant.

Smith v E Bush; Harris v Wyre Forest DC

In the first case, the plaintiff applied for a building society mortgage to buy a house. The building society instructed the defendants to inspect the house and to report on its value. The defendants' valuer noticed that two chimney breasts had been removed but failed to check whether the chimneys above had been adequately supported. The valuation report stated that no essential repairs were necessary. The building society supplied a copy of the report to the plaintiff and she relied on it and purchased the house. The chimneys were not adequately supported and one of them later collapsed.

In the second case, the plaintiffs applied to the first defendant council for a mortgage to help them in buying a house. The council then instructed the second defendant, a valuer employed by the Council, to carry out an inspection. He recommended a mortgage subject to certain minor repairs. The valuer's report was not shown to the plaintiffs but they were later offered a mortgage by the council. Three years later, a further survey on the house revealed the need for structural repairs estimated to cost thousands of pounds. The property was considered to be both uninhabitable and thus unsaleable.

On appeal by the defendants in the first case and by the plaintiffs in the second case:

Lord Templeman: In *Harris v Wyre Forest District Council* [1988] QB 835, the Court of Appeal (Kerr and Nourse LJJ and Caulfield J) accepted an argument that the Act of 1977 did not apply because the council by their express disclaimer refused to obtain a valuation save on terms that the valuer would not be under any obligation to Mr and Mrs Harris to take reasonable care or exercise reasonable skill. The council did not exclude liability for negligence but excluded negligence so that the valuer and the council never came under a duty of care to Mr and Mrs Harris and could not be guilty of negligence. This construction would not give effect to the manifest intention of the Act but would emasculate the Act. The construction would provide no control over standard form exclusion clauses which individual members of the public are obliged to accept. A party to a contract or a tortfeasor could opt out of the Act of 1977 by declining in the words of Nourse LJ, at p 845, to recognise 'their own answerability to the plaintiff'. Caulfield J said, at p 850, that the Act 'can only be relevant where there is on the facts a potential liability'. But no one intends to commit a tort and therefore any notice which excludes liability is a notice which excludes a potential liability.

Kerr LJ, at p 853, sought to confine the Act to 'situations where the existence of a duty of care is not open to doubt' or where there is 'an inescapable duty of care'. I can find nothing in the Act of 1977 or in the general law to identify or support this distinction. In the result the Court of Appeal held that the Act does not apply to 'negligent misstatements where a disclaimer has prevented a duty of care from coming into existence;' per Nourse LJ, at p 848. My Lords this confuses the valuer's report with the work which the valuer carries out in order to make his report. The valuer owed a duty to exercise reasonable skill and care in his inspection and valuation. If he had been careful in his work, he would not have made a 'negligent misstatement' in his report.

Section 11(3) of the Act of 1977 provides that in considering whether it is fair and reasonable to allow reliance on a notice which excludes liability in tort, account must be taken of: 'all the circumstances obtaining when the liability arose or (but for the notice) would have arisen.'

Section 13(1) of the Act prevents the exclusion of any right or remedy and (to that extent) section 2 also prevents the exclusion of liability: 'by reference to notices which exclude the relevant obligation or duty.'

Nourse LJ dismissed section 11(3) as 'peripheral' and made no comment on section 13(1). In my opinion both these provisions support the view that the Act of 1977 requires that all exclusion notices which would in common law provide a defence to an action for negligence must satisfy the requirement of reasonableness.

The answer to the second question involved in these appeals is that the disclaimer of liability made by the council on its own behalf in the Harris case and by the Abbey National on behalf of the appellants in the Smith case, constitute notices which fall within the Unfair Contract Terms Act 1977 and must satisfy the requirement of reasonableness.

The third question is whether in relation to each exclusion clause it is, in the words of section 11(3) of the Act of 1977:

'fair and reasonable to allow reliance on it, having regard to all the circumstances obtaining when the liability arose or (but for the notice) would have arisen.'

The liability of the council for the breach by [the surveyor] of his duty of care to Mr and Mrs Harris arose as soon as Mr and Mrs Harris, in reliance on the valuation of £8,505, bought the house for £9,000. The liability of the appellants for the breach of their duty of care to Mrs Smith in their valuation arose as soon as Mrs Smith, on reliance of the valuation of £16,500, bought the house for £18,000. The damages will include the difference between the market value of the house on the day when it was purchased and the purchase price which was in fact paid by the purchaser in reliance on the valuation.

Both the present appeals involve typical house purchases. In considering whether the exclusion clause may be relied upon in each case, the general pattern of house purchases and the extent of the work and liability accepted by the valuer must be borne in mind.

Each year one million houses may be bought and sold. Apart from exceptional cases the procedure is always the same. The vendor and the purchaser agree a price but the purchaser cannot enter into a contract unless and until a mortgagee, typically a building society, offers to advance the whole or part of the purchase price. A mortgage of 80 per cent or more of the purchase price is not unusual. Thus, if the vendor and the purchaser agree a price of £50,000 and the purchaser can find £10,000, the purchaser then applies to a building society for a loan of

£40,000. The purchaser pays the building society a valuation fee and the building society instructs a valuer who is paid by the building society. If the valuer reports to the building society that the house is good security for £40,000, the building society offers to advance £40,000 and the purchaser contracts to purchase the house for £50,000. The purchaser, who is offered £40,000 on the security of the house, rightly assumes that a qualified valuer has valued the house at not less than £40,000.

At the date when the purchaser pays the valuation fee, the date when the valuation is made and at the date when the purchaser is offered an advance, the sale may never take place. The amount offered by way of advance may not be enough, the purchaser may change his mind, or the vendor may increase his price and sell elsewhere. For many reasons a sale may go off, and in that case, the purchaser has paid his valuation fee without result and must pay a second valuation fee when he finds another house and goes through the same procedure.

The building society which is anxious to attract borrowers and the purchaser who has no money to waste on valuation fees, do not encourage or pay for detailed surveys. Moreover, the vendor may not be willing to suffer the inconvenience of a detailed survey on behalf of a purchaser who has not contracted to purchase and may exploit minor items of disrepair disclosed by a detailed survey in order to obtain a reduction in the price.

The valuer is and, in my opinion, must be a professional person, typically a chartered surveyor in general practice, who, by training and experience and exercising reasonable skill and care, will recognise defects and be able to assess value. The valuer will value the house after taking into consideration major defects which are, or ought to be obvious to him, in the course of a visual inspection of so much of the exterior and interior of the house as may be accessible to him without undue difficulty. This appears to be the position as agreed between experts in the decided cases which have been discussed in the course of the present appeal. In *Roberts v J Hampson & Co* (1988) 2 EGLR 181, Ian Kennedy J, after hearing expert evidence, came to the following conclusions concerning a valuation commissioned by the Halifax Building Society. I have no doubt the case is of general application. The judge, referring to the Halifax Building Society valuation, as described in the literature and as described by expert evidence, said, at p 185:

'It is a valuation and not a survey, but any valuation is necessarily governed by condition. The inspection is, of necessity, a limited one. Both the expert surveyors who gave evidence before me agreed that with a house of this size they would allow about half-an-hour for their inspection on site. That time does not admit of moving furniture, or of lifting carpets, especially where they are nailed down. In my judgment, it must be accepted that where a surveyor undertakes a scheme valuation it is understood that he is making a limited appraisal only. It is, however, an appraisal by a skilled professional man. It is inherent in any standard fee work that some cases will colloquially be "winners" and others "losers", from the professional man's point of view. The fact that in an individual case he may need to spend two or three times as long as he would have expected, or as the fee structure would have contemplated, is something which he must accept. His duty to take reasonable care in providing a valuation remains the root of his obligation. In an extreme case ... a surveyor might refuse to value on the agreed fee basis, though any surveyor who too often refused to take the rough with the smooth would not improve his reputation. If, in a particular case, the proper valuation of a £19,000 house needs two hours work, that is what the surveyor must devote to it. The second aspect of the problem concerns moving furniture and lifting carpets. Here again, as it seems to me, the position that the law adopts is simple. If a surveyor misses a defect because its signs are hidden, that is a risk that his client must accept. But if there is specific ground for suspicion and the trail of suspicion leads behind furniture or under carpets, the surveyor must take reasonable steps to follow the trail until he has all the information which it is reasonable for him to have before making his valuation.'

In his reference to 'a scheme valuation' the judge was alluding to the practice of charging scale fees to purchasers and paying scale fees to valuers.

The valuer will not be liable merely because his valuation may prove to be in excess of the amount which the purchaser might realise on a sale of the house. The valuer will only be liable if other qualified valuers, who cannot be expected to be harsh on their fellow professionals, consider that, taking into consideration the nature of the work for which the valuer is paid and the object of that work, nevertheless he has been guilty of an error which an average valuer, in the same circumstances, would not have made and as a result of that error, the house was worth materially less than the amount of the valuation upon which the mortgagee and the purchaser both relied. The valuer accepts the liability to the building society which can insist on the valuer accepting liability. The building society seeks to exclude the liability of the valuer to the purchaser who is not in a position to insist on anything. The duty of care which the valuer owes to the building society is exactly the same as the duty of care which he owes to the purchaser. The valuer is more willing to accept the liability to the building society than to the purchaser because it is the purchaser who is vulnerable. If the valuation is worthless the building society can still insist that the purchaser shall repay the advance and interest. So, in practice, the damages which the valuer may be called upon to pay to the building society and the chances of the valuer being expected to pay, are less than the corresponding liability to the purchaser. But this does not make it more reasonable for the valuer to be able to rely on an exclusion clause which is an example of a standard form exemption clause operating in favour of the supplier of services and against the individual consumer.

Lord Griffiths: At common law, whether the duty to exercise reasonable care and skill is founded in contract or tort, a party is as a general rule free, by the use of appropriate wording, to exclude liability for negligence in discharge of the duty. The disclaimer of liability in the present case is prominent and clearly worded and on the authority of *Hedley Byrne & Co Ltd v Heller & Partners Ltd* [1964] AC 465, in so far as the common law is concerned effective to exclude the surveyors' liability for negligence. The question then is whether the Unfair Contract Terms Act 1977 bites upon such a disclaimer. In my view it does.

The Court of Appeal, however, accepted an argument based upon the definition of negligence contained in section 1(1) of the Act of 1977 which provides:

'For the purposes of this part of this Act, 'negligence' means the breach of any obligation, arising from the express or implied terms of a contract, to take reasonable care or exercise reasonable skill in the performance of the contract; (b) of any common law duty to take reasonable care or exercise reasonable skill (but not any stricter duty); (c) of the common duty of care imposed by the Occupiers' Liability Act 1957 or the Occupiers' Liability Act (Northern Ireland) 1957.'

They held that, as the disclaimer of liability would at common law have prevented any duty to take reasonable care arising between the parties, the Act had no application. In my view this construction fails to give due weight to the provisions of two further sections of the Act. Section 11(3) provides:

'In relation to a notice (not being a notice having contractual effect), the requirement of reasonableness under this Act is that it should be fair and reasonable to allow reliance on it, having regard to all the circumstances obtaining when the liability arose or (but for the notice) would have arisen.'

And section 13(1):

'To the extent that this Part of this Act prevents the exclusion or restriction of any liability it also prevents – (a) making the liability or its enforcement subject to restrictive or onerous conditions; (b) excluding or restricting any right or remedy in respect of the liability, or subjecting a person to any prejudice in consequence of his pursuing any such right or remedy; (c) excluding or restricting rules of evidence or procedure; and (to that extent) sections 2 and 5 to 7 also prevent excluding or restricting liability by reference to terms and notices which exclude or restrict the relevant obligation or duty.'

I read these provisions as introducing a 'but for' test in relation to the notice excluding liability. They indicate that the existence of the common law duty to take reasonable care, referred to in section 1(1)(b), is to be judged by considering whether it would exist 'but for' the notice excluding liability. The result of taking the notice into account when assessing the existence of a duty of care would result in removing all liability for negligent mis-statements from the protection of the Act. It is permissible to have regard to the second report of the Law Commission on Exemption Clauses (1975) (Law Com No 69) which is the genesis of the Unfair Contract Terms Act 1977 as an aid to construction of the Act. Paragraph 127 of that report reads:

'Our recommendations in this part of the report are intended to apply to exclusions of liability for negligence where the liability is incurred in the course of a person's business. We consider that they should apply even in cases where the person seeking to rely on the exemption clause was under no legal obligation (such as a contractual obligation) to carry out the activity. This means that, for example, conditions attached to a licence to enter on to land, and disclaimers of liability made where information or advice is given, should be subject to control ...'

I have no reason to think that Parliament did not intend to follow this advice and the wording of the Act is, in my opinion, apt to give effect to that intention. This view of the construction of the Act is also supported by the judgment of Slade LJ in *Phillips Products Ltd v Hyland (Note)* [1987] 1 WLR 659, when he rejected a similar argument in relation to the construction of a contractual term excluding negligence.

Were the disclaimers of responsibility 'reasonable' within s 11 of the 1977 Act?

Section 11(5) Unfair Contract Terms Act 1977, places the burden of proving 'reasonableness' on the party seeking to rely on a disclaimer or exclusion clause ie on the surveyor. In the cases of *Smith v E Bush* and *Harris v Wyre Forest DC* (above) the House of Lords ruled against the surveyor, principally because the houses were at the bottom end of the property market and because the surveyor could obtain liability insurance comparatively easily. The conclusion reached by the House of Lords on the question of 'reasonableness' was specifically confined to ordinary residential houses. Lord Griffiths, for example, stated that he would not commit himself in the case of more unusual property; and, in particular, the very expensive house, where different considerations might apply.

Smith v E Bush

Lord Griffiths: Finally, the question is whether the exclusion of liability contained in the disclaimer satisfies the requirement of reasonableness provided by section 2(2) of the Act of 1977. The meaning of reasonableness and the burden of proof are both dealt with in section 11(3) which provides:

'In relation to a notice (not being a notice having contractual effect), the requirement of reasonableness under this Act is that it should be fair and reasonable to allow reliance on it, having regard to all the circumstances obtaining when the liability arose or (but for the notice) would have arisen.'

It is clear, then, that the burden is upon the surveyor to establish that in all the circumstances it is fair and reasonable that he should be allowed to rely upon his disclaimer of liability.

I believe that it is impossible to draw up an exhaustive list of the factors that must be taken into account when a judge is faced with this very difficult decision. Nevertheless, the following matters should, in my view, always be considered.

(1) Were the parties of equal bargaining power? If the court is dealing with a one-off situation between parties of equal bargaining power the requirement of reasonableness would be more easily discharged than in a case such as the present where the disclaimer is imposed upon the purchaser who has no effective power to object.

(2) In the case of advice would it have been reasonably practicable to obtain the advice from an alternative source taking into account considerations of costs and time. In the present case it is urged on behalf of the surveyor that it would have been easy for the purchaser to have obtained his own report on the condition of the house, to which the purchaser replies, that he would then be required to pay twice for the same advice and that people buying at the bottom end of the market, many of whom will be young first-time buyers, are likely to be under considerable financial pressure without the money to go paying twice for the same service.

(3) How difficult is the task being undertaken for which liability is being excluded. When a very difficult or dangerous undertaking is involved there may be a high risk of failure which would certainly be a pointer towards the reasonableness of excluding liability as a condition of doing the work. A valuation, on the other hand, should present no difficulty if the work is undertaken with reasonable skill and care. It is only defects which are observable by a careful visual examination that have to be taken into account and I cannot see that it places any unreasonable burden on the valuer to require him to accept responsibility for the fairly elementary degree of skill and care involved in observing, following-up and reporting on such defects. Surely it is work at the lower end of the surveyor's field of professional expertise.

(4) What are the practical consequences of the decision on the question of reasonableness. This must involve the sums of money potentially at stake and the ability of the parties to bear the loss involved, which, in its turn,

raises the question of insurance. There was once a time when it was considered improper even to mention the possible existence of insurance cover in a lawsuit. But those days are long past. Everyone knows that all prudent, professional men carry insurance, and the availability and cost of insurance must be a relevant factor when considering which of two parties should be required to bear the risk of a loss. We are dealing in this case with a loss which will be limited to the value of a modest house and against which it can be expected that the surveyor will be insured. Bearing the loss will be unlikely to cause significant hardship if it has to be borne by the surveyor but it is, on the other hand, quite possible that it will be a financial catastrophe for the purchaser who may be left with a valueless house and no money to buy another. If the law in these circumstances denies the surveyor the right to exclude his liability, it may result in a few more claims but I do not think so poorly of the surveyor's profession as to believe that the floodgates will be opened. There may be some increase in surveyors' insurance premiums which will be passed on to the public, but I cannot think that it will be anything approaching the figures involved in the difference between the Abbey National's offer of a valuation without liability and a valuation with liability discussed in the speech of my noble and learned friend, Lord Templeman. The result of denying a surveyor, in the circumstances of this case, the right to exclude liability, will result in distributing the risk of his negligence among all house purchasers through an increase in his fees to cover insurance, rather than allowing the whole of the risk to fall upon the one unfortunate purchaser.

I would not, however, wish it to be thought that I would consider it unreasonable for professional men in all circumstances to seek to exclude or limit their liability for negligence. Sometimes breathtaking sums of money may turn on professional advice against which it would be impossible for the adviser to obtain adequate insurance cover and which would ruin him if he were to be held personally liable. In these circumstances it may indeed be reasonable to give the advice upon a basis of no liability or possibly of liability limited to the extent of the adviser's insurance cover.

It must, however, be remembered that this is a decision in respect of a dwelling-house of modest value in which it is widely recognised by surveyors that purchasers are in fact relying on their care and skill. It will obviously be of general application in broadly similar circumstances. But I expressly reserve my position in respect of valuations of quite different types of property for mortgage purposes, such as industrial property, large blocks of flats or very expensive houses. In such cases it may well be that the general expectation of the behaviour of the purchaser is quite different. With very large sums of money at stake prudence would seem to demand that the purchaser obtain his own structural survey to guide him in his purchase and, in such circumstances with very much larger sums of money at stake, it may be reasonable for the surveyors valuing on behalf of those who are providing the finance either to exclude or limit their liability to the purchaser.

Lord Templeman: Mr Hague, who has great experience in this field, urged on behalf of valuers generally, that it is fair and reasonable for a valuer to rely on an exclusion clause particularly an exclusion clause which is set forth so plainly in building society literature. The principal reasons urged by Mr Hague are as follows:

(1) The exclusion clause is clear and understandable and reiterated and is forcefully drawn to the attention of the purchaser.

(2) The purchaser's solicitors should reinforce the warning and should urge the purchaser to appreciate that he cannot rely on a mortgage valuation and should obtain and pay for his own survey.

(3) If valuers cannot disclaim liability they will be faced by more claims from purchasers some of which will be unmeritorious but difficult and expensive to resist.

(4) A valuer will become more cautious, take more time and produce more gloomy reports which will make house transactions more difficult.

(5) If a duty of care cannot be disclaimed the cost of negligence insurance for valuers and therefore the cost of valuation fees to the public will be increased.

Mr Hague also submitted that there was no contract between a valuer and a purchaser and that, so far as the purchaser was concerned, the valuation was 'gratuitous', and the valuer should not be forced to accept a liability he was unwilling to undertake. My Lords, all these submissions are, in my view, inconsistent with the ambit and thrust of the Act of 1977. The valuer is a professional man who offers his services for reward. He is paid for those services. The valuer knows that 90 per cent of purchasers in fact rely on a mortgage valuation and do not commission their own survey. There is great pressure on a purchaser to rely on the mortgage valuation. Many purchasers cannot afford a second valuation. If a purchaser obtains a second valuation the sale may go off and then both valuation fees will be wasted. Moreover, he knows that mortgagees, such as building societies and the council, in the present case, are trustworthy and that they appoint careful and competent valuers and he trusts the professional man so appointed. Finally, the valuer knows full well that failure on his part to exercise reasonable skill and care may be disastrous to the purchaser. If, in reliance on a valuation, the purchaser contracts to buy for £50,000 a house valued and mortgaged for £40,000 but, in fact worth nothing and needing thousands more to be spent on it, the purchaser stands to lose his home and to remain in debt to the building society for up to £40,000.

In *Yianni v Edwin Evans & Sons* [1982] QB 438, Mr and Mrs Yianni decided that if the Halifax Building Society would agree to advance £12,000, they would buy a house for £15,000, otherwise they would let the house go as they had no money apart from £3,000. The house was valued by a valuer on behalf of the Halifax at £12,000, an advance of this amount was offered and accepted and the house was bought and mortgaged. Mr and Mrs Yianni then discovered that the house needed repairs amounting to £18,000. Park J, at p 445, found on evidence largely derived from the chief surveyor to the Abbey National, that the proportion of purchasers who have an independent survey is less than 15 per cent; that purchasers rely on the building society valuation; purchasers trust the building societies; each purchaser knows that he has paid a fee for someone on behalf of the society to look at the house:

'the intending mortgagor feels that the building society, whom he trusts, must employ for the valuation and survey competent qualified surveyors; and, if the building society acts upon its surveyor's report, then there can be no good reason why he should not also himself act upon it. The consequence is that if, after inspection by the building society's surveyor, an offer to make an advance is made, the applicant assumes that the building society has satisfied itself that the house is valuable enough to provide suitable security for a loan and decides to proceed by accepting the society's offer. So, if Mr Yianni had had an independent survey, he would have been exceptional in the experience of the building societies and of those employed to carry out surveys and valuations for them.'

Park J, following the *Hedley Byrne* case [1964] AC 465, concluded at pp 454–455, that a duty of care by the valuers to Mr and Mrs Yianni would arise if the valuers knew that their valuation:

'in so far as it stated that the property provided adequate security for an advance of £12,000, would be passed on to the plaintiffs, who, notwithstanding the building society's literature and the service of the notice under section 30 of the Building Societies Act 1962, in the defendants' reasonable contemplation would place reliance upon its correctness in making their decision to buy the house and mortgage it to the building society ... These defendants are surveyors and valuers. It is their profession and occupation to survey and make valuations of houses and other property. They make reports about the condition of property they have surveyed. Their duty is not merely to use care in their reports, they have also a duty to use care in their work which results in their reports ... Accordingly, the building society's offer of £12,000, when passed on to the plaintiffs, confirmed to them that 1, Seymour Road was sufficiently valuable to cause the building society to advance on its security 80 per cent. of the purchase price. Since that was also the building society's view the plaintiffs' belief was not unreasonable.'

In *Yianni's* case [1982] QB 438, there was no exclusion of liability on behalf of the valuer. The evidence and the findings of Park J, which I have set out, support the view that it is unfair and unreasonable for a valuer to rely on an exclusion clause directed against a purchaser in the circumstances of the present appeals.

Mr Hague referred to a new Abbey National proposal resulting from a consideration of *Yianni's* case. The purchaser is offered the choice between a valuation without liability on the valuer and a report which, as Mr Hague agreed, did not involve any more work for the valuer but accepted that the valuer was under a duty to exercise reasonable skill and care. The fee charged for the report as compared with the fee charged for the valuation represents an increase of £100 for a house worth £20,000, and £150 for a house worth £100,000, and £200 for a house worth £200,000. On a million houses, this would represent increases of income to be divided between valuers, insurers and building societies, of about £150m. It is hardly surprising that few purchasers have chosen the report instead of the valuation. Any increase in fees, alleged to be justified by the decision of this House in these appeals, will no doubt be monitored by the appropriate authorities.

It is open to Parliament to provide that members of all professions or members of one profession providing services in the normal course of the exercise of their profession for reward shall be entitled to exclude or limit their liability for failure to exercise reasonable skill and care. In the absence of any such provision valuers are not, in my opinion, entitled to rely on a general exclusion of the common law duty of care owed to purchasers of houses by valuers to exercise reasonable skill and care in valuing houses for mortgage purposes.

In the Green Paper 'Conveyancing by Authorised Practitioners' see Cm 572, the Government propose to allow building societies, banks and other authorised practitioners to provide conveyancing services to the public by employed professional lawyers. The Green Paper includes the following relevant passages:

'3.10 There will inevitably be claims of financial loss arising out of the provision of conveyancing services. A bad mistake can result in a purchaser acquiring a property which is worth considerably less than he paid for it because, for example, the conveyancer overlooked a restriction on use or the planning of a new motorway. The practitioner will be required to have adequate professional indemnity insurance or other appropriate arrangements to meet such claims.'

Annex, paragraph 12: 'An authorised practitioner must not contractually limit its liability for damage suffered by the client as a result of negligence on its part.'

The government thus recognises the need to preserve the duty of a professional lawyer to exercise reasonable skill and care so that the purchaser of a house may not be disastrously affected by a defect of title or an encumbrance. In the same way, it seems to me there is need to preserve the duty of a professional valuer to exercise reasonable skill and care so that a purchaser of a house may not be disastrously affected by a defect in the structure of the house.

The public are exhorted to purchase their homes and cannot find houses to rent. A typical London suburban house, constructed in the 1930s for less than £1,000 is now bought for more than £150,000 with money largely borrowed at high rates of interest and repayable over a period of a quarter of a century. In these circumstances it is not fair and reasonable for building societies and valuers to agree together to impose on purchasers the risk of loss arising as a result of incompetence or carelessness on the part of valuers. I agree with the speech of my noble and learned friend, Lord Griffiths, and with his warning that different considerations may apply where homes are not concerned.

In the instant case of *Harris v Wyre Forest District Council*, I would allow the appeal of Mr and Mrs Harris, restore the order of the trial judge and order the costs of Mr and Mrs Harris to be borne by the council. In the case of *Smith v Eric S. Bush*, I would dismiss the appeal with costs.

It is clear from *Smith v E Bush* and *Harris v Wyre Forest DC* that the surveyor will not normally escape liability by relying on a disclaimer of responsibility. The only other option open to him is to ensure that he is not negligent in conducting the valuation, which begs the question of what his duty of care to the mortgagor involves. A surveyor is, in general terms, expected to carry out his task with the reasonable care and skill to be expected of a person in his profession. Translating this general duty into more concrete terms, however, is another matter. This point was not in issue in *Yianni's* case, where negligence was not disputed, but was relevant in the case of *Roberts v J Hampson & Co* [1989] 2 All ER 504, a case stated to be 'of general application' in *Smith v E Bush* (see Lord Templeman's speech in *Smith v E Bush*).

Surveyors complain that this imposes upon them a duty which they do not have time to do, namely to move furniture or to lift carpets, some of which will have been professionally laid; vendors are not particularly happy to have their carpets pulled up, and surveyors risk embarrassment if they have to do this in front of the vendor. The decision in *Roberts v J Hampson & Co*, however, makes it clear that a surveyor is only expected to lift carpets and move furniture if there are grounds for doing so ie because of a reasonable suspicion of more extensive problems. The standard of care required of surveyors is therefore not particularly burdensome.

A comprehensive list of 'dos and don'ts' for the surveyor's benefit is impossible to compile, but the cases mentioned earlier have been helpful to some degree in suggesting certain things which a surveyor is expected to do. It may be sufficient, however, if the surveyor, on suspecting that a particular problem exists, advises on insurance cover against that problem (see *Eley v King & Chasemore* [1989] NLJ 791).

Does it make any difference as to the existence and extent of the surveyor's duty if the case against him is pleaded in contract rather than in the tort of negligence? The answer to this question must be 'no', since the surveyor is placed under a duty of reasonable care and skill as an implied term of his contract by virtue of s 13 Supply of Goods and Services Act 1982. This duty requires the same standard of professionalism as does the common law duty of care in negligence, which gives the purchaser the option of suing the surveyor with whom he has contracted either in contract or in the tort of negligence (such concurrent liability was recognised in a different context in *Midland Bank Trust Co Ltd v Hett, Stubbs & Kemp (a firm)* [1979] Ch 384).

Recent regulations have made it more difficult for surveyors to rely on contractual terms in their favour as against the 'consumer' who uses the services of the surveyor. The Unfair Terms in Consumer Contracts Regulations 1994 (SI 1994/3159), which came into force on 1 July 1995, will affect the law relating to surveyors in that the regulations apply to non-individually negotiated terms in a contract for the supply of a service between a 'consumer' and a supplier of that service.

Under reg 5(1), an 'unfair term' as defined in reg 4(1) (requiring 'good faith') will not be binding on a consumer, although the remaining part of the contract will survive 'if it is capable of continuing in existence without the unfair term' (see reg 5(2)). Where a consumer obtains a private survey, the Regulations will therefore apply to terms in the contract which were not individually negotiated. Where, however, the prospective mortgagor relies exclusively on a valuation carried out on behalf of the prospective mortgagee, negligence liability will continue to be the main source of liability as between the surveyor and the prospective mortgagor. At the same time, however, there will be a contract between the prospective mortgagee and the prospective mortgagor by which the former provides the latter with a service, namely, the valuation of the property through an independent surveyor. This contract could itself be affected by the Regulations, although the Regulations are more likely to have a significant impact in practice on the subsequent loan agreement and the mortgage charge between the mortgagee and mortgagor (see Chapter 13).

THE MEASURE OF DAMAGES

Cost of cure versus difference in value

Given that a surveyor may be held liable towards a mortgagor for negligence, an important question has to be 'What is the measure of damages that the surveyor has to pay?'

There are at least two possible approaches to this question. One is to take the difference between the value of the house as given in the surveyor's report and its value if the condition had been accurately reported on at the time of the valuation ('difference in value'); the other is to award to the plaintiff the amount which it would cost to have the repairs carried out ('cost of cure'). The latter, however, is often a much higher figure than the former, although carrying out the necessary work may add comparatively little to the overall value of the house. The question of the appropriate basis of damages in a contractual action against a surveyor has now been resolved; but there would seem to be no difference in principle on this issue between a contractually based action against a surveyor and one framed in the tort of negligence.

In *Perry v Sidney Phillips & Son (a firm)* [1982] 1 WLR 1297; [1982] 3 All ER 705, the Court of Appeal overruled the judge at first instance, who had awarded damages based on the cost of repairs, and substituted the 'difference in value' figure; but in that case, the plaintiff had sold the house (for which he had paid £27,000) for £43,000 before the appeal had been heard. This left in some doubt what the decision would have been had the plaintiff retained the house and wished to carry out the remedial work, but the Court of Appeal hinted that the 'difference in value' would be the normal basis of an award of damages against a surveyor.

The doubts arising from the hints of the Court of Appeal have now been resolved in *Watts & another v Morrow* [1991] 4 All ER 937. In that case, the Court of Appeal decided that a surveyor would only be liable for the lower 'difference in value' amount, and not the cost of cure, if the contract of survey was an ordinary one which contained no special terms. However, this does leave open the possibility that a different basis of award might apply if the contract in question contained 'special' terms, though precisely which special terms might have this effect is left unstated.

Watts and another v Morrow

The plaintiffs purchased a house in reliance on a survey prepared by the defendant. The plaintiffs later discovered substantial defects which had not been mentioned in the defendant's report. The plaintiffs carried our repairs to remedy the defects. The plaintiffs then brought an action claiming the cost of these repairs.

Ralph Gibson LJ: *The contest on the main issue: diminution in value or cost of repairs?*

> Before describing the submissions which have been made on this appeal it is necessary to refer to the decisions of this court in *Philips v Ward* [1956] 1 All ER 874, [1956] 1 WLR 471 and *Perry v Sidney Phillips & Son (a firm)* [1982] 3 All ER 705, [1982] 1 WLR 1297, to which detailed reference has been made in the submissions of counsel. In *Philips v Ward* the plaintiff, in reliance upon a negligent report by a surveyor, purchased in June 1952 for £25,000 an Elizabethan manor house farm consisting of a house, two cottages and some land. The surveyor failed to report that the timbers of the house were badly affected by death watch beetle and worm so that the only course was to replace the roof by a new roof and to rebuild the timbers etc. The market value of the property in its actual condition was £21,000. After moving into the house with his family the plaintiff found that it would require an additional expenditure of £7,000 at 1952 prices to put the property into the condition in which it had been described in the report. The plaintiff claimed, among other heads of claim, the cost of repairs ruling at the date of trial. The official referee awarded £4,000, namely the difference between the value of the property as it should have been described and its value as described. This court (Denning, Morris and Romer LJJ) held that the proper measure of damages was the difference in money between

the value of the property in the condition described and its value as it should have been described, namely £4,000. It is necessary to set out some passages in the judgments. It has been common ground on this appeal that the diminution in value rule is more accurately to be expressed as the difference between the price paid and the value in its true description, at least where no point is taken, as in this case, that the plaintiff chose to pay above market value.

Denning LJ (as he then was) said ([1956] 1 All ER 874 at 875-876, [1956] 1 WLR 471 at 473):

'I take it to be clear law that the proper measure of damage is the amount of money which will put the plaintiff into as good a position as if the surveying contract had been properly fulfilled (see *British Westinghouse Electric & Manufacturing Co Ltd v Underground Electric Rys Co of London Ltd* [1912] AC 673 at 689, [1911-13] All ER Rep 63 at 69 *per* Viscount Haldane LC). Now if the [surveyor] had carried out his contract, he would have reported the bad state of the timbers. On receiving that report, the plaintiff either would have refused to have anything to do with the house, in which case he would have suffered no damage, or he would have bought it for a sum which represented its fair value in its bad condition, in which case he would pay so much less on that account. The proper measure of damages is therefore the difference between the value in its assumed good condition and the value in the bad condition which should have been reported to the client. We were referred to the cases where a house is damaged or destroyed by the fault of a tortfeasor. These cases are, I think, different. If the injured person reasonably goes to the expense of repairing the house, the tortfeasor may well be bound to pay the cost of repair, less an allowance because new work takes the place of old: see *Lukin v Godsall* ((1795) Peake Add Cas 15, 170 ER 178); *Hide v Thornborough* ((1846) 2 Car&Kir 250, 175 ER 103). In other cases, the tortfeasor may only have to pay the value of the house: see *Moss v Christchurch Rural District Council* ([1925] 2 KB 750). It all depends on the circumstances of the case: see *Murphy v Wexford County Council* ([1925] 2 IR 230). The general rule is that the injured person is to be fairly compensated for the damage he has sustained, neither more nor less'.

Later in his judgment Denning LJ said ([1956] 1 All ER 874 at 876, [1956] 1 WLR 471 at 474):

'So also in this action, if the plaintiff were to recover from the surveyor £7,000, it would mean that the plaintiff would get for £18,000 (£25,000 paid less £7,000 received) a house and land which were worth £21,000. That cannot be right. The proper amount for him to recover is £4,000.'

Morris LJ said ([1956] 1 All ER 874 at 878, [1956] 1 WLR 471 at 475-476):

'In my judgment, the damages to be assessed were such as could fairly and reasonably be considered as resulting naturally from the failure of the defendant to report as he should have done ... It is said, however, that [the official referee] was not warranted in proceeding on the basis ... of the difference between the value of the property as it was described in the defendant's report and its value as it should have been described. In my view, however, that was the correct basis on the facts of this case.'

Romer LJ, after giving the same reasons for holding that the diminution in value was the correct measure of damages, said ([1956] 1 All ER 874 at 879, [1956] 1 WLR 471 at 478):

'It may well be that if, on learning of the real condition of the house, he had decided to leave and re-sell, he would have been entitled to recover from the defendant in addition to the £4,000, his costs and expenses of moving in and moving out and of the re-sale. As, however, he elected to stay, after all the facts had become known to him, this point does not arise.'

In *Perry v Sidney Phillips & Son (a firm)* [1982] 3 All ER 705, [1982] 1 WLR 1297 the surveyor failed to observe serious defects, including a leaking roof and a septic tank with an offensive smell. The plaintiff could not afford major repairs and executed only minor repairs himself. At the date of the trial the plaintiff was still occupying the house as his home. The judge awarded damages assessed in respect of repairing the defects as at the date of trial in 1981. Between the date of the trial and the hearing of the appeal the plaintiff sold the property for £43,000. He had paid £27,000 in 1976 in reliance upon the negligent report. It was acknowledged by the plaintiff that the sale of the house without repairs having been executed made it difficult to support the award based upon the cost of repairs and his contention was that damages should be assessed on the basis of the difference in market value of the property as between its value taking into account the defects for which the judge found liability established and its value in the condition the defendants reported it to be either on the basis of values at the date of the report or at the date of judgment.

Lord Denning MR, after reference to the measure of damages for breach of contract to build a house, or to do repairs to it, or in respect of damage done to it (see *Dodd Properties (Kent) Ltd v Canterbury City Council* [1980] 1 All ER 928, [1981] 1 WLR 433), continued ([1982] 3 All ER 705 at 708, [1982] 1 WLR 1297 at 1301):

' ... where there is a contract by a prospective buyer with a surveyor under which the surveyor agrees to survey a house and make a report on it, and he makes it negligently and the client buys the house on the faith of the report, then the damages are to be assessed at the time of the breach, according to the difference in price which the buyer would have given if the report had been carefully made from that which he in fact gave owing to the negligence of the surveyor. The surveyor gives no warranty that there are no defects other than those in his report. There is no question of specific performance. The contract has already been performed, albeit negligently. The buyer is not entitled to remedy the defects and charge the cost to the surveyor. He is only entitled to damages for the breach of contract or for negligence. That was so decided by this court in *Philips v Ward* [1956] 1 All ER 874, [1956] 1 WLR 471, followed in *Simple Simon Catering Ltd v Binstock Miller & Co* (1973) 228 EG 527.'

Oliver LJ said ([1982] 3 All ER 705 at 710, [1982] 1 WLR 1297 at 1304):

'The position, as I see it, is simply this, that the plaintiff has been misled by a negligent survey report into paying more for the property than that property was actually worth. The position, as I see it, is exactly the same as that which arose in *Philips v Ward* ... and in the subsequent case of *Ford v White & Co* [1964] 2 All ER 755, [1964] 1 WLR 885 ... I see nothing ... which justifies the proposition ... that damages are to be assessed on the basis of some hypothetical value at the date of the trial because the plaintiff has chosen, as he did in this case, to retain the property and not to cut his loss by reselling it. The right measure of damage is the measure suggested in both *Philips v Ward* and *Ford v White & Co*, which is simply the difference between what the plaintiff paid for the property and its value at the date when he obtained it.'

Kerr LJ reserved his view as to whether in a case like this the approach by way of cost of repairs is necessarily right since the point had not been argued.

Mr Jackson QC, in support of the contention that the judge was wrong in law in failing to apply the diminution in value rule, submitted that this case on the facts cannot be validly distinguished from, and should therefore be decided in accordance with, the decision of this court in *Philips v Ward* by awarding no more than the sum of £15,000, together with interest. *Philips v Ward* was, he submitted, a decision in which, upon analysis of the ordinary relationship between the purchaser of a dwelling-house and the surveyor advising him as to the condition of that house, this court was applying, and not failing to apply, what has been called the 'overriding rule' of restitution in relation to damages, that is as stated by Lord Blackburn in *Livingstone v Rawyards Coal Co* (1880) 5 App Cas 25, or as stated by Lord Haldane LC in the *British Westinghouse Electric Co Ltd* case [1912] AC 673, [1911–13] All ER Rep 63, to which Denning LJ referred to in his judgment in *Philips v Ward*. That was recognised by this court in the *County Personnel* case [1987] 1 All ER 289 at 297, [1987] 1 WLR 916 at 925, where, in a passage cited by Judge Bowsher in his judgment in this case, Bingham LJ said, after reference to the overriding rule of restitution:

> 'on the authorities as they stand the diminution in value rule appears almost always, if not always, to be appropriate where property is acquired following negligent advice by surveyors. Such cases as *Philips v Ward* [1956] 1 All ER 874, [1956] 1 WLR 471, *Pilkington v Wood* [1953] 2 All ER 810, [1953] Ch 770, *Ford v White & Co* [1964] 2 All ER 755, [1964] 1 WLR 885 and *Perry v Sidney Philips & Son (a firm)* [1982] 3 All ER 705, [1982] 1 WLR 1297 lay down that rule ... '

In commenting upon the judge's findings of fact with reference to the plaintiffs' decision not to resell but to carry our repairs Mr Jackson submitted that, since on the plaintiff's expert evidence the value of the house in its true condition in August 1987 was £185,000 (£7,500 more than the plaintiffs had paid in April 1987), the plaintiffs could have sold, have paid the sums wasted on fees etc and have been in the same financial position in August 1987 as immediately before exchange of contracts. This point was made, as I understood the argument, not in order to justify application of the diminution in value rule (which was submitted to be correctly applied irrespective of the financial consequences on resale), nor to criticise the finding that it was reasonable for the plaintiffs not to resell (it was conceded that it was reasonable if the plaintiffs wished so to act for their own purpose), but to demonstrate the consequences of the application of the rule to either course of conduct which the plaintiffs might have chosen to follow.

Mr Jackson drew to the court's attention a large number of cases decided since *Philips v Ward* in which the diminution in value rule had been applied. He submitted that in those cases where the diminution in value rule had not been applied, and where there was no justification on the facts for not applying it, the decisions were wrong, including, in his submission, *Hipkins v Jack Cotton Partnership* [1989] 1 EGLR 157 (Scott Baker J) and *Syrett v Carr & Neave* [1990] 2 EGLR 161 (Judge Bowsher).

For the plaintiffs Mr Naughton QC submitted that the judge was right in his conclusion for the reasons given by him. The judge had correctly applied the overriding rule of restitution. This court, it was said, in *Philips v Ward* [1956] 1 All ER 874, [1956] 1 WLR 471 had not laid down any particular rule which the judge was required to follow so as to prevent application of that overriding rule: he referred to *Admiralty Comrs v Chekiang (owners)* [1926] AC 637, [1926] All ER Rep 114 and to *Admiralty Comrs v Susquehanna (owners), The Susquehanna* [1926] AC 255, [1926] All ER Rep 124 for support for the proposition that a rule cannot be laid down which will apply to the measure of damages in cases of a particular category if application of the rule in a particular case in that category will result in departing from the rule of restitution.

The substance of Mr Naughton's submission on the facts of this case was: the plaintiffs had bought the house in reliance upon the report of the defendant as to its condition; the house was not in the condition described; in consequence the plaintiffs spent £33,961 to put the house in the condition in which, on reading the defendant's report, they believed the house to be; and, therefore, if the damages be limited to £15,000, in accordance with the diminution in value rule, the overriding rule of restitution is not satisfied.

Mr Naughton was willing to concede that the principle in *Philips v Ward*, in so far as it can be regarded as a *prima facie* rule for the measure of damages in a claim against a negligent surveyor, is applicable in, but, he said, only in, a case where it is clear that the plaintiffs would have bought the house anyway, ie even if it had been accurately described by the surveyor. He referred to and relied upon *Hayes v James & Charles Dodd (a firm)* [1990] 2 All ER 815, a case of negligent advice by solicitors as to the existence of a necessary right of way for the use of land for a motor repair business by the clients who bought that land. Properly advised, the clients would not have bought the premises. Staughton LJ referred to such a case as a 'no-transaction' case and contrasted it with a case where the claimant would still have bought the property if he had been correctly advised as to its condition, which he referred to as a 'successful-transaction' case (at 818–819). In that case, the plaintiffs recovered damages on the basis that it was a 'no-transaction' case and damages were awarded in the amount of the capital expenditure thrown away in the purchase of the business and the expenses incurred in extricating themselves from the purchase. He relied also on *Steward v Rapley* [1989] 1 EGLR 159, where, he submitted, in a claim against a negligent surveyor, Staughton LJ again held that in a 'no-transaction' case the cost of repairs, as contrasted with the diminution in value, may be the appropriate measure of damage.

Mr Naughton made detailed submissions designed to show that, if these plaintiffs, on discovering the defects missed by the defendant, had decided to sell the house, the damages which they would have suffered, and which would have been recoverable from the defendant, would have been substantial and probably greater than the £33,961, the cost of repairs. In outline, those damages, it was said, would have included at least £8,733 for agent's commission and solicitor's fees on resale, removal costs, solicitor's fees and stamp duty on a replacement purchase, the loss on resale, which would have been £17,250, the costs of seeking an alternative property, the increase in cost of the replacement house in the sum of at least £25,800, being 15% on £172,000, and the wasted cost of borrowing the purchase price of the house which Mr Naughton put at £1,000 per month from completion in April 1987 until resale at earliest some months after August 1987, when Mr Wadey's report was received. The points made by reference to these potential losses on resale were, as I understood the argument, primarily intended to answer the submission made by Mr Jackson and then to show, firstly, that the award of the cost of repairs at £33,900 is thus shown to be moderate and not excessive, secondly, that the nature and extent of such damages upon resale had been left out of account in the reasons given by the members of this court in *Philips v Ward* [1956] 1 All ER 874, [1956] 1 WLR 471 and, thirdly, by demonstrating the unreality of any suggestion that the plaintiffs could sensibly have chosen to sell the house instead of deciding to repair it, to make good the judge's ruling that the plaintiffs are entitled to recover the cost of repairs because, as in *Syrett's* case, the plaintiffs had had no real opportunity of cutting their losses by reselling.

I have given no more than a brief summary of Mr Naughton's argument, in which he referred to a number of cases and to the comments made in textbooks.

The argument followed the reasoning in Judge Bowsher's judgment in *Syrett's* case and the suggestion made in Dugdale and Stanton *Professional Negligence* (2nd edn, 1989) para 20.34, where it was submitted that if, being correctly advised, the plaintiff would have withdrawn the natural measure of his loss is to indemnify him against the loss incurred as a result of acquiring the property that the correct measure of damage, despite the decision in *Philips v Ward*, is the cost of repair provided that it is 'reasonable for him to retain the property and incur the cost of repairs', and that such an award does not 'amount to a surveyor warranting the quality of the building, it merely reflects the losses which the plaintiff incurs and needs to be indemnified against'.

The reasoning of Judge Bowsher in *Syrett's* case, and the argument based upon the alleged potential unfairness of the application of the diminution in value rule, particularly in cases of the purchase of dwelling-houses by purchasers of limited means, makes it necessary to try to test the ruling in *Philips v Ward* by reference to basic principles in a variety of possible situations. In the end, I have reached the conclusion that the defendant is right in his contentions on this issue and that, on the facts of this case, the financial loss of the plaintiffs is in law limited to the diminution in value of £15,000 with interest thereon. My reasons are as follows.

The task of the court is to award to the plaintiffs that sum of money which will so far as possible, put the plaintiff into as good a position as if the contract for the survey had been properly fulfilled: see Denning LJ in *Philips v Ward* [1956] 1 All ER 874 at 875, [1956] 1 WLR 471 at 473. It is important to note that the contract in this case, as in *Philips v Ward*, was the usual contract for the survey of a house for occupation with no special terms beyond the undertaking of the surveyor to use proper care and skill in reporting the condition of the house.

The decision in *Philips v Ward* was based upon that principle; in particular, if the contract had been properly performed the plaintiff either would not have bought, in which case he would have avoided any loss, or, after negotiation, he would have paid the reduced price. In the absence of evidence to show that any other or additional recoverable benefit would have been obtained as a result of proper performance, the price will be taken to have been reduced to the market price of the house in its true condition because it cannot be assumed that the vendor would have taken less.

The cost of doing repairs to put right defects negligently not reported may be relevant to the proof of the market price of the house in its true condition: see *Steward v Rapley* [1989] 1 EGLR 159; and the cost of doing repairs and the diminution in value may be shown to be the same. If, however, the cost of repairs would exceed the diminution in value, then the ruling in *Philips v Ward*, where it is applicable, prohibits recovery of the excess because it would give to the plaintiff more than his loss. It would put the plaintiff in the position of recovering damages for breach of a warranty that the condition of the house was correctly described by the surveyor and, in the ordinary case, as here, no such warranty has been given.

It is clear, and it was not argued to the contrary, that the ruling in *Philips v Ward* may be applicable to the case where the buyer has, after purchase, extricated himself from the transaction by selling the property. In the absence of any point on mitigation, the buyer will recover the diminution in value together with costs and expenses thrown away in moving in and out and of resale: see Romer LJ in *Philips v Ward* [1956] 1 All ER 874 at 879, [1956] 1 WLR 471 at 478. I will not here try to state the nature or extent of any additional recoverable items of damage.

The damages recoverable where the plaintiff extricates himself from the transaction by resale are not necessarily limited to the diminution in value plus expenses. The consequences of the negligent advice and of the plaintiff entering into the transaction into which he would not have entered if properly advised may be such that the diminution in value rule is not applicable. An example is *County Personnel (Employment Agency) Ltd v Alan R Pulver & Co (a firm)* [1987] 1 All ER 289, [1987] 1 WLR 916, a case of solicitors' negligence, where the plaintiff recovered the capital losses caused by entering into the transaction.

It is also clear, and again there was no argument for the plaintiffs to the contrary, that, if the plaintiff would have bought the house anyway, if correctly advised, the ruling in *Philips v Ward* is applicable: the fact that after purchase he discovers that the unreported defects will cost more than the diminution in value does not entitle him to recover the excess. That is, again, because, if the contract had been performed properly, he would have negotiated and, absent proof of a different outcome, would have done no better than reduction to the market value in true condition.

It was rightly acknowledged for the plaintiffs that proof that the plaintiff, properly advised, would not have bought the property does not by itself cause the diminution in value rule to be inapplicable. It was contended, however, that it becomes inapplicable if it is also proved that it is reasonable for the plaintiff to retain the property and to do the repairs. I cannot accept that submission for the following reasons.

(i) The fact that it is reasonable for the plaintiff to retain the property and to do the repairs seems to me to be irrelevant to determination of the question whether recovery of the cost of repairs is justified in order to put the plaintiff in the position in which he would have been if the contract, ie the promise to make a careful report, had been performed. The position is no different from that in *Philips v Ward*: either the plaintiff would have refused to buy or he would have negotiated a reduced price. Recovery of the cost of repairs after having gone into possession, that is to say in effect the acquisition of the house at the price paid less the cost of repairs at the later date of doing those repairs, is not a position into which the plaintiff could have been put as a result of proper performance of the contract. Nor is that cost recoverable as damages for breach of any promise by the defendant because, as stated above, there was no promise that the plaintiff would not incur any such cost.

(ii) In the context of the contract proved in this case, I have difficulty in seeing when or by reference to what principle it would not be reasonable for the purchaser of a house to retain it and to do the repairs. He is free to do as he pleases. He can owe no duty to the surveyor to take any cheaper course. The measure of damages should depend, and in my view does depend, upon proof of the sum needed to put the plaintiff in the position in which he would have been if the contract was properly performed, and a reasonable decision by him to remain in the house and to repair it, upon discovery of the defects, cannot alter that primary sum, which remains the amount by which he was caused to pay more than the value of the house in its condition.

(iii) If the rule were as contended for by the plaintiffs, what limit, if any, could be put on the nature and extent of the repairs of which the plaintiff could recover the cost? Mr Naughton asserted that the cost of repairs awarded in this case was no more than putting the house in the condition in which, on reading the report, they believed the house to be. That, however, contains no relevant standard of reasonableness because, again, the defendant did not warrant that description to be true. To argue that to award damages on that basis is not to enforce a warranty never given but merely to 'reflect the losses which the plaintiffs have incurred' seems to me to be a circular statement.

(iv) I have considered whether the reasonableness of the amount which a plaintiff might recover towards the cost of repairing unreported defects in excess of the diminution in value might be determined by reference to the amount which the plaintiff could recover if he sold the property, ie the diminution in value plus any other recoverable losses and expenses. Such a limit was not contended for by Mr Naughton. It has the apparent attraction of enabling a plaintiff who chooses to retain the property to recover as much as he would recover if he chose to sell it. It seems to me, however, to be impossible to hold that such is the law in the case of such a contract as was made in this case. The plaintiff must, I think, prove that the loss which he claims to have suffered was caused by the breach of duty proved and he cannot do that by proving what his loss would have been in circumstances which have not happened.

It is necessary to test the conclusion which I have reached as set out above by examining *Hipkins v Jack Cotton Partnership* [1989] 2 EGLR 157 and *Syrett v Carr & Neave* [1990] 2 EGLR 161, which Mr Jackson submitted were wrongly decided.

In *Hipkin's* case Scott Baker J held that application of the diminution in value rule would manifestly not do justice in that particular case. On applying that rule the damages would have been £8,900 with interest from the summer of 1981. The cost of repairs which the plaintiff was held reasonably to have carried out in 1985, after advice in 1982 to 'wait and see', was £14,211. I accept that, if I am right in the conclusion which I have described above, there is no valid ground of distinction reported in *Hipkin's* case and that, therefore, the award on the facts found should have been £8,900 with interest.

Next, in *Syrett's* case the reasoning of Judge Bowsher may be summarised, I think, as follows. He held that it was to be inferred that in *Philips v Ward* the purchaser, on discovering the defect on moving in, had the choice between selling the property at its true value, making a loss which was less than the then cost of repairs, or of doing the repairs. To award in those circumstances the cost of doing the repairs would have been to give him a benefit to which he was not entitled in the absence of a warranty from the surveyor as to the state of the property. There was, however, no such giving of a benefit to which the plaintiff was not entitled on the facts in *Syrett's* case, because instant resale would not, at that date, have left the purchaser with a loss less than the cost of repairs and, more importantly, the purchaser had no reason to make an instant sale of the property because she did not know of the defect until two years after moving in. Similarly in *Perry v Sidney Phillips & Son (a firm)* [1982] 3 All ER 705, [1982] 1 WLR 1297, the unreported defects were discovered soon after moving in and, in that case also, the plaintiff had a choice of either cutting his loss by reselling or undertaking the necessary repairs. Since, however, the plaintiff in *Syrett's* case was unaware of the unreported defects until two years after the purchase, she was entitled to the cost of repairs because she had not had an opportunity of cutting her losses about the date of purchase and had acted reasonably throughout.

With respect to the judge, I do not find that reasoning to be convincing and, in my view, the decision in *Syrett's* case was wrong. It is true that both in *Philips v Ward* and in *Perry's* case the plaintiff, on discovering the unreported defects, had the choice of selling or undertaking the necessary repairs. This court held that whichever choice was made, the primary sum for damages was the diminution in value together with any expenses etc caused by the breach. There is, however, nothing to suggest that it was the existence of that choice or opportunity at any particular time which caused the proper measure of damages to be stated as the diminution in value. Since that statement was expressly explained by reference to putting the plaintiff in the position in which he would have been if the contract had been properly performed, and since that concept is not affected by the subsequent date of discovery of breach, the fact that in *Syrett's* case the claimant did not discover the breach until two years after purchase seems to me to be irrelevant to the measure of damages as based upon the diminution in value. I would, however, reserve with reference to this point the question as to the date at which the diminution in value is to be calculated. Upon discovering the breach the plaintiff can decide whether on that ground to sell. In *Philips v Ward* [1956] 1 All ER 874 at 878, [1956] 1 WLR 471 at 475-476 the measure of damages was stated by Morris LJ as the difference between the value of the property as it was described in the negligent report and its value as it should have been described in 1952. If the unreported defects had been discovered three years later, and if the value of the property in either state had increased by 25% as a result of inflation of house prices, it seems to me to be arguable that this measure of damage should be taken as the difference between the values so increased ie £5,000, being £31,250 less £26,250. No such point was raised in this case.

Next, as to the grounds of decision in *Syrett's* case, if (in the case of the ordinary contract) an award of the cost of repairs to a plaintiff who discovers the defects on moving in is to give to him a benefit to which he is not entitled (and I agree that it is – see *Philips v Ward*), it is no less the giving of a benefit to which the plaintiff is not entitled to award him the cost of repairs when he discovers the defects years after moving in: the principle that an award of the cost of repairs is a benefit to which the plaintiff is not entitled depends upon the terms of the contract between the plaintiff and the surveyor and not upon the time of discovery of the unreported defects.

Lastly, in *Syrett's* case the opportunity to 'cut losses' at about the date of sale, which it was held was denied to the claimant in *Syrett's* case, is, as I understand it, the opportunity to decide to sell and to suffer the loss of the diminution in value which would be recoverable. If the plaintiff decided instead to do the repairs he would incur any additional cost over this diminution in value as a result of his own decision; but, if he did not discover the defects until two years later, having been deprived of that earlier opportunity, he becomes, it is said, entitled to the full cost of repairs and not, be it noted, only the amount by which the cost of repairs may be shown to have increased since the date of purchase. As I have said above, however, the opportunity to sell on discovery of the defects was not the reason for holding in *Philips v Ward* that the measure of damages was the diminution in value: that holding resulted from the application of the basic principle of restitution to the terms of the contract between the claimant and the surveyor. Delay in discovery of the defects does not affect that application of that principle. A decision to remain and to carry out repairs after such delayed discovery cannot, in my judgment, alter the proper measure of damages.

One further matter must, I think, be examined. It is, I think, clear law that where a claimant is caused to enter into a transaction in consequence of negligent advice, as in the case of a surveyor employed under the ordinary contract, the claimant may be entitled to all the losses incurred as a result of entering into the transaction where he would not have entered into the transaction if properly advised and the losses are caused by entry into the transaction and by extrication from it. An example in the case of a solicitor's advice is, as I have mentioned above, *County Personanel (Employment Agency) Ltd v Alan R Pulver & Co* (a firm) [1987] 1 All ER 289, [1987] 1 WLR 916. Can the claim of these plaintiffs to the cost of repairs properly be put on the same basis, ie as damages caused by entering into a transaction in reliance on the bad advice, and, if not, why not? On this part of the argument, Mr Naughton referred to a number of matters and, in particular, to the fact that it is in many cases unrealistic to measure the damages of the purchaser by reference to the value of the property where it is not his intention to resell the house but to live in it and resale is impossible for reasons unconnected with value in the market. If the buyer is caused to buy a house by a negligent report which does not warn him of the existence of defects, and which he must cause to be repaired in order to live in the house in the condition in which he expected it to be, why is not the cost of repairs a loss resulting from entering into the transaction just as much as the payments recovered in the *County Personnel* case? Since such a buyer has no intention of selling – he is repairing his home, not an article of commerce – any addition to the value of the house, it was said, will not be at once realised and he is not in truth thereby getting any advantage beyond what he reasonably thought he was getting when he relied upon the surveyor's advice.

I recognise the force of these points so far as concerns the position of such an unfortunate claimant. From his point of view, it would, indeed, be better if the surveyor could be treated as having warranted that no repairs, beyond those described as indicated in the survey report, would be required within some period of time. No such warranty, however, was given in this case, or said to have been given, and, in the absence of such a warranty, there is no basis for awarding the cost of repairs.

I would, therefore, hold that the judgment for £33,961, the cost of repairs, must be set aside and that, in substitution therefore, judgment should be entered for financial loss in the sum of £15,000 with interest at 15% from the date of payment until judgment. I understand it to be common ground that payment is to be taken as having been made as to £1,500, from the date of payment of the deposit of £17,750 on the making of the contract, and as to the balance of £13,500 at the date of completion, based upon the proportion of the excess payment of £15,000 to the total sum agreed to be paid. If I am wrong in my understanding I would wish to hear counsel upon that matter. I shall deal later in this judgment with my reasons for confirming the rate of interest at 15% as awarded by the judge.

The decision in *Watts & another v Morrow* (above) has been described as 'bad news' for victims of a surveyor's negligence. 'Of course owners should get compensation based on the cost of repair. If the courts cannot get it right the issue will have to be settled by Parliament' (*per* David Tench, Consumers Association).

The victim will have to pay the extra cost required for the repairs out of his own pocket if not insured against such a loss. Many insurance companies are now refusing to pay for problems that a surveyor should have picked up on a valuation because these are considered as 'pre-inception' problems ie in existence before the insurance policy was taken out; but the surveyor will have liability insurance to cover any damages that may be awarded against him. The home owner then faces the situation in which he either pays for the repairs himself, perhaps having to borrow even more money to do so, or remains living in the property with the defects present until he can find someone who is willing to buy it – usually, at a 'knock-down' price and with a consequent loss to the vendor. The odds are now heavily stacked against the home owner who has relied on the professional expertise of the surveyor.

Unfortunately for the home owner, *Watts & another v Morrow* (above) has adopted a commercial approach to what is essentially a human situation, namely, the purchase of a house to live in.

Damages for distress and inconvenience

A purchaser who discovers that his house has rising damp, woodworm, rot or subsidence can be placed under a great deal of stress as a result of such a discovery. The cost of remedying these sort of defects is enormous, but the cost is not the only problem. Remedial work may involve the purchaser and his family having to find alternative accommodation whilst the work is done. The stress which this can place on family life should never be underestimated. Should not, therefore, damages be awarded to compensate for such distress and inconvenience, in addition to the 'difference in value'?

In the law of contract, damages have been allowed for vexation and annoyance, but only in limited circumstances, such as where the contract itself was for enjoyment or where the contract involved action to be taken for the relief of anxiety. In *Perry v Sidney Phillips & Son (a firm)* (see earlier), and *Roberts v J Hampson & Co* (see earlier) the court allowed a claim for damages for distress, etc. In *Watts & another v Morrow*, however, the Court of Appeal reduced an award from £4,000 to £750 to each plaintiff under the heading of 'distress and inconvenience', and purported to lay down a general principle for an award of damages under this head. The Court of Appeal stated that an award of damages could only be made for the distress caused by the physical consequences of the breach of contract, and not for the fact that the plaintiff has suffered distress and anxiety at having purchased a defective house, ie moving out whilst remedial work is done will attract damages under this head, but the worry of having a less valuable property will not.

Watts & another v Morrow

Ralph Gibson LJ: *General damages: the award for 'distress and inconvenience'*

For the defendant Mr Jackson submitted that, on the facts of this case, the plaintiffs were entitled to no award under this head but that, if any sum was due, the award was plainly excessive and far greater than sums commonly awarded, in accordance with *Perry v Sidney Phillips & Son (a firm)* [1982] 3 All ER 705, [1982] 1 WLR 1297, as 'modest' compensation. His contention was that, in a contract of this nature, general damages are not recoverable for mere mental distress, but are recoverable only for the enduring of physical discomfort and inconvenience, in the measuring of which regard may properly be had to mental reaction to such discomfort. He further criticised the judge's conclusion on this part of the case on the ground that the judge did not make any finding as to the nature or extent of any physical discomfort which had been caused by the defendant's breach of contract as contrasted with physical discomfort caused by the plaintiffs' decision to carry out substantial additional repairs and refurbishment.

Mr Naughton submitted that it was decided by the decision of this court in *Perry's* case that damage for mental distress can be recovered against a negligent surveyor in the ordinary case and that such a contract is in the same category as contracts for the provision of a holiday: see *Jarvis v Swans Tours Ltd* [1973] 1 All ER 71, [1973] QB 233 and *Jackson v Horizon Holidays Ltd* [1975] 3 All ER 92, [1975] 1 WLR 1468. The misery and discomfort experienced by the claimants in the position of these plaintiffs is not, he said, linked to the cost of the works carried out or to the time taken to complete them. The hardship should be seen as subjective and that is best assessed by the judge who heard the evidence. The fact that this was the second home for hard-working and stressed individuals should be seen as increasing the proper compensation and not as reducing it. Further, the fact that the house was expensive, and that the use of it for relaxation could be regarded as costing the interest on the price paid, would justify a larger award in comparison with an award in respect of a cheaper house.

As to the law, it is, in my judgment, clear that the plaintiffs were not entitled to recover general damages for mental distress not caused by physical discomfort or inconvenience resulting from the breach of contract. It is true that in *Perry's case* [1982] 3 All ER 705 at 709, [1982] 1 WLR 1297 at 1302–1303 Lord Denning MR justified the award of damages for anxiety, worry and (ie 'modest compensation') by reference to the holiday cases of *Jarvis v Swans Tours Ltd* and *Jackson v Horizon Holidays Ltd* and to *Heywood v Wellers (a firm)* [1976] 1 All ER 300, [1976] QB 446, a solicitor's case. I do not, however, accept that *Perry's* case is authority for that proposition. It is, I think, clear that, in that case, the award of damages, which was upheld, was for–

> 'vexation, that is the discomfort and so on suffered by the plaintiff as a result of having to live for a lengthy period in a defective house which for one reason or another was not repaired over the period between the acquisition by the plaintiff and the date of the trial.'

(See [1982] 3 All ER 705 at 710, [1982] 1 WLR 1297 at 1307 *per* Oliver LJ). Further, in *Perry's* case [1982] 3 All ER 705 at 712, [1982] 1 WLR 1297 at 1307 Kerr LJ said:

> '... it should be noted that the deputy judge has awarded these [damages for vexation and inconvenience] not for the tension or frustration of a person who is involved in a legal dispute in which the other party refuses to meet its liabilities. If he had done so, it would have been wrong, because such aggravation is experienced by almost all litigants. He awarded these damages because of the physical consequences of the breach, which were all foreseeable at the time.'

Mr Jackson's submission is, I think, correct. In *Bailey v Bullock* [1950] 2 All ER 1167 Barry J, in a case of solicitor's negligence, held that damages for inconvenience and discomfort could be recovered for the solicitor's failure to get possession of premises for his client but not damages for annoyance and mental distress. So holding he relied upon the judgment of Scott LJ in *Groom v Crocker* [1938] 2 All ER 394 at 415, [1939] 1 KB 194 at 224, where *Addis v Gramaphone Co Ltd* [1909] AC 488, [1908–10] All ER Rep 1 was held to be a conclusive authority against general damages for injury to reputation or feelings. Barry J contrasted that decision with that of *Hobbs v London and South Western Rly Co* (1875) LR 10 QB 111, [1874–80] All ER Rep 111, where damages for physical inconvenience were upheld for breach of a contract of carriage.

In *Jarvis's* case it was held that the old authorities excluding damages for disappointment of mind were out of date and that damages for mental distress can be recovered in contract in a proper case. One such proper case was held there to be breach of a contract for a holiday or of a contract to provide entertainment and enjoyment. Breach of a contract of carriage, where vexation may be caused, was distinguished from breach of a contract for a holiday where the provision of pleasure is promised.

Again, in *Heywood v Wellers (a firm)* [1976] 1 All ER 300, [1976] QB 446 damages were awarded against a negligent solicitor for failure to obtain protection for his client against molestation, and in particular for the client's distress, because the solicitors were employed to protect the client from molestation, which was causing distress. In *Hayes v James & Charles Dodd (a firm)* [1990] 2 All ER 815 at 826 Purchas LJ, with reference to a claim to damages for mental distress in a claim against a surveyor, said:

> 'I agree with the approach adopted by Staughton LJ reflecting, as it does, the judgment of Dillon LJ in *Bliss v South East Thames Regional Health Authority* [1987] 1 CR 700 at 718, namely that damages of this kind are only recoverable when the subject-matter of the contract or duty in tort is to provide peace of mind or freedom from distress.'

If, then, the plaintiffs, for breach of a contract of this nature, are entitled only to damages in respect of physical discomfort or inconvenience resulting from the breach, it is clear, as in *Perry's* case, that such damages are recoverable where, as contemplated by the defendant, the plaintiffs move into the property and live there in physical discomfort because of the existence of unreported defects such as an evil-smelling cesspit or a leaking roof. But what of physical discomfort caused not by the defects but by the process of repairing them in a case where, as here, the surveyor has not warranted that there are no defects? Thus, in this case, there was no discomfort caused by any defect in the roof: it was replaced before it leaked or collapsed. Mr Jackson, rightly, I think, did not contend that damages for physical discomfort are not recoverable where caused by the carrying out of repairs to negligently unreported defects even though the surveyor is not in law liable for the cost of those repairs. The concession seems to me to be rightly made provided it is shown that the parties contemplated that, upon the plaintiff occupying the house as his home in reliance upon the report, he would in fact have to live there while the repairs are done and it is reasonable for him to do so. We do not have to decide whether, if the plaintiff has to rent other accommodation during the carrying out of repairs, such costs will be recoverable in the absence of any contractual warranty as to the existence of defects requiring repairs, and I would reserve my decision upon it.

In his judgment, Judge Bowsher, after reference to *Hayes v James & Charles Dodd (a firm)* and to *Perry's* case, held that a negligent surveyor of a residential property, which he has undertaken to survey for a prospective purchaser who intends to live there, may be liable to his client in damages to compensate him for 'inconvenience and distress arising out of living in the property, not out of litigation about it' (see 24 Con LR 125 at 145). Judge Bowsher continued that that seemed to him to be the case whether the position be rationalised by reference to 'special relationship' or 'a contract to provide peace of mind or freedom from distress'.

A prospective buyer of a house goes to a surveyor, said Judge Bowsher, not just to be advised on the financial advisability of one of the most important transactions of his life, but also to receive reassurance that, when he buys the house, he will have 'peace of mind and freedom from distress'.

It is clear, I think, that the judge was regarding the contract between these plaintiffs and the defendant as a contract in which the subject-matter was to provide 'peace of mind or freedom from distress' within the meaning of Dillon LJ's phrase in *Bliss's* case [1987] 1 CR 700 at 718 cited by Purchas LJ in *Hayes v*

Dodd [1990] 2 All ER 815 at 826. That, with respect, seems to me to be an impossible view of the ordinary surveyor's contract. No doubt house buyers hope to enjoy peace of mind and freedom from distress as a consequence of the proper performance by a surveyor of his contractual obligation to provide a careful report, but there was no express promise for the provision of peace of mind or freedom from distress and no such implied promise was alleged. In my view, in the case of the ordinary surveyor's contract, damages are only recoverable for distress caused by physical consequences of the breach of contract. Since the judge did not attempt to assess the award on that basis this court must reconsider the award and determine what it should be.

For my part, I accept that the award was excessive even if the judge had directed himself correctly. It was very substantially more than the awards made in similar cases apart from the award by the same judge in *Syrett v Carr & Neave* [1990] 2 EGLR 161. The other cases to which we were referred for this purpose included the following and I have listed the amount of the award together with the amount adjusted for inflation since the date of the award: *Roberts v J Hampson & Co (a firm)* [1989] 2 All ER 504, [1990] 1 WLR 94: £1,500 (£1,890); *Cross v Martin & Mortimer* [1989] 1 EGLR 154: £1,000 (£1,260); *Steward v Rapley* [1989] 1 EGLR 159: £2,000 (£2,520); *Bigg v Howard Son & Gooch* [1990] 1 EGLR 173: £1,600 (£ 1,744) and *Hipkins v Jack Cotton Partnership* [1989] 2 EGLR 157: £750 (£877). In the first three cases the award stated was to two plaintiffs. In each case the award was in respect of a period of inconvenience and discomfort in the claimants' home.

The judge accepted the evidence of the plaintiffs in full. The period of physical discomfort caused by the carrying out of work extended over eight months. It started in September 1987 when work to the roof began and was completed in October. The time taken in performing that work is not more exactly proved. Scaffolding was around the house. Work in respect of unreported defects began again in 1988 and was done under separate quotations before the several dates stated in para (xiv) above ending in October 1988. The periods of physical discomfort were limited to visits to the house at weekends, most but not all weekends over the relevant time. Some of the matters complained of were clearly not caused by the breach of contract – for example the interference with the use of bath and WC caused by work to the plumbing, which the plaintiffs chose to carry out at the same time as repair to the flooring.

Further, as explained in the judgment, the plaintiffs, finding that they had sufficient money to do so, decided to carry our work going far beyond the works the subject of the action. The judge held that the distress and inconvenience alleged by the plaintiffs was not to be discounted at all because he accepted, as sensible and well founded, the explanation by Mr Watts of his decision. For my part, while I have no doubt that it was a sensible and well founded decision for Mr Watts to do all the other work which he had decided to do at the same time as the repairs in respect of unreported defects, it does not seem to me thereby to be demonstrated that the physical discomfort and inconvenience throughout the period of work was caused by the failure to report those defects. It is clear that by 1987 the plaintiffs' earnings had risen and were rising. They decided that they would decorate and refurbish the house to a high standard. The need to do the repairs to unreported defects was not the reason why all the work was done when it was done. Indeed the need to carry out the unreported defects was seen by Mr Watts as delaying the process of refurbishment in the course of which the repairs of many other defects, of which there was no failure to give warning, were carried out. It is difficult, in my judgment, to be confident as a matter of probability that such physical discomfort as there was over the period of six months in 1988 was caused by the breach of contract of the defendant as contrasted with the decision of the plaintiffs to refurbish and redecorate the house. It is not clear to me that in any real sense the plaintiffs had to live in the house at weekends: their decision to do so appears to have resulted largely from their view that it was necessary for them to supervise personally all the work which they were having done.

The judge, however, accepted the plaintiffs' evidence and was not caused to doubt that all their complaints were caused by that breach of contract. It does not seem that the factual basis for the plaintiffs' claims to general damages was examined in any close detail at the trial. The right course, in my view, is for this court, accepting and applying the principle that damages for mental distress resulting from the physical consequence of such a breach of contract should be modest, to accept the judge's finding that, during the weekends over a period of eight months, there was discomfort from the physical circumstances of living in the house caused by the presence of the plaintiffs during the carrying out of repairs in respect of unreported defects. I reject the submission that, in comparing the proper awards in other cases of discomfort in a plaintiff's only home, there should be allowed, in respect of discomfort at weekends in an expensive second home, a comparatively larger sum. The proper approach is to fix a modest sum for the amount of physical discomfort endured having regard to the period of time over which it was endured. I would not take into account, as did the judge, in fixing the general damages, anything in respect of the plaintiffs' expenditure on a holiday in Scotland. There was no claim to loss of use. Any vexation in respect of taking a holiday away from the second home is not associated with physical discomfort in that home.

I would award to each plaintiff, since it has not been suggested that there is any basis for distinguishing between them, general damages in the sum of £750.

It could be pointed out that a prospective house buyer hires a surveyor precisely in order to give himself peace of mind when buying a house. No one wants a house which will require substantial repairs and the consequent inconvenience these will cause unless they, first of all, know the full extent of what is required, and, secondly, get some allowance for it in their purchase price. Treating the situation as a commercial one when the whole purpose of the contract is to avoid distress and inconvenience can only be described as a 'grave mistake' on the part of the Court of Appeal.

It would appear to make no difference whether the action is framed in contract or in negligence, since in *Roberts v Hampson* (see earlier) damages were awarded for distress and inconvenience in a negligence action. Will the court, however, award damages for distress and inconvenience on a more generous basis in negligence than in contract after the decision in *Watts v Morrow*?

THE LEGAL POSITION OF THE BUILDING SOCIETY OR OTHER MORTGAGEE

Some building societies have their own 'in-house' surveyors, as do most local authorities lending on the security of former council houses under the 'right to buy' provisions of the Housing Act 1985. (There is no longer a right to a local authority mortgage on a council house, following the enactment of s 107 Leasehold Reform, Housing and Urban Development Act 1993.) Other lenders get an independent firm of surveyors to do all their valuations. The legal liability of the building society will depend on whether an 'in-house' surveyor is used or whether an independent surveyor is called in.

Use of 'in-house' surveyors

A building society which employs an 'in-house' surveyor will be vicariously liable for that surveyor's negligence. In *Beaton & another v Nationwide Anglia Building Society* [1990] *The Times*, 8 October the Building Society employed an 'in-house' surveyor who was negligent. The Building Society tried to escape liability for the negligence by relying on a written notice given by the Building Society to the prospective mortgagor under the Building Societies Act. This notice stated that the making of the advance implied no warranty that the purchase price was reasonable, but the court (Queen's Bench Division) held that the notice did not relieve the building society of its vicarious liability for the negligent valuation carried out by a member of its staff.

In *Stevenson v Nationwide Building Society* [1984] 272 EG 663, it had been held that the inclusion of a disclaimer by the Building Society in its survey form was effective to prevent the Building Society from being liable for the negligence of one of its own staff valuers. This case, however, must now be considered as unreliable, since not only did it arise before *Smith v E Bush* was decided, but the Unfair Contract Terms Act 1977, though referred to, received little attention in the case and the plaintiff was also an estate agent who would be in a better position to look after himself than the average house buyer.

A Local Authority which uses an 'in-house' surveyor to value a council house on which it proposes to lend under the 'right to buy' provisions of the Housing Act 1985 will similarly be vicariously liable for the surveyor's negligence.

Use of an independent surveyor

The position of the building society which hires an independent surveyor to provide a valuation remains uncertain. The building society will have a contract with the prospective mortgagor under which the Society must exercise reasonable care and skill, eg in selecting the surveyor (see s 13 Supply of Goods and Services Act 1982), but the possibility of any contractual remedy against the Society for the negligence of the surveyor is remote on the basis that people are not normally liable for the negligence of their independent contractors (see also the discussion by Lord Griffiths in *Smith v E Bush* [1989] 2 WLR 790 at 814).

One other possibility remains, however, and that concerns the society's liability in negligence for any statements it may itself make to the mortgagor. Although a 'long-shot', the possibility of such liability was not ruled out in *Beresford v Chesterfield Borough Council & another* [1989] *The Times*, 14 August. In that case the valuation report by an independent surveyor was sent by the building society to the mortgagor on its own headed notepaper and therefore appeared as if it was the report of the Society itself. The Court of Appeal refused to strike out the claim against the building society as showing no cause of action but did not rule on whether the Society was in the event liable to the mortgagor.

Parker LJ indicated that there were formidable difficulties in the way of the success of such a claim, and the case certainly provides no general authority for holding a building society liable in other circumstances for the negligence of an independent valuer.

A local authority which chooses to use an independent surveyor should be in the same legal position in this respect as a building society.

LIMITATION PERIOD APPLICABLE TO ACTIONS AGAINST SURVEYORS

Any action against a surveyor, whether in contract or in tort, must be brought within the appropriate limitation period. Subject to the effect of the Latent Damage Act 1976, the period of limitation is set out in ss 2 and 5 Limitation Act 1980 (for actions in tort and contract respectively).

Limitation Act 1980

2. **Time limit for actions founded on tort**

    An action founded on tort shall not be brought after the expiration of six years from the date on which the cause of action accrued.

5. **Time limit for actions founded on simple contract**

    An action founded on simple contract shall not be brought after the expiration of six years from the date on which the cause of action accrued.

These provisions beg the question of when a cause of action against a surveyor accrues. This issue was discussed in a business context in a contractually based action against a surveyor in *Secretary of State v Essex, Goodman and Suggitt* [1986] 2 All ER 69. In that case it was decided that a cause of action accrued against a surveyor from the date on which the plaintiff acted on the negligently prepared report. Logically this was the only date from which a cause of action could be said to arise, since a surveyor is employed to find out whether defects already exist in a house or building and any loss can therefore only arise at the point at which reliance is placed on the surveyor's report. The same conclusion would logically follow if the action were in negligence rather than contract.

The Latent Damage Act 1976 extends the limitation period for the bringing of an action in tort (but not for actions in contract) in certain defined and limited circumstances. It provides that an action in respect of latent damage (other than personal injury) must be brought within an overall 'longstop' period, which is 15 years from the date of the defendant's negligence, but allows the plaintiff a three year period as from the 'starting date' if this would extend beyond the normal six year period of limitation. The 'starting date' is complicatedly defined in the Act as the earliest date on which the plaintiff had a right to bring an action and both knew of the fact or damage, the identity of the defendant and that the damage was caused by that defendant's negligence. The requirement of causation here between the latent damage itself and the defendant's negligence is likely to render the provisions of the 1986 Act redundant when applied to surveyors; but to be on the safe side, surveyors are advised to insure themselves against negligence liability for the full 15-year period.

CHAPTER 13

MORTGAGES AND THE HOME OWNER

INTRODUCTION

In this chapter, we shall be considering the mortgage relationship as it affects the owner occupier. The last half-century has seen the emergence of 'a property-owning, particularly a real-property-mortgaged-to-a-building-society-owning-democracy' (*per* Lord Diplock in *Pettitt v Pettitt* [1970] AC 777, 824). The proportion of households now in owner-occupation is in excess of 67%, of which almost all are subject to some form of mortgage liability.

Mortgage finance is a major factor in the lives of most households; the availability of mortgage finance, repayable over a long period has made the dream of home ownership a reality for many people, and the process has been encouraged by the measures of income tax relief, even though these have now been somewhat curtailed, made available to owner occupiers. In repayment mortgages, the monthly instalments paid by the mortgagor take the form of combined repayments of capital and interest; in endowment mortgages, the borrower's periodic payments are simply payments of interest, and the capital repayment is funded by a life assurance policy taken out by the mortgagor, calculated in such a way as to yield the capital sum due at the expiry of the mortgage term.

The existence of mortgage finance provides a means of capital accumulation, and enables upward mobility. The process has been accelerated over the last fifteen years by the operation of the 'right to buy' provisions in relation to council property, which has led to the transfer to the private sector of about one-sixth of the public sector housing stock.

The surge in owner-occupation has, however, led to some adverse effects. The years since the collapse of the housing market in the late 1980s have seen a surge in mortgage repossessions, which increased almost tenfold between 1983 and 1991 (from about 8,000 to over 75,000); also, the assumption on which the housing market has operated for many years – that of steadily increasing property values – came to a halt at the end of the 1980s, when severe falls in house prices, particularly in the South East, led to 'negative equity'. Some estimates suggested that over 1 million homes fell into this category.

INTEREST RATES

One of the most important factors in the mortgage is the level of interest rates charged by the mortgagee. Mortgage lenders depend for their funds upon the investment markets, which are often volatile in their behaviour.

Because of the volatility of the market, most institutional lenders lend their money on 'variable rate' mortgages, so that the interest rates chargeable to the borrower can be changed in line with market conditions. Although some institutional lenders are now offering a 'fixed rate' mortgage, these are often only 'fixed' for the first few years of their life; of course, whilst they protect the borrower against increases during that period necessitated by market conditions, they also have the disadvantage of excluding the borrower from the benefit of any advantageous falls in interest rates stemming from decline in interest levels in the market generally.

The normal procedure is for the mortgage to contain a clause requiring the mortgagor to pay interest at whatever rate the lender announces as applicable to his mortgages from time to time. The borrower thus enters into an open-ended commitment to pay whatever rate is stipulated by the mortgagee. In the case of owner occupiers, this possibility of an unforeseen increase in his housing costs can cause real hardship, and in cases of repayment mortgages the lender will sometimes offer the borrower the option of extending his mortgage term (eg from 20–25 years) so as to reduce the impact of the effect of such increases. In the case of an endowment mortgage, however, which is supported by a fixed-term insurance policy, this facility will not normally be available. These mortgages, with their possibility of capital appreciation, have become increasingly popular over recent years. Despite the open-ended nature of variable interest rates, it seems clear that there is nothing illegal about them by reason of their variability.

Although variability in itself is not an objection, the courts have long sought to control the effect of oppressive interest rates. There seems to be a long standing equitable tradition of tempering the wind to shorn lamb as exemplified in *Cityland and Property Holdings v Dabrah* [1968] Ch 166, where the court held an interest rate of 19% imposed in a mortgage of residential property to be 'unconscionable' and reduced it to a 'reasonable' rate of 7%. In this case there was a clear disparity of bargaining power between the lender and the borrower, and the borrower was clearly subjected to a degree of pressure to agree to the terms because he believed that he was faced with imminent eviction if he did not agree to the terms imposed by the lender. In reaching this decision the court was probably influenced by the existence of a parallel jurisdiction under the Moneylenders Acts 1900 and 1927 to set aside 'harsh and unconscionable' transactions.

The Moneylenders Acts have now been repealed by the Consumer Credit Act 1974. There are specific provisions in the 1974 Act which deal with 'extortionate' credit bargains, and these are the provisions most likely to be invoked in the mortgage relationship These provisions, though, have been disappointing in their effectiveness and the government has indicated, after a review of the provisions by the Office of Fair Trading, that it is minded to introduce amending legislation when the opportunity permits.

Provisions of the Consumer Credit Act relating to extortionate credit

Consumer Credit Act 1974

137(1) If the court finds a credit bargain extortionate it may re-open the credit agreement so as to do justice between the parties.

(2) In this section and sections 138 to 140–

(a) 'credit agreement' means any agreement between an individual (the 'debtor') and any other person (the 'creditor') by which the creditor provides the debtor with credit of any amount; and

(b) 'credit bargain'–

    (i) where no transaction other than the credit agreement is to be taken into account in computing the total charge for credit, means the credit agreement; or

    (ii) where one or more other transactions are to be so taken into account, means the credit agreement and those other transactions, taken together.

138(1) A credit bargain is extortionate if it–

(a) requires the debtor or a relative of his to make payments (whether unconditionally, or on certain contingencies) which are grossly exorbitant; or

(b) otherwise grossly contravenes ordinary principles of fair dealing.

(2) In determining whether a credit bargain is extortionate, regard shall be had to such evidence as is adduced concerning–

(a) interest rates prevailing at the time it was made;

(b) the factors mentioned in subsections (3) to (5); and

(c) any other relevant considerations.

(3) Factors applicable under subsection (2) in relation to the debtor include–

(a) his age, experience, business capacity and state of health; and

(b) the degree to which, at the time of making the credit bargain, he was under financial pressure, and the nature of that pressure.

(4) Factors applicable under subsection (2) in relation to the creditor include–

(a) the degree of risk accepted by him, having regard to the value of any security provided;

(b) his relationship to the debtor; and

(c) whether or not a colourable cash price was quoted for any goods or services included in the credit bargain.

(5) Factors applicable under subsection (2) in relation to a linked transaction include the question how far the transaction was reasonably required for the protection of debtor or creditor, or was in the interest of the debtor.

139(1) A credit agreement may, if the court thinks just, be re-opened on the ground that the credit bargain is extortionate–

(a) on an application for the purpose made by the debtor or any surety to the High Court, county court or sheriff court; or

(b) at the instance of the debtor or a surety in any proceedings to which the debtor and creditor are parties, being proceedings to enforce the credit agreement, any security relating to it, or any linked transaction; or

(c) at the instance of the debtor or a surety in other proceedings in any court where the amount paid or payable under the credit agreement is relevant.

(2) In reopening the agreement, the court may, for the purpose of relieving the debtor or a surety from payment of any sum in excess of that fairly due and reasonable, by order–

   (a) direct accounts to be taken, or (in Scotland) an accounting to be made, between any persons;

   (b) set aside the whole or part of any obligation imposed on the debtor or a surety by the credit bargain or any related agreement;

   (c) require the creditor to repay the whole or part of any sum paid under the credit bargain or any related agreement by the debtor or a surety, whether paid to the creditor or any other person;

   (d) direct the return to the surety of any property provided for the purposes of the security; or

   (e) alter the terms of the credit agreement or any security instrument.

(3) ... (4) ... (5) ... (5A) ... (6) ... (7) ...

The courts have shown caution in their interpretation of these provisions. Many of the bargains which fall to be challenged under these provisions could readily be characterised as 'unwise' or 'imprudent'; but this is not enough, and the very factors which may go to make the bargain 'unwise', such as the presence of a higher than usual interest rate, may stem from the very factors which increase the risk so far as the lender is concerned, like the inexperience of the lender. Thus in *Ketley v Scott* [1980] CCLR the court declined to interfere with an interest rate of 48%, when the borrower sought a loan from a money-lender at short notice to enable completion of the purchase of residential property, which the borrower had agreed to but without having taken any steps to ensure that the requisite finance was available. Further factors diminishing sympathy for the debtor were the misrepresentations which he had made about his financial position.

(For a more detailed discussion of these provisions in their application to domestic mortgages, see *Davies v Directloans Ltd* [1986] 1 WLR 823.)

CONSUMER CREDIT ACT PROTECTION

The Consumer Credit Act 1974 marked a major advance in the law relating to all aspects of consumer credit in the UK. Though details of many aspects of this legislation lie outside the scope of this work, there are some provisions of the Act which affect the mortgage relationship, especially in relation to mortgages granted by secondary lenders such as banks and second-mortgage companies.

Inapplicability of the Act to many domestic mortgages

The main sphere of operation of the Act is in relation to what are called 'regulated agreements'. Agreements with individuals which are not 'regulated agreements' fall within the classification under the Act of 'exempt agreements' (see s 16 of the Act). Loans in excess of £15,000 are not regulated agreements (s 8(2)) and this provision operates to take very many mortgages outside the operation of the Act. In addition, the category of 'exempt agreements' listed in s 16 of the Act includes loans for the purchase of land granted by building societies and insurance companies 'specified' by the Secretary of State. The net effect of all this is that most 'purchase money' mortgages, characteristically granted by building societies and insurance companies, will be 'exempt' and thus outside the control of the Act.

What the Act does catch, however, and what it was certainly intended to catch, is the second mortgage market; this area of the market, sorely in need of regulation, has been dominated by non-institutional lenders, who have over the years exploited vulnerable borrowers, who have often been tempted into mortgage transactions as a means of escape from what are seen to be insurmountable financial problems, or to gratify some desire to expand money on holidays or other consumables. Some of the creditors operating in this sector of the market have characteristically directed the thrust of their advertising at those who would not be thought to be acceptable risks by established financial institutions, or who have a bad credit record by reason of county court judgments or similar defaults.

Advertising controls under the Consumer Credit Act

In a pamphlet entitled 'Security Risks' published in 1987 the National Consumer Council drew attention to shortcomings in the marketing of 'second mortgages' by secondary lenders. The tenor of the advertisements was that borrowers were being wooed by seductive advertisements which made it clear that the existence of a poor credit record (such as the presence of county court judgments) would not be a bar to a loan if the debtor was a home owner. These loans, characteristically, were secured by a second mortgage over the debtor's home. Although these loans, under the advertising regulations then in force, had to be advertised as 'secured' loans, the significance of the description was all too often lost on the debtor, who might fail to appreciate that there was a risk of loss of a home in the event of a default in maintaining the payments due under the loan. As a result of this concern, the government amended the advertising regulations under the Consumer Credit Act. Under the current regulations (the Consumer Credit Advertisements Regulations 1989), any advertisements for loans secured on property, in addition to the usual requirements about the disclosure of interest rates (APRs: Annual Percentage Rate of Charge) have to contain a 'Government Health Warning', which states: 'Your home is at risk if you do not keep up repayments on a mortgage or other loan secured on it'.

The above requirement applies to all advertisements of mortgage facilities, whether or not the proposed loan will amount to a 'regulated agreement' under the Consumer Credit Act. The legality of the requirement to insert a 'Government Health Warning', though challenged by secondary lenders as *ultra vires*, was accepted as being lawful by the Court of Appeal in *R v Secretary of State for Trade and Industry ex p First National Bank* [1990] *The Times*, 7 March.

Licensing control under the Consumer Credit Act

One of the main features of the machinery provided by the Consumer Credit Act is a system of licensing control of lenders. In general, a licence is required to carry on a consumer credit business, which is defined in s 189 of the Act as a business which 'comprises or relates to the provision of credit under regulated consumer credit agreements' (s 21).

Building societies, and others who lend under 'exempt agreements' are not caught by this provision, because of the nature of their agreements; but secondary lenders are clearly within its terms. The penalties for unlicensed trading are severe; besides criminal penalties (s 39), agreements made by unlicensed lenders are *prima facie* unenforceable at the suit of the lender, unless the Director-General of Fair Trading can be persuaded to make an order in favour of the unlicensed trader permitting enforcement 'as if' the trader had been duly licensed (s 40).

These rules, however, only catch those who lend 'in the course of a business'. A retired hotelier, who, as a private individual from time to time lent money by way of mortgage at normal interest rates to debtors selected by his own solicitor was held not to require a licence (*Wills v Wood* [1984] CCLR 7).

Formalities control under the Consumer Credit Act

There are special provisions under the Consumer Credit Act relating to the formalities of entering into mortgages which are 'regulated agreements'. Though the Act contains elaborate provisions relating to the 'right to cancel' many types of consumer credit transactions, it was thought inappropriate for these provisions to apply to mortgages, because of the complications that might arise under the Land Registry systems for the priority of mortgages. Instead of a right of cancellation, a special regime for the formality of land mortgages is provided by s 58 of the Act. The essence of this scheme is that before entering into the mortgage, the creditor has to send to the debtor an advance copy of the agreement, which contains a prominent indication of the debtor's right to withdraw without penalty from the prospective agreement. Having sent the advance copy, the creditor must then allow the debtor a period of at least seven days 'undisturbed contemplation' of the prospective agreement before sending the formal copy for execution by the debtor. Failure to observe these requirements will mean that the agreement will be 'improperly executed' under s 65 of the Act. If an agreement is 'improperly executed' it is unenforceable by the creditor unless the court makes an 'enforcement order' permitting the creditor to enforce the agreement as if it was properly executed.

OTHER PROTECTION FOR MORTGAGORS: THE UNFAIR TERMS IN CONSUMER CONTRACTS REGULATIONS 1994

On 1 July 1995, the Unfair Terms in Consumer Contracts Regulations came into force. These Regulations implement EC Directive 93/13/EEC on unfair terms in consumer contracts. With certain exceptions, the Regulations apply to any terms which have not been individually negotiated in a contract for the supply of goods or services between a consumer and a seller or supplier. The Regulations may have a significant impact on the law relating to mortgages. The loan element of a mortgage is a 'service' contract to which the Regulations would appear to apply. But what is less clear is whether the mortgage charge itself is also covered. It has been suggested by the Department of Trade and Industry that 'given the close relationship with the terms concerning the loan, it would be prudent to assume that the mortgage charge falls within the scope of the Regulations'. On that basis, those terms in a mortgage of residential property, which have not been individually negotiated, will now be subject to a test of 'good faith'.

Regulation 4(1) defines an 'unfair term' as any term which, contrary to the requirement of good faith, causes a significant imbalance in the parties' rights and obligations under the contract to the detriment of the consumer. Any such 'unfair term' is not binding on the consumer. Schedule 2 to the Regulations contains a list of certain matters which are to be taken into account in deciding whether a particular term passes the test of 'good faith'. These include, *inter alia*, the strength of the bargaining position between the parties and the extent to which the supplier has dealt fairly and equitably with the consumer.

The Regulations, however, still leave all the existing UK consumer protection legislation intact. An interesting issue which may therefore arise in this context is the relationship between the test of 'good faith' in the Regulations and the test applied from the relevant provisions in the Consumer Credit Act 1974 in their application to mortgages.

REMEDIES OF THE MORTGAGEE

One of the most important factors in the mortgage relationship is the issue of the remedies of the mortgagee in the event of default by the mortgagor. Over the last few years the incidence of mortgage default has increased dramatically; one of the main factors leading to this increase was the escalation of interest rates at the end of the 1980s.

In the event of a default, the lender can sue as an action in debt for the amount due; this remains a possibility if the property is sold (for less than the mortgage debt) where there is negative equity (ie the value of the property is less than the value of the debt). This may mean that an owner occupier is saddled with a burden of continuing debt, even though he has already lost his home.

Besides the possibility of an action to recover the debt, the mortgagee has certain rights and remedies against the property; one effect of the mortgage transaction is to give the creditor rights over the property itself, usually in the form of a 'charge by way of legal mortgage' (see s 87 Law of Property Act 1925). This 'charge by way of legal mortgage' will give the mortgagee rights to take possession of the property and, in the last resort, to sell it in satisfaction of his debt. If the debt is so large that the proceeds of sale do not cover the debtor's liability, the mortgagee is able to pursue the debtor for the balance outstanding.

This right to sue for the balance due is governed by the general law, and owes nothing to any special feature of the law of mortgages as such. It is particularly relevant in cases of 'negative equity'; if a mortgaged house is sold for less than the amount due under the mortgage, there is nothing to prevent the mortgagee seeking to recover any shortfall from the former mortgagor.

The mortgagee's rights of possession and sale, however, are distinctive features of the law of mortgages, and it is to these that we now turn.

Possession

Traditionally, it has always been said that the creation of a mortgage, which vests a legal right in the mortgagee, has the consequence that it is the mortgagee and not the mortgagor who is entitled to possession of the property. This may be the legal position; but it is doubtful whether it represents reality, or, indeed, the wishes of most lenders.

The apparently absolute right of the mortgagee to possession may be limited by the express terms of the contract with the mortgagor, and there are hints in the (non-domestic) case of *Esso Petroleum Co Ltd v Alstonbridge Properties Ltd* [1975] 1 WLR 1474 that such a renunciation of a right to possession save where there has been a default will sometimes be implied.

There are also other limitations imposed by law. One of these limitations is contained in general principles, as enunciated in *Quennell v Maltby* [1979] 1 WLR 318; the other is the statutory limitation derived from the Administration of Justice Acts 1970–73.

The common law inhibition: Quennell v Maltby [1979] 1 WLR 318

In this case, Lord Denning MR in the Court of Appeal declared that there was a power in the court to restrain a mortgagee's claim for possession of the mortgaged property 'except where it is sought *bona fide* and reasonably for the purpose of enforcing the security and then only subject to such conditions as the court thinks fit to impose'. This pronouncement was probably not necessary for the decision in the case, which could have been decided in the same way on other, less controversial grounds (see [1979] CLJ 257 (Pearce) and [1979] Conv 266). This course was indeed favoured by the two other members of the Court of Appeal (Bridge and Templeman LJJ). However, it seems to have acquired a respectability in its adoption by the Law Commission as one of its proposals for the reform of the Law of Mortgages (see para 3.4 of the Law Commission Report Transfer of Land-Land Mortgages Law Com No 204, November 1991).

The statutory regime: Administration of Justice Acts 1970–73

In practice, so far as the owner occupier of a dwelling-house is concerned, the most important protection against arbitrary exercise of the right to possession by a mortgagee is to be found in the Administration of Justice Acts 1970–73.

The history of these provisions

In the years after the Second World War, faced with the exigencies of the housing shortage, Masters of the Chancery Division who were hearing mortgagees' possession actions would grant a temporary stay to enable a hard-pressed mortgagor to sort out his financial affairs and repay any arrears due under a mortgage. This merciful discretion, described by one of the leading Chancery Masters as being the exercise of a function more akin 'to that of a social worker rather than a Judge' (see Master Ball (1961) 77 LQR 331) received its quietus with the decision of Russell J in *Birmingham Citizens Permanent Building Society v Caunt* [1962] Ch 883.

The removal of the benevolent jurisdiction to grant a stay in such cases was deplored by the Payne Committee on the Enforcement of Judgment Debts (1969). The Committee, noting the encouragement of the trend towards owner-occupation by persons of modest means, recommended that the courts should be empowered 'subject to proper safeguards, to extend to the mortgagor the same protection in relation to the continued occupation of the house as would be given to a tenant of a property of similar rateable value'. This recommendation was eventually implemented by the Administration of Justice Acts. The original Act, in 1970, was found to contain a significant flaw, and amending legislation was passed in 1973.

Administration of Justice Act 1970

36(1) Where a mortgagee under a mortgage of land which consists of or includes a dwelling-house brings an action in which he claims possession of the mortgaged property, not being an action for foreclosure in which a claim for possession of the mortgaged property is also made, the court may exercise any of the powers conferred on it by subsection (2) below if it appears to the court that in the event of its exercising the power the mortgagor is likely to be able within a reasonable period to pay any sums due under the mortgage or to remedy a default consisting of a breach of any other obligation arising under or by virtue of the mortgage.

(2) The court–

(a) may adjourn the proceedings, or

(b) on giving judgment, or making an order, for delivery of possession of the mortgaged property, or at any time before the execution of such judgment or order, may–

(i) stay or suspend execution of the judgment or order, or

(ii) postpone the date for delivery of possession,

for such period or periods as the court thinks reasonable.

(3) Any such adjournment, stay, suspension or postponement as is referred to in subsection (2) above may be made subject to such conditions with regard to payment by the mortgagor of any sum secured by the mortgage or the remedying of any default as the court thinks fit.'

(4) ... (5) ... (6) ...

Administration of Justice Act 1973

Extension of powers of court in action by mortgagee of dwelling-house

8(1) Where by a mortgage of land which consists of or includes a dwelling-house, or by any agreement between the mortgagee under such a mortgage and the mortgagor, the mortgagor is entitled or is to be permitted to pay the principal sum secured by instalments or otherwise to defer payment of it in whole or in part, but provision is also made for earlier payment in the event of any default by the mortgagor or of a demand by the mortgagee or otherwise, then for purposes of section 36 of the Administration of Justice Act 1970 (under which a court has power to delay giving a mortgagee possession of the mortgaged property so as to allow the mortgagor a reasonable time to pay any sums due under the mortgage) a court may treat as due under the mortgage on account of the principal sum secured and of interest on it only such amounts as the mortgagor would have expected to be required to pay if there had been no such provision for earlier payment.

(2) A court shall not exercise by virtue of subsection (1) above the powers conferred by section 36 of the Administration of Justice Act 1970 unless it appears to the court not only that the mortgagor is likely to be able within a reasonable period to pay any amounts regarded (in accordance with subsection (1) above) as due on account of the principal sum secured, together with the interest on those amounts, but also that he is likely to be able by the end of that period to pay any further amounts that he would have expected to be required to pay by then on account of that sum and of interest on it if there had been no such provision as is referred to in subsection (1) above for earlier payment.

(3) ... (4) ... (5) ... (6) ...

For an illustration of the operation of these provisions, and also their limitations, see *Target Home Loans Ltd v Clothier* (1992) 25 HLR 48, *First National Bank v Syed* [1991] 2 All ER 250, and *Cheltenham & Gloucester BS v Grant* (1994) 26 HLR 703, which stresses the point that the likelihood of the debtor being able to pay off the arrears within a reasonable period is fundamentally one for the trial judge, and that appellate courts will normally be reluctant to interfere with the decision of the judge at first instance.

Target Home Loans Ltd v Clothier

Nolan LJ: ... The history of the matter is that by a legal charge dated July 28, 1988, made between the plaintiffs and the defendants, the defendants charged their home, 'Honeycroft', to secure the repayment of a loan of £225,000. The repayment was to be made with interest at the initial rate of 9.2 per cent per annum. Repayments were to be made monthly on the third day of each month. The monthly payments were duly made until July 3, 1990, whereupon they ceased. No further regular payments have been made since then. When the matter came before the district judge he adjourned it to the first open date after 56 days. Against that order the plaintiff appealed to the court of Mr Recorder Cole.

When the matter came both before the district judge and the learned recorder they had to consider the claim for possession that was made by the plaintiffs in the light of the relevant provisions of the Administration of Justice Acts of 1970 and 1973. Those are conveniently summarised in the judgment of Sir John Pennycuick in the case of the *Royal Trust Company of Canada v Markham* [1975] 3 All ER 433 at p 437. He first quoted section 36 of the Administration of Justice Act 1970 ...

Sir John Pennycuick continued:

' ... under that section, which applies alike to non-instalment and to instalment mortgages, the court is given a limited power to suspend execution of an order for possession. I will come back to the words of that section in a moment.'

That section gave rise to a difficulty in that, in order that the condition of likelihood of payment should be satisfied, on the face of the words used the mortgagor had to satisfy the court that he was likely to be able to pay not only arrears of interest or arrears of instalments but also the principal sum due under the mortgage: see *Halifax Building Society v Clarke* [1973] Ch 307. It is as a result, I think, of that decision that a further provision was enacted by the Administration of Justice Act 1973. Section 8 of that Act reads as follows:

(Nolan LJ referred to Section 8 and continued:)

A little later down the same page (by now p 438 of the report) his Lordship dealt with the suggestion that the court was unable to have regard to the possibility of the property being sold and thus producing the means of discharging both the existing accrued instalments and also further liabilities under the mortgage. As to that, he said:

'I ought, however, to mention ground 4, namely that the judge was wrong in law in taking into account as evidence of likelihood the defendants' proposal to pay such sums by selling the property, such proposal being repugnant to and/or incompatible with an order for possession. I do not think that that ground can be supported. Section 36 is expressed in perfectly unqualified terms; and I see no justification for writing into the section words which are not there, such as, "otherwise than by way of a sale of the property".'

Browne LJ at p 439 said:

'I also agree with Sir John that, for the reasons he has given, it is not possible to accept counsel's submission that in a proper case the court could not stay or suspend an order to enable a property to be sold. I suppose that in all probability this would only be done where there was clear evidence that a sale was going to take place in the near future and that the price would cover all the sums due to the mortgagee for capital and interest. But in such circumstances, and if the court thought it proper, in my view there would be jurisdiction to make such an order.'

How did matters stand when the case came before the learned recorder? His judgment says this:

'In his Defence of November 28, 1991, the Defendant, who has appeared unrepresented, and I assume appears on behalf of himself and of his wife, in a handwritten defence did not dispute the claim and stated that they were "actively pursuing finance to discharge the debt to date in full and have made further arrangements to ensure payments of the mortgage for the immediate future". That is the language of pious hope, not based on fact. It continues that they are "hopeful of selling part of the garden to our neighbour for £40,000 with the balance of the monies being met today from a near relative". That is again a hope completely unfulfilled as Mr Clothier did not pay a half-penny piece.'

I should add that immediately before that passage the recorder mentioned that the particulars of claim, dated October 4, 1991, had put the arrears at that date in the sum of £46,422.18. His judgment continued:

'On April 7, 1992, Mr Summerfield of the plaintiff's Solicitors swore an Affidavit and attached to that Affidavit is an exhibit which sets out the arrears as at April 3, 1992, as being £64,579.96. It is correct to record that Mr Clothier has not paid so much as a half penny towards the mortgage since his last payment on the July 3, 1990. Not only were payments not properly paid, no part of them was paid.'

Then at the foot of the next page of his judgment the recorder summarises the position in law in this way:

'The court may adjourn the proceedings, suspend execution of any judgment or postpone delivery of possession if it appears that the mortgagor is likely to be able to repay the sums due within a reasonable time. In so far as I am aware there is no reported case which sets out what a reasonable time may be. As a matter of common sense it should not be so short as to be negligible or so long as to defeat the mortgagor's rights.'

The recorder continued:

'Today (April 15, 1992) Mr Clothier produced a draft for £10,000 and he also produced on Monday correspondence with a Mr Popat which at least shows on the face of it that Mr Popat would purchase some of the land at the bottom of Mr Clothier's garden for £44,000/£48,000. This agreement is not completed due to the failure of Mr Popat to agree to a planning condition that a suitable line of trees should be planted. Mr Clothier says that Mr Popat is willing to do so and that planning permission will be given within 2 months. This would mean that a further £40,000 can be paid towards the mortgage debt.

Mr Clothier says that perhaps his sister-in-law may have other sums which can help to defray this debt. I am not convinced that Mr Clothier is the most reliable of witnesses and I suspect that he confuses the actual with what is desirable when giving his evidence. Nonetheless I have a discretion and I think I am extending it to very near its permissible limit ... I am adjourning this matter for 4 months to enable planning permission to he obtained to enable the sale of the plot of land to be completed. But, in respect of this adjournment, it will be granted on one condition that there is an undertaking given by Mr Clothier to the Court that the whole of the sale proceeds be paid into Court within 3 days of receipt of those proceedings to await their ultimate disposal.'

I would make two comments on those passages from the judgment. The first is based on the arithmetic of the evidence before the learned recorder. Mr Clothier, faced with arrears at that stage of £64,579.96, having made no payments since July 3, 1990, produced before the recorder a draft for £10,000 and correspondence showing on the face of it a prospective purchase of his land by Mr Popat for at most £48,000, a total (ignoring costs of sale) of £58,000. Apart from the suggestion that perhaps Mr Clothier's sister-in-law may have other sums which would help to defray the debt, which the learned assistant recorder was not prepared to treat as a matter of weight, there was no evidence whatever before the recorder of Mr Clothier being likely to discharge the sums due under the mortgage within a reasonable time. I quote again from the judgment of Sir John Pennycuick in the Markham case at p 438F, where he says:

'"Likelihood" is a question of fact, to be determined by the judge on the evidence before him.'

I am bound to say that for my part I can see no evidence to justify the view taken by the judge in granting the adjournment of the case as he did. That is my first comment on that passage in the judgment.

The second goes to its consequences. As I read what the judge said, what he had in mind was that if planning permission were to be given within two months, an adjournment of four months would not only enable planning permission to be obtained but would also enable the plot of land to be sold. Otherwise there was little point in his coupling the four-month adjournment with Mr Clothier's undertaking to pay over the whole of the sale proceeds of the land within three days. What in the event has happened now on July 30, 1992, three and a half months later? We are told that planning permission was indeed granted on May 20. That is over two months ago. There is no evidence that the proposed deal with Mr Popat is any nearer to occurring. There is, however, new evidence before us in the form of an affidavit by Mr Clothier which speaks of other possible ways of raising money. They consist of a proposed sale and a proposed letting of the house. I think it would be sufficient if I confine myself to the evidence concerning the possibility of a sale, because, although there is evidence concerning the possibility of a letting, that would require the consent of the mortgagees unless it were in itself to constitute a breach of the terms of the mortgage entitling the mortgagees to claim possession, and the mortgagees have made it plain that, having regard to the history of the matter and the risk of letting into the house a tenant who might give trouble and whom they might be unable to evict, they are unwilling to give their consent to a letting.

What then of a possible sale? Mr Clothier exhibits a letter from a firm of estate agents in Weybridge which says this:

'We confirm that we are instructed by Mr and Mrs Clothier in connection with the sale of the above property. We were first instructed on January 22, 1992, and have been actively marketing the property since then. Mr and Mrs Clothier have been persistent in their inquiries and have kept us under considerable pressure to sell the property. Unfortunately a sale has not yet been agreed and recently the price of the property was, on our advice, reduced to £495,000.

As a result, there have been several applicants interested in the property during the last few days, and this morning we received an initial offer of £450,000 from a Mr & Mrs T Jones who will require a mortgage in the region of £50,000 and have no property to sell, and therefore sound to be very good applicants. Naturally we are attempting to increase this offer because it is substantially less than the asking price. We are quite satisfied that the property will be sold very shortly either to this applicant or to another. 'Honeycroft' is one of the most desirable properties in the area and has been kept to a very high standard of decoration and repair by Mr & Mrs Clothier.'

I mean no disrespect to the estate agency profession when I offer the suggestion that they would win by a distance any competition between members of different professions for optimism. Any such letter must be viewed with reserve if it is to form the basis of a decision involving real money. It is also, as Miss Bell for the mortgagees points out, a little surprising that after all this time, with the lapse of regular payments over two years ago, we should on the day of this hearing be presented with evidence of very recent interest in the property and of the prospects of a sale at a price which, although no doubt disappointing in comparison with prices obtainable two or three years ago, is still a substantial offer and one which exceeds not only the amount owing to the plaintiffs but also the amount secured by way of a second charge on the property amounting to about £130,000 in favour of Mr and Mrs Clothier's bankers.

Miss Bell submits that just as the learned recorder was wrong to grant the adjournment when the evidential basis for it was lacking, so here in this court precisely the same position obtains even when regard is had to the new evidence. She says that there would be no certainty of the mortgagees getting their money or of Mr Clothier being put back in funds to meet his obligations unless an immediate order for possession is granted and the sale of the property is put in hand by the mortgage company.

Mr Brilliant has raised a number of points to the contrary effect. He submits, first, that although the plaintiffs undoubtedly claimed immediate possession in their original particulars of claim, they were evidently prepared to concede before the recorder that this was a case in which the recorder had a discretion: in other words, they were prepared to concede that there was evidence of a sufficient likelihood of the defendants being able to pay off the amounts due under the mortgage for the recorder to be entitled to make the order which he did. Mr Brilliant rightly accepts that jurisdiction cannot be created by agreement, but says in effect that here there was a concession as to the evidence available and in consequence the learned recorder was not and indeed this court is not in a position to contemplate making an order for immediate possession.

With respect, I do not think that argument can run. In the first place, although the notice of appeal to the recorder was couched in the terms that 'the plaintiff wishes to apply ... for an Order for possession to be granted suspended on such terms as the Court thinks fit', the grounds of appeal were in fact that suspension or adjournment would fail to comply with the conditions of the Administration of Justice Act 1970 and the Act of 1973. The phrase 'suspended on such terms' does not seem to me to be clear enough to be capable of committing the plaintiffs to the proposition that there was evidence which would justify the recorder in holding that he had a discretion under the Acts if in fact no such evidence existed. Just as jurisdiction cannot be created by agreement, so evidence and matters of fact cannot be created by agreement where they do not exist. Therefore, in my judgment it was open to the recorder and it is open to this court to make the order for immediate possession which was originally sought by the mortgagees ...

Mr Clothier has suffered badly in his business as a result of the recession. No one suggests that he is a dishonest man. But the fact remains that during the last two years he has failed to meet his mortgage commitments. On the evidence there is no way in which he is going to meet them except by the sale of this house. That leads directly to the question: Is there a prospect of an early sale? If so, is it better in the interests of all concerned for that to be effected by him and his wife or by the mortgage company? If the view is that the prospects of an early sale for the mortgagees as well as for Mr Clothier are best served by deferring an order for possession, then it seems to me that that is a solid reason for making such an order but the deferment should be short.

I would for my part propose an order granting possession in three months time. If in that time Mr and Mrs Clothier have not succeeded in discharging the whole of their indebtedness to the plaintiffs, they will lose possession. It would be open to them if they were unable to meet that deadline to come back to the court. I can only express the firm view in the light of the history of this matter and from what we have heard today that there should be no further deferment and if Mr and Mrs Clothier are unable to find a buyer and to pay off their debts within three months, then without doubt the time will have come for the mortgage company to be given possession. But I would propose an order for possession in three months for those reasons.

Hollis J agreed.

Cheltenham & Gloucester BS v Grant

Nourse LJ: ... By a legal charge dated November 13, 1989 the defendants, Alexander Tony Grant and his then wife Norma Ann Grant, charged by way of legal mortgage in favour of Portsmouth Building Society the dwelling-house known as 47 Queensway, Newton Abbot, Devon in order to secure the payment to the society by instalments of the principal sum of £30,000, interest thereon and all other moneys payable in accordance with the society's conditions. On March 12, 1991 the benefit of the legal charge was transferred to the plaintiff, Cheltenham and Gloucester Building Society.

The monthly instalments payable under the mortgage fell into arrear. In April 1993, at which time the instalments in arrear were said to amount to £2,902.75, the plaintiff commenced proceedings in the county court claiming possession of the property and payment. The proceedings came before Mrs District Judge Meredith on June 23, 1993, at which stage there was before the court an affidavit sworn by one of the plaintiff's senior litigation clerks stating that, as at June 16, first, the current monthly payment due on the first of each month was £312.41, together with an insurance premium due on the like date of £12.59, making a total of £325; secondly, that the amount of the monthly payments in arrear was £2,974.06; thirdly, that the total amount remaining due under the legal charge was £37,763.59; fourthly, that the last payment made under it was £177.48 on May 28, 1993, being the monthly amount payable by the Department of Social Security in respect of income support to which reference will be made hereafter. No evidence had been put in by or on behalf of the defendants ...

For present purposes it is agreed that the court has no power to suspend an order for possession of a dwelling-house made in favour of a mortgagee except under section 36 of the Administration of Justice Act 1970 and section 8 of the Administration of Justice Act 1973. The power is a discretionary power which can be exercised only if it appears to the court, in other words that it is satisfied, that if the order is suspended the mortgagor is likely to be able within a reasonable period to pay the arrears due under the mortgage, together, it is implicit, with the current instalments accruing due thereafter.

The first point taken by Mr Phillips, for the plaintiff, is that the court can only be satisfied for that purpose by evidence given by or on behalf of the mortgagor. He says, correctly, that no such evidence was given in either of the courts below. Therefore, he submits, the judges of those courts were wrong to have acted on the basis merely of the information given to them informally by those representing Mr Grant. I reject this submission. It is not the function of this court to lay down rigid rules as to how busy district and county court judges should satisfy themselves of what they have to be satisfied for the purposes of sections 36 and 8. It must be possible for them to act without evidence, especially where, as here, the mortgagor is present in court and available to be questioned and no objection to the reception of informal material is made by the mortgagee. Clearly, it will sometimes be prudent for the mortgagor to put in an affidavit before the hearing. Moreover, if the mortgagee submits that the truth of what the court is told should not be accepted without evidence, then evidence will normally be necessary. In the absence of such a submission it must be for the judge to decide whether or not to act on the basis of informal material.

Mr Phillips' much stronger point is that here there was really no material, formal or informal, on which it was possible for Judge Jones to be satisfied that Mr Grant was likely to be able, within a reasonable period, to pay off the instalment arrears and keep up with the payment of the current instalments. He says that the judge did not say what a reasonable period was for this purpose and therefore must be taken not to have asked himself that question, a fact demonstrated by the open-ended nature of the order he affirmed. He places great emphasis on the undoubted fact, as the figures show, that the current payments from the Department of Social Security fell short of what was needed to discharge the monthly payments of £325 by at least £147.50 per month or £1,770 per annum. He says that the evidence, such as it was, of Mr Grant's prospects of future employment contained in paragraph (e) of the note of the hearing before the district judge was wholly inadequate. In the circumstances, submits Mr Phillips, the judge's decision was plainly wrong.

These are without doubt powerful submissions. By the time that the matter came before the judge, the plaintiff's further evidence had shown that the district judge's view that there was a £10,000 equity in the property could not be sustained. The judge gave two reasons for his decision, the second being that if Mr Grant was properly advised and remortgaged at a more appropriate rate of interest, then the plaintiff would receive its money in full. As to that reason, the judge evidently thought that the rate of interest was inappropriate because it was fixed at two per cent above the plaintiff's base rate from time to time. I am not prepared to say that the second reason was an inadequate one. But it was certainly one which was speculative in the sense that it must have been, on any footing, doubtful whether Mr Grant in his then circumstances would have been able to find another lender to grant him a mortgage, certainly a mortgage at a lower rate of interest.

That leaves us with the judge's first reason which was, I think, his substantial reason. He was of the view that payments could be made within a reasonable period of time. If that is taken literally, it means that payments could start to be made within a reasonable period of time. If that is what the judge meant, it would not have been sufficient. The arrears would have had to be paid off within a reasonable period. However, I do not think that the judge's words, as expressed in the note, can be taken literally. I am certain that Judge Jones had very clearly in mind the test he had to apply. So I read him as saying that he was satisfied that Mr Grant was likely to be able, within a reasonable period, to pay off the instalment arrears and to keep up with the current instalments.

What then of Mr Phillips' point that the judge did not say what he took as a reasonable period? That is a powerful point. But I think we must proceed on the footing that, having affirmed the district judge's decision with its provision for a review at the end of a year, Judge Jones intended that that should be the period in question more or less.

What then of his apparent satisfaction that Mr Grant's prospects of employment were sufficiently favourable to make it likely that he would be able to make those payments within that period? Here I think we must treat the approach of the district judge as having been the approach of Judge Jones. From the questions which she asked Mr Grant, as recorded in the note, it is clear that she was proceeding on the footing that he would be able to obtain employment within the one-year period. It is, I am bound to say, right to point out that Mr Grant's proposals were extremely unspecific. But what the district judge and, we must assume, the judge intended to do was to give Mr Grant the opportunity of 'getting on to his feet again', as she put it. The provision for the matter to be reviewed at the end of the year was no doubt included in order to see whether Mr Grant had been able to take that opportunity or not.

As I say, there is great force in Mr Phillips' submissions. I have had very grave doubts as to whether the decision of Judge Jones can be upheld by this court. But in the end I am unable to say that it was plainly wrong. It may well be that another judge would have taken the opposite view. But the discretion in this case was entrusted to this judge, and in the light of the comparatively slight information we have as to what went on before him at the end of the day I am unable to say that his decision was plainly wrong.

The final question is whether we ought to make some order for payment. As a matter of principle I do not understand why a mortgagee who is owed moneys, the amount of which is either proved or agreed, should not be entitled to an order for payment as well as an order for possession. With orders in this form it is a very well established practice to suspend the order for payment upon precisely the same terms as the order for possession. With respect to the learned district judge, I do not understand the practice she appeared to support. However, there was no appeal to the judge against her refusal to make an order for payment and we are told today by Mr Pawlak, for Mr Grant, that he and his clients are not satisfied as to the amount now owing. Without objection, a further affidavit has been put in on behalf of the plaintiff bringing the state of the account up to date. Irrespective of the attitude of Mr Grant, I do not think it would be appropriate for us to make an order for payment in the circumstances of this case. It is a matter which can easily be taken up if and when there is a review at the end of the year period.

In the result, I would dismiss this appeal.

Wall J agreed.

The court also has power in such cases to make a money judgment for the amount due, which may be of assistance to the lender in the event of the property being one of 'negative equity' (see *Cheltenham & Gloucester BS v Grattidge* (1993) 25 HLR 454).

In *National & Provincial Bank v Lloyd* [1996] 1 All ER 630, the court stated that it was able to defer the grant of possession of mortgaged property where there was clear evidence that the mortgagor would be able to complete a proposed sale within a specified period, even though that might be a year hence.

There are two further matters which need to be considered in this context; the protection for the mortgagor's spouse, and the position of tenants.

The mortgagor's spouse

Early authorities under the Administration of Justice Acts, such as *Hastings & Thanet Building Society v Goddard* [1970] 1 WLR 1544 suggested that there was no onus on a mortgagee to inform a deserted wife of her husband's default on payments under a mortgage which affected the family home, even though the provisions of the Matrimonial Homes Act in force at that time extended to the wife a statutory right to maintain the payments due under the mortgage. The position has now been partly ameliorated by provisions in the Matrimonial Homes Act 1983, which gives a spouse (whether or not a Class F land charge has been registered) a right to be joined as a party in any possession proceedings unless the court is satisfied that there is some 'special reason' against joinder (s 8). This will enable a wife to present a case for consideration under s 36. Furthermore, if a Class F land charge has been registered by a spouse, the spouse has a right to be made a party to any possession proceedings.

Tenants

In a few cases a tenancy may be binding on the mortgagee (if for instance, it was created before the mortgage). In most cases, though, the power to grant a tenancy will be excluded by the terms of the mortgage, and it now seems clear, following *Britannia Building Society v Earl & Amin* [1990] 1 WLR 422 that a tenant cannot claim the protection of the Act (see Barnsley [1991] JSWL 220).

Britannia Building Society v Earl

McCowan LJ: This is an appeal against a judgment of his Honour Judge Dobry QC given in the Bloomsbury County Court on 17 February 1989 whereby he ordered that the second defendants give up possession of premises known as 12A Stuart Tower, Maida Vale, London W9 within 28 days of the date of his order.

The respondents to this appeal (the plaintiffs in the action) were the mortgagees of the premises under a mortgage deed between themselves and the mortgagor, one Anthony John Earl, who was the first defendant in the action. The mortgage deed was dated October 1985 and the total amount advanced was £43,630. By the date of the hearing of the action the mortgage payments due to the plaintiffs from the first defendant were in the region of £5,000. The first defendant did not contest the claim for possession and was, indeed, neither present nor represented before the judge.

However, after the plaintiffs had brought the proceedings, at that stage against the first defendant alone, it was discovered that two brothers called Amin were in occupation of the premises and they were joined as second defendants. They are the appellants before this court. It emerged, and these facts were not in dispute before the judge, that a bare three weeks after entering into the mortgage deed the first defendant let the premises to the second defendants, who have lived there ever since and paid rent to the first defendant for so doing in accordance with their tenancy. The first they heard of these proceedings, or that the tenancy had been granted to them after the date of the mortgage and in breach of it, was when they were served with a notice that the warrant of possession was about to be executed. They promptly applied for the warrant to be suspended (and the registrar of the court so ordered) and that they be joined as second defendants.

Their tenancy was for nine months from 25 October 1985. It is not in dispute that, after the expiry of that period, as between the first and second defendants, the second defendants became statutory tenants.

On the other side of the coin, however, these facts were undisputed: (1) the mortgage deed pre-dated the tenancy agreement, (2) the mortgage deed prohibited any purported letting of the property without the consent of the plaintiffs and (3) no such consent was sought or obtained by the first defendant.

In those circumstances, three arguments were advanced on behalf of the second defendants before the judge. One of those has been abandoned before us. Of the two that remain, the first is put like this. It is said that by reason of being statutory and not contractual tenants a possession order can only be made against the second defendants under the provisions of s 98 of the Rent Act 1977, irrespective of whether proceedings are brought by the landlords or by the mortgagees as holders of the title paramount. It is necessary that I should have regard to certain sections of the 1977 Act.

(McCowan LJ referred to ss 1 and 2(1) Rent Act 1977 and continued:)

I need not read further in that section, but I turn to s 98 of the 1977 Act. Subsection (1) reads:

> 'Subject to this Part of this Act, a court shall not make an order for possession of a dwelling-house which is for the time being let on a protected tenancy or subject to a statutory tenancy unless the court considers it reasonable to make such an order and either (a) the court is satisfied that suitable alternative accommodation is available for the tenant or will be available for him when the order in question takes effect, or (b) the circumstances are as specified in any of the Cases in Part I of Schedule 15 to this Act.'

... The plaintiffs ... rely on the decision of the Court of Appeal in *Dudley and District Benefit Building Society v Emerson* [1949] 2 All ER 252, [1949] Ch 707. In that case the court held that a contractual tenancy granted by a mortgagor after the date of the mortgage which excluded the mortgagor's statutory power of leasing was liable to be defeated by the assertion by the mortgagees of their paramount title. At the beginning of his judgment Evershed MR said ([1949] 2 All ER 252 at 253, [1949] Ch 707 at 711-712):

'The matter is by no means free from serious difficulty, and it is surprising that there has been no similar case before the court since the rent restriction legislation first operated. The point, put in its briefest form, is this: Can a person in occupation of premises within the monetary limits prescribed by the Rent Restrictions Acts by virtue of a contract of tenancy between himself and a mortgagor claim the protection of those Acts against a mortgagee claiming to assert his rights as mortgagee, where, by the terms of the mortgage, the Law of Property Act 1925, s 99(1), has been expressly excluded? The learned judge, Vaisey J, came to the conclusion that such a tenant could claim protection, and it is with natural diffidence that I find I have reached a different conclusion.'

He continued ([1949] 2 All ER 252 at 257, [1949] Ch 707 at 718):

'The question has been debated whether the result would be the same if the mortgagor had determined the contractual tenancy, which he, undoubtedly, created between himself and the second defendant, so that, at any rate as between himself and the second defendant, a statutory tenancy had arisen. I prefer for my part to express no view whether the result would be different if the second defendant could say: "My right to remain here is not by virtue of any contract or any estate which I derive from the mortgagor, but is by virtue of the statutory right to possession which, as between me and the mortgagor, the Rent Acts have conferred." Counsel for the second defendant suggested that in that event the mortgagees could not succeed in ousting the second defendant, but I must not be taken to assent to that. As I have said, I find it unnecessary to decide it. It may be that there is an anomaly, but I am certainly not satisfied that, if there had been a statutory tenancy created in the way I have indicated, that would have been necessarily sufficient to defeat the mortgagees' rights.'

I turn next to the concluding paragraph of the judgment of Somervell LJ, where he said ([1949] 2 All ER 252 at 260, [1949] Ch 707 at 723):

'The only point on which I would like to add a word relates to the last argument of counsel for the second defendant. It was suggested, and I think probably rightly, that, if the mortgagor in a case like this sought to get possession as against someone to whom he had let the mortgaged property in the circumstances which we are considering, that person, if the property was a dwelling-house separately let, could assert as against the mortgagor the benefits conferred by the Rent and Mortgage Interest Restrictions Acts, and, if he did so successfully, he would become a statutory tenant. It is unnecessary to decide what would be the position if a mortgagee, as against someone who had reached that position, sought to assert the right which the mortgagees are asserting in this case. All I want to say is that at the moment I do not feel that there would be any anomaly in coming to the same conclusion in those circumstances, although counsel for the second defendant submitted that there would be. Therefore, that part of the argument did not affect me in the conclusion to which I have come with regard to the other points. For these reasons, I think that this appeal must be allowed.'

Jenkins LJ agreed with the other two judgments.

The court was also referred to *Bolton Building Society v Cobb* [1965] 3 All ER 814, [1966] 1 WLR 1, where it was held that the Protection from Eviction Act 1964 did not protect a tenant in a situation comparable to the present as against the mortgagee.

Against this the second defendants argue that a statutory tenancy is different in kind from a contractual tenancy and, accordingly, that a mortgagee's title paramount puts the mortgagee in no better position than the mortgagor. In support of this proposition they rely on passages in the judgments in *Jessamine Investment Co v Schwartz* [1976] 3 All ER 521, [1978] QB 264. Giving the first judgment Sir John Pennycuick said, referring to the provisions of the Rent Act 1968 ([1976] 3 All ER 521 at 526-527, [1978] QB 264 at 270–271):

> 'The provisions now contained in s 3(1) have been the subject of a long line of judicial authorities which establish that the statutory tenant has no estate as tenant, but a personal right to retain the property. That right is held not only against his immediate lessor but also against persons under whom the immediate lessor derives his title, as well, of course, as persons claiming under the immediate lessor. See in this connection *Keeves v Dean* [1924] 1 KB 685 at 690, [1923] All ER Rep 12 at 14 in the Court of Appeal, *per* Bankes LJ where he said: "The person who so seeks to assign has come to be known as a 'statutory tenant', and I think it is a pity that that expression was ever introduced. It is really a misnomer, for he is not a tenant at all; although he cannot be turned out of possession so long as he complies with the provisions of the statute, he has no estate or interest in the premises such as a tenant has. His right is a purely personal one ..." and *per* Scrutton LJ ([1924] 1 KB 685 at 694, [1923] All ER Rep 12 at 17): "This case is another stage in the unwelcome task which Parliament has imposed upon the Courts of defining the position of the statutory tenant. My Lord has objected to his being called by that name, on the ground that he is not a tenant at all. But it is a convenient expression, and, although it is true that before the passing of these Acts no one would have spoken of a person who after the expiry of his tenancy remained in possession against the will of his landlord as a tenant, Parliament has certainly called him a tenant, and he appears to me to have something more than a personal right against his landlord. I take it that he has a right as against all the world to remain in possession until he is turned out by an order of the Court, and that he could maintain trespass against any person who entered the premises without his permission. However, it does not much matter what he is called so long as it is clear that one is speaking of a person who holds over after the expiry of his tenancy against his landlord's will."'

Sir John Pennycuick continued ([1976] 3 All ER 521 at 528, [1978] QB 264 at 272–273):

> 'Counsel for the freeholder asserted what is certainly true, that, always assuming s 18 to be inapplicable, there is in such circumstances no relation of tenancy between the freeholder and the former sub-tenant. But then a statutory tenancy does not involve such a relation, and indeed its existence negatives such a relation in the strict sense. The relation is rather what has been described as a status of irremovability, that status being enjoyed on terms analogous to those of a tenancy. I do not see any reason why this personal status of irremovability should be regarded as inconsistent with the new interest of the sub-tenant under his possessory title.'

I turn next to a passage in the judgment of Stephenson LJ ([1976] 3 All ER 521 at 531, [1978] QB 264 at 276):

> 'By provisions which are conceded to be no different in effect from s 3(1) of the 1968 Act, Mrs Schwartz was, and would continue to be, the statutory

tenant of this house if and so long as she occupied it as her residence, and the house was and continued to be subject to her statutory tenancy. She could lose her statutory tenancy, and the house could lose the burden of being subject to it, if she ceased to occupy it as her residence or if she was ordered out of occupation by the court on one of the grounds (including non-payment of rent lawfully due) set out in s 10 of, and the relevant provisions of Sch 3 to, the 1968 Act. She could also lose her statutory tenancy if the character of her occupation became inconsistent with her occupation of the house as her residence by virtue of her statutory tenancy. Without some such change she retained her status of irremovability, not only against Mrs David but against all the world.'

Counsel for the respondents points out that *Dudley and District Benefit Building Society v Emerson* [1949] 2 All ER 252, [1949] Ch 707 was not cited before that court.

However, from the passages in the judgments to which I have referred counsel for the second defendants argues that a statutory tenant enjoys no more than a personal right, a status of irremovability good against the whole world. The lack of a legal estate, he says, is demonstrated in a number of ways. For example a statutory tenant has no interest in land capable of assignment or testamentary disposition, a statutory tenancy cannot pass to the tenant's trustee in bankruptcy and the ordinary law as to joint tenancy is not applied in its full strictness to a statutory tenancy: see *Lloyd v Sadler* [1978] 2 All ER 529, [1978] QB 774.

However, counsel conceded that what his argument entailed, looking at the facts of the present case, was that in the course of the nine months of the contractual tenancy, at which time the second defendants were protected tenants under s 1 of the 1977 Act, they would have had no right to possession as against the plaintiffs. But, on his argument, once the nine months were up and the second defendants became statutory tenants, the plaintiffs could no longer recover possession from them. I am bound to say I find this quite illogical.

Counsel for the second defendants spoke of s 98 of the 1977 Act (to which I have already referred) as providing a complete code for recovery of possession of dwelling-houses. It is to be noted, however, that this section equates 'protected' and 'statutory tenancy' so far as security of tenure is concerned. Yet he is asking this court to make a profound distinction between them as against mortgagees in the circumstances here obtaining ...

Our attention was drawn by counsel for the plaintiffs to some words of Templeman LJ in *Quennell v Maltby* [1979] 1 All ER 568 at 572, [1979] 1 WLR 318 at 323:

'The lease to the statutory tenant was made by the landlord after the date of the mortgage without the consent of the bank and was therefore in breach of the landlord's covenant contained in the mortgage. That lease was binding on the landlord but void against the bank. On expiry of the lease the tenant became a statutory tenant as against the landlord but not as against the bank.'

Counsel for the plaintiffs concedes that the point was not argued there, but nonetheless it is a very persuasive authority and I respectfully follow it. I am, therefore, quite unpersuaded by the first point of counsel for the second defendants. His second point is put by him as an alternative to the first. it revolves around the words of s 36 of the Administration of Justice Act 1970 ...

Counsel for the second defendants further relies on the definition of 'mortgagor' in s 39(1) of that Act. This reads: '"mortgagor" and "mortgagee" includes any person deriving title under the original mortgagor or mortgagee."'

Counsel further placed reliance on *Tarn v Turner* (1888) 39 ChD 456. The headnote reads:

'Prior to the Conveyancing Act 1881, a mortgagor, without the consent of his mortgagee, contracted in writing to grant T a lease of the mortgaged premises for a term of years. T entered into possession under the contract, and subsequently, on notice from the mortgagee, paid rent to him. The mortgagee having refused to concur in the lease to T: Held (affirming the judgment of Kekewich J), that T was entitled to redeem the mortgage.'

Fry LJ said (at 468):

'Therefore, it appears to me that according to the general law of the land a person who claims as lessee under a mortgagor after the mortgage, and has thereby derived an interest in the equity of redemption, has the right to redeem.' ...

It seems to me that, having regard to the characteristics of a statutory tenant (which is the foundation of the argument of counsel for the second defendants under his first point), a statutory tenant has not got an estate or interest in the land. In any event, counsel agrees that he is not suggesting that the second defendants should redeem the mortgage. They ask only that the court should adjourn the action for such period as it thinks reasonable, subject to it being likely that sums due under the mortgage would be paid within a reasonable time. He says that he relies on *Tarn v Turner* only as showing that a tenant is entitled to be treated as the mortgagor ...

Counsel for the plaintiffs submits that s 39(1), the definition section, only applies to assignment of the property and does not include tenants. He says that, if he is wrong about that and it does include tenants, it does not include statutory tenants who do not derive title at all. I would accept those submissions. But counsel has a further point if those are wrong. He says that the very existence of the tenancy in this case is a breach of an obligation arising under the mortgage. The only ground for seeking possession here against the mortgagor was the arrears, but unknown to the mortgagees there was another perfectly good ground, namely the breach of the covenant against leasing, of which breach the mortgagees were unaware.

This leads him to his third point. He submits that the power can only be exercised under s 36(1) if the breach can be remedied. The present default, he says, cannot be remedied save by the departure of the tenant. Counsel for the second defendants seeks to counter this by submitting that the words in s 36(1) 'any other obligation' should be construed as obligations 'affecting the mortgagee's security'. For my part, I see no justification for construing the phrase 'any other obligation' as if those words were added. 'Any other obligation', in my judgment, means what it says. Consequently, in my judgment, the second point of counsel for the second defendants fails.

I would therefore dismiss the appeal.

Butler-Sloss LJ agreed.

In a case such as this it is difficult not to feel some sympathy for a tenant who may be unaware on the limitations on his landlord's power to create tenancies, and who may have paid his rent in good faith and be unaware of the arrears which have accrued under the landlord's mortgage.

Sale

The most drastic of the mortgagee's remedies is his power of sale. If this power is exercised, the mortgagor's rights to the home are brought to an end; all that is left is his right to demand the surplus money left over after the payment of the costs and expenses of the sale and the satisfaction of the mortgage debt. There are detailed requirements which provide what has been described as 'a framework which imposes constraints of fairness on a mortgagee who is exercising his remedies over his security' (see *Palk v Mortgage Services Funding plc* [1993] 2 WLR 415).

The price

This is a matter which is of primary importance to the mortgagor, since the attainment of a full price may have a critical part to play in whether he is able to save anything from the wreckage at all. In some cases statute has intervened; a building society, for instance, is under a statutory duty to take reasonable care to ensure that the price achieved is the best price that can reasonably be obtained: see s 13(7) and Schedule 4 para 1(1)(a) Building Societies Act 1986.

Building Societies Act 1986

Schedule 4

1(1) Where any land has been mortgaged to a building society as security for an advance and a person sells the land in the exercise of a power (whether statutory or express) exercisable by virtue of the mortgage, it shall be his duty–

(a) in exercising that power, to take reasonable care to ensure that the price at which the land is sold is the best price that can reasonably be obtained, and

(b) within 28 days from the completion of the sale, to send to the mortgagor at his last-known address by the recorded delivery service of a notice containing the prescribed particulars of the sale.

There are provisions which make any attempt to exclude this obligation by express terms void (para (2)).

There are many mortgagees, however, which are not bound by the provisions of the Building Societies Act, such as banks and insurance companies. After initial hesitation, it was confirmed by *Cuckmere Brick Co Ltd v Mutual Finance Ltd* [1971] Ch 949 that such mortgagees are also subject to a similar duty which, though expressed in varying terms, amounts to a duty of care to sell only for a proper market price. In that case a mortgagee who failed to refer to the existence of a planning permission when advertising the mortgaged property for sale was held liable to the mortgagor when the sale failed to realise enough to pay off the mortgage debt. Evidence was accepted that had reference been made to the planning permission in question it was likely that a wide range of bidders would have been attracted to the auction and that a significantly higher price would probably have been achieved. One has to bear in mind that a sale in these circumstances is a forced sale, and comparisons with other transactions in the market may be misleading. There is almost a presumption that the price actually realised is the 'proper' price, and an onus will be on any mortgagor seeking to contest the propriety of the sale to show that a higher price could have been achieved. It seems that any attempt to exclude liability for sale at an undervalue will fall foul of s 2(2) Unfair Contract Terms Act 1977, which would require any such attempted exclusion of liability to satisfy a test of 'reasonableness' (see *Bishop v Bonham* [1988] 1 WLR 742, 752).

The question of the extent of this duty was recently considered in *Parker-Tweedale v Dunbar Bank plc* [1991] Ch 12. In that case the Court of Appeal declined to permit a beneficial owner of the formerly mortgaged property to claim against a selling mortgagee for an allegedly improper exercise of the power of sale.

Parker-Tweedale v Dunbar Bank plc

Nourse LJ: ... The plaintiff submits that Dunbar, in exercising its power of sale over Ditchford, owed him, a beneficiary under a trust of which it had notice, an independent duty to take reasonable care to obtain a proper price over and above the duty which it admittedly owed to the wife as mortgagor. Counsel for Dunbar has at all times conceded that Dunbar believed that the plaintiff had a beneficial interest in Ditchford, in other words that it had notice that he had a beneficial interest under a trust of which the wife was the trustee. The plaintiff does not therefore have to make that point good. He argued that the larger his beneficial interest in Ditchford, the greater was the duty owed to him by Dunbar. He therefore sought to establish that Dunbar knew or ought to have known that he was solely entitled to the surplus proceeds of the sale of Ditchford after the mortgages on that property and Wilkes had been discharged. I am very doubtful whether, if there was a duty, it could vary in degree according to the extent of the beneficial interest of which the mortgagee had notice. Since I am satisfied that no duty was owed, it is unnecessary to explore that question further.

It was settled by the decision of this court in *Cuckmere Brick Co Ltd v Mutual Finance Ltd* [1971] 2 All ER 633, [1971] Ch 949 that a mortgagee, although he may exercise his power of sale at any time of his own choice, owes the mortgagor a duty to take reasonable care to obtain a proper price for the mortgaged property at that time. But there is no support, either in the authorities or on principle, for the proposition that where the mortgagor is a trustee, even a bare trustee, of the mortgaged property a like duty is owed to a beneficiary under the trust of whose interest the mortgagee has notice.

In seeking to support that proposition the plaintiff relied on the decision of this court in *Jarrett v Barclays Bank Ltd* [1946] 2 All ER 266, [1947] Ch 187. For reasons which were stated by Peter Gibson J and need not be repeated here, that case does not assist him. He also relied on the following passage in the judgment of Salmon LJ in *Cuckmere Brick Co Ltd v Mutual Finance Ltd* [1971] 2 All ER 633 at 643-644, [1971] Ch 949 at 966:

> 'Approaching the matter first of all on principle, it is to be observed that if the sale yields a surplus over the amount owed under the mortgage, the mortgagee holds this surplus in trust for the mortgagor. If the sale shows a deficiency, the mortgagor has to make it good out of his own pocket. The mortgagor is vitally affected by the result of the sale but its preparation and conduct is left entirely in the hands of the mortgagee. The proximity between them could scarcely by closer. Surely they are "neighbours". Given that the power of sale is for the benefit of the mortgagee and that he is entitled to choose the moment to sell which suits him, it would be strange indeed if he were under no legal obligation to take reasonable care to obtain what I call the true market value at the date of the sale.'

This reference to 'neighbours' has enabled the plaintiff to argue that the duty is owed to all those who are within the neighbourhood principle, ie to adapt the words of Lord Atkin in *Donoghue (or M'Alister) v Stevenson* [1932] AC 562 at 580–581, [1932] All ER Rep at 11–12, to all persons who are so closely and directly affected by the sale that the mortgagee ought reasonably to have them in contemplation as being so affected when he is directing his mind to the sale. Further support for the application of the neighbourhood principle in this context can be gained from the judgment of Lord Denning MR in *Standard Chartered Bank Ltd v Walker* [1982] 3 All ER 938 at 942, [1982] 1 WLR 1401 at 1415, where it was held that the duty to take reasonable care to obtain a proper price was owed to a surety for the mortgage debt as well as to the mortgagor himself.

In my respectful opinion it is both unnecessary and confusing for the duties owed by a mortgagee to the mortgagor and the surety, if there is one, to be expressed in terms of the tort of negligence. The authorities which were considered in the careful judgments of this court in *Cuckmere Brick Co Ltd v Mutual Finance Ltd* demonstrate that the duty owed by the mortgagee to the mortgagor was recognised by equity as arising out of the particular relationship between them. Thus Salmon LJ himself said ([1971] 2 All ER 633 at 644, [1971] Ch 949 at 967):

> 'It would seem, therefore, that many years before the modern development of the law of negligence, the courts of equity had laid down a doctrine in relation to mortgages which is entirely consonant with the general principles later evolved by the common law.'

The duty owed to the surety arises in the same way. In *China and South Sea Bank Ltd v Tan* ([1989] 3 All ER 839 at 841, [1990] 2 WLR 56 at 58) Lord Templeman, in delivering the judgment of the Privy Council, having pointed out that the surety in that case admitted that the moneys secured by the guarantee were due, continued:

> 'But the surety claims that the creditor owed the surety a duty to exercise the power of sale conferred by the mortgage and in that case the liability of the surety under the guarantee would either have been eliminated or very much reduced. The Court of Appeal [in Hong Kong] sought to find such a duty in the tort of negligence but the tort of negligence has not yet subsumed all torts and does not supplant the principles of equity or contradict contractual promises ... Equity intervenes to protect a surety.'

Once it is recognised that the duty owed by the mortgagee to the mortgagor arises out of the particular relationship between them, it is readily apparent that there is no warrant for extending its scope so as to include a beneficiary or beneficiaries under a trust of which the mortgagor is the trustee. The correctness of that view was fully established in the clear and compelling argument of counsel for Dunbar, who drew particular attention to the rights and duties of the trustee to protect the trust property against dissipation or depreciation in value and the impracticabilities and potential rights of double recovery inherent in giving the beneficiary an additional right to sue the mortgagee, a right which is in any event unnecessary.

The only exception for which counsel for Dunbar allowed was the special case where the trustee has unreasonably refused to sue on behalf of the trust or has committed some other breach of his duties to the beneficiaries, eg by consenting to an improvident sale which disables or disqualifies him from acting on behalf of the trust. In such a case the beneficiary is permitted to sue on behalf of the trust. This exception is established by a series of authorities, some of which were recently considered by the Privy Council in *Hayim v Citibank NA* [1987] AC 730. In delivering the judgment of their Lordships, Lord Templeman said (at 748):

> 'These authorities demonstrate that a beneficiary has no cause of action against a third party save in special circumstances which embrace a failure, excusable or inexcusable, by the trustees in the performance of the duty owed by the trustees to the beneficiary to protect the trust estate or to protect the interests of the beneficiary.'

It is important to emphasise that when a beneficiary sues under the exception he does so in right of the trust and in the room of the trustee. He does not enforce a right reciprocal to some duty owed directly to him by the third party.

As I have said, the plaintiff reached a settlement with the wife before the trial began. That meant that he could no longer pursue against her his claim that she had given her consent to the sale in breach of trust to him. But both here and below the argument proceeded on the footing that, if there was in truth a breach of trust, the plaintiff's settlement with the wife did not preclude him from suing Dunbar in right of the trust and in the place of the wife. Accordingly, the question which Peter Gibson J ultimately had to ask himself was whether there was a breach of trust by the wife in giving her consent to the sale.

That question was considered by the judge with great care. He stated his conclusion thus:

> 'In all the circumstances I reach the conclusion that the honest and well-intentioned decision of the wife to go ahead with the sale to Penbrook was a rational commercial decision in the reasonable belief that thereby she was ensuring that the property was sold at the best price, and £575,000 was a proper price. Accordingly there was no breach of trust by her in giving her consent. If that were wrong, I cannot find that Dunbar had notice of any impropriety by her.'

The judge accordingly held that just as the plaintiff had no cause of action against Dunbar as a beneficiary so he had no such cause of action in right of the trust. But it is to be observed that the essential basis of that holding, namely the finding that £575,000 was a proper price, would also have defeated the claim based on a duty owed directly by Dunbar to the plaintiff, had such a duty existed.

The judge then turned to the plaintiff's claim against Penbrook, which, in the light of his earlier findings, was bound to fail, it being impossible for a third party to have notice of a breach of duty which has never been committed either by the mortgagor or by the mortgagee. The plaintiff's arguments as against Penbrook were rejected by the judge and it is unnecessary for them to be repeated here. In this court we did not need to invite counsel to develop any arguments on behalf of Penbrook.

It remains for me to deal briefly with the principal grounds on which the plaintiff sought to impeach the judge's finding that £575,000 was a proper price. That finding derived in large part from the judge's view of the wife, who was accused by the plaintiff with what the judge thought was a wholly unfounded charge of malice. He thought that her evidence was given without rancour and in a fair-minded fashion. He was satisfied that she did her best to give her evidence to the fullest of her recollection, although she had some difficulty at times in recalling details. This is what the judge said about the wife's appreciation of her duty to obtain a proper price:

> 'I am satisfied by the evidence of Mr Pidgeon [of Messrs Baldock's, the wife's solicitor] and of the wife that throughout she was genuinely anxious to

obtain the very best possible price on a sale to anyone other than the plaintiff. She was content that he should be able to acquire Ditchford at "a ludicrously low price", as she put it, right up to the deadline on 27 May, in the hope that it would assist him to perform his maintenance obligations. She was also well aware that in the pending divorce proceedings capital might be ordered to be transferred from one spouse to the other, if less well off financially, so that a benefit to him might redound to her own benefit. But in relation to third party purchasers she wanted to obtain every penny possible as otherwise it would be, as she termed it "financial suicide".'

The plaintiff's complaints can be divided into two broad groups: those which are directed to saying that the property should have gone to auction and those which are directed to saying that, even if it was right to sell it by private treaty, it should not have been sold at the price and at the time at which it was sold to Penbrook.

Chief amongst the first group is the complaint that Cotswold's readiness to purchase the bulk of Ditchford at a price of £700,000 less than a week after it had been sold for £575,000 showed that the latter was not a proper price. The judge described that 'striking fact' as a matter for initial suspicion, but said that it had proved on investigation to have little relevance. The judge found that Mr Liddell of Cotswold had not indicated his willingness to pay any such price to anyone on 27 May and, further, that that price was not negotiated with Penbrook until after its acquisition of the property on 27 May. Moreover, Mr Liddell would not himself have attended the auction. A further complaint arose from the judge's finding, based on the evidence of two people who expressed their interest in Ditchford but did not bid or give an indication of their level of interest, a Mr Dean (the managing director of a property company) and a Mr Baggott (who, while primarily a butcher, was a partner with his son-in-law in a building development business), that they would both have attended the auction, had it been held, and that Mr Dean would have obtained Ditchford for £655,000. But, as the judge pointed out, the intentions of Mr Dean and Mr Baggott were known only to themselves and were kept to themselves.

In the second group, the plaintiff complains both that no response was made to a specific bid of £600,000 from a Mr Ratcliffe, a property developer, and that no approach was made by the agents to others who had expressed interest in the property, in order to see whether any of them would be prepared to go higher than £575,000. As to the first of these complaints, the judge, while thinking it regrettable that Messrs Clintons, Dunbar's solicitors, did not make any response, said that the evidence did not enable him to find that, if given the opportunity, Mr Ratcliffe would have exchanged contracts by the afternoon of 27 May at £600,000. Counsel for Dunbar also pointed to evidence which showed that Mr Pidgeon and the wife took into account a reasonable hope that agents' commission would not be payable on a sale to Penbrook, which had not been introduced by them, whereas it would certainly have been payable (at 31%) on a sale to Mr Ratcliffe. Since the judge did not refer to that evidence, I do not think that we should give it any special significance. But we still cannot go behind his inability to find that Mr Ratcliffe would have exchanged contracts by the afternoon of 27 May at £600,000.

The suggestion that the agents ought to have been asked to approach others who had expressed interest in the property before accepting Penbrook's offer of £575,000 is, at first sight, more impressive. The position there was that none of those interested who had mentioned figures had gone higher than £500,000. It was on that footing that on 26 May, on the agents' advice, Dunbar authorised them to put an offer of £495,000 on the property if it went to auction. However, it is possible that if those who had expressed interest, or some of them, had been approached by the agents with an indication that they might be able to purchase before the auction if they were prepared to go higher than £575,000 there would have been a positive response. The question is whether that failure to take that step amounted to a breach of duty.

The evidence on this point was not very extensive. I have already referred to what Mr Pidgeon said and thought. Mr Thomas (of Messrs Strutt & Parker, who acted on the sale) said that there was insufficient time to invite sealed bids and that a ringing round might not necessarily have produced the answer which was being looked for. The judge said:

> 'But the problem there was one of timing. The subject to contract agreement with Penbrook was reached on Wednesday, 25 May and Dunbar was made aware of it only that afternoon. Dunbar had, reasonably in my view, required any sale by private treaty to reach the stage of exchange of contracts by the end of Friday, 27 May, the latest date for enabling an orderly cancellation of the auction, as Mr Thomas confirmed, to take place, in view of the bank holiday on the following Monday. There is no evidence to suggest that anyone else could have reached the stage of exchange of contracts by that time. Penbrook was able to act quickly because its solicitor had already been engaged in the abortive negotiations between the plaintiff and Aylmer Securities Ltd [with which the plaintiff planned a subsale of a part of Ditchford which had a development potential].'

The judge added that the real choice was between proceeding with the sale to Penbrook and going to auction, a difficult decision over which it was clear to him that the wife had agonised. He went on to discuss the matter with great care, referring amongst other things to the advice of Mr Forsyth-Forrest and Mr Thomas that £575,000 was a good price for the property, each saying that he could not guarantee that it would fetch more at auction. He also referred to another factor in the wife's mind, which was that the plaintiff had threatened to 'sort out' the auction and he said that her unease over what he might do at an auction was not without foundation and could not be complained of by the plaintiff, who had caused it. The wife had said that she gave it all a great deal of thought and, bearing in mind what the agents had said about £575,000 being a good price, she decided to take the bird in the hand. The judge then stated his conclusion in the terms already quoted.

Although, as I have said, the last of the plaintiff's complaints was at first sight more impressive than the others, I do not in the end have any doubt that it would be quite impossible for this court to take a view of it different from that which was taken by the judge. I think that the judge was entitled to conclude that the problem of timing applied as much to a ringing round amongst those who had expressed interest as it did to an invitation to make sealed bids. There was in any event no guarantee that it would have produced a better result. In every other respect in which the plaintiff sought to impeach the judge's finding that £575,000 was a proper price, it transpired on an examination of the transcripts that there was ample evidence on which the finding could be made. In general, I would say that the whole of the plaintiff's attack on the central finding of the judge was an attempt to persuade this court to take the impermissible course of retrying the case on the transcripts of the evidence.

I would dismiss this appeal.

Sir Michael Kerr and Purchas LJ agreed.

In most cases it will be the mortgagee who seeks to sell and a mortgagor who seeks to resist sale; but sometimes these roles may be reversed. In *Palk v Mortgage Services Funding plc* [1993] 2 WLR 415, the mortgagor, faced with a mortgage debt of £358,000, was anxious to secure an immediate sale for £283,000, the best he could get in the depressed property market at that stage. The mortgagees wished to postpone sale, and in the interim to let the property on short-term leases until such time as the housing market recovered. This would lead to a situation where the borrowers' debt would be likely to increase at a staggering £30,000 per year. Holding for the borrowers, and directing a sale, the Court of Appeal in effect safeguarded the borrower from an open-ended liability for an ever increasing debt.

UNDUE INFLUENCE

One matter which has been the subject of much attention in recent years has been the extent to which, if at all, a mortgage or suretyship transaction into which a person has joined (and possibly conceded the postponement of their rights in accommodation) may be impugned on the grounds of undue influence or misrepresentation. Two decisions of the House of Lords on the matter have now clarified the situation.

In *Barclays Bank plc v O'Brien* (1993) 26 HLR 75 the House of Lords held that, in effect, a suretyship obligation entered into by a wife as a result of a husband's misrepresentation was held to be unenforceable. The Bank took the wife's surety obligation, to secure the debts of her husband's company, in circumstances where the Bank should at least have been put on enquiry, and should have taken steps to ensure that the wife's signature was the result of a free choice and in knowledge of the true facts. Having failed to make the proper enquiries, they were thus fixed with constructive notice of the misrepresentation. In the circumstances Mrs O'Brien was entitled, as against the Bank, to have the legal charge set aside.

Barclays Bank plc v O'Brien

Lord Browne-Wilkinson: My Lords, in this appeal your Lordships for the first time have to consider a problem which has given rise to reported decisions of the Court of Appeal on no less than 11 occasions in the last eight years and which has led to a difference of judicial view. Shortly stated the question is whether a bank is entitled to enforce against a wife an obligation to secure a debt owed by her husband to the bank where the wife has been induced to stand as surety for her husband's debt by the undue influence or misrepresentation of the husband ...

Policy considerations

The large number of cases of this type coming before the courts in recent years reflects the rapid changes in social attitudes and the distribution of wealth which have recently occurred. Wealth is now more widely spread. Moreover a high proportion of privately owned wealth is invested in the matrimonial home. Because of the recognition by society of the equality of the sexes, the majority of matrimonial homes are now in the joint names of both spouses. Therefore in order to raise finance for the business enterprises of one or other of the spouses, the jointly owned home has become a main source of security. The provision of such security requires the consent of both spouses.

In parallel with these financial developments, society's recognition of the equality of the sexes has led to a rejection of the concept that the wife is subservient to the husband in the management of the family's finances. A number of the authorities reflect an unwillingness in the court to perpetuate law based on this outmoded concept. Yet, as Scott LJ in the Court of Appeal rightly points out, although the concept of the ignorant wife leaving all financial decisions to the husband is outmoded, the practice does not yet coincide with the ideal [1993] QB 109 at 139. In a substantial proportion of marriages it is still the husband who has the business experience and the wife is willing to follow his advice without bringing a truly independent mind and will to bear on financial decisions. The number of recent cases in this field shows that in practice many wives are still subjected to, and yield to, undue influence by their husbands. Such wives can reasonably look to the law for some protection when their husbands have abused the trust and confidence reposed in them.

On the other hand, it is important to keep a sense of balance in approaching these cases. It is easy to allow sympathy for the wife who is threatened with the loss of her home at the suit of a rich bank to obscure an important public interest *viz* the need to ensure that the wealth currently tied up in the matrimonial home does not become economically sterile. If the rights secured to wives by the law renders vulnerable loans granted on the security of matrimonial homes, institutions will be unwilling to accept such security, thereby reducing the flow of loan capital to business enterprises. It is therefore essential that a law designed to protect the vulnerable does not render the matrimonial home unacceptable as security to financial institutions.

With these policy considerations in mind I turn to consider the existing state of the law. The whole of modern law is derived from the decision of the Privy Council in *Turnbull & Co v Duval* [1902] AC 429 which, as I will seek to demonstrate, provides an uncertain foundation. Before considering that case however, I must consider the law of undue influence which (though not directly applicable in the present case) underlies both *Duval's* case and most of the later authorities.

Undue influence ...

A person who has been induced to enter into a transaction by the undue influence of another ('the wrongdoer') is entitled to set that transaction aside as against the wrongdoer. Such undue influence is either actual or presumed. In *Bank of Credit and Commerce International SA v Aboody* [1990] 1 QB 923 at 953 the Court of Appeal helpfully adopted the following classification.

Class 1 Actual undue influence

In these cases it is necessary for the claimant to prove affirmatively that the wrongdoer exerted undue influence on the complainant to enter into the particular transaction which is impugned.

Class 2 Presumed undue influence

In these cases the complainant only has to show, in the first instance, that there was a relationship of trust and confidence between the complainant and the wrongdoer of such a nature that it is fair to presume that the wrongdoer abused that relationship in procuring the complainant to enter into the impugned transaction. In Class 2 cases therefore there is no need to produce evidence that actual undue influence was exerted in relation to the particular transaction impugned: once a confidential relationship has been proved, the burden then shifts to the wrongdoer to prove that the complainant entered into the impugned transaction freely, for example by showing that the complainant had independent advice. Such a confidential relationship can be established in two ways, *viz.*

Class 2(A)

Certain relationships (for example solicitor and client, medical advisor and patient) as a matter of law raise the presumption that undue influence has been exercised.

Class 2(B)

Even if there is no relationship falling within Class 2(A), if the complainant proves the *de facto* existence of a relationship under which the complainant generally reposed trust and confidence in the wrongdoer, the existence of such relationship raises the presumption of undue influence. In a Class 2(B) case therefore, in the absence of evidence disproving undue influence, the complainant will succeed in setting aside the impugned transaction merely by proof that the complainant reposed trust and confidence in the wrongdoer without having to prove that the wrongdoer exerted actual undue influence or otherwise abused such trust and confidence in relation to the particular transaction impugned.

As to dispositions by a wife in favour of her husband, the law for long remained in an unsettled state. In the 19th century some judges took the view that the relationship was such that it fell into Class 2(A), ie as a matter of law undue influence by the husband over the wife was presumed. It was not until the decisions in *Howes v Bishop* [1909] 2 KB 390 and *Bank of Montreal v Stuart* [1911] AC 120 that it was finally determined that the relationship of husband and wife did not as a matter of law raise a presumption of undue influence within Class 2(A). It is to be noted therefore that when the *Duval* case was decided in 1902 the question whether there was a Class 2(A) presumption of undue influence as between husband and wife was still unresolved.

An invalidating tendency?

Although there is no Class 2(A) presumption of undue influence as between husband and wife, it should be emphasised that in any particular case a wife may well be able to demonstrate that *de facto* she did leave decisions on financial affairs to her husband thereby bringing herself within Class 2(B), ie that the relationship between husband and wife in the particular case was such that the wife reposed confidence and trust in her husband in relation to their financial affairs and therefore undue influence is to be presumed. Thus, in those cases which still occur where the wife relies in all financial matters on her husband and simply does what he suggests, a presumption of undue influence within Class 2(B) can be established solely from the proof of such trust and confidence without proof of actual undue influence.

In the appeal in *CIBC Mortgages plc v Pitt* (judgment in which is to be given immediately after that in the present appeal) Mr Price for the wife argued that in the case of transactions between husband and wife, there was an 'invalidating tendency', ie although there was no Class 2(A) presumption of undue influence, the courts were more ready to find that a husband had exercised undue influence over his wife than in other cases. Scott LJ in the present case also referred to the law treating married women 'more tenderly' than others. This approach is based on dicta in early authorities. In *Grigby v Cox* (1750) 1 Ves Sen 517 Lord Hardwicke, whilst rejecting any presumption of undue influence, said that a court of equity 'will have more jealousy' over dispositions by a wife to a husband. In *Yerkey v Jones* (1939) 63 CLR 649 Dixon J (at pp 675 *et seq*) refers to this 'invalidating tendency'. He also refers to the court recognising 'the opportunities which a wife's confidence in her husband gives him of unfairly or improperly procuring her to become surety': see at p 677.

In my judgment this special tenderness of treatment afforded to wives by the courts is properly attributable to two factors. First, many cases may well fall into the Class 2(B) category of undue influence because the wife demonstrates that she placed trust and confidence in her husband in relation to her financial affairs and therefore raises a presumption of undue influence. Secondly, the sexual and emotional ties between the parties provide a ready weapon for undue influence: a wife's true wishes can easily be overborne because of her fear of destroying or damaging the wider relationship between her and her husband if she opposes his wishes.

For myself, I accept that the risk of undue influence affecting a voluntary disposition by a wife in favour of a husband is greater than in the ordinary run of cases where no sexual or emotional ties affect the free exercise of the individual's will.

Undue influence, misrepresentation and third parties

Up to this point I have been considering the right of a claimant wife to set aside a transaction as against the wrongdoing husband when the transaction has been procured by his undue influence. But in surety cases the decisive question is whether the claimant wife can set aside the transaction, not against the wrongdoing husband, but against the creditor bank. Of course, if the wrongdoing husband is acting as agent for the creditor bank in obtaining the surety from the wife, the creditor will be fixed with the wrongdoing of its own agent and the surety contract can be set aside as against the creditor. Apart from this, if the creditor bank has notice, actual or constructive, of the undue influence exercised by the husband (and consequentially of the wife's equity to set aside the transaction) the creditor will take subject to that equity and the wife can set aside the transaction against the creditor (albeit a purchaser for value) as well as against the husband: see *Bainbrigge v Browne* (1881) 18 ChD 188; *Aboody* (above) at p 973. Similarly, in cases such as the present where the wife has been induced to enter into the transaction by the husband's misrepresentation, her equity to set aside the transaction will be enforceable against the creditor if either the husband was acting as the creditor's agent or the creditor had actual or constructive notice.

Turnbull & Co v Duval

This case provides the foundation of the modern law: the basis on which it was decided is, to say the least, obscure. Mr Duval owed three separate sums to a firm, Turnbull & Co, including £1,000 owed to the Jamaican branch for beer. Turnbulls' manager and agent in Jamaica was a Mr Campbell. Mr Campbell was also an executor and trustee of a will under which Mrs Duval had a beneficial interest. Mr Campbell threatened to stop supplying beer to Mr Duval unless security was given for the debts owed and, with Mr Campbell's knowledge, a document was prepared under which Mrs Duval charged her beneficial interest under the will to secure the payment of all debts owed by Mr Duval to Turnbull, ie not only the money owed for beer but all the debts. Mr Duval put pressure on Mrs Duval to sign the document. She was under the impression that the document was to secure the beer debt only.

The trial judge in the Court of Appeal in Jamaica held that the security document should be set aside as against Turnbulls on the sole ground that Mr Campbell, as executor of the will, was in a fiduciary capacity *vis-à-vis* his beneficiary, Mrs Duval, and his employers could not uphold the security document unless they could show that Mrs Duval was fully aware of what she was doing when she entered into it and did it freely. The Privy Council dismissed Turnbulls' appeal, Lord Lindley expressing the ratio in these terms, at pp 434–435:

> 'In the face of such evidence, their Lordships are of opinion that it is quite impossible to uphold the security given by Mrs Duval. It is open to the double objection of having been obtained by a trustee from his *cestui que* trust by pressure through her husband and without independent advice, and of having been obtained by a husband from his wife by pressure and concealment of material facts. Whether the security could be upheld if the only ground for impeaching it was that Mrs Duval had no independent advice has not really to be determined. Their Lordships are not prepared to say it could not. But there is an additional and even stronger ground for impeaching it. It is, in their Lordships' opinion, quite clear that Mrs Duval was pressed by her husband to sign, and did sign, the document, which was very different from what she supposed it to be, and a document of the true nature of which she had no conception. It is impossible to hold that Campbell or Turnbull & Co are unaffected by such pressure and ignorance. They left everything to Duval, and must abide the consequences.'

The first ground mentioned by Lord Lindley (ie Campbell's breach of fiduciary duties) raises no problems. It is the second ground which has spawned the whole line of cases with which your Lordships are concerned. It raises two problems. The passage appears to suggest that Mr Duval had acted in some way wrongfully *vis-à-vis* his wife, and that Turnbulls who 'had left everything to Duval' were held liable for Duval's wrong. What was the wrongful act of Duval *vis-à-vis* his wife? Secondly, why did the fact that Turnbulls 'left everything to Duval' render them unable to enforce their security?

Duval's case: was the husband in breach of duty to his wife?

Thanks to the industry of counsel, we have seen the case lodged on the appeal to the Privy Council. The pleadings contain no allegation of undue influence or misrepresentation by Mr Duval. Mrs Duval did not in evidence allege actual or presumptive undue influence. The sole ground of decision in the courts below was Campbell's fiduciary position. There is no finding of undue influence against Mr Duval. No one appeared for Mrs Duval before the Privy Council. Therefore the second ground of decision sprung wholly from the Board and Lord Lindley's speech gives little insight into their reasoning.

For myself I can only assume that, if the Board considered that Mr Duval had committed a wrongful act *vis-à-vis* his wife, it proceeded on a mistaken basis. It will be remembered that in 1902 it had not been finally established that a presumption of undue influence within Class 2(A) did not apply as between husband and wife. The Board may therefore have been proceeding on the basis that the presumption of undue influence applied as between Mr and Mrs Duval. This was certainly one contemporary understanding of the *ratio decidendi*: see *Bishoffs Trustees v Frank* (1903) 89 LT 188. Alternatively, the Board may have been mistakenly applying the heresy propounded by Lord Romilly to the effect that when a person has made a large voluntary disposition the burden is thrown on the party benefiting to show that the disposition was made fairly and honestly and in full understanding of the nature and consequences of the transaction: see *Hoghton v Hoghton* (1852) 15 Beav 278. Although this heresy has never been formally overruled, it has rightly been regarded as bad law for a very long time: see the account given by Dixon J in *Yerkey v Jones* 63 CLR 649 at p 678 *et seq*. It is impossible to find a sound basis for holding that Mrs Duval was entitled to set aside the transaction as against her husband. How then could she set it aside as against Turnbulls?

Duval's case: was the creditor under a direct duty to the wife?

It is the lack of any sound basis for holding that Mr Duval was guilty of a legal wrong for which Turnbulls were indirectly held liable which has led to the theory that the creditor, Turnbulls, were themselves in breach of some duty owed by them as creditors directly to the surety, Mrs Duval. No one has ever suggested that in the ordinary case of principal and surety the creditor owes any duty of care to the surety: in the normal case it is for the surety to satisfy himself as to the nature and extent of the obligations he is assuming. Therefore, it is said, there must be some special feature of the case where a wife stands surety for her husband's debt which gives rise to some special duty. This is the explanation of the decision of *Duval's* case given by Dixon J in *Yerkey v Jones* (above) which, in turn, is the basis on which the Court of Appeal in the present case adopted the view that the law imposed on the creditor itself a duty to take steps to ensure not only that the husband had not used undue influence or made a misrepresentation but also that the wife had 'an adequate understanding of the nature and effect of what she was doing'. If this interpretation of *Duval's* case is correct, the law not only imposes on the creditor a duty *vis-à-vis* a particular class of surety where ordinarily there would be none but the extent of that duty is greater than that which, under the ordinary law, a husband would owe to his wife: a transaction between husband and wife cannot in the absence of undue influence or misrepresentation, be set aside simply on the ground that the wife did not fully understand the transaction.

Duval's case: 'they left everything to Duval and must abide the consequences'

These words provide the only guidance as to the circumstances which led the Board to set aside the surety agreement as against Turnbulls. In later cases the words have often been treated as indicating that Mr Duval (but not Turnbulls themselves) acted in breach of duty to Mrs Duval, that Mr Duval was Turnbulls' agent and that Turnbulls could not be in a better position than its agent. Quite apart from the difficulty of identifying what was the breach of duty committed by Mr Duval, the concept of Mr Duval having acted as agent for Turnbulls to procure his wife to become surety for the debt was artificial in *Duval's* case itself and in some of the later cases becomes even more artificial. As the Court of Appeal in this case point out, in the majority of cases the reality of the relationship is that, the creditor having required of the principal debtor that there must be a surety, the principal debtor on his own account in order to raise the necessary finance seeks to procure the support of the surety. In so doing he is acting for himself not for the creditor.

The subsequent authorities

The authorities in which the principle derived from the *Duval* case has been applied are fully analysed in the judgment of Scott LJ and it is unnecessary to review them fully again.

Scott LJ analyses the cases as indicating that down to 1985 there was no decision which indicated that the agency theory, rather than the special equity theory, was the basis of the decision in *Duval*. I agree. But that is attributable more to the application of the *Duval* principle than to any analysis of its jurisprudential basis. The only attempts to analyse the basis of the decision in *Duval's* case were the Australian decisions in *Bank of Victoria Ltd v Mueller* [1925] VLR 642 and the judgment of Dixon J in *Yerkey v Jones* (above). The former decision was reached by applying the Romilly heresy which, as I have already said, is bad law. The judgment of Dixon J undoubtedly supports the special equity theory.

From 1985 down to the decision of the Court of Appeal in the present case the decisions have all been based on the agency theory, ie that the principal debtor has acted in breach of duty to his wife, the surety, and that, if the principal debtor was acting as the creditor's agent but not otherwise, the creditor cannot be in any better position than its agent, the husband. In all the cases since 1985 the principal debtor has procured the agreement of the surety by a legal wrong (undue influence or misrepresentation). In all the cases emphasis was placed on the question whether the creditor was infected by the debtor's wrongdoing because the debtor was acting as the agent of the creditor in procuring the wife's agreement to stand as surety. I am unable to agree with Scott LJ that the decision in *Kings North Trust Ltd v Bell* [1986] 1 WLR 119 was not based on the agency theory: Dillon LJ at p 123F–G expressly makes it a necessary condition that the creditor has entrusted to the husband the task of obtaining his wife's signature.

However, in four of the cases since 1985 attention has been drawn to the fact that, even in the absence of agency, if the debtor has been guilty of undue influence or misrepresentation the creditor may not be able to enforce the surety contract if the creditor had notice, actual or constructive, of the debtor's conduct: see *Avon Finance Co Ltd v Bridger* [1985] 2 All ER 281 *per* Brandon LJ at p 287E; *Coldunell Ltd v Gallon* [1986] QB 1184 at 1201; *Midland Bank plc v Shephard* [1988] 3 All ER 17 at 23; *Bank of Credit and Commerce International SA v Aboody* [1990] 1 QB 923 at 973. As will appear, in my view it is the proper application of the doctrine of notice which provides the key to finding a principled basis for the law.

Accordingly, the present law is built on the unsure foundations of the *Duval* case. Like most law founded on obscure and possibly mistaken foundations it has developed in an artificial way, giving rise to artificial distinctions and conflicting decisions. In my judgment your Lordships should seek to restate the law in a form which is principled, reflects the current requirements of society and provides as much certainty as possible.

Conclusions

(a) Wives

My starting point is to clarify the basis of the law. Should wives (and perhaps others) be accorded special rights in relation to surety transactions by the recognition of a special equity applicable only to such persons engaged in such transactions? Or should they enjoy only the same protection as they would enjoy in relation to their other dealings? In my judgment, the special equity theory should be rejected. First, I can find no basis in principle for affording special protection to a limited class in relation to one type of transaction only. Secondly, to require the creditor to prove knowledge and understanding by the wife in all cases is to reintroduce by the back door either a presumption of undue influence of Class 2(A) (which has been decisively rejected) or the Romilly heresy (which has long been treated as bad law). Thirdly, although Scott LJ found that there were two lines of cases one of which supported the special equity theory, on analysis although many decisions are not inconsistent with that theory the only two cases which support it are *Yerkey v Jones* (63 CLR 649) and the decision of the Court of Appeal in the present case. Finally, it is not necessary to have recourse to a special equity theory for the proper protection of the legitimate interests of wives as I will seek to show.

In my judgment, if the doctrine of notice is properly applied, there is no need for the introduction of a special equity in these types of cases. A wife who has been induced to stand as a surety for her husband's debts by his undue influence, misrepresentation or some other legal wrong has an equity as against him to set aside that transaction. Under the ordinary principles of equity, her right to set aside that transaction will be enforceable against third parties (eg against a creditor) if either the husband was acting as the third party's agent or the third party had actual or constructive notice of the facts giving rise to her equity. Although there may be cases where, without artificiality, it can properly be held that the husband was acting as the agent of the creditor in procuring the wife to stand as surety, such cases will be of very rare occurrence. The key to the problem is to identify the circumstances in which the creditor will be taken to have had notice of the wife's equity to set aside the transaction.

The doctrine of notice lies at the heart of equity. Given that there are two innocent parties, each enjoying rights, the earlier right prevails against the later right if the acquirer of the later right knows of the earlier right (actual notice) or would have discovered it had he taken proper steps (constructive notice). In particular, if the party asserting that he takes free of the earlier rights of another knows of certain facts which put him on inquiry as to the possible existence of the rights of that other and he fails to make such inquiry or take such other steps as are reasonable to verify whether such earlier right does or does not exist, he will have constructive notice of the earlier right and take subject to it. Therefore where a wife has agreed to stand surety for her husband's debts as a result of undue influence or misrepresentation, the creditor will take subject to the wife's equity to set aside the transaction if the circumstances are such as to put the creditor on inquiry as to the circumstances in which she agreed to stand surety.

It is at this stage that, in my view, the 'invalidating tendency' or the law's 'tender treatment' of married women, becomes relevant. As I have said above in dealing with undue influence, this tenderness of the law towards married women is due to the fact that, even today, many wives repose confidence and trust in their husbands in relation to their financial affairs. This tenderness of the law is reflected by the fact that voluntary dispositions by the wife in favour of her husband are more likely to be set aside than other dispositions by her: a wife is more likely to establish presumed undue influence of Class 2(B) by her husband than by others because, in practice, many wives do repose in their husbands trust and confidence in relation to their financial affairs. Moreover the informality of business dealings between spouses raises a substantial risk that the husband has not accurately stated to the wife the nature of the liability she is undertaking, ie he has misrepresented the position, albeit negligently.

Therefore in my judgment a creditor is put on inquiry when a wife offers to stand surety for her husband's debts by the combination of two factors:

(a) The transaction is on its face not to the financial advantage of the wife; and

(b) there is a substantial risk in transactions of that kind that, in procuring the wife to act as surety, the husband has committed a legal or equitable wrong that entitles the wife to set aside the transaction.

It follows that unless the creditor who is put on inquiry takes reasonable steps to satisfy himself that the wife's agreement to stand surety has been properly obtained, the creditor will have constructive notice of the wife's rights.

What, then are the reasonable steps which the creditor should take to ensure that it does not have constructive notice of the wife's rights, if any? Normally the reasonable steps necessary to avoid being fixed with constructive notice consist of making inquiry of the person who may have the earlier right (ie the wife) to see if whether such right is asserted. It is plainly impossible to require of banks and other financial institutions that they should inquire of one spouse whether he or she has been unduly influenced or misled by the other. But in my judgment the creditor, in order to avoid being fixed with constructive notice, can reasonably be expected to take steps to bring home to the wife the risk she is running by standing as surety and to advise her to take independent advice. As to past transactions, it will depend on the facts of each case whether the steps taken by the creditor satisfy this test. However for the future in my judgment a creditor will have satisfied these requirements if it insists that the wife attend a private meeting (in the absence of the husband) with a representative of the creditor at which she is told of the extent of her liability as surety, warned of the risk she is running and urged to take independent legal advice. If these steps are taken in my judgment the creditor will have taken such reasonable steps as are necessary to preclude a subsequent claim that it had constructive notice of the wife's rights. I should make it clear that I have been considering the ordinary case where the creditor knows only that the wife is to stand surety for her husband's debts. I would not exclude exceptional cases where a creditor has knowledge of further facts which render the presence of undue influence not only possible but probable. In such cases, the creditor to be safe will have to insist that the wife is separately advised.

I am conscious that in treating the creditor as having constructive notice because of the risk of Class 2(B) undue influence or misrepresentation by the husband I may be extending the law as stated by Fry J in *Bainbrigge v Browne* (above) at p 197 and the Court of Appeal in the *Aboody* case (above) at p 973. Those cases suggest that for a third party to be affected by constructive notice of presumed undue influence the third party must actually know of the circumstances which give rise to a presumption of undue influence. In contrast, my view is that the risk of Class 2(B) undue influence or misrepresentation is sufficient to put the creditor on inquiry. But my statement accords with the principles of notice: if the known facts are such as to indicate the possibility of an adverse claim that is sufficient to put a third party on inquiry.

If the law is established as I have suggested, it will hold the balance fairly between on the one hand the vulnerability of the wife who relies implicitly on her husband and, on the other hand, the practical problems of financial institutions asked to accept a secured or unsecured surety obligation from the wife for her husband's debts. In the context of suretyship, the wife will not have any right to disown her obligations just because subsequently she proves that she did not fully understand the transaction: she will, as in all other areas of her affairs, be bound by her obligations unless her husband has, by misrepresentation, undue influence or other wrong, committed an actionable wrong against her. In the normal case, a financial institution will be able to lend with confidence in reliance on the wife's surety obligation provided that it warns her (in the absence of the husband) of the amount of her potential liability and of the risk of standing surety and advises her to take independent advice.

Mr Jarvis, for the bank, urged that this is to impose too heavy a burden on financial institutions. I am not impressed by this submission. The Report by Professor Jack's Review Committee on Banking Services: 'Law and Practice' (1989), (Cmnd 622), recommended that prospective guarantors should be adequately warned of the legal effects and possible consequences of their guarantee and of the importance of receiving independent advice. Pursuant to this recommendation, the Code of Banking Practice (adopted by banks and building societies in March 1992) provides in paragraph 12.1 as follows:

> 'Banks and building societies will advise private individuals proposing to give them a guarantee or other security for another person's liabilities that:

(i) by giving the guarantee or third party security he or she might become liable instead of or as well as that other person;

(ii) he or she should seek independent legal advice before entering into the guarantee or third party security.

Guarantees and other third party security forms will contain a clear and prominent notice to the above effect.'

Thus good banking practice (which applies to all guarantees not only those given by a wife) largely accords with what I consider the law should require when a wife is offered as surety. The only further substantial step required by law beyond that good practice is that the position should be explained by the bank to the wife in a personal interview. I regard this as being essential because a number of the decided cases show that written warnings are often not read and are sometimes intercepted by the husband. It does not seem to me that the requirement of a personal interview imposes such an additional administrative burden as to render the bank's position unworkable.

(b) Other persons

I have hitherto dealt only with the position where a wife stands surety for her husband's debts. But in my judgment the same principles are applicable to all other cases where there is an emotional relationship between cohabitees. The 'tenderness' shown by the law to married women is not based on the marriage ceremony but reflects the underlying risk of one cohabitee exploiting the emotional involvement and trust of the other. Now that unmarried cohabitation, whether heterosexual or homosexual, is widespread in our society, the law should recognise this. Legal wives are not the only group which are now exposed to the emotional pressure of cohabitation. Therefore if, but only if, the creditor is aware that the surety is cohabiting with the principal debtor, in my judgment the same principles should apply to them as apply to husband and wife.

In addition to the cases of cohabitees, the decision of the Court of Appeal in *Avon Finance Co Ltd v Bridger* (above) shows (rightly in my view) that other relationships can give rise to a similar result. In that case a son, by means of misrepresentation, persuaded his elderly parents to stand surety for his debts. The surety obligation was held to be unenforceable by the creditor *inter alia* because to the bank's knowledge the parents trusted the son in their financial dealings. In my judgment that case was rightly decided: in a case where the creditor is aware that the surety reposes trust and confidence in the principal debtor in relation to his financial affairs, the creditor is put on inquiry in just the same way as it is in relation to husband and wife.

Summary

I can therefore summarise my views as follows, Where one cohabitee has entered into an obligation to stand as surety for the debts of the other cohabitee and the creditor is aware that they are cohabitees:

1. The surety obligation will be valid and enforceable by the creditor unless suretyship was procured by the undue influence, misrepresentation or other legal wrong of the principal.

2. If there has been undue influence, misrepresentation or other legal wrong by the principal debtor, unless the creditor has taken reasonable steps to satisfy himself that the surety entered into the obligation freely and in knowledge of the true facts the creditor will be unable to enforce the surety obligation because he will be fixed with constructive notice of the surety's right to set aside the transaction.

3. Unless there are special exceptional circumstances, a creditor will have taken such reasonable steps to avoid being fixed with constructive notice if the creditor warns the surety (at a meeting not attended by the principal debtor) of the amount of her potential liability and of the risks involved and advises the surety to take independent legal advice.

I should make it clear that in referring to the husband's debts I include the debt of a company in which the husband (but not the wife) has a direct financial interest.

The decision of this case

Applying those principles to this case, to the knowledge of the bank Mr and Mrs O'Brien were man and wife. The bank took a surety obligation from Mrs O'Brien secured on the matrimonial home, to secure the debts of a company in which Mr O'Brien was interested but in which Mrs O'Brien had no direct pecuniary interest. The bank should therefore have been put on inquiry as to the circumstances in which Mrs O'Brien had agreed to stand as surety for the debt of her husband. If the Burnham branch had properly carried out the instructions from Mr Tucker of the Woolwich branch, Mrs O'Brien would have been informed that she and the matrimonial home were potentially liable for the debts of a company which had an existing liability of £107,000 and which was to be afforded an overdraft facility of £135,000. If she been told this, it would have counteracted Mr O'Brien's misrepresentation that the liability was limited to £60,000 and would last for only three weeks. In addition according to the side letter she would have been recommended to take independent legal advice.

Unfortunately Mr Tucker's instructions were not followed and to the knowledge of the bank (through the clerk at the Burnham branch) Mrs O'Brien signed the documents without any warning of the risks or any recommendation to take legal advice. In the circumstances the bank (having failed to take reasonable steps) is fixed with constructive notice of the wrongful misrepresentation made by Mr O'Brien to Mrs O'Brien. Mrs O'Brien is therefore entitled as against the bank to set aside the legal charge on the matrimonial home securing her husband's liability to the bank. For these reasons I would dismiss the appeal with costs.

This decision was followed and applied at first instance by Judge Rich QC, sitting as an additional judge of the Chancery Division, in *Goode Durrant Administration v Biddulph* (1994) 26 HLR 625 and by the Court of Appeal in *TSB Bank plc v Camfield* (1994) 27 HLR 329, where it was held that a bank was totally unable to enforce a legal charge entered into by a wife to stand surety as a result of her husband's misrepresentations.

If, however, the wife had been made properly aware of the significance of what she was signing, even though the advice she had received was not in the strict sense independent, it may be that the bank will have taken sufficient steps to make the charge enforceable. Thus, in *Banco Exterior v Mann* (1995) 27 HLR 329, a majority of the Court of Appeal held that a bank was entitled to enforce a wife's undertaking that her rights in the matrimonial home should be postponed to those of the bank. She had signed the documents after receiving advice from a solicitor. The solicitor was in fact the solicitor to the husband's company, but the bank was held to be entitled to rely on the fact that the solicitor felt able to give this advice without any conflict of duty or interest. This was held to be enough to amount to 'reasonable steps' to avoid being fixed with constructive notice of the alleged undue influence exercised by the husband. A similar decision was also reached in *Midland Bank v Serter* (1995) 27 HLR 647.

These cases should be contrasted, however, with *CIBC Mortgages v Pitt* (1993) 26 HLR 90. In that case a joint mortgage by Mr & Mrs Pitt was held to be enforceable against Mrs Pitt, notwithstanding the undue influence exercised by

Mr Pitt over Mrs Pitt. Here the bank had no actual notice of the undue influence. Unlike O'Brien, where the transaction was manifestly disadvantageous to Mrs O'Brien, this was a joint advance to Mr and Mrs Pitt, and there was nothing in the transaction to suggest that it was not for their joint benefit.

CIBC Mortgages v Pitt

Lord Browne-Wilkinson: ... (Having considered the question of manifest disadvantage, and having decided that cases of Class 1 (actual undue influence) no longer required proof of manifest disadvantage, continued:)

Notice

Even though, in my view, Mrs Pitt is entitled to set aside the transaction as against Mr Pitt, she has to establish that in some way the plaintiff is affected by the wrongdoing of Mr Pitt so as to be entitled to set aside the legal charge as against the plaintiff.

The Court of Appeal in the present case treated themselves as bound by the Court of Appeal decision in *O'Brien*. They were unwilling to distinguish *O'Brien* on the ground that the instant case is one of a loan to the husband and wife jointly whereas *O'Brien* was a surety case ...

Applying the decision of this House in *O'Brien* Mrs Pitt has established actual undue influence by Mr Pitt. The plaintiff will not however be affected by such undue influence unless Mr Pitt was, in a real sense, acting as agent of the plaintiff in procuring Mrs Pitt's agreement or the plaintiff had actual or constructive notice of the undue influence. The judge has correctly held that Mr Pitt was not acting as agent for the plaintiff. The plaintiff had no actual notice of the undue influence. What, then, was known to the plaintiff that could put it on inquiry so as to fix it with constructive notice?

So far as the plaintiff was aware, the transaction consisted of a joint loan to husband and wife to finance the discharge of an existing mortgage on 26 Alexander Avenue, and as to the balance to be applied in buying a holiday home. The loan was advanced to both husband and wife jointly. There was nothing to indicate to the plaintiff that this was anything other than a normal advance to husband and wife for their joint benefit.

Mr Price, for Mrs Pitt, argued that the invalidating tendency which reflects the risk of there being Class 2(B) undue influence was, in itself, sufficient to put the plaintiff on inquiry. I reject this submission without hesitation. It accords neither with justice nor with practical common sense. If third parties were to be fixed with constructive notice of undue influence in relation to every transaction between husband and wife such transactions would become almost impossible. On every purchase of a home in the joint names, the building society or bank financing the purchase would have to insist on meeting the wife separately from her husband, advise her as to the nature of the transaction and recommend her to take legal advice separate from that of her husband. If that were not done, the financial institution would have to run the risk of a subsequent attempt by the wife to avoid her liabilities under the mortgage on grounds of undue influence or misrepresentation. To establish the law in that sense would not benefit the average married couple and would discourage financial institutions from making the advance.

What distinguishes the case of the joint advance from the surety case is that, in the latter, there is not only the possibility of undue influence having been exercised but also the increased risk of it having in fact been exercised because, at least on its face the guarantee by a wife of her husband's debts is not for her financial benefit. It is the combination of these two factors that puts the creditor on inquiry.

For these reasons I agree with the Court of Appeal on this issue and would dismiss the appeal. Mrs Pitt is legally aided but, subject to affording the Legal Aid Board an opportunity to be heard, I would order her costs of this appeal to be paid out of the Legal Aid Fund.

On undue influence, see also *Midland Bank v Greene* (1995) 27 HLR 350; *Bank of Baroda v Rayerel* (1995) 27 HLR 387 and *Halifax Building Society v Brown* (1995) 27 HLR 511.

CHAPTER 14

OWNER OCCUPIERS AND THE FINANCIAL CRISIS

INTRODUCTION

This chapter is concerned with the protection which the law gives to the owner occupier in a time of financial crisis. One of the features of life during the last two decades in England and Wales has been the increasing incidence of financial failure. This is partly a product of the recession within the economy, and partly a result of the stresses to which the Housing Market itself has been subject, with interest rates rising rapidly since a 'low' in 1987, before falling back into single figures. Redundancy for breadwinners has clearly had a major impact on the incidence of mortgage arrears, as has the level of breakdown of marriage.

In many cases, where a person becomes the victim of financial crisis, the only substantial asset available for the satisfaction of his creditors will be his family home. At the same time, the law has to strike a balance between the rights of the creditors and the accommodation needs of the family of the debtor.

One form which financial crisis will often take is an increase in mortgage arrears. The rights of the debtor/mortgagor in this situation are covered by the provisions of the Administration of Justice Acts 1970 and 1973, and are considered in detail elsewhere (see Chapter 13). In this chapter the main concern will be to outline the provisions of the law relating to bankruptcy and charging orders as they affect owner occupiers and their families. It will be seen that the law seeks to strike a balance between the competing claims of the creditors and the family of the debtor.

Bankruptcy tends to occur in close association with such devastating events as redundancy, business failure, or marital breakdown. 'Eviction from the family home ... may be a disaster not only to the debtor himself ... but also to those who are living there as his dependants who may not, and often do not, have any legal or beneficial rights in the property which they can enforce' (Insolvency Law and Practice (Report of the Review Committee chaired by Sir Kenneth Cork) Cmnd 8558 (1982), para 1116). The current law on personal bankruptcy is contained in the Insolvency Act 1986 (henceforth 'the 1986 Act'), which was passed with the intention of partially implementing the recommendations of the Cork Committee (Report of the Review Committee (above)).

The basic principle of insolvency law remains that (with a few limited exceptions) the property of the bankrupt vests in his trustee in bankruptcy, who has to administer the estate of the bankrupt and realise as much as he can for the benefit of the creditors (s 305 of the 1986 Act). It has always been realised, however, that a further aim of the bankruptcy code has been to enable the individual debtor to achieve his rehabilitation as a useful and productive member of society. Certain assets necessary for this purpose are accordingly exempted from vesting in the trustee and are allowed to be retained by the debtor. These principles remain at the core of the 1986 Act.

At the same time, the legislation is designed to make a modest attempt to alleviate the hardships involved for those who are dependent on the debtor but not responsible for his bankruptcy. To this extent, at least, the provisions of the Act represent an advance from the position before the Act. The basic provisions in the 1986 Act are reproduced below.

Insolvency Act 1986

283. Definition of a bankrupt's estate

(1) A bankrupt's estate ... comprises–

(a) all property belonging to or vested in the bankrupt at the commencement of the bankruptcy; and

(b) any property which by virtue of any of the following provisions of this Part is comprised in that estate or is treated as falling within the preceding paragraph.

(2) Subsection (1) does not apply to–

(a) such tools, books, vehicles and other items of equipment as are necessary to the bankrupt for use personally by him in his employment business or vocation;

(b) such clothing, bedding, furniture, household equipment and provisions as are necessary for satisfying the basic domestic needs of the bankrupt and his family ...

(3) Subsection (1) does not apply to–

(a) property held by the bankrupt on trust for any other person ...

[Section 284 also operates to make void any purported disposition of property by the bankrupt, unless the disposition is made with the consent of the court or is subsequently ratified by the court.]

306. Vesting of bankrupt's estate in trustee

(1) The bankrupt's estate shall vest in the trustee immediately on his appointment taking effect or, in the case of the official receiver, on his becoming trustee.

(2) Where any property which is, or is to be, comprised in the bankrupt's estate vests in the trustee (whether under this section or under any other provision of this Part), it shall so vest without any conveyance, assignment, or transfer.

On bankruptcy, the house in which the debtor is living with his wife and family (or more often, the residual value of such a house after repayment of the mortgage debt) is frequently the major asset of a debtor. As such, the debtor's creditors will normally seek a sale of the house so that their claims can be satisfied, at least in part, out of the proceeds of sale. But changing houses is not easy, and to buy a house without the proceeds of sale from another is even more difficult. Eviction from the family home may thus be a disaster not only to the bankrupt himself but also to those who are living there as his dependants. As the Cork Committee stated in its report (at para 1118):

> It would be clearly wrong to allow a debtor or his family to continue to live in a lavish style at the expense of the debtor's creditors for an extended period. Nevertheless considerable personal hardship can be caused to the debtor's family by a sudden or premature eviction, and we believe it to be consonant with present social attitudes to alleviate the personal hardships of those who are dependent on the debtor but not responsible for his insolvency, if this can be

achieved by delaying for an acceptable time the sale of the family home. We propose therefore to delay, but not to cancel enforcement of the creditors' rights.

One of the major innovations of the 1986 Act has been the granting of certain rights of occupation (in some circumstances) to the bankrupt himself, which may lead to a postponement of the sale of the bankrupt's house. These rights are not automatic, however, and depend upon the bankrupt satisfying certain qualifying conditions. This protection applies both if the property is the sole property of the bankrupt and if the property is jointly owned (in which case only his beneficial interest vests in his trustee in bankruptcy: see ss 283 and 306 above).

It should be noted, however, that the protection of the bankrupt's right of occupation is not self-standing; it depends upon the presence of children – though they do not need to be the bankrupt's own children, so long as they are living in the house in question with him. The protection is not available for the childless bankrupt, nor one whose children have grown up (unless he has, for instance, resident grandchildren). The Cork Committee recommended that similar interim protection should be generated by the presence of other family members – for instance aged parents, living in the house as part of a family arrangement – but this was not accepted by the legislature.

The necessary condition mentioned above is that the bankrupt himself had the right to occupy a dwelling-house by virtue of some estate or interest, and that 'any persons under the age of 18 with whom that person (ie the bankrupt) had at some time occupied that dwelling-house had their home with that person at the time when the bankruptcy petition was presented and at the commencement of the bankruptcy' (s 337(1)).

Insolvency Act 1986

337 This section applies where–

(a) a person who is entitled to occupy a dwelling-house by virtue of a beneficial estate or interest is adjudged bankrupt; and

(b) any persons under the age of 18 with whom that person had at some time occupied that dwelling-house had their home with that person at the time when the bankruptcy petition was presented and at the commencement of the bankruptcy.

(2) Whether or not the bankrupt's spouse (if any) has rights of occupation under the Matrimonial Homes Act 1983–

    (a) the bankrupt has the following rights as against the trustee of his estate–

        (i) if in occupation, a right not to be excluded or evicted from the dwelling-house or any part of it, except with the leave of the court,

        (ii) if not in occupation, a right with the leave of the court to enter into and occupy the dwelling-house, and

    (b) the bankrupt's rights are a charge, having the like priority as an equitable interest created immediately before the commencement of the bankruptcy, on so much of his estate or interest in the dwelling-house as vests in the trustee.

(3) The Act of 1983 has effect, with the necessary modifications, as if–

    (a) the rights conferred by paragraph (a) of subsection (2) were rights of occupation under the Act;

(b) any application for leave such as is mentioned in that paragraph were an application for an order under section 1 of that Act; and

(c) any charge under paragraph (b) of that subsection on the estate or interest of the trustee were a charge under that Act on the estate or interest of a spouse.

(4) Any application for leave such as is mentioned in subsection (2)(a) or otherwise by virtue of this section for an order under section 1 of the Act of 1983 shall be made to the court having jurisdiction in relation to the bankruptcy.

(5) On such application the court shall make such order under section 1 of the Act of 1983 as it thinks just and reasonable having regard to the interests of the creditors, to the bankrupt's financial resources, to the needs of the children, and to all the circumstances of the case other than the needs of the bankrupt.

(6) Where such an application is made after the end of the period of one year beginning with the first vesting (under Chapter IV of this Part) of the bankrupt's estate in a trustee, the court shall assume, unless the circumstances of the case are exceptional, that the interests of the bankrupt's creditors outweigh all other considerations.

The general effect of these provisions is that (assuming that the 'children condition' is satisfied) any attempt by the trustee in bankruptcy to realise the value of the family home by a sale will have to be preceded by an application to the court for the termination of the bankrupt's rights of occupation. The court will then have a discretion whether or not to terminate the bankrupt's rights of occupation. The Cork Committee thought it essential that the court should have a wide discretion, as circumstances can vary greatly.

The statutory provisions, however, represent a watering down (by confining the statutory protection to those who satisfy the 'children condition') of the Cork Committee recommendations, which suggested that the court should give primary consideration 'to the welfare of dependent children, to the circumstances of the wife, and to the situation of dependent parents who are resident in the family dwelling' (para 1129). Also, the statutory limit on the court's discretion for a year was introduced against the majority opinion of the Cork Committee, who thought that there was no case for such a time limit.

It remains to be seen what sort of 'exceptional circumstances' will suffice to preserve the rights of occupation of the bankrupt once the first year has elapsed. Some assistance might be derived from the pre-1986 joint ownership cases, where occasionally the courts have been able to find 'exceptional circumstances' to justify the postponement of a sale, when a trustee in bankruptcy has applied for an order for sale under s 30 Law of Property Act 1925. These cases are further considered below.

It is a familiar concept of the law of implied, constructive and resulting trusts that periodical payments in respect of the outgoings of property can sometimes give rise to a beneficial interest in favour of the person making the payments. To preclude the generation of any further beneficial interest in favour of a bankrupt who makes payments of this sort, s 338 provides:

Where any premises comprised in a bankrupt's estate are occupied by him (whether by virtue of the preceding section or otherwise) on condition that he makes payments towards satisfying any liability arising under a mortgage of the premises or otherwise towards the outgoings of the premises, the bankrupt does not, by virtue of those payments, acquire any interest in the premises.

In cases where there is a delay because of these provisions, the trustee in bankruptcy can take steps to protect the interests of creditors by applying for an order on the property under s 313 of the Act:

(1) Where any property consisting of an interest in a dwelling-house which is occupied by the bankrupt or by his spouse or former spouse is comprised in the bankrupt's estate and the trustee is, for any reason, unable for the time being to realise that property, the trustee may apply to the court for an order imposing a charge on the property for the benefit of the bankrupt's estate.

(2) If on an application under this section the court imposes a charge on any property, the benefit of that charge shall be comprised in the bankrupt's estate and is enforceable, up to the value from time to time of the property secured, for the payment of any amount which is payable otherwise than to the bankrupt out of the estate and of interest on that amount at the prescribed rate.

Prior to the introduction of the 1986 Act, a spouse's rights of occupation under the Matrimonial Homes Act 1983 did not bind a trustee in bankruptcy. The position has now been changed as a result of s 337 Insolvency Act 1986.

Insolvency Act 1986

337(1) ...

(2) Where a spouse's rights of occupation under the Act of 1983 are a charge on the estate or interest of the other spouse, or of trustees for the other spouse, and the other spouse is adjudged bankrupt–

(a) the charge continues to subsist notwithstanding the bankruptcy and, subject to the provisions of that Act, binds the trustee of the bankrupt's estate and persons deriving title under that trustee; and

(b) any application for an order under section 1 of that Act shall be made to the court having jurisdiction in relation to the bankruptcy ...

(3) ...

(4) On such an application ... the court shall make such order under section 1 of the Act of 1983 ... as it thinks just and reasonable having regard to–

(a) the interests of the bankrupt's creditors;

(b) the conduct of the spouse or former spouse, so far as contributing to the bankruptcy;

(c) the needs and financial resources of the spouse or former spouse;

(d) the needs of any children; and

(e) all the circumstances of the case other than the needs of the bankrupt.

(5) Where such an application is made after the end of the period of one year beginning with the first vesting under Chapter IV of this Part of the bankrupt's estate in a trustee, the court shall assume, unless the circumstances of the case are exceptional, that the interests of the bankrupt's creditors outweigh all other considerations.

This provision, like the corresponding provision relating to the rights of occupation of the bankrupt himself, only gives the spouse, in effect, a breathing space for a year. This 'breathing space' depends upon the discretion of the court, and many factors may influence the court in the exercise of this discretion, including for instance, the conduct of the spouse in so far as it may have contributed to the bankruptcy. Thus, a spouse whose spendthrift habits may have contributed to the bankruptcy may have difficulty in persuading a court to allow rights of occupation to continue. The spouse's ability to find alternative accommodation may also be relevant. Paragraph (e) might make it possible for the needs of other relatives of the bankrupt to be taken into account. Thereafter, absent 'exceptional circumstances', the voice of the creditors will prevail. Again, the pre-1986 joint ownership cases may afford some guidance as to what will amount to special circumstances.

Many houses which become involved in bankruptcy procedures are jointly owned – characteristically by a bankrupt and his spouse and these cases (all of which precede the Insolvency Act 1986) have presented the courts with the greatest difficulties in balancing the interests of the creditors and the dependants of the bankrupt. Where a house is jointly owned, from the moment of acquisition the property will be subject to a trust for sale. On bankruptcy, the beneficial interest of the bankrupt (but not his legal interest – see s 283 above) vests in the trustee in bankruptcy. In such cases it is clear that the interests of the creditors will be best protected by a speedy sale, under the provisions of s 30 Law of Property Act 1925. Two separate question arise:

(1) Has the trustee in bankruptcy *locus standi* to apply for a sale?

(2) If so, should a sale be ordered?

The first issue was resolved in *Re Solomon* [1967] Ch 573 where it was established that a bankruptcy trustee has *locus standi* to apply for a sale. In that case freehold property was held by Solomon and his wife jointly. Solomon deserted his wife, and was adjudicated bankrupt some years later. The trustee in bankruptcy applied to the court for an order for sale of the property, but this was resisted by the wife on the grounds, *inter alia*, that the trustee had no *locus standi* to apply for a sale under s 30. This argument was rejected by Goff J. As to the second issue, the nature of the conflict between the trustee in bankruptcy and the dependants of the bankrupt was neatly summarised by Goff J in Re [1985] 1 All ER 5, when he said:

> In my judgment, there exist in equity two conflicting claims: on the one hand the wife, as part owner of the house asks: why should she as co-owner be turned out merely because her husband, the other co-owner, is bankrupt? On the other hand the trustee in bankruptcy says he is not only entitled to realise the husband's interest but is bound by statute to do so' (at p 7).

Holding that the guiding principle was not 'whether the trustee or the wife is being reasonable, but in all the circumstances of the case whose voice in equity ought to prevail', he held that a sale should be ordered.

It seems clear from the authorities (especially *Re Citro* (below at p 468) that, in general terms, no distinction ought to be made between a case where the property is still being enjoyed as a matrimonial home and one where it is not. The general approach of the court in such cases can be discerned from the decision in *Re Bailey* [1977] 2 All ER 26.

Re Bailey

Megarry V-C: This is an appeal from a decision of Judge MacManus QC on 15th July 1976, sitting in bankruptcy in the Tunbridge Wells County Court. There has really been only one point in the appeal, namely, what is to be the date of sale of the former matrimonial home.

The sequence of events can be stated shortly. The husband and the wife married in 1950. In May 1960 the only child of the marriage, a son, Alan, was born, and he is therefore now some 16 years and five months old. In April 1963 the 66 Sedgmoor Road, Flackwell Heath, Buckinghamshire (which stands, we were told, some 31 miles from High Wycombe) was purchased by the husband and the wife. Under the conveyance the house was conveyed to them to hold on trust for sale for themselves as joint tenants; and it has been accepted on both sides before us that they are equally entitled in equity to the proceeds of sale. There is a mortgage which leaves an equity worth some £12,000. In March 1971 the husband left his wife and child. Later that year, in August, an order was made in the magistrates' court whereby the wife was given custody of the son; and a maintenance order was made. On 11th March 1974 the wife petitioned for divorce. On 5th May a decree nisi was made on the ground of the husband's desertion, and on 28th June the decree was made absolute.

In those proceedings no property adjustment order was made, so that nothing was done to affect the house which is in issue before us. Just under a year later, on 13th June 1975, the husband was adjudicated bankrupt on his own petition. His statement of affairs, lodged later that month, showed that there were gross debts of rather over £4,000, of which a little over £2,000 were ranking debts, and that his assets consisted of about £200 and his half-share in the house. The house is accordingly a most important factor for his creditors in his bankruptcy.

The trustee in bankruptcy instituted these proceedings in the county court on 6th May 1976, seeking an order for the sale of the house under s 30 of the Law of Property Act 1925; and on 15th July, as I have said, the judge gave his judgment ... Put shortly, his order was that the wife ... should pay £3,000 to the trustee in bankruptcy before the 1st October of this year, and, if she did this, the sale of the house was to be postponed until 1st May 1977. If, as proved to be the case, she did not pay this sum of money, then the order for sale was to take effect on 1st November 1976; and that is accordingly the effective order. Before us there was some evidence that the wife had made efforts to raise the £3,000 referred to in the order, but had been quite unable to do so. She is plainly of modest means.

The dispute has largely revolved around the question of the son's education. At the moment he is engaged in preparing for some O-levels which he is due to re-sit in November 1976, but at the same time he has embarked on a course of studies for his A-levels, which he is due to take in the summer of 1978. It has been the contention of counsel for the wife that the sale should be postponed until August 1978 in order that the son's preparations for his examinations that summer shall not be disturbed. This has been opposed by counsel for the trustee in bankruptcy. It will be observed that if the wife had been able to pay the £3,000, and had done so, the judge's order would have resulted in a sale which was neither an immediate sale nor a postponement until after the son's examinations; and counsel for the trustee in bankruptcy said that he would have felt himself at least in difficulty in supporting that part of the order. However, that does not arise.

We have had put before us a considerable wealth of authorities, some on bankruptcy, some on the general matrimonial law. The main bankruptcy authorities put before us were *Re Solomon*, *Re Turner* and *Re Densham*. It is plain from these cases that there is considerable authority in support of the proposition that there is no automatic rule, but that it is the duty of the court to exercise a proper discretion in deciding whether to order a sale or not, and that in exercising that discretion the court is under a duty to consider all the circumstances of the case. Those, in a sense, are truisms. The matter was put shortly by Goff J in *Re Turner*: 'In my judgment, the guiding principle in the exercise of the court's discretion is not whether the trustee or the wife is being reasonable but, in all the circumstances of the case whose voice in equity ought to prevail.' He pointed out that the wife asked why, as co-owner, she should be turned out merely because the other co-owner was bankrupt, but that the trustee had a statutory duty which gave him a strong claim. It was this duty that on the facts of the case made the trustee's the voice which ought to prevail in equity.

Apart from *Re Densham*, the cases have concerned husband and wife, and the claims of children have not been before the Court. In *Burke v Burke*, which was a matrimonial case in the Court of Appeal not involving bankruptcy, Buckley LJ expressed the view that the interests of the children in a husband and wife case were interests which were only incidentally to be taken into consideration, as affecting the equities as between husband and wife: and *Re Densham* applied that view in bankruptcy. Under a trust for sale in which the husband and wife are entitled equally the children, of course, are not beneficiaries. However, it has been forcefully argued before us by counsel for the wife that that approach has now to be reconsidered in the light of the decision of a different Division of the Court of Appeal in *Williams v Williams*. That, again, was not a bankruptcy case, but a husband and wife case. There, Lord Denning MR emphasised that where a house had been bought as a home for the family to be brought up in, then in disputes between husband and wife as to whether the home should be sold, great weight had to be given to the interests of the family as a whole. The decision of the trial judge in that case was said to have gone back to the older view related to property rights, without giving effect to the modern view which requires regard to be paid to the needs of the family as a whole before a sale of the house is ordered. In that case the wife and the four sons were living in the house, the youngest son being only 13.

Let me accept for the purposes of this appeal that the view of one Division of the Court of Appeal, based as it was on the approach that the Matrimonial Proceedings and Property Act 1970 and the Matrimonial Causes Act 1973 had transformed the law, has rightly displaced the views of another Division of the Court of Appeal in *Burke v Burke*, also decided after those statutes had been passed. Assume that, and yet one must bear in mind that these were decisions within the sphere of matrimonial property concerning the proper disposition of the property rights of husband and wife under statutory provisions giving a very wide discretion to the court to adjust those property rights as was thought proper. They were not cases in which matters of commercial obligation arose, as in the case of bankruptcy. In bankruptcy one must, of course, consider the claims of the creditors as asserted through the trustee in bankruptcy. The fact that bankruptcy has a somewhat special position in relation to property rights in a matrimonial home is brought out by two Acts to which counsel for the trustee in bankruptcy made reference, namely, the Matrimonial Homes Act 1967, s 2(5), and the Matrimonial Causes Act 1973, s 39. I do not propose to read these sections; but they make it plain that bankruptcy has, in relation to the matrimonial home, its own claim to protection.

I return in a sense to the point where I started. There is a discretion in this court which has to be exercised on proper grounds. One has to weigh, on the one hand, the claims of the trustee in bankruptcy and the creditors; against those, one must put into the scales all that can properly be put there on behalf of the other spouse of the marriage and any children. In this case the creditors and the trustee clearly have a strong claim to the realisation of the husband's share in this house, which is the only real asset in the bankruptcy. If the sale is postponed, then it is true that the creditors will, if the assets suffice (as apparently they will), receive the statutory interest; but under s 33(8) of the Bankruptcy Act 1914 that is unhappily still a mere four per cent.

So far as the wife is concerned, the sale of this property would give her a substantial capital sum. Her half-share in equity, after discharging the mortgage on the property, would be of the order of some £6,000 or more. As against that, £6,000 is not a very large sum with which to seek some other home, and she would plainly have the difficulties of finding somewhere else to live with her son. So far as the son is concerned, he is not, as I have mentioned, a beneficiary under the trust for sale at all.

The evidence about the interference with his educational prospects is very slight. It seems improbable that he would have to move from his school. Other accommodation would be more likely to be obtained within the catchment area of his school than elsewhere. It is, after all, some eighteen months or so before the actual examinations at A-level will have to be taken, and there is nothing to suggest that there are any special circumstances, apart from the inevitable disruption of having to move one's home, that will affect his prospects in education.

Putting these competing interests into the balance on one side and the other, and looking at the facts of the case as a whole, the only conclusion I can reach is that the claims of the wife and the son do not suffice to outweigh the claims of the trustee in bankruptcy to an immediate sale of this house. When I say 'immediate sale' I am not suggesting that it should be sold tomorrow. The precise terms of any order will have to be settled after any further submissions by counsel have been heard; but I cannot think that this is a case that in any way justifies postponing the sale until the summer of 1978. Accordingly, I would dismiss this appeal.

Walton J agreed.

In the later case of *Re Holliday* [1980] 3 All ER 385, the court was prepared (exceptionally) to postpone a sale. One of the major difficulties with this case is that although there is a general acceptance of its exceptional character, it is not altogether clear just what there is about it to make it exceptional. In *Re Holliday* the property was a former matrimonial home, in which the deserted wife of the debtor (bankrupt on his own petition) continued to reside with the three children of the marriage, aged, at the relevant time, 15, 11 and seven. Buckley LJ said:

We have to consider all the circumstances of the case, and consider whether it is right and proper that the house should be sold now for the benefit of the creditors of the debtor, or whether it is right and proper that it should be retained unsold, the wife being allowed to continue to reside there with her children.

The only creditors, or the only creditors that call for consideration in the bankruptcy, are the debtor's former solicitors, to whom he owes a sum of approximately £1,260 for costs, the debtor's bank, to whom he owes something of the order of £5,000, and the wife's mother, to whom the debtor owes approximately £250 in respect of a loan. The wife's mother is not anxious to press for early repayment ...

In these circumstances the wife finds herself saddled with the burden of providing a proper home for her children, which she would be incapable of doing out of her own resources ... This seems to me to afford the wife strong and justifiable grounds for saying that it really would be unfair to her, at this juncture and in these circumstances, to enforce the trust for sale. Of course, the creditors are entitled to payment as soon as the debtor is in a position to pay them. They are entitled to payment forthwith; they have an unassailable right to be paid out of the assets of the bankrupt. But in my view, when one of those assets is an undivided share in land in respect of which the debtor's right to a sale is not an absolute right, that is an asset in the bankruptcy which is liable to be affected by the interest of any other party interested in the land, and if there are reasons which seem to the court to be good reasons for saying that the trust for sale of the land should not be immediately enforced, then that is an asset of the bankruptcy which is not immediately available because it cannot be immediately realised for the benefit of the creditors. Balancing the interest of the creditors and the interest of the wife ... in my view the right attitude for the court to adopt is that the house should not be sold at the present juncture.

A significant factor in this decision may be that the debtor was made bankrupt on his own petition (though the same was true of *Bailey*) and that it was unlikely that the postponement of the payment of the debts would cause any great hardship to any of the creditors. Later cases, however, have stressed the exceptional nature of the decision in *Re Holliday*, for example, *Re Lowrie* [1981] 3 All ER 353.

In *Re Lowrie* the presence of young children, who would be rendered homeless by the sale, was not regarded as a sufficiently exceptional circumstance to justify the refusal of an order for sale:

It is a normal circumstance and is the result, the all too obvious result, of a husband having conducted the financial affairs of the family in a way which has led to bankruptcy ... It is going to be incredibly hard and incredibly bad luck on the co-owner, the wife, who is in most cases a totally innocent person who has done nothing to bring about the bankruptcy. Of course, as against that, one has to realise that she has been enjoying over whatever period it may be the fruits of the debts which the bankrupt has contracted and which debts are not at the moment being paid. So that although it may be very bad luck on her, she at any rate has had some enjoyment of the fruits which led to the bankruptcy' (*per* Walton J).

Concurring in the decision, Goulding J drew attention to the hardship to creditors in having to wait for their money in times of high interest rates and depreciating currency.

In *Re Citro* [1990] 3 WLR 880 two brothers, Domenico and Carmine Citro, were declared bankrupt in 1985 (hence the Insolvency Act 1986 did not apply). Their only assets were their half shares of the beneficial interests they had in their respective matrimonial homes. Domenico was judicially separated from his wife, Mary, and she lived in their home with three children, the youngest being 12. Carmine lived in his home with his wife Josephine and their three children, the youngest being 10.

The trial judge (Hoffman J) purported to follow *Re Holliday* and postponed sale until the youngest child of each family attained the age of 16 years. A majority of the Court of Appeal reversed his decision. Nourse LJ (with whom

Bingham LJ, feeling himself to be constrained by authority, regretfully concurred) was not prepared to find that exceptional circumstances existed so as to justify a postponement of sale.

Re Citro

Nourse LJ: Where a spouse who has a beneficial interest in the matrimonial home has become bankrupt under debts which cannot be paid without the realisation of that interest, the voice of the creditors will usually prevail over the voice of the other spouse and a sale of the property ordered within a short period. The voice of the other spouse will only prevail in exceptional circumstances. No distinction is to be made between a case where the property is still being enjoyed as the matrimonial home and one where it is not.

What then are exceptional circumstances? As the cases show, it is not uncommon for a wife with young children to be faced with eviction in circumstances where the realisation of her beneficial interest will not produce enough to buy a comparable home in the same neighbourhood, or indeed elsewhere. And, if she has to move elsewhere, there may be problems over schooling and so forth. Such circumstances, while engendering a natural sympathy in all who hear of them, cannot be described as exceptional. They are the melancholy consequences of debt and improvidence with which every civilised society has been familiar. It was only in *Holliday* that they helped the wife's voice to prevail, and then only, as I believe, because of one special feature of that case. One of the reasons for the decision given by Sir David Cairns in *Re Holliday* was that it was highly unlikely that postponement of payment of the debts would cause any great hardship to any of the creditors ... It must indeed be exceptional for creditors in a bankruptcy to receive 100p in the £ plus statutory interest in full and the passage of years before they do so does not make it any less exceptional. On the other hand, without that special feature, I cannot myself see how the circumstances in *Re Holliday* could fairly have been treated as exceptional. I am confirmed in that view by the belief that it would be shared by Balcombe J, who in *Harman v Glencross* [1986] 1 All ER 545 said that the decision in *Re Holliday* was very much against the run of the recent authorities. I would not myself have regarded it as an exceptional circumstance that the husband had presented his own bankruptcy petition, even 'as a tactical move'. That was not something of the creditors' choosing and could not fairly have been held against them. I do not say that in other cases there might not be other exceptional circumstances. They must be identified if and when they arise.

If *Re Holliday* is put on one side, are the bankruptcy cases, all of which were decided at first instance or in the Divisional Court in Bankruptcy, consistent with the principles stated in *Jones v Challenger*? I will take first the case where the property is no longer being enjoyed as the matrimonial home, either because the marriage has been dissolved or because the bankrupt spouse has gone to live elsewhere and the marriage is dead in fact if not in law. The decisions in this category are *Re Solomon* and *Re Bailey*. Here it is clear that there is no inconsistency because, even if he was not bankrupt, the husband would usually be entitled to demand a sale. His trustee in bankruptcy cannot be in any worse position than he himself.

The more interesting question is whether there is an inconsistency in the case where the property was still being enjoyed as a matrimonial home, as it was in *Boydell v Gillespie* (1970) 216 EG 1505, *Re Turner* [1974] 1 WLR 1556, *Re Densham* [1975] 1 WLR 1519, and *Re Lowrie*. It would have been open to the wife in each of those cases to argue that the secondary purpose was still existing, that the husband's beneficial interest to which the trustee had succeeded was, in the words of Buckley J in *Re Holliday* 'an asset in the bankruptcy which is liable to be affected by the interest of any other party interested in that land' and that the trustee had no greater right to demand a sale than the husband himself. That argument may have been advanced in *Boydell v Gillespie* and I think it likely that Goff J had it in mind in Re Turner. Perhaps it was unfortunate that there the husband and wife had represented themselves, because after that the point appeared to have got lost. In none of the decisions is there to be found any overt consideration of the argument or any reasoned explanation of its rejection. They simply assume that there is no distinction between the two cases ...

Having been puzzled by the point myself and having thought it right to consider it, I have come to a clear conclusion that the assumption made in the earlier decisions is correct. Shortly stated, my reasoning is this. In the husband and wife cases exemplified by *Jones v Challenger* it is held that neither spouse has a right to demand a sale of the property while the purpose of its enjoyment as a matrimonial home still exists. In order to be so enjoyed it must be occupied by the spouses jointly. As a matter of property law, the basis of their joint occupation is their joint ownership of the beneficial interest in the home. Although the vesting of one of their interests in a trustee for creditors does not in itself destroy the secondary purpose of the trust, the basis for their joint occupation has gone. It must, I think, be implicit in the principle of *Jones v Challenger* that the secondary purpose can only exist while the spouses are not only joint occupiers of the home but joint owners of it as well.

I am therefore of the opinion that the earlier authorities, as I have summarised them, correctly state the law applicable to the present case. Did Hoffman J correctly apply it to the facts which were before him? I respectfully think that he did not. First, for the reasons already stated, the personal circumstances of the two wives and their children, although distressing, are not by themselves exceptional. Secondly, I think that he erred in fashioning his orders by reference to those which might have been made in the Family Division in a case where bankruptcy had not supervened. That approach, which tends toward treating the home as a source of provision for the children, was effectively disapproved by the earlier and uncontroversial part of the decision of this court in *Re Holliday*. Thirdly, he did not ask himself the critical question whether a further postponement of the payment of their debts would cause hardship to the creditors. It is only necessary to look at the substantial deficiencies referred to earlier in this judgment to see that it would. Since then a further 18 months' interest has accrued and the trustee has incurred the cost of these proceedings as well.

Sir George Waller, dissenting, held that the trial judge had correctly followed the decision in *Holliday*. He thought that greater weight should be given to the educational interests of the children, as had been done in *Holliday*.

The exceptional nature of the decision in *Re Holliday* was also stressed in *Harman v Glencross* (below p 476) where it was said to be 'very much against the run of the recent authorities' and that 'it represented the high water mark for the protection of the wife and children'.

In the light of these authorities, it is not easy to reach any firm conclusion about the nature of 'exceptional circumstances' which will justify postponement of a sale (or which could, presumably, be invoked to justify a prolongation of the 'rights of occupation' of a bankrupt or his spouse under the provisions of ss 336 and 337 Insolvency Act 1986). In particular, although Nourse LJ in *Re Citro* seems to have regarded the 'exceptional circumstance' in *Re Holliday* as being the lack of hardship to the creditors, Walton J in *Re Lowrie* seems to be placing at least equal stress on the self-induced nature of the bankruptcy. On the other hand, Sir George Waller in *Re Citro* seems to have regarded the educational needs of the children as of great importance, and claims to have found authority for this approach in the earlier decision of *Re Holliday*. It seems likely, however, that even after the enactment of the Insolvency Act 1986, the earlier authorities will still be regarded as relevant as indicated by Nourse J in *Re Citro*.

It is probably right that the courts should not seek to define too exhaustively the nature of such 'exceptional circumstances', as cases can vary infinitely. The fact that a bankruptcy is self-sought may be material (but not conclusive) – compare *Bailey* and *Holliday* above. Educational needs of children may be relevant but again not conclusive – compare *Bailey* and *Holliday* once more. The fact that creditors can, without hardship, wait for their money may be relevant.

The state of health of an occupying relative will rarely be decisive – see *Re Densham* [1975] 3 All ER 735, 738, and *Re Toobman* [1982] *The Times*, 3 March, unless perhaps, there is a course of medical treatment which needs to be completed and which will be completed in a finite time. The sole exception seems to be the case of *Re Mott* [1987] CLY 212, where a house was jointly owned by a mother and a son; the son was declared bankrupt, and a sale was postponed on account of the mother's poor state of health.

One example which might justify postponement is given in *Re Bailey* above. Where the house had been specially adapted to cater for the needs of (for instance) a handicapped child, it was said that the 'court would hesitate long before making an immediate order for sale' (at 33). A further example of a deferment of a sale can be found in *Re Gorman* [1990] 1 All ER 717. In that case, the ex-wife of the bankrupt had a claim pending against her former solicitors who had failed to apply for a property adjustment order when the divorce was made absolute. If the claim was successful, she might have been in a position to purchase the share of the trustee in bankruptcy. The court was thus prepared to postpone the sale until the negligence claim was finally determined. Likewise, in *Re Pittortou* (see later) a sale was deferred to enable the calculation of the value of the trustee in bankruptcy's interest, so that the possibility of a purchase by the ex-wife could be investigated.

The division of the proceeds of sale, if the bankrupt obtains an order for sale, may also be affected by the 'equity of exoneration'. This rule operates where A and B, joint owners of property, jointly mortgage that property to secure the debts of A. In this case B is entitled to require that the debt be discharged, as far as possible, out of the equitable interest of A. The rule, however, depends upon the intention of the parties; it only applies where the court can properly infer an intention on the part of the joint mortgagors that the indebtedness should primarily be discharged from A's share.

The operation of this principle can be illustrated by *Re a debtor (No 24 of 1971)* [1976] 2 All ER 1010. This was a case where Marley junior wished to set up in business, but, lacking the capital to do so, he approached his father, Marley senior, for assistance, which he agreed to provide. Marley senior conveyed his home into the joint names of Marley junior and himself, and they jointly mortgaged the property to Barclays Bank to secure Marley junior's business overdraft. The business failed, and eventually Marley junior became bankrupt. Marley senior contended that he was entitled to have the indebtedness to the bank debited to Marley junior's share of the property; if this was done, the trustee's interest was minimal and Marley senior contended that he should be given a chance to purchase the trustee in bankruptcy's share. Foster J (with whom Fox J agreed) accepted this contention, with the result that Marley senior was able to fend off a sale by purchasing the trustee in bankruptcy's interest.

The rule, however, depends upon the intention of the parties and the court must be satisfied that the debts so secured are genuinely those of one of the joint mortgagors. In *Re Pittortou* [1985] 1 All ER 285 the position was more complex.

Re Pittortou

Pittortou and his wife were jointly entitled to a matrimonial home. Mr Pittortou had an account at the National Westminster Bank, which he used, at least in part, to finance his business. Drawings on this account were also made for the household expenses of the family, and also for the support of Mr Pittortou's mistress. Pittortou and his wife executed a mortgage of the matrimonial home to the Bank to secure an overdraft on this account. Pittortou became divorced, and was eventually declared bankrupt. His wife sought, by invoking the equity of exoneration, to have the husband's liabilities thrown primarily upon the husband's beneficial interest.

Scott J: In my view, payments made out of the bankrupt's National Westminster Bank account for the benefit of the Pittortou family are of a character as to make it impossible to impute to the parties the intention that as between the husband and the wife the payments should be regarded as falling only on the share in the mortgaged property of the husband. In my view the equity of exoneration should be confined to payments out of the account which do not have the character of payments made for the joint benefit of the household ... payments made by the bankrupt purely for business purposes and, a fortiori, any payments made by him for the purposes of the second establishment [with his mistress] it seems he was supporting, should as between the bankrupt and the wife be treated as charged primarily on the bankrupt's half share in the mortgaged property.

Scott J then ordered an enquiry as to which sums paid out of the account fell into these categories. Any sale was deferred until the result of the enquiries was known, as it might then become possible for Mrs Pittortou to purchase the trustee in bankruptcy's share.

Even with the enhanced protection provided by the Insolvency Act, English law falls a long way short of the 'homestead' legislation which is in force in many jurisdictions within the Commonwealth and in many common law jurisdictions within the United States. The general principle of this legislation is that some part of the debtor's land, if it amounts to a family home, is exempt from seizure in bankruptcy. In some cases, as in New Zealand, homestead status depends upon registration (which creditors are entitled to oppose); in other cases, as in certain states in the United States, mere occupation as a family home will operate to create the exemption. Where it applies, it has the effect of preserving the family home throughout the financial vicissitudes of life, and represents a policy decision to give protection to the family unit against disruption.

One of the problems with which the law of bankruptcy has to grapple is the possibility that a debtor may seek to render his property safe from seizure in bankruptcy by transferring his interest to a third party. Many of the safeguards provided by bankruptcy jurisdiction for the interests of creditors would be negated if such transfers were automatically effective. The Insolvency Act contains provisions designed to deal with this problem. In one case, the transaction becomes impeachable because of the time at which it was made; in the other case, the timing of the transaction is irrelevant but the transaction becomes liable to attack because of the fraudulent purpose of the debtor which underlies the transaction.

Section 339 Insolvency Act 1986 is concerned with transactions at an undervalue within a specified period before the bankruptcy.

Insolvency Act 1986

339(1) Subject as follows in this section and sections 341 and 342, where an individual is adjudged bankrupt and he has at a relevant time (defined in section 341) entered into a transaction with a person at an undervalue, the trustee of the bankrupt's estate may apply to the court for an order under this section.

(2) The court shall, on such an application, make such order as it thinks fit for restoring the position to what it would have been if that individual had not entered into that transaction.

(3) ... an individual enters into a transaction with a person at an undervalue if—

(a) he makes a gift to that person or he otherwise enters into a transaction with that person on terms that provide for him to receive no consideration;

(b) he enters into a transaction with that person in consideration of marriage; or

(c) he enters into a transaction with that person for a consideration the value of which, in money or money's worth, is significantly less than the value, in money or money's worth, of the consideration provided by the individual.

341. 'Relevant time' under s 339

(1) ... the time at which an individual enters into a transaction at an undervalue ... is a relevant time if the transaction is entered into ...

(a) ... at a time in the period of five years ending with the day of the presentation of the bankruptcy petition on which the individual is adjudged bankrupt ...

(2) Where an individual enters into a transaction at an undervalue ... at a time mentioned in paragraph (a) (not being ... a time less than 2 years before the end of the period) ... that time is not a relevant time for the purposes of section 339 ... unless the individual—

(a) is insolvent at that time; or

(b) becomes insolvent in consequence of the transaction ...

but the requirements of this subsection are presumed to be satisfied, unless the contrary is shown, in relation to any transaction at an undervalue which is entered into by an individual with a person who is an associate of his (otherwise than by reason only of being his employee).

The effect of these provisions is that all transactions at an undervalue within two years of the presentation of the bankruptcy petition are open to attack; those within the two to five year time band are vulnerable only if the debtor was at that time insolvent, but in the case of a disposition to an associate (which would include a member of the debtor's family: s 435), such insolvency is presumed. Insolvency in this context includes the inability to pay debts as they fall due, or where the value of the debtor's assets is less than the amount of his liabilities, taking into account contingent and prospective liabilities. The power of the court to make an order under s 339 includes a power to require any property transferred as part of the transaction to be vested in the trustee of the bankrupt's estate as part of that estate.

Transactions defrauding creditors – without reference to a time limit – are covered by s 423, replacing earlier provisions in s 172 Law of Property Act 1925.

Insolvency Act 1986

423(1) This section relates to transactions entered into at an undervalue (defined in similar terms to s 339 above).

(2) Where a person has entered into such a transaction, the court may, if satisfied under the next subsection, make such order as it thinks fit for–

(a) restoring the position to what it would have been if the transaction had not been entered into; and

(b) protecting the interests of persons who are the victims of the transaction.

(3) In the case of a person entering into such a transaction, an order shall only be made if the court is satisfied that it was entered into by him for the purpose–

(a) of putting assets beyond the reach of a person who is making, or may at some time make, a claim against him; or

(b) of otherwise prejudicing the interests of such a person in relation to the claim which he is making or may make.

The operation of these provisions can be seen in *Moon and others v Franklin* [1990] *The Independent*, 22 June. In that case Franklin was a certified accountant who was faced with professional negligence claims and certain criminal proceedings. He transferred his house by way of gift to his wife. This transfer was held to be a transaction at an undervalue. Although Franklin contended that his motive in making the transfer was wholly unconnected with the claims made against him, and that it was unpremeditated, the judge was prepared to find that the purpose of the transaction was putting the assets beyond the reach of the claimants. He made an order restraining any dealing with the house.

CHARGING ORDERS

A charging order represents another way in which financial crisis can lead to lack of security of tenure in the home. The basic idea of a charging order is that a debt, hitherto unsecured, is converted at the creditor's request into a debt secured on the debtor's home. The main importance of this conversion is that the creditor then attains rights in the home; in certain circumstances these rights may be given effect to by the process of a forced sale of the house at the instance of the creditor, and the payment of the creditor's debt out of the proceeds of sale. Although the debtor may be entitled to the remainder of the proceeds of sale after payment of the debt in question, these proceeds may be insufficient to enable him to buy an alternative home.

Charging orders were originally made under s 13 Judgments Act 1838, later re-enacted with amendments in s 35 Administration of Justice Act 1956 and s 141(1) County Courts Act 1959, but the procedure under those Acts proved to be defective and many amendments were made by the Charging Orders Act 1979. One of the effects of these amendments is to make charging orders available to creditors in a greater number of cases than hitherto.

The first essential is that the creditor must be entitled to a judgment debt, either in the High Court or county court.

Charging Orders Act 1979

1(1) Where, under a judgment or order of the High Court or a county court, a person (the 'debtor') is required to pay a sum of money to another person (the 'creditor') then, for the purpose of enforcing that judgment or order, the appropriate court may make an order in accordance with the provisions of this Act imposing on any such property of the debtor as may be specified in the order a charge for securing the payment of any money due or to become due under the judgment or order ...

(3) An order under subsection (1) above is referred to in this Act as a 'charging order'.

Even where there is a judgment debt, the making of a charging order is not automatic. In deciding whether to make a charging order the court is required to consider all the circumstances of the case, including the personal circumstances of the debtor and whether any other creditor of the debtor would be unduly prejudiced by the making of the order (s 1(5) of the 1979 Act). If the creditor's application is successful the usual procedure is first to make a charging order nisi, which may then be converted, on further application by the creditor, into a charging order absolute. The making of a charging order – even a charging order absolute – does not immediately effect the payment of the debt. What it does do is to give the creditor *locus standi* to apply for a sale of the property which is the subject of the charging order. The creditor thus becomes, in effect, a mortgagee of the property in question.

The effect of these provisions was illustrated in *Midland Bank plc v Pike and another* [1988] 2 All ER 434. In that case the Midland Bank obtained a judgment against Mr Pike for £55,000 as an unsecured debt. The Bank obtained a charging order nisi, followed by a charging order absolute, over the matrimonial home jointly owned by Mr and Mrs Pike. Shortly thereafter the Bank applied for an order for sale of the property. The Master rejected the Bank's application, holding that it had no *locus standi* to apply for such a sale. This decision was rejected by Edward Nugee QC, sitting as a judge of the High Court.

Jointly owned homes

One of the major difficulties which has arisen with charging orders is their application to jointly owned property, especially matrimonial homes. In *Irani*

Finance Ltd v Singh [1971] Ch 59 it was held that a beneficial interest under a trust for sale, not being an 'interest in land' (as required by s 35 Administration of Justice Act 1956), could not be made the subject of a charging order under the 1956 Act. This meant that many houses, being jointly owned, were beyond the reach of a charging order. This defect was remedied by s 2 of the 1979 Act, which made it clear that a beneficial interest under a trust for sale was 'property' of a debtor to which a charging order could be made to attach. It was recognised as having had this effect by Russell J in *National Westminster Bank Ltd v Stockman* [1981] 1 All ER 800.

The making of a charging order involves an exercise of judicial discretion. In a report which preceded the 1979 Act, the Law Commission noted that there was a tendency for the court to accede almost automatically to a judgment creditor's request for a charging order. The Law Commission thought that this should be rectified, partly because a charging order could give undue priority (as against other creditors) to the successful creditor, but also because there was a risk that charging orders might be granted in cases where it was unfair to the debtor.

These considerations led to the enactment of s 1(5) of the 1979 Act, which gives the court a full discretion in deciding whether to accede to an application to grant a charging order. Nevertheless, the general principle remains that, if a judgment creditor seeks a charging order, in the absence of special circumstances a charging order will be granted and made absolute. In the commercial case of *Roberts Petroleum Ltd v Bernard Kenny Ltd (in liquidation)* [1982] 1 All ER 685, in the Court of Appeal Lord Bernard referred to the principle that a judgment creditor was entitled to have recourse to all or any of the means of execution prescribed by the relevant rules of court, and said that the burden of showing cause why a charging order should not be made absolute lay upon the debtor. The House of Lords, whilst reversing the decision on the facts, did not dissent from this principle.

Particular difficulties arise, however, where the claim to a charging order arises in respect of a jointly owned house (now, after the 1979 Act, susceptible to a charging order), especially if the circumstances are complicated by matrimonial proceedings between the owners of the house. In such a case the house may well be the only asset of the debtor against which the creditor can have recourse; but at the same time the court has to have regard to the claims of a spouse or ex-spouse, who may have a claim to a transfer of the house (as the only substantial matrimonial asset) in matrimonial proceedings. A case which illustrates these problems is *Harman v Glencross and another* [1984] 2 All ER 577 (Fam D), on appeal [1986] 1 All ER 545.

Harman v Glencross and another

Mr and Mrs Glencross jointly owned a matrimonial home. Mr Glencross was a business partner of Mr Harman. The marriage between the Glencrosses broke down and Mrs Glencross initiated divorce proceedings. While these proceedings were in progress Mr Harman obtained an unopposed money judgment against Mr Glencross. Harman then sought to enforce this by a charging order, and obtained a charging order absolute on 7 September 1981. In May 1983 the wife's application for ancillary relief in the divorce proceedings came before the Registrar, who also at the same time considered an application by the wife to vary or discharge the charging order, under s 3(5) of the 1979 Act. This provides: 'The court by which a charging order was made may at any time, on the application of the debtor or any person interested in any property to which the charging order relates, make an order discharging or varying the charging order.'

Although the issue before the court was an application under sub-s 3(5) to vary or discharge the charging order, the court was of the view that the same factors should be taken into account as would fall to be considered in the initial proceedings for the making of a charging order under s 1(5). (The wife had not been informed of the charging order proceedings, though the Court of Appeal accepted that she should have been so informed.)

At first instance, Ewbank J drew attention to the difficulties in balancing the interests of the creditor and the wife; he did not think that he would be helped by any presumption one way or the other, either in favour of the creditor or the wife. He held that the charging order should be postponed to any order the wife might subsequently obtain in the matrimonial proceedings.

The Court of Appeal dismissed an appeal by the creditor.

Balcombe LJ: This is an appeal from a judgment of Ewbank J dated 16 February 1984 ([1984] 2 All ER 577, [1985] Fam 49) whereby he dismissed an appeal from an order of Mr Registrar Angel ...

The first question which arises on this appeal is whether the wife had any *locus standi* to apply for the discharge or variation of the charging order absolute. This requires consideration of the provisions of the Charging Orders Act 1979. Previously the power of the High Court to make a charging order to enforce a judgment for the payment of money was contained in s 35(1) of the Administration of Justice Act 1956, which provided that the court could—

'impose on any such land or interest in land of the debtor as may be specified in the order a charge for securing the payment of any moneys due or to become due under the judgment ...'

The 1956 Act contained no provision for the discharge or variation of a charging order, but such power was conferred by RSC Ord 50, r 7 in its then form, at any rate in relation to a charge on securities under Ord 50, r 2.

In *Irani Finance Ltd v Singh* [1970] 3 All ER 199, [1971] Ch 59 this court held that the beneficial interest of a co-owner of land, which was necessarily an interest in the proceeds of sale of the land under an express trust for sale, or under the statutory trust for sale imposed by s 36(1) of the Law of Property Act 1925, was not an 'interest in land' within s 35 of the 1956 Act, and so could not be the subject of a charging order. After a report by the Law Commission on Charging Orders (Law Com no 74), the 1979 Act was passed ...

RSC Ord 50 is now in a new form to give effect to the provisions of the 1979 Act ...

In the present case it seems to me that the wife should have been given notice of the charging order nisi made on 17 August 1981 under Ord 50, r 2(1)(d), since the house was held on a statutory trust for sale, the charging order relates to the husband's interest under that trust and the wife was the only other trustee. She was also, in my judgment, for reasons which will become apparent, an 'interested person' under r 2(2). If she had been given such notice and had appeared on the restored hearing of the judgment creditor's application, counsel for the judgment creditor conceded that she would have been entitled to make representations under s 1(5) of the 1979 Act as to 'all the circumstances of the case' and at that stage to invite the court, having regard to her interest, either to make no charging order at all or to make it only subject to any order made by the divorce court on her application for a property adjustment order. It was no fault of the wife that she was deprived of this opportunity, and I agree with the judge's description of the argument of counsel for the judgment creditor on this point as unattractive (see [1984] 2 All ER 577 at 580, [1985] Fam 49 at 54). However, attractive or not, it must be considered on its merits, so I turn to consider s 3(5) of the 1979 Act.

For my part I agree with the judge that the phrase 'property to which the order relates' is wide enough to include the house in the present case. If the legislature had intended to refer to 'the property charged' or (as in Ord 50, r 7(1)) to 'the subject-matter of the charge', it could have done so. Where the property charged is a share in the proceeds of sale of land yet unsold, in my judgment the order relates ie stands in some relation to, that land.

But even if I were wrong in the construction I put on the words 'property to which the order relates' and they only bear the limited meaning of 'the property charged', nevertheless in my judgment the wife was at all material times 'interested' in the husband's half share of the proceeds of sale of the unsold house.

Counsel for the judgment creditor referred us to a number of authorities on the meaning of 'interest in' or having 'an interest in'. He accepted that, if the 'property to which the order relates' was the house, then the wife was interested in that property: see *Bull v Bull* [1955] 1 All ER 253 at 256, [1955] 1 QB 234 at 238 and *Williams & Glyn's Bank Ltd v Boland* [1980] 2 All ER 408 at 414-415, [1981] AC 487 at 507. But if, as he maintained the 'property to which the order relates' was only the husband's share of the proceeds of sale of the house, then he submitted that, as the wife had no proprietary right to that share, she was not 'interested' in it: see *Re No 39 Carr Lane, Acomb, Stevens v Hutchinson* [1953] 1 All ER 699, [1953] Ch 299. The mere fact that the wife had, by her application in the divorce proceedings, claimed that the husband's share should be transferred to her did not give her an interest in that share: see *Whittingham v Whittingham (National Westminster Bank Ltd intervening)* [1978] 3 All ER 805 at 814, [1979] Fam 19 at 21, although Stamp LJ made it clear that he was not speaking of the matrimonial home.

But where, as here, the wife was herself one of two legal owners of the house and having as such a right of occupation (and it seems to me that the same reasoning would apply if the property subject to the charging order was the matrimonial home owned by the husband alone but in which the wife had a right of occupation) under s1(1) of the Matrimonial Homes Act 1983 then in my judgment she is interested in the property to which the order relates even if that property is only the husband's share in the proceeds of sale of the house. After all, the purpose of the judgment creditor seeking a charging order is to enable him to realise the husband's share so as to satisfy his judgment debt. That will require a sale of the house, for which the judgment creditor will become entitled to apply under s 30 of the Law of Property Act 1925: see *Stevens v Hutchinson*. Although the wife will be entitled to resist that application, should it succeed and an order be made for the sale of the house, the wife will lose her rights of occupation. This by itself it sufficient to make her 'interested' in the husband's share in the context of s 3(5) of the 1979 Act.

I mention (only to reject) a further submission by counsel for the judgment creditor that the main purpose of s 3(5) of the 1979 Act was to resolve a doubt which, he submitted, existed under the 1956 Act and the old Ord 50 whether a charging order on land could be discharged once the judgment debt had been paid. This doubt arose from the wording of the old Ord 50, r 7. Whether or not this was a reason behind the enactment of s 3(5) seems to me to be irrelevant: the subsection is quite general in its wording and falls to be construed in accordance with the ordinary canons of construction, and there is no justification for limiting it in the manner proposed by counsel for the judgment creditor.

Accordingly I am satisfied that the wife had a *locus standi* to apply for a variation of the judgment creditor's charging order on the husband's share in the proceeds of sale of the house, and I turn to consider the next submission of counsel for the judgment creditor, namely that before us the matter is determined by the decision of this court in *First National Securities Ltd v Hegerty* [1984] 3 All ER 641, [1985] QB 850. The facts in *Hegerty* were similar to those of the present case in that there was there a matrimonial home owned jointly by the husband and the wife, a judgment obtained by a creditor against the husband and an application by the judgment creditor for a charging order nisi on the husband's interest in the house. The judgment creditor obtained a charging order nisi, but at that stage the wife was joined as a defendant and, when the matter came further before the master, he refused to make the order absolute and discharged the order nisi. The judgment creditor appealed to the judge, Bingham J, who allowed the appeal and made the charging order absolute. He rejected an application on behalf of the wife that the matter should be transferred to the Family Division so that the wife's interest in the property could be determined under Pt II of the Matrimonial Causes Act 1973 at the same time as the judgment creditor's claim for a charging order.

The judgment of Bingham J was given on 1 November 1982 (see [1984] 1 All ER 139, [1985] QB 850). The wife appealed, but her appeal was not heard until May 1984 and the judgment of the Court of Appeal was given on 6 July 1984. In the meantime, Ewbank J had given his judgment in this case on 16 February 1984, and the report of that judgment was available to this court in *Hegerty*. The first judgment in *Hegerty* was given by Sir Denys Buckley, who held that there were no sufficient grounds for holding that Bingham J was so clearly wrong in exercising his discretion as he did that this court should interfere with his decision. Accordingly, he was in favour of dismissing the appeal.

In the course of his judgment Sir Denys Buckley referred to the judgment of Ewbank J in this case, and to this pending appeal, and pointed out that there were differences between that case and this on the facts and the sequence of events, and in particular that the effect of the order of Mr Registrar Angel in this case (which Ewbank J affirmed) overrode the charging order but did not purport to discharge it. The decision of Ewbank J appeared to depend on his view of the nature and extent of the court's powers under the Matrimonial Causes Act 1973; the Court of Appeal, on the other hand, was exclusively concerned with whether Bingham J's exercise of his discretion under the 1979 Act should be disturbed (see [1984] 3 All ER 641 at 646, [1985] QB 850 at 865).

The second judgment in *Hegerty* was given by Stephenson LJ. He, too, was of the view that the court could not interfere with Bingham J's exercise of his discretion. However, he continued ([1984] 3 All ER 641 at 648, [1985] QB 850 at 867–868):

> 'But it would, I think, be wrong for this court to dismiss the appeal simply on the ground that the judge was entitled to exercise his discretion under the [Charging Orders Act 1979], as he did, because we are told by counsel on

both sides that there are a number of cases like the present in which guidance is required ... I have, however, come to the conclusion (1) that the court should not use its powers under Pt II of the 1973 Act to override the claims of a creditor seeking security for a debt by a charging order, (2) that it should not discharge or vary a charging order so as to prefer a wife's claim to such a creditor's, (3) that it can, and often should, postpone the enforcement of a charging order until the hearing of any application under s 30 of the 1925 Act, when the court can decide between the competing claims of wife and creditor ... I agree that the question whether *Harman v Glencross* [1984] 2 All ER 577, [1985] Fam 49 was rightly decided should await the appeal which we are told is pending in that case ... As at present advised I think that that decision was wrong; but that question, as I have indicated, will be decided when the appeal in *Harman's* case is heard.'

He, too, agreed that Bingham J's Order should be affirmed.

The third member of the court in *Hegerty*, O'Connor LJ, merely said that he agreed with both the previous judgments.

Counsel for the judgment creditor submits that the passage from the judgment of Stephenson LJ quoted above represented a separate ground for his decision, that it was supported by O'Connor LJ and that accordingly we are bound by it. That is wrong. As Sir Denys Buckley pointed out, the court in *Hegerty* was not concerned with the exercise of powers under the Matrimonial Causes Act 1973 but with the exercise of the court's discretion under the Charging Orders Act 1979. Accordingly, so far as Stephenson LJ was dealing with the use of powers under the 1973 Act, his judgment was necessarily obiter, while his observation that the court should not discharge or vary a charging order so as to prefer a wife's claim to that of the judgment creditor was also obiter, since he expressly disclaimed any intention to bind this court on this appeal. Any dicta of Stephenson LJ are, of course, entitled to be considered with the greatest respect, but for the reasons already given I am satisfied that we are not bound by the decision in *Hegerty* to allow this appeal and reverse the decision of Ewbank J.

So I come at last to the nub of this appeal: was the order of Mr Registrar Angel, affirmed by Ewbank J, postponing the judgment creditor's charging order to any order made in favour of the wife on her application for a property adjustment order a proper exercise of the court's discretion? Or, to put the question in another way: in considering 'all the circumstances' under s 1(5) of the 1979 Act, is the court entitled to take into account the interests of the wife, and, if so, what weight should it give to those interests as compared with those of the judgment creditor?

I start with the proposition that a judgment creditor is in general entitled to enforce a money judgment which he has lawfully obtained against a judgment debtor by all or any of the means of execution prescribed by the relevant rules of court: see *Roberts Petroleum Ltd v Bernard Kenny Ltd (in liq)* [1983] 1 All ER 564 at 571–572, [1983] 2 AC 192 at 207. However, this proposition is not absolute: it may be qualified where, as in the *Roberts Petroleum* case itself, the judgment creditor finds himself in competition with other creditors of the judgment debtor. Nevertheless, as Sir Denys Buckley said in *First National Securities Ltd v Hegerty* [1984] 3 All ER 641 at 646, [1985] QB 850 at 866: ' ... a judgment creditor, although not entitled to such an order as of right, is justified in expecting that such an order will be made in his favour ...'.

In the *Roberts Petroleum* case [1982] 1 All ER 685 at 690, [1982] 1 WLR 301 at 307, this court, Lord Brandon giving the leading judgment, set out under seven headings the principles which should be applied in deciding whether a charging order nisi should be made absolute. That statement was approved by the House of Lords in that case, although they disagreed with the application of the principles to the facts of the case. However, while it is correct to say, as Stephenson LJ did in *Hegerty* [1984] 3 All ER 641 at 647, [1985] QB 850 at 867, that–

> 'circumstances of the kind present in this case, namely an interest of the wife of a judgment debtor in the subject-matter of the execution and hardship to her or to their children if the principle [ie that quoted at the beginning of the preceding paragraph] is applied, are not among those set out or considered in Lord Brandon's statement of the principles,'

it is hardly surprising, since Lord Brandon was not considering this question. It is also correct that a wife's interest is not mentioned specifically in the 1979 Act, but there is no reason why it should be, since the court is required to consider 'all the circumstances of the case'.

Another point which the judge considered in favour of the judgment creditor in the present case was that if the business of Acorn Contractors had prospered the wife and children would have benefited, and it was said on behalf of the judgment creditor that, if the opposite happened and the business failed, the wife must bear the loss as well as everybody else.

Before leaving the consideration of the judgment creditor's position, there is one further point I should make. Not all judgment creditors are faceless corporations; indeed in the present case the judgment creditor is an individual. He, for reasons which doubtless appeared good to him and his advisers, chose to put in no evidence before the registrar or the judge as to his means but relied on what he asserted was his right to a charging order not postponed to any claim of the wife *ex debito justitiae*. If the court is entitled, under the 1979 Act or otherwise, to weigh the competing interests of the judgment creditor and the wife, then I can see no reason why, in a proper case, the judgment creditor should not be entitled to put in evidence of the hardship he would suffer if he were denied a charging order or if its enforcement were unduly postponed.

In considering the wife's position it is necessary to give separate attention to her rights of occupation and to her claim to have the husband's equitable share transferred to her.

In almost every case concerning a matrimonial home the wife will have a right of occupation, either, as here, because of her joint legal ownership or under the Matrimonial Homes Act 1983. Further, Parliament has looked with particular favour on a spouse's right to occupy the matrimonial home and has given it the status of an equitable interest (see s 2(1) of the 1983 Act) with consequential priority over subsequent equitable interests created by the other spouse (eg a charging order (see s 3(4) of the 1979 Act)) provided that the owner of the subsequent interest has notice and notice is given by registration of a Class F land charge or the equivalent notice on the title in the case of registered land.

Thus, in the case of a matrimonial home which is owned solely by the husband, the wife has the ability to protect her rights of occupation and to acquire priority over a charging order obtained by a judgment creditor of the husband. It would be peculiar if Parliament had intended that a wife who has a proprietary interest in the matrimonial home should have any less priority.

A spouse's rights of occupation under the Matrimonial Homes Act 1983 are brought to an end by the death of the other spouse or the termination (otherwise than by death) of the marriage: see s 2(4). However, even after the termination of the marriage, Parliament has shown a continued concern for the welfare of the minor children of the family, since the new s 25 of the Matrimonial Causes Act 1973, introduced by the Matrimonial and Family Proceedings Act 1984, admittedly since the hearing at first instance in the present case, provides that it shall be the duty of the court in deciding whether to exercise its powers under, *inter alia*, s 23 (financial provision orders), s 24 (property adjustment orders) and s 24A (orders for sale of property), and if, so, in what manner, to have regard to all the circumstances of the case, first consideration being given to the welfare (while a minor) of any child of the family who has not attained the age of 18. If the minor children are (as here) living with the wife, the loss of her right to occupy the matrimonial home could well be detrimental to their welfare, particularly if the funds available were inadequate to provide another home in its place.

Accepting as I do that the court is properly concerned to protect the wife's right to occupy the matrimonial home, the next question is how that right can be protected. In *Hegerty* [1984] 1 All ER 139 at 143, [1985] QB 850 at 856 at first instance, Bingham J held that the wife's right of occupation was adequately protected by the provisions of s 30 of the Law of Property Act 1925, since he accepted that the wife's possession of the house could not be disturbed until there had been an application under s 30 and a full hearing at which the wife's personal and family position could be investigated. As he put it: 'That is the stage for finally determining which of the competing voices is entitled in equity to prevail.' This view also found favour with Stephenson LJ in *Hegerty* [1984] 3 All ER 641 at 648, [1985] QB 850 at 868.

It must be remembered that the conveyancing device introduced by the Law of Property Act 1925 to deal with the joint ownership of real property is to impose an immediate binding *trust* for sale, with *power* to postpone sale, and to require the beneficial interests in the property to exist only in the proceeds of sale. If a person interested in the proceeds of sale wishes to ensure that the property is sold, so that his beneficial interest may be realised, he may apply to the court under s 30 of the Law of Property Act 1925, and under that section the court may make such order as it thinks fit. However, that discretion is a judicial discretion, and its exercise may be very much limited and controlled by the facts and circumstances of the case. Goff LJ reviewed the authorities in *Re Holliday (a bankrupt), ex p trustee of the bankrupt v The bankrupt* [1980] 3 All ER 385 at 391, [1981] Ch 405 at 415, and his summary of the law, with which Buckley LJ and Sir David Cairns agreed, was in the following terms:

> 'Where the property in question is a matrimonial home, then the provision of a home for both parties is a secondary or collateral object of the trust for sale (see *per* Devlin LJ in *Jones v Challenger* [1960] 1 All ER 785 at 787, [1961] 1 QB 177 at 181) and the court will not ordinarily order a sale if the marriage be still subsisting and no question of bankruptcy has supervened. Where, however, the marriage has come to an end by divorce or death of one of the parties, or is dead in fact, though still subsisting at law, then apart from any question how far the secondary or collateral object can be said to be still subsisting if there are young or dependent children, though there remains a discretion it is one in which, as I see it, some very special circumstances need to be shown to induce the court not to order a sale (see *Jones v Challenger* [1960] 1 All ER 785, [1961] 1 QB 177 and *Rawlings v Rawlings* [1964] 2 All ER 804, [1964] P 398).

He then considered *Williams (JN) v Williams (MA)* [1977] 1 All ER 28, [1976] Ch 278 and held that, if the case was not transferred to the Family Division for the wife's rights to be considered in an application for ancillary relief under the

Matrimonial Causes Act 1973, then the discretion should be exercised in accordance with the law as established and as he had adumbrated it (see [1980] 3 All ER 385 at 394, [1981] Ch 405 at 419).

In the very particular circumstances of that case, where the contest lay between the husband's trustee in bankruptcy and the wife, the court was prepared to make an order postponing the sale of the house for a limited period.

However, the decision in *Re Holliday* was very much against the run of the recent authorities: see eg *Re Bailey (a bankrupt), ex p the trustee of the bankrupt v Bailey* [1977] 2 All ER 26, [1977] 1 WLR 278 and Re *Lowrie (a bankrupt), ex p trustee of the bankrupt v The bankrupt* [1981] 3 All ER 353, in both of which an order for the immediate sale of the jointly-owned matrimonial home was made at the suit of the husband's trustee in bankruptcy; and in my view counsel for the wife was entitled to submit (as he did) that *Re Holliday* represented the high-water mark for the protection of the wife and children under s 30, a view which seems to underlie the decision of this court in *Thames Guaranty Ltd v Campbell* [1984] 2 All ER 585, [1985] QB 210, since in that case the court was not prepared to make an order which would expose the wife to the risk of proceedings under s 30.

In the present case Ewbank J considered whether to leave the wife to take her chances under s 30 and said ([1984] 2 All ER 577 at 583, [1985] Fam 49 at 58):

' ... I cannot help feeling that leaving a decision until an application under s 30 of the 1925 Act is made is failing to do justice to a wife. After all, under s 30 the only real question which the court is concerned with is how long is the wife to continue to have possession and not whether there should be a sale at all.'

In view of the state of the authorities to which I have referred above, this was a view which he was clearly entitled to take.

If, however, the wife's position is considered by the Family Division pursuant to her application for ancillary relief under the Matrimonial Causes Act 1973, then there are a number of ways in which her right to occupy the matrimonial home can be protected. First, the house can be settled on trust for sale (if it is not already so held) and the sale postponed until the youngest child attains the age of 17 or ceases full-time education, so as to enable the wife to provide a home for herself and the children until they are grown up. The proceeds of sale can then be divided in whatever proportions the court considers appropriate. This is the well-known *Mesher* order (see *Mesher v Mesher and Hall* [1980] 1 All ER 126) to which Ewbank J referred (see [1984] 2 All ER 577 at 583, [1985] Fam 49 at 57). The *Mesher* type of order has fallen out of favour of late, since its result is to throw the wife onto the housing market at a time of her life when she is unlikely to be able to secure adequate accommodation for herself, and the modern practice is to make an order to postpone the sale of the house until her death, remarriage, voluntary removal from the premises or becoming dependent on another man, although sometimes requiring her to pay an occupation rent after the youngest child has attained the age of 18: see eg *Harvey v Harvey* [1982] 1 All ER 693, [1982] Fam 83.

Although a *Mesher* order, or one of its variants, preserves the husband's interest in the matrimonial home and thus leaves something on which the judgment creditor's charging order can ultimately bite, the sale is likely to be so long postponed that, for practical purposes, the charging order will be of little value to the judgment creditor, whose natural wish is to recover his debt promptly. From the wife's point of view, a *Mesher* type order, or one of its variants, has its disadvantages. It leaves her linked financially with her husband, even though the modern practice, now enshrined in s 25A(1) of the Matrimonial Causes Act 1973, is to favour the 'clean break' whenever possible (see *Minton v Minton* [1979] 1 All ER 79, [1979] AC 593). Of greater importance, when considering the balance between the wife's rights and claims and those of the judgment creditor, an order which merely postpones the sale of the matrimonial home can leave her 'locked in' to the particular house which was the matrimonial home at the date of the break up of the marriage, and although family circumstances may render it desirable for her to be able to sell the house and move to a smaller house, or to a different district, she will be unable to do so if the result of a sale of the existing house, and the consequent division of the proceeds of sale, will leave her with insufficient funds to buy a new house.

It is for reasons such as these that an outright transfer of the husband's interest in the matrimonial home may be the appropriate way to protect fully the wife's right to have a roof over the heads of herself and the children, and it was, of course, such an order that the registrar made (and the judge affirmed) in the present case. Indeed, one of the points made in support of the wife's case, and accepted by the judge (see [1984] 2 All ER 577 at 584, [1985] Fam 49 at 59), was that if the charging order absolute stood and was followed by a sale she would not have enough money left to rehouse herself and the children. However, unless the transfer of the husband's share in the house to the wife is necessary to give her adequate protection so that she may have a home for herself and the children, it is difficult to see why the judgment creditor's undoubted rights should not take preference to the wife's claim to a transfer of property order.

One point made on behalf of the judgment creditor by counsel seemed to me initially to have considerable substance. He referred us to s 39 of the Matrimonial Causes Act 1973, which provides that the fact that a transfer of property had to be made in order to comply with a property adjustment order shall not prevent the transfer being a settlement of property to which s 42(1) of the Bankruptcy Act 1914 applies. Section 42(1) of the 1914 Act provides, so far as material, that any settlement of property, not made in favour of a purchaser in good faith and for valuable consideration, shall, if the settlor becomes bankrupt within two years after the date of the settlement, be void against the trustee in bankruptcy.

So, submitted counsel for the judgment creditor, there was little point in transferring the husband's share in the house to the wife, when all the judgment creditor has to do is to make him bankrupt, when the transfer of property order will be void as against the trustee in bankruptcy. However, in the present case the wife gave up her claim for periodical payments, and it seems to me that this constituted valuable consideration on her part which would preclude a trustee in bankruptcy of the husband from maintaining that the transfer of property order was void as against him: see *Re Abbott (a bankrupt), ex p the trustee of the property of the bankrupt v Abbott* [1982] 3 All ER 181, [1983] Ch 45. Certainly the contrary is not so clear as to support counsel's contention that it was here pointless to order the transfer of the husband's share in the house to the wife, and thereby override the judgment creditor's charging order. I accept, however, that were the facts different this could be an argument open to a judgment creditor in a similar type of case. Two other points were made to Ewbank J on behalf of the wife. These were that the judgment creditor had notice of the divorce petition on 15 January 1981, before he served his writ in the Queen's Bench Division, and that the wife had filed her notice of application for transfer of property before the writ. In this respect the present case differs significantly from the facts in *Hegerty*, where the judgment creditor had started his action and obtained judgment in default and a charging order nisi all before the wife had filed her divorce petition. If a judgment creditor obtains his charging order nisi after the wife has filed her divorce petition (which will usually contain a prayer for ancillary relief), then unless the court which hears the application to make the charging order absolute is satisfied that the wife's rights will be adequately protected by the court's discretion under s 30 of the Law of Property Act 1925, bearing in mind the limitations of that section mentioned above, it seems to me that it will normally be appropriate to take the course taken in the present case, and to transfer the judgment creditor's application for a charging order to the Family Division so that it may be heard by the court hearing the wife's application for ancillary relief.

The other points made to Ewbank J on behalf of the wife, the generality of which he accepted without indicating the weight he attached to any particular point, may be dealt with briefly.

(1) She had been previously cheated by her husband. The judge did not expressly decide this issue of fact, but in any event it can have little or no significance when weighed in the balance against the rights of the judgment creditor.

(2) She was not a party to the debt incurred by the husband and never agreed to the debt being incurred.

(3) The judgment creditor could, if he had wished, have asked for the debt to be made a charge on the house before he advanced the money.

(4) The judgment creditor was the partner of the husband and knew of the husband's wife and children and home.

Points (2), (3) and (4) are all points which it was legitimate for the judge to consider. The judge also considered (only to reject) a point made by the wife about her inability to gain priority over the judgment creditor by registering her claim as a *lis pendens*. Finally, he considered the point that the effect of a charging order absolute would (on the figures) be to transfer the whole of the husband's interest in the house to the judgment creditor, leaving the wife with nothing to claim against in the divorce proceedings. The judgment creditor, if the charging order absolute were discharged, would still have his judgment debt. However, since the husband had no assets other than his share in the house, without a charging order, or some other method of reaching that share (eg bankruptcy), that judgment debt was likely to be worthless. Counsel for the judgment creditor was justified in saying that this point was merely restating the problem: on the figures in this case it was all or nothing.

Finally, it is to be noted that the judge considered the possibility of making a *Mesher* type of order, but observed that this was not a solution for which the judgment creditor had asked.

At the end of this all too lengthy analysis of the position, I am satisfied that there are no grounds for holding that the judge was wrong in the manner in which he exercised his discretion so as to entitle this court to interfere.

That is sufficient to dispose of this appeal, but I am conscious that this is a point which is likely to come up with increasing frequency and, further, that it is apparent that I do not agree with the dicta of Stephenson LJ in *Hegerty*. In those circumstances, I think it right to set out how I conceive the court should deal with a similar problem when next it occurs.

(1) Where a judgment creditor has obtained a charging order nisi on the husband's share in the matrimonial home and his application to have that order made absolute is heard before the wife has started divorce proceedings, there is, of course, no other court to which the application for the charging order absolute can be transferred, the wife having no competing

claim to the husband's share. In those circumstances it is difficult to see why the court should refuse to make the charging order absolute, and the wife's right of occupation should be adequately protected under s 30 of the Law of Property Act 1925: See Goff LJ in *Re Holliday* [1980] 3 All ER 385 at 391, [1981] Ch 405 at 415.

(2) Where the charging order nisi has been made after the wife's petition, then on the application for a charging order absolute the court should consider whether the circumstances are such that it is proper to make the charging order absolute even before the wife's application for ancillary relief has been heard by the Family Division. There will, of course, be cases (such as *Llewellin v Llewellin* [1985] CA Bound Transcript 640, which we heard immediately after this appeal) where the figures are such that, even if the charging order is made absolute and then the charge is realised by a sale of the house, the resultant proceeds of sale (including any balance of the husband's share after the judgment debt has been paid) will be clearly sufficient to provide adequate alternative accommodation for the wife and children.

(3) Unless it appears to the court hearing the application for the charging order absolute that the circumstances are so clear that it is proper to make the order there and then, the usual practice should be to transfer the application to the Family Division so that it may come on with the wife's application for ancillary relief and one court can then be in a position to consider all the circumstances of the case.

When considering the circumstances, the approach of the court should be to recall the statement of Sir Denys Buckley in *Hegerty* [1984] 3 All ER 641 at 646, [1985] QB 850 at 866, that a judgment creditor is justified in expecting that a charging order over the husband's beneficial interest in the matrimonial home will be made in his favour. The court should first consider whether the value of the equity in the house is sufficient to enable the charging order to be made absolute and realised at once, as in *Llewellin*, even though that may result in the wife and children being housed at a lower standard than they might reasonably have expected had only the husband's interests been taken into account against them. Failing that, the court should make only such order as may be necessary to protect the wife's right to occupy (with the children where appropriate) the matrimonial home. The normal course should then be to postpone the sale of the house for such period only as may be requisite to protect the right of occupation, a *Mesher* type of order, again bearing in mind that the court is holding the balance, not between the wife and the husband, but between the wife and the judgment creditor. If the judgment creditor asks, even in the alternative to his claim to an immediate order, for a *Mesher* type of order, then it seems to me that it would require exceptional circumstances before the court should make an order for the outright transfer of the husband's share in the house to the wife, thereby leaving nothing on which the judgment creditor's charging order can bite, even in the future.

Finally, the court should consider whether there is any point in denying the judgment creditor his charging order if the wife's rights of occupation could, in any event, be defeated by the judgment creditor making the husband bankrupt.

(4) Once the charging order absolute has been made, it would normally require some special circumstance, eg where (as here) the wife had no proper opportunity to put her case before the court, for the court to set the charging

order aside under s 3(5) of the 1979 Act and thereby deprive the judgment creditor of his vested right.

I would dismiss this appeal.

Fox and Mustill LJJ delivered concurring judgments.

In this case the creditor had adopted an 'all-or-nothing' approach, asking for his charging order to take immediate effect. The court hinted at the possibility of a Mesher type order, which the court might more readily grant. This possibility was further considered, and the hint accepted, in the later case of *Austin-Fell v Austin-Fell and another* [1990] 2 All ER 455, where the effect of the charging order was postponed until the children of the marriage attained maturity.

Austin-Fell v Austin-Fell and another

The property concerned was a matrimonial home jointly owned by Mr and Mrs Austin-Fell, occupied at the time of the proceedings by Mrs Austin-Fell and the two daughters of the marriage, then aged 10 and eight. The creditor was Midland Bank plc, who had obtained judgment against Mr Austin-Fell in respect of an overdraft, and who sought to enforce this judgment debt by means of a charging order. In divorce proceedings, the wife claimed the transfer of the husband's beneficial interest in the former matrimonial home. The registrar formed the view that adequate security of accommodation could only be provided for the wife by giving her the entire beneficial interest in the property and dismissing the bank's application for a charging order on the property.

The bank appealed from the order of the registrar. Commenting on *Harman v Glencross* (above) Waite J said:

Although the circumstances of Harman's case involved a similar tripartite dispute between husband, wife and judgment creditor regarding the beneficial interests in a former matrimonial home, they included two notable features which are not to be found in the present case. One was that the judgment debt in *Harman's* case represented a very much higher proportion when measured against the total beneficial interest of the property. The equity in the property was £22,400. A half interest would therefore be £11,200. The judgment debt was £13,000. A charge on the husband's half interest would therefore have exhausted that interest entirely ... The comparable figures in the present case are ... £60,000 for the net equity ... £30,000 for a half share and £10,000 for the judgment debt.

The second distinctive feature of *Harman v Glencross* was that the judgment creditor adopted an 'all or nothing' approach to the enforcement of his security; it should either be imposed as a charge with immediate effect or not imposed at all. He did not ask for the alternative option to be considered of a postponement of his charge's enforceability to a later date. Although Fox LJ indicated that this was the solution he personally would have favoured ... there was no criticism by the Court of Appeal of Ewbank J's decision to treat that option as not being open to the court in that case for the simple reason that it had not been requested by the judgment creditor.

It would ... in my judgment be an exercise of discretion unfairly harsh to the wife and unduly favourable to the judgment creditor to force her at this stage to move to another area, or to a different part of the country altogether, in search of cheaper housing, and to leave behind her mother, her pupils, and the schools which have become familiar to her girls, all for the sake of ensuring immediate payment of the bank's debt ...

The right of occupation to be protected is not in the ordinary way to be permanent occupation ... Where, as here, the creditor asks, in the alternative to immediate enforcement, for a Mesher type of order, such an order ought not to be refused save in exceptional circumstances. The circumstances of the present case certainly include unusual features. The remarkable resilience and determination shown by the wife in recovering from the consequences and shock of the husband's business failure is one of them. They cannot, however, in my judgment be described as exceptional in the sense in which that term is used in the guideline ...

A postponed enforcement order represents the fairest balance between the competing claims of wife and creditor, in the endeavour which the court has to make to give some effect to both ...'

In both *Harman v Glencross* and *Austin-Fell v Austin-Fell* the divorce petition was presented before the attempt to secure the charging order. In those cases where the charging order is made before the commencement of divorce proceedings, it seems that the wife's rights will be left to her right to resist a sale under section 30 of the Law of Property Act.

The unfortunate effects of these decisions have been highlighted by another commentator:

Regard must be had to the times when the charging order was obtained and when the divorce petition was issued. In other words, the wife who thinks her husband has large debts and may be unable to meet them, must file a divorce petition first as a preventative measure; something that seems contrary to any sensible view of the matrimonial legislation. Moreover, a husband who sees a divorce coming and who wishes to make his wife's petition as unpleasant as possible, will run up large debts, default in their payment, not oppose judgment and rely on the creditors moving swiftly under the Charging Orders Act 1979 to overtrump any potential claim by the wife to his (the husband's) property (Clarke (1986) All ER Annual Review 186).

AMENDMENTS FOR THE FUTURE

The Family Law Act 1996 in Part IV, will replace the Matrimonial Homes Act 1983 as from a date to be announced. As from that date, references in this chapter to the Matrimonial Homes Act 1983 should be taken to be references to the Family Law Act 1996. Similarly, the Trusts of Land and Appointment of Trustees Act 1996 will, in ss 14 and 15, replace s 30 of the Law of Property Act 1925. Section 15 now includes the matters which are to be relevant in determining applications for an order under s 14 (the replacement for s 30 of the 1925 Act). These express in statutory form the consideration which the court was taking into account under s 30. However, s 15 does not apply to an application by a trustee in bankruptcy under the new s 335A of the Insolvency Act 1986 (concerning rights under trusts of land) which is added by Schedule 3, para 23 of the 1996 Act. Such an application is to be made to the court having jurisdiction in relation to bankruptcy. On such an application, the court is to make such order as it thinks just and reasonable, having regard to the interests of the creditors, the conduct (so far as contributin to the bankruptcy), needs and financial resources of the spouse or former spouse, the needs of any children and all the circumstances other than the needs of the bankrupt. Again, there is the one year provision, after which, apart from 'exceptional circumstances'. the interests of the creditors will outweigh all other considerations.

CHAPTER 15

HOMELESSNESS

INTRODUCTION

Homelessness has been described as 'one of the most pernicious social problems' (see D Hughes, *Public Sector Housing Law*, 2nd edn, Chapter 6, p 159). It has become a social problem approaching mammoth proportions. The number of people 'sleeping rough' has increased tremendously over the last few years. Large cities, such as Manchester, Glasgow and Bristol, as well as London, have seen the numbers of homeless people grow to such numbers that the authorities and voluntary organisations cannot cope and in consequence the formation of self-help groups (see, for example, the work of 'Giroscope' in Hull), aimed at reducing the problem by largely co-operative methods, has occurred. Nevertheless, many cities now have large numbers of homeless people on the streets. 'Cardboard City' in London is now merely the tip of the iceberg; and we are witnessing scenes on our streets reminiscent of times when Charles Dickens wrote novels describing the social problems of his time.

In 1970, approximately 8,000 people were accepted as homeless by Councils in England, but in 1988, that figure had increased to 108,000 per year. In 1990, the figure for Britain as a whole was 168,850; but in the first half of 1991 the figure for England alone was 73,900.

The homeless have often been treated as the 'undeserving poor' who should be put into workhouses rather than offered charity and welfare assistance. Workhouses and the Poor Law were abolished in 1948 when the National Assistance Act was passed, but Local Authorities were given only limited duties of providing the homeless with temporary shelter. Local Authorities were reluctant to do anything practical in terms of temporary accommodation unless a mother and her dependent children were homeless; the result was that families were often split up. The problems of homelessness and the splitting up of families became particularly acute in the 1960s. The televised documentary 'Cathy Come Home' led to public outrage and the formation of voluntary organisations aimed at eradicating homelessness. Despite good work by such organisations as 'Shelter' and the Campaign for the Homeless and Roofless (CHAR), homelessness remains an acute social and political problem.

It is against this background that this chapter will discuss the present law relating to homelessness.

The present legislation stems from the Housing (Homeless Persons) Act, 1977, which resulted from public pressure following the documentary 'Cathy Come Home' and the formation of 'Shelter' as a pressure group. The 1977 Act stemmed from a Private Members' Bill promoted by Stephen Ross. The aim of the Bill was twofold:

1 To transfer responsibility for housing homeless people from Local Authority Social Services Departments to their Housing Departments; and

2 To replace the duty to provide temporary accommodation with a range of duties which depended on various criteria, such as 'priority need'.

The slender government majority was such that the Local Authority lobby was able to enlist mainly Opposition support and obtain considerable concessions. In its rough passage through Parliament, the Bill was transformed into an 'obstacle course' which a homeless person had to negotiate before being owed the full duty to be provided with permanent accommodation.

The 1977 Act was re-enacted as Part III of the Housing Act 1985. However, the Housing 1996, replaced the provisions contained in the Housing Act 1985 and also, in doing so, made amendments to the law on homelessness.

Part VII of the 1996 Act lays down the criteria which have to be satisfied before a local Housing Authority owes an eligible applicant the full duty under the Act:

1 he/she has to be homeless;

2 he/she has to be in priority need;

3 he/she has to be homeless unintentionally; and

4 he/she has to have a local connection with the Local Authority applied to.

The notion of 'eligibility' under the Act is dealt with later.

It should be noted that Part VII of the 1996 Act is due to come into force in January 1997. It should also be noted that the cases referred to in this chapter pre-date the coming into force of the 1996 Act and that references in those cases are to the previous legislation.

The relevant sections of the 1996 Act provide as follows:

PART VII

Homelessness

Homelessness and threatened homelessness

175. (1) A person is homeless if he has no accommodation available for his occupation, in the United Kingdom or elsewhere, which he–

(a) is entitled to occupy by virtue of an interest in it or by virtue of an order of a court,

(b) has an express or implied licence to occupy, or

(c) occupies as a residence by virtue of any enactment or rule of law giving him the right to remain in occupation or restricting the right of another person to recover possession.

(2) A person is also homeless if he has accommodation but–

(a) he cannot secure entry to it, or

(b) it consists of a moveable structure, vehicle or vessel designed or adapted for human habitation and there is no place where he is entitled or permitted both to place it and to reside in it.

(3) A person shall not be treated as having accommodation unless it is accommodation which it would be reasonable for him to continue to occupy.

(4) A person is threatened with homelessness if it is likely that he will become homeless within 28 days.

176. Accommodation shall be regarded as available for a person's occupation only if it is available for occupation by him together with–

(a) any other person who normally resides with him as a member of his family, or

(b) any other person who might reasonably be expected to reside with him.

References in this Part to securing that accommodation is available for a person's occupation shall be construed accordingly.

177. (1) It is not reasonable for a person to continue to occupy accommodation if it is probable that this will lead to domestic violence against him, or against–

(a) a person who normally resides with him as a member of his family, or

(b) any other person who might reasonably be expected to reside with him.

For this purpose 'domestic violence', in relation to a person, means violence from a person with whom he is associated, or threats of violence from such a person which are likely to be carried out.

(2) In determining whether it would be, or would have been, reasonable for a person to continue to occupy accommodation, regard may be had to the general circumstances prevailing in relation to housing in the district of the local housing authority to whom he has applied for accommodation or for assistance in obtaining accommodation.

(3)...

178. (1) For the purposes of this Part, a person is associated with another person if–

(a) they are or have been married to each other;

(b) they are cohabitants or former cohabitants;

(c) they live or have lived in the same household;

(d) they are relatives;

(e) they have agreed to marry one another (whether or not that agreement has been terminated);

(f) in relation to a child, each of them is a parent of the child or has, or has had, parental responsibility for the child.

(2) If a child has been adopted or has been freed for adoption by virtue of any of the enactments mentioned in s 16(1) of the Adoption Act 1976, two persons are also associated with each other for the purposes of this Part if–

(a) one is a natural parent of the child or a parent of such a natural parent, and

(b) the other is the child or a person–

(i) who has become a parent of the child by virtue of an adoption order or who has applied for an adoption order, or

(ii) with whom the child has at any time been placed for adoption.

(3) In this section–

'adoption order' has the meaning given by section 72(1) of the Adoption Act 1976;

'child' means a person under the age of 18 years;

'cohabitants' means a man and a woman who, although not married to each other, are living together as husband and wife, and 'former cohabitants' shall be construed accordingly;

'parental responsibility' has the same meaning as in the Children Act 1989; and

'relative', in relation to a person, means–

(a) the father, mother, stepfather, stepmother, son, daughter, stepson, stepdaughter, grandmother, grandfather, grandson or granddaughter of that person or of that person's spouse or former spouse, or

(b) the brother, sister, uncle, aunt, niece or nephew (whether of the full blood or of the half blood or by affinity) of that person or of that person's spouse or former spouse,

and includes, in relation to a person who is living or has lived with another person as husband and wife, a person who would fall within paragraph (a) or (b) if the parties were married to each other.

General functions in relation to homelessness or threatened homelessness

179. (1) Every local housing authority shall secure that advice and information about homelessness, and the prevention of homelessness, is available free of charge to any person in their district.

(2) The authority may give to any person by whom such advice and information is provided on behalf of the authority assistance by way of grant or loan.

(3) A local housing authority may also assist any such person–

(a) by permitting him to use premises belonging to the authority,

(b) by making available furniture or other goods, whether by way of gift, loan or otherwise, and

(c) by making available the services of staff employed by the authority.

180. (1) The Secretary of State or a local housing authority may give assistance by way of grant or loan to voluntary organisations concerned with homelessness or matters relating to homelessness.

(2)..., (3)....

Application for assistance in case of homelessness or threatened homelessness

183. (1) The following provisions of this Part apply where a person applies to a local housing authority for accommodation, or for assistance in obtaining accommodation, and the authority have reason to believe that he is or may be homeless or threatened with homelessness.

(2) In this Part–

'applicant' means a person making such an application,

'assistance under this Part' means the benefit of any function under the following provisions of this Part relating to accommodation or assistance in obtaining accommodation, and

'eligible for assistance' means not excluded from such assistance by section 185 (persons from abroad not eligible for housing assistance) or section 186 (asylum seekers and their dependants).

(3) Nothing in this section or the following provisions of this Part affects a person's entitlement to advice and information under section 179 (duty to provide advisory services).

184. (1) If the local housing authority have reason to believe that an applicant may be homeless or threatened with homelessness, they shall make such inquiries as are necessary to satisfy themselves–

(a) whether he is eligible for assistance, and

(b) if so, whether any duty, and if so what duty, is owed to him under the following provisions of this Part.

(2) They may also make inquiries whether he has a local connection with the district of another local housing authority in England, Wales or Scotland.

(3) On completing their inquiries the authority shall notify the applicant of their decision and, so far as any issue is decided against his interests, inform him of the reasons for their decision.

(4) If the authority have notified or intend to notify another local housing authority under section 198 (referral of cases), they shall at the same time notify the applicant of that decision and inform him of the reasons for it.

(5) A notice under subsection (3) or (4) shall also inform the applicant of his right to request a review of the decision and of the time within which such a request must be made (see section 202).

(6) Notice required to be given to a person under this section shall be given in writing and, if not received by him, shall be treated as having been given to him if it is made available at the authority's office for a reasonable period of collection by him or on his behalf.

Eligibility for assistance

185. (1) A person is not eligible for assistance under this Part if he is a person from abroad who is ineligible for housing assistance.

(2) A person who is subject to immigration control within the meaning of the Asylum and Immigration Act 1996 is not eligible for housing assistance unless he is of a class prescribed by regulations made by the Secretary of State.

(3) The Secretary of State may make provision by regulations as to other descriptions of persons who are to be treated for the purposes of this Part as persons from abroad who are ineligible for housing assistance.

(4) A person from abroad who is not eligible for housing assistance shall be disregarded in determining for the purposes of this Part whether another person–

    (a) is homeless or threatened with homelessness, or

    (b) has a priority need for accommodation.

186. (1) An asylum-seeker, or a dependant of an asylum-seeker who is not by virtue of section 185 a person from abroad who is ineligible for housing assistance, is not eligible for assistance under this Part if he has any accommodation in the United Kingdom, however temporary, available for his occupation.

(2) For the purposes of this section a person who makes a claim for asylum–

    (a) becomes an asylum-seeker at the time when his claim is recorded by the Secretary of State as having been made, and

    (b) ceases to be an asylum-seeker at the time when his claim is recorded by the Secretary of State as having been finally determined or abandoned.

(3) For the purposes of this section a person–

    (a) becomes a dependant of an asylum-seeker at the time when he is recorded by the Secretary of State as being a dependant of the asylum-seeker, and

    (b) ceases to be a dependant of an asylum-seeker at the time when the person whose dependant he is ceases to be an asylum-seeker or, if it is earlier, at the time when he is recorded by the Secretary of State as ceasing to be a dependant of the asylum-seeker.

(4) In relation to an asylum-seeker, 'dependant' means a person–

(a) who is his spouse or a child of his under the age of eighteen, and

(b) who has neither a right of abode in the United Kingdom nor indefinite leave under the Immigration Act 1971 to enter or remain in the United Kingdom.

(5) In this section a 'claim for asylum' means a claim made by a person that it would be contrary to the United Kingdom's obligations under the Convention relating to the Status of Refugees done at Geneva on 28 July 1951 and the Protocol to that Convention for him to be removed from, or required to leave, the United Kingdom.

Interim duty to accommodate

188. (1) If the local housing authority have reason to believe that an applicant may be homeless, eligible for assistance and have a priority need, they shall secure that accommodation is available for occupation pending a decision as to the duty (if any) owed to him under the following provisions of this Part.

(2) The duty under this section arises irrespective of any possibility of the referral of the applicant's case to another local housing authority (see sections 198 to 200).

(3)...

The authority may continue to secure that accommodation is available for the applicant's occupation pending a decision on a review.

189. (1) The following have a priority need for accommodation–

(a) a pregnant woman or a person with whom she resides or might reasonably be expected to reside;

(b) a person with whom dependent children reside or might reasonably be expected to reside;

(c) a person who is vulnerable as a result of old age, mental illness handicap or physical disability or other special reason, or with whom such a person resides or might reasonably be expect to reside;

(d) a person who is homeless or threatened with homelessness as a result of an emergency such as flood, fire or other disaster.

(2)..., (3)..., (4)...

Duties to persons found to be homeless or threatened with homelessness

190. (1) This section applies where the local housing authority are satisfied that an applicant is homeless and is eligible for assistance but are also satisfied that he became homeless intentionally.

(2) If the authority are satisfied that the applicant has a priority need, they shall –

(a) secure that accommodation is available for his occupation for such period as they consider will give him a reasonable opportunity of securing accommodation for his occupation and

(b) provide him with advice and such assistance as they consider appropriate in the circumstances in any attempts he may make to secure that accommodation becomes available for his occupation.

(3) If they are not satisfied that he has a priority need, they shall provide him with advice and such assistance as they consider appropriate in the

circumstances in any attempts he may make to secure that accommodation becomes available for his occupation.

191. (1) A person becomes homeless intentionally if he deliberately does or fails to do anything in consequence of which he ceases to occupy accommodation which is available for his occupation and which it would have been reasonable for him to continue to occupy.

(2) For the purposes of subsection (1) an act or omission in good faith on the part of a person who was unaware of any relevant fact shall not be treated as deliberate.

(3) A person shall be treated as becoming homeless intentionally if–

(a) he enters into an arrangement under which he is required to cease to occupy accommodation which it would have been reasonable for him to continue to occupy, and

(b) the purpose of the arrangement is to enable him to become entitled to assistance under this Part,

and there is no other good reason why he is homeless.

(4) A person who is given advice or assistance under section 197 (duty where other suitable alternative accommodation available), but fails to secure suitable accommodation in circumstances in which it was reasonably to be expected that he would do so, shall, if he makes a further application under this Part, be treated as having become homeless intentionally.

192. (1) This section applies where the local housing authority–

(a) are satisfied that an applicant is homeless and eligible assistance, and

(b) are not satisfied that he became homeless intentionally,

but are not satisfied that he has a priority need.

(2) The authority shall provide the applicant with advice and such assistance as they consider appropriate in the circumstances in any attempts he may make to secure that accommodation becomes available for his occupation.

193. (1) This section applies where the local housing authority are satisfied that an applicant is homeless, eligible for assistance and has a priority need, and are not satisfied that he became homeless intentionally.

This section has effect subject to section 197 (duty where other suitable accommodation available).

(2) Unless the authority refer the application to another local housing authority (see section 198), they shall secure that accommodation is available for occupation by the applicant.

(3) The authority are subject to the duty under this section for a period of two years ('the minimum period'), subject to the following provisions of this section.

After the end of that period the authority may continue to secure that accommodation is available for occupation by the applicant, but are not obliged to do so (see section 194).

(4) The minimum period begins with–

(a) if the applicant was occupying accommodation made available under section 188 (interim duty to accommodate), the day on which he was notified of the authority's decision that the duty under this section was owed to him;

(b) if the applicant was occupying accommodation made available to him under section 200(3) (interim duty where case considered for referral but not referred), the date on which he was notified under subsection (2) of that section of the decision that the conditions for referral were not met;

(c) in any other case, the day on which accommodation was first made available to him in pursuance of the duty under this section.

(5)..., (6)..., (7)..., (8)...

(9) A person who ceases to be owed the duty under this section may make a fresh application to the authority for accommodation or assistance in obtaining accommodation.

194. (1) Where a local housing authority have been subject to the duty under section 193 in relation to a person until the end of the minimum period, they may continue to secure that accommodation is available for his occupation.

(2) They shall not do so unless they are satisfied on a review under this section that–

(a) he has a priority need,

(b) there is no other suitable accommodation available for occupation by him in their district, and

(c) he wishes the authority to continue securing that accommodation is available for his occupation;

and they shall not continue to do so for more than two years at a time unless they are satisfied on a further review under this section as to those matters.

The review shall be carried out towards the end of the minimum period, or subsequent two year period, with a view to enabling the authority to make an assessment of the likely situation at the end of that period.

(3) They shall cease to do so if events occur such that, by virtue of section 193(6) or (7), they would cease to be subject to any duty under that section.

(4)..., (5)..., (6)....

195. (1) This section applies where the local housing authority are satisfied that an applicant is threatened with homelessness and is eligible for assistance.

(2) If the authority–

(a) are satisfied that he has a priority need, and

(b) are not satisfied that he became threatened with homelessness intentionally,

they shall take reasonable steps to secure that accommodation does not cease to be available for his occupation.

This subsection has effect subject to section 197 (duty where other suitable accommodation available).

(3) Subsection (2) does not affect any right of the authority, whether by virtue of a contract, enactment or rule of law, to secure vacant possession of any accommodation.

(4) Where in pursuance of the duty under subsection (2) the authority secure that accommodation other than that occupied by the applicant when he made his application is available for occupation by him, the provisions of section 193(3) to (9) (period for which duty owed) and section 194 (power exercisable after minimum period of duty) apply, with any necessary modifications, in relation to the duty under this section as they apply in relation to the duty under section 193.

(5) If the authority–

    (a) are not satisfied that the applicant has a priority need, or

    (b) are satisfied that he has a priority need but are also satisfied that he became threatened with homelessness intentionally,

they shall furnish him with advice and such assistance as they consider appropriate in the circumstances in any attempts he may make to secure that accommodation does not cease to be available for his occupation.

196. (1) A person becomes threatened with homelessness intentionally if he deliberately does or fails to do anything the likely result of which is that he will be forced to leave accommodation which is available for his occupation and which it would have been reasonable for him to continue to occupy.

(2) For the purposes of subsection (1) an act or omission in good faith on the part of a person who was unaware of any relevant fact shall not be treated as deliberate.

(3) A person shall be treated as becoming threatened with homelessness intentionally if–

    (a) he enters into an arrangement under which he is required to cease to occupy accommodation which it would have been reasonable for him to continue to occupy, and

    (b) the purpose of the arrangement is to enable him to become entitled to assistance under this Part,

and there is no other good reason why he is threatened with homelessness.

(4) A person who is given advice or assistance under section 197 (duty where other suitable alternative accommodation available), but fails to secure suitable accommodation in circumstances in which it was reasonably to be expected that he would do so, shall, if he makes a further application under this Part, be treated as having become threatened with homelessness intentionally.

Duty where other suitable accommodation available

197. (1) This section applies if the local housing authority would be under a duty under this Part–

    (a) to secure that accommodation is available for occupation by an applicant, or

    (b) to secure that accommodation does not cease to be available for his occupation,

but are satisfied that other suitable accommodation is available for occupation by him in their district.

(2) In that case, their duty is to provide the applicant with such advice and assistance as the authority consider is reasonably required to enable him to secure such accommodation.

(3) The duty ceases if the applicant fails to take reasonable steps to secure such accommodation.

(4) In deciding what advice and assistance to provide under this section, and whether the applicant has taken reasonable steps, the authority shall have regard to all the circumstances including–

    (a) the characteristics and personal circumstances of the applicant, and

    (b) the state of the local housing market and the type of accommodation available.

(5) For the purposes of this section accommodation shall not be regarded as available for occupation by the applicant if it is available only with assistance beyond what the authority consider is reasonable in the circumstances.

(6) Subsection (1) does not apply to the duty of a local housing authority under–

section 188 (interim duty to accommodate in case of apparent priority need),

section 190(2)(a) (limited duty to person becoming homeless intentionally), or

section 200(1), (3) or (4) (interim duties where case is considered for referral or referred).

Referral to another local housing authority

198. (1) If the local housing authority would be subject to the duty under section 193 (accommodation for those with priority need who are another local not homeless intentionally) but consider that the conditions are met for referral of the case to another local housing authority, they may notify that other authority of their opinion.

The authority need not consider under section 197 whether other suitable accommodation is available before proceeding under this section.

(2) The conditions for referral of the case to another authority are met if–

    (a) neither the applicant nor any person who might reasonably be expected to reside with him has a local connection with the district of the authority to whom his application was made,

    (b) the applicant or a person who might reasonably be expected to reside with him has a local connection with the district of that other authority, and

    (c) neither the applicant nor any person who might reasonably be expected to reside with him will run the risk of domestic violence in that other district.

(3) For this purpose a person runs the risk of domestic violence–

    (a) if he runs the risk of violence from a person with whom he is associated, or

    (b) if he runs the risk of threats of violence from such a person which are likely to be carried out.

(4) The conditions for referral of the case to another authority are also met if–

    (a) the applicant was on a previous application made to that other authority placed (in pursuance of their functions under this Part) in accommodation in the district of the authority to whom his application is now made, and

    (b) the previous application was within such period as may be prescribed of the present application.

(5) The question whether the conditions for referral of a case are satisfied shall be decided by agreement between the notifying authority and the notified authority or, in default of agreement, in accordance with such arrangements as the Secretary of State may direct by order.

(6) ... (7) ...

199. (1) A person has a local connection with the district of a local housing authority if he has a connection with it–

(a) because he is, or in the past was, normally resident there, and that residence is or was of his own choice,

(b) because he is employed there,

(c) because of family associations, or

(d) because of special circumstances.

(2) A person is not employed in a district if he is serving in the regular armed forces of the Crown.

(3) Residence in a district is not of a person's own choice if–

(a) he becomes resident there because he, or a person who might reasonably be expected to reside with him, is serving in the regular armed forces of the Crown, or

(b) he, or a person who might reasonably be expected to reside with him, becomes resident there because he is detained under the authority of an Act of Parliament.

(4)..., (5)....

200. (1) Where a local housing authority notify an applicant that they intend to notify or have notified another local housing authority of their opinion that the conditions are met for the referral of his case to that other authority–

(a) they cease to be subject to any duty under section 188 (interim duty to accommodate in case of apparent priority need), and

(b) they are not subject to any duty under section 193 (the main housing duty),

but they shall secure that accommodation is available for occupation by the applicant until he is notified of the decision whether the conditions for referral of his case are met.

(2) When it has been decided whether the conditions for referral are met, the notifying authority shall notify the applicant of the decision and inform him of the reasons for it.

The notice shall also inform the applicant of his right to request a review of the decision and of the time within which such a request must be made.

(3) If it is decided that the conditions for referral are not met, the notifying authority shall secure that accommodation is available for occupation by the applicant until they have considered whether other suitable accommodation is available for his occupation in their district.

If they are satisfied that other suitable accommodation is available for his occupation in their district, section 197(2) applies; and if they are not so satisfied, they are subject to the duty under section 193 (the main housing duty).

(4) If it is decided that the conditions for referral are met, the notified authority shall secure that accommodation is available for occupation by the applicant until they have considered whether other suitable accommodation is available for his occupation in their district.

If they are satisfied that other suitable accommodation is available for his occupation in their district, section 197(2) applies; and if they are not so satisfied, they are subject to the duty under section 193 (the main housing duty).

(5) The duty under subsection (1), (3) or (4) ceases as provided in that subsection even if the applicant requests a review of the authority's decision (see section 202).

The authority may continue to secure that accommodation is available for the applicant's occupation pending the decision on a review.

(6) Notice required to be given to an applicant under this section shall be given in writing and, if not received by him, shall be treated as having been given to him if it is made available at the authority's office for a reasonable period for collection by him or on his behalf.

Right to request review of decision

202. (1) An applicant has the right to request a review of–

(a) any decision of a local housing authority as to his eligibility for assistance,

(b) any decision of a local housing authority as to what duty (if any) is owed to him under sections 190 to 193 and 195 to 197 (duties to persons found to be homeless or threatened with homelessness),

(c) any decision of a local housing authority to notify another authority under section 198(1) (referral of cases),

(d) any decision under section 198(5) whether the conditions are met for the referral of his case,

(e) any decision under section 200(3) or (4) (decision as to duty owed to applicant whose case is considered for referral or referred), or

(f) any decision of a local housing authority as to the suitability of accommodation offered to him in discharge of their duty under any of the provisions mentioned in paragraph (b) or (e).

(2) There is no right to request a review of the decision reached on an earlier review.

(3)..., (4).....

206. (1) A local housing authority may discharge their housing functions under this Part only in the following ways–

(a) by securing that suitable accommodation provided by them is available,

(b) by securing that he obtains suitable accommodation from some other person, or

(c) by giving him such advice and assistance as will secure that suitable accommodation is available from some other person.

(2) A local housing authority may require a person in relation to whom they are discharging such functions–

(a) to pay such reasonable charges as they may determine in respect of accommodation which they secure for his occupation (either by making it available themselves or otherwise), or

(b) to pay such reasonable amount as they may determine in respect of sums payable by them for accommodation made available by another person.

211. (1) This section applies where a local housing authority have reason to believe that–

(a) there is danger of loss of, or damage to, any personal property of an applicant by reason of his inability to protect it or deal with it, and

(b) no other suitable arrangements have been made or are being made.

(2) If the authority have become subject to a duty towards the applicant under section 188 (interim duty to accommodate),

500

section 190, 193 or 195 (duties to persons found to be homeless or threatened with homelessness), or

section 200 (duties to applicant whose case is considered for referral or referred),

then, whether or not they are still subject to such a duty, they shall take reasonable steps to prevent the loss of the property or prevent or mitigate damage to it.

(3) ... (4) ... (5) ... (6) ...

General provisions

214. (1) It is an offence for a person, with intent to induce a local housing authority to believe in connection with the exercise of their functions under this Part that he or another person is entitled to accommodation or assistance in accordance with the provisions of this Part, or is entitled to accommodation or assistance of a particular description–

(a) knowingly or recklessly to make a statement which is false in a material particular, or

(b) knowingly to withhold information which the authority have reasonably required him to give in connection with the exercise of those functions.

(2) If before an applicant receives notification of the local housing authority's decision on his application there is any change of facts material to his case, he shall notify the authority as soon as possible.

The authority shall explain to every applicant, in ordinary language, the duty imposed on him by this subsection and the effect of subsection (3).

(3) A person who fails to comply with subsection (2) commits an offence unless he shows that he was not given the explanation required by that subsection or that he had some other reasonable excuse for non-compliance.

(4) ...

Homeless

The first criteria which the eligible applicant has to satisfy is that he or she is homeless' or threatened with homelessness.

The Code of Guidance for Local Authorities (3rd edn, 1991), issued under the 1995 Act, provides in Chapter 5 some guidelines for determining whether a person satisfies this criteria, but the Code is not a legislative document and is not binding on Local Authorities. Section 182 of the 1996 Act provides for the issuing of Guidance by the Secretary of State and a new Code of Guidance is therefore likely to be issued in due course.

Put in simple terms, an applicant is homeless if there is no accommodation in the United Kingdom or elsewhere which they can reasonably occupy together with anyone else who normally lives with them as a member of their family or in circumstances in which it is reasonable for that other person to do so. A person is threatened with homelessness if it is likely that he will become homeless within the next 28 days.

A local authority must investigate each case of alleged threatened homelessness; but, so long as their decision is not 'unreasonable', it will not be quashed. (See *R v Decorum Borough Council, ex p M Taverner* (1989) 21 HLR 123.)

People who live in temporary or emergency accommodation are considered to be homeless; this includes women living in a 'battered wives' refuge or those living in a night shelter. (See *R v London Borough of Ealing, ex p Sidhu* (1983) 2 HLR 41, and *Williams v Cynon Valley Borough Council* [1980] LAG Bull 16.)

The quality of any existing accommodation is now relevant to deciding whether a person is 'homeless' within s 175. Section 14 of the Housing and Planning Act 1986 removed the unfortunate results of the House of Lords' decision in *Pulhofer v Hillingdon London Borough Council* [1986] 1 All ER 467. In *Pulhofer*, a family was living in temporary accommodation in a guest house on a bed and breakfast basis. Their facilities consisted of a single bedroom; there was no means of cooking food or of washing clothes. The House of Lords upheld the Local Authority's decision that the family were not homeless, because they had accommodation, even if it was totally inadequate for their needs. This scandalous and appalling decision prompted the government to amend s 58 of the 1985 Act by the introduction of subss (2A) and (2B), ('The *Pulhofer* Amendments') which introduced a criterion of 'reasonableness' of the continued occupation of any existing accommodation. These amendments have now been incorporated as ss 175(3) and 177(2) of the 1996 Act. The *Pulhofer* amendments had a considerable effect on subsequent cases. This can be seen in the following three cases in particular:

- *R v Kensington & Chelsea Royal London Borough Council, ex p Hammell* [1989] 1 All ER 1202;

- *R v Broxbourne, ex p Willmoth* (1990) 22 HLR 118; and

- *R v Westminster City Council, ex p Alouat* (1989) 21 HLR 477.

In the *Hammell* case, Mrs Hammell was the tenant of a council flat in Scotland but had fled to London to avoid violence and harassment from her husband, from whom she was separated. The violence had taken place outside the home; the Chelsea RLBC ignored it in arriving at its decision that Mrs Hammell was not homeless, as the council flat in Scotland was still available to her. The Council, however, was in error because it had failed to take adequate account of the *Pulhofer* amendments and the violence committed outside the flat:

R v Kensington and Chelsea Royal LBC, ex p Hammell

Parker LJ: In cases such as this the application for judicial review is in effect asserting that a public law right which is entitled to protection (see Lord Diplock in the passage I have quoted) has been invaded in that a wrong decision has been made. It may be that as a matter of discretion the court on the hearing of the application for judicial review, while accepting the submission, will not grant the relief claimed, but that the applicant is asserting that a right in public law has been invaded I regard for myself as being beyond all argument.

In my view there is clearly jurisdiction to grant relief whenever leave to move for judicial review is given and it is clear from *Pulhofer v Hillingdon London BC* [1986] 1 All ER 467, [1986] AC 484 that leave will only be given in limited circumstances. Those circumstances, I entirely accept, must involve the applicant in showing a strong prima facie case; that is said in clear terms in *De Falco v Crawley BC* [1980] 1 All ER 913, [1980] QB 460. I accept also that, unlike in the ordinary case where the balancing on the matter of convenience is between the two parties directly concerned, in all, or most, cases where the application is for judicial review, a very important consideration will be the public interest involved; that matter is dealt with in *Sierbien v Westminster City Council* (1987) 151 LG Rev 888.

With these matters in mind it is now necessary to examine in some detail the events which occurred on 12 and 13 April 1988 and the consequences of such events. But first I refer to s 58 of the Housing Act 1985 ...

In the present instance the duty of the council, it being plain that there was accommodation which Mrs Hammell and her children were entitled to occupy, was as follows: (1) to make inquiries necessary to satisfy themselves that 24 Menteith Court was accommodation which it would be reasonable for Mrs Hammell to continue to occupy and (2) to house her and her children until they had completed such inquiries and so decided. It is to be noted that the section requires a positive decision to be made by the council that the accommodation is accommodation which it would be reasonable for her to continue to occupy.

I go now to the council's documents to see in more detail what happened. The formal form of application signed by Mrs Hammell is followed by internal notes by the council's offices. The form filled in by Mrs Hammell reveals her present address, which is her sister's address. It reveals the names and dates of birth of her three children. It reveals the name of her tenanted property in Scotland, 24 Menteith Court, Alloa and her previous address, which had been the matrimonial home which had had to be sold during the course of the proceedings leading to the divorce and as a result of which sale she was granted a tenancy of 24 Menteith Court. There is a page which refers to medical details, but I find nothing on that of significance.

I come now to the notes of what happened when Mrs Hammell came for interview and thereafter. The notes relating to the day on which she came for interview are headed with the date, 12 April 1988, and are in these terms:

> 'Is at present living with sister at Adair Tower for 10 weeks – she is now asking her to leave. She has got a council tenancy in Alloa but has left there because of violence & harassment from ex-husband. M/S Hammell separated from her husband & was rehoused by Alloa. Unfortunately he has now moved in with someone else opposite where M/S Hammell lives. Her ex-husband not only harasses her himself [but sends] friends around to do the same. She has not got a telephone & cannot raise the alarm when he comes around. When she came to England she went to SHAC [the Shelter Housing Action Centre] & they advised her to go to [Hammersmith and Fulham housing authority] or [Royal Borough of Kensington and Chelsea housing authority] & seek NMS transfer.'

NMS refers to a national mobility scheme, which is of no statutory force but which is operated by many of the councils in England, Wales and Scotland, enabling council tenants for various reasons to be transferred from one area to another. The notes continue, setting out the name of Mrs Hammell's solicitor in Alloa and reporting the facts that she had told Mr Ashton that she had been advised by her solicitor that in order to obtain an injunction she would need a witness; that she apparently went to Hammersmith and Fulham, who suggested the emergency national mobility scheme and that she should not give up the tenancy but should go to Scotland to fill up the forms. She in fact went to Scotland for the day pursuant to that advice, filled in forms and then returned. The note continues:

'Came back & saw [Hammersmith and Fulham] & they said no connection (NMS for them suggested [Royal Borough of Kensington and Chelsea housing authority]) as staying there. Came here checked nothing had come to us. Discovered Clackmannan [District Council] had lost papers. Served notice.'

That requires a word of explanation. On her arrival in this country on 26 January 1988 Mrs Hammell very sensibly went to the shelter housing action centre. They advised her immediately to go to Scotland and apply for a transfer under the national mobility scheme. She did so. Having done so she lodged her papers with them and returned to London. That was a day trip which took place on 28 January. Thereafter, while waiting for a communication, nothing occurred until on 31 March, addressed to her sister's flat, she received a notice of abandonment relating to the tenancy at 24 Menteith Court. That no doubt surprised her. She sought again assistance from the housing action centre. They communicated with Clackmannan District Council and explained to them that they must have had the application, or they would not otherwise have known that the proper place to find her was at her sister's address, whereupon they suspended the operation of the abandonment notice.

There is recorded at the bottom of the first page of these notes the following by Mr Ashton:

'Spoke to Sue ... Lucking about case. She said violence was from outside the home & she considered it reasonable for her to return & [seek] legal assistance to protect herself and her interests.'

That concludes the notes of 12 April and it is not surprising that, on the basis of what he there recorded, Mr Ashton concluded that there was no reason to believe that she might be homeless and have a priority need. Indeed had he not so concluded, the decision would, as it seems to me, have been wholly irrational or *Wednesbury* unreasonable (see *Associated Provincial Picture Houses Ltd v Wednesbury Corp* [1947] 2 All ER 680, 1 [1948] 1 KB 223), but it is accepted that the conclusion was so reached. Thereupon it became the council's duty to make the inquiries and to provide accommodation ...

The notice itself can be attacked on a number of grounds. In the first place the reason given was on its face bad in law. It would have been good in law until the enactment of s 58(2A) by s 14 of the Housing and Planning Act 1986, but the result of that was that before the council could determine that she was not homeless, they had to reach a positive decision that it would be reasonable for her and her children to continue to occupy 24 Menteith Court, Alloa.

Secondly it can be attacked because there was material to show that the background reason was that violence was outside the home and therefore did not matter. That again would no doubt have been a sufficient reason had it not been for the enactment of sub-s (2A) of s 58, because under s 58(3)(b) of the 1985 Act there is provision that a person is homeless if he has accommodation but it is probable that occupation of it will lead to violence from some other person residing in it. But since it is now the position that the test is reasonableness of occupation, it cannot be right in law to suggest, as the council appear to believe, that the violence outside the home is not at least a very important factor going to the question of whether it is reasonable to occupy. There used to be, and indeed may still be among the many complications of the criminal law, an offence known as watching and besetting, which is something quite sufficient to render life intolerable to somebody, albeit nothing takes place within the premises themselves.

Thirdly, it can be attacked on the ground that the real reason, albeit a bad one, was that the violence was outside the home and not the reason stated.

Fourthly, it can be attacked on the ground that the inquiries that the council were obliged to make were insufficient to fulfil their statutory duty and that no reasonable council could, on the result of those inquiries, have supposed either (a) that the inquiries were sufficient, or (b) that they justify a conclusion that it would be reasonable for Mrs Hammell and her family to go back to 24 Menteith Court. As to this last matter, one asks: what did they know? They knew that Clackmannan District Council had confirmed that the house was available. They knew that there had been an injunction. They knew that Clackmannan District Council were going to investigate the matter of harassment. They had from a solicitor the observation that he was not surprised that the council were likely to reject the suggestion that Mrs Hammell was homeless. But they also knew that the solicitor had not seen her for at least six months. For my part I cannot regard anything which the solicitor said, other than confirmation of the legal position that she could not get an injunction without a witness and that there had been no application for breach of the earlier injunction, as being of the slightest significance.

On the basis of those notes, one would perhaps have expected that the council, having initiated quite properly, and very speedily, as they are encouraged to do, the inquiries which the statute obliges them to make would have pursued them. Instead the council stopped at a point when everything indicated the necessity of obtaining from Clackmannan District Council the result of their inquiries into the matter of harassment. But that did not occur either before or after issue of the s 64 purported notice. Since 14 April it appears that the council have not inquired of Clackmannan District Council how their inquiries are going and what they have found. It was submitted by counsel for the council that the respondent council are not obliged to make CID-type inquiries. I would readily accept that. But this is not a case of CID-type inquiries. Having properly approached the people who could most readily ascertain whether Mrs Hammell's account was right and whether the degree of harassment was such as she described, they then took no further action, save that they ascertained just before the hearing before us began that nothing further had occurred since 13 April.

The position may now be analysed. Mrs Hammell had on 12 April acquired a private right. That was a private right to be provided with accommodation on a temporary basis.

It was accepted by counsel for the council, quite rightly, that that right, so long as it existed, could be enforced by a mandatory injunction. That injunction would, albeit limited in point of time, have been a final rather than an interim injunction. The duty of the council was plain at that point of time. Mrs Hammell could, in my view, only be deprived of the right that she had then acquired by a decision validly taken by the council after they had fulfilled their duty to make necessary inquiries that it was reasonable for her to go back to Scotland and occupy the accommodation in Alloa. She had a public right to have that decision properly undertaken. Until that time, had the council originally provided accommodation and then purported to take it away, she could in my view have set up the invalidity of the purported s 64 decision as an answer to any attempt to remove her. She has to have a strong *prima facie* case that the council's duty was not fulfilled and that their decision was bad in law. In my view she succeeds. She has raised not only a serious question to be tried within *American Cyanamid Co v Ethicon Ltd* [1975] 1 All ER 504, [1975] AC 396, not only a strong *prima facie* case, which, on the basis of *De Falco v Crawley BC* [1980] 1 All ER 913, [1980] QB 460, is enough, but in my view a very strong *prima facie* case. She is entitled to protection with regard to her public law right to have the necessary inquiries made and the decision thereon properly made and also in the meantime to protection of her private right on the basis that she may show, when the case comes to trial, that it has been sought wrongly to take it away from her.

Had the *Hammell* case been decided before the *Pulhofer* Amendments, then in all probability the Council's decision would have been upheld. A similar situation occurred in *R v Broxbourne, ex p Willmoth* (below). In that case, the applicant had had a relationship with Willmoth, by whom she had two children. Willmoth had lived with her in her council accommodation in Hackney from time to time but had assaulted her on a number of occasions, as a result of which she had obtained non-molestation orders against him. After he left the flat on a permanent basis, Willmoth continued to be violent towards the applicant in the street. The applicant therefore left the area and finally applied to the respondent authority as a homeless person. The authority turned down her application on the basis that she still had a tenancy of council accommodation in Hackney. Again, the Council had failed to take adequate account of the *Pulhofer* Amendments.

R v Broxbourne Borough Council, ex p Willmoth

Megaw LJ: ... There is no doubt, and it is not in dispute in this case, that s 58(2A) does bring about the obligation on the housing authority to take into consideration the particular physical or mental needs or requirements of the particular applicant who claims to be homeless in deciding whether or not the claim for homelessness is justified. But it is said that the decision in *Puhlhofer's* case also showed that all that could be looked at was that which was to be found by way of living-room and amenities within the compass of the four walls of the particular accommodation which is available to the applicant.

Puhlhofer's case, in my opinion, does not say, or imply, anything of the sort. On the contrary, properly viewed, it shows, as it were by way of anticipation, that under the new provisions of subs 58(2A), which has since been enacted, the words 'it is accommodation which it would be reasonable for him to continue to occupy' are not necessarily or solely confined to looking at the actual quality of the accommodation within the four walls of the house or the room or the flat which is the accommodation available. It may be the duty of the housing authority to consider also circumstances, matters, and factors which may fall outside the limited consideration of the actual quality of the physical accommodation itself. That, in my judgment, is clear from the speech of Lord Brightman in *Puhlhofer's* case. Lord Brightman, in the passage to which I shall refer, was, of course, not dealing with s 58(2A), which had not then been enacted. He was dealing with s 17 of the 1985 Act which is a section dealing with 'intentional homelessness'. But the words which Lord Brightman used in connection with that section are highly relevant to the construction of the new subs 58(2A) because substantially identical words are used in the two provisions. I have read the words of s 58(2A) – 'unless it is accommodation which it would be reasonable for him to continue to occupy'. The relevant words of s 17, considered in *Puhlhofer's* case, are 'accommodation which is available for his occupation and which it would have been reasonable for him to continue to occupy'. At p 516, letter D, Lord Brightman makes it clear that those words, 'which it would have been reasonable for ' him to continue to occupy,' would involve taking into consideration, in a proper case, factors which fell outside the actual limits of the accommodation itself and outside the mere quality of that accommodation. Lord Brightman said:

'Or the accommodation which he occupied may have been up a flight of stairs, which was no longer within the physical capacity of the homeless person; so the local authority may consider that it was reasonable for him to have ceased to occupy it.'

It is quite impossible, in my view, to say that the new words enacted by Parliament following the words of section 17 in this context are restricted so that they apply only to, for example, violence or threats of violence by someone who is residing within the accommodation. Just as the difficulties created by a staircase or other approach to accommodation, to an applicant with physical infirmities, is relevant to reasonableness, so also are threats of violence, even though those threats come from one who is not resident in the accommodation.

The other limb of the argument put forward here is that if the new section 58(2A) had that wider meaning, it would make subsection (3) of section 58, which is one of the pre-existing sections, otiose. It would no longer, it is argued, have been necessary, when the Act was being amended, to continue to include a provision that a person is homeless if it is probable that his occupation of the accommodation would lead to violence to him from some other person residing in that accommodation. That, it is said, would necessarily be covered by the provisions of the new subsection (2A). It should be held, the argument runs, that there is here a clear indication that subsection (2A) cannot have been intended by Parliament to have as wide a meaning as I have stated, because, in that event, subsection (3) should and would have been repealed. In my view, that subsection is wrong for various reasons. I do not think that the effect of the true interpretation of section 58(2A) would be to make subsection (3) otiose. Further, even if it did, I do not think that the fact that that section in the original Act was not repealed at the time when this new subsection was introduced would be anything like sufficient to require the clear meaning of the words in the new subsection to be given a different and narrower meaning.

Therefore, apart from, or in addition to, the fact that, as I think, we are bound by a previous decision of this court to reject the argument based on the question of construction. I am satisfied that, if this court in the *ex p Hammell* case had had the argument put to it which was put today to us by Mr Straker, the decision in *ex p Hammell* would have been the same.

For those reasons I take the view that this appeal must be dismissed.

Finally, in *R v Westminster City Council, ex p Alouat* (earlier), the Council was held to be applying the wrong policy in concluding that, if a family were not statutorily overcrowded, they could not be homeless. The applicant and her family lived in accommodation which most people would regard as overcrowded, but which was not overcrowded within the meaning of Part X of the Housing Act 1985. To make matters worse, one of the children suffered from bed-wetting, making it difficult for that child to share a room with anyone else. The Council had decided that the family were not homeless as they had accommodation; and although conditions there left a lot to be desired, that accommodation was not statutorily overcrowded. The court, however, quashed the council's decision on an application for judicial review.

Applicants who have accommodation which it would be reasonable for them to continue to occupy may still be considered as constructively homeless if their circumstances fall within s 175(2)(a) or (b) of the 1996 Act. This covers the tenant who has been unlawfully evicted by his landlord and the traveller who cannot find a place on a site designated under the Caravan Sites Act 1968 on which to place his caravan. But if a tenant cannot be evicted without a court order and before a certain date which is more than 28 days into the future, then the authority may take the view that an applicant is not homeless because they have accommodation which it would be reasonable for them to continue to occupy until a court order is obtained (see *R v London Borough of Croydon, ex p Jarvis* (1994) 26 HLR 194).

In considering whether an applicant is homeless, the local authority have to consider the entire family unit and not just the applicant (see s 176).

Status of applicant

An application by a dependent child of young age may be turned down, not on the grounds that the child is not homeless, but on the grounds that they are not in priority need as a result of a 'special reason' making them vulnerable: see *Garlick v Oldham MBC and related appeals* [1993] 2 All ER 65:

'If a family has lost its right to priority treatment through intentional homelessness the parent cannot achieve the same result through the back door by an application in the name of a dependent child; if he could it would mean that the disqualification of intentional homelessness had no application to families with dependent children. If this had been the intention of Parliament it would surely have said so' (*per* Lord Griffiths at page 70, para d, [1993] 2 All ER 65).

However, if a local housing authority have turned down an application from parents of young children in need on the ground of intentionality, the housing authority may be required to reconsider the matter by the county council when it receives a request under s 27 of the Children Act, 1989, to assist the family in securing accommodation (see *R v Northavon District Council, ex p Smith The Times*, 4 August 1993).

An application by a mentally or physically incapacitated adult may also be turned down if the applicant is so disabled that they are incapable of forming the intention to make an application or to know that an application is being made on their behalf by authorising an agent to do so (see *Garlick v Oldham MBC and related appeals* [1993] 2 All ER 65). As people who are mentally incapacitated are classified as 'vulnerable' under Part VII of the Housing Act, 1996, this decision seems a little worrying. However, such a person would be owed a duty by the local authority under other legislation: see National Assistance Act 1948, s 21(1). Those people who are vulnerable by reason of mental incapacity may also be housed through an application made by their 'carer' in the community if such a carer were themselves made unintentionally homeless and in priority need; and s 189(1)(c) gives the carer such priority need.

A local housing authority is entitled to decide whether an applicant is an illegal immigrant and therefore whether no duty to house such a person is owed under Part VII of the 1996 Act (see *R v Secretary of State for the Environment, ex p Tower Hamlets London Borough Council* [1993] 3 WLR 32; [1993] 3 All ER 439).

As a result of the *Pulhofer* Amendments, now incorporated into the 1996 Act, and the case-law which has followed, the definition and interpretation of 'homeless' is relatively satisfactory. But the 'hurdle' of 'priority need' unfortunately leaves a lot to be desired; as, indeed, does the 'hurdle' of 'intentional homelessness.'

Priority need

The full duty is only owed to those people who are not only homeless but are also in priority need and are not intentionally homeless. The definition of priority need is set out in s 189 of the 1996 Act.

This lists four categories of people who are to be regarded as being in priority need:

- a pregnant women or a person with whom she resides or might reasonably be expected to reside;

- a person with whom dependent children reside or might reasonably be expected to reside;

- a person who is vulnerable due to one or more of various listed factors; and

- a person who is either homeless or threatened with homelessness as a result of an emergency, such as a fire or flood. (On which, see *R v Bristol City Council, ex p Bradic* (1995) 27 HLR 584.)

A notable exception from these four categories are the single homeless who are without dependent children and who are neither pregnant nor residing with a pregnant person. Unless these single people are considered to be 'vulnerable', then they fall outside the categories of 'priority need'.

There are several different types of single homeless people. The young single homeless probably form the largest group. These are often people who have left home in search of work or who have left after the breakdown of a family relationship. It is these sort of young people who too often end up on the streets of our major cities, sleeping in squalid conditions in squats, under bridges, or on park benches.

A second group of single homeless people consists of middle-aged persons, who are unemployed and dependent on charity for the basic necessities of life; these people often live on the streets by day and either 'sleep rough' or stay in temporary refuges or shelters at night.

A further 'group' of single homeless are a miscellaneous category of people who, through economic factors, such as unemployment or debt, find themselves without anywhere to live. Both young and middle-aged single people alike fall into this category.

Of the categories which are covered by s 189(1), pregnancy needs little explanation. The relevant date for this purpose is the date when the local authority's decision is made and not the date of the application. The Code of Guidance states that all pregnant women should be included, regardless of the length of time they have been pregnant.

If a pregnant woman suffers a miscarriage after making an application but before her case has been assessed, the authority should still consider whether she continues to be vulnerable. She must, of course, inform the authority of her change of circumstances.

The category of 'dependent children' mentioned in subsection (1)(b) is not confined to children who are subject to a legal custody order; it is sufficient if the children in question are *de facto* living with the applicant (see *R v Ealing London Borough Council, ex p Sidhu* (1983) 2 HLR 41, 45 and *R v London Borough Council, ex p Vagliviello* (1990) 22 HLR 392). A temporary stay with relatives, however, may be treated as a case where the children in question are reasonably expected to reside with their parents. If a parent has 'staying access' to a child, that child may be treated as residing with the other parent. In *R v Port Talbot Borough Council, ex p McCarthy* (1991) 23 HLR 207, a parent who enjoyed only staying access to his child was not considered to be in priority need:

R v Port Talbot Borough Council, ex p McCarthy

Butler-Sloss LJ: It is suggested that the effect of the joint custody order in itself is an indication that the children should reside with both parents. In so far as Mr Watkinson has put that forward in his skeleton argument ... he, I think, accepts that that is an inappropriate way of looking at a joint custody order, because the effect of the order is that care and control is always awarded to one parent, in this case the mother, and that is the parent with whom the children reside. In that way it bears a great resemblance to a custody order to one parent with access to the other, the purpose of joint custody being to give both parents a greater say in the future welfare of the children, rather than to have any effect upon the extent to which the children will or will not reside with the parent who does not have care and control. That is a matter of family law and not of housing law, but it is undoubtedly a matter which the Housing Authority will give its mind to, as it quite clearly did in this case. The purpose of care and control or custody is to indicate the principal residence of the children. Children normally reside with one parent and visit the other parent either daily or to stay. Mr Watkinson's very short point effectively put forward is that while accepting that it is a question of degree as to whether staying access is to be treated as residence, the Housing Authority in this case did not ask the correct question. They recognised that the children were residing with one parent but they did not put their mind to whether or not the children might reasonably be expected to reside with one parent at the same time as residing with the first one, that is to say four days with one parent and three with the other. Such an arrangement is not one that would be likely to be made in custody proceedings, and indeed there are decisions in the family law fields which clearly indicate that it would be considered by a court an unsuitable order to shuttle children from one parent to the other in this way. The duty of the local authority is to consider whether children might reasonably be expected to reside with their father. That was the question they considered. Mr Watkinson has attacked the wording of the letter and on the face of it, it is fair to say, it does not set out all the matters which they would have had in mind and it appears that the wording of it has to some extent been elided. But they implicitly say that they have, as they undoubtedly would have done, taken into account the facts of this case and were considering whether the children might reasonably be expected to reside with their father and were considering the reasonableness of that situation. As I have already said, an agreement as to staying access does not equal residence.

In the case the local authority have obviously taken into account all the relevant factors and have asked the right question. They have come to a conclusion that this is not a case where the children might reasonably be expected to reside with the father in these circumstances. This of course is not a lawyer's letter, it is a letter for and on behalf of the Borough Environmental and Housing Services

Officer. It might have been more felicitously expressed for the purpose of litigation. But it does undoubtedly, in my judgment, encompass all the necessary matters that this Housing Authority had to take into account. I would not like it thought that they are obliged to assume that children should reside with two parents as a normal arrangement. They would be entitled to take into account that the children reside with one parent and visit the other parent.

There may be exceptional circumstances where children might reside with both parents, but it would certainly be unlikely to be the normal arrangement.

For those reasons I would refuse this renewed application for leave to move.

The Code of Guidance states that Local Authorities should normally treat, as dependent children, all children under 16, and all children aged 16 to 18 who are in, or are about to begin, full-time education or training or who are for other reasons unable to support themselves and who live at home. In *R v Royal Borough of Kensington and Chelsea, ex p Amarfio* (1995) 27 HLR 543, however, an applicant's 16 year old son who was in receipt of a weekly allowance on a youth training scheme, was held not to be in full time educational training for this purpose.

'Vulnerability' of an applicant has proved the most difficult category of priority need. The Code of Guidance, in addition to including frail persons over the age of 60 and mentally or physically disabled persons for special consideration, also includes young people at risk from violence or sexual abuse at home, those with learning difficulties, juvenile offenders and those who are vulnerable to drug or alcoholic abuse or to prostitution. In addition, victims of violence or abuse or sexual and/or racial harassment are mentioned amongst those who 'for any other special reason' might be considered as vulnerable.

Three cases decided on grounds of vulnerability illustrate the courts' approach to this issue:

- *R v Waveney Borough Council, ex p Bowers* [1983] QB 238;
- *R v Bath City Council, ex p Sangermano* (1985) 17 HLR 94; and
- *R v London Borough of Lambeth, ex p Carroll* (1988) 20 HLR 142.

In *R v Waveney BC, ex p Bowers*, the applicant was a 59 year old alcoholic who had received a severe head injury which left him in a disorientated and confused state. The authority rejected his application on the grounds, *inter alia*, that he was not in priority need. On an appeal from an application for judicial review, the Court of Appeal allowed the applicant's appeal by holding that he was vulnerable, not because of alcoholism, but due to the brain damage which he had received in an accident:

R v Waveney Council, ex p Bowers

Waller LJ: The question we have to consider is whether or not the applicant is vulnerable and secondly whether the vulnerability is as a result of old, mental illness or handicap or physical or other special reason. Dealing first with the meaning of 'vulnerable', vulnerable literally means 'may be wounded' or 'susceptible of injury' (see the *Concise Oxford Dictionary*, 6th edn (1976) p 1305). In our opinion, however, vulnerable in the context of this legislation means less able to fend for oneself so that injury or detriment will result when a less vulnerable man will be able to cope without harmful effects.

To ascertain the degree of vulnerability guidance is provided by the code. The Code of Guidance suggests that a man above the age of 65 should be treated as vulnerable. Taken literally this would mean that a healthy man of 64 would not be vulnerable while the same man at 65 would be. It is of course merely a guide but it is an indication of the degree of vulnerability which is contemplated by the Act of 1977.

The code goes on in para 2.12 (c)(i) to indicate frailty, poor health or vulnerability for any other reason as reasons for treating a man as vulnerable by reason of old age even below the age of 65. The code then in para 2.12 (c)(ii) considers mental fitness or handicap or physical disability and says:

'This includes those who are blind, deaf, dumb or otherwise substantially disabled mentally or physically. Authorities are asked to take a wide and flexible view of what constitutes substantial disability, recognising that this will depend on individual circumstances.'

This paragraph starts by stating forms of disability which would necessarily create vulnerability of a much greater degree than reaching the age of 65, but then goes on to recommend a flexible approach. The Code of Guidance is of great assistance to those who have to make decisions under these provisions, but although it is authorised under s 12 of the Act of 1977, it must be read within the framework of s 2(1).

There can be no question here but that the applicant is vulnerable. The judge accepted that there was a degree of vulnerability. Furthermore it is reasonably clear that the degree of vulnerability increased as a result of a serious accident with severe brain injury in the early summer of 1980. Before that, although he had a drink problem, the applicant was able to cope, living in lodgings. Since the accident nobody will give him lodging and all those who have considered his case take the view that he needs either 'support' or 'help' or 'a degree of shelter' or 'sheltered accommodation'.

When approaching the test of vulnerability it is necessary to look at other examples. A pregnant woman is an obvious example, old age is another, although the vulnerability of a man aged 65 is not quite so obvious. An individual who is deaf or dumb is another. In this case if the applicant's problems arose solely because of his drink problem, it would be very difficult to say that his condition arose from mental illness or handicap, etc, but it is not the sole cause.

It would appear from the affidavit of the local authority that particular reliance was placed on the words 'substantially disabled mentally or physically' in the Code of Guidance and that led them to the conclusion that accommodation only had to be provided for those in substantial need. It was also suggested in the course of argument that the case had to be brought within one or other of the categories mentioned in s 2(1)(c).

In our judgment this was not the correct approach. The first question which has to be considered is whether or not there is vulnerability. If there is vulnerability, then does it arise from those matters which are set out within s 2(1)(c)? It may not arise from any single cause but it may arise from a combination of those causes.

In this case, the applicant's age was a factor but the brain injury was another important factor. Whether the brain injury is described as mental handicap or whether it is to be put into the category of other special reason is immaterial. If it had not been for the accident the applicant would not have had a priority need, at any rate until he reached the age of 65, but the accident made, in our judgment, the whole difference. We have no doubt that if the case had been approached in this way by the local authority they would have come to the conclusion that the applicant did have a priority need. We have great sympathy with the local authority in applying this section and the Code of Guidance to the facts of this case. It is important to draw a distinction between those cases solely due to the problems of drink where the case will normally not come within the provisions of s 2, and the facts of this case where an accident causing brain damage to a man of 59 has been an important factor.

We allow this appeal and hold that the applicant is homeless and has a priority need within the meaning of s 2 of the Act of 1977.

R v Bath City Council, ex p Sangermano

Hodgson J: This application is put in two ways. First of all, it is put that the local authority did not consider two relevant questions, namely the subnormality of the applicant and what effect upon that subnormality the question of her difficulty or impossibility of communicating in the English language might have. Whilst it is not specifically mentioned in the grounds, I would myself add, as I have said, it seems to me that they were plainly also misdirecting themselves in taking into account her arrears of rent record. It seems to me clear, not only from the two decision letters but also indeed from paragraphs 16 and 17 of Mr Cross's evidence, that the meeting in fact did not pay any regard at all to the evidence of subnormality which was before them in the evidence of Dr Boughton.

Section 2(1)(c) plainly draws a distinction between mental illness that is some psychotic illness and mental handicap. It seems to me plain that when the Act speaks of mental handicap, it is not speaking of illness but it is speaking either of subnormality or severe subnormality and from all the material before me it seems clear that this local authority was not making any distinction between mental illness and subnormality.

It is contended with some justification that these proceedings, even now, do not make the applicant's case clear in the grounds of application because, instead of mentioning specifically mental handicap, the grounds mention 'other difficulties', but what those other difficulties were is absolutely plain from the solicitors' letters and I do not think that there is any real substance in that objection.

It is also said that had it been made clear in the application itself, then the local authority might have thought it necessary to obtain medical evidence as to the degree of this lady's subnormality itself. I think there is nothing in that objection because the evidence in the medical report they had clearly stated that she was subnormal, and if they had had some doubts as to the degree of subnormality, then the duty was upon them to make the inquiries if they wanted to do so. As I have said, if one reads the solicitors' letters and the medical evidence supplied, it is plain that either they ought to have accepted that this lady was subnormal or, if they were not sure about the degree of the subnormality or whether it was present at all they ought to have made inquiries, which they did not do. It seems to me, therefore, clear that in the ways I have described the local authority did not properly instruct itself in coming to the decision which it did and was in error in law in that respect. Secondly, it is said that the conclusion to which the local authority arrived was unreasonable in the *Wednesbury* sense of unreasonableness. Looking at all the material which was before the meeting, it seems to me that had they properly instructed themselves they could not reasonably have come to any conclusion other than that this lady was vulnerable, within the meaning of section 2(1)(c) of the Act – vulnerable either because of mental handicap or because of another special reason being the combination of mental handicap and extreme language difficulty.

I have been cautioned against appearing in this judgment to be laying down any general principles and I do not do so. Clearly language difficulties on their own could not possibly amount to another special reason within section 2(1)(c), nor should I be seen or thought to be saying that merely because an applicant comes within the category of subnormality, as set out in the Mental Health Act, to which legislation I think plainly Parliament had regard in the framing of section 2(1)(c), that of itself would necessarily amount to vulnerability. I can conceive of cases where somebody, although in the medical category or the Mental Health Act category of subnormal would not, in terms of the Housing (Homeless Persons) Act be vulnerable, but I have no doubt that in this case when you get a lady with her record of incompetence who is subnormal and who is incapable of, on the evidence, articulating properly either in English or indeed in Italian, then you have someone who, properly instructing itself no local authority could, in the special circumstances of this case, come to any conclusion other than that she is vulnerable within the meaning of section 2(1)(c).

Finally, in *R v London Borough of Lambeth, ex p Carroll*, an application for judicial review on behalf of a man in his late forties was successful under the 'vulnerability' category. In that case, a single man, who regularly drank six or seven pints of beer a day, had also suffered a fractured skull in a car accident, as a result of which he had double vision. The local authority obtained the medical opinion of a doctor who never saw the applicant. The doctor's opinion was based on what the applicant's GP had said, but the GP had not seen the applicant for some time. The doctor's opinion that the applicant was not vulnerable was accepted by the local authority. Judicial review was granted on the basis that the authority had failed to perform its duties to make inquiries necessary to satisfy itself whether the applicant had a priority need. The case illustrates the well-established administrative law principle that a decision-making authority cannot delegate the task of decision-making to someone who is not empowered to make that decision on its behalf. The local authority must make its own decision and not blindly accept medical or other opinion without question.

(On vulnerability and epilepsy, see also *R v Sheffield City Council, ex p Leek* (1994) 26 HLR 669; see also *Ortiz v City of Westminster* (1995) 27 HLR 364 (CA), applicant an alcoholic and drug addict.)

Duty owed to those found not to be in priority need

Where there is homelessness but no priority need, s 190(3) of the 1996 Act imposes upon a local authority merely the duty to provide the applicant with advice and such assistance as is considered to be appropriate for the purposes of the applicant attempting to find accommodation for himself. The Code of Guidance suggests that local authorities should provide up to date lists of reasonable bed and breakfast and boarding houses and hostels in the area. In addition, the authority should interview each applicant and counsel him on the local accommodation options open to them, on housing benefit and other financial assistance; where appropriate, referring them to other specialist agencies. In practice, however, it is not unknown for the local authority to do little more than provide the applicant with a list of local bed and breakfast accommodation, or of those housing associations which might be prepared to help or the address of local accommodation agencies.

It is understandable that local housing authorities do not wish to see people 'queue-jumping' on the Housing Waiting List; but the present legislation fails to take adequate account of the changes in Social Security laws and the sad reality of family breakdown and unemployment.

Intentional homelessness

The concept of intentional homelessness has been one of the major problems of the legislation. The original Bill in 1977 contained no provision for intentionality, but the Parliamentary lobby forced through amendments which are now contained in s 191 of the 1996 Act. Local Councils, amongst others, feared that the legislation might otherwise become a 'Rogue's Charter', enabling people to jump the queue on the housing waiting list.

A person is intentionally homeless if he deliberately does or fails to do anything as a result of which he ceases to occupy accommodation which was available to him and which it would have been reasonable for him to continue to occupy. Since the House of Lords' decision in *R v London Borough of Brent, ex p Awua* (1995) 27 HLR 453, the available accommodation which was lost need not have been 'settled' in order for there to be a finding of intentionality.

A finding of intentional homelessness requires a positive answer to three questions:

- Was accommodation available to the applicant?
- Was it reasonable for the applicant to continue to occupy that accommodation?
- Was there a deliberate act or omission on the applicant's part, as a result of which that accommodation was lost?

The Code of Guidance stresses that, in general, the following should not be considered as a deliberate act or omission:

(a) if there is reason to believe that the applicant is incapable of managing his own affairs eg through age, mental illness or handicap;

(b) if the applicant was forced to sell their home through mortgage arrears or to vacate tenanted property through rent arrears and where they have suffered genuine financial difficulties even after claiming all benefits that they were entitled to claim;

(c) if an applicant, as owner occupier, was faced with foreclosure or possession proceedings to which there was no defence, sells before the mortgagee recovers possession through the courts or surrenders the property to the lender.

The Code adds that the following are acts or omissions which may be considered as deliberate:

(i) if the applicant chooses to sell their home in circumstances where they are not at risk of losing it or where they lose it as a result of a wilful and persistent refusal to pay rent or mortgage instalments when they had the money to do so (see *R v London Borough of Southwark, ex p Davise* (1994) 26 HLR 677);

(ii) if the applicant, in disregard of proper advice from qualified persons, has neglected his affairs;

(iii) if the applicant has voluntarily given up accommodation in this country or abroad which it would have been reasonable for him to continue to occupy (see *R v London Borough of Ealing, ex p Sukhija* (1994) 26 HLR 726);

(iv) if the applicant has been evicted due to anti-social behaviour (see, for example, *R v Westminster City Council, ex p Reid* (1994) 26 HGLR 690, where it was said that this issue depends upon whether the eviction is the reasonable result of the anti-social behaviour, in that case, violence against one of the applicant's sons); or

(v) if the applicant has voluntarily resigned from a job with tied accommodation where it would have been reasonable to remain in that employment.

This is by no means an exhaustive list but is given by way of example only. As mentioned earlier, the Code is not binding on local authorities; and cases involving the voluntary surrender of keys to Building Societies have caused particular problems.

Acts committed in good faith, in ignorance of a relevant fact (eg that full entitlement to Housing Benefit had not been claimed or that the prospects of the success of a business venture were very small do not amount to deliberate acts for this purpose (see s 191(2) and *R v Exeter City Council, ex p Tranckle* (1994) 26 HLR 244). If it is established that the applicant was ignorant of a relevant fact, the authority must not ask whether that ignorance was unreasonable but whether it was in good faith, since there is a distinction in this context between honest blundering and dishonesty. A fraudulent act can never be in good faith within the terms of s 191(2) (see *R v London Borough of Barnet, ex p Rughooputh* (1993) 25 HLR 607). Whenever bad faith is being attributed to an applicant, that is usually (though not necessarily) a matter which should be put to him. (See *R v London Borough of Tower Hamlets, ex p Rouf* (1991) 23 HLR 460, *R v London Borough of Hammersmith & Fulham, ex p Lusi & Lusi* (1991) 23 HLR 260 and *Hobbs v London Borough of Sutton* (1994) 26 HLR 132, *R v London Borough of Wandsworth, ex p Onwudiwe* (1994) 26 HLR 302.)

The question of 'infectious intentionality', which affects the applicant, will be dealt with later in this chapter.

The concept of intentional homelessness has led to a vast amount of case-law. The leading decision is that of the House of Lords in *Din v Wandsworth London Borough Council* [1983] 1 AC 657, [1981] 3 All ER 881:

Din v LB of Wandsworth

Lord Wilberforce: The appellants are married with four children; there is no doubt that they would fall into a potential priority class. In 1977 the whole family moved, from Croydon, into accommodation at 56 Trinity Road, Wandsworth, accommodation which was suitable for the whole family to occupy. This belonged, under a lease, together with a shop, to a relative, Mr Jaswail. Mr Din entered into a loose partnership with Mr Jaswail dealing with Pakistani food, but Mr Din retained his existing employment with Airfix Products Ltd. In April 1978 Mr Jaswail withdrew from the business. The landlord of the premises accepted rent from Mr Din without prejudice, but arrears of rent mounted up and Mr Din came to be in financial difficulties. In June 1979 Mrs Din went to the housing aid centre in Wandsworth and was put on the waiting list for accommodation. She was advised that before she could be helped she would have to wait for a court order for possession to be made against her. Mr Din was similarly advised on 2 July 1979. On 28 August 1979 the appellants vacated the premises; no court proceedings had been initiated against them, and no demand for vacant possession had been made. I do not think that there is any doubt that this action was deliberate and intentional and fell within the provisions of s 17. They then went to live with Mr Jaswail in a flat at Upminster; this was crowded accommodation. Mr Din hoped to get employment with Ford Motors at Dagenham; in this he was unsuccessful. In November 1979 he returned to his previous job with Airfix and took a room in Wandsworth. In December 1979 the appellants were asked to leave the Upminster flat. On 20 December 1979 the appellants applied to the respondents as homeless persons under the 1977 Act. The respondents made appropriate inquiries and on 4 January 1980 notified the appellants that they were satisfied that the appellants' homelessness was 'intentional'. The reasons given were that the appellants left 56 Trinity Road, Wandsworth after they had been advised on two occasions to remain in occupation until the owner sought a court order; they disregarded this advice and moved to Upminster knowing this to be only temporary accommodation.

As I have stated, the appellants later started proceedings in the county court. As to this procedure I have reservations. The local authority is, under the Act, carrying out statutory functions, and is required to make a decision based on findings of fact (being 'satisfied' as set our above). Its decision can be the subject of judicial review (see above), but county courts have no power to make this. A procedure achieving, in effect, the same result by county court action appears to have been approved by the Court of Appeal in *De Falco v Crawley Borough Council* [1980] 1 All ER 913, [1980] QB 460 and was not challenged in this case, so for the purposes of this appeal I will, under reservation, assume its validity. The evidence at the trial amplifies the facts in some respects and I am prepared to take it into consideration.

In his evidence Mr Din said that the only reason that compelled him to quit the place (56 Trinity Road) was the rate demand (he was scared) and said later that the main reason why he left was that he could also be at a new place but his move was prompted by his fear. Mr Godbold, an officer of the respondents, confirmed that this was what Mr Din told the housing centre. Mr Bruneau, head of the housing department, said that the reason why the local authority generally insisted on a court order was because of the 'impossible shortage' of accommodation. A few weeks are of extreme importance on financial grounds and as affecting the pressure on the stock. He did not accept that it was inevitable for the applicant to leave 56 Trinity Road in June 1979. In December he 'accepted on the evidence that they had no chance of making the accommodation pay' and 'on what I knew – whatever the time factor they would have had to have left.' In December. 'I accepted there was no possibility of him staying.' The impression, as regards time, of this evidence is to be noted.

So how does the matter stand? If one takes the words of the statute, the local authority have to be satisfied that the applicant became homeless intentionally (s 17). Under s 4(2)(b) their duty is limited to advice and assistance if 'they are satisfied ... that [the applicants] became homeless ... intentionally'. The time factors here are clearly indicated: at the time of decision (the present), the local authority must look at the time (the past) when the applicants became homeless and consider whether their action *then* was intentional in the statutory sense. If this was the right approach there could only be one answer: when the Dins left

56 Trinity Road their action was intentional within s 17, and the local authority were entitled to find that it would have been reasonable for them to continue to occupy 56 Trinity Road.

The appellants' argument against this is as follows. Whatever the position may have been in July 1979 when they left 56 Trinity Road, at the time of the decision in December 1979 they would have been homeless in any event; the original cause of homelessness (even if intentional) had ceased to operate. For s 17 to apply there must be a causal nexus between the intentional action and the homelessness subsisting at the time of the decision. On the facts of the case there was not, so that the decision was wrong in law. I am unable to accept this argument.

1   It cannot be reconciled with the wording of the Act. This is completely and repeatedly clear in concentrating attention on when the appellants became homeless and requiring the question of intention to be ascertained as at that time. To achieve the result desired by the appellants it is either necessary to distort the meaning of 'in consequence of which he ceases to occupy' (s 17(i)) or to read in a number of words.

   These are difficult to devise. Donaldson LJ suggests adding at the end of s 17(1) 'and still to occupy'; the appellants, as an alternative, 'to the date of his application'. Both are radical, and awkward, reconstructions of the section.

2   Such an interpretation, or reconstruction, of the Act is not called for by any purposive approach. As I have pointed out, the Act reflects a complex interplay of interests. It confers great benefits on one category of persons in need of housing, to the detriment of others. This being so, it does not seem unreasonable that, in order to benefit from the priority provisions, persons in the first category should bring themselves within the plain words. Failure to do so involves, as Mr Bruneau pointed out, greater expense for a hard pressed authority, and greater pressure on the housing stock.

3   The appellants' interpretation adds greatly to the difficulties of the local authority's task in administering this Act. It requires the authority, as well as investigating the original and actual cause of homelessness, to inquire into hypotheses as to what would have happened if the appellants had not moved, hypotheses involving uncertain attitudes of landlords, rating authorities, the applicants themselves and even intervening physical events. The difficulty of this is well shown by the singularly imprecise and speculative evidence given as to what was likely to have happened in December 1979 set out above. This approach almost invites challenge in the courts, all the more if it is open to applicants to litigate the whole state of facts with witnesses, de novo, in the county court, but still significantly if the applicants are limited to judicial review. On the other hand the respondents' contention involves a straightforward inquiry into the circumstances in which the appellants became homeless.

4   The appellants' argument is not assisted by *Dyson v Kerrier District Council* [1980] 3 All ER 313, [1980] 1 WLR 1205. There (as here) the applicant intentionally surrendered available accommodation in order to go to precarious accommodation (a 'winter letting') from which she was ejected and so became homeless. It was held (in my opinion, rightly) that she had become homeless in consequence of her intentional surrender. This does not in any way support an argument that a subsequent hypothetical cause should be considered to supersede an earlier actual cause. It merely decides

that a disqualification for priority by reason of an intentional surrender is not displaced by obtaining temporary accommodation. As pointed out by Ackner LJ in the Court of Appeal, it can be displaced by obtaining 'settled' accommodation.

5   It does not follow from accepting the respondents' argument that occupants who move before a notice to quit takes effect will be held to be intentionally homeless. Such cases are likely to be covered by s 1(3) referred to above.

I agree therefore with the majority of the Court of Appeal in holding that the present case falls squarely within the provisions of the Act as to intentional homelessness and that there is no justification for reading these provisions otherwise than in their natural sense.

In the result the local authority was entitled to decide, on the facts, that the appellants became intentionally homeless. I would dismiss this appeal.

Lord Bridge took a more humane and common sense view of the situation in his powerful dissenting judgement. He considered that the couple had merely bowed to the inevitable in leaving their accommodation before being legally evicted:

'Provided always that it can be demonstrated ... that by a certain date a man was bound to be evicted from his home, it offends common sense to hold that the cause of his homelessness after that date was that he chose to leave of his own volition before that date ...' (*per* Lord Bridge at page 897, paragraph j of [1981] 3 All ER).

This decision places people who cannot afford to pay their mortgage in a dilemma. Do they wait to be evicted by a possession order, or do they try to sell the house now, and recoup as much of their 'equity' as possible? The mortgagor who does sell before being evicted runs the risk that his homelessness may be considered as intentional, whilst the mortgagor who waits to be evicted will only be considered as intentionally homeless if the circumstances leading to his default show that he can be faulted. The latter, however, does run the risk of getting deeper into debt. Many people have been faced with this dilemma in recent years because they bought their houses on high mortgages before interest rates soared to 15% and house prices fell. Even though interest rates have since fallen, house prices have still dropped and increased unemployment has meant that there are still many people unable to meet their mortgage commitments.

A local housing authority should not insist that a person exhausts their legal remedies or wait to be evicted before leaving existing accommodation. In *R v London Borough of Hillingdon, ex p Tinn* (1988) 20 HLR 305, for example, Mr Justice Kennedy, in a non-homelessness case, commented on intentional homelessness; he said that, as a matter of common sense, it could not be reasonable for a person to continue to occupy accommodation when they could no longer discharge their fiscal obligations in relation to that accommodation without so restraining their resources as to deprive themselves of the ordinary necessities of life. Whilst *obiter*, this opinion shows a common sense attitude towards the plight of those thrown into financial turmoil by changes in their economic circumstances. The Code of Guidance also states that, in the case of tenants, local authorities should not require tenants to fight possession proceedings where the landlord has a certain prospect of success, such as an action for recovery of property let on an assured shorthold tenancy and where the fixed term of that tenancy has ended. See para 10:12, 3rd edn and on which see also *R v London Borough of Newham, ex p Ugbo* (1994) 26 HLR 263.

Was accommodation available?

The first question which the Local Housing Authority must ask is whether there was accommodation available which the applicant could have occupied. In *R v Westminster City Council, ex p Khan* (1991) 23 HLR 230, for example, the applicant had informed the Immigration Authority that she intended to live with a relative in Nottingham; but she never actually lived there before that house was sold. For a period of three months, however, the house had been available to her. She therefore had accommodation which was available. The test in the legislation is not whether the accommodation was actually occupied, but whether it was available for occupation.

Was it reasonable for the applicant to continue to occupy the available accommodation?

The Code of Guidance states that, in deciding whether it could have been reasonable for someone to continue to occupy available accommodation, authorities may be required to carry out a balancing act, and should therefore have regard to all relevant factors, including the applicant's reasons for leaving that accommodation. The Code adds that it will normally be reasonable for someone to leave available accommodation if they are the victim of domestic violence or threats of violence from inside or outside the home, and that the failure to exhaust legal remedies should not automatically render such an applicant as intentionally homeless. The loss of tied accommodation should also not be regarded as intentional if the employment was lost through no fault of the applicant. Although the Code is only for the guidance of local housing authorities, a failure to have regard to it may lead to a decision being quashed (see *R v London Borough of Newham, ex p Bones* (1992) 25 HLR 357).

If the local housing authority consider that the applicant is intentionally homeless because it was reasonable for him or her to continue to occupy available accommodation, then it must give to the applicant reasons which are intelligible and which convey to the applicant why their application has been rejected in such a way that if an error of reasoning is disclosed, then the applicant can take such steps as may be indicated (see *R v London Borough of Croydon, ex p Graham* (1994) 26 HLR 286).

Was there a deliberate act or omission?

In *Din* (above), the House of Lords said that the question of whether there was a deliberate act or omission had to be answered by reference to the time when the applicant had left the relevant accommodation.

In *R v London Borough of Barnet, ex p O'Connor* (1990) 22 HLR 486, it was held that substantial mortgage default by a family, who had no hope of ever being able to pay instalments on the several mortgages which they had taken out on their house, amounted to deliberate conduct. In times of economic recession, and when interest rates have gone as high as 15% before falling back into single figures, payment of the mortgage must therefore be priority ahead of other debts, such as on Visa and Departmental Store Cards. It is not uncommon for a Local Housing Authority to reject a homelessness application on the ground that an individual did have the means to pay the mortgage, so it is important for couples to realise that default is a serious business in more ways than one. Handing in the keys to the Lender voluntarily also can be considered as a deliberate act, since there is a procedure under the Administration of Justice Acts 1970 and 1973 for defending possession proceedings commenced by mortgagees (see Chapter 13 on Mortgages and the Home Owner).

The chain of causation

Prior to the *Din* case, the Court of Appeal in *Dyson v Kerrier District Council* [1980] 1 WLR 1205, [1980] 3 All ER 313, had held that a woman who had occupied a council flat in Huntingdon in which she could have expected to remain, was intentionally homeless by reason of her leaving that flat for accommodation (an off – season holiday let) which gave her no statutory protection against eviction. Eight months after she had moved from Huntingdon, she had been evicted from the new accommodation; the local authority were held entitled to look back into her previous accommodation history in reaching its conclusion that she had become intentionally homeless. Looking behind the immediate cause down the chain of intentionality is therefore acceptable (see also *De Falco v Crawley Borough Council* [1980] QB 460, and *Lambert v Ealing London Borough Council* [1982] 1 WLR 550).

One of the problems of going back beyond the immediate cause of homelessness is to know how far back it is legitimate to go and exactly what can be taken into account. Since the House of Lords' decision in *R v London Borough of Brent, ex p Awua* (1995) 27 HLR 453, there is no clear indication of how far back the authority may look. See *R v Islington London Borough Council, ex p Hassan* (1995) 27 HLR 485.

In *R v London Borough of Newham, ex p Campbell* (1994) 26 HLR 183, it was reiterated that in determining whether an applicant is intentionally homeless, the question is one of 'cause and effect'. In that case, the applicant had failed to pay the rent but had also been subject to violence and sexual harassment. The authority's sexual harassment policy was to make two reasonable offers of accommodation, but the applicant was refused accommodation under the homeless legislation on grounds of intentional homelessness. It was said that the deliberate act of failing to pay rent could not be divorced from the subsequent abandonment of occupation due to sexual harassment and personal violence from the applicant's partner. However, the only possible conclusion which the authority could have come to on the evidence in that case was that the sexual harassment and violence were not the dominant cause of the loss of the accommodation to the applicant; her application for relief was therefore refused (see also *R v Wandsworth Borough Council, ex p Oteng* (1994) 26 HLR 413).

'Purging' intentional homelessness

The chain of causation may be broken if the applicant has obtained 'settled' accommodation at a later stage which 'purges' earlier intentional homelessness. 'Settled' accommodation may take the form of a tenancy which will last for a minimum of one year, but there is no 'hard and fast' rule here. Short-term lets, such as a 'holiday let' or a 'winter let', and other temporary arrangements (eg staying with members of the family on a temporary basis or being accommodated in a homeless hostel as a step in the progression towards permanent accommodation), however, will not be treated as 'settled accommodation' and cannot therefore purge intentional homelessness (see *R v Wycombe District Council, ex p Holmes* (1990) 22 HLR 150 (*cf R v Swansea District Council, ex p Evans* (1990) 22 HLR 467), *Dyson v Kerrier District Council* (*supra*), *Lambert v Ealing London Borough Council* [1982] 1 WLR 550, *R v London Borough of Merton, ex p Ruffle* (1989) 21 HLR 361).

The formation of a new family unit by the applicant may also purge earlier intentional homelessness.

Behaviour outside the housing context

Most of the cases on intentional homelessness involve the loss of accommodation, either voluntarily (for a case where a poltergeist was the alleged reason for vacating accommodation, see *R v Nottingham County Council, ex p Costello* (1989) 21 HLR 301) or compulsorily as a result of acts or omissions, such as through non-payment of rent or mortgage instalments or through being a nuisance or annoyance to neighbours. Conduct outside the housing context, however, may also be taken into account. In *R v Hammersmith and Fulham London Borough Council, ex p P* (1990) 22 HLR 21, for example, criminal activity consisting of robbery, burglary and stealing cars was taken into account. In that case, six families had occupied settled accommodation in a 'no go' area of Belfast. The IRA had made threats to kill or injure these families if they did not get out of Belfast quickly, since they were thought to have been involved in criminal activities which had attracted the attention of the IRA. All six families left Northern Ireland and came to London, where they applied as homeless persons to the Hammersmith and Fulham London Borough Council. The court held that five of the six families were intentionally homeless, because they had been engaged in the sort of anti-social and criminal activities which were likely to attract the attention of the IRA. The sixth family was not proved to have been involved in such activities.

The problem of immigrant families and eligibility

The question of whether accommodation abroad is relevant to intentional homelessness arose before the 1996 Act in a number of cases involving immigrants. Immigrants have posed particular problems under the 'intentional homelessness' category. In *R v Hillingdon London Borough Council, ex p Islam* (1982) 1 HLR 107, [1981] 3 All ER 901, for example, the House of Lords were faced with a situation in which a man from Bangladesh had been living and working in London since 1965 marrying a woman in Bangladesh in 1968. His wife and children lived in Bangladesh for a number of years before applying to come to England. The husband moved from existing one-roomed accommodation to accommodation which was inadequate to house both himself and his family, who were still awaiting entry clearance. The husband was subsequently joined by his family, but they were eventually evicted from their accommodation.

The London Borough of Hillingdon, to which the husband applied, considered that the applicant was intentionally homeless because he had arranged for his family to leave accommodation in Bangladesh which it would have been reasonable for them to continue to occupy. The House of Lords ruled that as Mr Islam had never lived with his wife and family in Bangladesh, there was no evidence to suggest that this was available accommodation, nor could he be deemed to be in occupation of that accommodation through the agency of his wife and children.

Other cases, however, have been less generous to immigrants. In *De Falco v Crawley Borough Council* [1981] 1 All ER 913, for example, an Italian family who had lived in Naples were considered to be intentionally homeless, since they had left accommodation in Italy to seek employment in England. Similarly, in *Lambert v Ealing Borough Council* [1982] 2 All ER 394, a bookseller from Grenoble, in France, was held to be intentionally homeless as he had left accommodation in France in order to come to England for the better education of his children.

Eligibility

The Housing Act, 1996, in s 185, provides that persons from abroad who do not qualify for housing assistance will no longer be eligible for assistance with the provision of accommodation under the Homelessness legislation. Under s 186(1) of the new Act, an asylum-seeker who falls outside s 185 is also ineligible for assistance if he has any accommodation in the UK available for his occupation. This, however, does not exclude *all* those from abroad from eligibility.

'Infectious' intentionality

An applicant may be tainted with the intentional homelessness of another member of the family unit; this is not automatic but will depend on the circumstances of each individual case. If, for example, the applicant has done his or her best to dissociate themselves from the acts or omissions of another member of the family, or to dissuade that other person, then the applicant may not be 'tarred with the same brush'.

In *R v North Devon District Council, ex p Lewis* [1981] 1 All ER 27, a farm labourer voluntarily left his employment, as a result of which he had to give up tied accommodation. His cohabitee applied to the local housing authority for assistance, but her application was turned down on the basis that she had acquiesced in the man's decision to give up his job and was therefore tainted with his intentional homelessness such as to make herself intentionally homeless:

Lewis v North Devon DC

Woolf J: In support of their approach, the housing authority contends that an absurd position would be created if a husband or a man living with a woman could intentionally make the family homeless and then the wife or woman concerned could make an application and, because she, rather than he, makes the application, the family would be treated differently from the way it would have been treated if he made the application. This would result in his obtaining benefits under the Act which it was never intended that he should receive because he had rendered himself intentionally homeless.

The test whether a person is intentionally homeless or not is contained in s 17. [See Section 60 of the 1985 Act] ...

Section 4 makes it clear that it is not for the applicant to show that he did not become homeless intentionally; it is for the housing authority, as a result of its inquiries, to satisfy itself that the applicant became homeless or was threatened with homelessness intentionally.

Homelessness is defined in s 1(1) [See Section 58 of the 1985 Act] ...

That definition and a number of other provisions of the Act make it clear that in looking into an application under the Act the housing authority has to have regard to what I will loosely describe as the family unit. I draw attention to ss 2(1)(a) and (c), 2(2), 5(1)(a)(i) and (ii) and 16 ...

Those provisions make it clear that it is the policy of the Act to keep families together where possible. Such a policy is not surprising in an Act of Parliament passed in 1977.

As it is to the family unit that the housing authority is to have regard, it would be readily understandable if Parliament had provided expressly that the application should be made by the family unit and the question should be whether or not the family should be regarded as having become homeless intentionally. However, as is conceded on behalf of the housing authority, there are no express words which provide that where a man and a woman are living together, if one of the couple became homeless intentionally, the other should be treated as being homeless intentionally. The Act does not place any express limitation on who can make an application or how many applications can be made.

The main argument on behalf of the housing authority was that s 17 must be read as though it provided that, for the purposes of the Act, a person becomes homeless if he, or a person who resides with him or who could reasonably have been expected to reside with him, became homeless intentionally. Such a construction of s 17, in my view, is not possible. It is inconsistent with the wording of s 17 as a whole.

Clearly Parliament could have chosen to treat a woman who lived with a man who had become homeless intentionally as though she was tainted by his conduct. This would have been hard on her but would have avoided his obtaining benefits to which he was not entitled in his own right. Alternatively Parliament could have adopted the approach that, albeit the man was undeserving, because the woman was not herself homeless intentionally, he was to benefit because she was entitled to the additional rights of a person who was not homeless intentionally and she could only obtain those rights if he benefited as well. The literal wording of s 17 indicates that it was the second alternative that Parliament intended and such a result is not so wholly unreasonable that I feel compelled to read into the Act words which are not there so as to arrive at the opposite conclusion.

This construction does not mean that a housing authority should close its eyes to the conduct of the other members of the of the family unit. On the contrary, in my view, the fact that the Act requires consideration of the family unit as a whole indicates that it would be perfectly proper in the ordinary case for the housing authority to look at the family as a whole and assume, in the absence of material which indicates to the contrary, where the conduct of one member of the family was such that he should be regarded as having become homeless intentionally, that that was conduct to which the other members of the family were a party.

So, for example, where the husband is a tenant and gives notice in circumstances where he is properly to be regarded as having become homeless intentionally, the wife, even though she was not the tenant and she did not give notice, can be regarded in the same way. In normal circumstances this would be treated as a joint decision. If, however, at the end of the day, because of material put before the housing authority by the wife, the housing authority is not satisfied that she was a party to the decision, it would have to regard her as not having become homeless intentionally.

In argument the housing authority drew my attention to the difficulties which could arise in cases where the husband spent the rent on drink. If the wife acquiesced to his doing this then it seems to me it would be proper to regard her, as well as him, as having become homeless intentionally. She had failed to do something the likely result of which failure would be that she would be forced to leave the accommodation which was available for her occupation as provided by s 17. If, on the other hand, she had done what she could to prevent the husband spending his money on drink instead of the rent then she had not failed to do anything and it would not be right to regard her as having become homeless intentionally.

Turning therefore to the facts of this case, the finding of the housing authority stated that Mrs Lewis had acquiesced in Mr Hopkins's decision to terminate his employment knowing the accommodation was tied to Mr Hopkins's employment. Having come to that conclusion it was perfectly proper to take the view that Mrs Lewis was herself intentionally homeless.

It was argued on behalf of Mrs Lewis before me, that the housing authority could not reasonably come to a conclusion that she had acquiesced in this decision of Mr Hopkins. However , on the material before the authority, I do not regard that contention as being right. There was ample material before the housing authority on which it could come to the conclusion which it did, and the decision which the housing authority came to in this case, which I regard as being perfectly proper, indicates that perhaps the difficulties, which the housing authority fear might be caused by what I regard as the proper construction of s 17, are not quite as great as it fears.

Because the housing authority approached the matter properly by looking at Mrs Lewis's conduct, this application must be dismissed.

In *R v West Dorset District Council, ex p Phillips* (1985) 17 HLR 336, however, a wife was considered not to be tainted with her husband's conduct, which consisted of spending the rent money on drink, because she had made strenuous efforts to dissuade him from continuing his drinking habits.

(See, also, *R v Eastleigh Borough Council, ex p Beattie (No 2)* (1984) 17 HLR 168 and *R v Mole Valley District Council, ex p Burton* (1988) 20 HLR 479.)

It must be stressed, however, that it is the applicant's conduct which is being called into question in these situations, and not directly that of another member of the family unit.

If an applicant has a priority need but is intentionally homeless, then the local housing authority must provide the applicant with temporary accommodation and give advice and assistance. If the applicant is unintentionally homeless, however, the authority must secure that accommodation is made available to the applicant, though not necessarily from its own housing stock (see s 206 of the 1996 Act). The accommodation has to be suitable, however; and the authority must have regard for the particular circumstances of the applicant and his family (see *R v Brent London Borough, ex p Omar* (1991) 23 HLR 446, *R v London Borough of Southwark, ex p Solomon* (1994) 26

HLR 693, *R v London Borough of Newham, ex p Gentle* (1994) 26 HLR 466 and *R v London Borough of Lambeth, ex p Walters* (1994) 26 HLR 170). This includes the accommodation being at a rent which the applicant can afford (see *R v London Borough of Tower Hamlets, ex p Kaur, Ali et al* (1994) 26 HLR 597). Section 176 of the 1996 Act deals with the meaning of 'accommodation available for occupation' and refers to accommodation available both by the applicant and any other person who might reasonably be expected to reside with him. In *R v London Borough of Newham, ex p Dada* (1995) 27 HLR 502, this was held not to include an unborn child.

Local connection

An applicant may have a local connection with a local authority other than the one to whom he has applied. The case may then be referred to that other authority under s 198 of the 1996 Act. A local connection is defined in s 199 as a connection which a person has with an area:

- because he/she is or was in the past normally resident in it of their own free choice (this excludes prisoners from having a local connection with the area in which they are imprisoned);
- because he/she is employed in it;
- because of family associations; or
- because of any special circumstances.

If the referring authority considers that the homelessness of the applicant is intentional, the other authority must normally accept that finding.

In *R v Tower Hamlets, ex p Camden* (1989) 21 HLR 197, Tower Hamlets had taken the view that Mr Miah, from Bangladesh, was intentionally homeless as he had left accommodation in Bangladesh. Camden, however, took a different view when he applied to it to be housed but then referred the matter back to Tower Hamlets under the local connection procedure. The court held that a transferee authority was normally obliged to accept the findings of the transferor authority, unless the latter had reached its decision after obtaining inadequate evidence. On the facts, Camden had not launched proper inquiries; hence its decision was flawed.

In *R v Newham, ex p Tower Hamlets* (1990) 22 HLR 298, Tower Hamlets had again taken the view that the applicant, a Mr Uller, also from Bangladesh, was intentionally homeless as he had accommodation in Bangladesh. Mr Uller then presented himself as homeless to Newham, who made a finding that he was unintentionally homeless, but then invoked the local connection procedure and sent him back to Tower Hamlets. The decision of the referring authority was quashed since Newham had not made sufficient inquiries. Mr Uller must have felt like a football, being kicked from one local housing authority to another and back again (see also *R v London Borough of Harrow, ex p Carter* (1994) 26 HLR 32).

The Code of Guidance suggests that authorities should only consider transferring an applicant under the local connection procedure once satisfied that the applicant is both homeless, in priority need and not intentionally homeless.

If a person is found to be homeless, in priority need and unintentionally homeless, but has no connection with any other local housing authority in Britain, then the applicant is entitled to be provided with suitable accommodation in the area of the authority to which he has applied.

The enquiry process

A local housing authority has to make inquiries on the question of homelessness, priority need and intentional homelessness. These are not expected to be CID-type inquiries, but must be adequate. It is up to the authority to make the inquiries and not for the applicant to provide a detailed history of all relevant facts. The authority must provide adequate facilities. In *R v Camden London Borough Council, ex p Gillan* (1989) 21 HLR 114, for example, the local authority's homeless persons section was open for limited hours as a result of cut-backs in spending forced upon the authority by 'rate-capping'. The authority was held to be in breach of its duty under the legislation to provide adequate facilities for homeless persons to present themselves as such (see also *R v Royal Borough of Kensington & Chelsea, ex p Kassam* (1994) 26 HLR 455).

Where an applicant applies to the authority for accommodation, the duty to make inquiries applies only where the authority have reason to believe that at least the applicant may be threatened with homelessness; the authority cannot take a decision on this issue before the statutory definition is fulfilled and hence cannot determine before this time whether the applicant is tainted with intentionality (see *R v Rugby Borough Council, ex p Hunt* (1994) 26 HLR 1).

The authority, as a public body, must give the applicant a fair hearing and should not reach a decision adverse to the applicant unless there are adequate grounds for doing so.

The authority must notify the applicant in writing of its decision on each of homelessness, priority need and intentional homelessness, and give adequate reasons for its decision.

An applicant also has certain duties cast upon him. The applicant must be truthful in his application, etc if he is to avoid committing a criminal offence, and inform of any changes in his circumstances that might affect the authority's decision (see s 214).

Enforcement procedures

Under s 202 of the 1996 Act, an applicant has the right to request a review of his case in defined circumstances, and may then appeal to the county court on a point of law if dissatisfied with the decision on review (see s 204).

The main tool for enforcing the duties of local housing authorities under the earlier homelessness legislation has been by means of Judicial Review (see Order 53). This is a means of application to the High Court by which the Court can quash the decision of the local housing authority on administrative law grounds.

In *Pulhofer* (see earlier) the House of Lords considered that applications for Judicial Review should be discouraged. Despite this, however, there were a large number of such applications each year. In *Cocks v Thanet District Council* [1982] 3 All ER 1135, the court stated that the proper remedy for challenging decisions on homelessness was by way of Judicial Review rather than by a claim, for example, for damages (see also *Ali v Tower Hamlets London BC* [1992] 3 All ER 512).

The cost and amount of time spent on challenging local housing authority decisions through Judicial Review was prohibitory in a lot of cases unless the applicant was lucky enough to get a Law Centre to take their case on. A quicker and cheaper remedy could have been provided through a Housing Appeals Tribunal system, independent of the local authority, similar to the Rent Tribunal. That, however, has not been done. Instead, the new legislation has gone for internal review as the first means by which an applicant can have his/her case reconsidered. A review of its own decision by the local housing authority is not necessarily a truly independent review mechanism, and despite the right of appeal to the county court, there remains the problem that the county court may not be as good a means of dealing with homelessness issues as the previous High Court Judicial Review procedure.

Despite the trojan work of voluntary bodies, Law Centres and others, Homelessness is still a big social problem. It seems that organisations like Shelter, which were formed to deal with what was thought to be a temporary problem, will be around for many years to come, finances permitting. A cynic might be forgiven for concluding that the 1996 Act and its predecessors have had and will continue to have little real impact on homelessness in Britain. Hard-pressed authorities with over-stretched staff and inadequate financial resources are finding it difficult to cope with the increasing number of homelessness applications. There is little wonder that a finding of intentional homelessness has become increasingly common.

THE FUTURE – THE HOUSING ACT 1996 – SUMMARY OF CHANGES

As mentioned earlier in this chapter, Part VII of the 1996 Housing Act replaced Part III of the 1985 Act. Most of the provisions of the 1985 Act have been re-enacted, but with some changes. Amongst those changes are the following:

1   All local housing authorities are to make available advisory services to help prevent homelessness (s 179).

2   Unintentionally homeless persons in priority need will continue to be entitled to assistance if there is no suitable alternative accommodation available to them within the authority's area (ss 193 and 197).

3   Section 196 extends the meaning of 'intentionally homeless' to cover situations where a person enters an agreement which results in him/her losing accommodation and with the sole intention of taking advantage of the homelessness legislation.

4   The duty to accommodate, once established, will run for a minimum of two years (s 193). After that, the authority must satisfy themselves that the person remains entitled under the legislation (s 194). The DOE have stated

that this proposal 'will remove any uncertainty' caused by the decision in the *Awua* case.

5   A dissatisfied applicant may require a review of his case by the authority (s 202).

Other changes have been mentioned in more detail in the relevant part of the text of this chapter.

Housing agencies fear that the proposals will greatly increase homelessness. (Guardian Education, 5 March 1996). Shelter has pointed out that the private rented sector tends to be the most expensive, having the worst standards of accommodation and with the least security. This may be worsened by other changes which are incorporated in the Act relevant to security of tenure under the Housing Act 1988. Changes in housing benefit will also be likely to combine with the worst aspects of the proposed changes with the probable result of increasing homelessness.

INDEX